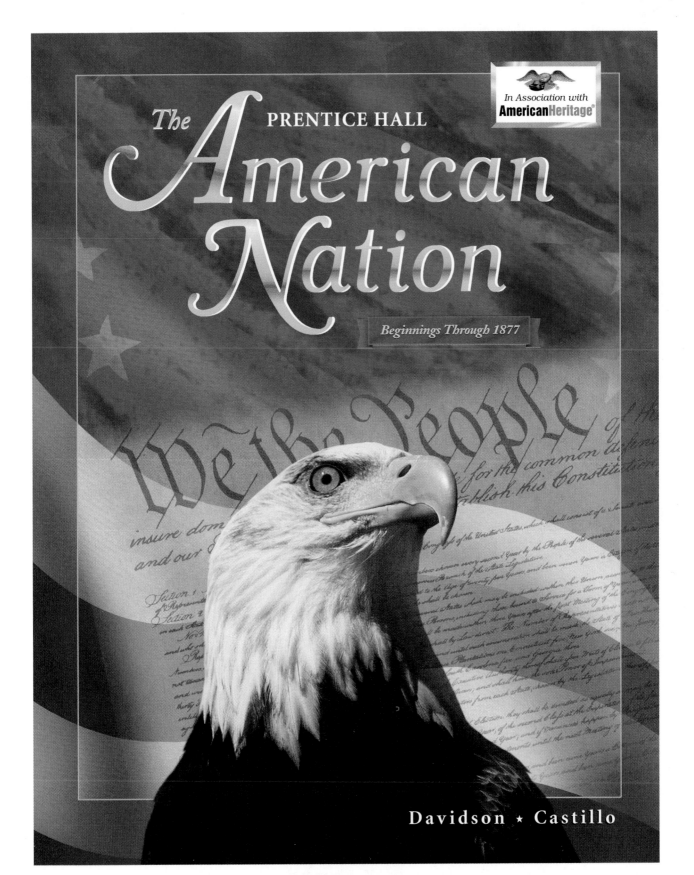

The PRENTICE HALL

American Nation

Beginnings Through 1877

In Association with **American Heritage®**

Davidson ★ Castillo

PRENTICE HALL

Upper Saddle River, New Jersey
Needham, Massachusetts

Authors

James West Davidson is coauthor of *After the Fact: The Art of Historical Detection* and *Nation of Nations: A Narrative History of the American Republic.* Dr. Davidson has taught at both the college and high school levels. He has also consulted on curriculum design for American history courses. Dr. Davidson is an avid canoeist and hiker. His published works on these subjects include *Great Heart,* the true story of a 1903 canoe trip in the Canadian wilderness.

Pedro Castillo teaches American history at the University of California, Santa Cruz, where he also co-directs the Chicano-Latino Research Center. He has earned a Rockefeller Foundation Research Fellowship and two Senior Fulbright-Hayes Lectureships in Latin America. Dr. Castillo's published works on American history and Chicano Latino history include *Mexico en Los Angeles* and *An Illustrated History of Mexican Los Angeles.*

AmericanHeritage® *American Heritage* magazine was founded in 1954, and it quickly rose to the position it occupies today: the country's preeminent magazine of history and culture. Dedicated to presenting the past in incisive, entertaining narratives underpinned by scrupulous scholarship, *American Heritage* today goes to more than 300,000 subscribers and counts the country's very best writers and historians among its contributors. Its innovative use of historical illustration and its wide variety of subject matter have gained the publication scores of honors across more than forty years, among them the National Magazine Awards.

Acknowledgments and Illustration Credits begin on page 652.

PRENTICE HALL

Copyright © 2000 by Prentice-Hall, Inc., Upper Saddle River, New Jersey 07458. All rights reserved. No part of this book may be reproduced or transmitted in any form or by any means, electronic or mechanical, including photocopying, recording, or by any information storage and retrieval system, without permission in writing from the publisher.

Printed in the United States of America.

ISBN 0-13-434902-4

1 2 3 4 5 6 7 8 9 10   02 01 00 99 98

Upper Saddle River, New Jersey   Needham, Massachusetts

Program Reviewers

◄ *Statue of a New England Puritan*

▲ *Anasazi pottery*

UNIT 2   A Nation Is Born   128

▲ *Early American flag*

▼ *Quill and inkwell used at the Constitutional Convention*

★ **v**

UNIT 3 The Nation Takes Shape 240

▲ *Thomas Jefferson*

The Louisiana Purchase ➤

▲ *Women factory workers*

▲ African American preacher

▲ Conestoga wagon

▲ *Civil War army caps*

▲ *Emancipation Proclamation*

Reference Section

Special Features

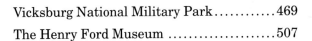

AmericanHeritage MAGAZINE

★ *With the editors of* American Her-*itage* magazine as your guides, you see and read about special sites where American history happened.

HISTORY HAPPENED HERE

▲ *The Erie Canal*

  Linking ...

★ *The Linking features use engaging visuals to make historical connections.*

Why Study History?

★ *These high-interest features show how history is relevant to American life today and to your life in particular.*

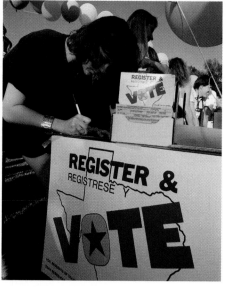

▲ *Because you will choose our nation's leaders*

Viewpoints:
Source Readings in American History

★ *Eyewitness accounts, historical documents, and literature selections provide you with different viewpoints on American history.*

Eyewitness Accounts

Historical Documents

★ *Learn and practice valuable skills: Critical Thinking; Managing Information; Communication; and Maps, Charts, and Graphs.*

▲ *Using the Internet*

Charts, Graphs, and Time Lines

Continued ▶

Charts, Graphs, and Time Lines (continued)

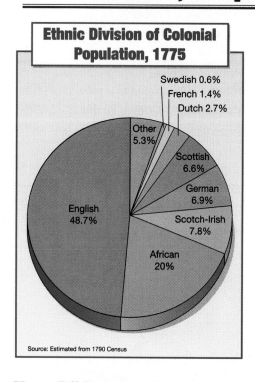

Ethnic Division of Colonial Population, 1775

Swedish 0.6%
French 1.4%
Dutch 2.7%
Other 5.3%
Scottish 6.6%
German 6.9%
Scotch-Irish 7.8%
English 48.7%
African 20%

Source: Estimated from 1790 Census

Graphic Organizers

School Enrollment, 1840–1870

Number of Students (in millions)

Year

Source: *American Education, The National Experience, 1783–1876,* by Lawrence A. Cremin

Maps and Geography Activities

Geography Activities

Geographic Atlas

The War in the West

Key
American forces
British forces
American victories
Forts
0 100 200 Miles
0 100 200 Kilometers

About This Book

The American Nation is organized into 5 units and 19 chapters. The Table of Contents lists units, chapters, sections, and special features.

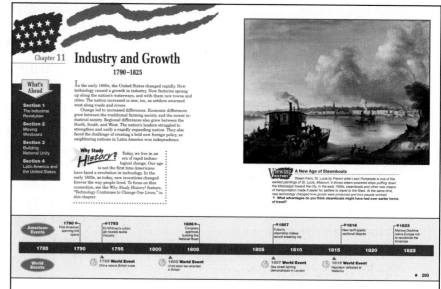

IN EACH UNIT

- **Unit Opener** a two-page introduction to the contents and major theme of the unit.
- **History Through Literature** a two-page excerpt from a work of American literature.

IN EACH CHAPTER

- **Chapter Opener** a two-page introduction that includes a time line and chapter summary.
- **As You Read** an introduction to each section, including questions to guide your reading and lists of vocabulary terms and people.
- **Section Reviews** questions and activities that test your understanding of each section.
- **Skills for Life** a lesson that helps you to learn, practice, and apply a useful skill.
- **Linking…** Past and Present, or United States and the World, or History and Technology is a visual feature that shows interesting connections.
- **Biographies** portraits of and information about key people in American history.
- **Interdisciplinary Connections** footnotes that give connections to Geography, Economics, Civics, Arts, or Science.
- **Maps, Graphs, and Charts** visual tools that help you understand history and practice important skills.
- **Chapter Review and Activities** two pages to help you review key terms and ideas and practice valuable skills, with these special features:
    - *Using Primary Sources,* a primary source excerpt with questions that help you recognize different points of view.
    - *Activity Bank,* includes Interdisciplinary, Career Skills, Citizenship, and Internet activities.
    - *Eyewitness Journal,* writing activity that lets you take on different historical roles.
    - *Critical Thinking and Writing,* questions and exercises that go beyond recall.

SPECIAL FEATURES

- Why Study History? This feature demonstrates the relevance of history to American life today and to your life in particular.
- **AmericanHeritage® Magazine History Happened Here** The editors of *American Heritage* magazine are your guides to interesting historic sites throughout the nation.

VIEWPOINTS: SOURCE READINGS IN AMERICAN HISTORY

- Located after the last unit, two readings per chapter, including eyewitness accounts, historical documents, and literature selections.

REFERENCE SECTION

- Includes an Atlas, a Gazetteer, a Glossary, the Declaration of Independence, the Constitution of the United States, information about the fifty states, information about the Presidents, and an Index.

Researching on the Internet

THE INTERNET

The **Internet** includes millions of business, governmental, educational, and individual computers on the World Wide Web. Using programs called browsers, Internet users can find out what sites are available on the Web and then access those sites.

SEARCHING THE INTERNET

There are two basic ways to find information on the Internet. The first is to go directly to the Net site that contains the information you want. Each site has an address, called a **URL,** or Universal Resource Locator. (For example, http://www.phschool.com is the URL of the Prentice Hall Web site.) Of course, this method works only if you know the appropriate URL.

The second way is to use a **search engine,** such as Infoseek or Yahoo! Type the key words representing the topic you want to research. The search engine will then scan the Internet and list sites that pertain to your topic.

Whichever method you choose, you will encounter sites containing **hyperlinks.** These appear as colored or underlined text or as icons. Hyperlinks act as doorways to other documents at the same Web site or others. When you click your mouse on hyperlinked text or graphics, an entirely new document appears on your screen.

Pay careful attention to the source of the information you find. Is the source a government agency, or a university, or a private company, or an individual? Not all sources are equally accurate or reliable in what they present.

See us on the Internet

http://www.phschool.com

At Prentice Hall's Web site, you will find current event updates, social studies links, and other resources to help you learn about American history.

TIPS FOR SUCCESSFUL SEARCHES

Focus your search. Because the Internet contains so much, it is easy to "wander off" into other parts of the Internet and forget about the information that you are trying to locate. To avoid this problem, establish a specific research goal before you begin.

Make bookmarks for useful Web sites. A bookmark is a note to your computer to "remember" the location of a Web site. Later, you can reach any bookmarked site with a simple click of your mouse.

Use specific key words. If your key words are too general, your search might turn up thousands of Net sites. Make your key words specific. Many search engines have useful tips on searching with key words.

Seek guidance from teachers and parents. Ask a teacher, parent, or librarian for help in evaluating whether Web sites and information are reliable and appropriate to your research.

Unit 1

Early Heritage of the Americas

Viewing UNIT THEMES — A Meeting of Different Cultures

George Catlin, an American artist of the 1800s, painted LaSalle Claiming Louisiana for France, April 9, 1682. As Native Americans watch, newly arrived French explorers gather around a flag and a cross. Encounters and exchanges between Europeans and Native Americans helped form the roots of American society. ★ **In addition to Europeans and Native Americans, what other people have helped shape American society?**

Unit Theme **Origins**

Over thousands of years, Native Americans formed diverse societies throughout North America. In the 1500s and 1600s, Europeans and Africans began to arrive in the Americas. The blending and clashing of these three cultures helped shape the nature of modern American life.

Along the Atlantic coast of North America, settlers from England established 13 colonies. English political traditions would form the basis for the American government today.

How did people of the time view American origins? They can tell you in their own words.

★ ★

VIEWPOINTS ON AMERICAN ORIGINS

❝ Roots have spread out from the Tree of the Great Peace, one to the north, one to the east, one to the south, and one to the west. ❞
Treaty forming an alliance among Iroquois nations (1500s)

❝ The people are a collection of diverse nations in Europe as French, Dutch, Germans, Swedes, Danes, Finns, Scotch, Irish, and English. ❞
William Penn, founder of Pennsylvania (1685)

❝ A democracy...is when...power is lodged in a council consisting of all the members and where every member has the privilege of a vote. ...Every man has the privilege freely to deliver his opinion concerning the common affairs. ❞
John Wise, Massachusetts minister (1717)

★ ★

History AND YOU

Activity Writing to Learn The peoples who first settled in North America came from many different backgrounds. Think about your school and your community. Then, make a list of the things that can help different people to live together without conflict.

Chapter 1

Focus on Geography
Prehistory–Present

The United States of America is blessed with a beautiful, diverse, and valuable natural environment. In this chapter, you will study geography in general and the geography of our nation in particular. You will learn about the landforms, physical regions, natural resources, and climates of the United States.

Several tools will aid you in your study. Geographers have developed five themes to help you understand the relationship between geography and history. Various kinds of maps will also prove useful.

Why Study History?

In the months ahead, you will see how geography has influenced the history, the government, and the economy of the United States. You will also study how people's actions affect the natural environment. You can learn about the vital importance of one natural resource and how you can help preserve it by reading this chapter's *Why Study History?* feature, "We All Need Water."

American Events			🔴 **1500s** Early encounters between Europeans and Native Americans		🔴 **1600s** Growing numbers of enslaved Africans in the Americas
Prehistory	**1500**		**1600**		**1700**

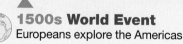 **1500s World Event**
Europeans explore the Americas

World Events

Viewing HISTORY
The View From Space

This picture was taken by a satellite in orbit around the Earth. You are looking directly at North America. The colors are enhanced to highlight the Earth's physical features. Green represents lowlands and orange represents highlands.

★ **What other continents are visible in this satellite photograph?**

1800s ●
Migration to the
Pacific Coast
increases

1900s ●
Industrialization
affects the natural
environment

Present ●
Efforts to
protect the
environment
increase

1700	1800	1900	Present

▲
1700s World Event
European states struggle for
control of North America

▲
1800s World Event
Millions of immigrants move
to the United States

★ **3**

1 ★ Five Themes of Geography

As You Read

Explore These Questions
- What are the five themes of geography?
- How do people and their natural environment interact?
- What are some causes and effects of the movement of people?

Define
- geography
- history
- latitude
- longitude
- irrigate

SETTING the Scene If you read almost any newspaper, you will find stories about the land around you. One story might argue that building a dam will be harmful to a river. Another might announce the discovery of oil. To understand these and other issues, we need to understand geography.

Geography and History

Geography is the study of people, their environments, and their resources. Geographers ask how the natural environment affects the way we live and how we, in turn, affect the environment. By showing how people and the land are related, geography helps to explain both the past and the present.

Geography is closely linked to history. **History** is an account of what has happened in the lives of different peoples. Both historians and geographers want to understand how the characteristics of a place affect people and events.

To help show the connection between geography and history, geographers have developed five themes. The themes are location, place, interaction between people and their environment, movement, and region.

Location

Where did this event happen? Where is this place? Both historians and geographers often ask such questions. Finding the answers involves the geographic theme of location.

Exact location

As you study American history, you will sometimes need to know the absolute, or exact, location of a place. For example, where, exactly, is Washington, D.C., the nation's capital?

To describe the exact location of Washington, D.C., geographers use a grid of numbered lines on a map or globe that measure latitude and longitude. Lines of **latitude** measure distance north and south from the Equator. Lines of **longitude** measure distance east and west from the Prime Meridian, which runs through Greenwich (GREHN ihch), England.

The exact location of Washington, D.C., is 39 degrees (°) north latitude and 77 degrees (°) west longitude. In writing, this location is often shortened to 39°N/77°W. The Gazetteer in the Reference Section of this book provides the exact location of many important places in American history.

Relative location

Sometimes it is more useful to know the relative location of a place, or its location in relation to some other place. Is Washington, D.C., on the east or west coast of the United States? Is it north or south of Richmond, Virginia? These questions involve relative location.

Knowing relative locations will help you see the relationship between places. Is a place located near a lake, river, or other source of water and transportation? Is it inland or on the coast? Answers to such ques-

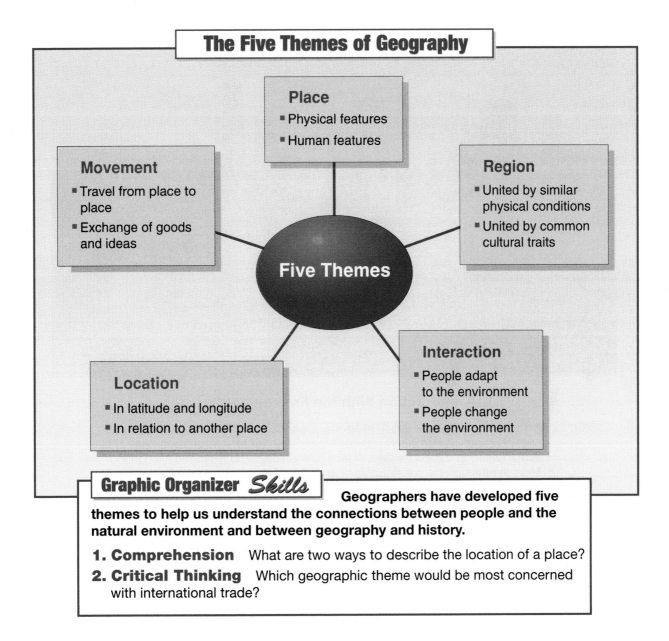

The Five Themes of Geography

Place
- Physical features
- Human features

Movement
- Travel from place to place
- Exchange of goods and ideas

Region
- United by similar physical conditions
- United by common cultural traits

Five Themes

Location
- In latitude and longitude
- In relation to another place

Interaction
- People adapt to the environment
- People change the environment

Graphic Organizer *Skills*   Geographers have developed five themes to help us understand the connections between people and the natural environment and between geography and history.

1. **Comprehension** What are two ways to describe the location of a place?
2. **Critical Thinking** Which geographic theme would be most concerned with international trade?

tions help explain why cities grew where they did. Chicago, Illinois, for instance, developed at the center of water, road, and railroad transportation in the Midwest.

Place

A second geography theme is place. Geographers generally describe a place in terms of both physical and human features.

The physical features of a place include climate, soil, plant life, animal life, and bodies of water. For example, New England has a hilly terrain, a rocky coast, and many deep harbors. Because of these physical features,

early Native Americans of the region turned to fishing for a living.

People help to shape the character of a place through their ideas and actions. The human features of a place include the kinds of houses people build as well as their means of transportation, ways of earning a living, languages, and religions.

Think of the human features of the American frontier. In the forests of the frontier, early settlers built log cabins. On the grassy plains, where trees were scarce, some settlers built their homes out of sod, clumps of earth, and grass.

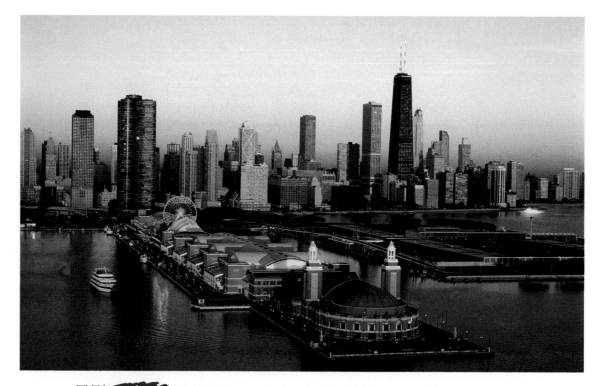

Viewing HISTORY

Interaction With the Environment

Chicago is one of several major cities that dot the shores of Lake Michigan. Before people interacted with the natural environment, only dense forests encircled the lake. Notice how Chicago has extended into Lake Michigan through the construction of large piers. ★ **How might lakeshore cities like Chicago have a negative impact on the natural environment?**

Interaction

Interaction between people and their environment is a third theme of geography. Throughout history, people have adapted to and changed their natural environment.

For example, ancient hunters in the Americas learned to plant seeds and grow food crops. This adaptation greatly affected their lives. No longer did they have to move from place to place in search of food.

Connections With Geography

Agriculture was impossible in the arid Imperial Valley of southeastern California until irrigation canals were built in the 1900s. The canals bring water from the Colorado River. Today, the Imperial Valley is a very productive farming region.

Later, Native Americans in the Southwest found ways to **irrigate,** or bring water to, the desert. They dug ditches that channeled water from the Salt and Gila rivers. In this way, they were able to change arid, unproductive land into farmland.

In the 1860s, railroad builders in the United States changed the natural environment in order to improve transportation. They wanted to link the Atlantic and Pacific coasts. The railroad workers blasted through mountains and built bridges across rivers. When the project was completed, a railroad line stretched across the nation, linking the eastern and western parts of the United States.

Today, advanced technology allows people to alter their environment dramatically. People have invented ways to take oil from beneath the ocean floor. They have cut down forests to build communities. They have wiped out pests that destroy crops. Such changes have brought great benefits. They have also created new problems, such as air and water pollution.

Movement

A fourth geographic theme involves the movement of people, goods, and ideas. Movement occurs because people and resources are scattered unevenly around the globe. To get what they need or want, people travel from place to place. As they meet other people, they exchange ideas and technology as well as goods.

History provides many examples of the movement of people and ideas. The first people who came to the Americas were hunters following animal herds. Much later, people from all over the world moved to the United States in search of political and religious freedom. They brought with them customs and beliefs that have helped shape American life.

Today, the movement of goods links the United States with all parts of the world. For example, American producers ship goods such as grain and computers to Europe and Africa. Meanwhile, we rely on materials such as oil and tin from other parts of the world.

Region

Geographers study regions. A region is an area of the world that has similar, unifying characteristics. The characteristics of a region may be physical, such as its climate or landforms. For example, the Great Plains is considered a region because it has fairly level land, very hot summers, very cold winters, and little rainfall. The Pacific Coast region, meanwhile, is known for its rugged mountains, dense forests, and scenic ocean shore.

A region's characteristics may also be human and cultural. San Francisco's Chinatown is a region because Chinese Americans there have preserved their language and culture. In New York City, Broadway is a theater district where many plays are performed. In Chicago, the Loop is a downtown area where there are office buildings and museums.

A region can be any size. It can be as large as the United States or as small as a neighborhood. Within one city, there could be several regions. For example, there may be a parkland area known for its natural beauty. There may be a residential area where people live in homes and apartments. There also may be a business district, occupied mostly by office buildings and stores.

★ Section 1 Review ★

Recall
1. **Define** **(a)** geography, **(b)** history, **(c)** latitude, **(d)** longitude, **(e)** irrigate.

Comprehension
2. Briefly describe the five themes of geography.
3. **(a)** Describe two examples of how the natural environment can affect the way people live. **(b)** Give two examples of problems that can result when people change the natural environment.

4. How has the movement of people helped shape American life?

Critical Thinking and Writing
5. **Synthesizing Information**   How does the picture of the New England coast on page 17 illustrate the theme of place?
6. **Understanding Causes and Effects**   How does modern technology affect the movement of people, goods, and ideas?

★ ★

Activity   **Using Geographic Themes** Use the five themes of geography to describe the neighborhood, community, or state in which you live. Develop your description by writing one or two sentences for each of the five themes.

Maps and Mapmaking

As You Read

Explore These Questions
- What different types of maps do people use?
- How do latitude and longitude help us to locate places?
- Why are today's maps more accurate than maps of the past?

Define
- globe
- cartographer
- map projection
- hemisphere
- standard time zone

Identify
- Equator
- Prime Meridian

SETTING the Scene In a tiny Indian fishing village in the early 1600s, a small group gathered around Samuel de Champlain. They watched closely as the French explorer pointed to the shore and then drew a sweeping line on a deerskin spread out on the ground. The line represented the coastline where they stood. Quickly, the Native American chief drew other lines on the informal map. A young man added piles of rocks to represent the village and nearby settlements.

Champlain and the Native Americans he met on Cape Ann in Massachusetts did not understand each other's languages. Yet they found a way to communicate. Together, they created a map of the local area. Champlain later used the map to aid him in exploring the Massachusetts coast. People today use maps, too, to help them locate places, judge distances, and follow routes.

Maps and Globes

To locate places, geographers use maps and globes. A map is a drawing of the Earth's surface. A **globe** is a sphere with a map of the Earth printed on it. Because a globe is the same shape as the Earth, it shows sizes and shapes accurately.

Geographers often use flat maps rather than globes.

Unlike a globe, a flat map of the world allows you to see all of the Earth's surface at one time. It is easier to handle and can show more detail. Still, a flat map has the disadvantage that it distorts, or misrepresents, some parts of the Earth.

Map Projections

Mapmakers, or **cartographers,** have developed dozens of different map projections. **Map projections** are ways of drawing the Earth on a flat surface.

Each map projection has benefits and disadvantages. Some projections show the sizes of landmasses correctly but distort their shapes. Others give continents their true shapes but distort their sizes. Still other projections distort direction or distances.

Mercator projection

In 1569, Gerardus Mercator developed the Mercator projection, the best map of its day. For hundreds of years, sailors depended on the Mercator map. Mercator himself boasted of his map:

66 If you wish to sail from one port to another, here is a chart, and a straight line on it, and if you follow this line carefully you will certainly arrive at your destination. 99

A globe is a map of the world.

A Mercator map shows the true shapes of landmasses, but it distorts size, especially for places that are far from the Equator. On a Mercator map, for example, Greenland appears as big as all of South America, even though South America is more than eight times larger!

Robinson projection

Today, many geographers use the Robinson projection. It shows the correct sizes and shapes of landmasses for most parts of the world. The Robinson projection also gives a fairly accurate view of the relationship between landmasses and water.

Kinds of Maps

Maps are part of our daily lives. You have probably read road or bus maps. On television, you have seen weather maps and maps of places in the news.

As you study history, you will use various maps. Examine the Geographic Atlas in the Reference Section of this book. There, you will find maps showing national and state boundaries as well as the physical features and natural resources of the United States.

Each kind of map serves a specific purpose. A political map shows boundaries that people have set up to divide the world into countries and states. A physical map shows natural features, such as mountains and rivers. A population map lets you see how many people live in a particular area. An economic map shows how people of a certain region make a living. A natural resource map helps you see links between the resources of an area and the way people use the land.

Still other kinds of maps include election maps, product maps, and battle maps. These maps also help you to see the connections between geography and history.

Map Projections

Robinson Projection

Mercator Projection

Geography *Skills*   Map projections make it possible for mapmakers to show a round world on a flat map.

1. **Location**   Use the map on page 10 to locate: **(a)** North America, **(b)** Africa, **(c)** Asia.
2. **Place**   How does North America appear differently on the two projections?
3. **Critical Thinking**   On the Mercator map, which areas are most distorted?

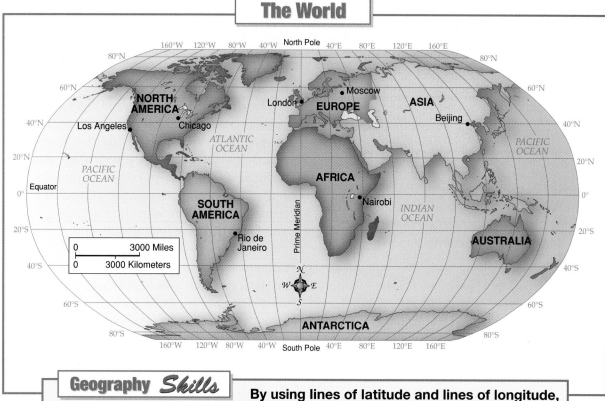

The World

By using lines of latitude and lines of longitude, one can locate any specific place in the world.

1. Location On the map, locate: **(a)** Atlantic Ocean, **(b)** Pacific Ocean, **(c)** Europe, **(d)** North America, **(e)** Africa.

2. Location Which city is located at about 55°N/35°E?

3. Critical Thinking Which continents lie entirely in the Northern Hemisphere?

Latitude and Longitude

Most maps and globes include lines of latitude and lines of longitude. The lines form a grid, making it possible to locate places exactly. Each latitude and longitude line on the grid is measured in degrees (°).

Latitude

Look at the map of the world, above. Notice that lines of latitude run east and west. As you have read, lines of latitude measure distances north and south from the Equator.

The **Equator** is an imaginary line that lies at 0° latitude. It divides the Earth into two halves, called **hemispheres.**

The Northern Hemisphere lies north of the Equator. In the Northern Hemisphere, lines of latitude are numbered from 1°N to 90°N, where the North Pole is located.

The Southern Hemisphere lies south of the Equator. There, lines of latitude are numbered from 1°S to 90°S, where the South Pole is located.

Longitude

Lines of longitude on a map or globe run north and south between the two poles. They measure distances east and west from the **Prime Meridian,** which lies at 0º longitude and runs through the Royal Observatory in Greenwich, England. Unlike lines of latitude, lines of longitude are not parallel to each other. They converge at the North Pole and South Pole. The distance between longitude lines is greatest at the Equator. The distance

Skills FOR LIFE

| Critical Thinking | Managing Information | Communication | **Maps, Charts, and Graphs** |

Reading a Map

How Will I Use This Skill?

Maps are not used just to study history and geography. They can also help you plan a trip, understand current events, or find out about the weather. Knowing how to read a map can keep you from getting lost, or help you find your way again.

LEARN the Skill

You can read a map by following these three steps:

❶ Identify the topic of the map. The **title** will tell you the subject of the map. The **key** explains the meanings of the map's symbols and colors.

❷ Look at a map's **scale** to determine distances between places. The scale shows you how many inches on the map equal how many actual miles or kilometers.

❸ Study the **directional arrow** to identify north, south, east, and west on a map.

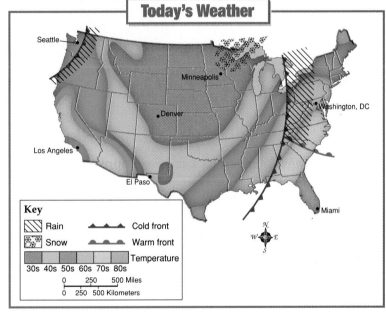

PRACTICE the Skill

Use the steps above and the map on this page to answer the following questions.

❶ (a) What is the title of the map? (b) How is a cold front shown on the map? (c) According to the color key, what is today's temperature in Los Angeles? In Denver?

❷ (a) On the scale, how many miles are represented by 3/4 of an inch?

(b) What is the approximate distance from Washington, DC, to Miami in miles? In kilometers?

❸ (a) What is the northernmost city shown on the map? (b) What direction would you travel from El Paso to reach a place where it is snowing?

APPLY the Skill

With a group of classmates, create a map of your classroom. Include a title, plus a key that explains what symbols represent doors, windows, desks, and other features. Use a compass or the sun to determine north, south, east, and west. Use a tape measure to measure the room and create a scale.

Viewing HISTORY Early Map of the Americas

This 1595 map distorts the true shapes of North America and South America. Gerardus Mercator, the map's creator, refers to the Americas as New India. Maps of the 1500s may not have been totally accurate, but they were very artistic. ★ **Why are today's maps much more accurate than those of several centuries ago?**

between the lines decreases as they approach and finally meet at the poles.

Lines of longitude are numbered from 1° to 179° east or west longitude. The line of longitude at 180° lies on the opposite side of the world from the Prime Meridian.

The circle formed by the Prime Meridian and 180° divides the Earth into the Eastern and Western hemispheres. The Eastern Hemisphere includes most of Europe, Africa, and Asia. The Western Hemisphere includes North America and South America.

Locating places

To locate places, you must combine latitude and longitude. Look at the map on page 10. Chicago is located north of the Equator at about 42°N latitude. It lies west of the Prime Meridian at about 88°W longitude. Its location is 42°N/88°W. Use the United States map in the Reference Section to find the exact location of your state capital.

Time Zones

Lines of longitude are also used to help us know what time it is around the world. When it is 11 A.M. in Miami, Florida, it is 8 A.M. in Portland, Oregon. In Lagos, Nigeria, it is 5 P.M.

Why does time differ from place to place? The answer is that the Earth rotates on its axis. As the Earth moves, the sun appears to rise in some places and to set in others. Throughout the world, people determine time by this rising and setting of the sun.

To make it easier to tell time around the world, a system of **standard time zones** was set up in 1884. Under this system, the world was divided into 24 times zones. Standard time is measured from the Prime Meridian, which runs through Greenwich, England.

When it is noon in Greenwich, it is before noon (A.M.) in places west of Greenwich. It is after noon (P.M.) in places east of Greenwich.

$ Connections With Economics

In the United States, the Daylight Saving Time system provides people with more usable hours of daylight. From April to October, clocks are set ahead one hour. The total amount of daylight remains the same, but more daylight hours are available for outdoor activities in the late afternoon and evening.

If you travel east from Greenwich across Europe, Africa, or Asia, you add one hour as you move through each time zone.

Making Accurate Maps

The oldest surviving map in the world today was created by an ancient cartographer on a clay tablet sometime around 2300 B.C. Ever since, geographers have worked to make maps more accurate.

Early mapmaking

Early cartographers relied on information from sailors and travelers as well as legends to create their maps. As a result, their maps included many errors. Five hundred years ago, European mapmakers did not even know that North America and South America existed!

Since the 1500s, mapmaking has improved greatly. Daring sailors gained information about uncharted lands. Explorers studied ocean currents and wind patterns around the world. Scientists learned more about the Earth itself.

Using satellites

Today, mapmakers depend on computers and satellites. By taking photographs from space, satellites provide information that no one on the ground can furnish. As a result, maps are more accurate than ever before.

Launched in 1972, Landsat 1 was the first satellite specially designed to study the Earth's surface from space. The unmanned spacecraft took pictures from about 570 miles (900 km) above the Earth. Each photo showed a land area that an airplane would need 1,000 pictures to depict. Within two years, Landsat photographed more than 80 percent of the Earth's surface.

Images from Landsat 1 and later satellites provided extraordinary help to mapmakers. They revealed uncharted islands. They enabled scientists to see entire mountain ranges and drainage basins at a single glance. They allowed surveys of remote areas, such as the polar regions and oceans. Based on these images, cartographers corrected old maps and mapped some places for the first time.

Today, geographers rely on satellites for more and more information about the Earth. Geographers can use satellite information to chart changes in population density and economic activity. They can also learn more about weather patterns, vegetation, pollution, and mineral resources.

★ Section 2 Review ★

Recall

1. **Locate** (a) North America, (b) South America, (c) Asia, (d) Arctic Ocean.
2. **Identify** (a) Equator, (b) Prime Meridian.
3. **Define** (a) globe, (b) cartographer, (c) map projection, (d) hemisphere, (e) standard time zone.

Comprehension

4. Why does a globe show the Earth more accurately than a flat map?

5. How can we use latitude and longitude to find the exact location of a place?
6. How have satellites made maps more accurate than ever before?

Critical Thinking and Writing

7. **Applying Information** Describe some of the special features of a road map.
8. **Understanding Causes and Effects** Before the 1500s, why were European maps of the world very inaccurate?

★ ★

History AND YOU

Activity **Making a Weather Map** You are the meteorologist for a local television news program. Make a map of your region, showing your forecast for tomorrow's weather conditions. You may wish to use the map on page 11 as a model.

3 ★ American Lands and Climates

As You Read

Explore These Questions

- What are the eight physical regions of the United States?
- How are rivers and lakes important to the United States?
- What are the major climates of North America?

Define

- isthmus
- mountain
- elevation
- hill
- plain
- plateau
- tributary
- weather
- climate
- precipitation
- altitude
- El Niño

SETTING the Scene North America is the world's third largest continent. As the World map in the Reference Section shows, the Atlantic Ocean washes the eastern shore of North America. The Pacific Ocean laps at its western shore. To the north lies the icy Arctic Ocean. To the south, an **isthmus** (IHS muhs), or narrow strip of land, links North America to South America.

North America has many different features. For example, one of the world's highest mountains, Mount McKinley, is in Alaska. Yet one of the lowest points on the Earth is in Death Valley, California. You will find many examples of contrast as you read more about the American land.

Types of Landforms

North America has many landforms, or natural features. There are high mountains, rolling hills, and long rivers. There are grassy plains, dense forests, and barren deserts. Within these different landscapes are four basic landforms: mountains, hills, plains, and plateaus (pla TOHZ).

Mountains are high, steep, rugged land. They rise to an **elevation,** or height, of at least 1,000 feet (300 m) above the surrounding land. Few people live on steep mountainsides. Yet people often settle in valleys between mountains.

Hills are areas of raised land that are lower and more rounded than mountains. Farming is often possible on hilly land. Therefore, more people live in hilly areas than on mountains.

Plains are broad areas of fairly level land. Few plains are totally flat. Most are gently rolling. Plains do not usually rise much above sea level. People often settle on plains because it is easy to build farms, roads, and cities on the level land.

Plateaus are plains that range from a few hundred to many thousand feet above sea level. With enough rain, plateaus can be good for farming. Mountains surround some plateaus. Such plateaus are often very dry because the mountains cut off rainfall.

Mountains, hills, plains, and plateaus are only a few of the special words that geographers use. For definitions of other geographic terms, you may refer to the Dictionary of Geographic Terms on pages 24–25.

Physical Regions of North America

The landforms of North America form seven major physical regions. The United States also includes an eighth region, the Hawaiian Islands in the Pacific Ocean. (See the map on page 19.)

The seven physical regions of North America offer great

The red fox is native to North America.

14 ★ Chapter 1

contrasts. In some regions, the land is fertile. There, farmers plant crops and reap rich harvests. Other regions have natural resources such as coal and oil.

Pacific Coast

The westernmost region of North America is the Pacific Coast. It includes high mountain ranges that stretch from Alaska to Mexico. In the United States, some of these western ranges hug the Pacific Ocean. The Cascades and Sierra Nevada* stand a bit farther inland. Some important cities of the Pacific Coast are Seattle, Portland, San Francisco, and Los Angeles.

An important feature of the Pacific Coast region is the San Andreas Fault. This is a

---

*Sierra (see EHR uh) is the Spanish word for mountain range. Nevada is Spanish for snowy. Spanish explorers were the first to see these snow-covered mountains.

600-mile (970 km) fracture in the Earth's crust. It runs through California from northwest to southeast. Movement of the Earth's crust along this fault causes earthquakes.

In 1906, a powerful earthquake shook the city of San Francisco. The tremors and fires that followed destroyed thousands of buildings and killed some 700 people. In 1994, another strong earthquake caused significant damage and loss of life in Los Angeles.

Intermountain region

East of the coast ranges is the Intermountain region. It is a very rugged region of mountain peaks, high plateaus, deep canyons, and deserts. The Grand Canyon, which is more than 1 mile (1.6 km) deep, and the Great Salt Lake are natural features of this region. Salt Lake City and Phoenix are among the few major cities of the Intermountain region.

Viewing HISTORY — Mount Rainier

The beauty of the Cascade Mountains can be seen at Mount Rainier National Park in the state of Washington. In spring, colorful wildflowers and evergreen trees contrast sharply with Mount Rainier's snowcap. ★ **In what physical region are the Cascades located?**

Rocky Mountains

The Rocky Mountains stretch from Alaska through Canada into the United States. They include the Bitterroot Range in Idaho and Montana, the Big Horn Mountains in Wyoming, and the Sangre de Cristo Mountains in Colorado and New Mexico. In Mexico, the Rocky Mountains become the Sierra Madre (MAH dray), or mother range.

The Rockies include some of the highest peaks in North America. Many peaks are more than 14,000 feet (4,200 m) high. Throughout history, people have described the mountains' rugged beauty and grandeur.

The Rockies, however, were a serious barrier to settlement of the United States. When settlers moved west in the 1800s, crossing the Rockies posed great hardships. Some people decided to stay and live in the Rockies. Today, Denver is a major city in the region.

Interior Plains

Between the Rockies in the West and the Appalachian Mountains in the East is a large lowland area called the Interior Plains. The dry western part of the Interior Plains is called the Great Plains. The eastern part is called the Central Plains.

According to scientists, a great inland sea once covered the Interior Plains. Today, some parts are rich in coal and petroleum.* Other parts offer fertile soil for farming and grassland for raising cattle. Chicago and Dallas are major cities on the Interior Plains.

Appalachian Mountains

The Appalachian Mountains run along the eastern part of North America. They stretch from Canada in the North to Georgia and Mississippi in the South. The Appalachians have different names in different places. For example, the Green Mountains, Alleghenies, and Great Smokies are all part of the Appalachian Mountains.

The Appalachians are lower and less rugged than the Rockies. The highest Appalachian peak is Mt. Mitchell in North Carolina, which is 6,684 feet (2,037 m) high. Still, early European settlers had a hard time crossing these heavily forested mountains.

Canadian Shield

The Canadian Shield is a lowland area that lies mostly in eastern Canada. The

---

*The Natural Resources map in the Reference Section shows where natural resources are located.

Viewing HISTORY

Interior Plains

Plains cover much of the central United States. They stretch from the Mississippi River to the Rocky Mountains and from Texas (shown at right) to Montana. The region is ideal for raising cattle. ★ **Why is this region ideal for raising cattle?**

▼ *Texas longhorn*

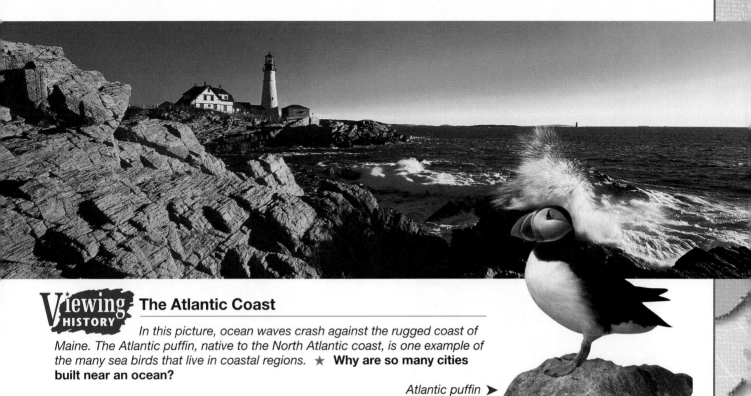

Viewing HISTORY

The Atlantic Coast

In this picture, ocean waves crash against the rugged coast of Maine. The Atlantic puffin, native to the North Atlantic coast, is one example of the many sea birds that live in coastal regions. ★ **Why are so many cities built near an ocean?**

Atlantic puffin ➤

southern part extends into the United States. The region was once an area of high mountains. The mountains were worn away to low hills and plains. The Canadian Shield lacks topsoil for farming, but it is rich in minerals.

Coastal Plains

The region called the Coastal Plains is a fairly flat, lowland area that includes the Atlantic Plain and the Gulf Plain. The Atlantic Plain lies between the Atlantic Ocean and the foothills of the Appalachians. The Atlantic Plain is narrow in the North, where Boston and New York City are located. It broadens in the South to include all of Florida.

Another part of the Coastal Plains is the Gulf Plain, which lies along the Gulf of Mexico. The Gulf Plain has large deposits of petroleum. New Orleans and Houston are major cities of the Gulf Plain.

Hawaiian Islands

The Hawaiian Islands lie far out in the Pacific, about 2,400 miles (3,860 km) west of California. There are eight large islands and many small islands.

The islands are the visible tops of volcanoes that erupted through the floor of the Pacific Ocean. Some volcanoes are still active. Mauna Loa, on the island of Hawaii, is an active volcano that rises 13,680 feet (4,170 m) above sea level.

Rivers and Lakes

Great river systems crisscross North America. They collect runoff water from rains and melting snows and carry it into the oceans.

The mighty Mississippi

The Mississippi and Missouri rivers make up the longest and most important river system in the United States. This river system carries water through the Interior Plains into the Gulf of Mexico.

Many **tributaries,** or streams and smaller rivers, flow into the Mississippi-Missouri river system. Among these tributaries are the Ohio, Tennessee, Arkansas, and Platte rivers. These and other rivers provide water for the rich farmlands of the Interior Plains.

The Mississippi River also serves as a means of transportation. Today, barges carry freight up and down the river. As in the past, people travel by boat on the river.

The mighty Mississippi has inspired many admiring descriptions. Among them is this one from the 1937 film *The River:*

> 66 The Mississippi River runs to the Gulf.
> Carrying every drop of water, that flows down two thirds of the continent,
> Carrying every brook and rill, rivulet and creek,
> Carrying all the rivers that run down two thirds of the continent.
> The Mississippi runs to the Gulf of Mexico. 99

The Colorado River

The Colorado River is another important river. It begins in the Rocky Mountains and flows through Colorado, Utah, Arizona, and Nevada. It forms the border between California and Arizona as it flows toward the Gulf of California. Smaller rivers feed into the Colorado. These include the Green River and the San Juan River.

The Colorado River created the Grand Canyon in Arizona. For millions of years, the river rushed over layers of rock, carving a deeper and deeper channel. Today, the Grand Canyon is one mile (1.6 km) deep and 18 miles (29 km) wide in some places.

There are several dams along the course of the Colorado River. These dams hold back the flow of the river. They help provide water and electricity to the people of the Southwest.

International borders

The Rio Grande and the St. Lawrence River serve as political boundaries. The Rio Grande is part of the border between the United States and Mexico. The St. Lawrence is part of the border with Canada.

Five large lakes, called the Great Lakes, also form part of the border between the United States and Canada. The Great Lakes are Superior, Michigan, Huron, Erie, and Ontario. Today, canals connect the Great Lakes, forming a major inland waterway that is important for commerce.

Weather and Climate

North America has a variety of weather patterns and climates. **Weather** is the condition of the Earth's atmosphere at any given time and place. It may be hot or cold, rainy or dry, or something in between.

Climate is the average weather of a place over a period of 20 to 30 years. Two main aspects of climate are temperature and **precipitation** (pree sihp uh TAY shuhn), or water that falls in the form of rain, sleet, hail, or snow.

Several factors affect climate. One factor is distance from the Equator. Lands near the Equator usually are hot and wet all year. Lands near the North and South poles are cold all year. **Altitude,** or height above sea

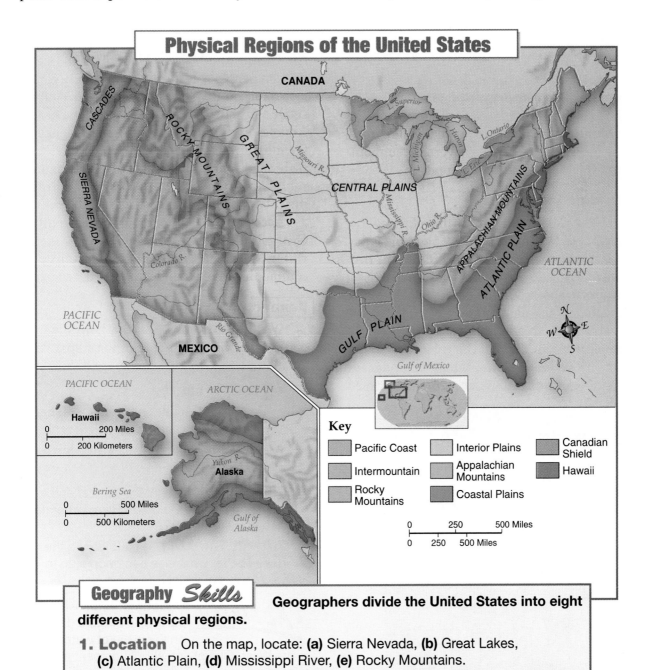

Physical Regions of the United States

Key

- Pacific Coast
- Intermountain
- Rocky Mountains
- Interior Plains
- Appalachian Mountains
- Coastal Plains
- Canadian Shield
- Hawaii

Geography Skills Geographers divide the United States into eight different physical regions.

1. **Location** On the map, locate: **(a)** Sierra Nevada, **(b)** Great Lakes, **(c)** Atlantic Plain, **(d)** Mississippi River, **(e)** Rocky Mountains.
2. **Region** Through what three physical regions does the Mississippi River flow?
3. **Critical Thinking** Why do you think more people live on the Pacific Coast than in the Rocky Mountains?

Why Study History?

Because We All Need Water

★ ★

Historical Background

In the past century, the demand for water has risen greatly. More and more water is diverted from rivers to serve people's needs. As a result, some major rivers throughout the world have begun to run dry.

Connections to Today

The Colorado River is one of those rivers. (See page 18.) Today, the Colorado rarely empties into the Pacific Ocean. Instead, it gradually shrinks until its last traces evaporate in the desert heat of Mexico.

Today, the demand for Colorado River water is greater than the supply. In 1922, an agreement divided the river's water among seven western states. Other agreements guaranteed water rights to Native Americans and Mexico. Now, more than 20 million people rely on the Colorado River.

Colorado River water disputes are often settled in court. Large cities such as Los Angeles and San Diego frequently accuse farmers of wasting water through old-fashioned irrigation methods. The farmers reply that cities are overbuilding and drawing too much water.

According to California Congressman George Miller, "The heart of the West is water. . . . It will be the most important commodity in dictating the future."

Connections to You

We all need water. You can help save water by taking these and other steps.

- Take short showers.
- Fix leaky faucets.
- Do only full loads in the dishwasher and clothes washer.
- Wash automobiles and water lawns infrequently.

1. Comprehension   Why do past agreements on sharing Colorado River water not meet today's needs?

2. Critical Thinking   In addition to the ideas above, what else can people do to help conserve water?

 Debating   Work with a partner to stage a debate on the issue of water rights in the West. One of you should present a farmer's viewpoint. The other should present a city official's viewpoint.

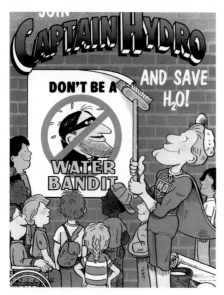

In California, this poster urges young people to conserve water.

The Philippines

United States

Weather Connections

Conditions around the world can affect your weather. Mount Pinatubo (above, left), a volcano in the Philippines, erupted in 1991. Gases and dust blocked some of the sun's rays and lowered temperatures in much of the world. In North America, though, the eruption led to a milder than average winter. ★ **What is the average winter like in the area where you live?**

level, also affects climate. In general, highlands are cooler than lowlands. Other factors that influence climate include ocean currents, wind currents, and mountains.

In the Pacific Ocean, wind and ocean currents interact to create the cyclical phenomenon called the El Niño (ehl NEEN yoh) Southern Oscillation. The temperature of Pacific Ocean water plays a major role in the phenomenon. During an El Niño period, the surface water of the eastern Pacific Ocean warms. During a La Niña (lah NEEN yah) period, ocean surface temperatures cool.

The Southern Oscillation affects weather patterns in nearly three quarters of the world. In the United States, for example, the warm ocean water of an El Niño helps to cause frequent and powerful storms in California and the Southwest. In Northeastern states, meanwhile, El Niño usually contributes to milder than normal winters.

North American Climates

The United States has 10 major climates. Look at the map on page 22 to see the locations of these climates.

Marine

The strip of land from southern Alaska to northern California is sometimes called the Pacific Northwest. This region has a mild, moist marine climate, with warm summers and cool winters. Moist winds from the Pacific Ocean bring mild temperatures and moisture that condenses and falls as rain or snow. The Pacific Northwest has many forests. This makes it the center of the lumber industry.

Mediterranean

Much of California has a Mediterranean climate. Winters are mild and wet. Summers are hot and dry. Farmers and fruit growers

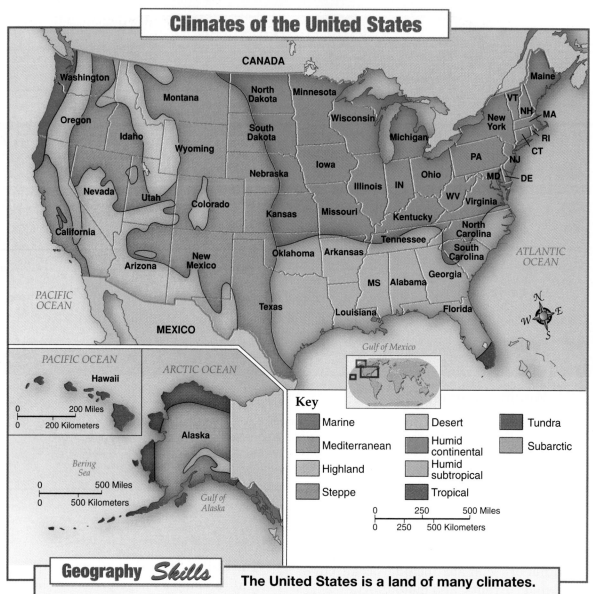

Climates of the United States

Key

Marine	Desert	Tundra
Mediterranean	Humid continental	Subarctic
Highland	Humid subtropical	
Steppe	Tropical	

Geography Skills

The United States is a land of many climates.

1. Location   On the map, locate: **(a)** New York, **(b)** Ohio, **(c)** Arizona.

2. Place   What states have three or more different climates?

3. Critical Thinking   **(a)** Identify a state or part of a state where water is probably scarce. **(b)** Why is water in such short supply there?

must often irrigate the land. Because of the climate, this region produces crops that cannot be grown anywhere else in the country. For example, it produces almost all the nation's almonds, walnuts, olives, apricots, dates, and figs.

Highland

In the Cascades, Sierra Nevada, and Rocky Mountains, a highland climate brings cooler temperatures. Conditions in a highland climate vary according to altitude. For example, Mount Rainier in the state of Washington, at over 14,000 feet (4,200 m) above sea level, is snow-capped all year. During the spring and summer, runoff from melting snows provides water to the major rivers of the West. Many people vacation in the mountains so they can participate in winter sports. In summer, vacationers come to the mountains to escape the heat and enjoy the cool highland temperatures.

Desert and steppe

Much of the southwestern United States has a desert climate, with hot days and cold nights. This dry region stretches as far east as the Rockies. In the deserts of Nevada, Arizona, and southeastern California, there is almost no rainfall. In many areas, people irrigate the land so that they can grow crops.

East of the Rockies are the Great Plains. They have a steppe climate with limited rainfall. Summers are hot and winters are cold. Huge herds of buffaloes once grazed on the short grasses of the Great Plains. In the 1800s, settlers brought cattle to graze on the plains.

Humid continental

The Central Plains and the northeastern United States have a humid continental climate. This climate, with mild summers and cold winters, has more precipitation than the steppe. Tall prairie grasses once covered the Central Plains. Today, American farmers raise much of the world's food in this region.

At one time, the humid continental climate supported forests that covered much of the northeastern United States. Early European settlers cleared forests to build settlements and to grow crops. However, many forests remain, and the lumber industry thrives in some areas.

Tropical and humid subtropical

Southern Florida and Hawaii, located near the Equator, have tropical climates. The hot, humid conditions make these regions good for growing such crops as pineapples and citrus fruits. The warm tropical temperatures are also ideal for the tourism industry.

The southeastern United States has a humid subtropical climate. Warm temperatures and regular rainfall make this region ideal for growing crops such as cotton, soybeans, and peanuts.

Tundra and subarctic

Northern and western coastal regions of Alaska have a tundra climate. It is cold all year round. The rest of Alaska and northern Canada have a subarctic climate with long, cold winters and short summers. Farming is limited to a small fertile valley in southern Alaska. Almost one third of Alaska is covered by forest. Therefore, logging and the production of paper pulp are important industries.

★ Section 3 Review ★

Recall

1. **Locate** (a) North America, (b) Pacific Coast, (c) Intermountain region, (d) Rocky Mountains, (e) Interior Plains, (f) Appalachian Mountains, (g) Mississippi River, (h) Great Lakes.
2. **Define** (a) isthmus, (b) mountain, (c) elevation, (d) hill, (e) plain, (f) plateau, (g) tributary, (h) weather, (i) climate, (j) precipitation, (k) altitude, (l) El Niño.

Comprehension

3. Name the eight physical regions of the United States and describe one feature of each region.

4. How do rivers and lakes benefit the economy of the United States?
5. Describe the climate of the region where you live.

Critical Thinking and Writing

6. **Drawing Conclusions** Do you think more people live in the Appalachian Mountains or in the Rocky Mountains? Why?
7. **Making Decisions** If you could live anywhere in the United States, which physical region and climate would you choose? Explain.

★ ★

Activity **Making a Chart** You are the graphic designer for a popular vacation and travel magazine. Create a chart that lists and describes the 10 major climates of the United States.

volcano

lake

hill

gulf

cape

strait

island

archipelago

Dictionary of Geographic Terms

The list below includes important geographic terms and their definitions. Sometimes, the definition of a term includes an example in parentheses. An asterisk (*) indicates that the term is illustrated above.

altitude   height above sea level.

*archipelago   chain of islands. (Hawaiian Islands)

basin   low-lying land area that is surrounded by land of higher elevation; land area that is drained by a river system. (Great Basin)

*bay   part of a body of water that is partly enclosed by land. (San Francisco Bay)

canal   waterway made by people that is used to drain or irrigate land or to connect two bodies of water. (Erie Canal)

*canyon   deep, narrow valley with high, steep sides. (Grand Canyon)

*cape   narrow point of land that extends into a body of water. (Cape Cod)

climate   pattern of weather in a particular place over a period of 20 to 30 years.

*coast   land that borders the sea. (Pacific Coast)

coastal plain   lowland area lying along the ocean. (Gulf Plain)

continent   any of seven large landmasses on the Earth's surface. (Africa, Antarctica, Asia, Australia, Europe, North America, South America)

continental divide   mountain ridge that separates river systems flowing toward opposite sides of a continent.

*delta   land area formed by soil that is deposited at the mouth of a river. (Mississippi Delta)

desert   area that has little or no moisture or vegetation. (Painted Desert)

directional arrow   arrow on a map that always points north.

downstream   in the direction of a river's flow; toward a river's mouth.

elevation   the height above sea level.

fall line   place where rivers drop from a plateau or foothills to a coastal plain, usually marked by many waterfalls.

foothills   low hills at the base of a mountain range.

*gulf   arm of an ocean or sea that is partly enclosed by land, usually larger than a bay. (Gulf of Mexico)

hemisphere   half of the Earth. (Western Hemisphere)

*hill   area of raised land that is lower and more rounded than a mountain. (San Juan Hill)

*island   land area that is surrounded by water. (Puerto Rico)

Figure labels: source of a river, mountain, plain, canyon, valley, plateau, river, tributary, isthmus, bay, delta, mouth of a river, coast, peninsula, sea

*isthmus narrow strip of land joining two large land areas or joining a peninsula to a mainland. (Isthmus of Panama)

*lake body of water surrounded entirely by land. (Lake Superior)

latitude the distance in degrees north and south from the Equator.

longitude the distance in degrees east or west from the Prime Meridian.

marsh lowland with moist soils and tall grasses.

*mountain high, steep, rugged land that rises sharply above the surrounding land. (Mount McKinley)

mountain range chain of connected mountains. (Allegheny Mountains)

*mouth of a river place where a river or stream empties into a large body of water.

ocean any of the four largest bodies of salt water on the Earth's surface. (Arctic, Atlantic, Indian, and Pacific Oceans)

*peninsula piece of land that is surrounded by water on three sides. (Delmarva Peninsula)

piedmont rolling land along the base of a mountain range.

*plain broad area of fairly level land that is generally close to sea level.

*plateau large area of high, flat, or gently rolling land.

prairie large area of natural grassland with few or no trees or hills.

*river large stream of water that empties into an ocean or lake or another river. (Pecos River)

*sea large body of salt water that is smaller than an ocean. (Caribbean Sea)

sea level average level of the ocean's surface from which the height of land or depth of the ocean is measured.

*source of a river place where a river begins.

steppe flat, treeless land with limited moisture.

*strait narrow channel that connects two larger bodies of water. (Straits of Florida)

*tributary stream or small river that flows into a larger stream or river.

upstream in the direction that is against a river's flow; toward a river's source.

*valley land that lies between hills or mountains. (Shenandoah Valley)

*volcano cone-shaped mountain formed by an outpouring of lava—hot, liquid rock—from a crack in the Earth's surface. (Mount St. Helens or Mauna Loa)

weather condition of the air at any given time and place.

Review and Activities

★ Sum It Up ★

Section 1 Five Themes of Geography
▶ Geography is the study of people, their environments, and their resources.
▶ The five themes of geography help show the connection between geography and history.
▶ The five themes of geography are location, place, interaction, movement, and region.

Section 2 Maps and Mapmaking
▶ Each type of map projection has advantages and disadvantages.
▶ Latitude and longitude lines on maps enable us to locate places exactly.
▶ The use of computers and satellites has made modern mapmaking more accurate than the mapmaking of centuries ago.

Section 3 American Lands and Climates
▶ Mountains, plains, and many other types of landforms can be found in North America.
▶ There are eight major physical regions in the United States.
▶ Rivers and lakes provide many benefits to the people of the United States.
▶ A variety of factors interact to produce weather and climate conditions.
▶ The United States has 10 major climates.
▶ The climate of a region helps to determine some of the economic activities that take place in the region.

CD-ROM Review For additional review of the major ideas of Chapter 1, see *Guide to the Essentials of American History* or *Interactive Student Tutorial CD-ROM,* which contains interactive review activities, graphic organizers, and practice tests.

◻ Reviewing the Chapter

Define These Terms
Match each term with the correct definition.

Column 1
1. history
2. latitude
3. longitude
4. cartographer
5. precipitation

Column 2
a. lines measuring distance east and west from the Prime Meridian
b. a mapmaker
c. lines measuring distance north and south from the Equator
d. an account of what has happened in people's lives
e. water that falls as rain, sleet, or snow

Explore the Main Ideas
1. How do geographers generally describe place?
2. How do people interact with their environment?
3. Why do all flat maps distort the shapes of continents and oceans?
4. Locate and describe three physical regions of the United States.
5. Why is the Mississippi River such an important waterway?
6. Locate and describe three climates found in the United States.

◻ Geography Activity

Match the letters on the map with the following places:
1. North America, **2.** South America, **3.** Atlantic Ocean, **4.** Pacific Ocean, **5.** Isthmus of Panama, **6.** Great Lakes.
Location What ocean lies to the east of North America?

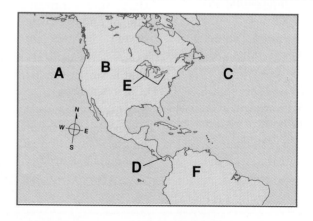

☐ Critical Thinking and Writing

1. **Applying Information** Using the themes of geography, **(a)** describe the special geographic characteristics of the place where you live, **(b)** describe an example of how people in your community have adapted to or changed the natural environment.

2. **Evaluating Information** Which is more reliable: a map of North America from the 1500s or a map of North America from the 1900s? Explain the reasons for your choice.

3. **Synthesizing Information** Look at the picture of Mount Rainier that appears in Section 3 of this chapter. **(a)** Describe the physical region in which Mount Rainier is located. **(b)** Describe the climate of that region.

4. **Exploring Unit Themes** **Origins** How can the climate of a region affect people's economic activities in that region?

☐ Using Primary Sources

In 1845, Lansford W. Hastings wrote a guide for people traveling to the West. In it he made the following predictions:

> ❝ The time is not distant, when those wild forests, trackless plains, untrodden valleys . . . will present one grand scene of continuous improvements . . . when those vast forests shall have disappeared before the hardy pioneer; those extensive plains shall abound with innumerable herds of domestic animals; those fertile valleys shall groan under the weight of their abundant products. ❞

Source: *The Emigrants' Guide to Oregon and California,* Lansford W. Hastings, 1845.

Recognizing Points of View **(a)** What changes did Hastings expect from human interaction with the environment? **(b)** How did he feel about the predicted changes?

ACTIVITY BANK

▶ Interdisciplinary Activity

Exploring the Arts Do research to find a song or poem about an American river. Read or sing the composition to the class. Then lead a group discussion on what the song or poem says about the river.

▶ Career Skills Activity

Cartographers On a large sheet of paper, create a map of the United States. On the map, draw and label the 50 states. Then label the major physical regions and landforms of the United States.

▶ Citizenship Activity

Using a Political Map Find a map that shows the Congressional districts in your state. Identify the district in which you live. Through research, find out the name of your district's representative in Congress. If an issue or question concerns you, you can write about it to your Congressperson and ask for a response.

Internet Activity

Use the Internet to find the official site of NASA (National Aeronautics and Space Administration). There you will find images of the Earth taken by satellites orbiting the Earth. Select a picture that interests you and, if possible, print it out. In a written report, describe what the picture shows and explain why the picture might be useful to a cartographer.

EYEWITNESS Journal

You are traveling across the United States from somewhere on the Atlantic Coast to somewhere on the Pacific Coast. List all the states that you are traveling through. Also, list and describe all the physical regions that you are crossing.

Chapter 2 The First Americans

Prehistory–1600

Thousands of years ago, hunters from Asia followed herds of wild animals to the Americas. As they gradually spread through North and South America, they developed a variety of cultures. The economic activities, religious beliefs, and societies of these first Americans reflected the environments in which they lived, from the icy north to the dry desert of the Southwest. Farther south, in Mexico and Central and South America, several great civilizations arose.

The world of these first Americans changed dramatically after Europeans reached American shores. At the same time, aspects of Native American culture spread to other parts of the globe.

Why Study History?

European settlers adapted many Native American customs. These included sports, such as lacrosse. Today, as in the past, sports play a role in society that goes far beyond just having fun. To focus on this connection, see this chapter's *Why Study History?* feature, "Sports Are Important in Our Culture."

American Events

300–900 Mayan cities flourish in Mexico and Central America

1100–1200 Anasazis build cliff dwellings in Southwest

Prehistory   1000   1200

World Events

30,000–15,000 Years Ago World Event
Hunters from Asia cross land bridge to the Americas

1013 World Event
Danish Vikings conquer England

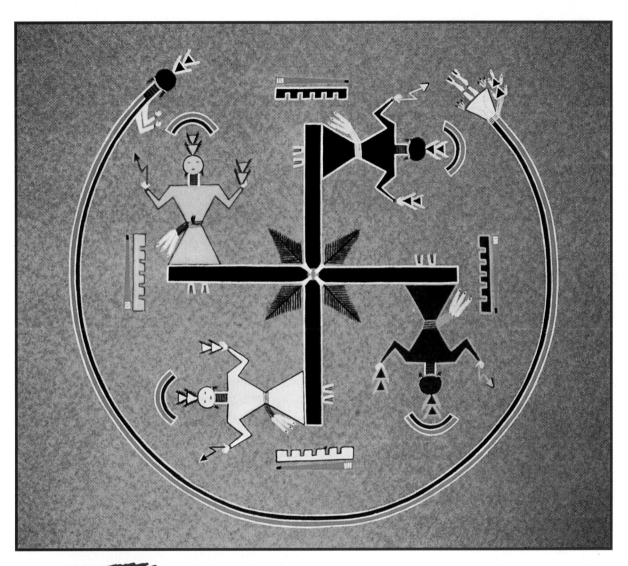

Native American Art

Viewing HISTORY

The Navajos used sand paintings in healing and religious ceremonies. This painting shows a whirlwind, or tornado, as people on spinning logs. Navajo culture arose in the American Southwest. Dozens of other Native American cultures emerged in the varied environments of North and South America. ★ **How does this painting reflect the desert environment of the Navajos?**

1400s ●
Aztecs build powerful empire in Mexico

Early 1500s ●
Incas control the largest empire in the Americas

┌─●**1570s**
Peoples of the Eastern Woodlands form the Iroquois League to promote peace

1200   **1400**   **1600**

1300s World Event
West African kingdom of Mali reaches its height

1492 World Event
Columbus reaches the Americas

★ **29**

1 Early People and Cultures

As You Read

Explore These Questions
- Where did the first Americans come from?
- How do archaeologists learn about the past?
- How did early people adapt to the desert Southwest?

Define
- glacier
- artifact
- archaeology
- culture
- adobe
- pueblo
- drought

Identify
- Native American
- Mound Builder
- Hohokam
- Anasazi

SETTING the Scene Crouched low, the small band of hunters crept slowly forward. Ahead, a herd of bison grazed at the edge of a swamp. At a signal, the hunters leaped up, shouting loudly. The startled herd stampeded into the swamp. As the bison struggled in the deep mud, the hunters hurled their spears.

Scenes much like this one took place on the Great Plains more than 10,000 years ago. Tracking herds of bison or woolly mammths, skillful hunters were among the first people to settle the Americas. Over many thousands of years, their descendants spread out across two continents. In the process, they developed many different ways of life.

Woolly mammoth bones found in Arizona

The First Americans Migrate From Asia

Like other early people, the first Americans left no written records to tell us where they came from or when they arrived. However, scientists have found evidence to suggest that the first people reached the Americas sometime during the last ice age.

The last ice age

According to geologists, the Earth has gone through four ice ages. The last one took place between 100,000 and 10,000 years ago.

During the last ice age, thick sheets of ice, called **glaciers,** spread out from the arctic regions. Almost one third of the Earth was buried under these sheets of ice. In North America, glaciers stretched across Canada and reached as far south as Kentucky.

As they moved, glaciers changed the lands they covered. They pushed soil, rocks, and huge boulders across the land. They created islands such as Long Island, New York, as well as Nantucket and Martha's Vineyard off the coast of Massachusetts. Water from melting glaciers drained into channels, creating rivers such as the Missouri.

Crossing the land bridge

Because glaciers locked up water from the oceans, sea levels fell. As a result, land that had been under water was uncovered. In the far north, a land bridge joined Siberia in northeastern Asia to Alaska in North

America. Today, this land bridge is under the Bering Strait.

Scientists think that the first Americans were probably hunters. Traveling in small bands, they followed herds of woolly mammoth, bison, and other game across the land bridge. Some groups may have wandered along the southern coast of the land bridge, catching fish and sea mammals.

Experts date the arrival of these first Americans anywhere from 30,000 to 15,000 years ago. Once they reached the Americas, the continuing search for better hunting grounds led the newcomers across the land. Over thousands of years, they spread out through North America, Central America, and South America.

Adapting to new conditions

About 12,000 years ago, the ice age ended. Temperatures rose around the globe. Glaciers melted, and the ocean once more covered the land bridge. At about the same time, the woolly mammoths and mastodons died out.

The people of the Americas adapted to the new conditions. They hunted smaller animals, gathered wild berries and grains, and caught fish.

Then, about 5,000 years ago, some people learned to grow crops such as corn, beans, and squash. Farming changed those people's lives. People who farmed no longer had to move constantly in search of food. Instead, they built the first permanent villages in the Americas. As farming methods improved, villagers produced more food. In turn, the increased food supply allowed populations to grow.

Studying the First Americans

Today, experts in many fields are working to develop a clearer picture of the first Americans. Some are studying the remains of ancient people of northeast Asia. They hope to learn how these Asian people might be related to the first Americans.

Other experts are analyzing the languages of Native American groups today. **Native Americans** are the descendants of the

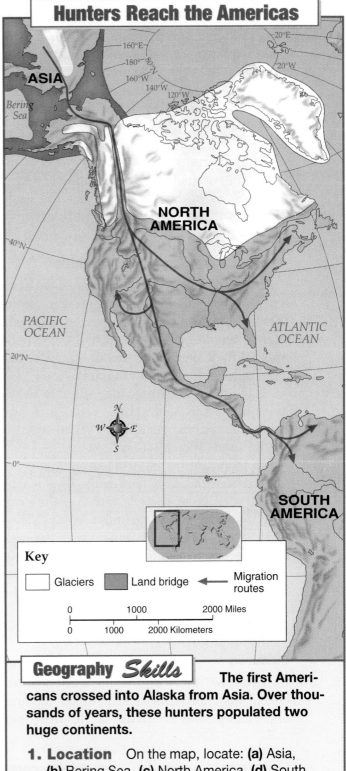

Hunters Reach the Americas

Geography Skills
The first Americans crossed into Alaska from Asia. Over thousands of years, these hunters populated two huge continents.

1. **Location** On the map, locate: **(a)** Asia, **(b)** Bering Sea, **(c)** North America, **(d)** South America.

2. **Movement** In which direction did early hunters travel from Asia to reach North America?

3. **Critical Thinking** Why do you think many of the first Americans continued to travel southward after crossing the land bridge?

first people to reach the Americas thousands of years ago. Through the study of Native American languages, scholars are trying to trace how these people spread out across the Americas.

Still other scholars are examining stone tools, weapons, baskets, and carvings found across the Americas. Objects such as these made by humans are called **artifacts** (AHRT uh faktz). Artifacts are the building blocks of **archaeology** (ahr kee AHL uh jee), the study of evidence left by early people in order to find out about their way of life.

Artifacts provide valuable clues

By studying artifacts, archaeologists can learn much about the people who made them. A finely carved arrowhead suggests that a people knew how to make weapons and hunt. Woven plant fibers suggest that they were skilled basket makers.

Each object can provide valuable information. At the same time, each new find raises questions such as, "When was it made?" and "Who made it?"

In laboratories, experts use technology to analyze new finds. By testing the level of carbon in a piece of pottery or bone, they can date it to within a few hundred years. They might study kernels of ancient corn through a microscope to find out about the climate in which it grew. They might compare clay pots from different areas to find out about the people who made them.

Forming theories about ancient cultures

From artifacts and other evidence, archaeologists form theories about the cultures of ancient people. A **culture** is the entire way of life that a people has developed. It includes their homes, clothing, economy, arts, and government. It also includes the customs, ideas, beliefs, and skills that they pass on from generation to generation.

Often, very little evidence survives about an ancient people. Sometimes, archaeologists find evidence in unexpected places, through sheer luck. A flood might wash away a river bank and uncover ancient bones. A bulldozer clearing land might dig up a buried campsite. Each new find or new method of studying ancient artifacts helps to fill in the story of early Americans.

In their search for evidence about the past, archaeologists often dig up ancient sites. In recent years, however, they have grown more aware of the need to respect Native American landmarks and traditions. Government officials, too, have become more respectful of Native American concerns. Some laws have been passed to protect Native American burial grounds.

The Mound Builders

Among the artifacts that archaeologists have found in North America are thousands of earthen mounds. The mounds are scattered across a region stretching from the Appalachian Mountains to the Mississippi Valley and from Wisconsin to Florida. Scholars call the people who built these earthworks **Mound Builders.** The Mound Builders lived at various times from about 3,000 years ago until the 1700s. The two main groups were the Hopewells and the Mississippians.

Purpose of the mounds

The mounds served different purposes. The first mounds were burial grounds, probably for important leaders. Inside the mounds, archaeologists have found carved pipes, stone sculptures, and copper weapons, tools, and ornaments. They have also found shells from the Gulf of Mexico and turquoise from the Southwest. This evidence shows that the Mound Builders traded with people from other parts of North America.

Some mounds were used for religious ceremonies. They are shaped like pyramids

Connections With Geography

In the southwestern United States, geography has helped archaeologists study early cultures. The dry climate has preserved baskets, bags, sandals, nets, and other items dating back approximately 2,000 years. In a damper climate, many of these items might have rotted away.

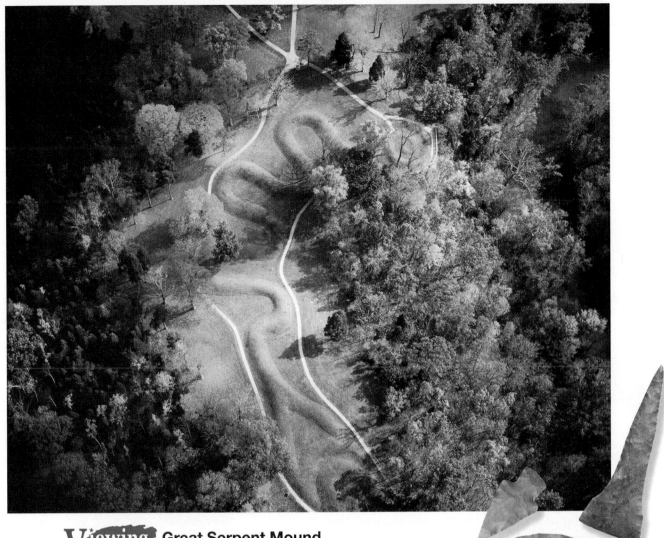

Great Serpent Mound

The ancient Americans known as the Mound Builders left behind thousands of mounds. One of the largest is the Great Serpent Mound, shown here. It twists across the Ohio landscape for more than 1,200 feet (365 m). ★ **Why do you think present-day archaeologists are eager to examine early burial mounds?**

▲ *Flints found at Great Serpent Mound*

with flat tops. On the flat surfaces, the people built temples and homes for the ruling class.

More than 2,000 years ago, Hopewell builders created the twisting Great Serpent Mound in present-day Ohio. From above, it looks like a snake with a coiled tail. The meaning of this and other animal-shaped mounds remains a mystery.

Monk's Mound

Some time between 700 and 1500, the Mississippians built a large city at Cahokia (kah HOH kee ah), in present-day Illinois. As many as 30,000 people may have lived there at one time. Over the years, the Cahokians moved tons of soil, basketload by basketload, to build Monk's Mound. This vast platform mound covers 16 acres—equal to $14^{1}/_{2}$ football fields! Hundreds of other smaller mounds stand nearby.

The Mississippians built a wooden fence around Cahokia. Beyond this fence, they placed circles of evenly spaced posts. Some archaeologists think the posts served as a kind of calendar. From the top of Monk's Mound, rulers could see the shadows cast by the posts. Shorter shadows announced the

HISTORY HAPPENED HERE

Mesa Verde National Park

The cliff dwellings at Mesa Verde were abandoned more than 700 years ago. Yet these spectacular buildings still stand. They remind us of the skill of Native Americans who carved entire villages out of the canyons and cliffs of southwest Colorado. Cliff Palace (left) is the largest complex at Mesa Verde. It contains more than 200 rooms, with sections up to four stories tall. The park also has a museum where you can see many Anasazi artifacts.

★ **To learn more about this historic site, write:** *Superintendent, Mesa Verde National Park, Colorado 81330.*

◀ *Clay cup from Mesa Verde*

coming of spring. Longer ones showed that autumn was near. To farming people like the Mississippians, knowing when to plant and when to harvest crops was important.

Early Cultures of the Southwest

Through careful study, archaeologists have also learned much about the early people of the American Southwest. This desert region may seem like a poor place to farm. Annual rainfall is only 5 to 10 inches (13 to 25 cm). In the daytime, temperatures can soar above 100° Fahrenheit (38°C). Cactus and sagebrush cover the desert floor.

Still, at least 3,000 years ago, people in the Southwest learned to grow crops such as corn. In time, several major farming societies, including the Hohokams (hoh HOH kahmz) and Anasazis (ah nuh SAH zeez), made their homes there.

The **Hohokams** lived in present-day southern Arizona. About 2,000 years ago,

they developed ways to turn the dry desert into fertile farmland. They dug a vast system of irrigation ditches to bring water to dry land. The irrigation ditches channeled water from the Salt and Gila rivers into fields that then produced corn, squash, and beans.

In the late 1800s, archaeologists began to study thousands of abandoned stone buildings that dotted the Southwest. Most were built between 750 and 1300.

Who built these structures? Archaeologists asked the Navajos, the Native Americans who live in the region today. The Navajos replied that the mounds were built by the Anasazis. In the Navajo language, Anasazi means "ancient one."

Anasazi pueblos

As the Hohokams did, the **Anasazis** farmed the desert by using irrigation. The Anasazis built large, multistoried houses.

Walls were made of stone and sun-dried bricks, called **adobe.** When the Spanish explored the Southwest in the early 1500s, they called these houses **pueblos** (PWEHB lohz), or villages. Similar in some ways to modern apartment buildings, pueblos could shelter hundreds of families.

Anasazi pottery

At Pueblo Bonito, in New Mexico's Chaco Canyon, a giant house was once home to 1,000 people. Its 800 rooms are tiny, but the Anasazis spent much of their time in sunny, outdoor courtyards. The house has no stairways or hallways. To reach rooms on the upper floors, people climbed steep ladders.

Cliff dwellings

Sometime between 1,000 and 800 years ago, some Anasazis sought protection from warlike neighbors. To make their villages harder to attack, they built adobe houses along the cliffs that dotted the region. Toeholds cut into the rock let the Anasazis climb up and down the cliff walls. On top of the cliffs, they planted corn and other crops.

A network of roads connected Anasazi villages. Along these roads, traders carried cotton, sandals made from yucca leaves, and blankets woven from turkey feathers. Some Anasazi traders headed into present-day Mexico to trade with people there.

In the late 1200s, the Anasazis abandoned most of their villages. Archaeologists think that a **drought,** or long dry spell, hit the region. One legend speaks of such a disaster:

> 66 Snow ceased in the north and the west; rain ceased in the south and the east; the mists of the mountains above were drunk up; the waters of the valleys below were dried up.... Our ancients who dwelt in the cliffs fled ... when the rain stopped long, long ago. 99

Later, some of the Anasazis may have gone back to their homes. Most, however, became part of other cultures. Today, descendants of these early people preserve traditions of the ancient Anasazi culture.

★ Section 1 Review ★

Recall

1. **Identify** (a) Native American, (b) Mound Builder, (c) Hohokam, (d) Anasazi.
2. **Define** (a) glacier, (b) artifact, (c) archaeology, (d) culture, (e) adobe, (f) pueblo, (g) drought.

Comprehension

3. How did ancient people first arrive in the Americas?
4. Describe three kinds of evidence that archaeologists study.

5. (a) How did the Hohokams farm the desert? (b) Why did the Anasazis abandon their villages?

Critical Thinking and Writing

6. **Applying Information** Review the subsection The First Americans Migrate From Asia on page 30. How does the information in this subsection support the idea that geography affects history?
7. **Recognizing Points of View** Why have archaeologists and Native Americans sometimes clashed over the digging up of burial grounds?

★ ★

History AND YOU

Activity **Writing a Survival Plan** Unplug that computer! Circumstances have forced you to live for a year in the desert Southwest. Write a plan explaining how you might adapt to your environment, as early Native Americans did. Consider all your options!

People of North America

★ ★

As You Read

Explore These Questions
- Why did many different cultures develop in North America?
- What ways of life did Native Americans develop?
- What role did religion play in the lives of Native Americans?

Define
- culture area
- tribe
- igloo
- kayak
- potlatch
- kiva
- hogan
- travois
- tepee
- long house
- clan
- sachem

Identify
- Inuit
- Pueblo
- kachina
- Apache
- Navajo
- Natchez
- Iroquois
- League of the Iroquois

 SETTING the Scene When Italian explorer Christopher Columbus reached the Americas in 1492, he thought he had reached the East Indies, a group of islands off the coast of Asia. He called the people he met "los Indios," or "the Indians." Soon, all Europeans were calling the people of the Americas Indians. By the time they realized Columbus's error, they were used to the term.

The name Indian is misleading for another, more important, reason. Native Americans do not belong to a single group. In Columbus's time, as now, Native Americans included many different people with many distinct cultures. In North America alone, Native Americans spoke hundreds of languages. Their cultures also varied greatly, from simple to highly complex.

Culture Areas and Tribes

The map on page 39 shows the 10 major culture areas of North America, north of Mexico. A **culture area** is a region in which people share a similar way of life.

Within each culture area, there were many different tribes. A **tribe** is a group of villages or settlements that shares common customs, language, and rituals. Members of a tribe saw themselves as a distinct people who shared the same origin. Throughout history, tribal organizations have played an important role in Indian life.

The tribe felt a strong bond with the land, plants, and animals in the region where they lived. As they hunted animals or raised crops or gathered wild plants, members of the tribe tried to keep a balance with the forces of the natural world. Their religious ceremonies and daily customs were designed to help them maintain that balance.

People of the Far North

Two culture areas, the Arctic and Subarctic, stretched across the far northern part of North America. In both regions, people adapted to harsh climates. In the Arctic, winter temperatures drop to −30° Fahrenheit (−34° C). Snow stays on the ground much of the year.

Arctic

Frozen seas and icy, treeless plains made up the world of the **Inuits,** the people of the Arctic.* The Inuits used all the limited re-

---

*Inuit, meaning "humans," was the Arctic people's name for themselves. Neighboring people, the Crees, called the Inuits "Eskimos," or "Eaters of Raw Meat."

sources of their environment in order to survive. In summer, they collected driftwood from the ocean shores to make tools and shelters. In winter, they built igloos, or houses of snow and ice. Lamps filled with seal oil kept the igloos warm even in the most bitter cold. Inuit women made warm clothing out of furs and waterproof boots out of sealskins.

Because food was scarce, the Inuits could not live in the same place all year round. In winter, large bands set up camp at a favorite spot near the sea. There on the thick sea ice, they hunted for seals. In spring, they paddled kayaks (KI aks), or small skin boats, to spear seals, whales, or walruses. When the summer came, they moved inland in smaller bands to hunt caribou or to fish in inland rivers and lakes.

Inuit religious beliefs reflected their close ties to the natural world. Inuits believed that each animal had a spirit. Before the hunt, they offered gifts to the animal they hoped to catch. After a successful hunt, they sang songs of praise and thanks to the animals.

Subarctic

Like their Arctic neighbors, the people of the Subarctic faced a severe environment. They, too, moved from place to place, hunting moose and caribou or fishing in rivers and

Viewing HISTORY — In the Frozen Arctic

In the Arctic region, Inuit hunters moved across an icy landscape in search of food. Inuit carvings reflect the importance of the seals, walruses, and polar bears they depended on for survival. ★ **How did Inuits find shelter during the Arctic winter?**

Inuit carving of a walrus

oceans. They fashioned caribou and rabbit skins into robes and leggings. When Europeans arrived, many Subarctic peoples supplied furs to traders.

People of the Northwest Coast

The people of the Northwest Coast enjoyed a favorable climate and abundant food supplies. They gathered rich harvests of fish from the sea. Sea creatures provided more than just food. In some areas, people caught shellfish, called dentalia, to use as money. The longer the string of dentalia shells, the greater was the value.

In autumn, the rivers were full of salmon. To show their gratitude, the people returned salmon skeletons to the water. They believed that the Salmon Beings would grow new bodies and continue to provide food. The fishers of one Northwest Coast group, the Kwakiutls (kwah kee OOT 'lz), chanted this prayer of thanks when they caught their first fish of the year:

66 We have come to meet alive,
Swimmer,
do not feel wrong about what I have
    done to you,
friend Swimmer,
for that is the reason why you came,
that I may spear you,
that I may eat you,
Supernatural One, you, Long-Life-
    Giver, you Swimmer.
Now protect us, me and my wife. 99

The Northwest Coast people also benefited from nearby forests. They cut down tall cedar trees and floated the timber by water to their villages. There, they split the tree trunks into planks for houses and canoes. From the soft inner bark, they made rope, baskets, and clothes. The forests also were home to deer, moose, and bears that the people hunted for meat and hides.

With plenty of food, the people of the Pacific Northwest could stay in one place. They built permanent villages and prospered from trade with nearby groups.

Within a village, families gained status according to how much they owned. Families sometimes competed for rank. To improve their standing, they held a **potlatch,** or ceremonial dinner, to show off their wealth. The family invited many guests and gave everyone presents. The more the family gave away, the more respect it earned. At one potlatch, which took years for the family to prepare, gifts included 8 canoes, 54 elk skins, 2,000 silver bracelets, 7,000 brass bracelets, and 33,000 blankets!

Other People of the West

Climates and resources varied in other parts of the West. As people adapted to these environments, they developed very different cultures.

Great Basin

The Great Basin lies in the dry Intermountain region of the United States. With little water, few plants or animals survived. As a result, Great Basin people like the Utes (yootz) and Shoshones (shoh SHOH neez) had to spend most of their time looking for food. They hunted rabbits or dug for roots in the desert soil.

Because the land offered so little, only a few related families traveled together in search of food. They had few possessions beyond digging sticks, baskets, and other tools or weapons needed for hunting. When they camped, they built temporary shelters out of willow poles and reeds.

Plateau

The people of the Plateau lived between two mountain ranges: the Rocky Mountains to the east and the Cascades to the west. Their main source of food was fish from rivers, like the Columbia and Fraser, or from smaller streams. They also hunted and gathered roots, nuts, and berries. In winter, they lived in earth houses that were partly underground. In summer, they set up lodges, temporary shelters made by placing rush mats over cottonwood frames.

Some groups traded with the Northwest Coast people and were influenced by their way of life. Others, like the Nez Percés (NEHZ PER sihz), adopted customs from the peoples of the Great Plains.

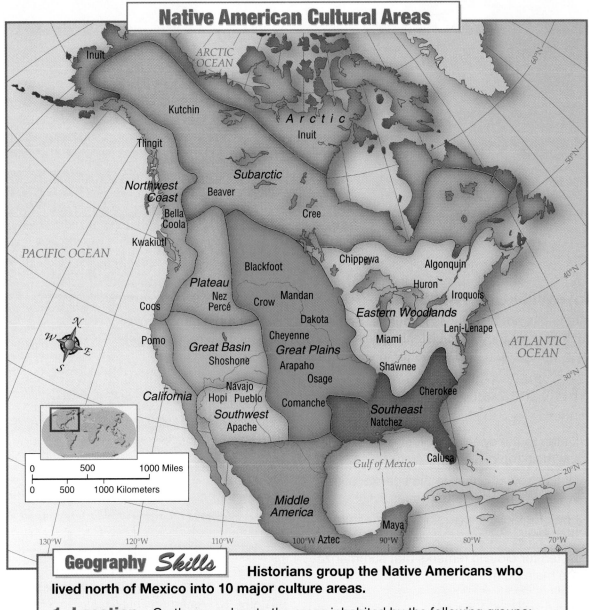

Native American Cultural Areas

Geography Skills

Historians group the Native Americans who lived north of Mexico into 10 major culture areas.

1. **Location**   On the map, locate the areas inhabited by the following groups: **(a)** Iroquois, **(b)** Inuit, **(c)** Pomo, **(d)** Hopi, **(e)** Shoshone.
2. **Place**   Name two groups that lived in the coldest regions of North America.
3. **Critical Thinking**   In which culture areas could Native Americans probably depend on the sea for food? Explain.

California

Differences in climate and resources helped create diverse cultures in California. Coastal people fished in the ocean and rivers. In the northern valleys, people hunted deer, rabbits, and elk or collected berries and nuts. In the southeast desert, small bands lived much like the people of the Great Basin.

For many Californians, like the Pomos, acorns were the basic food. Women harvested the nuts in autumn and later pounded them into flour. Both women and men among the Pomos were skilled at weaving baskets, which they decorated with fine designs.

People of the Southwest

The **Pueblos,** the Spanish name for people of the Southwest, were descended from the Anasazis. They included such groups as the Hopis, Acomas, Zuñis, and Lagunas. By

Skills FOR LIFE

| Critical Thinking | Managing Information | Communication | Maps, Charts, and Graphs |

Listening

How Will I Use This Skill?

Listening is not as easy as it sounds. Statistics show that most people miss much of what they hear. Listening clearly will help you follow directions, get along with people, and do better in school and on the job.

LEARN the Skill

Use these steps to practice listening skills:

❶ Listen to the opening words to determine the main topic.

❷ Notice how changes in the speaker's voice emphasize certain ideas.

❸ Look for facial expressions and gestures that stress important ideas.

❹ Listen for closing remarks that summarize the main point.

PRACTICE the Skill

Native American groups passed along tales like the one at right. Work with a partner. One partner reads the tale aloud, while the other listens and answers the following questions.

❶ What is the main topic of the story?

❷ What changes in voice helped you understand the story?

❸ Did the speaker use any gestures?

❹ How do the closing words summarize the story?

APPLY the Skill

Select a partner. Give each other brief descriptions of yourselves. Then, introduce your partner to the class. See how accurate you are.

> 66 *Listen, and learn why the rabbit has long ears. When the world was new, the rabbit had short ears. Back then, many, many moons ago, the rabbit and the eagle argued a lot. One day, in anger, the eagle grabbed the rabbit and flew it to her nest high in the trees. She gave the rabbit to her baby eagles as a toy.*
>
> *The baby eagles enjoyed chasing and tugging at the rabbit. One time, the rabbit got hurt. In a fit of rage, he killed all the baby eagles. The rabbit became frightened. He knew the mother eagle would look for him. He tried to disguise himself by taking feathers from the tiny eagles and stuffing them in his ears, stretching them very long. He then ran away and tried to hide himself in a hole of a fallen birch tree.*
>
> *When the eagle saw what happened, she searched for the rabbit for revenge. She saw the ears showing out of the tree and was ready to attack when she remembered an old tradition of covering the dead with birch bark. She thought the rabbit was dead, and so she flew away.*
>
> *Later, the eagle realized her mistake. To this day, the eagle still hunts the rabbit. Now you know why the rabbit has long ears and hides from the eagle.* 99

Kachina Dolls

To the Hopis of the Southwest, kachina dolls represented the spirits of the natural world. To create figures like these required great skill and care. For example, the kachina on the left is made of wood, cotton, fur, horsehair, feathers, shell, horn, and stone. ★ **Why do you think Hopi craftworkers took such care to create kachina dolls?**

1500, only the Hopis still farmed on clifftops as the Anasazis had done. Other groups lived in villages along the Rio Grande and its tributaries.

Pueblo way of life

Like their ancestors, the Pueblos built adobe houses and grew corn, beans, and squash. Their religious beliefs reflected the importance of farming. Most Pueblo villages had a kiva, or underground chamber, where men held religious ceremonies. Through prayers and other rituals, they tried to please the spirits of nature, such as wind, rain, and thunder.

At planting or harvest time, the Hopis and Zuñis held ceremonies to ensure rainfall and good crops. In the villages, cries rang out: "The kachinas are coming!" **Kachinas,** or masked dancers, represented the spirits. If the dance was pleasing to the spirits, they would return as rain to water the next season's crops.

The Pueblos traced their family lines through their mothers. This custom gave women special importance. When a man married, he went to live with his wife's family. Also, Pueblo wives owned most of the family property.

Navajos and Apaches

About 1500, two new groups reached the Southwest: the **Apaches** and the **Navajos.** Both groups lived as hunters, but they often raided Pueblo fields for food.

In time, the Navajos accepted many Pueblo ways. They began to farm and to build hogans, or houses made of mud plaster over a framework of wooden poles. The Apaches, however, continued to follow herds of buffalo and the other game they hunted. They traded dried buffalo meat and animal skins to the Pueblos in exchange for corn and woven cloth.

People of the Great Plains

Centuries ago, vast grasslands extended across the Great Plains from the Rocky Mountains to the Mississippi River. Because there were few trees, Plains people built their homes of sod, chunks of thickly matted grass.

Farming and hunting

Some Plains people farmed along river banks. In spring, women broke up the soft ground using hoes made from animal bones. They then planted corn, beans, squash, and sunflowers.

Large herds of animals grazed on the Plains, including buffalo, antelope, elk, deer, and bighorn sheep. Plains people hunted the animals on foot. In winter, men hunted near the village. In summer, however, they often traveled for miles in search of buffalo and other animals. They carried their belongings with them on a **travois** (truh VOY), or sled, pulled by dogs.

Each village had a ruling council that included the best hunters. The chief was respected by other council members because he spoke well and judged wisely.

Viewing HISTORY — Clothing From the Great Plains

On the Great Plains, Comanche hunters followed herds of deer and antelope. They ate the deer meat and used the hides to make clothing, like this woman's buckskin dress. ★ **In what other ways did Plains people make use of the animals they hunted?**

A new way of life

During the 1700s, the way of life of the Plains people changed. They began to catch and tame wild horses that appeared on the Plains. These horses descended from animals brought to the Southwest by Spanish settlers some 200 years earlier. Until then, there had been no horses in North America. A Blackfoot tale describes their reaction to seeing horses for the first time:

> 66 After a time, a woman said, 'Let's put a travois on one of them just like we do on our small dogs.' They made a larger travois and attached it to one of the gentler horses. It didn't kick or jump. They led the horse around with the travois attached. Finally, a woman mounted the horse and rode it. 99

Soon, Plains people became skillful riders. Because they could travel farther and faster than before, they raised fewer crops. They hunted more, moving often to follow huge herds of buffalo that roamed the plains. They also began to live in **tepees,** cone-shaped tents made of buffalo hides that could be carried easily on a travois.

People of the Southeast

The Southeast was home to more Native Americans than any other region. A warm

climate, fertile soil, and plentiful rain helped Southeast people produce good crops.

Most people lived in villages and farmed nearby land. They built their homes from saplings, or young trees. They split the trees into strips and wove them to make a frame for walls. Then, they plastered the walls with a mixture of clay and dry grass.

Farming and religion

Men and women had clearly defined roles in the community. Men cleared the land and hunted deer and other animals. Women planted, weeded, and harvested the crops. Among rows of corn, they planted beans that climbed up the cornstalks. They also grew squash, pumpkins, and sunflowers.

Most religious ceremonies were linked to farming. The most important, the Green Corn Ceremony, took place in midsummer, when the corn ripened. It marked the end of the year. Celebrations lasted several days. The highlight, on the last day, was the lighting of the sacred fire followed by a dance around its flames. With this event, the new year began.

Natchez society

One Southeast group, the **Natchez** (NACH ihz), hunted, fished, and farmed along the fertile coast of the Gulf of Mexico. They divided the year into 13 months. Each month

Connections With Civics

While warrior chiefs led most Plains Indian societies, the Cheyennes had a complex civil, or nonmilitary, government. The ruling council included representatives from the 10 main Cheyenne bands. Any warrior chief sent to the council had to resign his military power.

Linking History and Technology

PUEBLO

The walls are made of sandstone blocks plastered with adobe.

Kivas are rooms used for religious ceremonies.

Winter cooking room

Storage room

Sleeping room

Roofs are used as a center for work and socializing.

Drainspouts and splash blocks keep moisture away from roofs and walls.

TEPEE

Lodge poles

Smoke flaps

Buffalo sinew

Buffalo hide

Inner lining

Wooden stakes

The entrance almost always faced the rising sun in the east.

LONG HOUSE

Storage shelves

The stockade provided protection from enemies.

Each fire was shared by two families on either side of the center aisle.

Sleeping benches

The support posts divided the long house into separate rooms.

Elm bark walls

Iroquois ➤ cradleboard

Native American Dwellings

Native Americans developed a wide variety of dwellings to suit their different environments. Shown here are a pueblo from the Southwest, a tepee from the Great Plains, and a long house from the Eastern Woodlands. ★ **Describe one way each type of dwelling reflects the local environment.**

was named after a food or animal that the Natchez harvested or hunted. Months included Strawberry, Little Corn, Mulberry, Deer, Turkey, and Bear.

Natchez religious beliefs centered on worship of the sun. Priests kept a fire going day and night in a temple dedicated to the sun. The Natchez believed that fire came from the sun.

The Natchez ruler, the Great Sun, was worshipped as a god. He lived atop a giant pyramid mound. The Great Sun's feet never touched the ground. He either was carried in a litter or walked on mats. Below the Great Sun were other members of his family, called Little Suns. Next came Nobles, then Honored People, and finally Stinkards, or commoners, who were the majority of the people.

Marriage laws ensured that membership in each class kept changing. By law, noble men and women had to marry Stinkards. Even the Great Sun chose a Stinkard as a wife. In this way, no one family could hold the position of Great Sun forever. In time, even descendants of a Great Sun became Stinkards.

People of the Eastern Woodlands

Many groups lived in the Eastern Woodlands. In the forests and open lands, they hunted deer, moose, and other game. They also planted crops of corn, pumpkins, and squash.

The Iroquois: a complex society

The most powerful people of this region were the **Iroquois** (IHR uh kwoi). They lived in present-day New York State.

The Iroquois called themselves House Builders. They built long houses out of wood poles sided with bark. A typical long house was about 150 feet (46 m) long and 20 feet (7 m) wide. A hallway, with small rooms

Viewing HISTORY · Iroquois Women at Work

In several Native American cultures, including the Iroquois, women were responsible for growing and gathering food. Here, Iroquois women collect sap to make maple sugar. ★ **In what culture region did the Iroquois live?**

on either side, ran the length of the long house. Each room was home to one family. Families living across from each other shared a fireplace in the hallway.

Women had a special place in Iroquois society. They owned all household property and were in charge of planting and harvesting. Like a Pueblo man, an Iroquois man moved in with his wife's family when he married. Iroquois women also shared in political power because they chose clan leaders. A **clan** was a group of two or more related families. If a clan leader did not do his job well, the women could remove him from his position.

League of the Iroquois

The Iroquois included five nations: the Mohawk, Seneca, Onondaga (ahn uhn DAW guh), Oneida (oh NI duh), and Cayuga (kay YOO guh). Each nation had its own ruling council.

Constant warfare disrupted the Iroquois nations. Around 1570, the nations formed an alliance to end the fighting. According to legend, a religious leader named Dekanawida (deh kan ah WEE dah) inspired Hiawatha, a Mohawk, to organize the alliance. It became known as the **League of the Iroquois.** According to Iroquois tradition, the founders of the League of the Iroquois made this promise:

> 66 We bind ourselves together by taking hold of each other's hands.... Our strength shall be in union, our way the way of reason, righteousness, and peace.... Be of strong mind, O chiefs. Carry no anger and hold no grudges. 99

Later, a sixth nation, the Tuscarora (tuhs kuh ROR uh), joined the League.

A council of 50 **sachems,** or specially chosen tribal leaders, met once a year to make decisions for the League. Again, Iroquois women chose the sachems. At meetings, the council discussed problems and voted on ways to solve them. Each nation had one vote. The council could take action only if all of the nations agreed. The League helped end warfare among the Iroquois nations, and gave them a united defense against their enemies.

★ Section 2 Review ★

Recall

1. **Identify** (a) Inuit, (b) Pueblo, (c) kachina, (d) Apache, (e) Navajo, (f) Natchez, (g) Iroquois, (h) League of the Iroquois.

2. **Define** (a) culture area, (b) tribe, (c) igloo, (d) kayak, (e) potlatch, (f) kiva, (g) hogan, (h) travois, (i) tepee, (j) long house, (k) clan, (l) sachem.

Comprehension

3. (a) Name two Native American cultures that developed in North America. (b) Explain how each adapted to its environment.

4. How did cultures that relied on farming for food differ from those that were mainly hunters?

5. How did religion play a major role in the everyday life of most Native American cultures?

Critical Thinking and Writing

6. **Synthesizing Information** Review the feature Linking History and Technology on page 43. (a) Which of the three kinds of home shown here would you expect to find in a culture that relied on hunting for its way of life? Explain. (b) Which would be most suited to a settled farming community? Explain.

7. **Linking Past and Present** The Iroquois League helped settle disputes and keep the peace. What institutions perform this role in American society today?

★ ★

Activity **Writing a Chant** Write a chant celebrating your links with the natural world. For example, you could express gratitude for the foods you eat, or for the type of weather you most enjoy. For one example of a chant, see the Kwakiutl chant on page 38.

3 ★ Great Civilizations in the Americas

As You Read

Explore These Questions

- Where did the Mayan, Aztec, and Incan civilizations flourish?
- What were the main achievements of these civilizations?
- How were religion and learning linked in Aztec society?

Define

- civilization
- hieroglyphics
- causeway
- chinampas
- absolute power
- terrace
- aqueduct
- surplus

Identify

- Maya
- Olmec
- Aztec
- Tenochtitlán
- Inca
- Cuzco

SETTING the Scene Some 1,500 years ago, large oceangoing canoes sped along the Caribbean coast of Mexico. Cutting swiftly through the blue waters of the Caribbean Sea, the canoes made an impressive sight. Even more impressive were the riches inside the canoes. Traders carried jade statues, turquoise jewelry, parrot feathers, cocoa beans, and other valuable goods across a wide area.

The canoes belonged to the **Mayas,** a people who flourished in Mexico and Central America. The Mayas were one of several Native American people who built great, complex societies in the ancient Americas.

The Earliest American Civilizations

A **civilization** is an advanced culture. Historians identify several basic features of early civilizations. Perhaps the most important is the building of cities. Other features include a well-organized government, a system of social classes, specialized jobs, a complex religion, and some method of keeping records.

The earliest known American civilization was that of the **Olmecs.** The Olmecs emerged in the forests along the Gulf of Mexico, around 3,500 years ago. Archaeologists know very little about the Olmecs. However, rich tombs and temples suggest a powerful class of priests and nobles stood at the top of Olmec society.

The most dramatic Olmec artifacts are the giant carved stone heads found near a religious center. Without the use of pack animals or wheeled vehicles, the Olmecs moved these colossal 40-ton stones from distant quarries. Olmec temples were decorated with designs of grinning snakes and dragons. Similar designs in later buildings suggest that the Olmec civilization influenced the later, more advanced Mayan civilization.

Vase showing a Mayan king

Mayan Civilization

Mayan civilization emerged about 3,000 years ago. It grew up in the rain forests of present-day Mexico and Guatemala. The rain forests were difficult and dangerous places to live. Poisonous snakes hung from trees. Jaguars and other wild animals prowled the forest floor. Disease-carrying insects infested the swamps.

From earlier people, the Mayas learned to grow corn and to build stone structures. With much work, they cleared the jungle and drained the swamps.

On the cleared land, they grew corn to feed a growing population. They lived in simple homes with mud walls and thatched roofs.

Great cities

In time, the Mayas built great cities in many parts of Mexico and Central America. Two of these cities were Tikal and Copán. Each city had its own ruler. Although rival cities sometimes fought, they also enjoyed times of peaceful trade. Roads that cut through the jungle linked inland cities to the coast.

Towering above the cities were huge stone pyramids. Atop each pyramid stood a temple. There, priests performed ceremonies to please the Mayan gods.

Social classes

Priests were at the top of Mayan society. Only priests had the knowledge to perform the ceremonies that the Mayas believed were necessary to guarantee good harvests and victory in battle.

Nobles, government officials, and warriors also enjoyed high rank. A visitor to a Mayan city could easily spot priests and nobles. They wore gold jewelry, fine headdresses, and colorful cotton garments. While most rulers were men, Mayan records and carvings indicate that sometimes women governed on their own or in the name of young sons.

Near the bottom of Mayan society was a large class of peasant farmers. Lowest of all were slaves. Slaves were generally prisoners of war.

Advances in learning

Mayan priests paid careful attention to the passage of time and to the pattern of daily events. By studying the sun and the stars, they tried to predict the future. In that way, they could honor the gods who controlled events, including harvests, trade, and hunts.

Concern with time and the seasons led the Mayas to explore astronomy and mathematics. With the knowledge they gained, they created an accurate 365-day calendar. They also developed an advanced number system that included the concept of zero.

Great Civilizations of the Americas

Key
Maya Aztec Inca

0   1000   2000 Miles
0   1000   2000 Miles

Geography *Skills*   The Mayas, Aztecs, and Incas built great civilizations in Central and South America.

1. **Location**   On the map, locate: **(a)** Maya civilization, **(b)** Aztec empire, **(c)** Incan empire, **(d)** Tenochtitlán, **(e)** Andes Mountains.
2. **Movement**   Which people would have been able to travel by way of the Caribbean Sea?
3. **Critical Thinking**   Why might the Incas have had trouble keeping their empire united?

To record their findings, Mayan priests invented a system of **hieroglyphics,** or writing that uses pictures to represent words and ideas. Not until recent years have scholars deciphered Mayan hieroglyphics. The Mayas carved records on stone columns or painted them on paper made from bark.

V iewing HISTORY · **Aztec Education**

Pictures in an Aztec book show how Aztec parents taught their children needed skills. At left, a father teaches his son how to gather firewood, paddle a canoe, and fish. The mother, at right, instructs her daughter in grinding grain and weaving cloth. ★ **How do we pass on important skills to young people today?**

Decline of the Mayas

About 850, the Mayas abandoned their cities, and the forests once more took over the land. For centuries, these "lost cities" of the Mayas remained hidden in the thick rain forests of Central America.

We are unsure why the cities were left to decay. Perhaps peasants rebelled against heavy taxes imposed by their rulers. Maybe farming wore out the soil. Even though their cities declined, the Mayan people survived. Today, more than 2 million people in southern Mexico and Guatemala speak Mayan languages.

Aztec Civilization

To the north of the Mayan cities, the **Aztecs** built a powerful empire. Until the 1300s, the Aztecs were wanderers, moving from place to place in search of food. Then,

according to legend, a god told the Aztecs to look for a sign. They were to search for an eagle perched on a cactus with a snake in its beak.* On that spot, the god instructed, the Aztecs should build their capital. After more wandering, the Aztecs found the eagle in swampy Lake Texcoco (tay SKOH koh), in central Mexico.

Tenochtitlán

The Aztecs built their capital, **Tenochtitlán** (tay noch tee TLAHN), on an island in the middle of Lake Texcoco. Aztec engineers built **causeways,** or raised roads, out of packed earth. Aztec causeways connected the island to the mainland.

Farmers learned to grow crops on the swampland. They dug canals and filled in

---

*Today, the eagle, snake, and cactus remain symbols of Mexico and appear on the Mexican flag.

parts of the lake. With long stakes, they attached reed mats to the swampy lake bottom. Then, they piled mud onto the mats and planted their crops. Aztec farmers harvested as many as seven crops a year on these **chinampas,** or floating gardens.

In the 1400s, the Aztecs expanded their power by conquering neighboring people. They adopted many beliefs and ideas from these defeated people.

Riches from trade and conquest turned Tenochtitlán into a large, bustling city. City marketplaces offered an abundance of goods. "There are daily more than 60,000 people bartering and selling," wrote a Spanish visitor in the 1500s.

Canoes darted up the canals that crisscrossed the city. Soldiers and merchants traveled the causeways between Tenochtitlán and the mainland. Drawbridges on the roads could be raised in case of attack.

Religion

Religion was central to Aztec life. Young men and women attended special schools where they trained to become priests and priestesses. Like the Mayas, Aztec priests studied the heavens and developed advanced calendars. They used these calendars to determine when to plant or harvest and to predict future events. The priests divided the year into 18 months. Each month was governed by its own god. Aztec books contained knowledge about the gods as well as special prayers and hymns.

The sun god was especially important. Each day, the Aztecs believed, the sun battled its way across the heavens. They compared the sun's battles to their own, calling themselves "warriors of the sun." To ensure a successful journey across the sky, the sun required human sacrifices. The Aztecs sacrificed tens of thousands of prisoners of war each year to please their gods.

A powerful empire

By 1500, the Aztecs ruled millions of people from the Gulf of Mexico to the Pacific Ocean. The emperor had **absolute power,** that is, he had total authority over the people he ruled. The Aztec emperor was treated

Aztec Society

Emperor
chosen by nobles and priests to lead in war

Priests
performed rituals, gave advice, and ran schools

Nobles
served as officials, judges, and governors

Warriors
could become nobles by killing or capturing enemies

Merchants
often acted as spies for the empire

Artisans
passed skills on to their children

Farmers
made up most of the population

Slaves
were mostly captives or criminals

Graphic Organizer *Skills*

Like many other ancient civilizations, Aztec society was strictly divided into social classes.

1. **Comprehension** **(a)** Who occupied the highest position in Aztec society? **(b)** Which classes of people were equal to one another?

2. **Critical Thinking** How does this graphic organizer suggest the importance of warfare in Aztec society? Give two examples.

read in Chapter 3, in the 1520s, enemies of the Aztecs would help to destroy Tenochtitlán and end the Aztec empire.

Incan Civilization

Far to the south of the Aztec empire, the **Incas** united the largest empire in the Americas. By 1492, the Incan empire stretched for almost 3,000 miles (4,800 km) along the western coast of South America. (See the map on page 47.)

The Incan capital at **Cuzco** (KOOS koh) was high in the Andes Mountains. From there, the Incas ruled more than 10 million people living in coastal deserts, lowland jungles, and high mountains.

Farming

Like the Mayas and Aztecs, the Incas adapted customs and ideas from earlier cultures. Among them were the Moche, who lived along the Pacific coast of South America between about 250 and 700, and the Chimu people, who came after them.

Expanding on farming methods of these earlier Andean peoples, the Incas carved **terraces,** land shaped like wide steps, into the steep mountainsides. Sturdy stone walls kept the rains from washing the soil off the terraces. Stone **aqueducts,** or raised channels, carried water to the terraces from distant rivers. Most gardens produced two crops a year, including more than 100 varieties of potatoes.

The emperor, known as the Sapa Inca, controlled all the land and riches of the empire. Officials kept records of what each family in the empire produced. The government stored their **surplus,** or extra, crops in warehouses owned by the emperor. Incan officials used much of the food in these warehouses to feed the sick or victims of famine.

Engineering and medicine

The Incas perfected highly advanced building techniques. Their huge stone temples and forts showed their expert engineering skills. With only human labor, ropes, and wooden rollers, the Incas moved into place massive stones that weighed as much as 200 tons.

*B*iography **Pachacuti**

In 1438, Pachacuti rallied Incan forces to drive off an invasion. The Incas soon made him their leader. As founder of the Incan empire, Pachacuti devoted himself to uniting all the lands and people of Peru. He demanded that conquered people all speak one language, Quechua. He also turned the city of Cuzco into a magnificent capital. ★ **Why would Pachacuti think that one language would help unite his empire?**

almost like a god. Servants carried him from place to place on a litter. If the emperor did walk, nobles scattered flower petals in his path so that his feet never touched the ground. Ordinary people lowered their eyes when he passed.

Heavy taxes and the demand for human sacrifices fueled revolts among the neighboring people conquered by the Aztecs. Powerful Aztec armies, however, put down any uprising, taking even more prisoners to be sacrificed to the gods. One Aztec poet boasted:

66 Who could conquer Tenochtitlán? Who could shake the foundation of heaven? 99

In fact, the "foundation of heaven" was not as strong as the poet thought. As you will

Stonemasons chiseled each block so that it fit tightly to the next without any kind of cement. Even a knife blade could not fit between blocks. Incan buildings survived hundreds of earthquakes. Some remain standing today.

To unite and control their sprawling empire, the Incas built a complex network of roads. More than 19,000 miles (30,000 km) of roads linked all parts of the empire. Incan engineers carved roads through rock mountains and stretched rope bridges across deep gorges.

Teams of runners carried royal commands and news quickly across the empire. A runner from Cuzco, for example, would carry a message to a nearby village. From there, another runner would race to the next relay station. This system helped the emperor to control his people. If a runner brought news of a revolt, Incan armies could move swiftly along the network of roads to crush it.

Besides their success as farmers and engineers, the Incas made several important advances in medicine. They used quinine to treat malaria, performed successful brain surgery, and also discovered medicines to lessen pain.

Incan gold earrings

Religious beliefs

Like the Aztecs, the Incas worshipped the sun. The emperor, they believed, was descended from the sun god. A specially trained class of "chosen women of the sun" attended the emperor and performed religious rituals. To honor the sun, the Incas lined the walls of palaces and temples with sheets of gold. They called gold "the sweat of the gods." Nobles and priests adorned themselves with golden ornaments.

Very little Incan gold has survived. In the 1530s, as you will read, the Spanish rode up Incan highways to the golden city of Cuzco. The Incas, weakened by civil war and disease, were unable to fight off the invaders. The newcomers melted down the golden treasures of the Incan empire and sent them to Europe.

★ Section 3 Review ★

Recall

1. **Locate** (a) Mexico, (b) Guatemala, (c) Tikal, (d) Aztec empire, (e) Andes Mountains, (f) Incan empire.
2. **Identify** (a) Maya, (b) Olmec, (c) Aztec, (d) Tenochtitlán, (e) Inca, (f) Cuzco.
3. **Define** (a) civilization, (b) hieroglyphics, (c) causeway, (d) chinampas, (e) absolute power, (f) terrace, (g) aqueduct, (h) surplus.

Comprehension

4. (a) What civilizations emerged in present-day Mexico? (b) Where did the Incas build their civilization?

5. Describe one achievement of each of the following: (a) Mayas, (b) Aztecs, (c) Incas.
6. How was religion central to Aztec life?

Critical Thinking and Writing

7. **Synthesizing Information** Review the definition of a civilization on page 46. Then, choose one of the groups discussed in this section and explain why it should be considered a civilization.
8. **Comparing** Compare the major features of two of the civilizations discussed in the section. How are they similar? How are they different?

★ ★

Activity **Writing a Travel Plan** Next stop—Tenochtitlán! You are planning a trip through time to the Aztec capital. Write a list of the sights you want to see and the things you most want to do.

After 1492

As You Read

Explore These Questions
- How did the 1492 encounter with Europeans affect Native Americans?
- What is the Columbian Exchange?
- What elements of Native American culture did Europeans adopt?

Identify
- Viking
- Leif Erickson
- Vinland
- Christopher Columbus
- Taíno
- Columbian Exchange

SETTING the Scene Approximately 1,000 years ago, a group of seafaring men and women sailed across the Atlantic Ocean to settle on an island they called Vinland. There, they met local traders, who carried packs made of fur and skins. A witness wrote:

Figurehead of a Viking ship

66 Neither party could understand the other's language.... The Skraelings unslung their bales, untied them, and proffered their wares, and above all wanted weapons in exchange. 99

This meeting was one of the earliest encounters between Native Americans and Europeans. The "Skraelings" were Inuits. The settlers were **Vikings,** seafaring people from Scandinavia in Northern Europe.

The Viking settlement was brief and had no long-term effect on Native Americans. Then, in 1492, an expedition from Spain sailed into the Caribbean Sea. This time, the arrival of Europeans would have a dramatic impact on people throughout the Americas.

Early Contacts

For thousands of years, Native Americans had little knowledge of the world beyond their shores. Early contacts with outsiders were limited.

In 1001, Viking sailors led by **Leif Erickson** reached the northern tip of North America. They settled for a brief time in a flat, wooded territory they called **Vinland.** Today, many archaeologists believe that the Viking settlement was located in present-day Newfoundland, in Canada. The Vikings did not stay in Vinland long. No one is sure why they left. Viking stories, however, describe fierce battles with the Inuits.

There are also many stories about seafaring people from Asia reaching the Americas. Most experts agree that such voyages were very rare, if they occurred at all. Still, some believe that even after the last ice age ended, people continued to cross the Bering Sea from Asia into North America. Others claim that fishing boats from China and Japan blew off course and landed on the western coast of South America.

Encounter in 1492

If these early contacts did in fact take place, they had little impact either on Native Americans or the rest of the world. The encounter in 1492, however, changed history. Italian-born sailor **Christopher Columbus** led a Spanish fleet into the Caribbean. The voyage set off a chain of events whose effects are still felt throughout the world today. (You will read more about Christopher Columbus and other Europeans in Chapter 3.)

Columbus first landed in the Americas on a small Caribbean island. Friendly relations with the **Taínos** (TI nohz), the Native Americans he met there, did not last. Columbus and the Europeans who followed him were convinced that their culture was superior to that of the Indians. They claimed Taíno lands for themselves. They forced Taínos to work in gold mines, on ranches, or in Spanish households. Many Taínos died from harsh conditions. Others died from European diseases. Within 100 years of Columbus's arrival, the entire Taíno population had been destroyed.

The Taínos' experience with Europeans set a tragic pattern for Native Americans. That pattern was repeated again and again throughout the Americas.

Cultural Exchange

The 1492 encounter between Native Americans and Europeans had other effects. It started a worldwide exchange of goods and ideas that transformed people's lives around the globe. Because it began with Columbus, this transfer is known as the **Columbian Exchange.** It covered a wide range of areas, including food, medicine, government, technology, the arts, and language.

The exchange went in both directions. Europeans learned much from Native Americans. At the same time, Europeans contributed in many ways to the culture of the Americas. They introduced domestic animals such as chickens and horses. They also taught Native Americans how to use metals to make copper pots and iron knives.

Tragically, Europeans also brought new diseases to the Americas. Millions of Native Americans died of smallpox and other diseases to which they had no resistance.

Native American Influences

For their part, Native Americans introduced Europeans to new customs and ideas. Beginning with the encounter in 1492, elements of Native American culture gradually spread around the world.

Food and farming

Over thousands of years, Native Americans had learned to grow a variety of crops.

After 1492, they introduced Europeans to valuable food crops such as corn, potatoes, beans, tomatoes, manioc (a root vegetable), squash, peanuts, pineapples, and blueberries. Today, almost half the world's food crops come from plants that were first grown in the Americas.

Europeans carried the new foods with them as they sailed around the world. Everywhere, people's diets changed and populations increased. In South Asia, people used American hot peppers and chilies to spice their curries, or stews. Millions of Chinese peasants began growing sweet potatoes. Italians made sauces from tomatoes. People in West Africa grew manioc and maize.

 Potato Farming in South America

Farmers in the Andes first raised potatoes about 2,000 years ago. As a result of the Columbian Exchange, the potato has become an important part of people's diets around the world. ★ **Identify two other food crops that were first grown in the Americas.**

Why Study History?

Because Sports Are Important in Our Culture

★ ★

Historical Background

The athletes lined the playing field—nearly 1,000 young men in all. Each held a long pole topped with a web of leather netting. As the game began, they rushed up and down the mile-long field, trying to pass a ball over the other team's goal. Play was fast, dangerous, and exhausting. It might last well into the next day!

The players were Iroquois. They called the game baggataway. You know it by its French name: lacrosse.

The game was more than fun. The game taught young men agility, quick thinking, and teamwork—skills they would need as hunters or warriors. In fact, some called the game "the little brother of war." Each boy was assigned to a team at birth. The night before a match, villages held ceremonies with music, dancing, and speeches to cheer their team to victory.

Connections to Today

Today, lacrosse is popular in many American schools. Other sports we enjoy today were played by Native Americans. Field hockey and ice hockey developed partly from a sport known as the shinny game. Like Native Americans, we also compete in kayaking, canoeing, archery, swimming, wrestling, and foot races.

Connections to You

For us, as for Native Americans, sports are more than just fun. Athletics can improve your health and physical fitness.

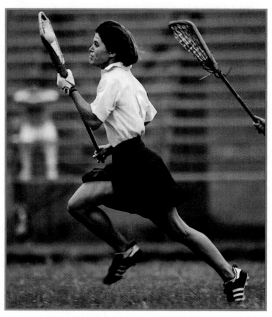

Modern lacrosse player

School pep rallies, like the pregame ceremonies of the Iroquois, encourage a sense of pride and community. Sports can also teach skills that you will use later in life. Today's sports emphasize teamwork, responsibility, and fair play.

1. **Comprehension** **(a)** Why did the Iroquois consider baggataway important? **(b)** How did they make sure each new generation learned the game?

2. **Critical Thinking** Choose a sport that is popular at your school. What kind of skills can that sport teach?

 Reporting on Sports Research the modern rules of lacrosse or one of the other sports mentioned above. Report on how that sport is played and why you think it has remained so popular today.

Language

Native American influences also show up in language. Europeans adopted words for clothing (poncho, moccasin, parka), trees (pecan, hickory), and inventions (toboggan, hammock). In an essay titled "The Indian All Around Us," historian Bernard DeVoto noted:

❝ Depending on what part of the country you are in, you may see a chipmunk, muskrat, woodchuck, or coyote. The names of all these animals are Indian words.... Twenty-six of our states have Indian names. ❞

Massachusetts, Alabama, Texas, Michigan, and Missouri are all Native American words. Many rivers bear Native American names, including the Mississippi, the Potomac, and the Monongahela.

Technology and medicine

Native Americans helped European settlers survive in North America. Besides showing the newcomers how to grow foods such as corn, Indians taught them hunting skills suitable to the American land. They led explorers on foot along Indian trails and paddled them up rivers in Indian canoes.

In the North, Indians showed Europeans how to use snowshoes and trap fur-bearing animals. Europeans also learned to respect Native American medical knowledge. Indians often treated the newcomers with medicines unknown to Europeans.

Other influences

As time went on, Native American cultures influenced the arts, sports, and even government. Today, Indian designs in pottery and leather work are highly prized. Americans play versions of such Indian games as lacrosse.

Some early leaders of the United States studied Native American political structures. Benjamin Franklin saw the League of the Iroquois as a model and urged Americans to unite in a similar way.

In time, all Native Americans felt the effects of European conquest. Still, despite attacks on their culture, Native Americans survived throughout the two continents. They preserved many traditions, including a respect for nature. Native Americans sought to live in harmony with the natural world. If that harmony was disrupted, they believed, misfortune would result. Today, many people have come to admire and share this concern for nature.

★ Section 4 Review ★

Recall

1. **Identify** **(a)** Viking, **(b)** Leif Erickson, **(c)** Vinland, **(d)** Christopher Columbus, **(e)** Taíno, **(f)** Columbian Exchange.

Comprehension

2. How did the arrival of Columbus affect the Taínos?
3. Describe two effects of the Columbian Exchange on Native Americans.

4. Name three ways that Native Americans influenced our culture today.

Critical Thinking and Writing

5. **Analyzing Information** Some historians think that Asians explored the Americas years before Columbus arrived. What kinds of evidence might prove that these historians are correct?
6. **Defending a Position** Do you think that the world was harmed or enriched by the Columbian Exchange? Defend your position.

Activity **Examining Exchange** List three items or activities in your life that were part of the Columbian Exchange. Write one or two sentences explaining how your life would be different without each item or activity.

Chapter 2 Review and Activities

★ Sum It Up ★

Section 1   Early People and Cultures
▶ The first Americans crossed a land bridge from Asia between 30,000 and 15,000 years ago.
▶ The first Americans adapted to the desert Southwest by learning to grow crops under dry conditions and building adobe houses.

Section 2   People of North America
▶ Native American cultures varied widely depending on geography.
▶ The religious beliefs of Native Americans reflected their close ties with the natural world.
▶ In the Eastern Woodlands, the five Iroquois nations formed a league to end warfare.

Section 3   Great Civilizations in the Americas
▶ The Mayan civilization boasted skill in astronomy, mathematics, and writing.
▶ The Aztecs of Mexico ruled a huge empire with millions of people.
▶ In South America, the Incas perfected advanced building techniques and built roads and bridges to unite their empire.

Section 4   After 1492
▶ Contact with Europeans had tragic consequences for Native Americans, as millions died of European diseases.
▶ The Columbian Exchange brought new products, technology, and ideas both to the Americas and to the rest of the world.

 CD-ROM Review For additional review of the major ideas of Chapter 2, see *Guide to the Essentials of American History* or *Interactive Student Tutorial CD-ROM*, which contains interactive review activities, graphic organizers, and practice tests.

▢ Reviewing the Chapter

Define These Terms

Match each term with the correct definition.

Column 1
1. culture
2. tribe
3. civilization
4. hieroglyphics
5. artifact

Column 2
a. group of villages or settlements that share common customs
b. advanced culture
c. object made by humans
d. complete way of life
e. writing that uses pictures

Explore the Main Ideas

1. What evidence suggests that early Native Americans traded with one another?
2. What was one important purpose of the religious ceremonies of Native Americans?
3. What role did women play in Iroquois society?
4. How did the Aztecs treat people captured in warfare?
5. **(a)** Describe one skill Native Americans learned from Europeans. **(b)** Identify two American products that Europeans adopted.

▢ Geography Activity

Match the letters on the map with the following places:
1. Mayan civilization, **2.** Aztec empire, **3.** Incan empire, **4.** Tenochtitlán, **5.** Tikal, **6.** Cuzco. **Interaction** How were the Aztecs able to grow crops on swampland?

⬜ Critical Thinking and Writing

1. **Understanding Chronology** **(a)** Place the following in correct chronological order: the height of the Mayan culture; the arrival of Columbus; the crossing of the land bridge; the founding of the League of the Iroquois. **(b)** How do you know that Columbus never ate tomato sauce when he was a boy?

2. **Linking Past and Present** Compare the communication technology of the Incas with our communication technology today.

3. **Analyzing Ideas** Review what you have read about Natchez society. **(a)** What was one advantage of the Natchez rule regarding marriage? **(b)** What was one disadvantage?

4. **Exploring Unit Themes** **Origins** Is it valuable for Americans to study early American cultures? Support your answer by citing examples from this chapter.

⬜ Using Primary Sources

Alvar Nuñez Cabeza de Vaca was an early Spanish explorer. He described the Yguazes people of the Gulf Coast region in this way:

> 66 These Indians are so accustomed to running that without rest or fatigue they follow a deer from morning to night. In this way they kill many. They pursue them until [the deer are] tired down, and sometimes overtake them in the race. Their houses are of matting, placed upon four hoops. They carry them on the back, and [move] every two or three days in search of food.... They are a merry people, considering the hunger they suffer; for they never cease, notwithstanding, to observe their festivities. 99

Source: *Original Narratives of Early American History: Spanish Explorers in the Southern United States*, 1959.

Recognizing Points of View **(a)** How did the Yguazes catch deer? **(b)** What does the writer think is interesting or surprising about the Yguazes?

ACTIVITY BANK

▶ Interdisciplinary Activity

Exploring the Arts Do research on traditional Native American designs from your region of the country. Then, use one of these designs in your own work of art.

▶ Career Skills Activity

Engineers Do research on Incan engineering. Make a model or draw a diagram of an Incan bridge. Prepare a report in which you compare the bridge with a modern bridge.

▶ Citizenship Activity

Forming a League Forming the League of the Iroquois required cooperation, organization, and commitment. Sketch out a plan for a league that would meet a need in your school. Suggest what kind of body would make decisions and what groups would need to be represented.

➤ Internet Activity

Use the Internet to find sites dealing with Native Americans in your state. Save the information you have found as a text file. Work with other members of your class to print out and bind the text files in an attractive format.

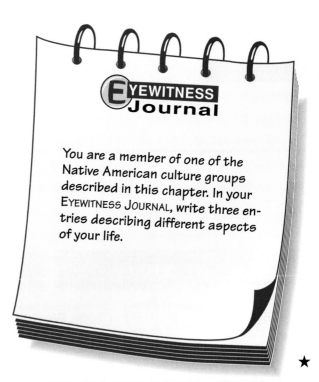

EYEWITNESS Journal

You are a member of one of the Native American culture groups described in this chapter. In your EYEWITNESS JOURNAL, write three entries describing different aspects of your life.

Chapter 3

A Meeting of Different Worlds 1100–1700

In the late 1400s, Europeans in search of trade sailed across the Atlantic and made contact with Native Americans. Soon, Spain and other nations established settlements in the Americas. The Europeans also began to bring enslaved Africans there. Gradually, Native American, European, and African peoples and cultures interacted to form a new way of life.

By the early 1600s, the nations of Europe were competing eagerly for wealth in the Americas. The Spanish built a large empire that spread over both North and South America. The French, Dutch, and English sought territory in North America. The English who settled at Jamestown and Plymouth brought with them traditions of political rights and freedoms.

What's Ahead

Why Study History?

Today, we take contact among different parts of the world for granted.
You can look at African art in European museums, or eat tacos in Japan. In the modern world, the pace of global exchange is much faster than it was 500 years ago. To focus on this connection, see this chapter's *Why Study History?* feature, "You Live in a Shrinking World."

American Events

1493 Columbus founds Spanish colony on Hispaniola

1521 Aztec empire falls to the Spanish

1100   **1400**   **1500**

World Events

 1100–1300s World Event
Christians go on Crusades to Holy Land

 1400s World Event
Prince Henry encourages exploration by sea

Crossing the Atlantic

This illustration by Johann Theodor de Bry shows Portuguese ships in an ocean filled with flying fish and sea monsters. Beginning in the late 1400s, European explorers and conquerors set sail across the Atlantic Ocean. Their voyages had a lasting impact, not only on Europe and the Americas, but on West Africa as well.

★ **How do you think illustrations like this affected European sailors as they sailed out into the Atlantic Ocean?**

1535	**1607**	**1620**	**1673**
Incan empire is controlled by the Spanish	Jamestown is founded by British colonists	Pilgrims arrive at Plymouth	French explore the Mississippi River

1500   **1600**   **1700**

1500s World Event
Protestant Reformation causes religious conflicts

1600s World Event
British East India Company trades in India

 59

Europeans Reach the Americas

As You Read

Explore These Questions
- How did the Crusades and the Renaissance change Europe?
- Why did Europeans look for new sea routes to Asia?
- What were the effects of Columbus's voyages?

Define
- monarch
- feudalism
- manor
- serf
- magnetic compass
- astrolabe
- caravel
- colony

Identify
- Middle Ages
- Crusades
- Renaissance
- Johannes Gutenberg
- Prince Henry
- Bartholomeu Dias
- Vasco da Gama
- Christopher Columbus

SETTING the Scene During the **Middle Ages,** the period in European history from about 500 to 1350, many Europeans thought of the world as a disk floating on a great ocean. The disk was made up of only three continents: Europe, Africa, and Asia.

Most Europeans knew little about the lands beyond their small villages. Even mapmakers called the waters bordering Europe the Sea of Darkness. Sailors who strayed into these waters often returned with tales of fearsome creatures: "One of these sea monsters," swore one sailor, "has horns, flames, and huge eyes 16 or 20 feet across."

Were such tales true? The few who wondered had no way of finding out. Most Europeans were not interested in the outside world because daily life was hard and their main concern was survival.

The Middle Ages

During the Middle Ages, weak European **monarchs,** or kings and queens, divided their lands among nobles. These nobles, or lords, had their own armies and courts but owed loyalty to a monarch. This system of rule by lords who owe loyalty to a monarch is called **feudalism** (FYOOD 'l ihz uhm).

Feudal life revolved around the manors of these powerful lords. The **manor** included the lord's castle, peasants' huts, and surrounding villages or fields. Most people on the manor were **serfs,** or peasants who worked for the lord and could not leave the manor without the lord's permission.

On the manor, people had to produce for themselves nearly everything they needed. There were few merchants and traders. Few roads or towns existed.

During the Middle Ages, all Christians in Western Europe belonged to the Roman Catholic Church. As a result, the Church had great influence.

A Changing Europe

Toward the end of the Middle Ages, conditions began to change. Religious wars led to increased trade with people in Asia and Africa. There was also a revival of learning in Europe.

The Crusades

To Christians, the city of Jerusalem in the Middle East was sacred because Jesus had lived and taught there. They referred to the city and other places in Palestine as the Holy Land. Jerusalem was also a holy place to Jews and Muslims.

From about 1100 to 1300, Christians and Muslims fought a series of religious wars for control of the Holy Land. Thousands of Christians from all over Europe joined in these wars, known as the **Crusades.** In the end, however, the Europeans failed to win control of the Holy Land.

Still, the Crusades had lasting effects for the Europeans. For the first time, large numbers of Europeans had traveled beyond the small towns of their birth. In the Middle East, they ate exotic foods, such as rice, oranges, and dates. They tasted ginger, pepper, and other spices that both improved the taste of food and helped preserve it. They bought shimmering silks and colorful rugs from Arab traders.

Italian merchants quickly realized that Europeans would pay handsome prices for these foreign goods. They therefore began a lively trade with Arab merchants in the Middle East.

The increase in trade led to an increase in knowledge. From the Arabs, Italian merchants learned about new instruments that made it easier to sail across large bodies of water. The **magnetic compass,** with a needle that always pointed north, helped ship captains sail a straight course. Another useful instrument was the **astrolabe** (AS troh layb). This tool made it possible for sailors to determine the positions of stars and figure out latitude at sea. Both the magnetic compass and the astrolabe helped make sailing less frightening.

A revival of learning

Increased trade and travel made Europeans curious about the wider world. Scholars translated ancient Greek, Roman, and Arab works. They then made discoveries of their own in fields such as art, medicine, astronomy, and chemistry. This burst of learning was called the **Renaissance** (REHN uh sahns), a French word meaning rebirth. It lasted from the late 1300s to about 1600.

The invention of the printing press helped to spread the Renaissance spirit. It was invented during the mid-1400s by German printer **Johannes Gutenberg** (GOOT uhn berg). Before Gutenberg's invention, there were few books because people had to copy them by hand. With the printing press, however, large numbers of books could be printed at low cost. As books became more available, more people learned to read. As reading increased, people learned more about the world around them.

Search for New Trade Routes

As trade brought new prosperity to Europe, kings and queens fought to increase their power. In England and France, rulers established greater authority over feudal lords. In Portugal and Spain, Christian monarchs drove out Arab Muslims who had conquered much of the area.

The rulers of England, France, Portugal, and Spain also looked for ways to increase their wealth. Huge profits could be made by trading with China and other Asian lands. However, Arab and Italian merchants controlled the trade routes across the Mediterranean Sea. Western European rulers would have to find another route to Asia.

Portugal led the way. In the early 1400s, **Prince Henry,** known as the Navigator, encouraged sea captains to sail south along the coast of West Africa. He founded an informal school to help sailors in their explorations.

Viewing HISTORY — Wealth and Knowledge

In his painting The Moneylender and His Wife, *Renaissance painter Quentin Metsys captured the spirit that was changing Europe in the 1400s and 1500s. Europeans wanted new wealth and knowledge. This spirit encouraged overseas trade and voyages of exploration.*
★ **How did Metsys communicate the ideas of wealth and knowledge in this painting?**

Columbus Reaches the Americas

The Spanish watched the Portuguese with envy because they, too, wanted a share of the rich Asian spice trade. In 1492, King Ferdinand and Queen Isabella agreed to finance a voyage of exploration by an Italian sea captain named **Christopher Columbus.** Columbus planned to reach the East Indies by sailing west across the Atlantic.

Across the Atlantic

In August 1492, Columbus set sail with three ships and a crew of about 90 sailors. As captain, he commanded the largest vessel, the *Santa María.* The other ships were the *Niña* and the *Pinta.*

After stopping briefly at the Canary Islands, the little fleet continued west into unknown territory. Fair winds sped them along, but a month passed without the sight of land. Some sailors began to grumble. They had never been beyond the sight of land for so long. Still, Columbus sailed on.

On October 7, sailors saw flocks of birds flying southwest. Columbus changed course to follow the birds. A few days later, crew members spotted tree branches and flowers floating in the water. At 2 A.M. on October 12, the lookout on the *Pinta* spotted white cliffs shining in the moonlight. *"Tierra! Tierra!"* he shouted. "Land! Land!"

At dawn, Columbus rowed ashore and planted the banner of Spain. Columbus called the local people Indians because he was convinced that he had reached the East Indies, in Asia. In fact, as you read in Chapter 2, he had reached the island home of the Taínos, in what are now called the West Indies. The West Indies lie off the coasts of North and South America. At the time, these continents were unknown to Europeans.

Riches for Spain

For three months, Columbus explored the West Indies. To his delight, he found signs of gold on the islands. Eager to report his success, he returned home to Spain.

Columbus gave King Ferdinand and Queen Isabella gifts of pink pearls and brilliantly colored parrots. The two Spanish

▲ Astrolabe

*B*iography **Christopher Columbus**

Christopher Columbus grew up in Genoa, one of the busiest seaports in Italy. As a young sailor, he heard how Portuguese sea captains were trying to reach the Indies and other parts of Asia by sailing around Africa. After studying Portuguese charts, Columbus formed his own idea. He would reach the Indies not by sailing south and east, but by sailing west. ★ **Was Columbus correct in thinking that he could reach Asia by sailing west? Explain.**

Under Henry's guidance, the Portuguese designed a new type of ship, the **caravel** (KAR uh vehl). With triangular sails and a steering rudder, the caravel enabled captains to sail against the wind.

Portuguese sailors gradually established a new route from Western Europe to Asia. In 1488, **Bartholomeu Dias** reached the southern tip of Africa. Then, in 1498, **Vasco da Gama** sailed around southern Africa and continued to India. (See the map on page 75.) Gradually, Portuguese ships pressed on to the East Indies, an island chain off the southeastern coast of Asia. This was the source of the trade in spices.

Why Study History?

Because You Live in a Shrinking World

★ ★

Historical Background

Among the Aztecs in Mexico 600 years ago, a typical meal included corn porridge, beans, tortillas, and tomato or pepper sauce. In Europe, meanwhile, most people ate dark bread, cheese, and cabbage or turnip soup.

Then in the 1500s, contacts grew between the Americas and the rest of the world. Europeans got their first taste of potatoes, corn, and cocoa from the Americas. Native Americans began eating wheat bread, bananas, and citrus fruit from Europe, Africa, and Asia.

Connections to Today

Our world continues to get smaller. Today, people around the world watch American movies and television shows. They wear American styles of clothing and listen to American forms of music. At the same time, new ideas and goods travel from other lands to become part of American culture. New dance styles have come from Latin America, new clothing fashions from France, and new advances in communication from Japan. Due to modern communication and transportation, exchanges take place more quickly than ever before.

Connections to You

You can see—and taste—examples of cultural exchange in the international foods aisle of your local supermarket. The chart above lists some foods from other lands that have become popular in the United States.

Food	Description	Place of Origin
borscht	Cold beet soup	Russia, Ukraine
chutney	Sauce or relish made of fruits, herbs, and spices	India
couscous	Tiny grains of wheat cooked until fluffy	North Africa
feta cheese	White, crumbly cheese	Greece
gazpacho	Chilled tomato soup	Spain
hummus	Spread made from chickpeas	Middle East
salsa	Hot sauce made from tomatoes, chilies, peppers, herbs, and spices	Mexico
egg rolls	Shredded vegetables in fried dough wrapper	China
sushi	Raw fish and rice, often wrapped in seaweed	Japan

Plate of tacos ➤

1. **Comprehension**
   (a) Name two foods that Native Americans introduced to Europeans.
   (b) Name two Mexican foods that are popular in the United States today.

2. **Critical Thinking** How do you think communication via the Internet affects cultural exchange today?

★ *Activity* **Planning a Food Festival** Working with other students, plan a festival of popular international foods. For ideas on what foods to include, visit your local supermarket or consult an international cookbook.

monarchs listened intently to his descriptions of tobacco, pineapples, and hammocks used for sleeping. Columbus also described the natives of the islands he had visited:

> 66 [They were] of a very acute intelligence...[but had] no iron or steel weapons....Should your majesties command it, all the inhabitants could be made slaves. 99

The Spanish monarchs were impressed. They gave Columbus the title of Admiral of the Ocean Sea. They also agreed to finance his future voyages.

Columbus made three more voyages to the West Indies. In 1493, on an island he called Hispaniola (present-day Haiti and the Dominican Republic), he founded the first Spanish colony in the Americas. A **colony** is a group of people who settle in a distant land and are ruled by the government of their native land. Columbus also explored Cuba and Jamaica and sailed along the coasts of Central America and northern South America. Wherever he went, he claimed the lands for Spain.

Columbus's lasting impact

For years, Columbus has been remembered as the bold sea captain who "discovered America." In at least one sense, he deserves that honor. Europeans knew nothing of the Americas before Columbus brought them news about this "new world." Today, however, we also recognize that other people "discovered" America long before Columbus. Still, his daring voyages initiated lasting contact among the peoples of Europe, Africa, and the Americas.

For Native Americans, though, the contact begun by Columbus resulted in tragedy. Columbus and other Europeans who came after him seized Indian lands. They forced native people to work in mines or on farms. Over the next 50 years, hundreds of thousands of Caribbean Indians died from harsh working conditions and European diseases.

For better or for worse, the voyages of Columbus signaled a new era for the Americas. Curious Europeans wanted to explore the lands across the Atlantic. They saw the Americas as a place where they could settle, trade, and grow rich.

★ **Section 1 Review** ★

Recall

1. **Locate** (a) Europe, (b) Middle East, (c) Asia, (d) Mediterranean Sea, (e) East Indies, (f) West Indies.
2. **Identify** (a) Middle Ages, (b) Crusades, (c) Renaissance, (d) Johannes Gutenberg, (e) Prince Henry, (f) Bartholomeu Dias, (g) Vasco da Gama, (h) Christopher Columbus.
3. **Define** (a) monarch, (b) feudalism, (c) manor, (d) serf, (e) magnetic compass, (f) astrolabe, (g) caravel, (h) colony.

Comprehension

4. Describe how each of the following changed life in Europe: (a) the Crusades, (b) the Renaissance.

5. Why did Western European rulers want to find new routes to Asia?
6. How did Columbus's voyages affect (a) Europeans, (b) Native Americans?

Critical Thinking and Writing

7. **Drawing Conclusions** In what way were the Crusades both a success and a failure?
8. **Recognizing Points of View** For many years, American schoolchildren were taught that Columbus "discovered America." In what way is this an accurate statement? In what way is the statement inaccurate?

★ ★

Activity **Writing a Contract** You are a legal expert in service to King Ferdinand and Queen Isabella. Draw up a contract explaining what your monarchs will provide to Christopher Columbus and what they expect from him in return.

2 ★ Spain Builds an Empire

As You Read

Explore These Questions
- How did Spain interact with Native American empires?
- How did Spain govern its lands in the Americas?
- Why was life difficult for the Native Americans who lived under Spanish rule?

Define
- conquistador
- pueblo
- presidio
- mission
- peninsulare
- creole
- mestizo
- encomienda
- plantation

Identify
- Vasco Núñez de Balboa
- Ferdinand Magellan
- Montezuma
- Hernando Cortés
- Francisco Pizarro
- Spanish borderlands
- Laws of the Indies
- Juan de Oñate
- Eusebio Francisco Kino
- Bartolomé de Las Casas

SETTING the Scene "What a troublesome thing it is to discover new lands. The risks we took, it is hardly possible to exaggerate." Thus said Bernal Díaz del Castillo, one of the many Spanish **conquistadors** (kahn KEES tuh dorz), or conquerors, who marched into the Americas in the 1500s. When asked why they traveled to the Americas, Díaz responded, "We came here to serve God and the king and also to get rich."

In their search for glory and gold, the conquistadors made Spain one of the richest nations in Europe. Soon, Spanish colonists followed the conquistadors and created a vast new empire in the Americas. However, the building of Spain's empire meant suffering and even death for Aztecs, Incas, and other Native Americans.

Early Explorations

After Columbus reached the West Indies, the Spanish explored and settled other islands in the Caribbean Sea. By 1511, they had conquered Puerto Rico, Jamaica, and Cuba. They also explored the eastern coasts of North America and South America. Like

Spanish sailing ship of the 1400s

Columbus, these explorers were searching for a western route to Asia.

Then, in 1513, an adventurer named **Vasco Núñez de Balboa** (bal BOH uh) plunged into the jungles of the Isthmus of Panama. Native Americans had told him that a large body of water lay to the west. With a party of Spanish and Indians, Balboa reached the Pacific Ocean after about 25 days. He stood in the crashing surf and claimed the ocean for Spain.

The Spanish had no idea how wide the Pacific was until a sea captain named **Ferdinand Magellan** (muh JEHL uhn) sailed across it. The expedition left Spain in 1519. After much hardship, it rounded the very stormy southern tip of South America and entered the Pacific Ocean. Crossing the Pacific, the sailors were forced to eat rats and sawdust when they ran out of food. Magellan himself was killed in a battle with the local people of the Philippine Islands off the coast of Asia.

Of five ships and about 250 crew members, only one ship and 18 sailors returned to Spain in 1522, three years after they set out.

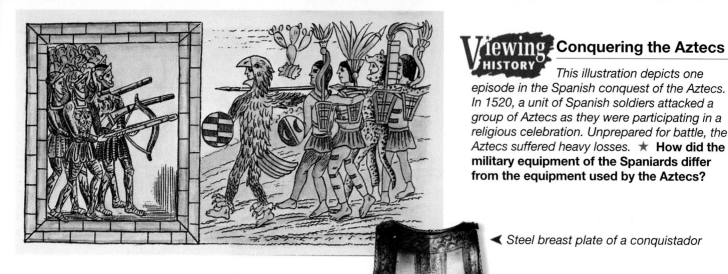

This illustration depicts one episode in the Spanish conquest of the Aztecs. In 1520, a unit of Spanish soldiers attacked a group of Aztecs as they were participating in a religious celebration. Unprepared for battle, the Aztecs suffered heavy losses. ★ **How did the military equipment of the Spaniards differ from the equipment used by the Aztecs?**

◄ *Steel breast plate of a conquistador*

These survivors were the first men to circumnavigate, or sail around, the world. In doing so, they had found an all-water western route to Asia. Their voyage made Europeans aware of the true size of the Earth.

Spanish Conquistadors

Meanwhile, Spanish colonists in the Caribbean heard rumors of gold and other riches in nearby Mexico. Spanish conquistadors began to dream of new conquests. The rulers of Spain gave conquistadors permission to establish settlements in the Americas. In return, conquistadors agreed to give Spain one fifth of any gold or treasure they captured.

Cortés conquers the Aztecs

In 1519, messengers brought disturbing news to **Montezuma** (mahn tuh ZYOO muh), the Aztec emperor who ruled over much of Mexico. They said that they had seen a large house floating on the sea. It was filled with white men with long, thick beards.

Montezuma thought that these strangers might be messengers of gods. Aztec sacred writings predicted that a powerful white-skinned god would come from the east to rule the Aztecs. The white strangers did come from the east, and they were certainly powerful. They wore metal armor and had weapons that spit fire. As the strangers neared Tenochtitlán (tay nawch tee TLAHN), the capital of the Aztec empire, Montezuma decided to welcome them as his guests.

The Spanish leader, **Hernando Cortés** (kor TEHZ), took advantage of Montezuma's invitation. Like other conquistadors, Cortés wanted power and riches. An Indian woman the Spanish called Doña Marina had told him about Aztec gold. With only about 600 soldiers and 16 horses, Cortés set out to seize the Aztecs' gold. On November 8, 1519, Cortés marched into Tenochtitlán. For the next six months, he held Montezuma prisoner.

Finally, the Aztecs attacked and drove out the Spanish, but the victory was brief. Aided by people whom the Aztecs had conquered, Cortés recaptured Tenochtitlán. In the end, the Spanish killed Montezuma and destroyed Tenochtitlán. The mighty Aztec empire had fallen.

Pizarro conquers the Incas

Another bold conquistador, **Francisco Pizarro** (pee ZAR oh), heard about the fabulous Incan empire while marching with Balboa across Panama. Pizarro decided to sail down the Pacific coast of South America with fewer than 200 Spanish soldiers. In 1532, he captured the Incan emperor Atahualpa (at ah WAHL pa) and much of his army. An Incan historian described the surprise attack:

❝ The Spaniards killed them all—with horses, with swords, with guns.... From more than 10,000 men, there did not escape 200. ❞

Later, the Spanish executed Atahualpa. The following year, Pizarro's army attacked

Cuzco, the Incan capital in present-day Peru. Without the leadership of Atahualpa, Incan resistance collapsed. By 1535, Pizarro controlled much of the Incan empire.

Reasons for Spanish victories

With only a handful of soldiers, the Spanish had conquered two great empires. There were several major reasons for the remarkable success that the Spanish enjoyed.

First, the Spanish had superior military equipment. They were protected by steel armor and had guns. Meanwhile, the Aztecs and Incas relied on clubs, bows and arrows, and spears. Also, the Native Americans had never seen horses. As a result, they were frightened by mounted Spanish soldiers.

Another factor was that the Native Americans offered weak resistance. The Aztecs were slow to fight because they thought the Spanish might be gods. The Incas were weak from fighting among themselves over control of their government.

Finally, the Indians fell victim to European diseases. Large numbers of Indians died from chicken pox, measles, and influenza. Some historians believe that disease alone would have ensured Spanish victory over the Indians.

Seeking Riches in the North

The Spanish search for treasure extended beyond the lands of the Aztecs and Incas. Moving north, conquistadors explored the area known as the **Spanish borderlands.** The borderlands spanned the present-day United States from Florida to California.

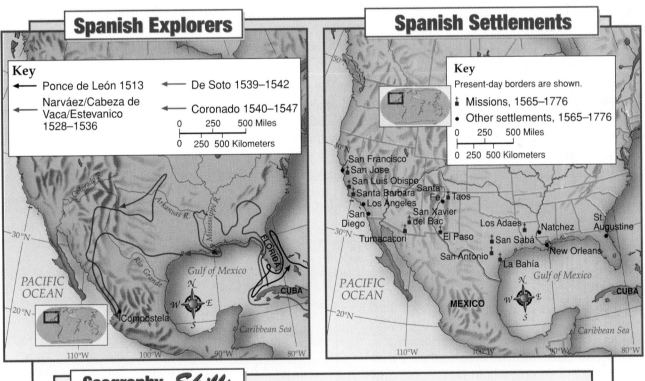

Geography Skills

Spanish conquistadors explored and conquered parts of North America in the 1500s. They mapped the routes that Spanish settlers later followed.

1. Location On the maps, locate: **(a)** Coronado's route, **(b)** De Soto's route, **(c)** St. Augustine, **(d)** San Antonio, **(e)** Santa Fe, **(f)** Los Angeles, **(g)** San Francisco.

2. Region What is the easternmost Spanish settlement shown on the maps?

3. Critical Thinking In what states of the present-day United States would you expect Spanish influence to be strong?

Juan Ponce de León (PAWN suh day lay AWN) traveled through parts of Florida in 1513, looking for a legendary fountain of youth. Indians claimed that anyone who bathed in its magical water would remain young forever. Ponce de León found no such fountain.

Spain in the Americas

Geography *Skills*

In the 1500s, Spain established a system for ruling its American colonies. The colonies were divided into the Viceroyalty of New Spain and the Viceroyalty of Peru.

1. **Location** On the map, locate: **(a)** Brazil, **(b)** West Indies, **(c)** Mexico City, **(d)** Lima.

2. **Region** Which viceroyalty included Mexico and Florida?

3. **Critical Thinking** Why was control of the Caribbean Sea important to Spain?

In 1528, Panfilo Narváez (nar VAH ehs) led an expedition that ended in disaster. A storm struck his fleet in the Gulf of Mexico. Narváez and many others were lost at sea. The rest landed on an island near present-day Texas. Native Americans captured the few survivors and held them prisoner. Álvar Núñez Cabeza de Vaca assumed leadership of the group, which included an enslaved African named Estevanico.

In 1533, Cabeza de Vaca, Estevanico, and two others finally escaped their captors. The four went searching for a Spanish settlement. Their astonishing journey did not end until 1536, when they reached a town in Mexico. They had traveled by foot more than 1,000 miles through the Southwest. (See the map on page 67.) They learned much about Native American ways. They also heard amazing tales about seven cities whose streets were paved with gold.

From 1539 to 1542, Hernando De Soto explored Florida and other parts of the Southeast. He was looking for the cities of gold and other treasures. In 1541, he reached the Mississippi River. De Soto died along the riverbank, without finding the riches he sought.

The conquistador Francisco Coronado (koh roh NAH doh) also heard about the seven cities of gold. In 1540, he led an expedition into the southwestern borderlands. He traveled through Mexico to present-day Arizona and New Mexico. Some of his party went as far as the Grand Canyon. Still, the Zuñi villages he visited had no golden streets.

Governing New Spain

The Spanish king decided to set up a strong system of government to rule his growing empire in the Americas. In 1535, the king divided his lands into New Spain and Peru. The borderlands were part of New Spain. He put a viceroy in charge of each region to rule in his name.

The viceroys enforced the **Laws of the Indies,** a code of laws that stated how the colonies should be organized and ruled. The Laws of the Indies provided for three kinds of settlements in New Spain: pueblos, presidios (prih SIHD ee ohz), and missions. Sometimes,

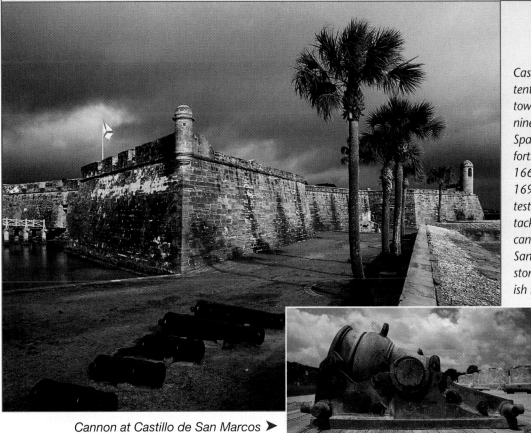

American Heritage
M A G A Z I N E

Castillo de San Marcos

Castillo de San Marcos was the tenth fort built to protect the town of St. Augustine. The first nine were built of wood. The Spanish decided to build a stone fortress after a pirate attack in 1668. The fort was completed in 1695 and survived its first major test in 1702 when it was attacked by the British. Today, you can cross a moat to Castillo de San Marcos and stand atop the stone walls that defended Spanish settlers some 300 years ago.

★ **To learn more about this historic site, write:** Castillo de San Marcos National Monument, 1 South Castillo Drive, St. Augustine, FL 32084.

Cannon at Castillo de San Marcos ➤

a large community included all three types of settlements.

Pueblos, or towns, were centers of farming and trade. In the middle of the town was a plaza, or public square. Here, townspeople and farmers gathered on important occasions. They also came to worship at the church. Shops and homes lined the four sides of the plaza.

Spanish rulers took control of Indian pueblos and built new towns as well. In 1598, **Juan de Oñate** (oh NYAH tay) founded the colony of New Mexico among the adobe villages of the Pueblo Indians. He used brutal force to conquer the Native Americans of the region. In 1609, Don Pedro de Paralta founded Santa Fé as the Spanish capital of New Mexico.

Presidios were forts where soldiers lived. Inside the high, thick walls of a presidio were shops, stables for horses, and storehouses for food. Most soldiers lived in large barracks. Soldiers protected the farmers who settled around the presidios. The first presidio in the borderlands was built in 1565 at St. Augustine, Florida. (See History Happened Here above.)

Missions were religious settlements run by Catholic priests and friars. Like other Europeans in the Americas, the Spanish believed they had a duty to convert Indians to Christianity. They often forced Indians to live and work on the missions.

Missionaries gradually moved into various parts of the Spanish borderlands. The first mission in Texas was founded at El Paso in 1659. In 1691, Father **Eusebio Francisco Kino** (KEE noh) crossed into present-day Arizona. He eventually set up 24 missions in the area. Missionaries also moved into California. By the late 1700s, a string of missions dotted the California coast from San Diego to San Francisco. (See the map on page 67.)

Biography — Sor Juana

Juana Inés de la Cruz was one of the most talented poets of New Spain. Because she was a girl, she was refused admission to the university in Mexico City. She entered a convent at age 16 and devoted herself to studying and writing poetry. She also wrote a spirited defense of women's right to an education. ★ **Besides women, what other people in New Spain were denied equal rights?**

Society in New Spain

The Laws of the Indies divided the people in Spanish colonies into four social classes: peninsulares (puh nihn suh LAH rayz), creoles (KREE ohlz), mestizos (mehs TEE zohz), and Indians.

Four social classes

At the top of the social scale were the **peninsulares.** Born in Spain, the peninsulares held the highest jobs in the colonial government and the Catholic Church. They also owned large tracts of land as well as rich gold and silver mines.

Below the peninsulares were the **creoles.** Creoles were people born in the Americas to Spanish parents. Many creoles were wealthy and well educated. They owned farms and ranches, taught at universities, and practiced

law. However, they could not hold the jobs that were reserved for peninsulares.

Below the creoles were the **mestizos,** people of mixed Spanish and Indian background. Mestizos worked on farms and ranches owned by peninsulares and creoles. In the cities, they worked as carpenters, shoemakers, tailors, and bakers.

The lowest class in the colonies was the Indians. The Spanish treated them as a conquered people. Under New Spain's strict social system, Indians were kept in poverty for hundreds of years.

A blending of cultures

By the mid-1500s, a new way of life had begun to take shape in New Spain. It blended Spanish and Indian ways.

Spanish settlers brought their own culture to the colonies. They introduced their language, laws, religion, and learning. In 1539, a printer in Mexico City produced the first European book in the Americas. In 1551, the Spanish founded the University of Mexico.

Native Americans also influenced the culture of New Spain. As you have read in Chapter 2, colonists adopted items of Indian clothing, such as the poncho and moccasins. Indians also introduced Spanish colonists to new foods, including potatoes, corn, tomatoes, and chocolate.

With the help of Indian workers, Spanish settlers built many fine libraries, theaters, and churches. The Indians used materials they knew well, such as adobe bricks. Sometimes, Spanish priests allowed Indian artists to decorate the church walls with paintings of harvests and local traditions.

Harsh Life for Indians

The colonists who came to the Americas needed workers for their ranches, farms, and mines. To help them, the Spanish government gave settlers **encomiendas** (ehn koh mee EHN dahz), or the right to demand labor or taxes from Native Americans living on the land.

Working in mines and plantations

During the 1500s, mines in Mexico, Peru, and other areas of the Americas made Spain

| Critical Thinking | Managing Information | Communication | Maps, Charts, and Graphs |

Reading a Line Graph

How Will I Use This Skill?

Graphs present statistics, or number facts, in a visual way. A line graph can show you at a glance how statistics change over time—from the population of the world to your batting average.

LEARN the Skill

You can read a line graph by following these four steps:

❶ Use the title to identify the subject of the graph. The source line will tell you where the information was found.

❷ Study the labels on the graph. The horizontal (or side-to-side) axis usually tells you the time period covered by the graph. The vertical (or up-and-down) axis tells you what is being measured.

❸ Practice reading the information on the graph. Line up the points on the graph with the horizontal and vertical axes to determine how much or how many of something there was at a given time.

❹ Draw conclusions about the information presented on the graph.

PRACTICE the Skill

Use the line graph on this page to answer the following questions.

❶ (a) What is the subject of the line graph? (b) What is the source of the information?

❷ (a) What time period is covered by the graph? (b) What is being measured?

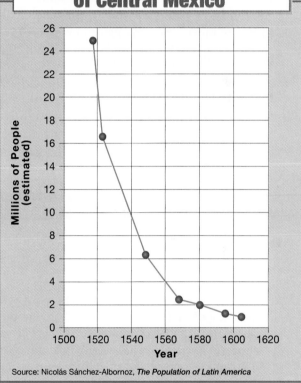

Native American Population of Central Mexico

Source: Nicolás Sánchez-Albornoz, *The Population of Latin America*

❸ About how many Native Americans lived in central Mexico before 1520? In 1580?

❹ Using the information on the graph, make a generalization about the Indian population of central Mexico.

APPLY the Skill

For the next week, keep track of the number of hours you spend each day performing a certain activity. Use your statistics to make a line graph.

rich. Spanish treasure ships laden with thousands of tons of gold and silver sailed regularly across the Atlantic.

The Spanish forced Native Americans to work in the gold and silver mines. In flickering darkness, Indians labored in narrow tunnels where they hacked out rich ores. Many died when tunnels caved in.

Meanwhile, on the islands of the West Indies, large numbers of Indians worked on **plantations,** or large estates farmed by many workers. They grew sugar cane and tobacco, which plantation owners sold in Spain at a huge profit.

Thousands of Native Americans died from overwork in mines and on plantations. As you have read, European diseases killed millions more. (See the graph on page 71.)

Las Casas seeks reform

These harsh conditions led one priest, **Bartolomé de Las Casas** (day lahs KAH sahs), to seek reform. Traveling through New Spain, Las Casas witnessed firsthand the deaths of Indians due to hunger, disease, and mistreatment. He was horrified by the terrible conditions that he saw:

66 The Indians were totally deprived of their freedom.... Even beasts enjoy more freedom when they are allowed to graze in the field. 99

Las Casas journeyed to Spain and asked the king to protect the Indians. In the 1540s, the royal government did pass laws prohibiting the enslavement of Native Americans. The laws also allowed Indians to own cattle and grow crops. However, few officials in New Spain enforced the new laws.

As the death toll among Native Americans rose, the Spanish looked for a new source of labor. Las Casas, still seeking to help the Indians, suggested that Africans be brought as slaves to replace Indian laborers. Unlike Indians, Africans did not catch European diseases, he said. Besides, they were used to doing hard farm work in their homelands. In the years ahead, Las Casas would regret the results of his suggestion.

★ Section 2 Review ★

Recall

1. **Locate** (a) Pacific Ocean, (b) Gulf of Mexico, (c) Florida, (d) New Spain.
2. **Identify** (a) Vasco Núñez de Balboa, (b) Ferdinand Magellan, (c) Montezuma, (d) Hernando Cortés, (e) Francisco Pizarro, (f) Spanish borderlands, (g) Laws of the Indies, (h) Juan de Oñate, (i) Eusebio Francisco Kino, (j) Bartolomé de Las Casas.
3. **Define** (a) conquistador, (b) pueblo, (c) presidio, (d) mission, (e) peninsulare, (f) creole, (g) mestizo, (h) encomienda, (i) plantation.

Comprehension

4. Why were a handful of Spanish soldiers able to conquer the empires of the Aztecs and Incas?

5. How did the Laws of the Indies regulate life in New Spain?
6. (a) In what ways was life harsh for Native Americans under Spanish rule? (b) How did Bartolomé de Las Casas try to help Indians?

Critical Thinking and Writing

7. **Making Generalizations** Based on what you have read in this section, make a generalization about the way Spain governed its colonies in the Americas.
8. **Recognizing Points of View** Why do you think the Spanish felt they had the right to force the Indians to work for them?

Activity **Creating a Chart** One of your friends has asked you for help understanding the social classes of Spain's American colonies. Help your friend by creating a chart that accurately illustrates the social structure that existed in New Spain.

Africans Come to the Americas

★ ★

As You Read

Explore These Questions
- Why were African states prosperous?
- How did the African slave trade change in the 1500s?
- What was the Middle Passage?

Define
- city-state
- kinship network
- Middle Passage

Identify
- Swahili
- Mansa Musa
- Affonso

SETTING the Scene In the late afternoon, the distant sound of a horn, blown repeatedly, interrupted the peace of a small West African village. Children ran toward the sound. *"Batafo! Batafo!"* they cried. "Traders!"

Soon the caravan arrived. The long line of porters and camels carried precious goods. Some brought sacks of salt or fish. Others had gold, fine fabrics, or jewelry. Some pushed slaves toward the village.

Trade had long played a vital role in African life. Complex trade routes across the Sahara, a vast desert, linked African villages and kingdoms. At first, Europeans played little or no role in this trade. After the 1400s, however, new trading patterns developed. They drew Africa into closer contact with both Europe and the Americas.

African States

Africa is a vast continent, the second largest on Earth. Across the continent, a wide variety of societies and cultures developed. By the 1400s, there were prosperous trading states in both East Africa and West Africa.

East Africa

On the coast of East Africa, where there were natural harbors, small villages grew

West African ivory carving, showing Portuguese traders

into busy trading centers. Gold from Zimbabwe, a powerful inland state, made its way to coastal cities such as Mogadishu, Kilwa, and Sofala. From the coastal cities, ships carried the gold and other valuable products up the African coast as well as to India. (See the map on p. 75.)

The profits from trade helped local rulers build strong city-states in East Africa. A **city-state** is a large town that has its own independent government.

As East Africans mingled with merchants from other lands, a rich variety of cultures developed. From Arab traders, many East Africans adopted the religion of Islam. The blend of cultures also gave rise to **Swahili,** a new language that used both Arab and African words.

West Africa

Several major trading states also emerged south of the Sahara in West Africa. Of these, two of the most important were Mali and Songhai.

Between 1200 and 1400, the kingdom of Mali reached its height. Its most famous ruler was the emperor **Mansa Musa.** In 1324, Mansa Musa journeyed from Mali across North Africa to Egypt and the Middle East. His wealth dazzled the Egyptians, who spread tales of his splendor as far as Europe. A Spanish map of the period shows a powerful Mansa Musa on his throne. The

Past

Present

African Art

In many African societies, elaborate masks were used in political, religious, and social ceremonies. At left is a mask of a West African king, carved by African artists several hundred years ago. At right, a similar mask is present during an American family's celebration of Kwanzaa. ★ **How else does this American family show pride in its African roots?**

mapmaker praised Mansa Musa's great wealth by writing these words on the map:

> 66 So abundant is the gold in his country that he is the richest and most noble king in all the land. 99

Later, in the 1400s, Songhai (SAWNG hi) became the most powerful kingdom in West Africa. Timbuktu, located on the Niger River, was one of Songhai's thriving cities. Timbuktu boasted over 100 schools, including a university.

$ Connections With Economics

Captain Theodore Canot, a European slave trader, witnessed the busy economy of the West African town of Timbo: "They weave cotton, work in leather, fabricate iron, . . . engage diligently in agriculture, and, whenever not laboriously employed, devote themselves to reading and writing."

Village and Family Life

Throughout Africa, most people lived in small villages and made a living by herding or farming. Many farmers worked the same land as their parents and grandparents before them. In rain forests close to the coast, farmers grew yams and other crops. In the grasslands, they raised millet, rice, and other grains. During the 1500s, Africans also began to grow corn, which had been introduced from the Americas.

Family relations played an important part in African life. Children had duties not only to their parents but also to aunts, uncles, and cousins. Grandparents received special respect. These kinds of close family ties are called a **kinship network.** Kinship ties encouraged a strong sense of community and cooperation.

African religions helped to stress the importance of kinship. Religious ceremonies honored ancestors and the spirits of the Earth. Farmers believed that by farming the land properly, they brought honor to their families.

The African Slave Trade

In Africa, as elsewhere around the world, slavery had been part of the social and economic system since ancient times. Most slaves in Africa were people who had been captured in war. African traders often transported and sold slaves as laborers. Muslim merchants also carried African slaves into Europe and the Middle East.

In many African societies, slaves were part of the community. They were treated as servants rather than property. According to a saying of the Ashanti people, "A slave who knows how to serve inherits his master's property." In time, slaves or their children might become full members of the society.

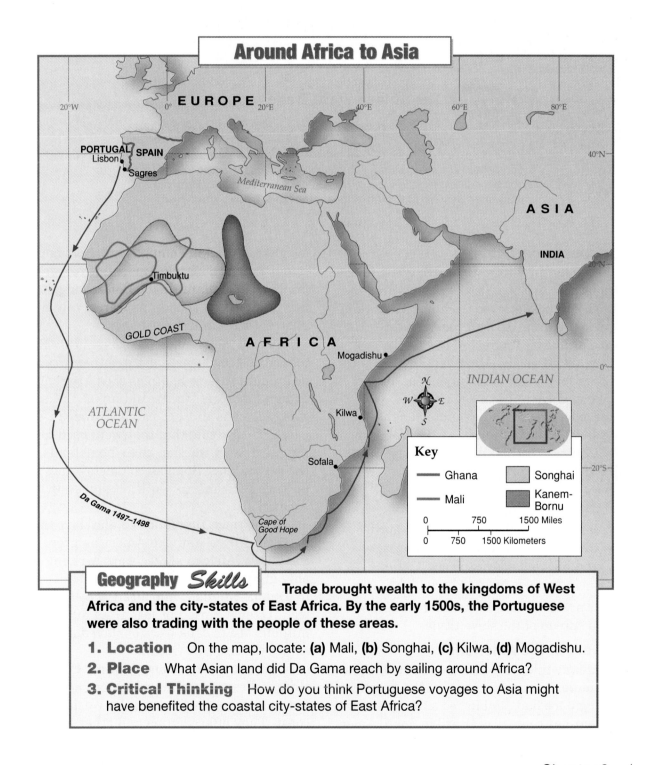

Around Africa to Asia

Geography Skills Trade brought wealth to the kingdoms of West Africa and the city-states of East Africa. By the early 1500s, the Portuguese were also trading with the people of these areas.

1. Location On the map, locate: **(a)** Mali, **(b)** Songhai, **(c)** Kilwa, **(d)** Mogadishu.

2. Place What Asian land did Da Gama reach by sailing around Africa?

3. Critical Thinking How do you think Portuguese voyages to Asia might have benefited the coastal city-states of East Africa?

Viewing **HISTORY** The African Slave Trade

Along the coast of West Africa, the Portuguese, French, Dutch, and English built forts from which they could participate in the profitable slave trade. African traders became wealthy by selling captives to the Europeans. The inset picture shows enslaved Africans in the West Indies, doing the backbreaking work of harvesting sugar cane. ★ **How did the plantation system in the Americas affect the African slave trade?**

Europeans participate

During the 1400s, the slave trade took a dramatic new turn. It was at this time that the Portuguese started trading with communities along the African coast. At first, they were primarily interested in gold, ivory and other trade goods. However, by 1500, the Portuguese were also buying as many as 2,500 enslaved Africans each year.

Some African leaders protested the growing slave trade. **Affonso,** a Christian king of the Central African kingdom of Kongo, wrote to the king of Portugal:

66 Merchants are taking every day our natives, sons of the land and sons of our nobles and vassals and our relatives, because the thieves and men of bad conscience...grab them and get them to be sold. 99

Such protests, however, could not stop the rapid spread of the slave trade.

Slavery in the Americas

Meanwhile, as you have learned, Spain was building a great empire in the Americas. Portugal too had established a colony—in the present-day country of Brazil in South Amer-ica. For a while, Spanish and Portuguese colonists forced Native Americans to work in mines and on plantations. Before long, however, thousands of Indians were dying from mistreatment and disease.

As you have read (see page 72), Bartolomé de Las Casas suggested that Africans be brought to New Spain as slaves to replace Indian laborers. Unlike Indians, Las Casas said, Africans did not catch European diseases. He also said that they were used to doing hard farm work in their homelands. In the early 1500s, Spanish colonists began importing Africans to work as slaves in the Americas.

In the years that followed, the slave trade between Africa and the Americas grew. By the 1600s, African slaves were arriving not only in Spanish and Portuguese colonies but in Dutch, English, and French colonies as well. Over a period of less than 400 years, millions of Africans were enslaved and sent across the Atlantic Ocean.

Slave traders from Spain, Portugal, Britain, France, and other western European nations set up posts along the West African coast. They offered guns and other goods in exchange for slaves. As the demand for slaves increased, Africans who lived along the coast made raids into the interior, seeking captives to sell to the Europeans. They marched their captives to the coast. There, the slaves were loaded aboard European ships headed for the Americas.

Some scholars today estimate that more than 10 million enslaved Africans were transported to the Americas between the 1500s and 1800s. The vast majority came from West Africa and most were sent to Brazil or the Caribbean. However, a total of more than 500,000 enslaved Africans would eventually arrive in the British colonies of North America. (You will read about the English colonies in Chapter 4.)

The Middle Passage

In the 1700s, English sailors began referring to the passage of slave ships west across the Atlantic Ocean as the **Middle Passage.** Below the decks of the slave ships, slaves were crammed tightly together on shelves. One observer noted that they were "rammed like [fish] in a barrel." They were "chained to each other hand and foot, and stowed so close, that they were not allowed above a foot and a half for each in breadth." The captives were allowed above deck to eat and exercise in the fresh air only once or twice a day.

Many enslaved Africans resisted, but only a few escaped. Some fought for their freedom during the trip. Others refused to eat or even jumped overboard to avoid a life of slavery. Olaudah Equiano (oh LAW dah ehk wee AH noh), an enslaved African, recalled an incident from his Middle Passage:

66 One day...two of my wearied countrymen who were chained together...jumped into the sea; immediately another...followed their example.... Two of the wretches were drowned, but [the ship's crew] got the other, and afterwards flogged him unmercifully for thus attempting to prefer death to slavery. 99

Records of slave ships show that about 10 percent of Africans loaded aboard ship for passage to the Americas died during the voyage. Many died of illnesses that spread rapidly in the filthy, crowded conditions inside a ship's hold. Others died of mistreatment. The Atlantic slave trade would last about 400 years. During that time, it may have caused the deaths of as many as 2 or 3 million Africans.

★ Section 3 Review ★

Recall

1. **Locate** (a) Mogadishu, (b) Kilwa, (c) Mali, (d) Songhai, (e) Timbuktu.
2. **Identify** (a) Swahili, (b) Mansa Musa, (c) Affonso.
3. **Define** (a) city-state, (b) kinship network, (c) Middle Passage.

Comprehension

4. (a) How did trade affect the culture of East Africa? (b) What were some of the achievements of Songhai?

5. How did the slave trade change after Europeans arrived in Africa?
6. Describe conditions on the Middle Passage.

Critical Thinking and Writing

7. **Comparing** How do traditional African kinship networks compare to American family ties today?
8. **Drawing Conclusions** Why do you think the antislavery protests of King Affonso and others were ignored by both Africans and Europeans?

★ ★

Activity **Writing a Short Story** Write a short story about a young African who is captured by slavers and transported across the Atlantic to the Americas. In your story, also describe the life that the African was forced to leave behind.

4 Colonizing North America

As You Read

Explore These Questions
- How did competition grow among European nations?
- How did trappers and missionaries help New France grow?
- How did the arrival of Europeans affect Native Americans in North America?

Define
- northwest passage
- Protestant Reformation
- missionary

Identify
- Jacques Cartier
- Henry Hudson
- Samuel de Champlain
- coureur de bois
- Jacques Marquette
- Robert de La Salle
- Peter Minuit
- New Netherland
- Algonquin

 In August 1497, the court of King Henry VII of England buzzed with excitement. Italian sea captain Giovanni Caboto and a crew of sailors from England had just returned from a 79-day Atlantic voyage. Caboto, called John Cabot by the English, reported that he had reached a "new-found island" in Asia where fish were plentiful.

Cabot was one of many Europeans who explored North America in the late 1400s and early 1500s. England, France, and the Netherlands all envied Spain's new empire. They wanted American colonies of their own.

Search for a Northwest Passage

Throughout the 1500s, European nations continued looking for new ways to reach the riches of Asia. They felt that Magellan's route around South America was too long. They wanted to discover a shorter **northwest passage,** or waterway through or around North America. (See the map on page 79.)

As you read above, John Cabot was confident he had found such a passage in 1497. He was mistaken. His "new-found island" off the Asian coast in fact lay off the shore of North America. Today, it is called Newfoundland and is the easternmost province of Canada.

In 1524, the French sent Giovanni da Verrazano (vehr rah TSAH noh), another Italian captain, in search of a northwest passage. Verrazano journeyed along the North American coast from the Carolinas to Canada. During the 1530s, **Jacques Cartier** (KAR tee YAY), also sailing for the French, sailed a good distance up the river that is now known as the St. Lawrence.

In 1609, the English sailor **Henry Hudson** sailed for the Dutch. His ship, the *Half Moon,* entered what is today New York harbor. Hudson continued some 150 miles (240 km) up the river that now bears his name.

The following year, Hudson made a voyage into the far north—this time for the English. After spending a harsh winter in what is now called Hudson Bay, Hudson's crew rebelled. They put Hudson, his son, and seven loyal sailors into a small boat and set it adrift. The boat and its crew were never seen again.

All these explorers failed to find a northwest passage to Asia. However, they succeeded in mapping and exploring many parts of North America. The rulers of western Europe began thinking about how to profit from the region's rich resources.

European Rivalries

As European nations began to compete for riches around the world, religious differences also heightened their rivalry. Until the 1500s, the Roman Catholic Church was the only church in western Europe. After that, however, a major religious reform movement split the Catholic Church and sharply divided Christians.

Catholics and Protestants

In 1517, a German monk named Martin Luther challenged many practices of the Catholic Church. Luther believed that the Church had become too worldly and greedy. He opposed the power of popes. He also objected to the Catholic teaching that believers needed to perform good works to gain eternal life. Luther argued that people could be saved only by their faith in God.

Luther's supporters became known as Protestants because of their protests against the Church. The **Protestant Reformation**, as the new movement was known, divided Europe. Soon, the Protestants themselves split, forming many different Protestant churches.

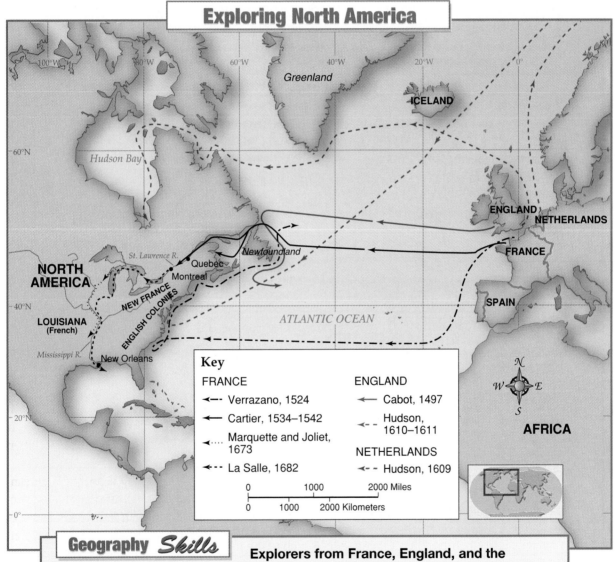

Exploring North America

Key

FRANCE
- ◄-- Verrazano, 1524
- ◄— Cartier, 1534–1542
- ◄···· Marquette and Joliet, 1673
- ◄-- La Salle, 1682

ENGLAND
- ◄— Cabot, 1497
- ◄-- Hudson, 1610–1611

NETHERLANDS
- ◄-- Hudson, 1609

Geography Skills Explorers from France, England, and the Netherlands competed to find a northwest passage to Asia. European states claimed ownership of the lands their explorers visited.

1. Location On the map, locate: **(a)** English Colonies, **(b)** New France.

2. Region What waterway was most important for travel through Louisiana?

3. Critical Thinking Why might you expect conflict between the French and English in North America?

As a result, religion divided the states of western Europe. In the late 1500s, Roman Catholic monarchs ruled Spain and France. Elizabeth I, a Protestant queen, ruled England. In the Netherlands, the Dutch people were mostly Protestant.

Rivalries in the Americas

As Europeans spread to the Americas, they brought their religious conflicts with them. Queen Elizabeth encouraged English adventurers to raid Spanish colonies and capture the treasure fleets of Catholic Spain.

European Explorers

Explorer	Achievements
For Portugal	
Bartolomeu Dias 1487–1488	Sailed around the southern tip of Africa
Vasco da Gama 1497–1498	Sailed around Africa to India
Pedro Álvares Cabral 1500	Reached Brazil
For Spain	
Christopher Columbus 1492–1504	Explored the West Indies and the Caribbean
Vasco Núñez de Balboa 1513	Sighted the Pacific Ocean
Juan Ponce de León 1508–1509, 1513	Explored Puerto Rico Explored Florida
Ferdinand Magellan 1519–1522	Led first expedition to sail around the world
Pánfilo de Narváez/Cabeza de Vaca/Estevanico 1528–1536	Traveled in the Spanish borderlands
Francisco Coronado 1540–1542	Explored southwestern North America
Hernando De Soto 1516–1520, 1539–1542	Explored Central America Led expedition to the Mississippi River
Juan Cabrillo 1542–1543	Explored west coast of North America
For England	
John Cabot 1497–1501(?)	Explored east coast of North America
Henry Hudson 1610–1611	Explored Hudson Bay
For the Netherlands	
Henry Hudson 1609	Explored east coast of North America and the Hudson River
For France	
Giovanni da Verrazano 1524	Explored east coast of North America, including present-day New York harbor
Jacques Cartier 1534–1542	Explored St. Lawrence River
Samuel de Champlain 1603–1615	Explored St. Lawrence River valley Founded Quebec
Jacques Marquette/Louis Joliet 1673	Explored along the Mississippi River
Robert de La Salle 1679–1682	Explored Great Lakes Reached the mouth of the Mississippi River

Chart Skills

Starting in the late 1400s, western European nations sent explorers to find new trades and to establish new colonies.

1. **Comprehension** (a) Name two explorers who worked for England. (b) What Frenchman explored the Great Lakes?

2. **Critical Thinking** What theory can you offer to explain why Henry Hudson sailed for two different countries?

Protestant England also competed with Catholic France for lands in North America.

Not all rivalries were religious, however. The Netherlands and England struggled against each other even though both were Protestant. They competed for control of land in North America and for economic markets all over the world.

New France

The first permanent French settlements, in what became known as New France, were founded by **Samuel de Champlain** (sham PLAYN). The first colony took root at Port Royal, Nova Scotia, in 1605. Three years later, Champlain led another group of settlers along the route Cartier had pioneered. On a rocky cliff high above the St. Lawrence River, Champlain built a trading post known as Quebec (kwi BEHK).

Economy of New France

Unlike Spain's empire in the Americas, the French empire had little gold or silver. Instead, the French profited from fishing, trapping, and trading.

Most French colonists were traders and trappers. Those who lived and worked in the woods became known as **coureurs de bois** (koo RYOOR duh BWAH), or runners of the woods. The French brought knives, kettles, cloth, and other items for trade with Native Americans. In return, the Native Americans gave them beaver skins and other furs that sold for high prices in Europe.

Coureurs de bois established friendly relations with the Native Americans. Many married Indian women. They learned trapping and survival skills from Native Americans. For example, Indians taught them how to make valuable tools such as snowshoes and canoes.

Missionary work

Catholic **missionaries** often came from Europe and traveled with the fur traders. The missionaries were determined to convert Native Americans to Christianity. They set up missions, drew maps, and wrote about the lands they explored. Life was difficult, espe-

Viewing HISTORY "Runner of the Woods"

To be a successful hunter and trapper in New France, a coureur de bois, or "runner of the woods," often relied on Native American skills and technology. For example, the snowshoes that Indians invented made it easier to travel through deep snow. ★ **What other skills did coureurs de bois learn from Indians?**

cially in winter. One priest recalled traveling through deep snow using Indian snowshoes:

> 66 If a thaw came, dear Lord, what pain!...I was marching on an icy path that broke with every step I took; as the snow softened...we often sunk in it up to our...waist. 99

Expansion to the Mississippi

French trappers followed the St. Lawrence deep into the heart of North America. Led by Indian guides, they reached the Great Lakes. Here, Indians spoke of a mighty river, which they called Mississippi, or "Father of the Waters."

In 1673, a French missionary, Father **Jacques Marquette** (mar KEHT), and a fur trader, Louis Joliet (JOH lee eht), set out with

A View of Manhattan

The Dutch built New Amsterdam on the southern tip of Manhattan Island. From a small town of fewer than 30 houses, the settlement grew into a busy port visited by ships from around the world. This painting shows New Amsterdam as it appeared in the 1600s. ★ **What does Manhattan Island look like today?**

Indian guides to reach the Mississippi. They followed the river for more than 700 miles (1,100 km) before turning back. In 1682, another explorer, **Robert de La Salle,** completed the journey to the Gulf of Mexico. La Salle named the region Louisiana in honor of the French king, Louis XIV.

To keep Spain and England out of Louisiana, the French built forts along the Mississippi. One fort, at the mouth of the river, was named New Orleans. New Orleans soon grew into a busy trading center. The French also built forts in the north along the Great Lakes. Among them was Fort Detroit, built by Antoine Cadillac near Lake Erie.

Government of New France

New France was governed much like New Spain. The French king controlled the government directly, and people had little freedom. A council appointed by the king made all decisions.

King Louis XIV was concerned that too few French were moving to the territories of New France. In the 1660s, therefore, he sent about a thousand farmers to the colony. The newcomers included many young women.

Despite Louis's efforts to increase the population of New France, the colony grew slowly. By 1680, only about 10,000 settlers lived in the colony. Of those, one third lived on farms along the St. Lawrence. Many more chose the life of the coureurs de bois, who lived largely free of government control.

New Netherland

Like the French, the Dutch hoped to profit from their discoveries in the Americas. In 1626, **Peter Minuit** (MIHN yoo wiht) led a group of Dutch settlers to the mouth of the Hudson River. There, he bought Manhattan Island from local Indians. Minuit called his settlement New Amsterdam. Other Dutch colonists settled farther up the Hudson River. The entire colony was known as **New Netherland.**

By the mid-1600s, New Amsterdam grew into a busy port. The Dutch welcomed people of many nations and religions to their colony. One Dutch governor boasted that more than 15 languages could be heard in the streets of New Amsterdam.

In 1655, the Dutch enlarged New Netherland by taking over the colony of New Sweden. The Swedes had established New Sweden along the Delaware River some 15 years earlier.

Rivalry over furs

Dutch traders sent furs to the Netherlands. The packing list for the first shipment included "the skins of 7,246 beaver, 853 otter, 81 mink, 36 cat lynx, and 34 small rats."

The Dutch and French became rivals in the fur trade. In this rivalry, the French were helped by the **Algonquin** (al GAHN kwihn) Indians. The Dutch made friends with the Iroquois. For many years, fighting raged among the Europeans and their Indian allies.

Dutch ways in North America

The Dutch brought many of their customs to New Netherland. They liked to ice-skate, and in winter the frozen rivers and ponds filled with skaters. Every year on Saint Nicholas's birthday, children put out their shoes to be filled with all sorts of presents. Later, "Saint Nick" came to be called Santa Claus.

Some Dutch words entered the English language. A Dutch master was a "boss." The people of New Amsterdam sailed in "yachts." Dutch children munched on "cookies" and went for rides through the snow on "sleighs."

Impact on Native Americans

The coming of Europeans to North America brought major changes for Native Americans. Once again, as in New Spain, European diseases killed millions of Indians. Rivalry over the fur trade increased Indian warfare because European settlers encouraged their Indian allies to attack one another. The scramble for furs also led to over-trapping. By 1640, trappers had almost wiped out the beavers on Iroquois lands in upstate New York.

The arrival of European settlers affected Native Americans in other ways. Missionaries tried to convert Indians to Christianity. Indians eagerly adopted European trade goods, such as copper kettles and knives, as well as muskets and gunpowder for hunting. Alcohol sold by European traders had a harsh effect on Native American life.

The French, Dutch, and English all waged warfare to seize Indian lands. As Indians were forced off their lands, they moved westward onto lands of other Indians. The conflict between Native Americans and Europeans would continue for many years.

★ Section 4 Review ★

Recall

1. **Locate** (a) Newfoundland, (b) St. Lawrence River, (c) Hudson Bay, (d) Quebec, (e) Mississippi River, (f) Louisiana.
2. **Identify** (a) Jacques Cartier, (b) Henry Hudson, (c) Samuel de Champlain, (d) coureur de bois, (e) Jacques Marquette, (f) Robert de La Salle, (g) Peter Minuit, (h) New Netherland, (i) Algonquin.
3. **Define** (a) northwest passage, (b) Protestant Reformation, (c) missionary.

Comprehension

4. Why did European nations compete for control of lands in North America?

5. (a) How did French trappers get along with Native Americans? (b) Why did missionaries often travel with the coureurs de bois?
6. How did competition between the French and Dutch affect the Algonquins and Iroquois?

Critical Thinking and Writing

7. **Comparing** (a) Describe one way in which New France was similar to New Spain. (b) Describe one way in which they were different.
8. **Inferring** How did missionaries help New France expand?

Activity **Making a Map** Suppose you can send a map back through time to French explorers of the 1600s. On your map, show how they can travel by land and water from Newfoundland through New France to the mouth of the Mississippi.

The First English Colonies

As You Read

Explore These Questions
- How did representative government take root in Virginia?
- Why did the Pilgrims start a colony in North America?
- How did Native Americans help the Plymouth Colony to survive?

Define
- charter
- representative government
- Magna Carta
- Parliament
- Mayflower Compact

Identify
- Sir Walter Raleigh
- John Smith
- Powhatan
- Pocahontas
- House of Burgesses
- Pilgrims
- Squanto

SETTING the Scene 66 If England possesses these places in America, Her Majesty will have good harbors, plenty of excellent trees for masts, good timber to build ships . . . all things needed for a royal navy, and all for no price. 99

Richard Hakluyt wrote these words to persuade Queen Elizabeth I of England to set up colonies in North America. Hakluyt explained a total of more than 30 arguments in favor of settlement. "We shall," Hakluyt concluded, "[stop] the Spanish king from flowing over all the face . . . of America."

Hakluyt's pamphlet, written in 1584, appealed to English pride. England's rival, Spain, had built a great empire in the Americas. England was determined to win a place there, too.

Settlement at Roanoke

The man who encouraged Hakluyt to write his pamphlet was **Sir Walter Raleigh,** a favorite of Queen Elizabeth. With the queen's permission, Raleigh raised money to outfit a colony in North America. In 1585, seven ships and about 100 men set sail across the Atlantic.

The colonists landed on Roanoke (ROH uh nohk), an island off the coast of present-day North Carolina. Within a year, the colonists ran short of food and quarreled with neigh-boring Native Americans. When an English ship stopped in the harbor, the weary settlers climbed aboard and sailed home.

In 1587, Raleigh asked John White, one of the original colonists, to return to Roanoke with a new group of settlers. This time, women and children went along, too. In Roanoke, one of the women gave birth to a baby girl named Virginia Dare. She was the first English child born in North America.

When supplies ran low, White returned to England, leaving behind 117 colonists. White planned to return in a few months. In England, however, he found the whole nation preparing for war with Spain. It was three years before he returned to Roanoke.

When White did reach Roanoke, he found the settlement strangely quiet. Houses stood empty. Vines twined through the windows and pumpkins sprouted from the earthen floors. White found the word CROATOAN, the name of a nearby island, carved on a tree.

 Connections With Science

In 1998, researchers from the University of Arkansas and the College of William and Mary theorized that the Roanoke settlers were victims of the region's worst drought in eight centuries. Their theory was based on the study of moisture-sensitive tree rings from 800-year-old cypress trees.

White was eager to investigate, but a storm was blowing up and his crew refused to make the trip. The next day, White stood sadly on board as the captain set sail for England. To this day, the fate of Roanoke's settlers remains a mystery.

Jamestown Colony

Nearly 20 years passed before England tried again to plant a colony. Then, in 1606, the Virginia Company of London received a charter from King James I. A **charter** is a legal document giving certain rights to a person or company. The charter gave the Virginia Company the right to settle lands to the north of Roanoke, between North Carolina and the Potomac River. The land was called Virginia. The charter guaranteed colonists of Virginia the same rights as English citizens.

A difficult start

In the spring of 1607, 105 colonists arrived in Virginia. They sailed into Chesapeake Bay and began building homes along the James River. They named their tiny outpost Jamestown, after their king, James I.

The colonists soon discovered that Jamestown was located in a swampy area. The water was unhealthy, and mosquitoes spread malaria. Many settlers suffered or died from disease.

Governing the colony also proved difficult. The Virginia Company had chosen a council of 13 men to rule the settlement. Members of the council quarreled with one another and did little to plan for the colony's future. By the summer of 1608, the Jamestown colony was near failure.

Starvation and recovery

Another major problem was starvation. Captain **John Smith,** a 27-year-old soldier and explorer, observed that the colonists were not planting enough crops. He complained that people wanted only to "dig gold, wash gold, refine gold, load gold." As they searched in vain for gold, the colony ran out of food.

Smith helped to save the colony. He set up stern rules that forced colonists to work if

Ætatis suæ 21. Aº. 1616.

*B*iography Pocahontas

Pocahontas, daughter of Powhatan, brought food to starving colonists at Jamestown. According to John Smith, she also saved him from an execution that her father had ordered. Later, Pocahontas converted to Christianity, married colonist John Rolfe, and moved to England. There, an artist painted this portrait of her in English dress.
★ **Why do you think the story of Pocahontas remains so popular today?**

they wished to eat. He also visited nearby Indian villages to trade for food. **Powhatan** (pow uh TAN), the most powerful chief in the area, agreed to sell corn to the English.

Peaceful relations between the English and Native Americans of the region were short-lived, however. Whenever the Indians did not agree to supply food voluntarily, the colonists used force to seize what they needed. On one occasion John Smith aimed a gun at Powhatan's brother until the Indians provided corn to buy his freedom. Incidents such as these led to frequent and bloody warfare. Peace was restored, for a brief time only, when the colonist John Rolfe married **Pocahontas,** daughter of Powhatan.

While the English were enjoying the peace, their economic difficulties resumed.

Virginia's House of Burgesses, shown at left, first met in 1619. It consisted of 22 representatives elected by "freemen" of the colony. In their first session, the burgesses passed laws against drunkenness and gambling and required colonists to attend church each Sunday. ★ **What people in Virginia could not elect burgesses?**

Problems arose soon after John Smith returned to England in 1609. For the next few years, the colony suffered terribly. Desperate settlers cooked "dogs, cats, snakes, [and] toadstools" to survive. To keep warm, they broke up houses to burn as firewood.

Tobacco and economic success

The Jamestown economy finally got on a firm footing after 1612, when colonists began growing tobacco. Europeans had learned about tobacco and pipe smoking from Native Americans. Although King James I considered smoking "a vile custom," the new fad caught on quickly. By 1620, England was importing more than 30,000 pounds (13,500 kg) of tobacco a year. At last, Virginians had found a way to make their colony succeed.

Representative Government

With Jamestown's economy improving, the Virginia Company took steps to establish a stable government in Virginia. In 1619, it sent a governor with orders to consult settlers on all important matters. Male settlers were allowed to elect burgesses, or representatives. The burgesses met in an assembly called the **House of Burgesses.** Together with the governor, they made laws for the colony.

The House of Burgesses marked the beginning of representative government in the English colonies. A representative gov-

ernment is one in which voters elect representatives to make laws for them.

The idea that people had political rights was deeply rooted in English history. In 1215, English nobles had forced King John to sign the Magna Carta, or Great Charter. This document said that the king could not raise taxes without first consulting the Great Council of nobles and church leaders. The Magna Carta established the principle, or basic idea, that English monarchs had to obey the laws of the land.

Over time, the rights won by nobles were extended to other English people. The Great Council grew into a representative assembly, called Parliament. By the 1600s, Parliament was divided into the House of Lords, made up of nobles, and an elected House of Commons. Only a few rich men had the right to vote. Still, the English had established that their king or queen must consult Parliament on money matters and must respect the law.

At first, free Virginians had even greater rights than citizens in England. They did not have to own property in order to vote. In 1670, however, the colony restricted the vote to free, male property owners.

Despite these limits, representative government remained important in Virginia. The idea took root that settlers should have a say in the affairs of the colony.

New Arrivals in Virginia

Virginia needed more people in order for the colony to grow and thrive. During the early years of the Jamestown Colony, only a few women chose to make the journey from England. There was also a need for more workers to help raise tobacco and other crops.

Women in Virginia

In 1619, the Virginia Company sent about 100 women to Virginia to help "make the men more settled." This first shipload of women quickly found husbands in Jamestown. The Virginia Company profited from the marriages because it charged each man who found a wife 150 pounds (68 kg) of tobacco.

Women did make the colony more settled. Still, life in Virginia remained a daily struggle. Women in Virginia were not allowed the right to vote throughout the colonial period. Women had to make everything from scratch—food, clothing, even medicines. Hard work and childbirth killed many at a young age.

The first Africans arrive

In 1619, a Dutch ship arrived at Jamestown with about 20 Africans. The Dutch sold the Africans to Virginians who needed laborers for growing tobacco. The colonists valued the agricultural skills that the Africans brought with them.

Two of the Africans, Antoney and Isabella, married after they arrived in Virginia. In 1624, they had a son, William. He was the first child of African descent to be born in the English colonies.

By 1644, about 300 Africans lived in Virginia. Some of them were slaves for life. Others worked as servants and expected one day to own their own farms. Some Africans did become free planters. For a time, free Africans in Virginia could own property, testify in court, and vote in elections. In 1651, Anthony Johnson owned 250 acres of land and employed five servants to help him work it.

Later in the 1600s, Virginia set up a system of laws allowing white colonists to enslave Africans. As slavery expanded, free Africans also lost rights. By the early 1700s, free African property owners could not vote.

Cause and Effect

Causes

- Europeans want more goods from Asia
- Muslims gain control of trade between Europe and Asia
- Rulers of European nations seek ways to increase their wealth
- European nations look for a sea route to Asia
- Columbus reaches the Americas

Exploration of the Americas

Effects

- Spain builds an empire in the Americas
- English, French, and Dutch set up colonies in North America
- Millions of Native Americans die from "European" diseases
- Slave traders bring enslaved Africans to the Americas
- Foods from the Americas are introduced into Europe

Effects Today

- The United States is a multicultural society today
- American foods, such as corn and potatoes, are important to people's diets around the world

Graphic Organizer *Skills*

Several hundred years ago, European exploration of the Americas affected Native Americans, Africans, and Europeans. The impact of this period is still felt today.

1. **Comprehension** How did economic factors lead to European exploration?
2. **Critical Thinking** Name some of the languages that are spoken by the people of North America and South America today.

Pilgrims Seek Religious Freedom

In 1620, another band of English settlers, the **Pilgrims,** sailed for the Americas. Unlike the Virginians or the Spanish, these colonists sought neither gold nor silver. All they wanted was to practice their religion freely.

In England, the Pilgrims belonged to a religious group known as Separatists. They were called that because they wanted to separate from the official church, the Church of England. The English government bitterly opposed this and took action against the Separatists. Separatists were fined, jailed, and sometimes even executed.

The Pilgrims' journey

In the early 1600s, a group of Separatists left England for Leyden, a city in the Netherlands. The Dutch allowed the newcomers to worship freely. Still, the Pilgrims missed their English way of life. They also worried that their children were growing up more Dutch than English.

A group of Pilgrims returned to England. Along with some other English people, they won a charter to set up a colony in Virginia. In September 1620, more than 100 men, women, and children set sail aboard a small ship called the *Mayflower*.

After a stormy two-month voyage, the Pilgrims landed on the cold, bleak shore of Cape Cod, in present-day Massachusetts. It was November 1620. Exhausted by the difficult sea voyage, the Pilgrims decided to travel no farther.

The Mayflower Compact

Before going ashore, the Pilgrims decided to establish rules for their new settlement. They gathered together and drew up the **Mayflower Compact.** The 41 men who signed it agreed to consult one another about laws for the colony and promised to work together to make the colony succeed:

> 66 We, whose names are underwritten…Having undertaken for the Glory of God, and Advancement of the Christian Faith…a voyage to plant the first colony in the northern parts of Virginia…do enact, constitute, and frame, such just and equal Laws…as shall be thought most [fitting] and convenient for the general Good of the Colony. 99

The First English Settlements

Geography *Skills*

In the late 1500s and early 1600s, English settlers established colonies in Roanoke, Jamestown, and Plymouth.

1. **Location**   On the map, locate: **(a)** Roanoke Island, **(b)** Jamestown, **(c)** Plymouth, **(d)** Virginia, **(e)** Massachusetts.

2. **Region**   What Native American peoples lived in the area around Plymouth?

3. **Critical Thinking**   How did the shape of the land around Plymouth provide a natural harbor for ships?

Early hardships

The Pilgrims named the colony Plymouth. They built their settlement on the site of a Native American village that had been abandoned because of disease. The colonists even found baskets filled with corn that they were able to eat.

However, the corn was not enough to get the Pilgrims through their first winter. The harshly cold season was also difficult to survive because the Pilgrims had not had enough time to build proper shelters. Nearly half the settlers perished of disease or starvation. The Pilgrims' religious faith was strong, however. They believed that it was God's will for them to remain in Plymouth.

Help from Native Americans

In the spring, the Pilgrims received help from neighboring Indians. A Pemaquid Indian, Samoset, had learned English from

▲ *The Pilgrims wore beaver hats such as this.*

earlier explorers sailing along the coast. He introduced the Pilgrims to Massasoit (MAS uh soit), chief of the local Wampanoag (wahm puh NOH ahg) Indians.

The Wampanoag who helped the Pilgrims most was named **Squanto.** Squanto brought the Pilgrims seeds of native plants—corn, beans, and pumpkins—and showed them how to plant them. He also taught the settlers to stir up eels from river bottoms and then snatch them with their hands. The grateful Pilgrims called Squanto "a special instrument sent of God."

In the fall, the Pilgrims had a very good harvest. Because they believed that God had given them this harvest, they set aside a day for giving thanks. In later years, the Pilgrims celebrated after each harvest season with a day of thanksgiving. Americans today celebrate **Thanksgiving** as a national holiday.

★ Section 5 Review ★

Recall

1. **Locate** **(a)** Roanoke Island, **(b)** Jamestown, **(c)** Cape Cod, **(d)** Plymouth.
2. **Identify** **(a)** Sir Walter Raleigh, **(b)** John Smith, **(c)** Powhatan, **(d)** Pocahontas, **(e)** House of Burgesses, **(f)** Pilgrims, **(g)** Squanto.
3. **Define** **(a)** charter, **(b)** representative government, **(c)** Magna Carta, **(d)** Parliament, **(e)** Mayflower Compact.

Comprehension

4. **(a)** What were the origins of representative government in the English colonies? **(b)** Which Virginia colonists were denied equal rights?

5. Why did the Pilgrims come to the Americas?
6. Describe two ways in which Squanto helped the Plymouth colonists.

Critical Thinking and Writing

7. **Linking Past and Present** In the 1600s, there was representative government in Jamestown. How do we have representative government in the United States today?
8. **Comparing** How were the reasons for founding Jamestown different from the reasons for founding Plymouth?

★ ★

Activity **Creating an Advertisement** You are an investor in the Virginia Company, and you want to encourage people to move to Virginia. Create an advertisement describing and illustrating the advantages of life in Virginia.

★ Sum It Up ★

Section 1 Europeans Reach the Americas
▶ During the Renaissance, Europeans grew interested in the world beyond Europe.
▶ European voyages to the Americas started a global exchange of products and ideas.

Section 2 Spain Builds an Empire
▶ Spanish conquistadors conquered the Aztecs and Incas and built a Spanish empire in the Americas.
▶ In time, the Spanish and Native American cultures began to blend together.

Section 3 Africans Come to the Americas
▶ By the 1400s, there were thriving trading communities in both East and West Africa.
▶ African and European traders worked together to supply millions of enslaved Africans for labor in the Americas.

Section 4 Colonizing North America
▶ European states, such as France and the Netherlands, were rivals for wealth and power in the Americas.
▶ Native Americans traded with Europeans, but also suffered from warfare and loss of lands.

Section 5 The First English Colonies
▶ The first English colonies in North America were at Jamestown and Plymouth.
▶ People in English colonies enjoyed English traditions of rights and freedoms.
▶ Native Americans helped the settlers of the Plymouth Colony survive their first difficult years in North America.

For additional review of the major ideas of Chapter 3, see *Guide to the Essentials of American History* or *Interactive Student Tutorial CD-ROM,* which contains interactive review activities, graphic organizers, and practice tests.

🗖 Reviewing the Chapter

Define These Terms
Match each term with the correct definition.

Column 1
1. Parliament
2. presidio
3. city-state
4. northwest passage
5. charter

Column 2
a. town that has its own independent government
b. legal document giving rights to a person or company
c. waterway through or around North America to Asia
d. English law-making body
e. fort where Spanish soldiers lived

Explore the Main Ideas
1. How did the Renaissance and Crusades cause Europeans to look beyond Europe?
2. Why did Spanish conquistadors go to the Americas?
3. How did the transatlantic African slave trade begin?
4. What role did Native Americans play in the building of **(a)** New France, **(b)** Plymouth Colony?
5. How did English political traditions affect government in **(a)** Virginia, **(b)** Plymouth?

🗖 Geography Activity

Match the letters on the map with the following places:
1. Africa, **2.** Asia, **3.** Europe, **4.** North America, **5.** East Indies, **6.** West Indies, **7.** South America. **Region** Why did Europeans want to reach Asia?

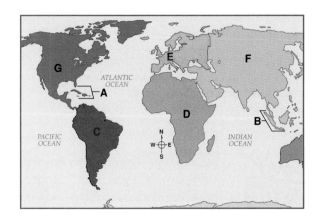

☐ Critical Thinking and Writing

1. **Linking Past and Present** How are Native American, African, and European influences evident today in the society and culture of the United States?

2. **Understanding Chronology** Place the following events in chronological order: **(a)** Columbus crosses the Atlantic, **(b)** the Renaissance begins, **(c)** Spain builds missions in borderlands, **(d)** Cortés conquers Aztecs.

3. **Recognizing Points of View** Describe how you think each of the following people might have felt about Bartolomé de Las Casas: **(a)** an enslaved Native American in New Spain, **(b)** a Spanish plantation owner, **(c)** a Portuguese slave trader, **(d)** King Affonso of Kongo.

4. **Exploring Unit Themes** **Origins** Choose one event or development discussed in this chapter. Explain why you think that event or development had an impact on the present-day United States.

☐ Using Primary Sources

In their rivalry for power in North America, Europeans enlisted the aid of Native American warriors. In 1687, the French planned an attack on the Iroquois, who were allies of the English.

   66 The Iroquois force consists of two thousand picked warriors—brave, active, more skillful in the use of the gun than our Europeans and all well armed.... If they be [surrounded] on both sides, all their plantations of Indian corn will be destroyed, their villages burnt, their women, children, and old men captured, and their warriors driven into the woods, where they will be pursued and [destroyed] by the other Indians. **99**

Source: *Memoir for the Marquis de Seignelay,* 1687, Department of Alfa-Information, University of Groningen, 1996.

Recognizing Points of View (a) How did the French plan to destroy the Iroquois? **(b)** Did the French respect the Iroquois? Explain.

ACTIVITY BANK

▶ Interdisciplinary Activity

Exploring the Arts Do research on Native American, European, or African art of the 1600s. In a presentation, display one or more copies of sample artwork. Explain how the art was created and discuss the meaning or symbolism of the art.

▶ Career Skills Activity

Biologists Prepare a fact sheet on an animal species that was hunted in the North American fur trade. Include information such as the animal's diet, habitat, and whether it is endangered today. Create drawings to illustrate your fact sheet.

▶ Citizenship Activity

Exploring Local Government In New Spain, the Spanish king appointed viceroys to make laws. In Virginia, the House of Burgesses made laws. Do research to learn how local laws are made in your community today. Present your findings in a chart.

Internet Activity

Review the maps on page 67. Some Spanish missions, pueblos, and presidios still stand today and are open to explore. Find Internet home pages dealing with those sites today. List the Internet addresses of the most interesting and informative sites. Share your list so others can visit, too.

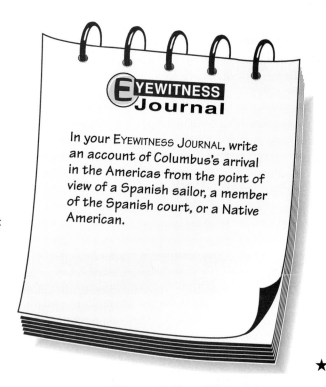

EYEWITNESS Journal

In your EYEWITNESS JOURNAL, write an account of Columbus's arrival in the Americas from the point of view of a Spanish sailor, a member of the Spanish court, or a Native American.

Chapter 4

The 13 English Colonies
1630–1750

In the 1600s and 1700s, English settlers founded 13 colonies on the eastern coast of what is now the United States. Many colonists came in search of new homes or a chance to earn a living. Others sought religious freedom. Over time, the various colonies developed different economies and ways of life.

Despite their differences, English settlers in all of the colonies came to develop an independent spirit and a tradition of self-government. This independence was strengthened by a religious movement called the Great Awakening and by new social and political ideas from Europe.

Why Study *History?*

The United States grew from the 13 English colonies. As a result, many of our traditions have English roots. One of the most important is representative government—the right to elect the people who govern us. To focus on this connection, see the *Why Study History?* feature, "You Have a Say in Government," in this chapter.

American Events

●1630
Puritans from England set up colony in Massachusetts

1675●
Metacom leads Native Americans against settlers in New England

●1682
William Penn founds colony of Pennsylvania

| 1630 | 1650 | 1670 | 1690 |

World Events

1660 World Event
Britain passes Second Navigation Act

1689 World Event
William and Mary sign English Bill of Rights

Colonial Life in Needlework

In England's North American colonies, women skilled at needle-work recorded details of their daily life. This sampler shows wealthy Bostonians in the mid-1700s. By this time, different ways of life had developed across the 13 English colonies. ★ **Do you think this sampler gives an accurate picture of colonial life? Why or why not?**

1700s
Plantations in the Southern Colonies rely on slave labor

1730s
Religious movement, known as the Great Awakening, sweeps through the colonies

1732
Georgia is founded as refuge for people jailed for debt

1690   1710   1730   1750

1700s World Event
Age of Enlightenment begins

1725 World Event
British Quakers speak out against slavery

1

The New England Colonies

★ ★

As You Read

Explore These Questions
- Why did the Puritans set up the Massachusetts Bay Colony?
- Who founded the colonies of Connecticut and Rhode Island?
- What was life like in the New England colonies?

Define
- toleration
- common
- Sabbath
- town meeting

Identify
- John Winthrop
- Puritans
- General Court
- Great Migration
- Thomas Hooker
- Fundamental Orders of Connecticut
- Roger Williams
- Anne Hutchinson
- Metacom

 April and May 1630 were cold, stormy months in the North Atlantic. Huddled below deck, colonists aboard the ship *Arbella* wondered if they had been foolish to sail to a new land. Their leader, however, had no doubts. **John Winthrop,** a lawyer and a devout Christian, assured them that their new colony would set an example to the world:

66 The Lord will make our name a praise and glory, so that men shall say of succeeding [colonies]: 'The Lord make it like that of New England.' For we must consider that we shall be like a City upon a Hill. The eyes of all people are on us. 99

The passengers on the *Arbella* were among more than 1,000 people who left England in 1630 to settle in North America. They set up their colony on Massachusetts Bay, north of Plymouth. Over the next 100 years, English settlers would build towns and farms throughout New England.

Puritans in Massachusetts

John Winthrop and his followers were part of a religious group known as **Puritans.** Unlike the Pilgrims, the Puritans did not want to separate entirely from the Church of England. Instead, they hoped to reform the church by introducing simpler forms of worship. They wanted to do away with many practices inherited from the Roman Catholic church, such as organ music, finely decorated houses of worship, and special clothing for priests.

Leaving England

The Puritans were a powerful group in England. Many were well-educated and successful merchants or landowners. Some sat in the House of Commons.

Charles I, who became king in 1625, disapproved of the Puritans and their ideas. He canceled Puritan business charters and had Puritans expelled from universities. He even had a few Puritans jailed.

By 1629, some Puritan leaders were convinced that England had fallen on "evil and declining times." They persuaded royal officials to grant them a charter to form the Massachusetts Bay Company. The company's bold plan was to build a new society in New England. They vowed to base their new society on biblical laws and teachings. Far from the watchful eye of the king, Puritans would run their colony as they pleased.

Some settlers joined the Massachusetts colonists for economic rather than religious reasons. In wealthy English families, the oldest son usually inherited his father's estate. With little hope of owning land, younger sons sought opportunity elsewhere. They were attracted to Massachusetts Bay because it offered cheap land or a chance to start a business.

Governing the colony

In 1629, the Puritans sent a small advance party to North America. John Winthrop and his larger party arrived the following year. Winthrop was chosen first governor of the Massachusetts Bay Colony, as the Puritan settlement was called.

Once ashore, Winthrop set an example for others. Although he was governor, he worked hard to build a home, clear land, and plant crops. One colonist wrote, "He so encouraged us that there was not an idle person to be found in the whole colony."

Under the charter, only stockholders who had invested money in the Massachusetts Bay Company had the right to vote. Most settlers, however, were not stockholders. They resented taxes and laws passed by a government in which they had no say.

Winthrop and other stockholders quickly realized that the colony would run more smoothly if a greater number of settlers could take part. At the same time, Puritan leaders sought to keep non-Puritans out of government. As a result, they granted the right to vote for governor to all men who were church members. Later, male church members also elected representatives to an assembly called the **General Court.**

Under the firm leadership of Winthrop and other Puritans, the Massachusetts Bay Colony grew and prospered. Between 1629 and 1640, some 15,000 men, women, and children made the journey from England to Massachusetts. This movement of people is known as the **Great Migration.** Many of the newcomers settled in Boston, which grew into the colony's largest town.

Settling Connecticut

In May 1636, a Puritan minister named **Thomas Hooker** led about 100 settlers out

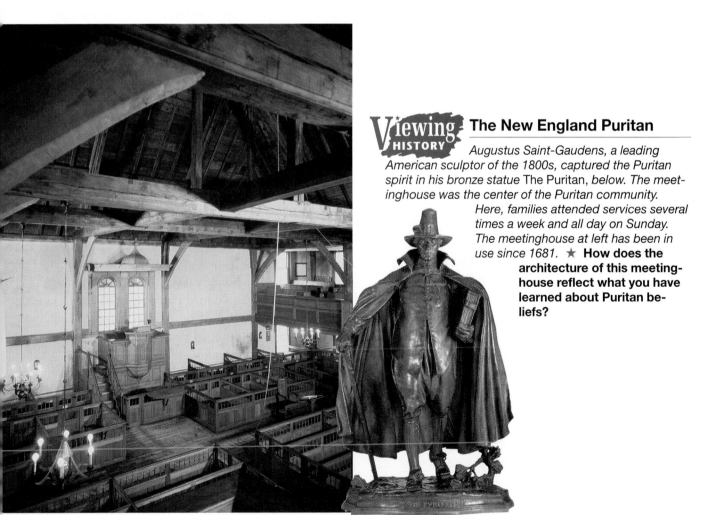

Viewing HISTORY **The New England Puritan**

Augustus Saint-Gaudens, a leading American sculptor of the 1800s, captured the Puritan spirit in his bronze statue The Puritan, *below. The meetinghouse was the center of the Puritan community. Here, families attended services several times a week and all day on Sunday. The meetinghouse at left has been in use since 1681.* ★ **How does the architecture of this meetinghouse reflect what you have learned about Puritan beliefs?**

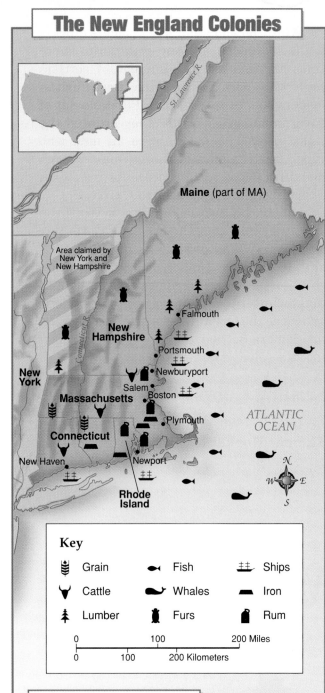

The New England Colonies

Maine (part of MA)

Area claimed by New York and New Hampshire

New Hampshire

New York

Massachusetts

Connecticut

New Haven

Newport

Rhode Island

Falmouth

Portsmouth

Newburyport

Salem

Boston

Plymouth

ATLANTIC OCEAN

N W E S

Key

🌾 Grain   🐟 Fish   ‡‡ Ships

⩔ Cattle   🐋 Whales   ▬ Iron

🌲 Lumber   Furs   Rum

0   100   200 Miles

0   100   200 Kilometers

Geography *Skills*

The New England colonies were among the first English settlements in North America. Major economic activities in the region included shipbuilding, fishing, and fur trapping.

1. **Location** On the map, locate: **(a)** Massachusetts, **(b)** Connecticut, **(c)** Rhode Island, **(d)** New Hampshire, **(e)** Boston, **(f)** Plymouth.

2. **Interaction** In which colonies did settlers mine iron ore?

3. **Critical Thinking** How did New England's geography encourage the growth of shipbuilding?

of Massachusetts Bay. Pushing west, they drove their cattle, goats, and pigs along Indian trails that cut through the forests. When they reached the Connecticut River, they built a town, which they called Hartford.

Hooker left Massachusetts Bay because he believed that the governor and other officials had too much power. He wanted to set up a colony in Connecticut with strict limits on government.

In 1639, the settlers wrote a plan of government called the **Fundamental Orders of Connecticut.** It created a government much like that of Massachusetts. There were, however, two important differences. First, the Fundamental Orders gave the vote to all men who were property owners, including those who were not church members. Second, the Fundamental Orders limited the governor's power. In this way, the Fundamental Orders expanded the idea of representative government in the English colonies.

In 1662, Connecticut became a separate colony, with a new charter granted by the king of England. By then, 15 towns were thriving along the Connecticut River.

Settling Rhode Island

Another Puritan who challenged the leaders of Massachusetts Bay was **Roger Williams.** A young minister in the village of Salem, Williams was gentle and good-natured. Most people, including Governor Winthrop, liked him. Williams's ideas, however, alarmed Puritan leaders.

Williams believed that the Puritan church had too much power in Massachusetts. In Williams's view, the business of church and state should be completely separate. The role of the state, said Williams, was to maintain order and peace. It should not support a particular church.

Williams also believed in religious toleration. Toleration means a willingness to let others practice their own beliefs. In Puritan Massachusetts, non-Puritans were not permitted to worship freely.

Puritan leaders viewed Williams as a dangerous troublemaker. In 1635, the General Court ordered him to leave Massachusetts. Fearing that the court would send him back to England, Williams fled to Narragansett Bay, where he spent the winter with Indians. In the spring, the Indians sold him land for a settlement. After a few years, it became the English colony of Rhode Island.

In Rhode Island, Williams put into practice his ideas about toleration. He allowed complete freedom of religion for all Protestants, Jews, and Catholics. He did not set up a state church or require settlers to attend church services. He also gave all white men the right to vote. Before long, settlers who disliked the strict Puritan rule of Massachusetts flocked to Providence and other towns in Rhode Island.*

Anne Hutchinson

Among those who fled to Rhode Island was **Anne Hutchinson.** A devout Puritan, Hutchinson regularly attended church services. After church, she and her friends gathered at her home to discuss the minister's sermon. At first, Hutchinson merely related what the minister had said. Later, she began to express her own views. Often, she seemed to criticize the minister's teachings.

Puritan leaders grew angry. They believed that Hutchinson's opinions were full of religious errors. Even worse, they said, a woman did not have the right to explain God's law. In November 1637, Hutchinson was ordered to appear before the General Court.

At her trial, Hutchinson answered all the questions put to her by General Winthrop and other members of the court. Time after time, she revealed weaknesses in their arguments. They could not prove that she had broken any Puritan laws or disobeyed any religious teachings.

Then, after two days of questioning, Hutchinson made a serious mistake. She told the court that God spoke directly to her, "By the voice of His own spirit to my soul." Members of the court were shocked. Puritans be-

*In 1763, Jewish settlers in Rhode Island built Touro Synagogue, the first Jewish house of worship in North America. It still stands today.

Biography — Anne Hutchinson

Anne Hutchinson was the respectable wife of a wealthy Boston merchant. She worked as a midwife, helping to deliver babies, and had 14 children of her own. When she questioned the authority of Puritan ministers, though, she was banished from the colony. Although Puritan leaders denounced her "bold spirit," today she is admired for her brave stand. ★ **How did Anne Hutchinson anger Puritan officials?**

lieved that God spoke only through the Bible, not directly to individuals. The court declared that Hutchinson was "deluded by the Devil" and ordered her out of the colony.

In 1638, Hutchinson, along with her family and some friends, went to Rhode Island. The Puritan leaders had won their case. For later Americans, however, Hutchinson became an important symbol of the struggle for religious freedom.

Conflict With Native Americans

From Massachusetts Bay, settlers fanned out across New England. Some built trading and fishing villages along the coast north of

Colonial Boston

This engraving shows a street near Boston harbor in the 1660s. By this time, fishing was already a vital part of the New England economy. The cod was so important that it even appeared in home decoration. ★ **Identify two other ways the sea played an important role in the economy of New England.**

▲ *Wooden cod from a Massachusetts home*

Boston. In 1680, the king made these coastal settlements into a separate colony called New Hampshire.

As more colonists settled in New England, they took over Native American lands. As a result, fighting broke out between white settlers and Indian nations of the region.

The largest conflict came in 1675. Wampanoag Indians, led by their chief, **Metacom,** attacked villages throughout New England. Other Indian groups soon allied themselves with the Wampanoags. Fighting lasted 14 months. Metacom and his allies destroyed 12 towns and killed more than 600 European settlers.

In the end, however, Metacom was captured and killed. The English sold his family and about 1,000 other Indians into slavery in the West Indies. Other Indians were forced from their homelands. Many of them died of starvation.

The pattern of English expansion followed by war between colonists and Indians was repeated throughout the colonies. It would continue for many years to come.

Life in New England

Puritans believed that people should worship and tend to local matters as a community. As a result, New England became a land of tightly knit towns and villages.

At the center of each village was the common, an open field where cattle grazed. Nearby stood the meetinghouse, where Puritans worshipped and held town meetings. Wooden houses with steep roofs lined the town's narrow streets.

Religion and family

The Puritans took their Sabbath, or holy day of rest, very seriously. On Sundays, no one was allowed to play games or visit taverns to joke, talk, and drink. The law required all citizens to attend church services, which on Sunday lasted all day.

During the 1600s, women sat on one side of the church and men on the other. Blacks and Indians stood in a balcony at the back. Children had separate pews, where an adult watched over them. If they "sported and played," they were punished.

The Puritans taught that children were a blessing of God. The average family had seven or eight children. The healthy climate allowed New Englanders to live long lives. Many reached the age of 70. As a result, children often grew up knowing both their parents and their grandparents.

Government

At town meetings, settlers discussed and voted on many issues. What roads should be built? How much should the schoolmaster be paid? Town meetings gave New Englanders a chance to speak their minds. This early experience encouraged the growth of democratic ideas in New England.

Puritan laws were strict. About 15 crimes carried the death penalty. One crime punishable by death was witchcraft. In 1692, Puritans in Salem Village executed 20 men and women as witches.

Economy

New England was a difficult land for colonists. The Puritans, though, believed that daily labor honored God as much as prayer. With hard work, they built a thriving way of life.

New England's rocky soil was poor for farming. After a time, however, settlers learned to grow many Native American crops, such as Indian corn, pumpkins, squash, and beans.

Although the soil was poor, the forests were full of riches. Settlers hunted wild turkey and deer, as well as hogs that they let roam free in the woods. In the spring, colonists collected sweet sap from sugar maple trees. Settlers also cut down trees and floated them to sawmills near ports such as Boston, Massachusetts, or Portsmouth, New Hampshire. These cities grew into major shipbuilding centers.

Other New Englanders fished the coastal waters for cod and halibut. When the fish were running, fishers worked tirelessly, seldom taking time to eat or sleep. Shellfish in New England were especially large. Oysters sometimes grew to be a foot long. Lobsters stretched up to 6 feet!

In the 1600s, New Englanders also began to hunt whales. Whales supplied oil for lamps, as well as ivory and other products. In the 1700s and 1800s, whaling grew into a big business.

Decline of the Puritans

During the 1700s, the Puritan tradition declined. Fewer families left England for religious reasons. Ministers had less influence on the way colonies were governed. Even so, the Puritans stamped New England with their distinctive customs and their dream of a religious society.

★ Section 1 Review ★

Recall

1. **Locate** (a) Massachusetts, (b) Connecticut, (c) Rhode Island, (d) New Hampshire.

2. **Identify** (a) John Winthrop, (b) Puritans, (c) General Court, (d) Great Migration, (e) Thomas Hooker, (f) Fundamental Orders of Connecticut, (g) Roger Williams, (h) Anne Hutchinson, (i) Metacom.

3. **Define** (a) toleration, (b) common, (c) Sabbath, (d) town meeting.

Comprehension

4. How did the Puritans govern the Massachusetts Bay Colony?

5. Explain why each of the following left the Massachusetts Bay Colony: (a) Thomas Hooker, (b) Roger Williams, (c) Anne Hutchinson.

6. How did the New England colonists make a living?

Critical Thinking and Writing

7. **Making Generalizations** Make a generalization about the role of religion in the Massachusetts Bay Colony. Give two examples to support your generalization.

8. **Making Inferences** Why do you think the Puritan leaders felt threatened by settlers who voiced opposing views?

★ ★

Activity **Writing a Letter** Go back in time! You are a young person living in Puritan New England about 1650. Write a letter to a friend in England, explaining what you like and what you do not like about life in New England.

The Middle Colonies

As You Read

Explore These Questions
- Why did William Penn start a colony in North America?
- Why were the Middle Colonies known as the Breadbasket Colonies?
- What was life like in the backcountry?

Define
- patroon
- proprietary colony
- proprietor
- royal colony
- cash crop
- backcountry

Identify
- Peter Stuyvesant
- William Penn
- Quakers
- Pennsylvania Dutch
- Breadbasket Colonies
- Great Wagon Road

SETTING the Scene In the summer of 1744, a doctor from the colony of Maryland traveled north to Philadelphia. Doctor Hamilton was amazed at the wide variety of people he met during his stay in that city. He wrote:

66 I dined at a tavern with a very mixed company of different nations and religions. There were Scots, English, Dutch, Germans, and Irish. There were Roman Catholics, Church [of England] men, Presbyterians, Quakers, . . . Moravians, . . . and one Jew. 99

By 1700, England had four colonies in the region directly south of New England. These colonies became known as the Middle Colonies because they were located between New England and the Southern Colonies. As Doctor Hamilton observed, the Middle Colonies had a much greater mix of people than either New England or the Southern Colonies.

New Netherland Becomes New York

As you read, the Dutch set up the colony of New Netherland along the Hudson River. In the colony's early years, settlers traded with Indians for

Dutch-style writing desk from colonial New York

furs and built the settlement of New Amsterdam into a thriving port.

To encourage farming in New Netherland, Dutch officials granted large parcels of land to a few rich families. A single land grant could stretch for miles. Indeed, one grant was as big as Rhode Island! Owners of these huge estates were called **patroons.** In return for the grant, each patroon promised to settle at least 50 European farm families on the land. Few farmers wanted to work for the patroons, however. Patroons had great power and could charge whatever rents they pleased.

Most settlers lived in the trading center of New Amsterdam. They came from all over Europe. Many were attracted by the chance to practice their religion freely.

Dutch colonists were mainly Protestants who belonged to the Dutch Reformed Church. Still, they permitted members of other religions—including Roman Catholics, French Protestants, and Jews—to buy land. "People do not seem concerned what religion their neighbor is," wrote a shocked visitor from Virginia. "Indeed, they do not seem to care if he has any religion at all."

By 1664, the rivalry between England and the Netherlands for trade and colonies was at its height. In August of that year, English warships entered New Amsterdam's harbor. **Peter Stuyvesant** (STI vuh sehnt), the governor of New Netherland, swore to defend the city. However, he had few weapons and little gunpowder. Also, Stuyvesant had made himself so unpopular with his harsh rule and heavy taxes that the colonists refused to help him. In the end, he surrendered without firing a shot.

King Charles II of England then gave New Netherland to his brother, the Duke of York. He renamed the colony New York in the duke's honor.

New Jersey

At the time of the English takeover, New York stretched as far south as the Delaware River. The Duke of York realized that it was too big to govern easily. He gave some of the land to friends, Lord Berkeley and Sir George Carteret. They set up a proprietary (proh PRI uh tuhr ee) colony, which they called New Jersey.

In setting up a **proprietary colony,** the king gave land to one or more people. These **proprietors** were free to divide the land and rent it to others. They made laws for the colony but had to respect the rights of colonists under English law.

Like New York, New Jersey attracted people from many lands. English Puritans mingled with French Protestants, Scots, Irish, Swedes, and Finns.

In 1702, New Jersey became a **royal colony,** that is, a colony under control of the English crown. The colony's charter protected religious freedom and the rights of an assembly that voted on local matters.

Pennsylvania

South of New Jersey, **William Penn** founded the colony of Pennsylvania in 1682. Penn came from a wealthy English family. King Charles II was a personal friend. At age 22, however, Penn shocked family and friends by joining the **Quakers,** one of the most despised religious groups in England.

The Quakers

Like Pilgrims and Puritans, Quakers were Protestant reformers. Their reforms went further than those of other groups, however. Quakers believed that all people—men and women, nobles and commoners—were equal in God's sight. They allowed women to preach in public and refused to bow or remove their hats in the presence of the nobility. Quakers spoke out against war and refused to serve in the army.

To most English people, Quaker beliefs seemed wicked. In both England and New England, Quakers were arrested, fined, or even hanged for their ideas. Penn became convinced that the Quakers must leave England. He turned to the king for help.

Charles II made Penn proprietor of a large tract of land in North America. The king named the new colony Pennsylvania, or Penn's woodlands.

*B*iography   **Peter Stuyvesant**

Peter Stuyvesant lost a leg fighting in the Caribbean. He fought just as hard when he became governor of New Netherland. Given almost total power, he imposed heavy taxes and punished lawbreakers with public whippings. When colonists demanded a voice in government, he replied that his authority came "from God." Still, Stuyvesant was powerless to stop England from taking over the colony. ★ **What are some advantages and disadvantages of having a strong ruler like Stuyvesant?**

The Middle Colonies

Key

🌾 Grain	⟨ Fish	🍶 Rum			
⋁ Cattle	🌲 Lumber	▬ Iron			

0   100   200 Miles
0   100   200 Kilometers

Geography *Skills*

The Middle Colonies were located to the south and west of New England and north of the Southern Colonies.

1. **Location** On the map, locate: **(a)** New York, **(b)** New Jersey, **(c)** Pennsylvania, **(d)** Delaware, **(e)** Hudson River, **(f)** Philadelphia, **(g)** Great Wagon Road.

2. **Movement** Identify two ways settlers could have traveled inland from the Atlantic Coast.

3. **Critical Thinking** Based on the map, why do you think Philadelphia would become a major trading center?

A policy of fairness

Penn thought of his colony as a "holy experiment." He wanted it to be a model of religious freedom, peace, and Christian living. Protestants, Catholics, and Jews went to Pennsylvania to escape persecution. Later, English officials forced Penn to turn away Catholic and Jewish settlers.

Penn's Quaker beliefs led him to speak out for fair treatment of Native Americans. Penn believed that the land belonged to the Indians. He said that settlers should pay for the land. Native Americans respected Penn for this policy. As a result, colonists in Pennsylvania enjoyed many years of peace with their Indian neighbors. One settler later remarked:

> 66 And as [Penn] treated the Indians with extraordinary humanity, they became very civil and loving to us.... As in other countries, the Indians were [angered] by hard treatment, which hath been the [cause] of much bloodshed, so the [opposite] treatment here hath produced love and affection. 99

The colony grows

Penn sent pamphlets describing his colony all over Europe. Soon, settlers from England, Scotland, Wales, the Netherlands, France, and Germany began to cross the Atlantic Ocean to Pennsylvania.

Among the new arrivals were large numbers of German-speaking Protestants. They became known as **Pennsylvania Dutch** because people could not pronounce the word Deutsch (DOICH), which means German.

Penn carefully planned a capital city along the Delaware River. He named it Philadelphia, a Greek word meaning "brotherly love." Philadelphia grew quickly. By 1710, a visitor wrote that it was "the most noble, large, and well-built city I have seen."

Delaware

For a time, Pennsylvania included some lands along the lower Delaware River. The region was known as Pennsylvania's Lower Counties.

Past

Present

A Simple Country Life

Today, in certain parts of Pennsylvania, horses and buggies are still a common sight, as they were in colonial days. The Amish, a Christian sect, came to Pennsylvania in the 1700s. Today, Amish families farm the land, use horses, and dress as plainly as their ancestors did.
★ **Why do you think the Amish chose Pennsylvania as their home?**

Settlers in the Lower Counties did not want to send delegates to a faraway assembly in Philadelphia. In 1701, Penn allowed them to elect their own assembly. Later, the Lower Counties broke away to form the colony of Delaware.

Life in the Middle Colonies

Farmers found more favorable conditions in the Middle Colonies than in New England. The broad Hudson and Delaware river valleys were rich and fertile. Winters were milder than in New England, and the growing season lasted longer.

A thriving economy

On such promising land, farmers in the Middle Colonies produced surpluses of wheat, barley, and rye. These were **cash crops,** or crops that are sold for money at market. In fact, the Middle Colonies exported so much grain that they became known as the **Breadbasket Colonies.**

Farmers of the Middle Colonies also raised herds of cattle and pigs. Every year, they sent tons of beef, pork, and butter to the ports of New York and Philadelphia. From there, the goods went by ship to New England and the South or to the West Indies, England, and other parts of Europe.

Encouraged by William Penn, skilled German craftsworkers set up shop in Pennsylvania. In time, the colony became a center of manufacturing and crafts. One visitor reported that workshops turned out "hardware, clocks, watches, locks, guns, flints, glass, stoneware, nails, [and] paper."

Settlers in the Delaware River valley profited from the region's rich deposits of iron ore. Heating the ore in furnaces, they purified it and then hammered it into nails, tools, and parts for guns.

Middle Colony homes

Farms in the Middle Colonies were generally larger than those in New England.

Skills FOR LIFE

| Critical Thinking | Managing Information | Communication | **Maps, Charts, and Graphs** |

Reading a Pie Graph

How Will I Use This Skill?

When you read textbooks, newspapers, or magazines, you will often find important statistics presented as part of a pie graph. A pie graph is in the shape of a circle that represents 100% of the group you are examining. Pie graphs present statistics in wedges, like pieces of a pie. The wedges represent percentages of the whole, helping you better compare the groups.

LEARN the Skill

You can learn to understand pie graphs by using the steps below.

❶ Identify the topic of the pie graph. Remember that the circle represents 100% of the group you are examining.

❷ Identify which groups are represented by the various wedges of the pie. Some groups which are few in number or not easily identified may be shown as "others."

❸ Compare the sizes of the various groups. The largest wedge will correspond to the largest group.

PRACTICE the Skill

Use the steps below to read the pie graph. The graph does not include Indians.

❶ (a) What is the topic of this graph? (b) What entire group does the circle as a whole represent?

❷ (a) List the population groups represented by the wedges. (b) Are all groups identified individually on the graph?

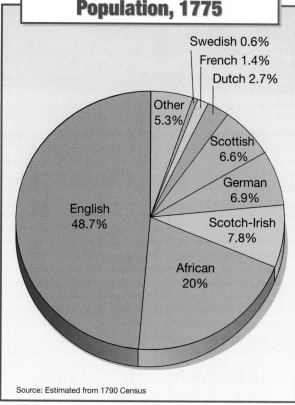

Ethnic Division of Colonial Population, 1775

Swedish 0.6%
French 1.4%
Dutch 2.7%
Other 5.3%
Scottish 6.6%
German 6.9%
Scotch-Irish 7.8%
English 48.7%
African 20%

Source: Estimated from 1790 Census

❸ (a) Which group made up the largest percentage of the colonial population? (b) What percentage of the population had Swedish roots? (c) What was the largest non-European group shown here?

APPLY the Skill

Take a poll to determine in which month each member of your class was born. Turn the numbers into percentages and show the information on a pie graph. To figure out percentages, divide the number in each group by the total number of the class.

Because houses tended to be far apart in the Middle Colonies, towns were less important. Counties, rather than villages, became centers of local government.

The different groups who settled the Middle Colonies had their own favorite ways of building. Swedish settlers introduced log cabins to the Americas. The Dutch used red bricks to build narrow, high-walled houses. German settlers developed a wood-burning stove that heated a home better than a fireplace, which let blasts of cold air leak down the chimney.

The Backcountry

In the 1700s, thousands of German and Scotch-Irish settlers arrived in Philadelphia. From there, they traveled west into the **backcountry,** the area of land along the eastern slopes of the Appalachian Mountains. Settlers followed an old Iroquois trail that became known as the **Great Wagon Road.**

To farm the backcountry, settlers had to clear thick forests. From Indians, settlers learned how to use knots from pine trees as candles to light their homes. They made wooden dishes from logs, gathered honey from hollows in trees, and hunted wild animals for food. German gunsmiths developed a lightweight rifle for use in forests. Sharpshooters boasted that the "Pennsylvania rifle" could hit a rattlesnake between the eyes at 100 yards.

Many of the settlers who arrived in the backcountry moved onto Indian lands. "The Indians...are alarmed at the swarm of strangers," one Pennsylvania official reported. "We are afraid of a [fight] between them for the [colonists] are very rough to them." On more than one occasion, disputes between settlers and Indians resulted in violence.

▼ *Wooden plow used in New York in the 1700s*

★ Section 2 Review ★

Recall

1. **Locate** (a) New York, (b) New Jersey, (c) Pennsylvania, (d) Philadelphia, (e) Delaware.
2. **Identify** (a) Peter Stuyvesant, (b) William Penn, (c) Quakers, (d) Pennsylvania Dutch, (e) Breadbasket Colonies, (f) Great Wagon Road.
3. **Define** (a) patroon, (b) proprietary colony, (c) proprietor, (d) royal colony, (e) cash crop, (f) backcountry.

Comprehension

4. What policies did William Penn follow in the Pennsylvania colony?

5. How did the land and climate help Middle Colonies farmers to prosper?
6. What did settlers have to do in order to farm the backcountry?

Critical Thinking and Writing

7. **Comparing** (a) How was Penn's "holy experiment" like the Puritan idea of a "city upon a hill"? (b) How was it different?
8. **Understanding Causes and Effects** Why do you think many settlers moved westward into the backcountry?

Activity **Creating a Pamphlet** Did you ever think about a career in advertising? Make up a pamphlet advertising the settlement of Pennsylvania like the ones that Penn sent to countries all over Europe. Encourage people to move to Pennsylvania by describing its economy and society.

3 The Southern Colonies

★ ★

As You Read

Explore These Questions
- Why were the Southern Colonies founded?
- What two ways of life developed in the Southern Colonies?
- Why did slavery become important in the South?

Define
- indigo
- debtor
- buffer
- plantation
- slave code
- racism

Identify
- Mason-Dixon Line
- Lord Baltimore
- Act of Toleration
- Bacon's Rebellion
- James Oglethorpe
- Mary Musgrove
- Tidewater

 In 1763, two English mathematicians, Charles Mason and Jeremiah Dixon, began to survey the 244-mile boundary between Pennsylvania and Maryland. The boundary had been in dispute since 1681.

For four years, Mason and Dixon carefully laid stone markers on the border between the two colonies. The sides of the markers facing Pennsylvania were inscribed with the letter *P*. The sides facing Maryland were inscribed with the letter *M*. In 1767, the two men completed the **Mason-Dixon Line.**

The Mason-Dixon Line was more than just the boundary between Pennsylvania and Maryland. It also divided the Middle Colonies from the Southern Colonies. Below the Mason-Dixon Line, the Southern Colonies developed a way of life different in many ways from that of the other English colonies.

Maryland

In 1632, Sir George Calvert persuaded King Charles I to grant him land for a colony in the Americas. Calvert had ruined his career in Protestant England by becoming a Roman Catholic. Now, he planned to build a colony where Catholics could practice their religion freely. He named the colony Maryland in honor of Queen Henrietta Maria, the king's wife.

Calvert died before his colony could get underway. His son Cecil, **Lord Baltimore,** pushed on with the project.

Settling the colony

In the spring of 1634, 200 colonists landed along the upper Chesapeake Bay, across from England's first southern colony, Virginia. The land was rich and beautiful. In the words of one settler:

ὦ The soil is dark and soft, a foot in thickness, and rests upon a rich and red clay. Every where there are very high trees.... An abundance of springs afford water.... There is an [endless] number of birds.... There is [nothing] wanting to the region. 🚙

Maryland was truly a land of plenty. Chesapeake Bay was full of fish, oysters, and crabs. Across the bay, Virginians were already growing tobacco for profit. Maryland's new settlers hoped to do the same.

Remembering the early problems at Jamestown, the newcomers avoided the swampy lowlands. They built their first town, St. Mary's, in a healthful location.

As proprietor of the colony, Lord Baltimore appointed a governor and a council of advisers. He gave colonists a role in government by creating an elected assembly. Eager to attract settlers to Maryland, Lord Baltimore made generous land grants to anyone who brought over servants, women, and children.

A few women took advantage of Lord Baltimore's offer of land. Two sisters, Margaret and Mary Brent, arrived in Maryland in

1638 with nine male servants. In time, they set up two plantations of 1,000 acres each. Later, Margaret Brent helped prevent a rebellion among the governor's soldiers. The Maryland assembly praised her efforts, saying that "the colony's safety at any time [was better] in her hands than in any man's."

Religious toleration

To ensure Maryland's continued growth, Lord Baltimore welcomed Protestants as well as Catholics to the colony.

Later, Lord Baltimore came to fear that Protestants might try to deprive Catholics of their right to worship freely. In 1649, he asked the assembly to pass an **Act of Toleration.** The act provided religious freedom for all Christians. As in many colonies, this freedom did not extend to Jews.

Bacon's Rebellion

Meanwhile, settlers continued to arrive in Virginia, lured by the promise of profits from tobacco. Wealthy planters, however, controlled the best lands near the coast. Newcomers had to push farther inland, onto Indian lands.

As in New England, conflict over land led to fighting between settlers and Indians. After several bloody clashes, settlers called on the governor to take action against Native Americans. The governor refused. He was unwilling to act, in part because he profited from his own fur trade with Indians. Frontier settlers were furious.

Finally, in 1676, Nathaniel Bacon, an ambitious young planter, organized angry men and women on the frontier. He raided Native American villages. Then, he led his followers to Jamestown and burned the capital.

The uprising, known as **Bacon's Rebellion,** lasted only a short time. When Bacon died suddenly, the revolt fell apart. The governor hanged 23 of Bacon's followers. Still, he could not stop English settlers from moving onto Indian lands along the frontier.

The Carolinas

South of Virginia and Maryland, English colonists settled in a region which they called

The Southern Colonies

Key

⌇ Rice		🌾 Grain		🌲 Lumber	
▲ Indigo		🍃 Tobacco		▬ Iron	
🐂 Cattle		🐟 Fish		🍶 Rum	

0   100   200   300 Miles

0   100   200   300 Kilometers

Geography Skills   England's five Southern Colonies stretched along the Atlantic coast from Maryland to Georgia. Farm products and lumber were important to the economy of the region.

1. **Location**   On the map, locate: **(a)** Maryland, **(b)** Virginia, **(c)** North Carolina, **(d)** South Carolina, **(e)** Georgia, **(f)** Chesapeake Bay, **(g)** Charleston.

2. **Place**   Describe the area where cattle herding took place.

3. **Critical Thinking**   Compare this map to the maps on pages 96 and 102. **(a)** What crops were grown only in the Southern Colonies? **(b)** Why do you think such products were not grown farther north?

This engraving from 1734 is the earliest known picture of Savannah, Georgia. English colonists carved the settlement out of a forest on the banks of the Savannah River. ★ **Based on this picture, how can you tell that building Savannah was hard work?**

caped into the forests. Planters then turned to slaves from Africa. By 1700, the majority of people coming to Charleston were African men and women brought there against their will.

The northern area of Carolina had fewer slaves. Differences between the two areas led to division of the colony into North Carolina and South Carolina in 1712.

Georgia

The last of England's 13 colonies was carved out of the southern part of South Carolina. **James Oglethorpe,** a respected English soldier and energetic reformer, founded Georgia in 1732. He wanted the new colony to be a place where **debtors,** or people who owed money they could not pay back, could make a new start.

A haven for debtors

Under English law, the government could imprison debtors until they paid what they owed. If they ever got out of jail, debtors often had no money and no place to live. Oglethorpe offered to pay for debtors and other poor people to travel to Georgia. "In America," he said, "there are enough fertile lands to feed all the poor of England."

In 1733, Oglethorpe and 120 colonists built the colony's first settlement at Savan-

the Carolinas. Settlement took place in two separate areas, one in the north and the other in the south.

In the northern part of the Carolinas, settlers were mostly poor tobacco farmers who had drifted south from Virginia. They tended to have small farms.

Farther south, a group of eight English nobles set up a larger colony. As proprietors, they received a grant of land from King Charles II in 1663. The largest settlement, Charles Town, grew up where the Ashley and Cooper rivers met. Later, Charles Town was shortened to Charleston.

Most early settlers in Charleston were English people who had been living in Barbados, a British colony in the Caribbean. Later, other immigrants arrived, including Germans, Swiss, French Protestants, and Spanish Jews.

Around 1685, a few planters discovered that rice grew well in the swampy lowlands along the coast. Before long, Carolina rice was a valuable crop traded around the world. Settlers in southern Carolina later learned to raise **indigo,** a plant used to make a valuable blue dye.

Carolina planters needed large numbers of workers to grow rice. At first, they tried to enslave local Indians. Many Indians died of disease or mistreatment, however. Others es-

Connections With Geography

Indigo was first grown in South Carolina by 17-year-old Eliza Lucas. She ran the family plantation while her father, an army colonel, served overseas. While away, Colonel Lucas sent his daughter seeds from all over the world. Eliza Lucas found that the West Indian indigo plant grew well in land that was bad for planting rice.

nah, above the Savannah River. Oglethorpe set strict rules for the colony. Farms could be no bigger than 500 acres, and slavery was forbidden.

At first, Georgia grew slowly. Later, however, Oglethorpe changed the rules to allow large plantations and slave labor. After that, the colony grew more quickly.

Rivalry with Spain

England hoped that Georgia would act as a buffer between the Carolinas and Spanish Florida. A **buffer** is a land located between two larger lands that reduces the possibility of conflict between them. Spain and England both claimed the land between South Carolina and Florida. Spain, aided by Creek allies, tried to force the English out. Oglethorpe and the Georgians held their ground.

A woman known as **Mary Musgrove** greatly helped Oglethorpe during this time. The daughter of a Creek mother and an English father, Musgrove spoke both Creek and English. She helped to keep peace between the Creeks and the settlers in Georgia. Musgrove's efforts did much to allow the colony of Georgia to develop in peace.

Two Ways of Life

Today, we often think of the colonial South as a land where wealthy planters lived in elegant homes, with large numbers of enslaved African Americans toiling in the fields. In fact, this picture is only partly true. As the Southern colonies grew, two distinct and different ways of life emerged—one along the Atlantic coast and another in the backcountry.

Tidewater plantations

The Southern Colonies enjoyed warmer weather and a longer growing season than the colonies to the north. Virginia, Maryland, and parts of North Carolina all became major tobacco-growing areas. Settlers in South Carolina and Georgia raised rice and indigo.

Colonists soon found that it was most profitable to raise tobacco and rice on large plantations. As you recall, a **plantation** is a large estate farmed by many workers. On these southern plantations, anywhere from 20 to 100 slaves did most of the work. Most slaves worked in the fields. Some were skilled workers, such as carpenters, barrel

Viewing HISTORY — Two Ways of Life

These pictures from the 1700s show two vastly different ways of life in the Southern Colonies. At left, wealthy planters enjoy a life of elegant leisure. At right, a woman in the backcountry fetches water for her daily chores. ★ **Who do you think fetched the water for the wealthy planters shown here?**

Viewing History

Slavery in the South

As the poster shows, colonial law permitted Africans to be bought and sold as property. The growth of slavery allowed southern colonists to work large plantations. The painting at right shows rows of slave cabins on a plantation in the Southern Colonies. ★ **Where did the slaves advertised on the poster come from? Where would they end up?**

makers, or blacksmiths. Still other slaves worked in the main house as cooks, servants, or housekeepers.

The earliest plantations were located along rivers and creeks of the coastal plain. Because the land was washed by ocean tides, the region was known as the **Tidewater.** The Tidewater's gentle slopes and rivers offered rich farmland for plantations.

Farther inland, planters settled along rivers. Rivers provided an easy way to move goods to market. Planters loaded crops onto ships bound for the West Indies and Europe. On the return trip, the ships carried English manufactured goods and other luxuries for planters and their families.

Most Tidewater plantations had their own docks, and merchant ships picked up crops and delivered goods directly to them. For this reason, few large seaport cities developed in the Southern Colonies.

Only a small percentage of white southerners owned large plantations. Yet, planters set the style of life in the South. Life centered around the Great House, where the planter's family lived. The grandest homes had elegant quarters for the family, a parlor for visitors, a dining room, and guest bedrooms.

In the growing season, planters decided which fields to plant, what crops to grow, and when to harvest the crops and take them to market. Planters' wives kept the household running smoothly. They directed house slaves and made sure daily tasks were done, such as milking cows.

The backcountry South

West of the Tidewater, life was very different. Here, at the base of the Appalachians, rolling hills and thick forests covered the land. As in the Middle Colonies, this inland area was called the backcountry. Attracted by rich soil, settlers followed the Great Wagon Road into the backcountry of Maryland, Virginia, and the Carolinas.

The backcountry was more democratic than the Tidewater. Settlers there were more likely to treat one another as equals. Men tended smaller fields of tobacco or corn or hunted game. Women cooked meals and fashioned simple, rugged clothing out of wool or deerskins.

The hardships of backcountry life brought settlers closer together. Families gathered to husk corn or help one another build barns. Spread out along the edge of the Appalachians, these hardy settlers felled trees, grew crops, and changed the face of the land.

Growth of Slavery

In the early years, Africans in the English colonies included free people and servants as well as slaves. Indeed, during the 1600s, even those Africans who were enslaved enjoyed some freedom. In South Carolina, for example, some enslaved Africans worked without supervision as cowboys, herding cattle to market.

Planters rely on slavery

On plantations throughout the Southern Colonies, enslaved Africans used farming skills they had brought from West Africa. They showed English settlers how to grow rice. They also knew how to use wild plants unfamiliar to the English. They made water buckets out of gourds, and they used palmetto leaves to make fans, brooms, and baskets.

By 1700, plantations in the Southern Colonies had come to rely on slave labor. Slaves cleared the land, worked the crops, and tended the livestock.

Limiting rights

As the importance of slavery increased, greater limits were placed on the rights of slaves. Colonists passed laws that set out rules for slaves' behavior and denied slaves their basic rights. These slave codes treated enslaved Africans not as human beings but as property.

Most English colonists did not question the justice of owning slaves. They believed that black Africans were inferior to white Europeans. The belief that one race is superior to another is called racism. Some colonists claimed that they were helping slaves by introducing them to Christianity.

A handful of colonists saw the evils of slavery. In 1688, Quakers in Germantown, Pennsylvania, became the first group of colonists to call for an end to slavery.

★ Section 3 Review ★

Recall

1. **Locate** (a) Maryland, (b) Virginia, (c) North Carolina, (d) South Carolina, (e) Georgia.
2. **Identify** (a) Mason-Dixon Line, (b) Lord Baltimore, (c) Act of Toleration, (d) Bacon's Rebellion, (e) James Oglethorpe, (f) Mary Musgrove, (g) Tidewater.
3. **Define** (a) indigo, (b) debtor, (c) buffer, (d) plantation, (e) slave code, (f) racism.

Comprehension

4. Why did their founders set up the colonies of (a) Maryland, and (b) Georgia?

5. How was life in the Tidewater different from life in the backcountry South?
6. What role did slaves play in the economy of the Southern Colonies by 1700?

Critical Thinking and Writing

7. **Applying Information** Review the definition of religious toleration. Did Maryland's Act of Toleration provide true religious toleration? Explain.
8. **Analyzing Ideas** How did the passage of slave codes in the colonies reflect racism?

★ ★

Activity **Creating Flashcards** Do you get confused about the 13 English colonies? Use the text, including the maps and charts, to create 13 flashcards. On one side, write the name of a colony. On the other, write three facts about that colony. You may later use these cards for review.

4 ★ Governing the Colonies

As You Read

Explore These Questions
- Why did England pass the Navigation Acts?
- What were colonial governments like?
- What rights did English colonists enjoy?

Define
- mercantilism
- import
- export
- triangular trade
- legislature
- bill of rights

Identify
- Navigation Acts
- Yankee
- Glorious Revolution
- English Bill of Rights

SETTING the Scene Philadelphia bustled with activity in 1750. Young farmers drove cattle, pigs, and sheep to market along narrow cobblestone streets. On the docks, sailors unloaded barrels of molasses from the West Indies, wines from Spain and Portugal, Dutch and English cloth, as well as spices, leather goods, tea, and coffee.

Philadelphia was the largest and busiest seaport in the colonies. Yet, by the 1700s, trade flourished all along the Atlantic coast. As trade increased, England began to take a new interest in its colonies.

England Regulates Trade

Like other European nations at the time, England believed that colonies existed for the benefit of the home country. This belief was part of an economic theory known as **mercantilism** (MER kuhn tihl ihz uhm). According to this theory, a nation became strong by building up its gold supply and expanding trade.

Because exports help a country earn money, mercantilists thought that a country should export more than it imports. **Imports** are goods brought into a country. **Exports** are goods sent to markets outside a country.

Beginning in the 1650s, the English Parliament passed a series of **Navigation Acts** that regulated trade between England and its colonies. The purpose of these laws was to ensure that only England benefited from colonial trade.

Under the new laws, only colonial or English ships could carry goods to and from the colonies. The Navigation Acts also listed certain products, such as tobacco and cotton, that colonial merchants could ship only to England. In this way, Parliament created jobs for English workers who cut and rolled tobacco or spun cotton into cloth.

The Navigation Acts helped the colonies as well as England. For example, the law encouraged colonists to build their own ships. As a result, New England became a prosperous shipbuilding center. Also, because of the acts, colonial merchants did not have to compete with foreign merchants because they were sure of having a market for their goods in England.

Still, many colonists resented the Navigation Acts. In their view, the laws favored English merchants. Colonial merchants often ignored the Navigation Acts or found ways to get around them.

Trading in Rum and Slaves

The colonies produced a wide variety of goods, and ships moved up and down the Atlantic coast in an active trade. Merchants from New England dominated colonial trade. They were known as **Yankees,** a nickname that implied they were clever and hardworking. Yankee traders earned a reputation for profiting from any deal.

Colonial merchants developed many trade routes. One route was known as the **triangular trade** because the three legs of the route formed a triangle. On the first leg, ships from New England carried fish, lumber, and other goods to the West Indies. There, Yankee traders bought sugar and molasses, a dark-brown syrup made from sugar cane. The ships then sailed back to New England, where colonists used the molasses and sugar to make rum.

On the second leg of the journey, ships carried rum, guns, gunpowder, cloth, and tools from New England to West Africa. In Africa, merchants traded these goods for slaves. On the final leg, ships carried enslaved Africans to the West Indies. With the profits from selling the enslaved Africans, traders bought more molasses.

Many New England merchants grew wealthy from the triangular trade. In doing so, they often disobeyed the Navigation Acts. Traders were supposed to buy sugar and molasses only from English colonies in the West Indies. However, the demand for molasses

The 13 English Colonies

Colony / Date Founded	Leader	Reasons Founded
New England Colonies		

■ Massachusetts
   Plymouth / 1620
   Massachusetts Bay / 1630
	
	William Bradford
	John Winthrop
		
		Religious freedom
		Religious freedom

■ New Hampshire / 1622	Ferdinando Gorges John Mason	Profit from trade and fishing
■ Connecticut / 1636	Thomas Hooker	Expand trade; religious and political freedom
■ Rhode Island / 1636	Roger Williams	Religious freedom
Middle Colonies		
■ New York / 1624	Peter Minuit	Expand trade
■ Delaware / 1638	Swedish settlers	Expand trade
■ New Jersey / 1664	John Berkeley George Carteret	Expand trade; religious and political freedom
■ Pennsylvania / 1682	William Penn	Profit from land sales; religious and political freedom
Southern Colonies		
■ Virginia / 1607	John Smith	Trade and farming
■ Maryland / 1632	Lord Baltimore	Profit from land sales; religious and political freedom

■ The Carolinas / 1663
   North Carolina / 1712
   South Carolina / 1712
	Group of eight
	proprietors
		Trade and farming; religious
		   freedom

■ Georgia / 1732	James Oglethorpe	Profit; home for debtors; buffer against Spanish Florida

Chart Skills

English settlers founded 13 separate colonies along the Atlantic coast of North America.

1. **Comprehension** **(a)** Identify two colonies founded by people seeking religious freedom. **(b)** Identify two colonies founded to expand trade.

2. **Critical Thinking** How long did it take for England to establish its American colonies?

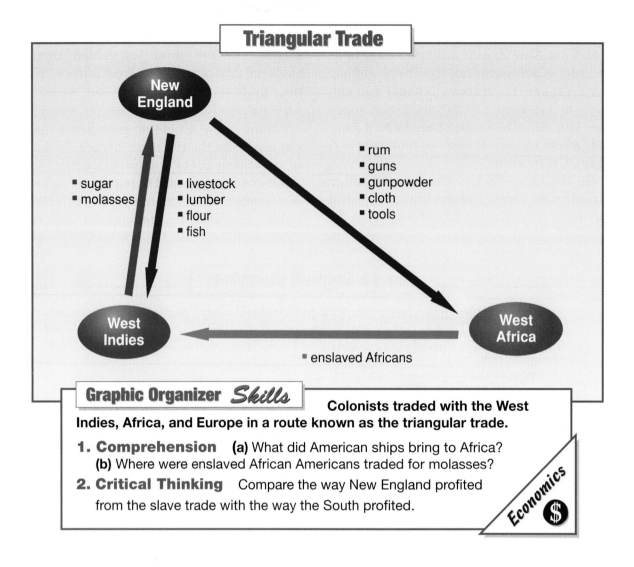

Triangular Trade

New England

- sugar
- molasses

- livestock
- lumber
- flour
- fish

- rum
- guns
- gunpowder
- cloth
- tools

West Indies

West Africa

- enslaved Africans

Graphic Organizer *Skills*   Colonists traded with the West Indies, Africa, and Europe in a route known as the triangular trade.

1. **Comprehension** **(a)** What did American ships bring to Africa? **(b)** Where were enslaved African Americans traded for molasses?

2. **Critical Thinking** Compare the way New England profited from the slave trade with the way the South profited.

Economics $

was so high that New Englanders smuggled in cargoes from the Dutch, French, and Spanish West Indies, too. Bribes made customs officials look the other way.

Political Life

Although each colony developed its own government, the governments had much in common. A governor directed the colony's affairs and enforced the laws. Most governors were appointed, either by the king or by the colony's proprietor. In Rhode Island and Connecticut, however, colonists elected their own governors.

Elected assemblies

Each colony also had a legislature. A **legislature** is a group of people who have the power to make laws. In most colonies, the legislature had an upper house and a lower

house. The upper house was made up of advisers appointed by the governor.

The lower house was an elected assembly. It approved laws and protected the rights of citizens. Just as important, it had the right to approve any taxes the governor asked for. This "power of the purse," or right to raise or spend money, was an important check on the governor's power. Any governor who ignored the assembly risked losing his salary.

The right to vote

Each colony had its own rules about who could vote. By the 1720s, however, all the colonies had laws that restricted the right to vote to white Christian men over the age of 21. In some colonies, only Protestants or members of a particular church could vote. All voters had to own property. Colonial leaders believed that only property owners knew what was best for a colony.

Why Study History?

Because You Have a Say in Government

★ ★

Historical Background

In 1295, King Edward I of England needed money for a war with France. To get the funds, he summoned Parliament, including representatives of the "common people," lords, and clergy. "What touches all should be approved by all," the king said. Over the years, the power of Parliament grew.

The idea of representative government passed on to England's American colonies. In 1619, King James I gave the Virginia colonists the right to form the House of Burgesses. Other colonies developed their own legislatures. Finally, the colonies became the United States of America. The English tradition of electing officials to make laws became the basis of American democracy.

Connections to Today

Today, Americans participate in government at many levels. On the national level, citizens elect representatives to Congress. Each state has its own legislature. In counties, cities, and towns, residents elect councils and boards to pass laws and make regulations. In some small towns, especially in New England, citizens still come together at town meetings to make their own laws.

Connections to You

Representative government affects you in a direct way. Do you attend a public school? If so, an elected school board probably governs your school district. School boards make decisions that affect everything from the books you use to your school's dress code and code of conduct.

You may also participate in representative government right now, by electing or serving on the student council. A student council may seem a long way from the English Parliament. Yet they are part of the same proud tradition.

1. Comprehension **(a)** How did the English tradition of representative government come to the colonies? **(b)** List two types of representative government in the United States today.

2. Critical Thinking "What touches all should be approved by all," said King Edward I. How do the king's words reflect one basic idea behind representative government?

★*Activity* **Writing a Speech** You have decided to run for a seat on your school's student council. Write a campaign speech. Describe what policies you would support. Explain why other students should elect you to be their representative.

Representative government begins early.

On election day, voters and their families gathered in towns and villages. Smiling candidates shook hands with voters and slapped them heartily on the back. In some areas, they offered to buy them drinks. When things quieted down, the sheriff called the voters together. One by one, he read out their names. Each man announced his vote aloud:

> 66 *Sheriff:* Mr. Blair, whom do you vote for?
> *Mr. Blair:* John Marshall.
> *Mr. Marshall:* Your vote is appreciated, Mr. Blair. 99

A bill of rights

Colonists took great pride in their elected assemblies. They also valued the rights the Magna Carta gave them as English subjects. (See page 86.)

Colonists won still more rights as a result of the **Glorious Revolution** of 1688. Parliament removed King James II from the throne and asked William and Mary of the Netherlands to rule. In return for Parliament's support, William and Mary signed the **English Bill of Rights** in 1689. A **bill of rights** is a written list of freedoms the government promises to protect.

The English Bill of Rights protected the rights of individuals and gave anyone accused of a crime the right to a trial by jury. Just as important, the English Bill of Rights said that a ruler could not raise taxes or an army without the approval of Parliament.

Limits on liberties

In many ways, English colonists in the Americas enjoyed more freedoms than the English themselves. More ordinary men could vote. Over time, colonial legislatures increased their power.

Still, the rights of English citizens did not extend to everyone in the colonies. Women had more rights in the colonies than in Europe, but far fewer rights than did free white males. A woman's father or husband was supposed to protect her. A married woman could not start her own business or sign a contract unless her husband approved it.

In most colonies, unmarried women and widows had more rights than married women. They could make contracts and sue in court. In Maryland and the Carolinas, women settlers who headed families could buy land on the same terms as men.

Africans and Native Americans in the colonies had almost no rights. Sadly, slavery existed side by side with the English liberties so many colonists held dear. The conflict between liberty and slavery would not be resolved until the 1860s.

★ Section 4 Review ★

Recall

1. **Identify** (a) Navigation Acts, (b) Yankee, (c) Glorious Revolution, (d) English Bill of Rights.
2. **Define** (a) mercantilism, (b) import, (c) export, (d) triangular trade, (e) legislature, (f) bill of rights.

Comprehension

3. List two ways that the Navigation Acts benefited (a) England, and (b) the colonies.

4. How were colonial governments organized?
5. Which colonists had the right to vote?

Critical Thinking and Writing

6. **Predicting Consequences** How do you think the Navigation Acts might affect future relations between England and the colonies? Explain.
7. **Analyzing Ideas** How did colonial legislatures reflect the tradition of self-rule?

Activity **Making a Decision** The time is 1750. You are a young person in Britain looking for success and freedom, so you plan to move to the American colonies. Write a letter to your parents explaining the reasons for your decision.

5 ★ A Changing Colonial Culture

As You Read

Explore These Questions
- What was the Great Awakening?
- How did colonists educate their children?
- How did new ideas spread through the colonies?

Define
- gentry
- middle class
- indentured servant
- public school
- tutor
- apprentice
- dame school
- libel

Identify
- Gullah
- Great Awakening
- Jonathan Edwards
- George Whitefield
- Enlightenment
- Benjamin Franklin
- John Peter Zenger

SETTING the Scene Benjamin Franklin of Philadelphia was a writer, scientist, businessman, and community leader. In 1743, he called on his fellow colonists to expand their cultural horizons:

66 The first drudgery of settling new colonies . . . is now pretty well over, and there are many in every province . . . [who have time] to cultivate the finer arts, and improve the common stock of knowledge. 99

Franklin invited colonists to join a society to promote "USEFUL KNOWLEDGE." Thus, the American Philosophical Society was born.

Franklin's new society was only one sign that the colonies were coming of age. By the mid-1700s, they had developed a culture that was truly new and American.

Social Classes

For the most part, colonists enjoyed more social equality than people in England did. Still, class differences existed. Like Europeans, colonial Americans thought it was only natural that some people ranked more highly than others.

Powdered wigs like this were the fashion for men of the gentry.

The gentry and the middle class

At the top of society stood the **gentry.** The gentry included wealthy planters, merchants, ministers, successful lawyers, and royal officials. They could afford to dress elegantly in the latest fashions from London.

Below the gentry were the **middle class.** The middle class included farmers who worked their own land, skilled craftsworkers, and some tradespeople. Nearly three quarters of all white colonists belonged to the middle class. They prospered because land in the colonies was plentiful and easy to buy. Also, laborers were in demand, and skilled workers received good wages.

Indentured servants

The lowest social class included hired farmhands, indentured servants, and slaves. **Indentured servants** signed contracts to work without wages for four to seven years for anyone who would pay their ocean passage to the Americas. When their term of service was completed, indentured servants received "freedom dues": a set of clothes, tools, and 50 acres of land. Because there were so few European women in the colonies, female indentured servants often shortened their terms of service by marrying.

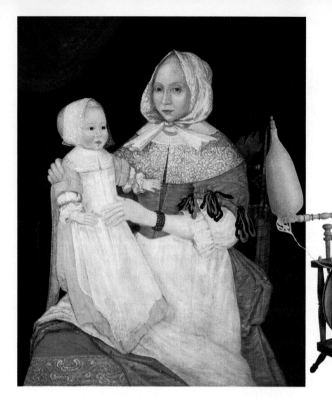

◄ *Colonial spinning wheel*

Thousands of men, women, and children came to North America as indentured servants. After completing their terms, some became successful and rose into the middle class.

Women's Work in the Colonies

From New Hampshire to Georgia, colonial women did many of the same tasks. A wife took care of her household, husband, and family. By the kitchen fire, she baked the family's meals. She milked cows, watched the children, and made clothing.

In the backcountry, wives and husbands often worked side by side in the fields at harvest time. With so much to be done, no one worried whether harvesting was proper "woman's work." A visitor described a backcountry woman's activities:

66 She will carry a gunn in the woods and kill deer, turkeys &c., shoot down wild cattle, catch and tye hoggs, knock down [cattle] with an ax, and perform the most manfull Exercises as well as most men. 99

In cities, women sometimes worked outside the home. A young single woman from a poorer family might work as a maid, a cook, or a nurse for one of the gentry. Other women were midwives, delivering babies. Still others sewed fine hats or dresses to be sold to women who could afford them. Learning such skills required many years of training.

Some women learned trades from their fathers, brothers, or husbands. They worked as butchers, shoemakers, or silversmiths. Quite a few women became printers. A woman might take over her husband's business when he died.

African Cultural Influences

By the mid-1700s, the culture of Africans in the colonies varied greatly. On rice plantations in South Carolina, slaves saw few white colonists. As a result, African customs

---

$ Connections With Economics

In 1733, some women in New York cited their economic achievements in a newspaper notice: "We are house keepers, pay our taxes, carry on trade and most of us are she merchants, and as we . . . contribute to the support of the government, we ought to be entitled to some of the sweets of it."

remained strong. For example, parents often chose African names for their children, such as Quosh or Juba or Cuff. In some coastal areas, African Americans spoke a distinctive combination of English and West African languages, known as **Gullah.**

In Charleston and other South Carolina port towns, more than half the population had African roots. Many of them worked along the docks, making rope or barrels or helping to build ships. Skilled craftsworkers made fine wooden cabinets or silver plates and utensils. Many of their designs reflected African artistic styles. Although most Africans in these towns were enslaved, many opened their own shops or stalls in the market. Some used their earnings to buy their own and their family's freedom.

In Virginia and Maryland, African traditions were weaker. Africans in the Chesapeake region were less isolated from white farmers and planters. Also, by the 1750s, the number of new slaves arriving in the region each year had begun to decline. Even so, many old customs survived. One traveler observed an African-style funeral. Mourners took part in a ceremony to speed a dead man's spirit to his home, which they believed was in Africa.

Fewer Africans lived in the Middle Colonies and New England. Most lived in such cities as Philadelphia, New York, and Newport. Often, the men outnumbered the women. As a result, the number of African families remained small.

The Great Awakening

In the 1730s and 1740s, a religious movement known as the **Great Awakening** swept through the colonies. Its drama and emotion touched women and men of all backgrounds and classes.

Powerful preachers

A New England preacher, **Jonathan Edwards,** set off the Great Awakening. In powerful sermons, Edwards called on colonists, especially young people, to examine their lives. He preached of the sweetness and beauty of God. At the same time, he warned listeners to heed the Bible's teachings. Otherwise, they would be "sinners in the hands of an angry God," headed for the fiery torments of hell. Edwards thundered:

> 66 O sinner! Consider the fearful danger you are in: it is a great furnace of wrath [anger], a wide and bottomless pit.... You hang by a slender thread, with the flames of divine wrath flashing about it, and ready every moment to singe it, and burn it asunder. 99

In 1739, when an English minister named **George Whitefield** arrived in the colonies, the movement spread like wildfire. Whitefield drew huge crowds to outdoor meetings from Massachusetts to Georgia. His voice rang with feeling as he called on sinners to repent. After hearing Whitefield speak, Jonathan Edwards's wife reported, "I have seen upwards of a thousand people hang on his words with breathless silence, broken only by an occasional half-suppressed sob."

Viewing HISTORY **Preserving African Culture**

In the colonies, African craftsworkers created much fine wooden furniture. Many of their works, such as this detail from a fireplace, were inspired by traditional African designs.

★ **In what colonies did African influences remain strongest?**

George Whitefield

George Whitefield's preaching drew huge crowds throughout the colonies. One witness reported, "He looked as if he was clothed with authority from the great God, and my hearing him preach gave me a heart wound." Whitefield also encouraged the building of American colleges such as Princeton.

★ **Why did some Americans oppose preachers like Whitefield?**

Impact of the Awakening

The Great Awakening aroused bitter debate. People who supported the movement often split away from their old churches to form new ones. Opponents warned that the movement was too emotional. Still, the growth of so many new churches forced colonists to become more tolerant of people with different beliefs.

The Great Awakening contributed in another way to the spread of democratic feelings in the colonies. Many of the new preachers were not as well educated as most ministers. They argued that book learning was less important than a heart filled with the holy spirit. Such teachings encouraged a spirit of independence. Many believers felt more free to challenge authority when their liberties were at stake. In years to come, many of the same colonists were willing to challenge the authority of British officials.

A Tradition of Education

Among the colonists, New Englanders were the most concerned about education. Puritans taught that all people had a duty to study the Bible. If colonists did not learn to read, how would they fulfill this duty?

New England

In 1647, the Massachusetts assembly passed a law ordering all parents to teach their children "to read and understand the principles of religion." They also required all towns with 50 or more families to hire a schoolteacher. Towns with 100 families or more also had to set up a grammar school to prepare boys for college.

In this way, Massachusetts set up the first **public schools,** or schools supported by taxes. Public schools allowed both rich and poor children to receive an education.

The first New England schools had only one room for students of all ages. Parents paid the schoolteacher with corn, peas, or other foods. Each child was expected to bring a share of wood to burn in the stove. Students who forgot would find themselves seated in the coldest corner of the room!

Middle and Southern Colonies

In the Middle Colonies, churches and individual families set up private schools. Because pupils paid to attend, only wealthy families could afford to educate their children.

In the Southern Colonies, people lived too far from one another to bring children together in one school building. Some planters engaged **tutors,** or private teachers. The wealthiest planters sent their sons to school in England. As a rule, slaves were denied education of any kind.

Apprentices and dame schools

Boys whose parents wished them to learn a trade or craft served as apprentices (uh PREHN tihs ehz). An **apprentice** worked for a master to learn a trade or a craft. For example, when a boy reached age 12 or 13, his parents might apprentice him to a master glassmaker. The young apprentice lived in the glassmaker's home for six or seven years. The glassmaker gave him food and clothing. He was also supposed to teach the boy how to read and write and provide him with religious training.

In return, the apprentice worked without pay in the glassmaker's shop and learned the skills he needed to set up his own shop. Boys were apprenticed in many trades, including papermaking, printing, and tanning.

In New England, some girls attended dame schools, or private schools run by women in their own homes. Most schools in the colonies accepted only boys, however. Girls learned skills from their mothers, who taught them to spin wool, weave, and embroider. A few learned to read and write.

An Age of Reason

During the 1600s, European scientists tried to use reason and logic to understand the world. They developed theories and then performed experiments to test them. In doing so, they discovered many laws of nature. The English scientist Isaac Newton, for example, explained the law of gravity.

The Enlightenment spreads

European thinkers of the late 1600s and 1700s believed that reason and scientific methods could be applied to the study of society. They tried to discover the natural laws that governed human behavior. Because these thinkers believed in the light of human reason, the movement that they started is known as the **Enlightenment.**

In the 13 colonies, the Enlightenment spread among better educated colonists. They included wealthy merchants, lawyers, ministers, and others who had the leisure to read the latest books from Europe.

Benjamin Franklin

The best example of the Enlightenment spirit in the 13 colonies was **Benjamin Franklin.** Franklin was born in 1706, the son of a poor Boston soap and candle maker. Although he had only two years of formal schooling, he used his spare time to study literature, mathematics, and foreign languages.

At age 17, Franklin made his way to Philadelphia. There, he built up a successful printing business. His most popular publication was *Poor Richard's Almanac.* Published yearly, it contained useful information and clever quotes, such as "Early to bed, early to rise, makes a man healthy, wealthy, and wise."

Viewing HISTORY — Education in the Colonies

Education and values were closely linked in the colonies. The picture at left shows apprentices learning beekeeping and carpentry. The writing around the picture praises the value of work. The New England primer, above, taught Bible tales and moral lessons along with the alphabet.

★ **Examine the page from the primer. What moral lesson is taught with the letter *Y*? What does this suggest about the Puritan attitude toward childhood?**

Colonial Williamsburg

In the 1700s, Williamsburg was one of the most important cities in Virginia. Today, it is one of the state's most popular attractions. As you walk down the restored streets, you can watch people bake bread, print newspapers, or make shoes as they did in colonial times.

★ *To learn more about this historic site, write:* Colonial Williamsburg Foundation, P.O. Box 627, Williamsburg, VA 23187.

◄ *A wigmaker in Colonial Williamsburg demonstrates her trade.*

Like other Enlightenment thinkers, Franklin wanted to use reason to improve the world around him. He invented practical devices such as a lightning rod, a smokeless fireplace, and bifocal glasses. As a community leader, Franklin persuaded Philadelphia officials to pave streets, organize a fire company, and set up the first lending library in the Americas. Franklin's inventions and his public service earned him worldwide fame.

Colonial Cities and the Spread of Ideas

While most colonists lived on farms, towns and cities strongly influenced colonial life. Through the great ports of Philadelphia, New York, Boston, and Charleston, merchants shipped products overseas. Towns and cities also served as the center of a busy trade between the coast and the growing backcountry.

Culture flourished in the cities. By the mid-1700s, all major colonial cities had their own theaters. City dwellers found entertainment at singing societies, traveling circuses, carnivals, and horse races.

Communication and the growth of newspapers

The growth of colonial cities helped new ideas to spread. The newest ideas from Europe appeared first in city drawing rooms and taverns. In 1704, John Campbell founded the *Boston News-Letter*, the first regular weekly newspaper in the English colonies. Within 50 years, each of the colonies except New Jersey and Delaware had at least one weekly paper.

The growth of colonial newspapers led to a dispute over freedom of the press. **John Peter Zenger** published the *Weekly Journal* in New York City. In 1734, he was arrested for publishing stories that criticized the governor. Zenger was put on trial for **libel,** the act of publishing a statement that may unjustly damage a person's reputation. Zenger's lawyer argued that, since the stories were true, his client had not committed libel. He told the jury:

> 66 By your verdict, you will have laid a noble foundation for securing to ourselves, our descendants, and our neighbors, the liberty both of exposing and opposing tyrannical power by speaking and writing truth. 99

The jury agreed and freed Zenger. Freedom of the press would later become recognized as a basic American right.

Improved travel

Newspapers often took several months to travel from one colony to another. Travel was

▲ *Connecticut tavern sign*

often slow and difficult. Roads were rough and muddy, and there were few bridges over streams and rivers. Worst of all, there were no road signs. Most colonists stayed close to home.

Colonists set up a postal system, but it was slow. In 1717, it took one month for a letter to travel from Boston to Williamsburg, Virginia. In the winter, delivery could take twice as long.

As the colonies grew, roads and mail service improved. Families built taverns along main roads and in towns and cities. Travelers stopped to rest and to exchange news and gossip with local people.

Along with the growth of cities, improved travel and communication created an active colonial culture. In cities, large numbers of people exchanged news and ideas that eventually spread throughout the colonies. In the years ahead, these ideas would help shape a revolution.

★ Section 5 Review ★

Recall

1. **Identify** (a) Gullah, (b) Great Awakening, (c) Jonathan Edwards, (d) George Whitefield, (e) Enlightenment, (f) Benjamin Franklin, (g) John Peter Zenger.
2. **Define** (a) gentry, (b) middle class, (c) indentured servant, (d) public school, (e) tutor, (f) apprentice, (g) dame school, (h) libel.

Comprehension

3. How did the Great Awakening contribute to the spread of democratic feelings in the colonies?

4. Why did the Puritans support public education?
5. In what ways was Benjamin Franklin an example of the Enlightenment spirit?

Critical Thinking and Writing

6. **Making Inferences** Why do you think there was greater social equality in the colonies than in England?
7. **Linking Past and Present** How did New England public schools compare with public schools today?

History AND YOU

Activity **Delivering an Editorial** You are a television reporter with a time machine. You have gone back to 1734 to report on the trial of John Peter Zenger. Write and deliver a one-minute editorial explaining why you think he should or should not be found guilty.

Review and Activities

★ Sum It Up ★

Section 1   The New England Colonies
▶ The Puritans went to New England to form a society where they could practice their religious beliefs.
▶ Life in New England was based on farming, hunting, and fishing.

Section 2   The Middle Colonies
▶ The Middle Colonies had a diverse mix of people, in part because they offered settlers religious freedom.
▶ The economy of the Middle Colonies was based on farming, but grew to include manufacturing as well.

Section 3   The Southern Colonies
▶ Two distinct ways of life emerged on Tidewater plantations and backcountry farms.
▶ As a plantation economy grew, slavery became firmly established in the Southern Colonies.

Section 4   Governing the Colonies
▶ The British passed laws to control colonial trade.
▶ Democratic traditions grew in the colonies, including representative government and protection of individual rights.

Section 5   A Changing Colonial Culture
▶ The Great Awakening inspired religious feeling and beliefs about equality.
▶ New England offered public education, while schools in the Middle and Southern colonies were usually private.

CD-ROM Review For additional review of the major ideas of Chapter 4, see *Guide to the Essentials of American History* or *Interactive Student Tutorial CD-ROM,* which contains interactive review activities, graphic organizers, and practice tests.

▢ Reviewing the Chapter

Define These Terms

Match each term with the correct definition.

Column 1
1. toleration
2. patroon
3. debtor
4. mercantilism
5. indentured servant

Column 2
a. owner of a huge estate in New Netherland
b. theory that a nation becomes strong by building its gold supply and expanding trade
c. willingness to let others practice their own beliefs
d. someone who promises to work for four to seven years in exchange for passage
e. someone who owes money

Explore the Main Ideas

1. How did the Fundamental Orders of Connecticut differ from the plan of government in Massachusetts?
2. How did a proprietary colony differ from a royal colony?
3. Why did Catholics and debtors want to move to North America?
4. What rights did English colonists have?
5. Describe the main social classes in the colonies.

▢ Geography Activity

Match the letters on the map with the following places:
1. New England Colonies, **2.** Middle Colonies, **3.** Southern Colonies, **4.** Massachusetts, **5.** Pennsylvania, **6.** Virginia.
Region   Name the five Southern Colonies.

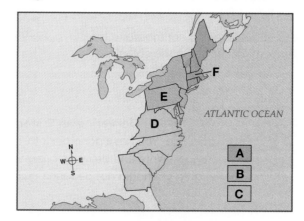

🔲 Critical Thinking and Writing

1. **Analyzing Ideas** "The Puritans came to America in search of religious freedom." **(a)** In what sense is this statement accurate? **(b)** In what sense is this statement inaccurate?

2. **Understanding Chronology (a)** Place the following events in the correct chronological order: Georgia is founded; colonists begin to plant tobacco; Jamestown is founded; Virginia settlers move inland. **(b)** Which of these events was the direct cause of Bacon's Rebellion?

3. **Linking Past and Present (a)** Reread the description of voting in the colonies on page 116. How does it differ from the way Americans vote today?

4. **Exploring Unit Themes Origins** What do you think are the two most important traditions the United States got from England? Explain your reasoning.

🔲 Using Primary Sources

The following notice appeared in Southern newspapers sometime in the 1730s:

> 66 Ran away some time in June last, from William Pierce of Nansemond County,... a convict servant woman named Winifred Thomas. She is a Welsh woman, short, black-haired and young; marked on the inside of her right arm with gunpowder, W.T., and the date of the year underneath. She knits and spins, and is supposed to be gone into North Carolina by the way of Cureatuck and Roanoke Inlet. Whoever brings her to her master shall be paid a [gold coin] besides what the law allows. 99

Source: *A Documentary History of American Industrial Society*, 1910.

Recognizing Points of View (a) What is the purpose of this advertisement? **(b)** Based on your reading, was Winifred Thomas a slave or an indentured servant? **(c)** What was Pierce's attitude toward Thomas?

ACTIVITY BANK

▶ Interdisciplinary Activity

Exploring Sciences Do research on the inventions of Benjamin Franklin. Create a display that explains how one of his inventions worked.

▶ Career Skills Activity

Playwrights Read more about the life of women in the British colonies. Write a short play in which a city woman, a backcountry woman, and the mistress of a plantation meet and compare their lives.

▶ Citizenship Activity

Learning About Education In this chapter you read about the beginnings of public education. One of the responsibilities of citizens is being informed about education in the community. Arrange to visit a meeting of a local school board or parent-teacher association. Write a report on your visit.

Internet Activity

Use the Internet to find sites dealing with William Penn. After you have done research to find out more about him, write a letter from Penn to the President of the United States today, advising the President on how to handle some of the challenges facing our nation. Use information from your research in your letter.

Ⓔ YEWITNESS Journal

You are a Puritan, a Pennsylvania Quaker, a plantation owner, or an enslaved African American. In your EYEWITNESS JOURNAL, describe a visit to another region in the British colonies and compare it with your own. Remember, your own viewpoint will be influenced by the colony in which you live.

History Through Literature

Hiawatha the Unifier

Iroquois Folk Tale

Introduction

People who accomplish heroic deeds often become the subject of legends. The following tale is a legend about Hiawatha. According to Iroquois tradition, Hiawatha helped form the League of the Iroquois around 1570. The following traditional tale appeared in a collection called *American Indian Myths and Legends*.

Vocabulary

Before you read the selection, find the meanings of these words in a dictionary: **untutored, eternal, devastation, tranquil, counselors, orators, recoil, strife, innumerable.**

From out of the north beyond the Great Lakes came wild tribes, fierce, untutored nations who knew nothing of the eternal law;* peoples who did not plant or weave baskets or fire clay into cooking vessels. All they knew was how to prey on those who planted and reaped the fruits of their labors. Fierce and pitiless, these strangers ate their meat raw, tearing it apart with their teeth. Warfare and killing were their occupation. They burst upon Hiawatha's people like a flood, spreading devastation wherever they went. Again the people turned to Hiawatha for help. He advised all the nations to assemble and wait his coming.

And so the five tribes came together at the place of the great council fire, by the shores of a large and tranquil lake where the wild men from the north had not yet penetrated. The people waited for Hiawatha one day, two days, three days. On the fourth day his gleaming white magic canoe appeared, floating, gliding above the mist....

When the sachems, elders, and wise men had seated themselves in a circle around the sacred fire, Hiawatha came before them and said:

"My children, war, fear, and disunity have brought you from your villages to this sacred council fire. Facing a common danger, and fearing for the lives of your families, you have yet drifted apart, each tribe thinking and acting only for itself. Remember how I took you from one small band and nursed you up into many nations. You must reunite now and act as one. No tribe alone can withstand our savage enemies, who care nothing about the eternal law, who sweep upon us like the storms of winter, spreading death and destruction everywhere.

"My children, listen well. Remember that you are brothers, that the downfall of one means the downfall of all. You must have one fire, one pipe, one war club....

"Onondagas, you are a tribe of mighty warriors. Your strength is like that of a giant pine tree whose roots spread far and deep so that it can withstand any storm. Be you the protectors. You shall be the first nation.

---

*The eternal law refers to the need to keep a balance between people and nature.

"Oneida, your men are famous for their wisdom. Be you the counselors of the tribes. You shall be the second nation.

"Seneca, you are swift of foot and persuasive in speech. Your men are the greatest orators among the tribes. Be you the spokesmen. You shall be the third people.

"Cayuga, you are the most cunning. You are the most skilled in the building and managing of canoes. Be you the guardians of our rivers. You shall be the fourth nation.

"Mohawk, you are foremost in planting corn and beans and in building longhouses. Be you the nourishers.

"Your tribes must be like the five fingers of a warrior's hand joined in gripping the war club. Unite as one, and then your enemies will recoil before you back into the northern wastes from whence they came. Let my words sink deep into your hearts and minds. Retire now to take counsel among yourselves, and come to me tomorrow to tell me whether you will follow my advice."

On the next morning the sachems and wise men came to Hiawatha with the promise that they would from that day on be as one nation. Hiawatha rejoiced. He gathered up the dazzling white feathers which the great mystery bird of the sky had dropped and gave the plumes to the leaders of the assembled tribes. "By these feathers," he said, "you shall be known as the Ako-no-shu-ne: the Iroquois." Thus with the help of Hiawatha, the Great Unifier, the mighty League of the Five Nations was born and its tribes held sway undisturbed over all the land between the great river of the west and the great sea of the east.

The elders begged Hiawatha to become the chief sachem of the united tribes, but he told them: "This can never be, because I must

Cap of an Iroquois Leader

Wooden caps like this one were traditionally worn by important members of the Iroquois League. The six-sided design on the band may symbolize the six nations that belonged to the League after the Tuscarora joined. ★ **What was the chief purpose of the Iroquois League?**

leave you. Friends and brothers, choose the wisest women in your tribes to be the future clan mothers and peacemakers. Let them turn any strife rising among you into friendship. Let your sachems be wise enough to go to such women for advice when there are disputes. Now I have finished speaking. Farewell."

At that moment there came to those assembled the sweet sound like the rush of rustling leaves and the song of innumerable birds. Hiawatha stepped into his white mystery canoe, and instead of gliding away on the waters of the lake, it rose slowly into the sky and disappeared into the clouds. Hiawatha was gone, but his teachings survive in the hearts of the people.

Analyzing Literature

1. Why did the Five Nations seek Hiawatha's help?
2. According to Hiawatha, why was each of the Five Nations important to the League as a whole?
3. **Synthesizing Information** (a) What final advice did Hiawatha give the sachems? (b) Based on your reading, did they follow this advice?

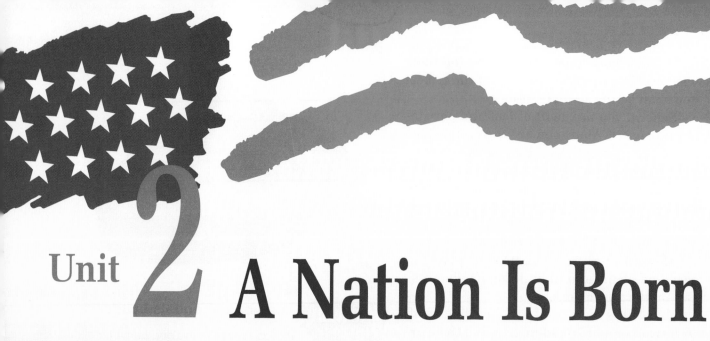

Unit 2
A Nation Is Born

Viewing UNIT THEMES Freedom of Religion: A Basic American Right

Since colonial days, American women have used the craft of quilt-making to express their values and depict their daily life. This detail from a New England quilt from the late 1700s portrays a church as the center of the community. Americans of the time expected their new government to safeguard freedom of religion. ★ **List two other freedoms that Americans enjoy.**

Unit Theme Rights and Liberties

In 1776, the 13 colonies declared their independence from Britain. One major reason was colonists' belief that Britain had violated their basic rights.

Later, American leaders worked to create a government. Many people in the United States demanded that the new government protect basic liberties, such as freedom of religion, freedom of the press, and the right to trial by jury.

How did Americans of the time feel about basic rights and liberties? They can tell you in their own words.

★ ★

VIEWPOINTS ON RIGHTS AND LIBERTIES

❝If we separate from Britain, what code of laws will be established? How shall we be governed so as to retain our liberties?❞

Abigail Adams, wife of John Adams (1775)

❝By reason of long bondage and hard slavery, we have been deprived of the profits of our labor or the advantage of inheriting estates from our parents as our neighbors the white people do.❞

Paul Cuffe, African American ship owner (1783)

❝Were it left to me to decide whether we should have a government without newspapers, or newspapers without a government, I should not hesitate a moment to prefer the latter.❞

Thomas Jefferson, Virginia political leader (1787)

★ ★

Activity **Writing to Learn** Turn to the First Amendment in the Reference Section and read the Constitution. List the freedoms guaranteed by the First Amendment. Then, choose one of those freedoms. Write a skit showing what life might be like if that freedom were not protected.

Chapter 5

The Road to Revolution

1745–1775

Between 1754 and 1760, competition for land led to a conflict between England and France that is now known as the French and Indian War. The British, with the help of American colonists and Indian allies, put an end to French power in North America.

After the war, Britain angered colonists by taxing them without giving them representation in Parliament. Over the next years, colonial protests grew stronger. Finally, in April 1775, British troops and colonial farmers clashed at the villages of Lexington and Concord in Massachusetts. The battles marked the start of the American Revolution.

Why Study History?

"Taxation without representation is tyranny!" This protest sparked a revolution in the 13 colonies. Today, American citizens have representation. Still, attempts to raise taxes always stir heated debate. To focus on this connection, look at the *Why Study History?* feature, "You Pay Taxes," in this chapter.

American Events

●1740s
Settlers cross
Appalachian
Mountains

1754 ●
French and
Indian War begins

1759 ●
British capture of
French Quebec is
turning point
of war

1745　　　　**1750**　　　　**1755**　　　　**1760**

World Events

1748 World Event
Britain and France fight for
control of trade in India

1756 World Event
Seven Years' War begins
in Europe

Viewing HISTORY

Protests in the Colonies

This 1774 engraving, The Bostonians Paying the Exciseman, *shows American colonists who have just tarred and feathered a British tax collector. While they force tea down the tax collector's throat, other colonists throw chests of British tea into Boston harbor. Violent protests like this one contributed to a split between Britain and its American colonists.* ★ **Do you think the artist who created this engraving had a favorable view of the Americans? Give reasons for your answer.**

●1763
Proclamation of 1763 closes western lands to further settlement

1773●
Boston Tea Party is punished by the Intolerable Acts

●1775
Fighting breaks out at Concord and Lexington

| 1760 | 1765 | 1770 | 1775 |

1763 World Event
Treaty of Paris ends French power in North America

1773 World Event
British Parliament passes Tea Act

Rivalry in North America

As You Read

Explore These Questions
- What European nations competed for land in North America?
- Why did the French build a system of forts?
- Why did Indian nations become involved in the struggle between France and England?

Identify
- Hurons
- Joseph Brant

 In June 1749, the governor of New France sent a group of men down the Ohio River. The men stopped from time to time to nail an engraved lead plate to a tree or to set one in the ground. These plates proclaimed that the fertile land of the Ohio Valley belonged to France.

About the same time, Christopher Gist, a Virginia fur trader, was also roaming the Ohio Valley. Gist worked for the Ohio Company, a group of English investors. King George II had given the company a huge tract of land in the valley. They sent Gist to find a good spot for settlement.

Gist chose a site where the Ohio and Allegheny rivers meet. On a rock beside the water, he carved these words:

> The Ohio Company
> FEBy 1751
> By Christopher Gist

Clearly, with two great powers claiming the same land, the stage was set for conflict. At stake was more than control of the Ohio River valley. France and England each hoped to drive the other nation out of North America altogether.

Competing Claims

By the mid-1700s, the major powers of Europe were locked in a worldwide struggle for empire. England, France, Spain, and the Netherlands competed for trade and colonies in far-flung corners of the globe. The English colonies in North America soon became caught up in the contest.

By the late 1600s, England had already taken over New York from the Dutch. Its two remaining rivals in North America were Spain and France. The major threat from Spain was in the West Indies and along the border between Georgia and Spanish Florida. England and Spain clashed often in these areas.

Spain also had settlements in present-day New Mexico, Texas, and Arizona. However, these settlements were located far away from England's colonies on the Atlantic coast. As a result, the English paid little attention to them.

The threat from France was much more serious to the English colonies. France claimed a vast area that stretched from the St. Lawrence River westward to the Great Lakes and southward to the Gulf of Mexico. To protect their land claims, the French built an extensive system of forts. (See the map on page 133.)

Connections With Geography

As the French explored and settled North American lands, they gave French names to forts, towns, and natural features. Familiar examples of these French names include *Detroit* (narrow water passage), *Des Moines* (belonging to the monks), *Baton Rouge* (red stick), and *Vermont* (green mountain).

Conflict in the Ohio Valley

At first, most English settlers were content to remain along the Atlantic coast. By the 1740s, however, traders from New York and Pennsylvania were crossing the Appalachian Mountains in search of furs. Pushing into the Ohio Valley, they tried to take over the profitable French trade with the Indians.

France was determined to stop the English from intruding on their territory. The Ohio River was especially important to the French because it provided a vital link between their lands in Canada and the Mississippi River. In 1751, the French government sent the following orders to its officials in New France:

66 Drive from the Ohio River any European foreigners, and do it in a way that will make them lose all taste for trying to return. 99

Native Americans Choose Sides

Native Americans had hunted animals and grown crops in the Ohio Valley for centuries. They did not want to give up the land to European settlers, French or English. One Native American protested to an English trader:

66 You and the French are like the two edges of a pair of shears. And we are the cloth which is to be cut to pieces between them. 99

Still, the growing conflict between England and France was too dangerous to ignore. Some Native Americans decided that the only way to protect their way of life was to take sides in the struggle.

Allies for the French

At the same time, both France and England tried to make Indian allies. The French expected the Indians to side with them. Most French in North America were trappers and traders, not farmers like the English. The French generally did not destroy Indian hunting grounds by clearing forests for

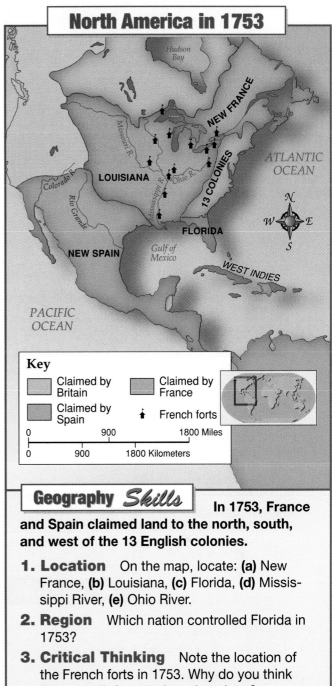

North America in 1753

Key
- Claimed by Britain
- Claimed by Spain
- Claimed by France
- French forts

0   900   1800 Miles
0   900   1800 Kilometers

Geography Skills   In 1753, France and Spain claimed land to the north, south, and west of the 13 English colonies.

1. **Location**   On the map, locate: **(a)** New France, **(b)** Louisiana, **(c)** Florida, **(d)** Mississippi River, **(e)** Ohio River.
2. **Region**   Which nation controlled Florida in 1753?
3. **Critical Thinking**   Note the location of the French forts in 1753. Why do you think France built forts at these locations?

farms. Also, many French trappers married Native American women and adopted their ways.

France built strong alliances with several Native American groups. As you read, the French gained the support of the Algonquins. (See page 83.) They also built friendly relations with the **Hurons.** The Hurons often served as negotiators between French traders and other Indian nations.

$\mathcal{B}$iography Joseph Brant

Known to the British as Joseph Brant, the Mohawk chief Thayendanegea was a valuable ally. He helped persuade the Iroquois nations to side with Britain in their struggle against the French. In later years, Brant became a Christian and helped translate the Bible into the Mohawk language. ★ **How does this painting show that Brant combined Native American and English cultures?**

Allies for the English

In contrast to the French, English settlers were mostly farm families. They ignored Indian rights when they cleared land for crops. Nor did they respect Indian ways. As the English moved onto their lands, the Indians fought back.

Still, in the end, England also found allies among Native Americans. The English won over the powerful Iroquois nations, who were old enemies of the Algonquins and the Hurons.

An English trader and official, William Johnson, helped gain Iroquois support for England. The Iroquois respected Johnson, and they listened carefully when he urged them to side with the English. Johnson was one of the few English settlers who had an Indian wife, Molly Brant. She was the sister of the Mohawk chief Thayendanegea, known to the English as **Joseph Brant.** Brant became a valuable ally for the English.

Some Indians supported the English because they charged lower prices for trade goods than the French did. Many Indians began to buy goods from English rather than French traders. The loss of Indian trade angered the French, who were determined to defend their claims in the Ohio Valley.

★ Section 1 Review ★

Recall

1. **Identify** (a) Hurons, (b) Joseph Brant.

Comprehension

2. Who were England's two main rivals in North America?

3. What steps did France take to protect its lands in North America?

4. (a) Why did the French expect Native Americans to side with them? (b) Why did some Indians side with the English?

Critical Thinking and Writing

5. **Applying Information** How did the rivalry among England, France, and Spain in North America reflect their worldwide struggle for power?

6. **Recognizing Points of View** Reread the statement by the Native American to the English trader on page 133. (a) What did the speaker mean by these words? (b) Do you think he felt that Native Americans could hold out against the British and French? Explain.

Activity **Writing a Speech** You are William Johnson. Write a speech in which you explain to the Iroquois why they should help the English instead of the French.

The French and Indian War

As You Read

Explore These Questions
- Why did the British and French go to war in North America?
- What advantages did each side have in the war?
- How did the Treaty of Paris affect North America?

Identify
- George Washington
- French and Indian War
- Albany Plan of Union
- Edward Braddock
- William Pitt
- James Wolfe
- Marquis de Montcalm
- Plains of Abraham
- Treaty of Paris

SETTING the Scene Captain Joncaire had just sat down to dinner on December 4, 1753, when a tall young man strode into the room. He introduced himself as Major **George Washington.** He said he had a letter from the English lieutenant governor of Virginia, Robert Dinwiddie, to the commander of the French forces in the Ohio Valley.

Joncaire told his visitor where the commander could be found. The captain then politely invited Washington to dine. As they ate, Joncaire boasted that France was determined to take full possession of the Ohio River valley. The remark made Washington pause. He knew that in the letter he was carrying, Dinwiddie warned the French to get out of the Ohio Valley!

For years, tensions had been building between the French and the English. By the 1750s, armed conflict seemed certain. The war that followed would forever change the balance of power in North America.

Fighting Begins

Three times between 1689 and 1748, France and Great Britain* had fought for power in Europe and North America. Each war ended with an uneasy peace.

In 1754, fighting broke out for a fourth time. The struggle that followed lasted until 1760. English settlers called the conflict the **French and Indian War** because it pitted them against France and its Native American allies.

Scuffles between France and Britain in the Ohio River valley triggered the opening shots of the French and Indian War. Young George Washington played a major role in this early phase of the conflict.

George Washington

At the time, George Washington was only 22 years old, but he was an able and brave soldier. Washington had grown up on a plantation in Virginia, the son of wealthy parents. Gifted at mathematics, he began working as a land surveyor at the age of 15. His job took him to frontier lands in western Virginia. In 1753, when Lieutenant Governor Dinwiddie wanted to warn the French out of Ohio, Washington offered to deliver the message. On this dangerous mission, the young officer narrowly escaped death.

After Washington returned, Dinwiddie promoted him to colonel. He also sent the young man west again. At the time, some wealthy Virginians claimed land in the upper Ohio Valley. To protect their claims, they urged the governor of Virginia to build a fort where the Monongahela and Allegheny rivers meet. (See the map on page 138.) Dinwiddie ordered Washington to take a party of 150 men and build the fort.

---

* In 1707, England and Scotland were officially joined into the United Kingdom of Great Britain. After that date, the terms *Great Britain* and *British* were used to describe the country and its people. However, the terms *England* and *English* were still used throughout much of the 1700s.

Conflict at Fort Necessity

In April 1754, Washington and his party headed for Ohio country. Along the way, they heard that the French had just completed Fort Duquesne (doo KAYN) at the fork of the Monongahela and Allegheny rivers. This was the very spot where Dinwiddie had ordered Washington to build a fort.

Determined to carry out his orders, Washington journeyed on. Indian allies revealed that a French scouting party was camped in the woods ahead. Marching quietly through the night, Washington surprised and scattered the French.

Washington's success was short-lived, however. Hearing that the French were plan-

ning to counterattack, he and his men quickly built a makeshift stockade. They named it Fort Necessity. A huge force of French and Indians surrounded the fort. Trapped and heavily outnumbered, the Virginians were forced to surrender. Soon after, the French released Washington, and he returned home to Virginia.

Despite Washington's defeat, the British quickly saw the importance of the skirmish. "The volley fired by this young Virginian in the forests of America," a British writer noted, "has set the world in flames."

The Albany Congress

While Washington was defending Fort Necessity, delegates from seven colonies gathered in Albany, New York. The delegates to the Albany Congress met for two reasons. They wanted to persuade the Iroquois to help them against the French. They also wanted to plan a united colonial defense.

The Iroquois refuse

Iroquois leaders listened patiently to the delegates, but they were wary of the request for help. The British and French "are quarreling about lands which belong to us," pointed out Hendrik, a Mohawk chief. "And such a quarrel as this may end in our destruction." In addition, the Iroquois believed that the French were stronger and had more forts than the British.

In the end, the Iroquois left without agreeing to help the British. At the same time, they did not join the French either.

Franklin's plan of union

The delegates in Albany knew that the colonists had to work together to defeat the French. Benjamin Franklin, the delegate from Pennsylvania, proposed the **Albany Plan of Union.** The plan was an attempt to create "one general government" for the 13 colonies. It called for a Grand Council made up of representatives from each colony. The council would make laws, raise taxes, and set up the defense of the colonies.

The delegates voted to accept the Plan of Union. When the plan was submitted to the colonial assemblies, however, not one ap-

Biography **George Washington**

Like many wealthy young Virginians, George Washington enjoyed dancing and horseback riding. At the same time, he worked hard managing the family plantation and later as a surveyor. After his defeats in the French and Indian War, Washington wrote, "I have been on the losing [side] ever since I entered the service." Little did he know that he would one day lead his country to independence.
★ **List two facts you know about Washington.**

proved it. None of the colonies wanted to give up any of its powers to a central council. The largest colony, Virginia, had not even sent a delegation to the Albany Congress! A disappointed Benjamin Franklin expressed his frustration at the failure of his plan:

66 Everyone cries a union is necessary. But when they come to the manner and form of the union, their weak noodles are perfectly distracted. 99

The Two Sides

At the start of the French and Indian War, the French had several advantages over the British. Because the English colonies could not agree on a united defense, 13 separate colonial assemblies had to approve all decisions. New France, on the other hand, had a single government that could act quickly when necessary. Also, the French had the support of many more Indian allies than the British did.

Britain, however, also had strengths. At the time, the population of the English colonies was about 15 times greater than that of New France. The English colonies were clustered along the coast, so they were easier to defend than the widely scattered French settlements. In addition, while most Indians sided with the French, the British did have some Indian allies. Finally, the British navy ruled the seas.

Early English Defeats

In 1755, General **Edward Braddock** led British and colonial troops in an attack against Fort Duquesne. Braddock was a stubborn man, called "Bulldog" behind his back. He knew how to fight a war in the open fields of Europe. However, he knew little about how to fight in the wilderness of North America. Still, the general boasted that he would sweep the French from the Ohio Valley.

Disaster for "Bulldog" Braddock

Braddock's men moved slowly because they had to clear a road through thick forests for their cannons and other heavy gear. George Washington, who went with Braddock, was upset by the slow pace. Indian scouts warned Braddock that he was headed for trouble. He ignored them.

As the British neared Fort Duquesne, the French and their Indian allies launched a surprise attack. Sharpshooters hid in the forest and picked off British soldiers, whose bright-red uniforms made them easy targets. Washington later wrote to his mother:

66 Our [forces] consisted of about 1,300 well-armed troops, chiefly of the English soldiers, who were struck with such a panic that they behaved with more cowardice than it is possible to conceive. The officers behaved gallantly in order to encourage their

JOIN, or DIE.

Viewing HISTORY A Call for Union

In 1754, Benjamin Franklin printed this famous cartoon in the Pennsylvania Gazette. *That year, Franklin drew up the Albany Plan of Union. However, his hopes for political unity among the 13 colonies did not succeed.*

★ **Summarize the main point of Franklin's cartoon in your own words.**

◄ *Model of Ben Franklin*

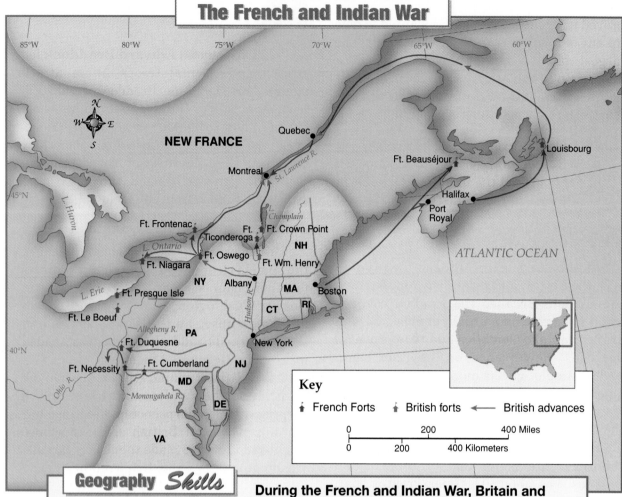

The French and Indian War

NEW FRANCE

ATLANTIC OCEAN

Key

⚑ French Forts   ⚑ British forts   ← British advances

0 ——— 200 ——— 400 Miles

0 — 200 — 400 Kilometers

Geography *Skills*

During the French and Indian War, Britain and France battled for control of North America. The conflict began in the Ohio River valley.

1. **Location** On the map, locate: **(a)** Fort Necessity, **(b)** Fort Duquesne, **(c)** Louisbourg, **(d)** Quebec, **(e)** Albany.
2. **Movement** About how many miles did advancing British forces travel from Louisbourg to Quebec?
3. **Critical Thinking** Based on the map, do you think naval power was important in fighting the French and Indian War? Explain.

men, for which they suffered greatly, there being nearly 60 killed or wounded—a large proportion out of the number we had! **"**

Braddock himself had five horses shot out from under him before he fell, fatally injured. Washington was luckier. He later reported that he "escaped without a wound, although I had four bullets through my coat."

Almost half the British were killed or wounded. Washington and other survivors returned to Virginia with news of Braddock's

defeat. Washington was now put in command of a small force of men. For the rest of the war, he had the almost impossible task of guarding the long Virginia frontier against Indian attack.

Further British setbacks

During the next two years, the war continued to go badly for the British. British attacks against several French forts ended in failure. Meanwhile, the French won important victories, capturing Fort Oswego on Lake Ontario and Fort William Henry on

Skills FOR LIFE

Critical Thinking	Managing Information	Communication	Maps, Charts, and Graphs

Reading a Time Line

How Will I Use This Skill?

A time line is a graphic organizer that lists events in chronological, or time, order. Using a time line can help you understand sequences and see relationships between events. You might find time lines, not only in history books, but also in magazine and newspaper articles about current events.

LEARN the Skill

At the start of each chapter in this book, you will find a two-page horizontal time line. It is organized from left to right, with the earliest date on the left. Some events may take place over several years. This will be indicated on the time line.

Time lines are divided into equal time periods. The total period of time from beginning to end is called the time span. Use the following steps to read a time line:

❶ Look at the first and last dates on the time line to determine the complete time span.

❷ Notice the intervals, or divisions, on the time line.

❸ Look at the specific events and dates listed.

❹ Determine if there is any relationship between events.

PRACTICE the Skill

Use the time line below to answer the following questions.

❶ (a) What is the earliest event shown? (b) What is the latest event? (c) What is the time span of the time line?

❷ How many years are there between dates on the time line?

❸ (a) What took place in 1755? (b) When did the fighting in North America end?

❹ (a) How would you describe the success of the British in the early years of the war? (b) What relation did the events of 1758 have to the events of 1760?

APPLY the Skill

Make a time line of important events in your life. Use your life up to this point as the time span. Include at least six events that you feel made a major difference in your life.

1754 Fighting begins

1755 French defeat Braddock

1758 British capture Louisbourg and Fort Duquesne

1760 British capture Montreal; fighting ends

1754   1756   1758   1760

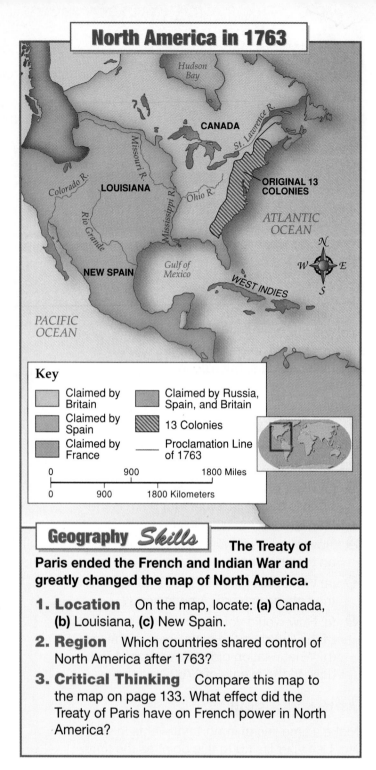

North America in 1763

Key

- Claimed by Britain
- Claimed by Spain
- Claimed by France
- Claimed by Russia, Spain, and Britain
- 13 Colonies
- Proclamation Line of 1763

0   900   1800 Miles
0   900   1800 Kilometers

Geography Skills   The Treaty of Paris ended the French and Indian War and greatly changed the map of North America.

1. **Location**   On the map, locate: **(a)** Canada, **(b)** Louisiana, **(c)** New Spain.
2. **Region**   Which countries shared control of North America after 1763?
3. **Critical Thinking**   Compare this map to the map on page 133. What effect did the Treaty of Paris have on French power in North America?

Lake George. (See the map on page 138.) To English colonists, the situation looked grim. In the words of Massachusetts minister Jonathan Edwards:

66 God indeed is remarkably frowning upon us every where; our enemies get up above us very high, and we are brought down very low: They are the Head, and we are the Tail. . . . What will become of us God only knows. 99

The Tide of Battle Turns

In 1757, **William Pitt** became the new head of the British government. Pitt was a bold leader. "I believe that I can save this nation and that no one else can," he declared with great confidence.

Pitt set out to win the war in North America. Once that goal was achieved, he argued, the British would be free to focus on victory in other parts of the world.* Pitt sent Britain's best generals to North America. To encourage colonists to support the war, he promised large payments for military services and supplies.

Under Pitt's leadership, the tide of battle turned. In 1758, Major General Jeffrey Amherst captured Louisbourg, the most important fort in French Canada. That year, the British also won more Iroquois support.

The Iroquois persuaded the Delawares at Fort Duquesne to abandon the French. Without the Delawares, the French could no longer hold the fort. Acting quickly, the British seized Fort Duquesne, which they renamed Fort Pitt after the British leader. The city of Pittsburgh later grew up on the site of Fort Pitt.

The Fall of New France

The British enjoyed even greater success in 1759. By summer, they had pushed the French from Fort Niagara, Crown Point, and Fort Ticonderoga (ti kahn duh ROH guh). Now, Pitt sent General **James Wolfe** to take Quebec, capital of New France.

Battle for Quebec

Quebec was vital to the defense of New France. Without Quebec, the French would be unable to supply their forts farther up the St. Lawrence River. Quebec was well de-

---

* By 1756, fighting between the French and British had broken out in Europe. There, it became known as the Seven Years' War. The British and the French also fought in India. In the early years of the war, the British suffered setbacks on every front.

fended, though. The city sat atop a steep cliff high above the St. Lawrence. An able French general, the **Marquis de Montcalm,** was prepared to fight off any British attack.

General Wolfe devised a bold plan to capture Quebec. He knew that Montcalm had only a few soldiers guarding the cliff because the French thought that it was too steep to climb. Late one night, Wolfe ordered British troops to move quietly in small boats to the foot of the cliff. Under cover of darkness, the soldiers swarmed ashore and scrambled to the top.

The next morning, Montcalm awakened to some shocking news. A force of 4,000 British troops were drawn up on the **Plains of Abraham,** a grassy field just outside the city.

Montcalm quickly marched out his own troops to meet the enemy. A fierce battle followed. When it was over, both Montcalm and Wolfe were dead. Moments before Wolfe died, a soldier gave him the news that the British had won. Wolfe reportedly whispered, "Now, God be praised, I will die in peace." On September 17, 1759, Quebec surrendered to the British.

Treaty of Paris

The fall of Quebec sealed the fate of New France. In 1760, the British took Montreal, and the war in North America ended. Fighting dragged on in Europe for several more years. Finally, in 1763, Britain and France signed the **Treaty of Paris,** officially bringing the long conflict to an end.

The Treaty of Paris marked the end of French power in North America. Under the treaty, Britain gained Canada and all French lands east of the Mississippi River. France was allowed to keep two islands in the Gulf of St. Lawrence, as well as its rich sugar-growing islands in the West Indies. Spain, which had entered the war on the French side in 1762, gave up Florida to Britain. In return, Spain received all French land west of the Mississippi. In addition, Spain gained the vital port city of New Orleans. Spain retained control of its vast empire in Central and South America.

After years of fighting, peace returned to North America. Yet, in a few short years, a new conflict would break out. This time, the struggle would pit Britain against its own 13 colonies.

★ Section 2 Review ★

Recall

1. **Locate** (a) Fort Necessity, (b) Fort Duquesne, (c) Louisbourg, (d) Quebec.
2. **Identify** (a) George Washington, (b) French and Indian War, (c) Albany Plan of Union, (d) Edward Braddock, (e) William Pitt, (f) James Wolfe, (g) Marquis de Montcalm, (h) Plains of Abraham, (i) Treaty of Paris.

Comprehension

3. What were the causes of the French and Indian War?
4. (a) List two strengths of the French in the French and Indian War. (b) List two strengths of the British.
5. (a) What lands did Britain gain under the Treaty of Paris? (b) How did the treaty affect French power in North America?

Critical Thinking and Writing

6. **Analyzing Ideas** (a) How would the Albany Plan of Union have helped the colonies fight the French? (b) Why do you think colonists rejected the Plan of Union?
7. **Linking Past and Present** How might your life be different if France, not England, had won the French and Indian War?

★ ★

Activity **Creating a Battle Plan** You are a British commander at the start of the French and Indian War. You know all of your strengths and weaknesses and those of your enemy. Examine the map on page 138. Then, write up a brief statement explaining why you think you should attack the French fort at Louisbourg.

3 A Crisis Over Taxes

As You Read

Explore These Questions
- What was the goal of the Proclamation of 1763?
- How did colonists protest British taxes?
- What was the Boston Massacre?

Define
- petition
- boycott
- repeal
- writ of assistance
- nonimportation agreement
- committee of correspondence

Identify
- Pontiac's War
- Proclamation of 1763
- Stamp Act
- Townshend Acts
- Sons of Liberty
- Daughters of Liberty
- Samuel Adams
- John Adams
- Mercy Otis Warren
- Patrick Henry
- Boston Massacre

SETTING the Scene As Britain celebrated the victory over France, a few officials expressed concern. Now that the French were no longer a threat, would the 13 colonies become too independent? Might they even unite one day against Britain? Benjamin Franklin scoffed at such an idea. He recalled the failure of the colonies to agree to his Albany Plan of Union:

66 If [the colonies] could not agree to unite for their defense against the French and Indians, . . . can it reasonably be supposed there is any danger of their uniting against their own nation? . . . I will venture to say, a union amongst them for such a purpose is not merely improbable, it is impossible. 99

Franklin was wrong. After the French and Indian War, new British policies toward the colonies aroused angry cries from Massachusetts to Georgia. Despite their differences, colonists began to move toward unity.

New Troubles on the Frontier

By 1760, the British had driven France from the Ohio Valley. Their troubles in the region were not over, however. For many years, fur traders had sent back glowing reports of the land beyond the Appalachian Mountains. With the French gone, English colonists eagerly headed west to claim the lands for themselves.

Clashes with Native Americans

Many Native American nations lived in the Ohio Valley. They included the Senecas, Delawares, Shawnees, Ottawas, Miamis, and Hurons. As British settlers moved into the valley, they often clashed with these Native Americans.

In 1762, the British sent Lord Jeffrey Amherst to the frontier to keep order. French traders had always treated Native Americans as friends, holding feasts for them and giving them presents. Amherst refused to do this. Instead, he raised the price of goods traded to Indians. Also, unlike the French, Amherst allowed English settlers to build farms and forts on Indian lands.

Discontented Native Americans found a leader in Pontiac, an Ottawa chief who had fought on the side of the French. An English trader remarked that Pontiac "commands more respect amongst these nations than any Indian I ever saw." In April 1763, Pontiac spoke out against the British, calling them "dogs dressed in red, who have come to rob [us] of [our] hunting grounds and drive away the game."

Pontiac's War

Soon after, Pontiac led an attack on British troops at Fort Detroit. He then called on other Indians to join the fight. A number of other nations responded. In a few months, they captured most British forts on the frontier. British and colonial troops struck back and regained much of what they had lost.

Pontiac's War, as it came to be called, did not last long. In October 1763, the French informed Pontiac that they had signed the Treaty of Paris. Because the treaty marked the end of French power in North America, the Indians could no longer hope for French aid against the British.

One by one, the Indian nations stopped fighting and returned home. "All my young men have buried their hatchets," Pontiac reportedly observed. By December, the British controlled the frontier.

Proclamation of 1763

Pontiac's War convinced British officials that they should stop British subjects from settling on the western frontier. To do this, the government issued the **Proclamation of 1763.** The proclamation drew an imaginary line along the crest of the Appalachian Mountains. Colonists were forbidden to settle west of the line. All settlers already west of the line were "to remove themselves" at once.

To enforce the law, Britain sent 10,000 troops to the colonies. Few troops went to the frontier, however. Most stayed in cities along the Atlantic coast.

The proclamation angered colonists. Some colonies, including New York, Pennsylvania, and Virginia, claimed lands in the West. Also, colonists had to pay for the additional British troops that had been sent to enforce the law. In the end, many settlers simply ignored the proclamation and moved west anyway.

One colonist who defied the Proclamation of 1763 was Daniel Boone. In 1767, Boone explored Kentucky, west of the Appalachians. Later, he led settlers through the Cumberland Gap along an old Indian path, renamed the Wilderness Road. Boone fought a number of battles against the Indians.

Britain Imposes New Taxes

The French and Indian War had plunged Britain deeply into debt. As a result, the tax bill for citizens in Britain rose sharply. The British prime minister, George Grenville, decided that colonists in North America should help share the burden. After all, he reasoned, it was the colonists who had gained most from the war.

Sugar Act

In 1764, Grenville asked Parliament to approve the Sugar Act, which put a new tax on molasses. Molasses, you will recall, was a valuable item in the triangular trade. (See page 114.)

Viewing HISTORY Pontiac's War

Despite a hard-fought struggle, Indian forces under Pontiac were unable to drive English settlers out of the Ohio Valley. More than 100 years later, Frederic Remington imagined this scene of Pontiac's warriors attacking Fort Detroit. Remington was a painter and sculptor who specialized in scenes of the American West. ★ **Why did Pontiac want to drive out the British?**

The Sugar Act replaced an earlier tax, which had been so high that any merchant who paid it would have been driven out of business. As a result, most colonial merchants simply avoided the tax by smuggling molasses into the colonies. Often, they bribed tax collectors to look the other way. The Sugar Act of 1764 lowered the tax. At the same time, the law made it easier for British officials to bring colonial smugglers to trial. Grenville made it clear that he expected the new tax to be paid.

Stamp Act

Grenville also persuaded Parliament to pass the **Stamp Act** of 1765. The act placed new duties on legal documents such as wills, diplomas, and marriage papers. It also taxed newspapers, almanacs, playing cards, and even dice.

All items named in the law had to carry a stamp showing that the tax had been paid. Stamp taxes were used in Britain and other countries to raise money. However, Britain had never required American colonists to pay such a tax.

"No Taxation Without Representation!"

When British officials tried to enforce the Stamp Act, they met with stormy protests. Riots broke out in Boston, New York City, Newport, and Charleston. Angry colonists threw rocks at agents trying to collect the unpopular tax. Some tarred and feathered the agents. In Boston, a mob burned an effigy, or likeness, of the English tax collector and then destroyed his home. John Adams, a Massachusetts lawyer, wrote:

66 Our presses have groaned, our pulpits have thundered, our legislatures have resolved, our towns have voted, the crown officers everywhere trembled. 99

The fury of the colonists shocked the British. After all, Britain had spent a great deal of money to protect the colonies against the French. Besides, people living in Britain were paying much higher taxes than the colonists were. Why, the British asked, were colonists so angry about the Stamp Act?

Colonists replied that the taxes imposed by the Stamp Act were unjust. The taxes, they claimed, went against the principle that there should be no taxation without representation. That principle was rooted in English traditions dating back to the Magna Carta. (See page 86.)

Colonists insisted that only they or their elected representatives had the right to pass taxes. Since the colonists did not elect representatives to Parliament, Parliament had no right to tax them. The colonists were willing to pay taxes—but only if the taxes were passed by their own colonial legislatures.

Moving toward unity

The Stamp Act crisis brought a sense of unity to the colonies. Critics of the law called for delegates from every colony to meet in New York City. There, the delegates would consider actions against the hated Stamp Act.

In October 1765, nine colonies sent delegates to what became known as the Stamp Act Congress. The delegates drew up petitions to King George III and to Parliament. A petition is a formal written request to someone in authority, signed by a group of people. In these petitions, the delegates rejected the Stamp Act and asserted that Parliament had no right to tax the colonies. Parliament paid little attention.

The colonists took other steps to change the law. They joined together to boycott British goods. To boycott means to refuse to buy certain goods and services. The boycott of British goods took its toll. Trade fell off by 14 percent. British merchants suffered. So, too, did British workers who made goods for the colonies.

Finally, in 1766, Parliament repealed, or canceled, the Stamp Act. At the same time, though, it passed a law asserting that Parliament had the right to raise taxes in "all cases whatsoever."

The Townshend Acts

In May 1767, Parliament reopened the debate over taxing the colonies. In a fierce exchange, George Grenville, now a member

▼ British tax stamp

▲ Teapot protesting the Stamp Act

Viewing HISTORY **Protesting the Stamp Act**

Tax collectors hoped to make a good living distributing stamps. Instead, they found themselves targets of violence. Here, protesters tie a tax collector to a pole and drive him through the streets on a cart. ★ **Why do you think many Americans were dismayed by the tactics used by tax protesters?**

of Parliament, clashed with Charles Townshend, the official in charge of the British treasury. "You are cowards, you are afraid of the Americans, you dare not tax America!" Grenville shouted.

"Fear? Cowards?" Townshend snapped back. "I dare tax America!"

The next month, Parliament passed the **Townshend Acts,** which taxed goods such as glass, paper, paint, lead, and tea. The taxes were low, but colonists still objected. The principle, they felt, was the same: Parliament did not have the right to tax them without their consent.

The Townshend Acts also set up new ways to collect taxes. Customs officials were sent to American ports with orders to stop smuggling. Using legal documents known as writs of assistance, the officers would be allowed to inspect a ship's cargo without giving a reason.

Colonists protested that the writs of assistance violated their rights as British citizens. Under British law, an official could not search a person's property without a good reason for suspecting the owner of a crime.

Arguing against the writs, Massachusetts lawyer James Otis commented:

> ❝ Now, one of the most essential branches of English liberty is the freedom of one's house. A man's house is his castle; and while he is quiet, he is as well guarded as a prince in his castle. This writ, if it should be declared legal, would totally [destroy] this privilege. Customhouse officers may enter our houses when they please. ❞

Colonial protests widen

Colonists responded swiftly and strongly to the Townshend Acts. From north to south, colonial merchants and planters signed nonimportation agreements. In these agreements, they promised to stop importing goods taxed by the Townshend Acts. The colonists hoped that the new boycott would win repeal of the Townshend Acts.

To protest British policies, some angry colonists formed the **Sons of Liberty.** From Boston to Charleston, Sons of Liberty staged

Why Study History?

Because You Pay Taxes

★ ★

Government by the People: NO NEW TAXES

Many Americans protest that their taxes are too high.

Historical Background

In the 1760s and 1770s, colonists charged that taxes levied on them by the British government were unfair because Americans did not elect representatives to Parliament. "No taxation without representation!" American patriots cried. In protest, they boycotted British goods and attacked tax collectors. They even tarred and feathered a few agents. The furor over taxes helped cause the American Revolution.

Connections to Today

Fortunately, we no longer tar and feather tax collectors, but many people do still object to taxes. The most frequent complaint is that taxes are too high. In the mid-1990s, the average American worked from January to May just to pay taxes!

The size of the tax bill is not the only complaint. Some people charge that the tax system is unfair. They say that the poor pay too much while the rich pay too little. Others say that the tax system is too complicated and that the rules are hard to understand. Recently, one sentence in a tax instruction was 436 words long

Taxes pay for essential services, such as fire protection.

—longer than the entire Gettysburg Address. As a result, nearly half of all Americans pay someone else to prepare their taxes.

Connections to You

If your state has a sales tax, you already pay taxes whenever you buy a taxable item. When you get a job, you will pay income taxes. Some day, you may pay property taxes on a home. As a voter, you will help to choose the legislators who decide our nation's tax laws.

Do you think taxes should be drastically reduced? Before you decide, remember that taxes pay for important services. Tax cuts could mean less money for national defense, health care, education, and transportation. There would also be less money for fire and police protection, recreation facilities, and the environment. So when you consider taxes, consider carefully.

1. **Comprehension** Describe three reasons some Americans complain about taxes today.

2. **Critical Thinking** Taxes spread the cost of services across the entire population. What are the benefits of this system? What are the disadvantages?

★*Activity* **Debating** Organize a classroom debate on taxes. One side should argue in favor of lower tax rates and the benefits to be gained from them. The other side should oppose tax cuts because of the possible negative effects on the community.

mock hangings of cloth or straw effigies dressed like British officials. The hangings were meant to show tax collectors what might happen to them if they tried to collect the unpopular taxes.

Some women joined the **Daughters of Liberty.** They paraded, signed petitions, and organized a boycott of fine British cloth. They urged colonial women to raise more sheep, prepare more wool, and spin and weave their own cloth. A slogan of the Daughters of Liberty declared, "It is better to wear a Homespun coat than to lose our Liberty."

Some Sons and Daughters of Liberty also used other methods to support their cause. They visited merchants and urged them to sign the nonimportation agreements. A few even threatened people who continued to buy British goods.

New Leaders Emerge

As the struggle over taxes continued, new leaders emerged in all the colonies. Men and women in New England and Virginia were especially active in the colonial cause.

In Massachusetts

Samuel Adams of Boston stood firmly against Britain. Sam Adams seemed an unlikely leader. He was a failure in business and a poor public speaker. Still, he loved politics. He was always present at Boston town meetings and Sons of Liberty rallies. Adams's greatest talent was organizing people. He knew how to work behind the scenes, arranging protests and stirring public support.

Sam's cousin John was another important Massachusetts leader. **John Adams** was a skilled lawyer. More cautious than Sam, he weighed evidence carefully before acting. His knowledge of British law earned him much respect.

Mercy Otis Warren also aided the colonial cause. Warren published plays that made fun of British officials. She formed a close friendship with Abigail Adams, the wife of John Adams. The two women used their pens to spur the colonists to action. They also called for greater rights for women in the colonies.

In Virginia

Virginia contributed many leaders to the struggle against taxes. In the House of Burgesses, George Washington joined other Virginians to protest the Townshend Acts.

A young lawyer, **Patrick Henry,** became well known as a violent critic of British policies. His speeches in the House of Burgesses moved listeners to both tears and anger. Once, Henry attacked Britain with such fury that some listeners cried out, "Treason!" Henry boldly replied, "If this be treason, make the most of it!"

Britain Takes Action

Port cities such as Boston and New York were centers of protest. In New York, a dispute arose over the Quartering Act. Under

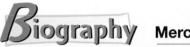 **Mercy Otis Warren**

Mercy Otis Warren's anger was inflamed when her brother, James Otis, was struck on the head by an English officer and suffered permanent brain damage. Warren used her pen and sharp wit to stir feelings against the British. In plays like The Blockheads, *she ridiculed British officials. Warren's home in Massachusetts became a meeting place for colonists who opposed British policies.* ★ **How do writers influence public opinion today?**

Viewing HISTORY — The Boston Massacre

Paul Revere's engraving of the Boston Massacre helped whip up colonial fury against the British. In fact, the picture is very inaccurate. No British officer ever gave an order to fire, as shown here. The redcoats, faced with an unruly mob, fired on their own. Revere also shows seven American dead, when there were actually five. ★ **Why do you think Revere distorted the event in his engraving?**

that law, colonists had to provide housing, candles, bedding, and beverages to soldiers stationed in the colonies. When the New York assembly refused to obey the law, Britain dismissed the assembly in 1767.

Britain also sent two regiments to Boston to protect customs officers from local citizens. To many Bostonians, the soldiers were a daily reminder that Britain was trying to bully them into paying unjust taxes. When British soldiers walked along the streets of Boston, they risked insults or even beatings. The time was ripe for disaster.

The Boston Massacre

On the night of March 5, 1770, a crowd gathered outside the Boston customs house. Colonists shouted insults at the "lobster-backs," as they called the redcoated British who guarded the building. Then the Boston crowd began to throw snowballs, oyster shells, and chunks of ice at the soldiers.

The crowd grew larger and rowdier. Suddenly, the soldiers panicked. They fired into the crowd. When the smoke from the musket volley cleared, five people lay dead or dying. Among the first to die was Crispus Attucks, a black sailor who was active in the Sons of Liberty.

Colonists were quick to protest the incident, which they called the **Boston Massacre**. Boston silversmith Paul Revere stirred up anti-British feeling with an engraving that showed British soldiers firing on unarmed colonists. Sam Adams wrote letters to other colonists to build outrage about the shooting.

The soldiers were arrested and tried in court. John Adams agreed to defend them, saying that they deserved a fair trial. He wanted to show the world that the colonists believed in justice, even if the British government did not. At the trial, Adams argued that the crowd had provoked the soldiers. His arguments convinced the jury. In the end, the heaviest punishment any soldier received was a branding on the hand.

Samuel Adams later expanded on the idea of a letter-writing campaign like the one he had used to arouse colonists after the Boston Massacre. Adams formed a **committee of correspondence.** Members of the committee regularly wrote letters and pamphlets reporting on events in Massachusetts. Before long, committees of correspondence became a major tool of protest in every colony.

Samuel Adams

A Temporary Calm

By chance, on the very day of the Boston Massacre, Parliament voted to repeal most of the Townshend Acts. English merchants, harmed by the nonimportation agreements, had pressured Parliament to end the taxes. Still, King George III asked Parliament to retain the tax on tea. "There must always be one tax to keep up the right [to tax]," he argued. Parliament agreed.

News of the repeal delighted the colonists. Most people dismissed the remaining tax on tea as not important and ended their boycott of British goods. For a few years, calm returned. Yet the underlying issue—Britain's power to tax the colonies—remained unsettled. For the first time, the colonists were thinking more clearly about their political rights.

★ Section 3 Review ★

Recall

1. **Identify** **(a)** Pontiac's War, **(b)** Proclamation of 1763, **(c)** Stamp Act, **(d)** Townshend Acts, **(e)** Sons of Liberty, **(f)** Daughters of Liberty, **(g)** Samuel Adams, **(h)** John Adams, **(i)** Mercy Otis Warren, **(j)** Patrick Henry, **(k)** Boston Massacre.

2. **Define** **(a)** petition, **(b)** boycott, **(c)** repeal, **(d)** writ of assistance, **(e)** nonimportation agreement, **(f)** committee of correspondence.

Comprehension

3. **(a)** Why did Britain issue the Proclamation of 1763? **(b)** How did colonists respond to the Proclamation?

4. **(a)** What argument did the colonists use against British taxes? **(b)** How did colonists protest the taxes?

5. Describe the key events leading up to the Boston Massacre.

Critical Thinking and Writing

6. **Understanding Causes and Effects** Why did the French defeat in North America doom Pontiac's efforts to drive English settlers out of the Ohio Valley?

7. **Defending a Position** Do you think Britain had the right to tax the colonies? Defend your position.

Activity **Writing a Letter** Spread the word! You are a member of Sam Adams's committee of correspondence. Write a letter to other colonists in which you remind them of the injustice of British taxes and the actions of British officials and troops, and call for further protests.

The Fighting Begins

4

As You Read

Explore These Questions
- Why did Americans protest the Tea Act?
- How did Britain respond to the Boston Tea Party?
- Why did fighting break out at Lexington and Concord?

Define
- militia
- minuteman

Identify
- British East India Company
- Tea Act
- Boston Tea Party
- Intolerable Acts
- First Continental Congress

SETTING the Scene One night in July 1774, John Adams stopped at a tavern in eastern Massachusetts. After riding for more than 30 miles, he was hot and dusty, and his body ached with fatigue.

Adams asked the innkeeper for a cup of tea. The innkeeper, however, refused his request. She did not serve tea, she informed him. He would have to drink coffee instead.

Adams later praised the innkeeper's conduct. In a letter to his wife, Abigail, he wrote that tea must be given up by all colonists. He promised to break himself of the habit as soon as possible.

Why did colonists like John Adams give up tea? The answer was taxes. When Parliament decided to enforce a tea tax in 1773, a new crisis exploded. This time, colonists began to think the unthinkable. Perhaps the time had come to reject British rule and declare independence.

Uproar Over Tea

Tea was tremendously popular in the colonies. By 1770, at least one million Americans brewed tea twice a day. People "would rather go without their dinners than without a dish of tea," a visitor to the colonies noted.

Parliament passes the Tea Act

Most tea was brought to the colonies by the **British East India Company.** The company bought tea in southern Asia and sold it to colonial tea merchants. The merchants then sold the tea to the colonists. To make a profit, the merchants sold the tea at a higher price than they had paid for it.

In the 1770s, however, the British East India Company found itself in deep financial trouble. More than 15 million pounds of its tea sat unsold in British warehouses. Britain had kept a tax on tea as a symbol of its right to tax the colonies. The tax was a small one, but colonists resented it. They refused to buy English tea.

Parliament tried to help the East India Company by passing the **Tea Act** of 1773. The act let the company bypass the tea merchants and sell directly to colonists. Although colonists would still have to pay the tea tax, they would not have to pay the higher price charged by tea merchants. As a result, the tea itself would cost less than ever before.

To the surprise of Parliament, colonists protested the Tea Act. Tea merchants were angry because they had been cut out of the

Connections With Science

American physicians joined the protest against tea. They spread stories warning about tea's adverse effects on health. One doctor claimed that drinking tea would make one an invalid for life. Another said that tea weakened "the tone of the stomach, and therefore of the whole system, inducing tremors and spasmodic affections."

Disguised as Indians, some 50 or 60 Bostonians attacked British tea ships. A crowd watched silently as the colonists dumped tea into Boston harbor. British officials called the Boston Tea Party "the most wanton and unprovoked insult offered to the civil power that is recorded in history."

★ **Why did colonists attack the tea ships?**

◄ *Colonial tea caddy*

tea trade. If Parliament ruined tea merchants today, they warned, what would prevent it from turning on other businesses tomorrow?

Even tea drinkers, who would have benefited from the law, scorned the Tea Act. They believed that it was a British trick to make them accept Parliament's right to tax the colonies.

A new boycott

Once again, colonists responded to the new tax with a boycott. One colonial newspaper warned:

> 66 Do not suffer yourself to sip the accursed, dutied STUFF. For if you do, the devil will immediately enter into you, and you will instantly become a traitor to your country. 99

Daughters of Liberty and other women led the boycott. They served coffee or made "liberty tea" from raspberry leaves. At some ports, Sons of Liberty enforced the boycott by keeping the British East India Company from unloading cargoes of tea.

Boston Tea Party

Three ships loaded with tea reached Boston harbor in late November 1773. The colonial governor of Massachusetts, Thomas Hutchinson, insisted that they unload their cargo as usual.

Sam Adams and the Sons of Liberty had other plans. On the night of December 16,

they met in Old South Church. They sent a message to the governor, demanding that the ships leave the harbor. When the governor rejected the demand, Adams stood up and declared, "This meeting can do nothing further to save the country."

Adams's words seemed to be a signal. As if on cue, a group of men burst into the meetinghouse. Dressed like Mohawk Indians, they waved hatchets in the air. From the gallery above, voices cried, "Boston harbor a teapot tonight! The Mohawks are come!"

The disguised colonists left the meetinghouse and headed for the harbor. Others joined them on the way. In the cold, crisp night, under a nearly full moon, the men boarded the ships, split open the tea chests, and dumped the tea into the harbor. By 10 P.M., the **Boston Tea Party,** as it was later called, was over. Its effects would be felt for a long time to come.

Britain Strikes Back

Colonists had mixed reactions to the Boston Tea Party. Some cheered the action. Others worried that it would encourage lawlessness in the colonies. Even those who condemned the Boston Tea Party, though, were shocked at Britain's response.

Punishing Massachusetts

The British were outraged by what they saw as Boston's lawless behavior. In 1774, Parliament, encouraged by King George III,

❶ The type case held metal letters.

❷ Letters were placed in a composing stick to create lines of type.

❸ Lines of type were locked in a form to create a sheet of text.

❹ The form was inked with ink balls.

❺ The frisket kept the margins of the paper clean. It folded onto the tympan.

❻ The tympan held the paper. It folded onto the form.

❼ The form was slid under the platen.

❽ The press bar was pulled to lower the platen.

❾ The platen pressed the inked form against the paper.

❿ The printed page was removed and hung on a drying rack.

In Provincial Congrefs,
New-York, August 8th, 1775.
RESOLVED,

THAT the feveral Committees and Sub-Committees of the different Counties within this Colony, be directed immediately to purchafe or hire all the ARMS, with or without Bayonets, that are fit for prefent Service (on the Credit of this Colony) and to deliver them to the refpective Colonels in this Colony employed in the Continental Service, or their Order, for the Ufe of the Continental Army.

A true Copy from the Minutes,
ROBERT BENSON, Secry.

Colonial Printing Press

Colonial printers played a vital role in uniting colonists against the British. Besides publishing newspapers and magazines, they also printed letters and pamphlets that kept colonists informed of such developments as the Intolerable Acts. The drawing shows how a printing press of the time worked. ★ **Why would printing a document with this press be very time-consuming?**

Printing press owned by ➤
Benjamin Franklin

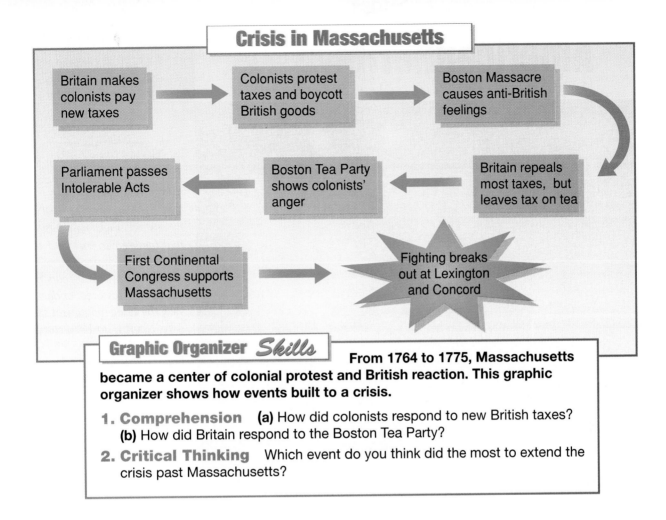

Crisis in Massachusetts

Britain makes colonists pay new taxes →

Colonists protest taxes and boycott British goods →

Boston Massacre causes anti-British feelings →

Britain repeals most taxes, but leaves tax on tea ←

Boston Tea Party shows colonists' anger ←

Parliament passes Intolerable Acts →

First Continental Congress supports Massachusetts →

Fighting breaks out at Lexington and Concord

Graphic Organizer *Skills* From 1764 to 1775, Massachusetts became a center of colonial protest and British reaction. This graphic organizer shows how events built to a crisis.

1. **Comprehension** **(a)** How did colonists respond to new British taxes? **(b)** How did Britain respond to the Boston Tea Party?
2. **Critical Thinking** Which event do you think did the most to extend the crisis past Massachusetts?

acted to punish Massachusetts. Colonists called the four laws they passed the **Intolerable Acts** because they were so harsh.

First, Parliament shut down the port of Boston. No ship could enter or leave the harbor—not even a small boat. The harbor would remain closed until the colonists paid for the tea.

Second, Parliament forbade Massachusetts colonists to hold town meetings more than once a year without the governor's permission. In the past, colonists had called town meetings whenever they wished.

Third, Parliament provided for customs officers and other officials charged with major crimes to be tried in Britain instead of in Massachusetts. Colonists protested that a dishonest official could break the law in the colonies and avoid punishment "by being tried, where no evidence can pursue him."

Fourth, Parliament passed a new Quartering Act. No longer would redcoats camp in tents on Boston Common. Instead, British commanders could force citizens to house troops in their homes.

Other colonies support Boston

The committees of correspondence spread news of the Intolerable Acts. They warned that the people of Boston faced hunger while their port was closed. People from other colonies responded quickly. Carts rolled into the city with rice from South Carolina, corn from Virginia, and flour from Pennsylvania.

In the Virginia assembly, a young lawyer named Thomas Jefferson suggested that a day be set aside to mark the shame of the Intolerable Acts. The royal governor of Virginia rejected the idea and dismissed the assembly. The colonists went ahead anyway. On June 1, 1774, church bells tolled slowly. Merchants closed their shops. Many colonists prayed and fasted all day.

In September 1774, colonial leaders called a meeting in Philadelphia. Delegates from 12 colonies gathered in what became

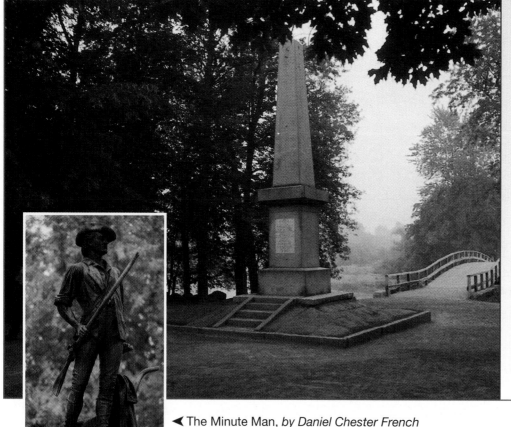

◄ The Minute Man, *by Daniel Chester French*

known as the **First Continental Congress.** Only Georgia did not send delegates.

After much debate, the delegates passed a resolution backing Massachusetts in its struggle. They agreed to boycott all British goods and to stop exporting goods to Britain until the Intolerable Acts were repealed. The delegates also urged each colony to set up and train its own militia (muh LIHSH uh). A **militia** is an army of citizens who serve as soldiers during an emergency.

Before leaving Philadelphia, the delegates agreed to meet again in May 1775. Little did they know that before then an incident in Massachusetts would change the fate of the colonies forever.

Lexington and Concord

In Massachusetts, newspapers called on citizens to prevent what they called "the Massacre of American Liberty." Volunteers known as **minutemen** trained regularly. Minutemen got their name because they kept their muskets at hand, prepared to fight at a minute's notice. Meanwhile, Britain built up its forces. More troops arrived in Boston, bringing the total number in that city to 4,000.

Early in 1775, General Thomas Gage, the British commander, heard a rumor that minutemen had a large store of arms in Concord, a village about 18 miles (29 km) from Boston. Gage planned a surprise march to Concord to seize the arms. (See the map on page 162.)

Sounding the alarm

On April 18, about 700 British troops quietly left Boston under cover of darkness. The Sons of Liberty were watching. As soon as the British set out, the Americans hung two lamps from the Old North Church in Boston. This signal meant that the redcoats were on the move.

Colonists who were waiting across the Charles River saw the signal. Messengers mounted their horses and galloped through the night toward Concord. One midnight rider was Paul Revere. "The British are coming! The British are coming!" shouted Revere as he passed through each sleepy village along the way.

"The shot heard round the world"

At daybreak on April 19, the redcoats reached Lexington, a town near Concord. On the village green, some 70 minutemen were waiting, commanded by Captain John Parker. The British ordered the minutemen to go home.

Outnumbered, the colonists began to leave. Suddenly, a shot rang out through the chill morning air. No one knows who fired it. In the brief struggle that followed, eight colonists were killed and one British soldier was wounded.

The British pushed on to Concord. Finding no arms in the village, they turned back to Boston. On a bridge outside Concord, they met 300 minutemen. Again, fighting broke out. This time, the British were forced to retreat. As they withdrew, colonial sharpshoot-ers took deadly aim at them from the woods and fields. Local women also fired at the British from their windows. By the time they reached Boston, the redcoats had lost 73 men. Another 200 British soldiers were wounded or missing.

News of the battles at Lexington and Concord spread swiftly. To many colonists, the fighting ended all hope of reaching an agreement with Britain. Only war would decide the future of the 13 colonies.

More than 60 years after the battles of Lexington and Concord, a well-known New England poet, Ralph Waldo Emerson, wrote a poem honoring the minutemen. Emerson's "Concord Hymn" begins:

> **❝** By the rude bridge that arched the flood,
> Their flag to April's breeze unfurled,
> Here once the embattled farmers stood,
> And fired the shot heard round the world. **❞**

The "embattled farmers" faced long years of war. At the war's end, though, the 13 colonies would stand strong and free as a new, independent nation.

★ Section 4 Review ★

Recall

1. **Locate** (a) Boston, (b) Concord, (c) Lexington.
2. **Identify** (a) British East India Company, (b) Tea Act, (c) Boston Tea Party, (d) Intolerable Acts, (e) First Continental Congress.
3. **Define** (a) militia, (b) minuteman.

Comprehension

4. (a) Why did Britain pass the Tea Act? (b) Why did the act anger colonists?
5. How did the Intolerable Acts help to unite the colonies?
6. Describe the events that led to the fighting at Lexington.

Critical Thinking and Writing

7. **Making Inferences** Do you think the organizers of the Boston Tea Party would have ended their protests against Britain if Parliament had repealed the tax on tea? Explain.
8. **Identifying Alternatives** (a) Do you think Parliament should have passed the Intolerable Acts in response to the Boston Tea Party? (b) What other actions might Parliament have taken in this situation?

★ ★

Activity **Writing a Poem** Today, as in the past, writers like Mercy Otis Warren often use their skills to comment on current events. You are a poet living in colonial Boston. Write a poem in which you tell about the Boston Tea Party, the Intolerable Acts, or the events of April 19, 1775.

Review and Activities

★ Sum It Up ★

Section 1 Rivalry in North America
▶ By the mid-1700s, England, France, Spain, and the Netherlands were competing for land and trade in North America.
▶ Native Americans were drawn into the struggle between the French and British in the Ohio Valley.

Section 2 The French and Indian War
▶ In 1754, the French and Indian War pitted the British against the French and their Indian allies.
▶ As a result of the French and Indian War, Britain won control of French land claims in North America.

Section 3 A Crisis Over Taxes
▶ Colonists objected to the Proclamation of 1763 because it forbade them to settle in lands west of the Appalachian Mountains.
▶ American colonists objected to Parliament's attempts to tax them without their consent.
▶ Colonists were outraged when British soldiers shot and killed Americans in the Boston Massacre.

Section 4 The Fighting Begins
▶ Conflict over taxes gradually increased until colonists staged the Boston Tea Party and Britain passed the Intolerable Acts.
▶ In April 1775, fighting between British troops and colonial minutemen marked the start of the American Revolution.

For additional review of the major ideas of Chapter 5, see *Guide to the Essentials of American History* or *Interactive Student Tutorial CD-ROM,* which contains interactive review activities, graphic organizers, and practice tests.

▢ Reviewing the Chapter

Define These Terms
Match each term with the correct definition.

Column 1
1. petition
2. boycott
3. repeal
4. committee of correspondence
5. militia

Column 2
a. refusal to buy certain goods and services
b. formal written request
c. army of citizens who serve as soldiers during an emergency
d. cancel
e. group that wrote letters and pamphlets reporting events in the colonies

Explore the Main Ideas
1. Why was the Ohio River especially important to the French before 1754?
2. Why did Pontiac call for war against British settlers?
3. How did the Daughters of Liberty protest the Tea Act?
4. How did the Intolerable Acts affect the port of Boston?
5. Describe the outcome of the battles of Lexington and Concord.

▢ Geography Activity

Match the letters on the map with the following locations:
1. Spanish lands in 1763, **2.** British lands in 1763, **3.** Original 13 English colonies, **4.** Mississippi River, **5.** Ohio River.
Location What body of water formed the western boundary of British lands in North America in 1763?

Critical Thinking and Writing

1. **Understanding Chronology** In 1763, Britain banned settlement west of the Appalachian Mountains. Why do you think it did not issue such a proclamation before the French and Indian War?

2. **Linking Past and Present** Why is English the most widely spoken language in the United States and Canada today?

3. **Exploring Unit Themes** **Origins** The principle that people must give their consent before they pay taxes goes back to ancient British law. How is it reflected in our government today?

4. **Ranking** Which of the Intolerable Acts do you think would have been most alarming to the Americans throughout the colonies? Explain your reasoning.

Using Primary Sources

In August 1765, Francis Bernard, the governor of Massachusetts, reported to England on a Stamp Act riot in Boston:

> 66 Toward evening some boys began to light a bonfire before the Town House, which is a usual signal for a mob. Before it was quite dark a great company of people gather together crying liberty and property, which is the usual notice of their intention to plunder and pull down a house. . . . They went to the house of Mr. Story, . . . broke into it and tore it all to pieces; and took out all the books and papers, among which were all the records of the Court of the Admiralty, and carried them to the bonfire and burned them. 99

Source: *The Annals of America,* Volume 2, 1976.

Recognizing Points of View **(a)** In the first sentence, what words does Bernard use to describe the protesters? **(b)** How does he view the protesters' use of the word *liberty*? **(c)** How do you think Samuel Adams would have responded to the governor's report?

ACTIVITY BANK

Interdisciplinary Activity

Exploring the Arts List five reasons for the colonists' anger with Britain. Based on your list, write a song of protest against British treatment. You can make up your own melody or write new words to an existing tune. Sing or play your song for the class.

Career Skills Activity

Scriptwriters Write a script dramatizing one of the events you have read about in this chapter. With a small group of students, perform your skit for the class.

Citizenship Activity

Testing Alternative Courses of Action Review the events of the Boston Tea Party. List reasons for citizens of the colonies to support the actions of the protesters. Then, list reasons for citizens to condemn the protesters' actions.

Internet Activity

Use the Internet to find sites dealing with one of the people you have read about in this chapter. Write a mini-biography of the person you have chosen. If possible, illustrate your biography with a picture downloaded from the Web site.

EYEWITNESS Journal

You are one of the following: a Native American in the Ohio Valley in 1750; Major George Washington in the 1750s; a Son or Daughter of Liberty in 1770; a minuteman on April 19, 1775. In your EYEWITNESS JOURNAL, describe the events of the time that have had the greatest effect on you.

The American Revolution

1775–1783

After Lexington and Concord, representatives of the colonies tried, without success, to find a peaceful solution to the conflict with Britain. In 1776, as the fighting spread, they called for separation from Britain. With the bold words of the Declaration of Independence, the United States became a nation.

The Americans now fought a life-and-death struggle for liberty. From New England, the major operations of the war gradually spread to the Middle States and the South. With help from France and other nations, the Americans defeated the British and won their war for independence.

Why Study
History?

On July 4, 1776, Americans declared their independence from British rule. Today, on every Fourth of July, we celebrate the Declaration of Independence and the ideals it proclaims. To learn more about how and why we celebrate, see this chapter's *Why Study History?* feature, "We Celebrate Our Independence."

American Events

●**1775**
Battle of Bunker Hill

●**1776**
Declaration of Independence is issued

●**1777**
American victory at Saratoga is turning point of war

| 1775 | 1776 | 1777 | 1778 | 1779 |

World Events

1778 World Event
France recognizes American independence

Viewing HISTORY — **A Nation Wins Its Independence**

This painting, Surrender of Lord Cornwallis, *is by John Trumbull, one of the greatest early American artists. It shows British troops surrendering to an American army at Yorktown, Virginia, in 1781. The Battle of Yorktown marked the end of the American Revolution. The six-year struggle freed the 13 colonies from British rule.*

★ **Why do you think Britain was unwilling to give up its colonies?**

1780
Patriots' victory at
King's Mountain
boosts morale

1781
British surrender
at Yorktown

1783
Britain recognizes
American inde-
pendence in the
Treaty of Paris

1779 **1780** **1781** **1782** **1783**

1779 World Event
Spain enters the war
against Britain

1782 World Event
War between British and
Marāthā people of India ends

★ 159

Early Battles

As You Read

Explore These Questions
- How did Americans pursue both war and peace in 1775?
- What were the advantages of each side as they entered the war?
- How did the Continental Army gain control of Boston?

Define
- refugee
- blockade
- mercenary

Identify
- Ethan Allen
- Green Mountain Boys
- Continental Army
- Olive Branch Petition
- Patriots
- Loyalists
- Battle of Bunker Hill
- Benedict Arnold

SETTING the Scene The events of April 19, 1775, left the British stunned. How had a handful of rebels forced 700 redcoats to retreat? That night, British soldiers grew even more uneasy as they watched rebels set up campfires all around Boston.

In the months ahead, the campfires remained. They were a clear sign that the quarrel between Britain and its colonies had blazed into war. Many colonists clung to hopes for a peaceful solution. Others were ready and eager to fight.

War or Peace?

On May 10, 1775, just a few weeks after the battles at Lexington and Concord, delegates from the colonies met at the Second Continental Congress in Philadelphia. Most who attended still hoped to avoid a final break with Britain. However, while they were meeting, the fighting spread.

Rebels take Ticonderoga

Ethan Allen, a blacksmith known for his fierce temper, followed a course of action rather than talk. Allen decided to lead a band of Vermonters, known as the **Green Mountain Boys,** in a surprise attack on Fort Ticonderoga, located at the southern tip of Lake Champlain. (See the map on page 162.) Allen knew that inside the fort were many cannons which the colonies badly needed.

In early May, the Green Mountain Boys crept quietly through the morning mists to Fort Ticonderoga. They quickly overpowered the guard on duty and entered the fort. Allen rushed to the room where the British commander slept. "Come out, you old rat!" he shouted. The commander demanded to know by whose authority Allen acted. "In the name of the Great Jehovah and the Continental Congress!" Allen replied.

The British commander surrendered Ticonderoga. With the fort, the Green Mountain Boys won a valuable supply of cannons and gunpowder. Allen's success also gave the Americans control of a key route into Canada.

Setting up an army

Then, in June, the Second Continental Congress took the bold step of setting up the **Continental Army.** John Adams proposed that George Washington of Virginia be appointed commander:

> 66 I [have] in mind for that important command...a gentleman whose skill and experience as an officer, whose independent fortune, great talents, and excellent universal character would command the [approval] of all America. 99

Tall and dignified, George Washington commanded the respect of all the delegates. They promptly voted to approve him as commander. Without wasting any time, the new general left Philadelphia to take charge of the forces around Boston.

A peace petition

Even though the delegates had created an army, they were not eager for war. After much debate, Congress decided to try to patch up the quarrel with Britain by sending the **Olive Branch Petition,** written by John Dickinson of Pennsylvania. In it, they declared their loyalty to King George and asked him to repeal the Intolerable Acts.

George III was furious when he heard about the petition. The colonists, he raged, were trying to begin a war "for the purpose of establishing an independent empire!" He blamed "wicked and desperate persons" in the colonies for the growing conflict. Rejecting the Olive Branch Petition, the king vowed to bring the rebels to justice.

The Opposing Sides

The rebels that King George III spoke of called themselves **Patriots.** They opposed aspects of British rule that they considered harsh and unjust. Most of the American colonists were Patriots.

In their war with Britain, the Patriots faced a powerful foe. They also had to struggle against a large number of colonists who chose to remain loyal British subjects.

American Patriots

It would take a great effort for the Patriots to overcome their disadvantages. Colonial forces were poorly organized and untrained. They had few cannons, little gunpowder, and no navy.

Yet the Patriots had some important advantages. Many Patriots owned rifles and were good shots. Also, they had a brilliant commander in George Washington. Another strength was that they would fight hard to defend their homes and property. Reuben Stebbins of Massachusetts was typical of many patriotic farmers. When the British approached, he rode off to battle. "We'll see who's goin' t' own this farm!" he cried.

The British

The British were a powerful foe. They had highly trained, experienced troops. Their navy was the best in the world. British ships could move soldiers quickly up and down the Atlantic coast. In addition, many colonists still supported the British.

Still, Britain was not without problems. Britain's armies were 3,000 miles (4,800 km) from home. News and supplies took months to travel from Britain to North America. Also, British soldiers risked attacks by colonists once they marched out of the cities into the countryside.

Viewing HISTORY: Rebels Take Ticonderoga

In May 1775, Ethan Allen and the Green Mountain Boys made a bold attack on Fort Ticonderoga. In this painting, Allen demands that the British commander surrender. ★ **Why was Fort Ticonderoga an important prize?**

The War for Independence Begins

CANADA

Quebec

Montreal

MONTGOMERY

St. Lawrence R.

ARNOLD

Kennebec R.

L. Champlain

Maine
(part of MA)

Crown Point

Ft. Ticonderoga

New
Hampshire

Connecticut R.

New
York

Hudson R.

ATLANTIC
OCEAN

Concord Lexington
Massachusetts Boston

HOWE
TO HALIFAX

New
Jersey

Connecticut

Rhode
Island

Key

← American forces   ← British forces

✶ American victories   ✶ British victories

0   50   100 Miles
0   50   100 Kilometers

Geography Skills

At the beginning of the War for Independence, most of the fighting took place in the northern colonies and in Canada.

1. **Location** On the map, locate: **(a)** Lexington, **(b)** Concord, **(c)** Boston, **(d)** Fort Ticonderoga, **(e)** Quebec.

2. **Movement** **(a)** Describe Arnold's route to Canada. **(b)** Describe Montgomery's route from Crown Point to Quebec.

3. **Critical Thinking** Based on the map, which American commander would have a harder time reaching Quebec? Explain.

American Loyalists

American colonists who remained loyal to Britain were known as **Loyalists** or Tories. It is estimated that they made up about 20 percent of the colonists. They included wealthy merchants and former officials of the royal government. However, some farmers and craftsworkers were also Loyalists. There were more Loyalists in the Middle States and the South than in New England.

Loyalists faced tough times during the American Revolution. Patriots tarred and feathered people known to favor the British. Many Loyalists fled to England or Canada. Others found shelter in cities controlled by the British. Those who fled lost their homes, stores, and farms.

The Fight for Boston

During the first year of conflict, much of the fighting was centered around Boston. About 6,000 British troops were stationed there. Colonial militia surrounded the city and prevented the British from marching out.

Battle of Bunker Hill

Even before Washington reached Boston, the Patriots took action. On June 16, 1775, Colonel William Prescott led 1,200 minutemen up Bunker Hill, across the river from Boston. From there, they could fire on British ships in Boston harbor. Prescott, however, noticed that nearby Breed's Hill was an even better position. He ordered his men to move there and dig defensive trenches.

At sunrise, the British general, William Howe, spotted the Americans. He ferried about 2,400 redcoats across the harbor to attack the rebels' position. Slowly, the British began to climb Breed's Hill. Each soldier carried a heavy pack that weighed about 125 pounds. Many of the British troops were exhausted even before the fighting began.

The Americans waited patiently as the British approached. The Patriots held their fire because they had very little gunpowder. Their commanders warned, "Don't shoot until you see the whites of their eyes!"

When the Americans finally fired, the British were forced to retreat. A second British attack was also turned back. On the

CHARLES TOWN

BOSTON

Viewing HISTORY — **The Fight for Boston**

In this painting of the Battle of Bunker Hill, British ships bombard the village of Charlestown, across the river from Boston. Meanwhile, British troops make the long march up Breed's Hill to attack the waiting Americans. ★ **Why was the Battle of Bunker Hill important to Americans?**

Drum carried ➤
at Bunker Hill

third try, the British succeeded in pushing over the top. They took both Bunker Hill and Breed's Hill, but paid a high price for their victory. More than 1,000 redcoats lay dead or wounded. American losses numbered only about 400.

The **Battle of Bunker Hill** was the first major battle of the Revolution. It proved that the Americans could fight bravely. However, it also showed that the British would not be easy to defeat.

The British leave Boston

Washington finally reached Boston a few weeks after the Battle of Bunker Hill. There, he found about 16,000 troops camped in huts and tents at the edge of the city. Their

weapons ranged from rifles to swords made by local blacksmiths.

General Washington quickly began to turn raw recruits into a trained army. His job was especially difficult because soldiers from different colonies mistrusted one another. "Connecticut wants no Massachusetts men in her corps," he wrote. And "Massachusetts thinks there is no necessity for a Rhode Islander to be introduced into her [ranks]." Slowly, Washington won the loyalty of his troops. They, in turn, learned to take orders and work together.

In January 1776, Washington had a stroke of good fortune. Soldiers arrived outside Boston with cannons they had dragged across the mountains from Fort Ticonderoga.

Washington had the cannons placed on Dorchester Heights, overlooking the harbor.

Once General Howe saw the American cannons in place, he knew that he could not hold Boston. In March 1776, he and his troops sailed from Boston to Halifax, Canada. About 1,000 American Loyalists went with the British. The Loyalists of Boston became **refugees,** people who flee their homes to seek refuge from war, persecution, or other hardships.

Although the British left New England, they had not given up. King George III ordered a **blockade** of all colonial ports. A blockade is the shutting off of a port to keep people or supplies from moving in or out. The king also used Hessian **mercenaries,** or troops for hire, from Germany to help fight the colonists.

March on Canada

While Washington's army was winning control of Boston, other Americans were launching an attack on Canada. The Americans hoped to get help from French Canadians, who were unhappy under British rule.

In the fall of 1775, two American armies moved north into Canada. (See the map on page 162.) Richard Montgomery led one army from Fort Ticonderoga to Montreal. He seized that city in November 1775. He then moved toward Quebec. **Benedict Arnold** led the second army north through Maine. He was supposed to join forces with Montgomery in Quebec.

Arnold and his troops had a terrible journey through the Maine woods in winter. Rainstorms followed by freezing nights coated their clothes with ice. Supplies ran so low that soldiers survived only by eating boiled bark and shoe leather. Finally, Arnold reached Quebec. However, he was disappointed to learn that most French Canadians did not support the Americans.

In a blinding snowstorm on December 31, 1775, the Americans attacked Quebec. Montgomery was killed, and Arnold was wounded. The Americans failed in their attempt to take the city. They stayed outside Quebec until May 1776, when the British landed new forces in Canada. At last, weakened by disease and hunger, the Americans withdrew, leaving Canada to the British.

★ Section 1 Review ★

Recall

1. **Locate** (a) Fort Ticonderoga, (b) Boston, (c) Montreal, (d) Quebec.
2. **Identify** (a) Ethan Allen, (b) Green Mountain Boys, (c) Continental Army, (d) Olive Branch Petition, (e) Patriots, (f) Loyalists, (g) Battle of Bunker Hill, (h) Benedict Arnold.
3. **Define** (a) refugee, (b) blockade, (c) mercenary.

Comprehension

4. (a) How did the Second Continental Congress pursue a peaceful settlement with Britain? (b) What steps did the Congress take to prepare for war with Britain?

5. (a) What advantages did the British have over the Patriots? (b) What advantages did the Patriots have?
6. How did Washington force the British to leave Boston?

Critical Thinking and Writing

7. **Understanding Causes and Effects** Explain two reasons for the American failure to capture Quebec.
8. **Making Inferences** Why did the Boston Loyalists feel that they had to go with the British to Canada?

★ ★

Activity **Making a Decision** You are an American in 1775. War between the rebels and the British seems certain! Decide whether you will become a Loyalist or a Patriot. Explain the facts and ideas that led to your decision.

2 Declaring Independence

Explore These Questions

- How did *Common Sense* influence the colonists?
- How did American Patriots respond to the Declaration of Independence?
- What are the main ideas of the Declaration of Independence?

Define

- traitor
- preamble
- natural rights

Identify

- *Common Sense*
- Thomas Paine
- Richard Henry Lee
- Thomas Jefferson
- Declaration of Independence

SETTING the Scene Many Americans had come to believe that Parliament did not have the right to make laws for the 13 colonies. After all, they argued, the colonists had their own elected legislatures. At the same time, however, most Americans still felt strong bonds of loyalty to Britain. Especially, they felt they owed allegiance to the king.

Then, in January 1776, a pamphlet titled **Common Sense** appeared on the streets of Philadelphia. "I offer nothing more than simple facts, plain arguments, and common sense," wrote its author, **Thomas Paine.** Though Paine had only recently arrived from England, he strongly supported the colonists in their quarrel with the king. In blunt words, he boldly urged the colonies to declare their independence.

Common Sense

In *Common Sense,* Thomas Paine tried to convince the colonists that they did not owe loyalty to George III or any other monarch. The very idea of setting up kings and queens was wrong, he said.

> 66 In England a King hath little more to do than to make war and give away [jobs]; which in plain terms, is to impoverish the nation. ... Of more worth is one honest man to society and in the sight of God, than all the crowned ruffians that ever lived. 99

Americans did not owe anything to England, either, Paine went on. If the English had helped the colonists, they had done so for their own profit. It could only hurt the Americans to remain under British rule:

> 66 Everything that is right or reasonable pleads for separation. ... 'Tis time to part. 99

Common Sense won many colonists to the idea of independence. In six months, more than 500,000 copies of the pamphlet were printed and sold. "*Common Sense* is working a powerful change in the minds of men," George Washington observed.

Moving Toward Independence

Paine's *Common Sense* affected many members of the Continental Congress. In June 1776, **Richard Henry Lee** of Virginia offered a resolution stating that "these United Colonies are, and of right ought to be, free and independent States."

Delegates faced a difficult decision. There could be no turning back once

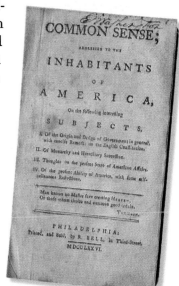

Common Sense by ➤ *Thomas Paine*

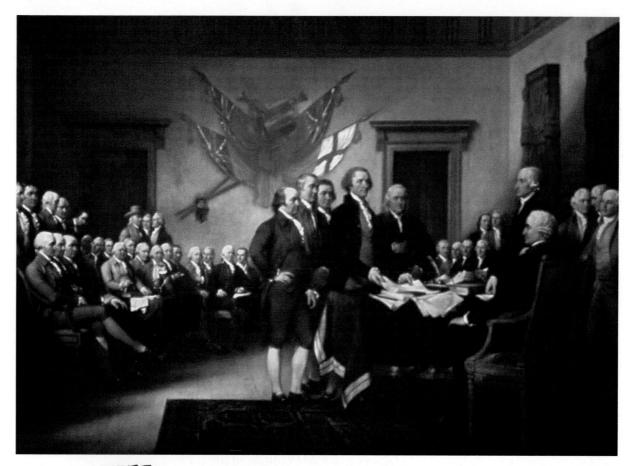

Viewing HISTORY **Signing the Declaration**

Thomas Jefferson labored many hours perfecting the Declaration of Independence. Here, Jefferson and other committee members present the Declaration to the Continental Congress. This painting, like the one on page 159, is by John Trumbull. ★ **What was the purpose of the Declaration of Independence?**

they declared independence. If they fell into British hands, they would be hanged as traitors. A **traitor** is a person who betrays his or her country.

The Congress took a fateful step. They chose a committee to draw up a declaration of independence. The committee included John Adams, Benjamin Franklin, Thomas Jefferson, Robert Livingston, and Roger Sherman. Their job was to tell the world why the colonies were breaking away from Britain.

The committee asked Jefferson to write the document. **Thomas Jefferson** was one of the youngest delegates. A quiet man, he spoke little at formal meetings. Among friends, however, he liked to sprawl in a chair with his long legs stretched out and talk for hours. His ability to write clearly and gracefully had earned him great respect.

The Declaration of Independence

In late June, Jefferson completed the declaration, and it was read to the Congress. On July 2, the Continental Congress voted that the 13 colonies were "free and independent States." Two days later, on July 4, 1776, the delegates accepted Jefferson's **Declaration of Independence,** making only a few minor changes.

John Hancock, president of the Continental Congress, signed the Declaration first. He penned his signature boldly, in large, clear letters. "There," he said, "I guess King George will be able to read that."

Copies of the Declaration were distributed throughout the colonies. Across the colonies, those who were Patriots greeted the

Why Study History?

Because We Celebrate Our Independence

★ ★

Historical Background

John Adams reacted proudly to the signing of the Declaration of Independence. He declared that the event "ought to be solemnized with pomp and parade, with shows, games, sports, guns, bells, bonfires, and illuminations, from one end of this continent to the other, from this time forward, forevermore."

In 1777, on the first anniversary of the Declaration of Independence, Philadelphia overflowed with excitement. A navy ship on the Delaware River sounded a 13-gun salute. Bells rang all day, bonfires burned in the streets, and fireworks lit up the evening sky. Following a dinner attended by members of Congress, American soldiers paraded through the city's streets.

Independence Day fireworks over Washington, D.C.

Connections to Today

Throughout the nation, we celebrate Independence Day in much the same way that people did in 1777. John Adams would feel right at home with our parties, picnics, athletic games, patriotic speeches, and American flags. Today's televised concerts, parades of large, decorated floats, and massive displays of community-sponsored fireworks would have been beyond his imagination, but certainly in keeping with his spirit.

Connections to You

How do you commemorate the Fourth of July? You may celebrate the day at the beach, at the park, or in your own backyard. Yet, no matter how you spend the Fourth of July, the reason for celebration remains the same—to honor the foresight and courage of our founders.

The Declaration of Independence that they issued spoke of equality. It also discussed the rights and freedoms that all people have and the responsibility of government to protect those rights and freedoms. During the Revolutionary War, Americans fought and died for those ideas. Today, you enjoy a democratic way of life based on those ideas.

1. **Comprehension** Describe three things that Philadelphians did in 1777 to commemorate Independence Day.

2. **Critical Thinking** How do the ideas in the Declaration of Independence still live on today?

 Activity It is 1776 and you are a member of the Continental Congress. Review the ideas contained in the Declaration of Independence. Write a short speech explaining to the Congress (your classmates) why they should sign it.

news of independence with joyous celebrations. In New York, Patriots tore down a statue of King George III. In Boston, the sound of cannons could be heard for hours.

The Declaration of Independence consists of a **preamble,** or introduction, followed by three main parts. (The complete Declaration of Independence is printed in the Reference Section.)

Natural rights

The first part of the Declaration stresses the idea of **natural rights,** or rights that belong to all people from birth. In bold, ringing words, Jefferson wrote:

> 66 We hold these truths to be self-evident, that all men are created equal, that they are endowed by their Creator with certain unalienable rights, that among these are life, liberty, and the pursuit of happiness. 99

According to the Declaration of Independence, people form governments in order to protect their natural rights and liberties. Governments can exist only if they have the "consent of the governed." If a government fails to protect the rights of its citizens, then it is the people's "right [and] duty, to throw off such government, and provide new guards for their future security."

British wrongs

The second part of the Declaration lists the wrongs committed by Britain. Jefferson condemned King George III for disbanding colonial legislatures and for sending troops to the colonies in times of peace. He complained about limits on trade and about taxes that had been imposed without the consent of the people. Jefferson listed many other wrongs to show why the colonists had the right to rebel. He also pointed out that the colonies had petitioned the King to correct these injustices. Yet they remained.

Independence

The last part of the Declaration announces that the colonies had become the United States of America. All political ties with Britain were cut. As a free and independent nation, the United States had the power to make alliances and trade with other countries.

★ Section 2 Review ★

Recall

1. **Identify** **(a)** *Common Sense,* **(b)** Thomas Paine, **(c)** Richard Henry Lee, **(d)** Thomas Jefferson, **(e)** Declaration of Independence.

2. **Define** **(a)** traitor, **(b)** preamble, **(c)** natural rights.

Comprehension

3. What arguments did Thomas Paine offer in favor of independence?

4. How did American Patriots react to the Declaration of Independence?

5. Describe the four parts of the Declaration of Independence.

Critical Thinking and Writing

6. **Analyzing Primary Sources** Review the excerpts from Thomas Paine's *Common Sense* that appear on page 165. Explain the meaning of those excerpts in your own words.

7. **Synthesizing Information** After the Declaration of Independence was issued, enslaved Africans sent petitions to state legislatures asking for freedom. How might they have used the Declaration of Independence to support their demands?

Activity **Writing a Document** You are Thomas Jefferson. Reports are coming in that many people cannot understand the Declaration of Independence because the language is too complex. Try to help them by rewriting the preamble, or first paragraph, in simpler language.

Fighting in the Middle States

Explore These Questions
- What defeats and hardships did the Americans suffer in the Middle States?
- Why was the Battle of Saratoga a turning point in the war?
- What help did the United States receive from other nations?

Define
- ally
- cavalry

Identify
- Battle of Long Island
- Nathan Hale
- Battle of Trenton
- John Burgoyne
- Battle of Saratoga
- Marquis de Lafayette
- Friedrich von Steuben
- Thaddeus Kosciusko

As You Read

Continental Army medicine chest

 SETTING the Scene It was early one morning in late June of 1776. Daniel McCurtin glanced out his window at New York harbor. He was amazed to see "something resembling a wood of pine trees trimmed." He watched the forest move across the water. Then, he understood. The trees were the masts of ships!

> 66 I could not believe my eyes...the whole bay was full of shipping as ever it could be. I declare that I thought all London was afloat. 99

Daniel McCurtin had witnessed the arrival of a large British fleet in New York. Aboard the ships were General Howe and his redcoats. Thus began a new stage in the war. Previously, most of the fighting of the American Revolution took place in New England. In mid-1776, the heavy fighting shifted to the Middle States. There, the Continental Army suffered through the worst days of the war.

The British Take New York

Washington, expecting Howe's attack, had led his forces south from Boston to New York City. His army, however, was no match for the British. Howe had about 34,000 troops and 10,000 sailors. He also had ships to ferry them ashore. Washington had fewer than 20,000 poorly trained troops. Worse, he had no navy.

In August, Howe's army landed on Long Island. In the **Battle of Long Island,** more than 1,400 Americans were killed, wounded, or captured. The rest retreated to Manhattan. The British followed. To avoid capture, Washington hurried north.

Throughout the autumn, Washington fought a series of battles with Howe's army. In November, he crossed the Hudson River into New Jersey. Pursued by the British, the Americans retreated across the Delaware River into Pennsylvania.

During the campaign for New York, Washington needed information about Howe's forces. **Nathan Hale,** a young Connecticut officer, slipped behind British lines and returned with the details. Soon after, the British captured Hale. They tried him and condemned him to death. As Hale walked to the gallows, he is said to have declared: "I only regret that I have but one life to lose for my country."

Despair and New Hope

Months of campaigning took a toll on the Continental Army. In December 1776, Washington described his troops as sick, dirty, and "so thinly clad as to be unfit for service." Every day, soldiers deserted. Washington

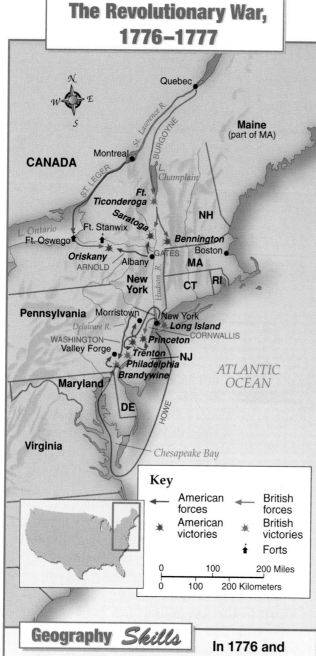

The Revolutionary War, 1776–1777

Key

← American forces
← British forces
✦ American victories
✦ British victories
⚓ Forts

0   100   200 Miles
0   100   200 Kilometers

Geography Skills

In 1776 and 1777, the Americans and British battled over a large area. The American victory at Saratoga marked a major turning point of the war.

1. **Location** On the map, locate: **(a)** Long Island, **(b)** New York City, **(c)** Trenton, **(d)** Hudson River, **(e)** Saratoga, **(f)** Valley Forge.

2. **Movement** How did the British use sea power to help them capture Philadelphia?

3. **Critical Thinking** How did Burgoyne and St. Leger use geography to help move their armies quickly toward Albany?

wrote to his brother: "I am wearied to death. I think the game is pretty near up."

The Crisis

Thomas Paine had retreated with the army through New Jersey. Once again, he took up his pen. This time, he wrote *The Crisis,* urging Americans to support the army.

> 66 These are the times that try men's souls. The summer soldier and the sunshine patriot will, in this crisis, shrink from the service of his country; but he that stands it *now* deserves the love and thanks of man and woman. 99

Grateful for Paine's inspiring words, Washington had *The Crisis* read aloud to his troops.

American victories in New Jersey

The Americans needed more than words to help their cause, however. General Washington decided on a bold move—a surprise attack on Trenton.

On Christmas night, Washington secretly led his troops across the icy Delaware River. Soldiers shivered as spray from the river froze on their faces. Once ashore, they marched through swirling snow. "Soldiers, keep by your officers," Washington urged.

Early on December 26, the Americans surprised the Hessian troops guarding Trenton and took most of them prisoner. An American summed up the **Battle of Trenton:** "Hessian population of Trenton at 8 A.M.—1,408 men and 39 officers; Hessian population at 9 A.M.—0."

British General Charles Cornwallis set out at once to retake Trenton and capture Washington. Late on January 2, 1777, he saw the lights of Washington's campfires. "At last we have run down the old fox," he said, "and we will bag him in the morning."

Washington fooled Cornwallis. He left the fires burning and slipped behind British lines to attack Princeton. There, the Continental Army won another victory. From Princeton, Washington moved to Morristown, where the army spent the winter. The victories at Trenton and Princeton gave the Americans new hope.

Viewing History

Victory at Princeton

This painting depicts the battle at Princeton, New Jersey, in January 1777. Victories at Trenton and Princeton boosted American morale. Still, difficult times lay ahead for Washington's troops. ★ **How was Washington able to surprise the British at Princeton?**

Turning Point of the War

In London, British officials were dismayed by the army's failure to crush the rebels. Early in 1777, General **John Burgoyne** (buhr GOIN) presented George III with a new plan for victory. If British troops cut off New England from the other colonies, he argued, the war would soon be over.

Burgoyne wanted three British armies to march on Albany, New York, from different directions. They would crush American forces there. Once they controlled the Hudson River, the British could stop the flow of soldiers and supplies from New England to Washington's army.

Britain's plan fails

Burgoyne's plan called for General Howe to march on Albany from New York City. George III, however, wanted Howe to capture Philadelphia first.

In July 1777, Howe sailed from New York to the Chesapeake Bay. (See the map on page 170.) Despite Washington's efforts to stop him, Howe captured Philadelphia. He then went on to defeat the Americans at the battles of Brandywine and Germantown. Howe then retired to comfortable quarters in Philadelphia for the winter. Washington retreated to Valley Forge, where he set up a makeshift camp.

Meanwhile, two other British armies under Burgoyne and Barry St. Leger (lay ZHAIR) marched from Canada toward Albany. St. Leger tried to take Fort Stanwix. However, Benedict Arnold drove him back with a strong American army.

Victory at Saratoga

Only Burgoyne was left to march on Albany. His army moved slowly because it had many heavy baggage carts to drag through the woods. To slow Burgoyne further, Patriots cut down trees to block the route and dammed up streams to create swampy bogs.

Despite these obstacles, Burgoyne retook Fort Ticonderoga. He then sent troops into Vermont to find food and horses. There, Patriots attacked the redcoats. At the Battle of

Bennington, they wounded or captured nearly 1,000 British.

Burgoyne's troubles grew. The Green Mountain Boys hurried into New York to help other American forces there. At the village of Saratoga, the Americans surrounded the British. When Burgoyne tried to break free, the Americans beat him back. Realizing he was trapped, Burgoyne surrendered his entire army to the Americans on October 17, 1777.

The American victory at the **Battle of Saratoga** was a major turning point in the war. It ended the British threat to New England. It boosted American spirits at a time when Washington's army was suffering defeats. Most important, it convinced France to become an **ally** of the United States. Nations that are allies work together to achieve some common goal.

Help from Europe

The Continental Congress had long hoped for French aid. In 1776, the Congress had sent Benjamin Franklin to Paris. His job was to persuade Louis XVI, the French king, to help the Americans with weapons and other badly needed supplies. The Congress also wanted France to declare war on Britain. France had a strong navy that could stand up to the British.

The French were eager to hurt Britain, but they were also cautious. France and Britain were rivals for power and France was still angry about their defeat by the British in the French and Indian War. However, Louis XVI did not want to help the Americans openly until he was sure they could win.

The American victory at Saratoga convinced France and other nations that the United States could stand up to Britain. In February 1778, France became the first nation to sign a treaty with the United States. In it, Louis XVI recognized the new nation and agreed to provide military aid. Later, the Netherlands and Spain also joined in the war against Britain. France, the Netherlands, and Spain all provided loans to the Americans.

Even before European nations provided aid to the United States, individual volunteers had been coming from Europe to join the American cause. Some became leading officers in the American army.

The **Marquis de Lafayette** (lah fee YEHT), a young French noble, brought trained

Saratoga: A Turning Point

Before
- France gives American rebels money and supplies but stays neutral.
- French king does not want to make commitment unless he is sure Americans will win.

American Victory at Saratoga

After
- Victory proves that Americans can win.
- France becomes official ally of the United States.
- France gives military and naval support.
- France declares war on Britain.

Graphic Organizer Skills   The American victory at the Battle of Saratoga was a major turning point in the War for Independence.

1. **Comprehension**   (a) How did France help the Americans before Saratoga? (b) How did France help them after Saratoga?
2. **Critical Thinking**   What do you think France hoped to gain by helping the Americans win independence?

soldiers to help the Patriot cause. Lafayette, who fought at Brandywine, became one of Washington's most trusted friends.

From the German state of Prussia came **Friedrich von Steuben** (STOO buhn). He helped train Washington's Continental troops to march and drill. Von Steuben had served in the Prussian army, considered the best in Europe.

Two Polish officers also joined the Americans. **Thaddeus Kosciusko** (kahs ee UHS koh), an engineer, helped build forts and other defenses. Casimir Pulaski trained **cavalry,** or troops on horseback.

Harsh Winter at Valley Forge

The victory at Saratoga and the promise of help from Europe did much to boost American morale. Nevertheless, Washington's ragged army still faced hard times. During the long, cold winter of 1777–1778, the Continental Army suffered severe hardships at Valley Forge in Pennsylvania.

The conditions at Valley Forge were terrible. American soldiers shivered in damp, drafty huts. Many slept on the frozen ground. They had little or no warm clothing. Some soldiers stood on guard wrapped only in blankets. Many had no shoes, so they wrapped bits of cloth around their feet. As the bitter winter wore on, soldiers suffered from frostbite and disease. An army surgeon from Connecticut wrote about the suffering:

66 There comes a Soldier, his bare feet are seen thro his worn-out stockings, his Breeches not sufficient to cover his nakedness...his whole appearance pictures a person forsaken & discouraged. 99

As news of the suffering at Valley Forge spread, Patriots from around the nation sent help. Women collected food, medicine, warm clothes, and ammunition for the army. Some women, like Martha Washington, wife of the commander, went to Valley Forge to help the sick and wounded.

The arrival of desperately needed supplies was soon followed by warmer weather. By the spring of 1778, the army at Valley Forge was more hopeful. Washington could not know it at the time, but the Patriots' bleakest hour had passed.

★ Section 3 Review ★

Recall

1. **Locate** **(a)** New York City, **(b)** Trenton, **(c)** Princeton, **(d)** Hudson River, **(e)** Albany, **(f)** Saratoga, **(g)** Valley Forge.
2. **Identify** **(a)** Battle of Long Island, **(b)** Nathan Hale, **(c)** Battle of Trenton, **(d)** John Burgoyne, **(e)** Battle of Saratoga, **(f)** Marquis de Lafayette, **(g)** Friedrich von Steuben, **(h)** Thaddeus Kosciusko.
3. **Define** **(a)** ally, **(b)** cavalry.

Comprehension

4. What problems did the Americans face during the campaign in the Middle States?

5. Describe three results of the Battle of Saratoga.
6. Why was help from France and other nations important to the Americans?

Critical Thinking and Writing

7. **Synthesizing Information** Reread the excerpt from *The Crisis* on page 170. **(a)** What did Paine mean by the words, "These are the times that try men's souls"? **(b)** What are "sunshine patriots"? **(c)** Why do you think Washington wanted Paine's words read to the troops?
8. **Drawing Conclusions** Why do you think Burgoyne's plan to cut the colonies in two by seizing Albany ended in failure?

★ ★

Activity **Reporting the News** You are a newspaper reporter during the American Revolution. Write a report on a major event or battle that took place in the Middle States. You may need to do some additional research to write an interesting and informative article.

Other Battlefronts

4

As You Read

Explore These Questions
- What were the major military events in the West?
- How did the South become the major battlefield of the war?
- How did women and African Americans take part in the war?

Define
- neutral

Identify
- George Rogers Clark
- Bernardo de Gálvez
- John Paul Jones
- Betsy Ross
- Molly Pitcher
- Peter Salem

 Flying Crow, a Seneca chief, looked sternly at the British officers who were seated before him. "If you are so strong, Brother, and they but a weak boy, why ask our assistance?"

Like many Native American leaders, Flying Crow did not want to become involved in a war between the "weak boy"—the United States—and Britain. Yet, Native Americans could not avoid the struggle.

Americans of various backgrounds played significant roles in the Revolution. Also, the American Revolution took place on many fronts. Fighting occurred not only in the North but also in the West and South. The war was also fought at sea.

The War in the West

When the Revolution began, most Indians tried to stay **neutral,** or uninvolved in the war. The British and Patriots, however, both sought Native American aid. In the end,

the British were more persuasive. They convinced many Native Americans that a Patriot victory would mean more white settlers crossing the Appalachians and taking Indian lands.

Native Americans help the British

In the South, the British gained the support of the Cherokees, Creeks, Choctaws, and Chickasaws. In the summer of 1776, a Cherokee force attacked dozens of settlements on the frontier. Only after hard fighting were Patriot militia able to drive the Native Americans into the mountains. Sporadic fighting continued throughout the war.

Fighting was equally fierce on the northern frontier. In 1778, Iroquois forces led by the Mohawk leader Joseph Brant joined with Loyalists in raiding frontier settlements in Pennsylvania and New York. The next year, Patriots retaliated by invading Iroquois lands. They destroyed dozens of Iroquois villages. They also ruined thousands of acres of crops.

Victory at Vincennes

Further west, in 1778, **George Rogers Clark** led Virginia frontier fighters against the British in the Ohio Valley. With help from Miami Indians, Clark captured the British forts at Kaskaskia and Cahokia.

Clark then plotted a surprise winter attack on the British fort at Vincennes. He led a small band 150 miles (240 km) through heavy rains, swamps, and icy rivers.

> **Connections With Civics**
>
> Unlike most other Iroquois, the Oneida Indians allied themselves with the Americans. The Congress thanked them in these words: "You stood forth in the cause of your friends and ventured your lives in our battles. While the sun and moon continue to give light to the world, we shall love and respect you."

When Clark's force reached the fort, they spread out through the woods to make their numbers appear greater than they really were. The British commander thought it was useless to fight so many Americans. He surrendered Vincennes in February 1779.

Spanish aid

On the southwestern frontier, Americans received help from New Spain. In the early years of the war, Spain was neutral. However, **Bernardo de Gálvez,** governor of Spanish Louisiana, favored the Patriots. He secretly supplied medicine, cloth, muskets, and gunpowder to the Americans. He also sent cattle from Texas to feed the Continental Army.

When Spain entered the war against Britain in 1779, Gálvez took a more active role. He seized British forts along the Mississippi River and the Gulf of Mexico. He also drove the British out of West Florida.

The War in the South

Scattered fighting had taken place in the South throughout the Revolution. In February 1776, North Carolina Patriots defeated a Loyalist army at the Battle of Moore's Creek Bridge. This battle is sometimes called the Lexington and Concord of the South.

After the British plan to conquer New York and New England failed, the South became the main battleground of the war. Sir Henry Clinton, the new British commander-in-chief, knew that many Loyalists lived in the southern backcountry. He hoped that if British troops marched through the South, Loyalists would join them.

At first, Clinton's plan seemed to work. In December 1778, the British seized Savannah, Georgia. A year and a half later, they took Charleston, South Carolina. Next, they crushed a Continental force at Camden, South Carolina. (See the map on page 179.) "I have almost ceased to hope," wrote Washington when he learned of the losses.

Fighting at Sea

At sea, the Americans could do little against the powerful British navy. British ships blockaded American ports. From time to time, however, a bold American captain captured a British ship.

The most daring American captain was **John Paul Jones.** In his most famous battle, in September 1779, Jones commanded the *Bonhomme Richard.* He was sailing in the North Sea near Britain when he spotted a large fleet of enemy merchant ships. They were guarded by a single warship, the *Serapis.* Jones attacked the *Serapis,* even though it was larger than the *Bonhomme Richard.*

In a furious battle, cannonballs ripped through the *Bonhomme Richard,* setting it on fire. The British commander called on

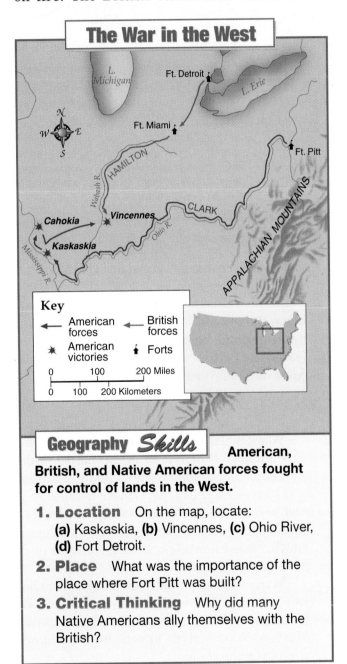

The War in the West

Geography Skills American, British, and Native American forces fought for control of lands in the West.

1. **Location** On the map, locate: (a) Kaskaskia, (b) Vincennes, (c) Ohio River, (d) Fort Detroit.
2. **Place** What was the importance of the place where Fort Pitt was built?
3. **Critical Thinking** Why did many Native Americans ally themselves with the British?

Past

Present

Women in Arms

During the American Revolution, few women took part in battle. Those who did became legendary. At left, Mary Ludwig Hays—known as "Molly Pitcher"—loads and fires a cannon. Today, thousands of American women serve on active duty in the United States military. Shown above are two female pilots aboard the aircraft carrier Eisenhower. ★ **Why do you think so many young women have volunteered to serve in the military?**

Jones to surrender. "I have not yet begun to fight!" Jones replied.

Jones sailed close to the *Serapis* so that his sailors could board the enemy ship. In hand-to-hand combat, the Americans defeated the British. Jones earned a hero's welcome on his return home.

Women in the War

Women also helped in the struggle for independence. When men went off to war, women took on added work. Some planted and harvested the crops. Others made shoes and wove cloth for blankets and uniforms. One woman, called "Handy Betsy the Blacksmith," was known for making cannons and guns for the army.

Many women joined their husbands who were serving in the army. The women cared for the wounded, washed clothes, and cooked. Martha Washington joined her husband whenever she could.

Some women achieved lasting fame for their activities in the war. **Betsy Ross** of Philadelphia sewed flags for Washington's army. Legend claims that she made the first American flag of stars and stripes.

A few women even took part in battle. During the Battle of Monmouth in 1778, Mary Ludwig Hays carried water to her husband and other soldiers. The soldiers called her Moll of the Pitcher or **Molly Pitcher.** When her husband was wounded, she took his place, loading and firing a cannon.

African Americans in the War

By 1776, more than a half million African Americans lived in the colonies. At first, the Continental Congress refused to let African Americans, whether free or enslaved, join the army. The British, however, offered freedom to any male slave who served the king. In response, Washington changed his policy and allowed free African Americans to enlist.

Joining the fight

It is estimated that about 5,000 African Americans fought against the British. At least nine black minutemen saw action at Lexington and Concord. One of them, Prince Estabrook, was wounded. Two others, **Peter Salem** and Salem Poor, went on to fight bravely at Bunker Hill.

Some African Americans formed special regiments. Others served in white regiments as drummers, fifers, spies, and guides. Thousands of black sailors also served on American ships. Whites recognized the courage of their African American comrades, as this eyewitness account shows:

> 66 Three times in succession, [African American soldiers] were attacked . . . by well-disciplined and veteran [British] troops, and three times did they successfully repel the assault, and thus preserve our army from capture. 99

Enslaved African Americans faced difficult choices. If they tried to flee to the British army to gain freedom, they risked being hanged by angry Patriots. If they joined the American army or continued to work on Patriot plantations, the British might capture and sell them.

Hoping for freedom

Black Patriots hoped that the Revolution would bring an end to slavery. After all, the Declaration of Independence proclaimed that "all men are created equal." In Massachusetts and elsewhere, enslaved African Americans sent petitions to lawmakers asking for freedom.

Some white leaders also hoped the war would end slavery. James Otis wrote that "the colonists are by the law of nature free born, as indeed all men are, white or black." Quakers in particular spoke out strongly against slavery.

By the 1770s, slavery was declining in the North, where a number of free African Americans lived. During the American Revolution, several states moved to make slavery illegal, including Massachusetts, New Hampshire, and Pennsylvania. Other states also began to debate the slavery issue.

★ Section 4 Review ★

Recall

1. **Locate** (a) Kaskaskia, (b) Cahokia, (c) Vincennes.
2. **Identify** (a) George Rogers Clark, (b) Bernardo de Gálvez, (c) John Paul Jones, (d) Betsy Ross, (e) Molly Pitcher, (f) Peter Salem.
3. **Define** neutral.

Comprehension

4. Describe the role that each of the following played in the war in the West: (a) Native Americans, (b) the Spanish.
5. How did the South replace the North as the major battlefield of the Revolution?

6. (a) How did women participate in the war effort? (b) Why did some African Americans join the British army?

Critical Thinking and Writing

7. **Understanding Causes and Effects** Read the following two statements. Then decide which is the cause and which is the effect. Explain your answer. (a) Many Native Americans sided with the British. (b) During the Revolution, settlers continued to push west of the Appalachians.
8. **Drawing Conclusions** How do you think the story of John Paul Jones's victory over the *Serapis* affected the attitudes of American Patriots?

Activity **Writing a Tribute** During the American Revolution, you are a member of a special awards committee in the Congress. Choose a person or group mentioned in this section who helped the American cause. Write a tribute praising the individual's or group's accomplishments.

Winning the War

★ 5

As You Read

Explore These Questions
- How did the Americans begin to win battles in the South?
- How did the Americans and French defeat the British at Yorktown?
- What were the terms of the Treaty of Paris?

Define
- guerrilla
- siege
- ratify

Identify
- Battle of King's Mountain
- Nathanael Greene
- Daniel Morgan
- Francis Marion
- Benedict Arnold
- Comte de Rochambeau
- Admiral de Grasse
- Battle of Yorktown
- Treaty of Paris

Powder horn

SETTING the Scene When he was only 16 years of age, Thomas Young set out with about 900 other Patriots to capture King's Mountain in South Carolina. Although most of the Patriots were barefoot, they moved quickly up the wooded hillside, shouldering their old muskets. They were determined to take the mountain from the Loyalists dug in at the top.

Whooping and shouting, Young and his comrades dashed from tree to tree, dodging bullets as they fired their own weapons. They climbed higher and higher toward the enemy lines. Suddenly, Thomas heard the frantic cry, "Colonel Williams is shot!"

❝ I ran to his assistance for I loved him as a father.... He revived, and his first words were, 'For God's sake boys, don't give up the hill!' ... [I] returned to the field to avenge his fate. ❞

Patriots Rally in the South

The Patriots succeeded in capturing King's Mountain on October 7, 1780. The victory boosted morale and breathed new life into the Patriot cause in the South. Jefferson called the **Battle of King's Mountain** "the turn of the tide."

The American Patriots in the South certainly needed the good news. General Clinton's redcoats had captured both Savannah and Charleston, forcing the American armies into retreat. Throughout the southern countryside, attacks by British troops and Loyalist militia had become especially destructive and brutal. One Loyalist officer boasted how the army was "destroying furniture, breaking windows, taking...cattle, horses, mules."

The Patriot victory at King's Mountain was only the first in a string of American victories in the South. In the months ahead, two able American generals helped to turn the tide against Cornwallis and his British army. The American generals were **Nathanael Greene** of Rhode Island and **Daniel Morgan** of Virginia.

 Connections With Geography

Geography helped the Patriots win at King's Mountain. To reach the Loyalists atop the ridge, the Patriots climbed through a forest that protected them from enemy fire. The Loyalists had a difficult downhill line of fire. One Patriot recalled how the Loyalists "overshot us altogether, scarce touching a man except those on horseback."

General Greene's ability as a military leader was perhaps second only to Washington's. In 1780, Greene took command of the Continental Army in the South. Making good use of his soldiers' knowledge of the local geography, Greene chose to fight only on ground that put the British at a disadvantage. When he retreated, he followed the easiest routes. He often arranged for boats to be waiting at river crossings. General Cornwallis wore out his soldiers trying to catch Greene's army.

In January 1781, General Morgan won an important battle at Cowpens, South Carolina. Morgan used a clever tactic to defeat the British. Morgan divided his soldiers into a front line and a rear line. He ordered the front line to retreat after firing just two volleys. The British, thinking the Americans were retreating, charged forward—straight into the devastating fire of Morgan's second rank. In this way, the Americans won the Battle of Cowpens.

Greene and Morgan had combined their armies when they fought Cornwallis at Guilford Court House, near present-day Greensboro, North Carolina. The battle was one of the bloodiest of the war. Though the Americans retreated, the British sustained great losses. One Englishman observed that "another such victory would destroy the British army." Cornwallis withdrew to the coastal town of Wilmington to rest and regroup his army.

Francis Marion of South Carolina added to British frustrations. He led a small band of militia, who often slept by day and traveled by night. Marion was known as the Swamp Fox. His soldiers used **guerrilla,** or hit-and-run, tactics to harass the British. They would appear suddenly out of the swamps, quickly attack, and then retreat back into the swamps.

Victory at Yorktown

Finally, Cornwallis gave up on his plan to take the Carolinas. In the spring of 1781, he moved his troops north into Virginia. He planned to conquer Virginia and cut off the Americans' supply routes to the South.

The War Ends in the South

Geography Skills The War for Independence came to a close in the South. After a string of defeats, the Americans gradually gained the upper hand. The last major battle was the American victory at Yorktown.

1. **Location** On the map, locate: **(a)** Savannah, **(b)** King's Mountain, **(c)** Guilford Courthouse, **(d)** Chesapeake Bay, **(e)** Yorktown.

2. **Region** Did the British have greater control over coastal or inland regions of the South?

3. **Critical Thinking** Why was it a mistake for Cornwallis to retreat to the Yorktown peninsula?

An American traitor

The British had achieved some success in Virginia, even before the arrival of Cornwallis. **Benedict Arnold,** formerly one of the Americans' best generals, was now leading British troops. Arnold captured and burned the capital city of Richmond. His forces raided and burned other towns as well.

Arnold had turned traitor to the American cause in September 1780, while commanding West Point, a key fort in New York. Arnold was resentful because he felt he had not received enough credit for his victories. He also needed money. He secretly agreed to turn over West Point to the British. The plot was uncovered by a Patriot patrol, but Arnold escaped to join the British.

Biography · James Armistead

Though enslaved, James Armistead faithfully served the Patriot cause as a spy. Under the direction of Lafayette, Armistead worked as a volunteer in the camps of Benedict Arnold and Lord Cornwallis. The information he gained contributed to the American victory at Yorktown. Later, after winning his freedom, Armistead changed his name to Lafayette. ★ **Why do you think Armistead decided to change his name to Lafayette?**

Arnold's act of treachery and his raids on towns in Connecticut and Virginia enraged the Patriots. Thomas Jefferson, governor of Virginia, offered a sizable reward in gold for his capture. Washington wrote orders that Arnold was to be hanged. Despite these efforts, Arnold was never captured.

Cornwallis trapped

Cornwallis hoped to meet with the same kind of success in Virginia that Arnold had. At first, things did go well. Cornwallis sent Loyalist troops to attack Charlottesville, where the Virginia legislature was meeting. Governor Thomas Jefferson and other officials had to flee.

American troops under Lafayette fought back by making raids against the British. Lafayette did not have enough troops to fight a major battle. Still, his strategy kept Cornwallis at bay.

Then, Cornwallis made a mistake. He refused an order from Sir Henry Clinton to send part of his army to New York. Instead, he retreated to Yorktown peninsula, a strip of land jutting into Chesapeake Bay. He felt confident that British ships could supply his army from the sea.

Washington saw an opportunity to trap Cornwallis on the Yorktown peninsula. He marched his Continental troops south from New York. With the Americans were French soldiers under the **Comte de Rochambeau** (roh shahm BOH). The combined army rushed to join Lafayette in Virginia.

Meanwhile, a French fleet under **Admiral de Grasse** was also heading towards Virginia. Once in Chesapeake Bay, De Grasse's fleet closed the trap. Cornwallis was cut off. He could not get supplies. He could not escape by land or by sea.

The British surrender

By the end of September, more than 16,000 American and French troops lay siege to Cornwallis's army of fewer than 8,000. A siege is the act of surrounding an enemy position in an attempt to capture it. Day after day, American and French artillery pounded the British.

For several weeks, Cornwallis held out. Finally, with casualties mounting and his

Skills
FOR LIFE

Understanding Causes and Effects

How Will I Use This Skill?

Some causes and effects are easy to see. A frost in Florida causes the price of orange juice to rise. An accident at a busy intersection leads the town to put up a new stop sign. Recognizing the relationship between causes and effects can help you understand what has happened and predict future events.

LEARN the Skill

❶ Identify the primary event or condition that you will examine.

❷ Determine which events had a role in causing the primary event.

❸ Determine which events occurred as a result of the primary event.

❹ Explain the relationship between causes and effects.

PRACTICE the Skill

At right are a list of events and a partially filled-in cause-and-effect chart. After reading this section, answer the following questions:

❶ What primary event is the focus of the chart?

❷ Which events on the list would you include in the chart as causes? Why?

❸ Which events on the list would you include in the chart as effects? Why?

❹ (a) Why was taxation one cause of the American Revolution? (b) Do you think the United States of America could have been formed without the American Revolution?

Cause and Effect

Causes

- Parliament taxes the colonies
- _____
- _____

The American Revolution

Effects

- United States of America is formed
- _____
- _____

George Washington emerges as national leader

Proclamation of 1763 stops colonists from moving west

Intolerable Acts set up harsh rule in Massachusetts

United States borders extend to Florida and Mississippi River

APPLY the Skill

Select an event that affected you. Create a chart that identifies at least two causes and two effects of that event.

North America in 1783

Key

- ☐ United States
- ☐ British colonies
- ☐ French colony
- ☐ Spanish colonies
- ☐ Disputed territory

0   900   1800 Miles

0   900   1800 Kilometers

Geography _Skills_   By the Treaty of Paris of 1783, Britain recognized the United States as an independent nation.

1. **Location**   On the map, locate: **(a)** United States, **(b)** Canada, **(c)** New Spain.
2. **Interaction**   What territory was claimed by both the United States and British Canada?
3. **Critical Thinking**   Compare this map with the map on page 140. According to the maps, what was the major difference between North America in 1763 and North America in 1783?

supplies running low, Cornwallis decided the situation was hopeless. The British had lost the **Battle of Yorktown.**

On October 19, 1781, the British surrendered their weapons to the Americans. The French and the Americans lined up in two facing columns. As the defeated redcoats marched between the victorious troops, a British army band played the tune "The World Turned Upside Down."

The Peace Treaty

The British thought that they could settle their disputes with the American colonies through a show of massive military strength. They were mistaken. In fact, British efforts to impose their will by force served only to alienate the colonists even more. Americans who suffered at the hands of British troops usually became strong supporters of the Patriots' fight for independence. In London, however, the defeat shocked the British. "It is all over," cried the British prime minister, Lord North. Left with no other choice, he agreed to peace talks.

The talks began in Paris in 1782. Congress sent Benjamin Franklin and John Adams, along with John Jay of New York and Henry Laurens of South Carolina, to work out a treaty. Because Britain was eager to end the war, the Americans got most of what they wanted.

Under the **Treaty of Paris,** the British recognized the United States as an independent nation. The borders of the new nation extended from the Atlantic Ocean to the Mississippi River. The southern border stopped at Florida, which was returned to Spain.

On their part, the Americans agreed to ask state legislatures to pay Loyalists for property they lost in the war. In the end, however, most states ignored Loyalist claims.

On April 15, 1783, Congress **ratified,** or approved, the Treaty of Paris. It was almost eight years to the day since the battles of Lexington and Concord.

Washington's Farewell

In December 1783, General Washington bid farewell to his officers at Fraunces Tavern in New York City. Colonel Benjamin Tallmadge recalled the event:

❝ Such a scene of sorrow and weeping I had never before witnessed
.... [W]e were then about to part from the man who had conducted us

through a long and bloody war, and under whose conduct the glory and independence of our country had been achieved. **99**

All along Washington's route home to Virginia, crowds cheered the hero of American independence. The new nation faced difficult days ahead. Americans would call on Washington to lead them once again.

Reasons for the American Victory

Geography had much to do with the American victory in the Revolutionary War. It was difficult for the British to send soldiers and supplies to a war several thousand miles from home. The Patriots they sought to conquer were spread over a very wide area. When the British captured coastal cities, American forces moved inland. The Americans knew the local geography. They knew the best routes and the best places to fight.

Flag of a new nation

Assistance from other nations also contributed to the American victory. Spanish forces attacked the British along the Gulf of Mexico and in the Mississippi Valley. French money helped pay for supplies. Most important was French military aid. Without French soldiers and warships, the Americans might not have won the Battle of Yorktown.

Victory over the British was also due to the patriotic spirit, determination, and fighting skill of the Patriots. Despite many setbacks in the early years of the war, the Americans battled on. As time passed, their devotion to liberty and their fighting ability both grew. Critically important, too, was the leadership of General Washington. By war's end, Washington's ability as a general was respected by Americans and British alike.

★ Section 5 Review ★

Recall

1. **Locate** (a) King's Mountain, (b) Savannah, (c) Charleston, (d) Cowpens, (e) Guilford Courthouse, (f) Yorktown.
2. **Identify** (a) Battle of King's Mountain, (b) Nathanael Greene, (c) Daniel Morgan, (d) Francis Marion, (e) Benedict Arnold, (f) Comte de Rochambeau, (g) Admiral de Grasse, (h) Battle of Yorktown, (i) Treaty of Paris.
3. **Define** (a) guerrilla, (b) siege, (c) ratify.

Comprehension

4. For each of the American military leaders that follow, describe a tactic that the leader used to defeat the British: (a) Greene, (b) Morgan, (c) Marion.

5. How did the Americans and French achieve victory over the British at Yorktown?
6. Describe the major points of the Treaty of Paris of 1783.

Critical Thinking and Writing

7. **Analyzing Ideas** Why do you think the British played "The World Turned Upside Down" when they surrendered at Yorktown?
8. **Understanding Causes and Effects** Describe three reasons why the Americans were able to defeat the British and win the American Revolution.

Activity **Writing a Song** You are a member of a fife and drum band in the Continental Army. General Washington has asked you to write the words for a lively tune that the soldiers can march to. The General wants the song to praise the daring exploits of American soldiers in the South.

★ Sum It Up ★

Section 1   Early Battles
▶ King George III rejected the Second Continental Congress's attempt to solve their conflict peacefully.
▶ The Americans captured Ticonderoga and Boston from the British, but lost a major battle in Canada.

Section 2   Declaring Independence
▶ In his pamphlet *Common Sense,* Thomas Paine argued that colonists did not owe loyalty to the king.
▶ The Continental Congress declared in 1776 that the American colonies had become the independent United States of America.

Section 3   Fighting in the Middle States
▶ The British gained contol of New York City and forced Washington's army into retreat.
▶ The American victory at Saratoga was the major turning point of the war.

Section 4   Other Battlefronts
▶ Fighting took place on many battlefronts, including the West and the high seas.
▶ Women aided the war effort by making needed goods, by caring for the wounded, and, in some cases, by fighting.

Section 5   Winning the War
▶ With help from the French, the Americans defeated the British army at Yorktown.
▶ By the Treaty of Paris, Britain recognized the United States as an independent nation.

 For additional review of the major ideas of Chapter 6, see *Guide to the Essentials of American History* or *Interactive Student Tutorial CD-ROM,* which contains interactive review activities, graphic organizers, and practice tests.

🖸 Reviewing the Chapter

Define These Terms
Match each term with the correct definition.

Column 1	Column 2
1. traitor	**a.** to approve
2. mercenary	**b.** a friend or supporter
3. ally	**c.** not taking sides in a war
4. neutral	**d.** hired soldier who fights for a foreign country
5. ratify	**e.** person who betrays his or her country

Explore the Main Ideas
1. In 1775, how did American Patriots offer peace, but prepare for war?
2. **(a)** How did *Common Sense* affect American colonists? **(b)** Describe three ideas contained in the Declaration of Independence.
3. Why did Thomas Paine write *The Crisis*?
4. In what ways was the Battle of Saratoga a major turning point of the war?
5. What role did African Americans play during the war?
6. **(a)** What advantages did the British have in the War for Independence? **(b)** Why were Americans able to win the war?

🖸 Geography Activity

Match the letters on the map with the following places: **1.** Boston, **2.** Trenton, **3.** Saratoga, **4.** Cowpens, **5.** Savannah, **6.** Yorktown. **Movement** Why was control of the Chesapeake Bay important to Cornwallis at Yorktown?

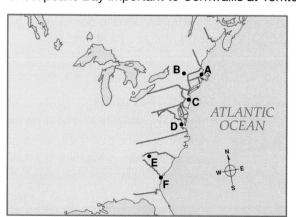

Critical Thinking and Writing

1. **Ranking**   In your opinion, what were the three biggest mistakes that British political and military leaders made between 1775 and 1783? Explain the reasons for your choices.

2. **Exploring Unit Themes**   **Rights and Liberties**   According to the Declaration of Independence, when do people have a right and duty to rebel against their government?

3. **Understanding Chronology**   **(a)** Arrange the following four events in chronological order: (1) British defeat at Yorktown, (2) American victory at Saratoga, (3) French entry into the war against Britain, (4) the signing of the Treaty of Paris. **(b)** Explain how each event helped to cause the next event.

4. **Linking Past and Present**   Today, the United States and Britain are close allies. Why do you think the two nations have such close ties?

Using Primary Sources

In 1776, General George Washington wrote to John Hancock, president of the Continental Congress, about the condition of the army:

66 To place any dependance upon Militia, is, assuredly, resting upon a broken staff. Men just dragged from the tender Scenes of domestick life; unaccustomed to the din of Arms; totally unacquainted with every kind of Military skill, which being followed by a want of confidence in themselves, when opposed to Troops regulary train'd, disciplined, and appointed, superior in knowledge, and superior in Arms, makes them timid, and ready to fly from their own shadows. 99

Source: *The Writings of George Washington from the Original Manuscript Sources: 1745–1799.*

Recognizing Points of View   **(a)** What was Washington's view of British soldiers? **(b)** What was his opinion of American militia? **(c)** What do you think Washington wanted from Congress?

ACTIVITY BANK

▶ Interdisciplinary Activity

Exploring Sciences   Do research to learn about medical treatments provided to sick and wounded soldiers of the American Revolution. Summarize your findings in a report and create illustrations of the medical instruments used at the time.

▶ Career Skills Activity

Graphic Artist   In a graphic organizer, show the role that each of the following played in the American Revolution: **(a)** Native Americans, **(b)** French, **(c)** women, **(d)** African Americans, **(e)** Spanish.

▶ Citizenship Activity

Honoring Good Citizenship   Create a "Nathan Hale Award" for a citizen of your community who has proudly made a sacrifice for the good of the United States. Working with classmates, hold a ceremony in which you explain why you are giving the award to the citizen you have chosen.

Internet Activity

Use the Internet to learn more about the activities of Nathan Hale, James Armistead Lafayette, or another spy of the Revolution. Based on what you learn, write a short fictional story about espionage in the American Revolution.

EYEWITNESS Journal

It is 1776 and you have just heard about the Declaration of Independence. Choose one of the following roles: Loyalist; Patriot; African American; Native American; British soldier; French government official; a woman whose husband, father, or son is a soldier in the war. In your EYEWITNESS JOURNAL, explain what the Declaration means for you and your future.

Chapter 7

Creating a Republic

1776–1791

After the American Revolution ended, the new nation struggled to create a workable government. At first, the states were knit together only by a loose set of laws. When this central government proved too weak, representatives of 12 states gathered in 1787. They created a new framework for government: the Constitution of the United States.

During nearly four exhausting months of debate, the representatives hammered out a set of laws that would make the nation strong, yet protect the rights of the people. After fiery arguments in each state, the Constitution was finally approved. It lives on as the framework of our government today.

Why Study History?

While the new nation was taking shape, American leaders were also creating many symbols and traditions. Today, as in the past, emblems such as the flag and the eagle bind the American people together. To focus on this connection, see the *Why Study History* feature, "National Symbols Unite Us," in this chapter.

American Events

●**1777**
Continental Congress completes the Articles of Confederation

1783 ●
Treaty of Paris formally ends the American Revolution

1776   **1780**   **1784**

World Events

1778 World Event
British Captain Cook becomes first European to reach Hawaii

1784 World Event
Emperor Joseph II forces Czec to use German language

Viewing HISTORY

Signing the Constitution

In 1787, representatives from 12 states gathered in Philadelphia to create a new national government. The result of their work was the Constitution, which still governs the nation today. This painting by Howard Chandler Christy shows delegates to the Constitutional Convention, including George Washington (standing right) and Benjamin Franklin (seated center). Washington served as the president of the Convention. ★ **Why do you think the representatives chose Washington as their president?**

1787 ●—
Northwest Ordinance
sets up method to
admit new states to
the United States

—●**1788**
The Constitution
is ratified

—●**1791**
Bill of Rights
guarantees
individual rights
and freedoms

1784　　　　　　　　　　**1788**　　　　　　　　　　**1792**

 ▲ **1785 World Event**
Russians settle in Aleutian
Islands off coast of Alaska

 ▲ **1789 World Event**
French Revolution begins

A Confederation of States

As You Read

Explore These Questions
- What ideas guided the new state governments?
- What problems did the nation face under the Articles of Confederation?
- How did the Northwest Ordinance benefit the nation?

Define
- constitution
- execute
- confederation
- ordinance
- economic depression

Identify
- Articles of Confederation
- Land Ordinance of 1785
- Northwest Ordinance
- Shays' Rebellion

SETTING the Scene In 1776, the Declaration of Independence created a new nation made up of 13 independent states. The former colonies, though, had little experience working together. In the past, Britain had made the major decisions. Now, the Americans set about the business of establishing 13 state governments. Furthermore, they hoped to create a central government that all the states would follow.

State Governments

In forming a government, most states wrote a constitution. A **constitution** is a document that sets out the laws and principles of a government. States created written constitutions for two reasons. First, a written constitution would spell out the rights of all citizens. Second, it would set limits on the power of government.

The new state governments were similar to the colonial governments. The states divided political power between an executive and a legislature. The legislature was elected by the voters to pass the laws. Most legislatures had an upper house, called a senate, and a lower house. All states except Pennsylvania had a governor who **executed,** or carried out, the laws.

Articles of Confederation

Virginia limited government power by including a bill of rights in its constitution. A bill of rights lists freedoms that the government promises to protect. Virginia's bill of rights protected freedom of religion and freedom of the press. It also guaranteed citizens the right to a trial by jury. Other states followed Virginia's example and included bills of rights in their constitutions.

Under the state constitutions, more people had the right to vote than in colonial times. To vote, a citizen had to be white, male, and over age 21. He had to own a certain amount of property or pay a certain amount of taxes.

For a time, some women in New Jersey could vote. In a few states, free black men could vote. In no state did enslaved African Americans have the right to vote.

A Weak Confederation

In 1776, as citizens were forming state governments, the Continental Congress was drafting a plan for the nation as a whole. Delegates believed that the colonies needed to be united by a central government in order to win independence.

It was difficult to write a constitution that all of the states would approve. They were reluctant to give up power to a national government. In 1776, few Americans saw themselves as citizens of one nation. Instead, they felt loyal to their own states. Also, people were fearful of replacing the "tyranny" of British rule with another strong government. Still, in 1777, after much debate, the Continental Congress completed the **Articles of Confederation**—the first American constitution. It created a confederation, or alliance of independent states.

Government under the Articles

Under the Articles of Confederation, the states sent delegates to a Confederation Congress. Each state had one vote in Congress. Congress could declare war, appoint military officers, and coin money. It was also responsible for foreign affairs. However, these powers were few compared with those of the states.

The Articles limited the powers of Congress and preserved the powers of the states. Congress could pass laws, but at least 9 of the 13 states had to approve a law before it could go into effect.

Congress had little economic power. It could not regulate trade between states nor could it regulate trade between states and foreign countries. It could not pass tax laws. To raise money, Congress had to ask the states for it. No state could be forced to contribute funds.

The new confederation government was weak. There was no president to carry out laws. It was up to the states to enforce the laws passed by Congress. There was no system of courts to settle disputes between states. The Articles created a very loose alliance of 13 states.

Dispute over western lands

A dispute arose even before the Articles of Confederation went into effect. Maryland refused to ratify the Articles unless Virginia and other states gave up their claims to lands west of the Appalachian Mountains. Maryland wanted these western lands turned over to Congress. In this way, the "landed" states would not become too powerful.

One by one, the states gave up their western claims. Only Virginia held out. However,

Claims to Western Lands

Geography Skills
By 1783, several states claimed land west of the Appalachians.

1. **Location** On the map, locate lands claimed by both New York and Virginia.
2. **Region** Which states had no claim to western lands?
3. **Critical Thinking** Why did Thomas Jefferson, a Virginian, persuade Virginia to give up its claims to western lands?

Thomas Jefferson and other leading Virginians saw a great need for a central government. They persuaded state lawmakers to give up Virginia's claims in the West. At last, in 1781, Maryland ratified the Articles of Confederation, and the first American government went into effect.

Viewing HISTORY — State Banknotes

During and after the American Revolution, each state issued its own money. The bills here came from Rhode Island and South Carolina.

★ **What problems might arise due to the fact that each state issued its own money?**

Troubles for the New Nation

By 1783, the United States had won independence. The new nation faced many challenges, however. From 1783 to 1787, Americans had reason to doubt whether their country could survive.

Conflicts between states

Despite its weaknesses, the Articles might have succeeded if the states could have put aside their differences and worked together. Many conflicts arose, however. New Hampshire and New York both claimed Vermont. Most states refused to accept the money of other states.

The Articles did not provide a way for states to settle such disputes. Noah Webster, a teacher from New England, warned:

66 So long as any individual state has power to defeat the measures of the other twelve, our pretended union is but a name, and our confederation, a cobweb. 99

Money problems

As a result of borrowing during the Revolution, the United States owed millions of dollars to individuals and foreign nations. Since Congress did not have the power to tax, it had no way to repay these debts. Congress asked the states for money, but the states had the right to refuse. Often, they did.

During the Revolution, the Continental Congress solved the problem of raising funds by printing paper money. However, the money had little value because it was not backed by gold or silver. Before long, Americans began to describe any useless thing as "not worth a Continental."

As Continental dollars became worthless, states printed their own paper money. This caused confusion. How much was a North Carolina dollar worth? Was a Virginia dollar as valuable as a Maryland dollar? As a result, trade became difficult.

Other nations take advantage

Foreign countries took advantage of the confederation's weakness. Britain, for example, refused to withdraw its troops from the Ohio Valley, as it had agreed to do in the Treaty of Paris. Spain closed its port in New Orleans to American farmers. This was a serious blow to western farmers, who depended on the port to ship their products to the East.

Organizing the Northwest Territory

Despite its troubles, Congress did pass important **ordinances,** or laws, concerning the Northwest Territory, the name for lands lying north of the Ohio River and east of the Mississippi. The principles established in these laws were later applied to other areas of settlement.

Townships and sections

The **Land Ordinance of 1785** set up a system for surveying and settling the Northwest Territory. The law called for the territory to be surveyed and then divided into townships.

Each township would have 36 sections. A section was 1 square mile and contained 640 acres. (See the diagram below.) Congress planned to sell sections to settlers for $640 each. One section in every township was set aside to support public schools.

A plan for new states

Another law, passed in 1787, was the **Northwest Ordinance.** It set up a government for the Northwest Territory, guaranteed basic rights to settlers, and outlawed slavery there. It also provided for the vast region to be divided into separate territories in the future.

Once a territory had a population of 60,000 free settlers, it could ask Congress to be admitted as a new state. The newly admitted state would be "on an equal footing with the original states in all respects whatsoever."

The Northwest Ordinance was the finest achievement of the national government under the Articles. It provided a way to admit new states to the nation. It guaranteed that new states would be treated the same as the original 13 states. In time, the states of Ohio, Indiana, Illinois, Michigan, and Wisconsin were created from the Northwest Territory.

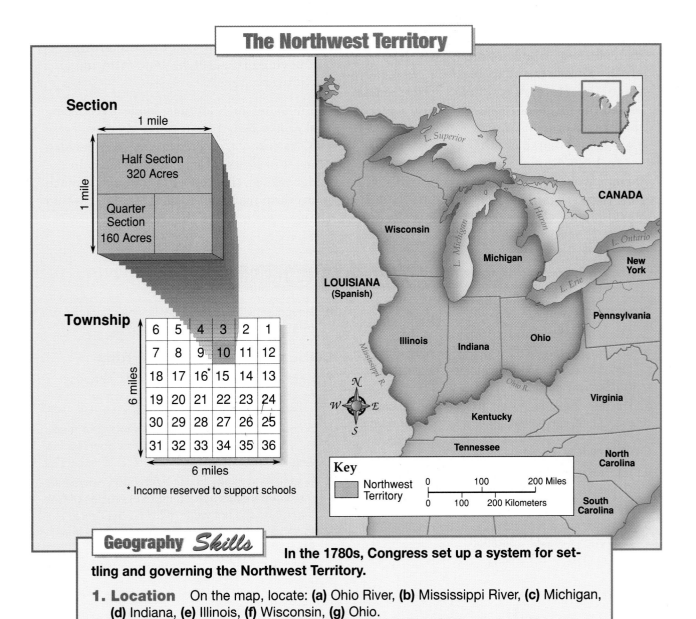

The Northwest Territory

Section

1 mile

Half Section
320 Acres

1 mile

Quarter Section
160 Acres

Township

6	5	4	3	2	1
7	8	9	10	11	12
18	17	16*	15	14	13
19	20	21	22	23	24
30	29	28	27	26	25
31	32	33	34	35	36

6 miles

6 miles

* Income reserved to support schools

Key
Northwest Territory

0   100   200 Miles
0 100   200 Kilometers

CANADA
L. Superior
L. Huron
L. Michigan
L. Ontario
L. Erie
Wisconsin
Michigan
New York
LOUISIANA (Spanish)
Pennsylvania
Illinois
Indiana
Ohio
Mississippi R.
Ohio R.
Virginia
Kentucky
Tennessee
North Carolina
South Carolina

Geography Skills   In the 1780s, Congress set up a system for settling and governing the Northwest Territory.

1. Location   On the map, locate: **(a)** Ohio River, **(b)** Mississippi River, **(c)** Michigan, **(d)** Indiana, **(e)** Illinois, **(f)** Wisconsin, **(g)** Ohio.

2. Place   What was the size of **(a)** a township, **(b)** a section?

3. Critical Thinking   Did the state of Wisconsin have public education when it joined the Union? Explain.

A Farmers' Revolt

While Congress dealt successfully with the Northwest Territory, it failed to solve its economic problems. After the Revolution, the nation suffered an economic depression. An **economic depression** is a period when business activity slows, prices and wages fall, and unemployment rises.

The depression hit farmers hard. During the Revolution, there had been high demand for farm products. To increase production, farmers had borrowed money for land, seed, animals, and tools. However, when the war ended and soldiers returned home, demand for farm goods weakened. Prices fell, and many farmers could not repay their loans.

In Massachusetts, matters worsened when the state raised taxes. The courts seized the farms of those who could not pay their taxes or loans. Angry farmers felt they were being treated unfairly.

In 1786, Daniel Shays, a Massachusetts farmer who had fought at Bunker Hill and Saratoga, organized an uprising. Nearly 2,000 farmers took part in **Shays' Rebel-lion.** They attacked courthouses and prevented the state from seizing farms. They even tried to capture an arsenal filled with guns. Finally, the Massachusetts legislature sent the militia to drive them off.

A Change Is Needed

Many Americans saw Shays' Rebellion as a sign that the Articles of Confederation did not work. George Washington warned that a terrible crisis was at hand:

66 No day was ever more clouded than the present.... I predict the worst consequences from a half-starved, limping government, always moving upon crutches and tottering at every step. 99

To avoid such a crisis, leaders from several states called for a convention to revise the Articles of Confederation. They decided to meet in Philadelphia in May 1787. In the end, however, this convention would do much more than just revise the Articles. It would change the course of the nation.

★ Section 1 Review ★

Recall

1. **Locate** Northwest Territory.
2. **Identify** (a) Articles of Confederation, (b) Land Ordinance of 1785, (c) Northwest Ordinance, (d) Shays' Rebellion.
3. **Define** (a) constitution, (b) execute, (c) confederation, (d) ordinance, (e) economic depression.

Comprehension

4. (a) How were the new state governments similar to the old colonial governments? (b) How were they different?
5. Describe three problems the nation faced under the Articles of Confederation.

6. How did the Northwest Ordinance affect the future growth of the United States?

Critical Thinking and Writing

7. **Analyzing Ideas** When Thomas Jefferson heard about Shays' Rebellion, he wrote: "The spirit of resistance to government is so valuable on occasion that I wish it to be always kept alive." Do you think Shays' Rebellion was good for the United States? Explain.
8. **Identifying Main Ideas** After only 10 years, many Americans agreed that the Articles of Confederation did not work. Why did the Articles fail to serve as a lasting constitution for the United States?

Activity **Drawing a Political Cartoon** You have been asked to create a political cartoon about Shays' Rebellion. The purpose is to help explain to younger students the reasons why farmers like Daniel Shays were angry and what happened as a result of their rebellion.

2 ★ The Constitutional Convention

★ ★

As You Read

Explore These Questions
- How did the Virginia Plan and the New Jersey Plan differ?
- How did the Great Compromise satisfy both large and small states?
- What compromises were made on the issue of slavery?

Define
- legislative branch
- executive branch
- judicial branch
- compromise

Identify
- Constitutional Convention
- James Madison
- Virginia Plan
- New Jersey Plan
- Roger Sherman
- Great Compromise
- Three-Fifths Compromise

◄ The Liberty Bell, a symbol of freedom, originally hung in the Pennsylvania State House.

 SETTING the Scene An air of mystery hung over the Pennsylvania State House in Philadelphia during the summer of 1787. Philadelphians watched as the nation's greatest leaders passed in and out of the building. Eleven years earlier, some of the same men had signed the Declaration of Independence there. What was going on now? Susannah Dillwyn wrote to her father about the excitement:

66 There is now sitting in this city a grand convention, who are to form some new system of government or mend the old one. I suppose it is a body of great consequence, as they say it depends entirely upon their pleasure whether we shall in the future have a congress. 99

What would this "grand convention" decide? No one knew. For almost four months, Americans waited for an answer.

The Convention Opens

On May 25, 1787, the **Constitutional Convention** opened in Philadelphia. Every state except Rhode Island sent representatives. Their mission was to revise the Articles of Confederation.

The 55 delegates gathered for the convention were a remarkable group. At age 81,

Benjamin Franklin was the oldest delegate. He was wise in the ways of government and human nature. George Washington was a representative from Virginia. Washington was so well respected that the delegates at once elected him president of the Convention.

Perhaps the best-prepared delegate to the Constitutional Convention was young **James Madison** of Virginia. For months, Madison had secluded himself on his father's plantation. There, he read many books on history, politics, and commerce. He arrived in Philadelphia with a case bulging with volumes of research.

Many delegates were young men in their twenties and thirties. Among them was Alexander Hamilton of New York. During the Revolution, Hamilton served for a time as Washington's private secretary. Hamilton despised the Articles of Confederation. "The nation," he wrote, "is sick and wants powerful remedies." The powerful remedy he prescribed was a strong national government.

When the Convention began, the delegates decided to keep their talks secret. They wanted to be able to speak their minds freely. They wished to explore issues and solutions without pressures from outside.

Biography Roger Sherman

Roger Sherman was a shoemaker, shopkeeper, surveyor, lawyer—and one of the most respected early leaders of the United States. Thomas Jefferson once said that Sherman "never said a foolish thing in his life." Sherman was one of only four people to sign both the Declaration of Independence and the Constitution. ★ **What major contribution did Roger Sherman make to the Constitutional Convention?**

To ensure secrecy, guards stood at the door. The windows were left closed to keep passersby from overhearing the debates. The closed windows made the room very hot, however. New Englanders in their woolen suits suffered terribly in the summer heat. Southerners, with clothing more suited to warm temperatures, were less bothered.

Hopelessly Divided

Soon after the meeting began, the delegates decided to do more than revise the Articles of Confederation. They chose instead to write an entirely new constitution for the nation. They disagreed, however, about what form the national government should take.

The Virginia Plan

Edmund Randolph and James Madison, both from Virginia, proposed a plan for the new government. This **Virginia Plan** called for a strong national government with three branches. The legislative branch would pass the laws. The executive branch would carry out the laws. The judicial branch, or system of courts, would decide if laws were carried out fairly.

According to the Virginia Plan, the legislative branch would consist of two houses. Seats in both houses would be awarded on the basis of population. Thus, in both houses, larger states would have more representatives than smaller ones. This differed from the Articles of Confederation, which gave every state, regardless of population, one vote in Congress.

The New Jersey Plan

Small states objected strongly to the Virginia Plan. They feared that the large states could easily outvote them in Congress. In response, supporters of the Virginia Plan said that it was only fair for a state with more people to have more representatives.

After two weeks of debate, William Paterson of New Jersey presented a plan that had the support of the small states. Like the Virginia Plan, the **New Jersey Plan** called for three branches of government. However, it provided for a legislature that had only one house. Each state, regardless of its population, would have one vote in the legislature.

The Great Compromise

For a while, no agreement could be reached. With tempers flaring, it seemed that the Convention would fall apart without adopting any plan. Finally, **Roger Sherman** of Connecticut worked out a compromise that he hoped would satisfy both large and small states. A compromise is a settlement in which each side gives up some of its demands in order to reach an agreement.

Sherman's compromise called for a two-house legislature. Members of the lower house, known as the House of Representatives, would be elected by popular vote. As

Skills FOR LIFE

Critical Thinking	Managing Information	Communication	Maps, Charts, and Graphs

Identifying Main Ideas

How Will I Use This Skill?

Every day you get huge quantities of information—from print materials, radio, television, the Internet, and other sources. Sometimes, excessive details make it easy to miss the main point. Learning to identify main ideas saves you time and makes it easier to understand the information you receive.

LEARN the Skill

When dealing with written information, such as in this textbook, use the structure that is provided. Take note of topic headings. In each paragraph, look for the main idea, usually found in a topic sentence at the beginning or end of the paragraph. Details and examples support the topic sentence. To identify main ideas, follow these steps.

❶ Identify main topic headings and subtopic headings.

❷ Identify the topic sentence found in each paragraph.

❸ Identify the supporting details in each paragraph. Determine how each relates to the topic sentence.

❹ Review the topic headings and main ideas of each paragraph to determine the main idea of the entire section or chapter.

PRACTICE the Skill

Review the subsection Hopelessly Divided on page 194.

❶ Identify the two subtopic headings under Hopelessly Divided.

❷ Identify the topic sentence of each of the five paragraphs in this subsection.

❸ Identify two supporting details from the first paragraph. How does each support the main idea?

❹ Review the main ideas of each paragraph. In your own words, restate the main idea of the entire subsection.

APPLY the Skill

Our mailboxes are often stuffed with business letters. Choose a letter from today's mail. Using the skills that you have learned, determine the main idea.

Quill and inkwell used at the Constitutional Convention

Independence Hall

For many, the birthplace of the United States is the old Pennsylvania State House, known today as Independence Hall. Here, the Declaration of Independence was signed, the Articles of Confederation were approved, and the Constitution was adopted. The site is now part of a national park. Visitors to the park can tour the building, learn about the Constitution, and see the Liberty Bell.

★ **To learn more about this historic site, write:** *Independence National Historical Park, 313 Walnut Street, Philadelphia, PA 19106.*

▲ *Chamber where the Constitution was debated*

the larger states wished, seats in the lower house would be awarded to each state according to its population.

Members of the upper house, called the Senate, would be chosen by state legislatures. Each state, no matter what its size, would have two senators. This part of Sherman's compromise appealed to the smaller states.

On July 16, the delegates narrowly approved Sherman's plan. It became known as the **Great Compromise.** Each side gave up some demands to preserve the nation.

Northern and Southern States Compromise

Just as there were disagreements between large and small states, there were also disagreements between northern and southern states. These disagreements concerned the issue of slavery. Would slaves be counted as part of a state's population? Would the slave trade continue to bring enslaved African Americans into the United States?

The Three-Fifths Compromise

Southerners wanted to include slaves in the population count even though they would not let slaves vote. If slaves were counted, southern states would have more representatives in the House of Representatives. Northerners argued that since slaves could not vote, they should not be counted.

Once again, the delegates compromised. They agreed that three fifths of the slaves in any state would be counted. In other words, if a state had 5,000 slaves, 3,000 of them would be included in the state's population count. This agreement became known as the **Three-Fifths Compromise.**

The slave trade

There was another disagreement over slavery. By 1787, some northern states had banned the slave trade within their borders. They urged that the slave trade be banned in the entire nation. Southerners warned that such a ban would ruin their economy.

In the end, the two sides compromised once more. Northerners agreed that Congress could not outlaw the slave trade for at least 20 years. After that, Congress could regulate the slave trade if it wished. Northerners also agreed that no state could stop a fugitive slave from being returned to an owner who claimed that slave.

Signing the Constitution

As summer drew to a close, the weary delegates struggled with other difficult questions. How many years should the President, head of the executive branch, serve? How should the courts be organized? Would members of Congress be paid?

Finally, on September 17, 1787, the Constitution was ready. Gathering for the last time, delegates listened quietly as Benjamin Franklin rose to plead that the document be accepted:

> 66 I doubt...whether any other Convention...may be able to make a better Constitution....I cannot help expressing a wish, that every member of the Convention, who may still have objections to it, would with me, on this occasion, doubt a little of his own infallibility, and...put his name to this instrument. 99

One by one, delegates came forward to sign the document. Of the 42 delegates remaining in Philadelphia, 39 signed the document. Edmund Randolph and George Mason of Virginia, along with Elbridge Gerry of Massachusetts, refused to sign. They felt that the new Constitution gave too much power to the national government.

The Constitution required each state to hold a state convention to decide if the plan for the new government should be accepted. Once 9 of the 13 states endorsed it, the Constitution would go into effect. Before that occurred, the new Constitution was discussed and debated in all the states.

★ Section 2 Review ★

Recall

1. **Identify** (a) Constitutional Convention, (b) James Madison, (c) Virginia Plan, (d) New Jersey Plan, (e) Roger Sherman, (f) Great Compromise, (g) Three-Fifths Compromise.
2. **Define** (a) legislative branch, (b) executive branch, (c) judicial branch, (d) compromise.

Comprehension

3. Why did New Jersey and other small states oppose the Virginia Plan?
4. (a) How did the Great Compromise satisfy large states? (b) How did it satisfy small states?
5. What compromise did the North and South reach on the slave trade?

Critical Thinking and Writing

6. **Defending a Position** James Madison said that "no Constitution would ever have been adopted by the Convention if the debates had been made public." Do you agree or disagree? Defend your position.
7. **Predicting Consequences** Some historians refer to the issue of slavery as the Constitutional Convention's "unfinished business." How do you think the issue of slavery would continue to divide North and South in the years after the Convention?

Activity **Writing a Letter** You are the editor of a Philadelphia newspaper in 1787. Decide whether you agree or disagree with the Convention's decision to keep its talks secret. Explain your viewpoint in a letter to the delegates of the Constitutional Convention.

3 A More Perfect Union

As You Read

Explore These Questions
- What ideas helped shape the Constitution?
- How did the framers of the Constitution divide power between the national government and the states?
- How did they limit the power of government?

Define
- republic
- separation of powers
- federalism
- electoral college
- checks and balances
- bill
- veto
- override
- impeach

Identify
- Magna Carta
- English Bill of Rights
- House of Burgesses
- Mayflower Compact
- Enlightenment
- John Locke
- Montesquieu

SETTING the Scene Jonathan Smith, a Massachusetts farmer, wanted to learn the results of the Constitutional Convention. During Shays' Rebellion, he had seen how weak government could lead to violence and tyranny. Smith noted:

> 66 When I saw this Constitution, I found that it was a cure for these disorders. It was just such a thing as we wanted. I got a copy of it and read it over and over. I had been a member of the convention to form our state constitution, and had learnt something of the checks and balances of power; and I found them all here. I formed my own opinion, and I was pleased with this Constitution. 99

The framers of the Constitution had designed a **republic,** a government in which citizens rule themselves through elected representatives. The Constitution outlined a new government that would be strong. At the same time, it protected the people from excessive power in government. As Smith hoped, it also prevented any one branch of government from becoming too powerful.

Origins of the Constitution

The framers of the Constitution were well-educated men. They were familiar with the traditions of British and American government. Many of them had read the latest works of Europe's leading political philosophers. In creating the Constitution, the framers made good use of their rich knowledge and experience.

British government

As you learned in Chapter 3, the **Magna Carta** limited the power of English rulers. The Magna Carta contained two basic ideas that helped to shape both British and American government. First, it stated that English nobles had certain rights—rights that were later extended to other classes of people as well. Second, the Magna Carta made clear that English monarchs themselves had to obey the law.

When King John signed the Magna Carta, he agreed not to raise taxes without first consulting the Great Council of nobles and church officials. Eventually, the Great Council grew into the representative body known as Parliament. Parliament consisted

Connections With Civics

Benjamin Franklin admired the government formed by Indian nations in the Iroquois League. The nations in the League governed their own affairs, but joined together for mutual defense.

of two bodies—the House of Lords and the House of Commons.

In the Magna Carta, King John was also forced to recognize that citizens had legal rights. One of the most important of these was the right to a trial by jury:

> 66 No freeman shall be arrested or imprisoned or dispossessed or . . . in any way harmed . . . except by the lawful judgment of his peers or by the law of the land. 99

In 1689, the **English Bill of Rights** went further in limiting the monarchy and protecting the rights of citizens. The document said that parliamentary elections should be held regularly. It reaffirmed the right to a trial by jury, while protecting people from excessive fines and cruel or unjust punishment. It allowed citizens to bear arms. It also affirmed the right of habeas corpus, the idea that no person could be held in prison without first being charged with a specific crime.

The American experience

Americans enjoyed a long tradition of elected representative government. In 1619, the Virginia colonists set up the **House of Burgesses.** Eventually, each of Britain's thirteen American colonies had its own representative legislature.

Another American tradition was having written documents that clearly identified the powers and limits of government. In 1620, the Pilgrim leaders at Plymouth drew up and signed the **Mayflower Compact,** the first document of self-government in North America. They agreed to "combine ourselves together in a civil body politic" in order to establish "just and equal laws." Each of the 13 colonies had a written charter granted by the monarch or Parliament.

The framers of the Constitution also drew on their own experiences. They were very familiar with the workings of the Second Continental Congress, the Articles of Confederation, and their own state governments. Much that went into the Constitution came from either the Articles or from one of the state constitutions.

The Enlightenment

The Constitution was also based on the ideas of the European **Enlightenment.** Enlightenment thinkers believed that people could improve society through the use of reason. Many of the Constitution's framers had read the works of Enlightenment thinkers, such as John Locke and the Baron de Montesquieu (MOHN tehs kyoo).

In 1690, **John Locke** published *Two Treatises on Government.* In it, he stated two important ideas.

First, Locke declared that all people had natural rights to life, liberty, and property. Second, he suggested that government is an agreement between the ruler and the ruled. The ruler must enforce the laws and protect the people. If a ruler violates the people's natural rights, the people have a right to rebel.

Biography Baron de Montesquieu

Montesquieu studied European, Chinese, and Native American governments. His ideas influenced the framers of the Constitution to divide government power among three separate branches. He said that "government should be set up so that one man need not be afraid of another." ★ **Why do you think the framers of the Constitution did not want to place all power into a single branch of government?**

The Federal System

Powers Delegated to the National Government

- Regulate interstate and foreign trade
- Set standard weights and measures
- Create and maintain armed forces
- Make copyright and patent laws
- Establish postal offices
- Establish foreign policy
- Create federal courts
- Coin money
- Declare war
- Admit new states

Shared Powers

- Provide for public welfare
- Administer criminal justice
- Charter banks
- Raise taxes
- Borrow money

Powers Reserved to the States

- Create corporation laws
- Regulate trade within state
- Establish and maintain schools
- Establish local governments
- Make laws about marriage and divorce
- Conduct elections
- Provide for public safety

Graphic Organizer Skills The system of federalism divides power between the national government and state governments.

1. Comprehension **(a)** List two powers shared by national and state governments. **(b)** List two powers reserved to the states.

2. Critical Thinking Why do you think the power to create and maintain armed forces was delegated to the federal government?

Civics

Locke's ideas were popular among Americans. The framers of the Constitution wanted to protect people's natural rights and limit the power of government. They saw the Constitution as a contract between the people and their government.

In 1748, the French thinker Baron de **Montesquieu** published *The Spirit of the Laws.* He urged that the power of government be divided among three separate branches: the legislative, executive, and judicial. This idea, known as the separation of powers, was designed to keep any person or group from gaining too much power.

Montesquieu stressed the importance of the rule of law. The powers of government, he said, should be clearly defined. This would prevent individuals or groups from using government power for their own purposes. In the Constitution, the framers set out the basic laws of the nation, defining and limiting the powers of the government.

A Federal System

The framers had to decide how to divide power between the national government and the states. Under the Articles of Confederation, states had more power than Congress. Under the Constitution, states delegated, or gave up, some of their powers to the national government. At the same time, the states reserved, or kept, other powers. This division of power between the states and the national government is called **federalism.**

Federal powers

The Constitution spells out the powers of the federal government. For example, only the federal government can coin money or declare war. The federal government can also regulate trade between the states and with other countries.

State powers

Under the Constitution, states have the power to regulate trade within their borders. They decide who can vote in state elections. They also have power to establish schools and local governments.

In addition, the Constitution says that those powers not clearly given to the federal government belong to the states or the people. This point pleased people who were afraid that the federal government might become too powerful.

Shared powers

The Constitution lists some powers that are to be shared by federal and state governments. Both governments, for example, can build roads and raise taxes.

The framers of the Constitution had to decide how the state governments and the federal government would settle disagreements. They did so by making the Constitution "the supreme law of the land." This means that the Constitution is the final authority in any dispute between the states and the federal government.

Separation of Powers

The framers of the Constitution set up a strong federal government. However, they also took steps to prevent any one branch from becoming too powerful. James Madison said that this was necessary in order to prevent tyranny:

> 66 The accumulation of all powers, legislative, executive, and judiciary, in the same hands, whether one, a few, or many…may justly be pronounced the very definition of tyranny. 99

To prevent such a tyranny, the framers relied on Montesquieu's idea of separation of powers. In the Constitution, they created three branches of government and then defined the powers of each.

The legislative branch

The legislative branch of government is Congress. Its main function is to make laws. Congress consists of the House of Representatives and the Senate. Members of the House are elected for two-year terms. Senators are elected for six-year terms.

Under the Constitution, voters in each state elect members of the House of Representatives. Delegates to the Constitutional Convention wanted the House to represent the interests of ordinary people.

At first, the Constitution provided for senators to be chosen by state legislatures. In 1913, this was changed. Today, senators are elected in the same way as House members.

Article 1 of the Constitution sets out the powers of Congress. These include the power to collect taxes and to regulate foreign and interstate trade. In foreign affairs, Congress has the power to declare war and to "raise and support armies."

The executive branch

Article 2 of the Constitution sets up the executive branch of government. It is headed by the President. The executive branch also includes the Vice President and any advisers appointed by the President. The President and Vice President serve four-year terms.

The President is responsible for carrying out all laws passed by Congress. The President is also commander in chief of the armed forces and is responsible for directing foreign relations. Over the years, the power of the presidency has greatly increased.

The judicial branch

Article 3 of the Constitution calls for a Supreme Court. The article also allows Congress to set up other federal courts. The Supreme Court and other federal courts hear cases that involve the Constitution or any laws passed by Congress. They also hear cases arising from disputes between two or more states.

Legislative Branch
(Congress)

Passes laws
Can override President's veto
Approves treaties and presidential
  appointments
Can impeach and remove President
  and other high officials
Creates lower federal courts
Appropriates money
Prints and coins money
Raises and supports the armed forces
Can declare war
Regulates foreign and interstate trade

Executive Branch
(President)

Carries out laws
Proposes laws
Can veto laws
Negotiates foreign treaties
Serves as commander in
  chief of the armed forces
Appoints federal judges,
  ambassadors, and other
  high officials
Can grant pardons to federal
  offenders

Judicial Branch
(Supreme Court and
Other Federal Courts)

Interprets laws
Can declare laws
  unconstitutional
Can declare executive
  actions unconstitutional

Chart *Skills*

The Constitution set up three branches of government. Each of the branches has its own powers.

1. **Comprehension** (a) Who heads the executive branch? (b) What is the role of the legislative branch?
2. **Critical Thinking** Based on this chart, describe the relationship between the judicial branch and the executive branch.

Civics

Electing the President

The framers of the Constitution wanted to ensure that the President would not become too strong. Some feared that a President elected directly by the people might become too independent of Congress and the states.

Others opposed direct election because they worried that voters would not know a candidate from outside their area. In the late 1700s, news traveled slowly. New Englanders would probably know little about a candidate from the South. A candidate from Pennsylvania might be unknown to voters in Vermont or Georgia.

As a result of these concerns, the Constitution calls for an **electoral college.** It is made up of electors from every state. Every four years, the electors vote for the President and Vice President of the United States.

The framers of the Constitution expected that the electors would be well informed and familiar with the national government. They believed that such people would choose a President and Vice President wisely.

Checks and Balances

The Constitution set up a system of **checks and balances.** Under this system, each branch of the federal government has some way to check, or control, the other two branches. The system of checks and balances is another way in which the Constitution limits the power of government. (See the chart on page 220.)

Checks on Congress

To do its work, Congress passes **bills,** or proposed laws. A bill then goes to the President to be signed into law. The President can check the power of Congress by **vetoing,** or rejecting, a bill.

The Supreme Court checks the power of Congress by reviewing laws. If a law violates the Constitution, the Court can declare the law unconstitutional.

Checks on the President

After the President vetoes a bill, Congress can **override,** or overrule the veto. To override a veto, two thirds of both houses of Congress must vote for the bill again. In this way, a bill can become law without the President's signature.

Congress has other checks on the President. The President appoints officials such as ambassadors to foreign countries and federal judges. The Senate must approve these appointments. The President can negotiate treaties with other nations; however, a treaty becomes law only if two thirds of the Senate approve it.

Congress also has the power to remove a President from office if it finds the President guilty of a crime or serious misbehavior. First of all, the House of Representatives must **impeach,** or bring charges against, the President. A trial is then held in the Senate. If two thirds of the senators vote for conviction, the President must leave office.

Checks on the courts

Congress and the President have checks on the courts. The President appoints judges, who must be approved by the Senate. If judges misbehave, Congress may remove them from office. Congress establishes the number of justices in the Supreme Court. Congress can also propose changes to the Constitution to overturn Court decisions.

A Living Document

The Constitution carefully balances power among the three branches of the federal government. It also divides power between the federal government and the states. This balance has helped keep it alive for more than 200 years, longer than any other written constitution in the world. The Constitution has lasted because it is a living document. As you will read, it can be changed to meet new conditions.

★ Section 3 Review ★

Recall

1. **Identify** **(a)** Magna Carta, **(b)** English Bill of Rights, **(c)** House of Burgesses, **(d)** Mayflower Compact, **(e)** Enlightenment, **(f)** John Locke, **(g)** Montesquieu.

2. **Define** **(a)** republic, **(b)** separation of powers, **(c)** federalism, **(d)** electoral college, **(e)** checks and balances, **(f)** bill, **(g)** veto, **(h)** override, **(i)** impeach.

Comprehension

3. Describe three traditions or ideas that helped to shape the Constitution.

4. Why did the framers of the Constitution set up a system of federalism?

5. Describe one check on each of the following: **(a)** Congress, **(b)** the President, **(c)** the courts.

Critical Thinking and Writing

6. **Analyzing Ideas** On page 200, you read that the framers "...saw the Constitution as a contract between the people and their government." What do you think is meant by this statement?

7. **Comparing** Was the national government stronger under the Articles of Confederation or the Constitution? Explain.

Activity **Summarizing** You have been shipwrecked on a far-off island! The islanders want to set up a government like that of the United States. Write a summary for them in which you explain the basic ideas behind the Constitution.

4 ★ Ratifying the Constitution

★ ★

As You Read

Explore These Questions
- What arguments did Americans raise for and against the Constitution?
- How can the Constitution be amended?
- What rights does the Bill of Rights protect?

Define
- ratify
- amend
- due process

Identify
- Federalist
- Antifederalist
- *The Federalist Papers*
- Bill of Rights

 SETTING the Scene In homes and in town squares across the nation, Americans discussed the new Constitution. Many supported it. Many others did not. Its critics especially worried that the Constitution had no bill of rights. In Virginia, Patrick Henry sounded the alarm:

66 Show me an age and country where the rights and liberties of the people were placed on the sole chance of their rulers being good men, without a consequent loss of liberty! 99

Was a bill of rights needed? Did the Constitution give too much power to the federal government? In the fall of 1787, citizens began to debate the document sentence by sentence. The Convention had done its work. Now the states had to decide whether or not to ratify the new frame of government.

The Constitution Goes to the Nation

The framers of the Constitution sent the document to Congress. With it, they sent a letter from George Washington, as president of the Constitutional Convention. In the letter, Washington described how the framers had struggled to make the Constitution meet the varied needs of the different states. He wrote:

66 In our deliberations, we kept steadily in view...the greatest inter-

ests of every true American. That [the Constitution] will meet the full and entire [approval] of every state is not perhaps to be expected; but each will doubtless consider that had her interest been alone consulted, the consequences might have been...disagreeable or [harmful] to others. 99

Washington warmly endorsed the document and called on Congress to support it. It was his belief, he said, that the Constitution would "promote the lasting welfare of that country so dear to us all, and secure her freedom and happiness."

The framers of the Constitution had set up a process for the states to decide on the new government. At least 9 of the 13 states had to **ratify,** or approve, the Constitution before it could go into effect. In 1787 and 1788, voters in each state elected delegates to special state conventions. These delegates then met to decide whether or not to ratify the Constitution.

⚛ Connections *With* Science

Today, the Constitution is publicly displayed. For protection against damage due to light, insects, and impurities in the air, each page is in a glass case filled with helium. Levels of light and humidity are carefully controlled.

Heated Debate

In every state, heated debates took place. Supporters of the Constitution called themselves **Federalists.** They called people who opposed the Constitution **Antifederalists.**

The Federalist position

The Federalists argued that the Articles of Confederation had produced an excessively weak central government. It had placed the nation in grave danger because it left too much power with the individual states. Disputes among the states, Federalists said, had made it too difficult for the Confederation government to function.

According to the Federalists, the Constitution gave the national government the authority to function effectively. At the same time, it still protected the rights of the individual states.

Among the best-known Federalists were James Madison, Alexander Hamilton, and John Jay. They wrote a series of essays, called *The Federalist Papers*, defending the Constitution. They used pen names, but most people knew who they were. Today, *The Federalist Papers* remains one of the best discussions of the political theory behind the American system of government.

The Antifederalist position

Antifederalists opposed the Constitution for many reasons. They felt that it made the national government too strong and left the states too weak. They thought that the Constitution gave the President too much power. Patrick Henry was among those who voiced such concerns:

> 66 This Constitution is said to have beautiful features, but...they appear to me horribly frightful.... Your President may become king... If your American chief be a man of ambition and abilities, how easy is it for him to render himself absolute! 99

Most people expected George Washington to be elected President. Antifederalists admired Washington, but they warned that future Presidents might lack Washington's

Biography — James Madison

Historians call James Madison the "Father of the Constitution" because much of the document was based on his ideas. When the Constitution was being debated, Madison was only in his 30s. He went on to serve the nation as a member of Congress, as Secretary of State, and as the fourth President of the United States . ★ **Was Madison a Federalist or an Antifederalist?**

honor and skill. For this reason, they said, the office should not be too powerful.

Need for a bill of rights

The chief argument used by Antifederalists against the Constitution was that it had no bill of rights. Americans had just fought a revolution to protect their freedoms. They wanted a bill of rights in the Constitution that spelled out basic freedoms such as freedom of speech and freedom of religion.

Federalists replied that the Constitution protected citizens very well without a bill of rights. Anyway, they argued, it was impossible to list all the natural rights of people. Antifederalists responded that if rights were not written into the Constitution, it would be easy to ignore them. Several state conventions refused to ratify the Constitution unless they received a firm promise that a bill of rights would be added.

When the Constitution was ratified, celebrations were held across the nation. Shown here is a celebration parade in New York City. The three-masted ship on the float represented the "ship of state." ★ **Why do you think Alexander Hamilton's name is displayed so visibly?**

The States Vote to Ratify

One by one, states voted to ratify the Constitution. Delaware was the first, in December 1787. In June 1788, New Hampshire became the ninth state to ratify. The new government could now go into effect.

Still, the future of the United States remained in doubt. It was important that all the states support the Constitution. However, New York and Virginia, two of the largest states, had not yet ratified the plan. In both states, Federalists and Antifederalists were closely matched.

In Virginia, Patrick Henry strongly opposed the Constitution. Henry charged that the document gave the government too much power. "There will be no checks, no real balances in this government," he cried. In the end, however, Washington, Madison, and other Virginia Federalists prevailed. In late June, Virginia approved the Constitution.

In New York, the struggle went on for another month. At last, in July 1788, the state convention voted to ratify. North Carolina ratified in November 1789. Rhode Island was the last state to approve the Constitution, finally doing so in May 1790.

The Nation Celebrates

Throughout the land, Americans celebrated the news that the Constitution was ratified. The city of Philadelphia set its festival for July 4, 1788. At sunrise, church bells rang. In the harbor, the ship *Rising Sun* boomed a salute from its cannons. Horses wore bright ribbons, and bands played popular tunes.

A festive parade filed along Market Street, led by soldiers who had fought in the Revolution. Thousands cheered as six colorfully outfitted horses pulled a blue carriage shaped like an eagle. Thirteen stars and stripes were painted on the front, and the Constitution was raised proudly above it.

That night, even the skies seemed to celebrate. The northern lights, vivid bands of color, lit up the sky above the city. Benjamin Rush, a Philadelphia doctor and strong supporter of the Constitution, wrote to a friend: "'Tis done. We have become a nation."

Adding a Bill of Rights

Americans voted in the first election under the Constitution in January 1789. As

Why Study History?

Because National Symbols Unite Us

★ ★

Historical Background

The Constitution changed a loose alliance of states into a more unified nation. It takes more than a document, however, to create a nation. Shared ideals and symbols also help to bring people together. In 1782, the bald eagle was declared a symbol of the United States by Congress.

The presidential seal

Today, the eagle and other symbols appear on the Great Seal of the United States and on the Seal of the President of the United States. On both seals, the American eagle holds an olive branch representing peace and a bundle of arrows representing military readiness. In its beak, it holds a scroll with the Latin phrase *"E pluribus Unum."* These words, which mean "Out of many, one," are our nation's motto. They refer to the union of states and to the union of the diverse American people.

Connections to Today

Almost 200 years after Congress declared it an American symbol, the American bald eagle was in serious trouble. Only about 400 breeding pairs of eagles remained in the lower 48 states. Hunting, loss of habitat, and pollution were some causes of the decline. In the 1960s, President John F. Kennedy made an urgent appeal. "The fierce beauty and proud independence of this great bird aptly symbolize the strength and freedom of America," he said, "and we shall have failed a trust if we allow the eagle to disappear."

The nation took action. Congress banned the use of DDT, an insecticide that damaged the birds' eggs. Also, it declared the eagle an endangered species. This step prohibited the hunting of eagles and protected their habitat. By the mid-1990s, the eagle population had recovered.

Connections to You

The bald eagle is only one of the emblems that represent you and all citizens of the United States. The foremost symbol of the nation is the American flag. Others include the Liberty Bell, the Statue of Liberty, and Uncle Sam. Such images have a long and interesting history as symbols of our nation.

1. **Comprehension** (a) Why was the bald eagle endangered in the 1960s? (b) How did government help the eagle to recover?

2. **Critical Thinking** Why do you think Congress chose the eagle as a symbol of the United States?

 Researching and Writing Conduct research to learn about the origins and meaning of the American flag, the Liberty Bell, or other symbols of the United States. Write an essay summarizing your findings.

Past

Present

Trial by Jury

Trial by jury is part of the nation's English heritage. Yet in colonial times, British officials sometimes suspended jury trials. Therefore, many Americans wanted the new Constitution to guarantee this right. The members of a jury promise to give an impartial verdict based on evidence. ★ **Turn to the Reference Section and read the Sixth Amendment. List three rights guaranteed to Americans accused of crimes.**

expected, George Washington was elected President, while John Adams was chosen Vice President.

The first Congress was made up of 59 representatives and 22 senators. It met in New York City, which was chosen as the nation's first capital. The first Congress quickly turned its attention to adding a bill of rights to the Constitution.

The amendment process

The framers had set up a way to **amend,** or change, the Constitution. They did not want people to make changes lightly, however. Thus, they made the process of amending the Constitution fairly difficult.

To start the amendment process, an amendment must be proposed. This can be done in two ways. Two thirds of both houses of Congress can vote to propose an amendment, or two thirds of the states can request special conventions to propose amendments.

Next, the amendment must be ratified. Three fourths of the states must approve the amendment before it becomes part of the Constitution.

In the more than 200 years since the Constitution was adopted, only 27 amendments have been approved. Ten of those amendments were added in the first years after the Constitution was ratified.

The first 10 amendments

The first Congress proposed a series of amendments to the Constitution of the United States in 1789. By December 1791, three fourths of the states had ratified 10 amendments. Those 10 amendments became known as the **Bill of Rights.**

James Madison, who wrote the amendments, insisted that the Bill of Rights does not give Americans any rights. People already have the rights listed in the amendments. They are natural rights, said Madison, that belong to all human beings. The Bill of Rights simply prevents the government from taking these rights away.

Protecting individual rights

The 10 amendments that make up the Bill of Rights ensure the basic freedoms of American citizens. The First Amendment guarantees individual liberties, including freedom of religion, freedom of speech, and freedom of the press. It also guarantees the right to assemble peacefully and the right to petition the government.

The next three amendments came out of the colonists' struggle with Britain. The Second Amendment guarantees the right of citizens to keep and bear arms. The Third Amendment was included because the framers remembered Parliament's efforts to make colonists house and feed British soldiers. The amendment prevents Congress from forcing citizens to quarter, or house, troops in their homes. The Fourth Amendment protects citizens from unreasonable searches and seizures. Before the Revolution, you will remember, British customs officials had often searched and seized the property of colonists without their permission.

The Fifth Amendment guarantees due process of law. **Due process** means that the government must follow the same fair rules in all cases brought to trial. Under the Fifth Amendment, the accused must be notified of the charges brought against him or her. The accused must also be given the chance to present a defense in court. Also, the government cannot require self-incriminating testimony nor may it try a defendant twice for the same crime if the defendant has already been acquitted.

Amendments 6 through 8 provide other protections for citizens accused of crimes. The Sixth Amendment guarantees a jury trial in criminal cases and the right to be defended by a lawyer. The Seventh Amendment requires jury trials in civil cases. The Eighth Amendment prevents judges from ordering "excessive bail" or imposing "cruel and unusual punishment" on a convicted criminal.

The Ninth Amendment assures that the rights listed in the Constitution are not the only ones that exist. The Tenth Amendment states that all powers not given to the national government and not denied to the states are reserved for the states or for the people. This assured that the power of the national government would be limited.

With the Bill of Rights in place, the new framework of government was complete. Over time, the Constitution became a living document that grew and changed along with the nation.

★ Section 4 Review ★

Recall

1. **Identify** **(a)** Federalist, **(b)** Antifederalist, **(c)** *The Federalist Papers,* **(d)** Bill of Rights.
2. **Define** **(a)** ratify, **(b)** amend, **(c)** due process.

Comprehension

3. **(a)** Why did Federalists favor ratification of the Constitution? **(b)** Why did Antifederalists oppose it?
4. Describe the process for adding amendments to the Constitution.

5. Describe three specific rights protected by the first 10 amendments to the Constitution.

Critical Thinking and Writing

6. **Defending a Position** Imagine that you are a citizen of the United States in 1789. Would you argue for or against the Constitution? How would you defend your position?
7. **Analyzing Ideas** **(a)** List five rights protected by the Bill of Rights. **(b)** Which do you think is most important? Explain.

★ ★

Activity **Making Illustrations** You are the illustrator for a handbook on the rights of American citizens. Draw a series of sketches to illustrate the rights that are guaranteed by the First Amendment.

Review and Activities

★ Sum It Up ★

Section 1 A Confederation of States
▶ During the American Revolution, most states wrote constitutions providing for a governor and legislature.
▶ The Articles of Confederation created a weak alliance of states.
▶ Under the Articles of Confederation, the government set up a system for forming and governing new territories.

Section 2 The Constitutional Convention
▶ The Constitutional Convention met in Philadelphia in 1787 to revise the nation's government.
▶ The delegates created the Constitution by making important compromises on several divisive issues.

Section 3 A More Perfect Union
▶ The framers of the Constitution drew ideas from British government, colonial and state governments, and the Enlightenment.
▶ A federal system divides power between the national and state governments.
▶ The separation of powers prevents any branch of government from becoming too strong.

Section 4 Ratifying the Constitution
▶ After many debates, the separate states approved the Constitution.
▶ The first 10 amendments form a Bill of Rights designed to protect the rights of individuals.

 CD-ROM Review For additional review of the major ideas of Chapter 7, see *Guide to the Essentials of American History* or *Interactive Student Tutorial CD-ROM,* which contains interactive review activities, graphic organizers, and practice tests.

⬛ Reviewing the Chapter

Define These Terms
Match each term with the correct definition.

Column 1	Column 2
1. constitution	a. system of courts
2. judicial branch	b. to bring charges against
3. republic	c. nation in which voters elect representatives to govern them
4. legislative branch	d. branch that passes laws
5. impeach	e. document that sets out the laws and principles of a government

Explore the Main Ideas
1. Describe three reasons for the failure of the Articles of Confederation.
2. **(a)** Why was the Great Compromise necessary?
   (b) Why was the Three-Fifths Compromise necessary?
3. Describe three ideas that shaped the Constitution.
4. What is one benefit of a federal system of government?
5. **(a)** Describe one reason why Federalists favored the Constitution. **(b)** Describe one reason why Antifederalists opposed it.

⬛ Chart Activity

Use the chart below to answer the following questions:
1. Which state was the first to ratify the Constitution?
2. Which state was the last? **Critical Thinking** In which three states was support for the Constitution strongest?

Ratification of the Constitution

State	Date	Vote
Delaware	Dec. 7, 1787	30–0
Pennsylvania	Dec. 12, 1787	46–23
New Jersey	Dec. 19, 1787	38–0
Georgia	Jan. 2, 1788	26–0
Connecticut	Jan. 9, 1788	128–40
Massachusetts	Feb. 6, 1788	187–168
Maryland	Apr. 28, 1788	63–11
South Carolina	May 23, 1788	149–73
New Hampshire	June 21, 1788	57–46
Virginia	June 25, 1788	89–79
New York	July 26, 1788	30–27
North Carolina	Nov. 21, 1789	184–77
Rhode Island	May 29, 1790	34–32

☐ Critical Thinking and Writing

1. **Understanding Chronology** Arrange the following documents in chronological order: **(a)** the Constitution, **(b)** Articles of Confederation, **(c)** the First Amendment, **(d)** Magna Carta, **(e)** Mayflower Compact.

2. **Making Inferences** Benjamin Franklin said that Americans had a republic, if they could keep it. Why do you think Franklin was unsure whether the government would last?

3. **Predicting Consequences** What do you think might happen if the government was not required to follow due process?

4. **Exploring Unit Themes** **Rights and Liberties** The nation has changed a great deal since 1787. Does the Bill of Rights still protect individual rights in the United States today? Explain.

☐ Using Primary Sources

During the American Revolution, Johann David Schoepf was a physician for Britain's Hessian troops. After the war, he traveled about the United States, recording his observations. Here, he comments on the government created by the Articles of Confederation:

> ❝ The Congress has neither the necessary weight nor the necessary solidity.... It was to be expected of a people so enthusiastic for liberty that they should grant their Congress only a shadow of dignity, and watch its proceedings with a jealous eye. ❞

Source: *Travels in the Confederation,* Johann David Schoepf, 1911.

Recognizing Points of View **(a)** Did Schoepf consider the new American Congress to be strong or weak? **(b)** Schoepf wrote that Americans watched Congress "with a jealous eye." What do you think he meant by this? **(c)** How do you think Schoepf's background affected his point of view?

ACTIVITY BANK

▶ Interdisciplinary Activity

Exploring Geography Find out more about the early settlement of one of the five states carved out of the Northwest Territory. Report on how people traveled there, what obstacles they faced, and how they lived. Include a map showing geographic features of the area.

▶ Career Skills Activity

Teachers Every immigrant who wants to become an American citizen has to learn about the Constitution. Suppose you were teaching a citizenship class. With a partner, prepare a presentation on one part the Constitution. Use visual aids such as diagrams and pictures in your presentation.

▶ Citizenship Activity

Identifying Community Issues The process of amending the Constitution often starts with a petition—a statement signed by many members of a community and presented to lawmakers to show public support for a change. Working with others in your class, choose a problem in your community. Prepare a petition that suggests a solution.

Internet Activity

On the Internet, find information on one of the leading figures at the Constitutional Convention. Write a brief biography of the person, noting especially his role in producing the Constitution.

EYEWITNESS Journal

You are a delegate to the Constitutional Convention. In your EYEWITNESS JOURNAL, describe the debate over the Virginia Plan and the New Jersey Plan. Also, describe the debates that took place over issues of slavery.

★ CIVICS OVERVIEW ★

Chapter 8

The Constitution at Work 1789–Present

The goal of the Constitution is to create a single, united nation with a fair government and system of laws. It ensures peace within the nation, provides for the defense of the country, and guarantees people's rights and liberties. The principles behind the Constitution include the people's right to rule themselves and the careful division of power among three separate branches of the government.

Changing the Constitution is not easy. For this reason, the basic framework of government has grown slowly. One key change over the centuries has been to extend the rights of citizenship to more and more Americans.

Why Study History?

As you study American history, you will see how different people won greater rights. Such rights carry with them responsibilities. Americans meet their responsibilities as citizens in many ways, such as voting or serving in the military. There are also individuals who see a problem in their community and work to solve it. To meet one such person, see this chapter's *Why Study History?* feature, "Citizens Have Responsibilities."

★ ★

American Events

1788 Constitution of the United States is ratified

1791 Bill of Rights is approved

1700   1750   1800   1850

World Events

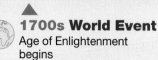 **1700s World Event**
Age of Enlightenment begins

 1789 World Event
French Revolution begins

Voting: A Right and a Responsibility

Voting is one of the most important duties of an American citizen. Two hundred years ago, only white male property owners over the age of 21 could vote in most states. Today, as this painting shows, every citizen over the age of 18 has the right to vote. ★ **List three other rights that American citizens enjoy.**

●**1870**
Fifteenth Amendment gives African American men the right to vote

●**1920**
Nineteenth Amendment gives women the right to vote

●**1971**
Twenty-sixth Amendment extends voting rights to Americans 18 to 21 years old

1850   **1900**   **1950**   **2000**

 1893 World Event
New Zealand is first nation to give vote to women

 1948 World Event
United Nations approves Universal Declaration of Human Rights

1

Goals of the Constitution

As You Read

Explore These Questions
- How does the national government help to unify the nation?
- What are the benefits of a national system of courts?
- How does the Constitution protect the basic rights of the people?

Define
- federal
- justice
- domestic tranquillity
- general welfare
- liberty

Identify
- Preamble
- Bill of Rights

SETTING the Scene In 1787, Benjamin Franklin was 81 years old. As long ago as the French and Indian War, he had urged the 13 colonies to unite for their mutual interest. Now, he was serving as the oldest delegate to the Constitutional Convention.

At the end of the convention, Franklin commented on the new Constitution. The document, he admitted, was not perfect:

66 When you assemble a number of men, to have the advantage of their joint wisdom, you inevitably assemble with those men all their prejudices, their passions, their errors of opinion, their local interests, and their selfish views.... It therefore astonishes me, Sir, to find this system approaching so near to perfection as it does. 99

Constitution of the United States
▼

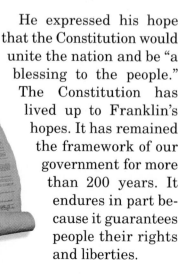

He expressed his hope that the Constitution would unite the nation and be "a blessing to the people." The Constitution has lived up to Franklin's hopes. It has remained the framework of our government for more than 200 years. It endures in part because it guarantees people their rights and liberties.

Ensuring liberty is just one of the main goals of the Constitution.

Preamble to the Constitution

The opening statement, of the Constitution is called the **Preamble.** In it the American people proudly announce that they have established the Constitution to achieve certain goals:

66 We the people of the United States, in order to form a more perfect Union, establish justice, ensure domestic tranquillity, provide for the common defense, promote the general welfare, and secure the blessings of liberty to ourselves and our posterity, do ordain and establish this Constitution for the United States of America. 99

As you read about these six goals, think about their importance to you.

"Form a More Perfect Union"

Under the Articles of Confederation, the United States was a loose alliance of independent, quarreling states. Many states acted like separate nations. One of the main goals of the framers of the Constitution was to get the states to work together as part of a single, united nation.*

---

* *E pluribus unum,* the official motto of the United States, also expresses this principle of unity. The Latin phrase means, "Out of many, one."

To achieve this goal of unity, the Constitution gives a broad range of powers to the national government. For example, only Congress—the national legislature—has the power to tax all the people. The President—the national executive—is responsible for carrying out all the laws of the nation. And **federal,** or national, courts enforce one system of law for the entire nation.

"Establish Justice"

A second goal of the Constitution is to establish **justice,** or fairness. Justice requires that the law be applied fairly to every American, regardless of that person's race, religion, gender, country of origin, political beliefs, or financial situation. The Constitution gives this task to a federal system of courts.

Federal courts deal with a broad range of issues. They hear cases involving the Constitution, national laws, treaties, foreign ambassadors, and ships at sea. They also decide disputes between individuals, between individuals and the national government, and between the states.

When federal courts decide cases, they must often interpret, or explain, the law. The Supreme Court, the highest court in the land, can rule that a law passed by Congress or a state legislature is not permitted by the Constitution.

Why is a national system of courts necessary? Without it, state or local courts would interpret national laws. Judges in some states might refuse to enforce national laws they did not like. Disputes about the meaning of certain laws would remain unsettled. Confusion, and even injustice, might result.

"Ensure Domestic Tranquillity"

In 1786, Daniel Shays marched on a Massachusetts courthouse with hundreds of protesters. Upon hearing about Shays' Rebellion, George Washington warned, "We are fast verging to [absence of government] and confusion!" The uprising made it clear that the national government must have the power to ensure **domestic tranquillity,** or peace at home.

Contents of the Constitution

Chart Skills The Constitution of the United States includes a preamble, 7 articles, and 27 amendments.

1. **Comprehension** (a) What is the subject of Article 4? (b) On what pages would you find the Bill of Rights?

2. **Critical Thinking** (a) Identify as many amendments as you can that deal with voting or elections. (b) Why do you think so many amendments are concerned with this issue?

Civics

"Provide for the Common Defense"

After the American Revolution, the United States had no armed forces to defend itself. Without an army, it could not force British troops to leave the western frontier. Without a navy, it could not prevent Spain from closing part of the Mississippi River to American trade.

The framers of the Constitution realized that armed forces are vital to a nation's survival. Military power helps not only to prevent attack by other nations, but also to protect economic and political interests.

The Constitution gives Congress the power to "raise and support Armies" and to "provide and maintain a Navy." Today, the armed forces include the army, navy, air force, marine corps, and coast guard.

At the same time, the Constitution establishes the principle that the military is under civilian, or nonmilitary, control. Article 2 of the Constitution states that the President is Commander in Chief of the armed forces. Thus, even the highest-ranking military officer must answer to an elected official.

"Promote the General Welfare"

The Constitution gives the national government the means to promote the **general welfare,** or well-being of all the people. The national government has the power to collect taxes. It also has the power to set aside money for programs that will benefit the people.

▲ Logo of the FDA

*B*iography Frances Kelsey

In the early 1960s, a prescription drug named thalidomide caused birth defects in hundreds of children in Europe and Canada. Thanks to Frances Kelsey (left), the drug was never sold in the United States. As an official at the Food and Drug Administration (FDA), Kelsey refused to approve thalidomide without more tests. For her work, Kelsey received a medal from President John Kennedy (right). ★ **How did Kelsey's work fulfill one of the goals of the Constitution?**

The Constitution gives the national government certain powers that allow it to keep the peace. State and local governments can use their own police to enforce national laws within their borders. When crime crosses state borders, however, national police agencies, such as the Federal Bureau of Investigation (FBI), can step in to help protect life and property.

Have you ever seen a news report about a civil emergency, such as a riot or a flood? If so, you probably saw the National Guard keeping the peace. The President can summon such aid if a state or community cannot or will not respond to the emergency.

$ Connections *With* Economics

Government spending for defense and the general welfare has grown dramatically. In 1795, government outlays totaled $7.5 million for a population of 4.6 million people—an average of $1.63 per person. In 1995, the government's outlays totaled $1.5 billion for a population of 263 million people—an average of $5.70 per person.

The workplace provides many examples of how the national government—often in cooperation with state governments—has acted to promote the general welfare. Factory owners are required to meet safety standards for work areas. Workers who are disabled or unemployed receive financial support. Thanks to the Social Security system, all workers are entitled to income upon retirement.

Another way in which the national government helps to promote the general welfare is by supporting education. Education helps to prepare people to become responsible citizens. It also provides tools and training for employment.

Support for education takes many forms. The national government pays for school nutrition programs in local school districts. Many students receive money to help pay the costs of a college education.

The national government also supports scientific research and development to improve the quality of life. For example, researchers at the National Institutes of Health lead the fight against many diseases. Scientists at the Department of Agriculture help farmers to improve their crops and develop better livestock.

"Secure the Blessings of Liberty"

Protection of liberty was a major reason that colonists fought the American Revolution. It is no wonder, then, that the framers made securing liberty a major goal of the Constitution. **Liberty** is the freedom to live as you please, as long as you obey the laws and respect the rights of others.

One way that the Constitution ensures liberty is by limiting the powers of government. For example, the **Bill of Rights,** the first 10 amendments to the Constitution, lists basic rights and freedoms that the government may not take away.

The Constitution provides yet another safeguard of liberty—the right to vote. The people select the leaders who make the laws. At the same time, they can remove from office those leaders who abuse their power.

The "blessings of liberty" have been extended to more Americans since the Constitution was written. Changes in the Constitution have been made to ensure that all Americans—no matter what their sex, religion, or race—have the same rights regarding voting, education, housing, employment, and other opportunities in life.

★ Section 1 Review ★

Recall

1. **Identify** **(a)** Preamble, **(b)** Bill of Rights.
2. **Define** **(a)** federal, **(b)** justice, **(c)** domestic tranquillity, **(d)** general welfare, **(e)** liberty.

Comprehension

3. **(a)** List two goals of the Constitution. **(b)** Describe one way that the national government helps to achieve each of these goals.
4. How does the national system of courts help to ensure justice for all Americans?

5. List two ways the Constitution safeguards the people's liberty.

Critical Thinking and Writing

6. **Evaluating Information** Which goal of the Constitution do you think is most important? Explain.
7. **Linking Past and Present** Are the goals of the nation today the same as those set out in the Preamble to the Constitution?

★ ★

Activity **Teaching Through Pictures** A fifth-grader in your school has to recite the Preamble to the Constitution in a speaking contest. When you hear him practice, you realize he doesn't understand what it means. Draw six pictures with captions that will explain the goals of the Constitution for him.

2 Five Principles of the Constitution

Explore These Questions

As You Read

- What are the five basic principles of the Constitution?
- Why do people adopt a system of representative government?
- How did the framers of the Constitution try to strike a balance between too much and too little government?

Define

- popular sovereignty
- representative government
- bill
- veto
- unconstitutional
- override

SETTING the Scene In 1787, when American leaders were struggling to create the new Constitution, every government in Europe was a monarchy. In most cases, a king or queen made, enforced, and interpreted the laws. Many European rulers would have agreed with Louis XIV, an earlier king of France. *"L'état, c'est moi,"* declared Louis. "I am the state."

Poster urging Americans to vote

The framers of the Constitution knew they had to set up a strong government. At the same time, they sought to keep power from falling into the hands of a privileged few. To achieve this delicate balance, they rested the Constitution on five basic principles: popular sovereignty, limited government, federalism, separation of powers, and checks and balances.

The People Rule

The first three words of the Constitution, "We the people," express the principle of **popular sovereignty.** According to this principle, the people hold the final authority in government.

The Constitution is a contract between the American people and their government. In it, the people grant the government the powers it needs to achieve its goals. At the same time, they limit the power of government by spelling out what the government may not do.

In a large society, not all citizens can take part directly in government. Instead, they exercise their ruling power indirectly by electing public officials to make laws and other decisions for them. This system is called **representative government.**

The people elect public officials by voting in free and frequent elections. Americans today have the constitutional right to vote for members of the House of Representatives (Article 1, Section 2) and for members of the Senate (Amendment 17). The people also elect the members of the electoral college, who, in turn, choose the President (Article 2, Section 1).

The right to vote has been gradually expanded over time. When the Constitution was ratified, only white men over age 21 who owned property could vote. Over the years, other Americans have won the right to vote. Today, all citizens are eligible to vote at the age of 18.

Limited Government

The framers of the Constitution had lived under the harsh rule of the British king. They feared tyranny, or cruel and unjust government. However, the failures of the Articles of Confederation made it clear that the national government had to be strong. How could the framers strike a balance between too much government and too little?

The answer was limited government. According to this principle, the government has only the powers that the people grant it. The Constitution clearly states the powers of the national government. It also states what powers the government does not have.

Guarantees of liberty

The most important limits on government are set out in the Bill of Rights. It guarantees that the government may not take away the individual freedoms of the people. These liberties include freedom of speech, freedom of the press, and freedom of religion.

The Ninth Amendment goes beyond these specific guarantees. It states that the people have rights that are not listed in the Constitution. The Tenth Amendment gives the states or the people any powers not formally granted by the Constitution to the national government.

Federalism

The framers of the Constitution created a strong central government. Yet they also wanted the states to retain much of their power. Like most Americans, they believed that state governments would best understand the special needs and concerns of their citizens. As one defender of the Constitution stated in 1788:

> 66 The two governments act in different manners, and for different purposes—the general government in great national concerns, in which we are interested in common with other members of the Union; the state legislature in our mere local concerns. 99

The principle of federalism divides power between the federal government and state governments. The federal government has the power to deal with national issues. The states have the power to meet local needs.

The Constitution delegates, or assigns, certain powers to the national government. Other powers are reserved, or left, to the states. Still other powers, sometimes called concurrent powers, are shared by the federal and state governments. The chart on page 202 shows how government powers are divided under federalism.

Powers of the states

The Constitution does not list the powers of the states. Instead, it says that all powers not specifically granted to the federal government are reserved to the states (Tenth Amendment). At the same time, it makes clear exactly what powers the states do not have (Article 1, Section 10).

In addition to the reserved powers, the Constitution makes several guarantees to the states. All states must be treated equally in matters of trade (Article 1, Section 9). Each state must respect the laws of other states (Article 4, Section 1). Perhaps most important, all states have representation in the national government.

State License Plates

Under federalism, each state makes its own traffic laws and issues its own drivers' licenses and car registrations. At the same time, a driver's license issued by one state is valid in every other state. ★ **Name two other powers reserved to the states.**

System of Checks and Balances

Executive Branch (President carries out laws) 	**Checks on the Legislative Branch** Can propose laws Can veto laws Can call special sessions of Congress Makes appointments Negotiates foreign treaties	**Checks on the Judicial Branch** Appoints federal judges Can grant pardons to federal offenders
Legislative Branch (Congress makes laws) 	**Checks on the Executive Branch** Can override President's veto Confirms executive appointments Ratifies treaties Can declare war Appropriates money Can impeach and remove President	**Checks on the Judicial Branch** Creates lower federal courts Can impeach and remove judges Can propose amendments to overrule judicial decisions Approves appointments of federal judges
Judicial Branch (Supreme Court interprets laws)	**Check on the Executive Branch** Can declare executive actions unconstitutional	**Check on the Legislative Branch** Can declare acts of Congress unconstitutional

Chart *Skills*

Through the system of checks and balances, each branch of government controls the powers of the other two.

1. **Comprehension** **(a)** Name one check the President has on Congress. **(b)** How can the Supreme Court check Congress?
2. **Critical Thinking** Why do you think the framers of the Constitution gave Congress so many checks on the power of the President?

Civics

The "law of the land"

Federalism creates a working partnership between the national government and the state governments. However, when a dispute arises between them, there is no doubt where the final authority lies. The Constitution is the "supreme law of the land" (Article 6, Section 2). Only federal courts can settle the dispute.

Separation of Powers

The framers wanted to prevent the abuse of power by one person or group. To do so, the Constitution divides the national government into three branches: the legislative, the exec-

utive, and the judicial. Each branch has its own powers and responsibilities. This division of the national government is known as separation of powers.

Article 1 of the Constitution sets up the legislative branch. This branch, called Congress, makes the laws. Congress has two houses: the House of Representatives and the Senate. Its many powers include the power to tax, to coin money, and to declare war.

Article 2 describes the executive branch, which carries out the laws. The President heads the executive branch and appoints officials to help carry out the duties of the office.

Article 3 creates the Supreme Court to head the judicial branch. The Supreme Court interprets and explains laws. Congress may set up lower courts as needed.

Checks and Balances

To prevent one branch of government from gaining too much power, the Constitution sets up a system of checks and balances. Each branch can check, or control, the power of the other two branches. (See the chart on page 220.)

Checks on Congress

Congress has the power to pass **bills,** or proposed laws. However, the President can influence the lawmaking process by proposing new bills or by pushing members of Congress to vote for or against a bill. The President can also check Congress by **vetoing,** or rejecting, a bill. The vetoed bill then goes back to Congress.

The Supreme Court has the power to rule whether a law is **unconstitutional,** or not permitted by the Constitution. The power to declare laws unconstitutional is one check the Supreme Court has on Congress. Any law declared unconstitutional by the Court cannot take effect.

Checks on the President

Congress has several checks on the powers of the President. For example, the President is commander in chief of the armed forces, but only Congress has the power to declare war. In addition, the President has the power to make treaties with foreign nations. However, the Senate must ratify all treaties.

Congress may also check the President by **overriding,** or setting aside, a presidential veto. In this way, a bill can become a law without the President's signature. Two thirds of each house must vote to override a veto. The Supreme Court can also check the President by declaring that an act of the President is unconstitutional.

Checks on the courts

Both the President and Congress have several checks on the power of the judicial branch. The President appoints all federal judges, while the Senate must approve the President's court appointments. In addition, Congress has the power to remove federal judges from office if they are found guilty of wrongdoing. Congress may also propose a constitutional amendment to overrule a judicial decision.

★ Section 2 Review ★

Recall

1. **Define** (a) popular sovereignty, (b) representative government, (c) bill, (d) veto, (e) unconstitutional, (f) override.

Comprehension

2. (a) Identify the five basic principles of the Constitution. (b) Describe two of them.
3. (a) Explain how representative government works. (b) Why do people in a democracy adopt this system?

4. (a) Why did the framers of the Constitution set up three branches of government? (b) How does the Constitution prevent any branch from becoming too powerful?

Critical Thinking and Writing

5. **Synthesizing Information** How are the principles of popular sovereignty and limited government related?
6. **Analyzing Ideas** Explain the following statement: The Constitution sets up a government of laws, not of people.

Activity **Making a Chart** Working with a partner or your class, create a chart that gives examples of ways in which the five basic principles of the Constitution protect you and your community.

3 A Living Document

As You Read

Explore These Questions
- What is the formal process for changing the Constitution?
- What is the purpose of the Bill of Rights?
- What informal changes have been made to the Constitution?

Define
- amendment
- precedent
- Cabinet
- judicial review

Identify
- First Amendment
- Fourth Amendment
- Sixth Amendment
- Elastic Clause
- Commerce Clause

SETTING the Scene The framers of the Constitution realized that the nation would grow and change. With this in mind, they created a living Constitution—one that could be altered and improved to meet new conditions and challenges as they arose. As George Washington commented:

66 I do not think we are more inspired, have more wisdom, or possess more virtue than those who will come after us. 99

Formal Changes to the Constitution

The framers spelled out a process for making **amendments,** or formal written changes, to the Constitution. Amending the Constitution is not easy, however. It requires two difficult steps: proposal and ratification. (See the chart on page 223.)

Proposing an amendment

Article 5 describes two methods for proposing amendments. Two thirds of each house of Congress can vote to propose an amendment. Or two thirds of the state legislatures can demand that Congress summon a national "convention for proposing amendments."

So far, only the first method—a vote by Congress—has been used. As experts have pointed out, the Constitution does not give guidelines for a national convention. Who should set the agenda? How should dele-gates be selected? Such questions probably would cause much delay and confusion.

Ratifying an amendment

Article 5 also outlines two methods of ratifying a proposed amendment. Either three fourths of the state legislatures or three fourths of the states meeting in special conventions must approve the amendment. Congress decides which method of ratification to use.

So far, only the Twenty-first Amendment was ratified by state conventions. All other amendments were ratified by state legislatures. In recent years, Congress has set a time limit for ratification. The limit today is seven years, but it may be extended.

The 27 Amendments

As you can see, the amendment process is a difficult one. Since 1789, more than 9,000 amendments have been introduced in Congress. Yet, only 27 amendments have been ratified!

The Bill of Rights

The original Constitution did not list basic freedoms of the people. In fact, several states refused to ratify the Constitution until they were promised that a bill of rights would be added. Those states wanted to ensure that the national government would not be able to take away people's basic freedoms.

The Bill of Rights, the first 10 amendments to the Constitution, was ratified in 1791. (See the chart on page 215.)

You will recognize many of the freedoms in the Bill of Rights. The **First Amendment** protects your right to worship and speak freely and to hold peaceful meetings. The **Fourth Amendment** protects you from "unreasonable" search and seizure of your home and property. The **Sixth Amendment** guarantees you the right to a trial by jury.

The protections of the Bill of Rights extend into many areas of your life. Suppose that you sent a letter to a newspaper criticizing the governor. Without the First Amendment protection of free speech, the governor might order your arrest. Without the Sixth Amendment, you might even be imprisoned for years without a trial.

Amendments 11 through 27

Only 17 amendments have been ratified since 1791. Several of these amendments reflect changing ideas about equality.

Amendments 13 through 15—the so-called Civil War amendments—were passed to protect the rights of former slaves. The Thirteenth Amendment ended slavery. The Fourteenth Amendment guaranteed citizenship and constitutional rights to African Americans. The Fifteenth Amendment guaranteed African Americans the right to vote.

Equality was also the goal of two later amendments. The Nineteenth Amendment gave women the right to vote. The Twenty-sixth Amendment set age 18 as the minimum voting age. The chart on page 215 lists Amendments 11 through 27. For more information about the amendments, refer to the page numbers shown on the chart.

Informal Changes

The language of the Constitution provides a general outline rather than specific details about the national government. Over time, this flexible language has allowed the government to adapt to the changing needs of the nation.

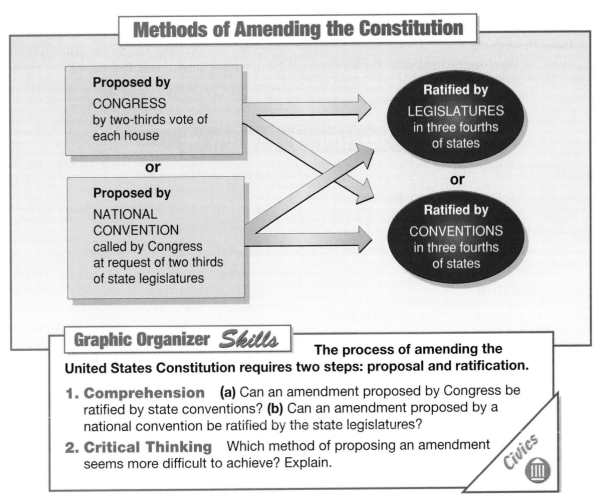

Methods of Amending the Constitution

Proposed by
CONGRESS
by two-thirds vote of each house

or

Proposed by
NATIONAL CONVENTION
called by Congress at request of two thirds of state legislatures

Ratified by
LEGISLATURES
in three fourths of states

or

Ratified by
CONVENTIONS
in three fourths of states

Graphic Organizer *Skills*   The process of amending the United States Constitution requires two steps: proposal and ratification.

1. **Comprehension** **(a)** Can an amendment proposed by Congress be ratified by state conventions? **(b)** Can an amendment proposed by a national convention be ratified by the state legislatures?

2. **Critical Thinking** Which method of proposing an amendment seems more difficult to achieve? Explain.

Civics

New powers for Congress

The framers knew that they could not foresee the future. To deal with this problem, Article 1, Section 8, Clause 18, gives Congress the power to make all laws that shall be "necessary and proper" to carry out the powers of the national government. This so-called **Elastic Clause** has allowed Congress to stretch its power to pass laws.

Still another clause of the Constitution has allowed Congress to extend its powers. Article 1, Section 8, Clause 3, gives Congress the power to "regulate" trade with other nations and between the states.

Armed with the **Commerce Clause** and the Elastic Clause, Congress has been able to keep pace with change. For example, it has passed laws that regulate the airline industry, television, nuclear energy, and genetic engineering.

A more powerful executive

The Constitution does not describe in detail the powers of the President. Some Presidents, however, have taken actions or made decisions that set a **precedent,** or example, for later Presidents.

George Washington set one such precedent. The Constitution does not state that the President may appoint a **Cabinet,** or group of close advisers. President Washington assumed the power to do so on his own. Every President since then has followed his lead.

In national emergencies, Presidents have expanded their constitutional role. During the Great Depression, President Franklin Roosevelt expanded the size and power of the executive branch to propose and carry out programs that would restore the national economy.

A broader role for the judiciary

The Supreme Court can decide whether acts of a President or laws passed by Congress are unconstitutional. This power is known as **judicial review.**

The Constitution does not list judicial review as a power of the judicial branch. Like the unstated powers of the President, judicial review is implied in the words and structure of the Constitution. Article 3, Section 2, states that the Supreme Court has the right to hear "all cases . . . arising under this Constitution." In the case of *Marbury* v. *Madison,* an early Supreme Court decision interpreted Article 3, Section 2, to mean that the Supreme Court has the right to decide whether any law violates the Constitution.

★ Section 3 Review ★

Recall

1. **Identify** **(a)** First Amendment, **(b)** Fourth Amendment, **(c)** Sixth Amendment, **(d)** Elastic Clause, **(e)** Commerce Clause.

2. **Define** **(a)** amendment, **(b)** precedent, **(c)** Cabinet, **(d)** judicial review.

Comprehension

3. Describe the process for amending the United States Constitution.

4. List four rights protected by the Bill of Rights.

5. **(a)** How did George Washington expand the powers of the President? **(b)** How did Franklin Roosevelt expand the President's powers during the Great Depression?

Critical Thinking and Writing

6. **Drawing Conclusions** Why do you think there have been more informal changes than formal changes to the Constitution?

7. **Defending a Position** Do you think the process of amending the Constitution should be made simpler? Defend your position.

★ ★

Activity **Writing an Essay** Choose one of the amendments described in this section. In a brief essay, describe your thoughts and feelings about that amendment and what it means to you.

4 ★ The National Government at Work

Explore These Questions
- What are the roles of Congress?
- What jobs does the President do?
- How is the federal court system organized?

Define
- appropriate
- standing committee
- joint committee
- impeach
- constituent
- executive agreement
- appeal
- opinion
- dissenting opinion

Identify
- House of Representatives
- Senate
- Supreme Court

SETTING the Scene On October 10, 1788, the last Congress under the Articles of Confederation transacted its final business. By September of the following year, the Presidential electors had chosen George Washington as the first President of the United States, the first Congress under the Constitution had met in New York City, and the Federal Judiciary Act had provided for the organization of the United States Supreme Court. The government of the United States, as set up by the Constitution, was in place.

More than 200 years later, Americans still live under this three-branched government set up by the Constitution. Each branch has its own clearly defined powers. Together, they provide us with a government of laws.

The Legislative Branch

Congress, the legislative branch of government, is made up of two houses: the House of Representatives and the Senate. Together, the two houses have the power to make the laws that govern all 50 states. At the same time, the states have a say in making those laws.

Two houses of Congress

The larger house, the **House of Representatives,** currently seats 435 members. The number of representatives for each state

The Congressional Record reports events in Congress. ➤

is determined according to that state's population. The more people who live in a state, the greater its number of representatives. Each state, however, is guaranteed at least one representative.*

Representatives serve for two-year terms. As a result, the entire House is up for election every even-numbered year. Congressional terms are numbered consecutively. The Congress that served from 1789 to 1791 is known as the First Congress. The Congress serving from 1999 to 2001 is the One Hundred Sixth Congress.

The **Senate,** the smaller house, has 100 members. Each state, no matter how large or small its population, has two senators. Senators serve for six-year terms. The terms are staggered, however. As a result, one third of the Senate are up for election every two years.

Powers of Congress

The chief job of Congress is to make the nation's laws. A new law first appears as a

---

*Guam, the Virgin Islands, American Samoa, and Washington, D.C., each elect a delegate to the House, while Puerto Rico elects a resident commissioner. However, these delegates are not voting members of the House.

Federal Officeholders

Office	Number	Term	Selection	Requirements
Representative	At least 1 per state; based on population	2 years	Elected by voters of congressional district	Age 25 or over Citizen for 7 years Resident of state in which elected
Senator	2 per state	6 years	Original Constitution—elected by state legislature Amendment 17—elected by voters	Age 30 or over Citizen for 9 years Resident of state in which elected
President and Vice President	1	4 years	Elected by electoral college	Age 35 or over Natural-born citizen Resident of U.S. for 14 years
Supreme Court Justice	9	Life	Appointed by President	No requirements in Constitution

Chart Skills The Constitution details the number, length of term, method of selection, and requirements for officeholders in the three branches of government.

1. Comprehension **(a)** At what age can you be elected to the Senate? The House of Representatives? **(b)** How long may a Supreme Court Justice remain in office?

2. Critical Thinking Why do you think the requirements for President and Vice President are the same?

Civics

proposal called a bill. The bill must be passed by both houses of Congress and signed by the President to become law. The chart on page 227 shows the steps a bill must pass through before becoming a law.

Congress has another equally important power. It decides what laws or programs will receive funds. The federal government cannot spend money on any program unless Congress **appropriates** it, or sets it aside for a special purpose. In this way, Congress controls how much money the government spends, whether for military aircraft, national highways, or school lunches.

Congressional committees

During the first session of Congress, 31 bills were proposed by both houses. Today, thousands of bills are introduced every year in Congress. Clearly, it would be impossible for each member of Congress to study and make recommendations about every bill. This job is reserved for committees.

The House of Representatives and the Senate each have **standing committees.** These are permanent committees assigned to study specific issues such as agriculture, labor, and energy. They are often broken up into subcommittees that examine certain problems in depth.

Congress may sometimes create a **joint committee,** or committees that include both House and Senate members. One of the most important kinds of joint committee is the conference committee. Its task is to settle differences between the House and the Senate versions of the same bill. Members of a conference committee try to find a middle ground and to agree on the language of the bill. Compromise is often difficult.

Skills FOR LIFE

Critical Thinking	Managing Information	Communication	Maps, Charts, and Graphs

Reading a Flowchart

How Will I Use This Skill?

A flowchart is a type of graphic organizer. It uses boxes and arrows to guide you step by step through a development or process. Learning to read a flowchart can help you understand even the most complicated processes—from programming a VCR to running for public office.

LEARN the Skill

❶ Identify the process described by the flowchart.

❷ Locate the starting point of the process. (This is the box with no arrow leading toward it.) Some flowcharts may have more than one starting point, since more than one part of a process is being tracked to the end point.

❸ Follow the steps of the process by following the arrows to the end point.

PRACTICE the Skill

❶ What process does the flowchart below describe?

❷ (a) Where can a bill be introduced? (b) Why are there two starting points on this flowchart?

❸ (a) What happens to a bill after it is introduced? (b) At what point in the process do the work of the Senate and the House come together? (c) What happens next?

APPLY the Skill

Create a flowchart to describe the steps of a process you know well. You might show how to play a game, how to repair something, or how to prepare a meal. Show your flowchart to some friends. See if they can understand the process by looking at your chart.

How a Bill Becomes a Law

Introduction	Committee Action	Floor Action	Enactment Into Law
Introduced in House	Referred to House committee	House debates and passes its form of bill	Conference committee reaches compromise on single form of bill
Introduced in Senate	Referred to Senate committee	Senate debates and passes its form of bill	
		House and Senate approve compromise	President signs bill into law

The United States Capitol Building

History is still happening at the Capitol Building. Since November 1800, the Capitol has been the meeting place of the United States Congress. Each year, millions of people visit the parts of the Capitol open to the public. If you have a pass from your representative or senator, you can even visit the House or Senate chambers and watch lawmakers in action. Funeral ceremonies for Presidents and other outstanding Americans are held in the Great Rotunda under the famous Capitol dome.

★ *To learn more about this historic site, write:* The Capitol, Washington, DC 19106.

◄ *The Capitol Building in Washington, D.C.*

Passing a bill requires the cooperation of many individuals. For example, a recent trade bill was 1,000 pages long. It required the efforts of 200 members of Congress, working in 17 subcommittees, to get it passed. Most bills introduced in Congress do not meet with such success. In fact, more than 90 percent of all the bills introduced are defeated in committees.

Other roles of Congress

Members of Congress have duties other than serving on committees and making laws. They also guard the public trust. For example, the House of Representatives can **impeach,** or bring a formal charge of wrongdoing against, the President or another federal official. The Senate acts as a court to try the accused. Congress also acts as a "watchdog" by supervising the way the executive branch carries out the laws.

Members of Congress must also respond to the special needs of their states. Responsible representatives and senators must remember their **constituents,** or the people who elected them. They do this by supporting bills that have a direct impact on the people "back home." Such bills might include promoting new post offices, improving highways, and helping to pay for local education programs.

The Executive Branch

The framers created an executive branch to carry out the laws. However, they left out details about the President's powers. They thought that Congress would be the central branch of government except in times of war and other emergencies. Over the years, the powers of the President have been increased or decreased, depending on the needs of the time. Still, Americans expect the President to fill certain roles.

Roles of the President

The main role of the President is to carry out the nation's laws. As chief executive, the President oversees the many departments, agencies, and commissions that help to accomplish this task.

The President directs the nation's foreign policy. Three important powers allow the President to influence relations with other countries. They are the powers to appoint ambassadors, make treaties, and enter into **executive agreements.** Executive agreements are informal agreements with other heads of state, usually dealing with trade. Unlike treaties, they do not require Senate approval.

The President is the highest-ranking officer in the armed forces. As commander in chief, the President can appoint and remove top military commanders. The President may also use the armed forces to deal with crises both at home and abroad. (However, only Congress has the power to declare war on another country.)

As the nation's chief legislator, the President suggests new laws and works for their passage. In this role, the President often meets with members of Congress to win their support. Sometimes, the President campaigns for public support through television or radio speeches and press conferences. The President also can use persuasion to oppose a bill. In this case, however, the President's most powerful weapon is the power to veto a bill.

The President is the living symbol of the nation. In this role, the President represents all American citizens at many occasions. For example, the President welcomes visiting foreign leaders, makes speeches to commemorate national holidays, and gives medals to national heroes. (See the photograph on page 216.)

The American people also see the President as the chief symbol of the condition of the nation, even though this responsibility is shared with Congress and the judiciary. In describing this situation, former President Jimmy Carter declared that "When things go bad you get entirely too much blame," and "when things go good, you get entirely too much credit."

Executive agencies and departments

The nation's laws cover a broad range of concerns—defense, housing, crime, and pollution, to name a few. To carry out these laws and to perform other duties, the President needs the help of millions of government workers and assistants.

Presidents at Work

Under the Constitution, the President commands the armed forces and directs foreign policy. At left, President Bill Clinton meets with Tony Blair, prime minister of Great Britain. Above, President George Bush visits American troops in Saudi Arabia. ★ **Describe two other roles of the President.**

The Supreme Court

Here, the 1998 Justices of the Supreme Court pose for an annual photograph. Standing, left to right, are Ruth Bader Ginsburg, David Souter, Clarence Thomas, and Stephen Breyer. Sitting, left to right, are Antonin Scalia, John Paul Stevens, Chief Justice William Rehnquist, Sandra Day O'Connor, and Anthony Kennedy.
★ **What kinds of cases does the Supreme Court hear?**

One group of assistants, the Executive Office, includes many agencies and individuals. They range from the Vice President to the Office of Management and Budget, which prepares the total budget of the United States.

The President's Cabinet, called secretaries, are the heads of executive departments. Today, the President relies on 14 executive departments—among them, the Departments of Defense, Commerce, Justice, Labor, and Energy. Each department has many concerns. For example, the Department of Agriculture deals with food quality, crop improvement, and nutrition. The Department of Transportation establishes rules for speed limits, automobile exhaust systems, and highway and vehicle safety.

More than 30 independent executive agencies also help the President carry out duties. For example, the Central Intelligence Agency (CIA) provides the President with secret information about the world's trouble spots. The National Aeronautics and Space Administration (NASA) is in charge of the nation's space program.

Eleven independent regulatory commissions enforce national laws. They establish rules, rates, and standards for trade, business, science, and transportation. For example, the Federal Trade Commission (FTC) enforced the federal law banning "false or misleading advertising" by ruling that ciga-rettes may not be advertised as "kind" to your throat.

Finally, there are government corporations. There are at least 60 government corporations today. They include the United States Postal Service, the Tennessee Valley Authority, and Amtrak.

The Judicial Branch

Article 3 of the Constitution gives the judicial power of the United States to the Supreme Court and to lower courts that Congress may set up. Under the Judiciary Act of 1789, Congress created the system of federal courts that still operates today.

Lower courts

Most federal cases are first heard in the district courts. These courts are located in more than 90 districts around the country. Cases brought to these courts may involve matters of criminal law, such as kidnapping and murder, or matters of civil law, such as bankruptcy and divorce. In district courts, decisions are made by either a judge or a jury, which is a panel of citizens.

Every citizen has the right to **appeal** a decision, or ask that it be reviewed by a higher court. These higher courts of appeal are called circuit, or appellate, courts. The United States has 13 circuit courts of appeal.

Circuit courts operate differently from district courts. A panel of three judges reviews each case. The judges decide if rules of trial procedure were followed in the original trial. If errors did occur, the circuit court may reverse, or overturn, the original decision. Or it may send back the case to the district court for a new trial.

Supreme Court

The **Supreme Court** is the highest court in the United States. Americans depend upon the Supreme Court to settle disputes, interpret the law, and protect their guaranteed rights. The Court is made up of a Chief Justice and eight Associate Justices. The President appoints the Supreme Court Justices, but Congress must approve the appointments. In about one out of five cases, Congress rejects the President's appointment and a new nomination must be made. Appointments to the Supreme Court are for life.

Only two kinds of cases can begin in the Supreme Court. One kind involves disputes between states. The other involves foreign ambassadors. In other cases, the Supreme Court serves as a final court of appeals. It hears cases that have been tried and appealed as far as law permits in lower courts.

The Supreme Court hears only issues about the Constitution, federal law, or treaties. It selects only about 120 cases from the 4,000 or more requests it receives each year. Most of the cases involve laws written in unclear language. The Court must decide what each law means, whom it affects, and whether it is constitutional.

A Supreme Court decision rests on a simple majority vote of at least five Justices. A member of the majority writes an **opinion,** or official statement of the legal reasons for the Court's decision. Sometimes, a member of the minority strongly disagrees with the majority ruling. That Justice may write a **dissenting opinion,** explaining the reasons for the disagreement. Justice Oliver Wendell Holmes, Jr., wrote so many dissenting opinions that he became known as the "Great Dissenter."

Supreme Court decisions are final. There are no other courts of appeal. If Congress strongly disagrees with a Supreme Court decision, however, it can take other action. It can pass a modified version of the law that will meet the Court's objections. Congress can also propose an amendment to the Constitution.

★ Section 4 Review ★

Recall

1. **Identify** (a) House of Representatives, (b) Senate, (c) Supreme Court.
2. **Define** (a) appropriate, (b) standing committee, (c) joint committee, (d) impeach, (e) constituent, (f) executive agreement, (g) appeal, (h) opinion, (i) dissenting opinion.

Comprehension

3. What are the two most important powers of Congress?
4. (a) How does the President influence legislation?

(b) What three powers enable the President to direct foreign policy?
5. (a) What is the role of circuit courts? (b) What is the role of the Supreme Court?

Critical Thinking and Writing

6. **Ranking** Review the subsection "Roles of the President." List the President's roles. Then rank the roles in order of importance. Be prepared to support your ranking.
7. **Analyzing Ideas** Why is it important for Congress to approve the President's choices for Supreme Court Justices?

Activity **Making a Diagram** Make a graphic organizer with three branches. Fill in the chart to show the roles of each branch of government and the smaller parts that make them up.

5 ★ Good Citizenship

★ ★

Explore These Questions

- How was the Bill of Rights limited?
- How did the Supreme Court use the Fourteenth Amendment to expand citizens' rights?
- What are the rights and responsibilities of citizens?

Define

- due process

Identify

- *Gideon* v. *Wainwright*

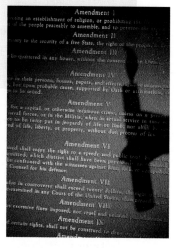

Plaque listing ➤
the Bill of Rights

SETTING the Scene Americans first proclaimed their rights in the Declaration of Independence. In it, they declared boldly:

> 66 All men are created equal; . . . they are endowed by their Creator with certain unalienable rights, that among these are life, liberty, and the pursuit of happiness. 99

Since the birth of the nation, Americans have struggled to reach this ideal of basic rights for all. They have learned, however, that along with the rights of citizenship come responsibilities.

Citizens' Rights

The Constitution originally protected some individual rights by limiting government actions. For example, Article 6, Section 3, prevents the government from making religion a requirement for public service. Article 1, Section 9, prohibits Congress from passing a law punishing an act that was not illegal at the time it was committed.

Bill of Rights

Many Americans, however, demanded a more specific list of rights. In response, the first Congress drew up and the states ratified the Bill of Rights.

Still, the Bill of Rights applied only to the federal government. States were free to restrict or deny basic rights of many people, in-cluding women, African Americans, and Asian Americans. At times, the federal government also restricted rights through laws and court decisions.

Fourteenth Amendment

An amendment passed in 1868 paved the way for a major expansion of rights. The Fourteenth Amendment states that persons born or naturalized in the United States are citizens of both the nation and their state. No state may limit the rights of citizens or deny citizens **due process,** or a fair hearing or trial. States are also forbidden to deny citizens "equal protection of the laws."

Over the years, the Supreme Court has decided that the Fourteenth Amendment's guarantee of due process and equal protection includes rights listed in the Bill of Rights. States cannot deny citizens the protections of the Bill of Rights.

For example, in the 1960s, the Supreme Court ruled that due process includes the Sixth Amendment right to representation by a lawyer. The case of *Gideon* **v.** *Wainwright* involved a poor Florida man who had been convicted of breaking and entering. The judge hearing the case had refused the defendant's request for a lawyer. The Supreme Court ruled that a state court must appoint a lawyer for any defendant who cannot afford to hire one.

232 ★ Chapter 8

What are basic rights?

As the Ninth Amendment states, the people have rights beyond those listed in the Constitution. Americans still strive to define these rights. Some people believe that a citizen's basic rights include the opportunity to get a good education and to find a job. Others argue that these rights are not guaranteed by the Constitution.

Citizens' Responsibilities

Like every citizen, you must do your part to safeguard your rights. At the same time, you must accept the civic responsibilities that are a part of living in a free and democratic society.

Know your rights

You cannot protect your rights unless you know what they are. Books, government pamphlets, and groups such as the League of Women Voters, the National Association for the Advancement of Colored People (NAACP), and the Legal Aid Society can give you information about your rights and the law.

You must also know the limits of your rights. A popular saying states, "Your right to swing your fist ends where my nose begins." As part of your civic responsibilities, you must respect the rights of others. After all, your rights are only as safe as your neighbor's. If you abuse or allow abuse of another citizen's rights, your own rights may be at risk someday.

Become involved

Good government depends on good leaders. Therefore, citizens have the responsibility to exercise their right to vote. A good citizen studies the candidates and the issues in order to make responsible choices.

Linking United States and the World

United States

South Africa

Getting Out the Vote

Voting is both a right and a responsibility. Yet, many take this right for granted. In 1996, only 48.8 percent of Americans who were eligible to vote actually voted. In 1994, when South Africa's black majority won the right to vote for the first time (right), 86.9 percent of eligible voters cast their ballots. ★ **Why do you think South Africans were so eager to vote? What point is the cartoon on the left making?**

Why Study History?

Because Citizens Have Responsibilities

★ ★

Historical Background

For many Americans, providing unpaid community service is an important civic responsibility. In the 1770s, cities like Boston and Philadelphia had volunteer fire departments. During the Revolution, thousands of Americans volunteered to serve in state militias. By the mid-1800s, women took a leading role in charitable organizations that cared for the sick and needy.

In April 1997, the Presidents' Summit for America's Future encouraged a national spirit of volunteerism. At the meeting, President Bill Clinton said good citizenship meant that you "serve in your community to help make it a better place."

Connections to Today

Adults are not the only volunteers. Young people can also find ways to serve their community. Consider, for example, the story of David Levitt.

David Levitt was a sixth grader in Florida when he read about Kentucky Harvest. This organization collected leftover food from restaurants and distributed it to people in need. David had an idea. He had seen how much unused food was thrown out in his school cafeteria. Why not start a similar program himself?

David presented his plan to the local school board and got permission to start a food distribution program. His first delivery was cartons of milk and bags of salad. Over the next few years, David sent more than 250,000 pounds of cafeteria leftovers to

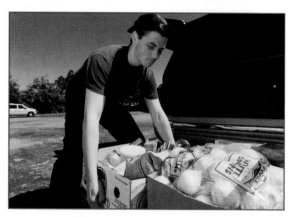

David Levitt collects food for the needy.

shelters and food banks all over Florida. While still in middle school, he was invited to the White House and awarded a medal for his volunteer work.

Connections to You

There are many ways for you to volunteer in your community. You can participate in a food or clothing drive. You can help clean up a neighborhood park. Perhaps you would like to tutor a younger child or help at a local hospital or senior citizen center. To learn more about these and other opportunities, look up community organizations in your local telephone directory.

1. **Comprehension** **(a)** How did President Clinton define good citizenship? **(b)** How did David Levitt help his local community?

2. **Critical Thinking** How might volunteering affect the cost of government?

Writing a Proposal Decide on a volunteer program that might be helpful in your community. Describe the benefits of the program and how it could be set up. Write your plan as a formal written proposal.

The First Amendment guarantees you the freedom to speak, write, sign petitions, and meet with others freely. You can use those freedoms not only to defend your rights but also to take a stand on political and community issues. It is important to remember that such expressions should be truthful and peaceful. Supreme Court Justice Oliver Wendell Holmes, Jr., once warned:

> 66 The most [strict] protection of free speech would not protect a man in falsely shouting fire in a theater and causing a panic. 99

Responsible citizens keep informed about national and community issues. In addition to reading newspapers, you can attend local meetings. At a town council meeting, for example, you might learn about proposed solutions to local health issues or pollution problems. Groups such as the League of Women Voters may sponsor debates by candidates for political office.

The Bill of Rights guarantees citizens the right to a trial by jury. Every citizen, in turn, has the responsibility to serve on juries when called. Serving on a jury is a serious duty. Jurors must take time out from their work and personal lives. Deciding the guilt or innocence of the accused can be difficult.

Civic Values

Citizens enter into a contract with the government. They give the government the power to make certain laws. In return, they expect government to protect the well-being of society. As part of this contract, the government has the power to set penalties if laws are broken.

Like other citizens, you have a responsibility to obey the laws and respect the rights of others. For example, you should not steal, damage property, or harm someone.

Volunteer

Responsible citizens offer their time and talents to help others and to improve the community. For example, you can join or start a group to clean up parks or to serve food to senior citizens. You can also take part in a walk-a-thon or bike-a-thon to raise money for a worthy cause. Many volunteer fire departments have junior divisions.

Defend the nation

At age 18, all men must report their name, age, and address to the government. In time of war, the government may call them to serve in the armed forces. Many young citizens feel the duty to enlist in the military on their own.

★ Section 5 Review ★

Recall

1. **Identify** *Gideon* v. *Wainwright.*
2. **Define** due process.

Comprehension

3. Why were some states able to ignore the guarantees of the Bill of Rights?
4. **(a)** What does the Fourteenth Amendment guarantee? **(b)** How did the Supreme Court expand the guarantees of this amendment?

5. List three responsibilities of citizenship.

Critical Thinking and Writing

6. **Analyzing Ideas** Reread the words of Justice Holmes, above. How does this statement relate to the need to balance the rights of the individual and civic responsibility?
7. **Solving Problems** Why must a citizen of a democracy learn how to compromise?

★ ★

Activity **Making a Poster** Help people in your school and community become better citizens. Create a poster that encourages people to do one of the following: know their rights, vote, become involved in government, volunteer in the community, or join the armed services.

★ Sum It Up ★

Section 1 Goals of the Constitution
▶ The goals of the Constitution include establishing justice, keeping peace at home, and defending the nation.
▶ The Constitution helps guarantee the rights and liberties of American citizens.

Section 2 Five Principles of the Constitution
▶ The five basic principles of the Constitution are popular sovereignty, limited government, federalism, separation of powers, and checks and balances.

Section 3 A Living Document
▶ The process for amending the Constitution was made difficult on purpose.
▶ Flexible language has allowed informal changes to the Constitution.

Section 4 The National Government at Work
▶ Congress, made up of the Senate and House of Representatives, makes the nation's laws.
▶ The duties of the President include carrying out the nation's laws, directing foreign policy, and commanding the armed forces.
▶ The judicial branch, headed by the Supreme Court, interprets the laws.

Section 5 Good Citizenship
▶ Over time, the protections of the Bill of Rights were extended to all Americans.
▶ Citizens have responsibilities, including obeying the law and voting.

CD-ROM Review For additional review of the major ideas of Chapter 8, see *Guide to the Essentials of American History* or *Interactive Student Tutorial CD-ROM,* which contains interactive review activities, graphic organizers, and practice tests.

▢ Reviewing the Chapter

Define These Terms
Match each term with the correct definition.

Column 1	Column 2
1. federal	a. proposed law
2. bill	b. put money aside
3. general welfare	c. set aside a veto
4. appropriate	d. national
5. override	e. well-being of all the people

Explore the Main Ideas
1. How may the government promote the general welfare?
2. Describe how the Constitution is a contract.
3. How does the Elastic Clause allow for informal changes in the Constitution?
4. Give three examples of checks and balances.
5. What rights and responsibilities do citizens have in the justice system?

▢ Chart Activity

Look at the chart and answer the following questions:
1. What percentage of Americans vote in presidential elections? In local elections? **2.** Are people more likely to know the names of their representatives or their senators? **Critical Thinking** Why do you think so few Americans attend public meetings? What can happen if citizens do not participate in government?

Political Participation and Awareness

Percentage of Americans who...	
Vote in presidential elections	50%
Vote in congressional elections	35–40
Know name of congressional representative	36
Know names of both U.S. senators	29
Occasionally contact local officials	28
Vote in local elections	10–30
Occasionally attend public meetings	19
Give money to candidate or party	13

Source: Selected polls, including Gallup, *Denver Post* Poll, University of Michigan, and *The New York Times, 1989.*

Critical Thinking and Writing

1. **Exploring Unit Themes** **Rights and Liberties** How might our government be different today if there were no Tenth Amendment?
2. **Understanding Chronology** **(a)** In what order did the following groups win the right to vote: women; people 18 to 21 years old; African American men? **(b)** Who could vote for President in 1964 who could not do so in 1960?
3. **Linking Past and Present** The federal government recently adopted rules about a new type of nationwide television broadcasting that will provide sharper, clearer pictures. Explain how the government gets its power to make such rules.
4. **Defending a Position** Why is keeping informed an important responsibility of citizenship? Give reasons and examples.

Using Primary Sources

Long after the Constitution was ratified, Thomas Jefferson commented:

> 66 As the [human mind] becomes more developed, . . . as new discoveries are made, . . . and manners and opinions changed with the change of circumstances, [constitutions] must advance also, and keep pace with the times. We might as well require a man to wear still the coat which fitted him when a boy, as civilized society to remain ever under the [government] of their . . . ancestors. 99

Source: *Patterns in American History,* ed. Alexander De Conde et al., 1965.

Recognizing Points of View **(a)** What did Jefferson think happens as time goes on? **(b)** How do you think he felt about the process of amending the Constitution? Explain.

ACTIVITY BANK

Interdisciplinary Activity

Exploring the Arts Find out more about the procedure of a courtroom. If possible, visit a courthouse or watch a trial on television. Then, with several classmates, write a script and conduct a mock trial.

Career Skills Activity

Fiction Writer Write a short story about what might happen if people had no political rights. Set the story in the United States or in another country.

Citizenship Activity

Holding a Panel Discussion Organize a panel discussion to consider a proposal for a new constitutional amendment. You might examine the idea of limiting the President to a single six-year term, changing the voting age, or another issue.

Internet Activity

Use the Internet to find sites dealing with the agencies of the United States government. Choose one agency and prepare a report on its activities. Questions you should answer are: When was the agency founded? What does it do? What branch does it serve? How many employees does it have? How much money does it spend every year?

EYEWITNESS Journal

You are the President of the United States. In three EYEWITNESS JOURNAL entries, describe some of the kinds of activities you have to perform and what you think about your job. Use information from the chapter to help think up events.

History Through **Literature**

Valley Forge

by Maxwell Anderson

Introduction

For 30 years, Maxwell Anderson was one of the most respected American playwrights. Many of his dramas were based on history. His 1934 play *Valley Forge* describes the hardships the Continental Army faced during the winter of 1777–1778. In this scene, George Washington hears some of the complaints of his troops.

Vocabulary

Before you read the selection, find the meanings of these words in a dictionary: **lenient, commissary, savvy, munitions.**

TEAGUE: General Washington!

WASHINGTON: What is it?

TEAGUE: These here new regulations about men going home. Going home without leave. They say it's seventy-five lashes if they catch you now. Why is that?

WASHINGTON: The traditional penalty for desertion is shooting at sunrise. We've been more lenient here.

TEAGUE: But look, General Washington, it don't make sense. It don't stand to reason—

NICK: Do you want to talk your neck into a rope?

WASHINGTON: Let him say what's on his mind.

TEAGUE: Well, here it is: I'm going hungry here and my woman's going hungry at home. You let me go home for the winter, and you won't have to feed me, and that relieves the commissary. I rustle some wild meat for the younguns and the old woman, and they don't starve and I don't starve. More'n that, everybody knows there's two or three thousand men gone home already for that same reason, and if they was here now they'd be chewing the bark off the second-growth birch like so many cottontails. I don't hold it against you and I don't hold it against anybody because I don't know who in thunder to hold it against, but there's nothing to eat here.

ALCOCK: Stow it, will you? The dog ate the stuff, and he isn't dead yet.

TEAGUE: It ain't that I'm afraid of a good fight. A good fight's ham and eggs to me. Me and my boy here, we make for home every winter when the grub gets scarce, and we come back every spring when the fighting starts. We're coming back next spring, and every spring, till we chase the...redcoats clear out of Chesapeake Bay, and across the Atlantic Ocean and right up a lamppost in London town! Fightin's fine, but sitting here and starving down to a hide and buttons—I don't savvy it.

WASHINGTON: What is your name, sir?

TEAGUE: Teague, sir. Teague's my name.

WASHINGTON: Well, Master Teague, if they catch you they'll give you seventy-five

The March to Valley Forge by William B. Trego shows General George Washington on horseback, reviewing his troops. At Valley Forge, Washington had to plead with local merchants and farmers for food supplies. ★ **Why does Trego show one of the soldiers taking off his hat to Washington?**

lashes, and that's a good deal to take and live. On the other hand you're quite right from your own angle, and if I were you I'd feel as you do.—But this you should know, sir: if you go home, and we all go home this winter, you won't need to bother about coming back in the spring. There'll be no fighting to come back to.—General Howe will march out of Philadelphia and take over these states of ours. If he knew now how many have deserted, how many are sick, how many unfit for duty on account of the lack of food and clothes and munitions, he'd come back in force and wring our necks one by one, and the neck of our sickly little revolution along with us.... What are we in this war for? Do we want to quit?

THE MEN: No, sir. No.

WASHINGTON: I can't blame you if you sound a bit half-hearted about it.

TEAGUE: I'm not half-hearted about it! Not me! I'm fighting to keep King George out of my backyard! I moved west three times to get away from his...tax-collectors, and every time they caught up to me! I'm sick of tax-collectors, that's why I'm in it!

WASHINGTON: Then it may be you're here in error, and the sooner you discover it the better. You'll get death and taxes under one government as well as another. But I'll tell you why I'm here, and why I've hoped you were here, and why it's seemed to me worthwhile to stick with it while our guns rust out for lack of powder, and men die around me for lack of food and medicine, and women and children sicken at home for lack of clothing and the little they need to eat.... [W]hat I fight for is your right to do what you please with your government and with yourselves without benefit of kings.—It's for you to decide, Master Teague—you, and your son, and the rest of you.... But if we lose you—if you've lost interest in this cause of ours—we've lost our war, lost it completely, and the men we've left lying on our battlefields died for nothing whatever—for a dream that came too early—and may never come true....

TEAGUE: I guess the old woman'll get along. She's brought in her own bear meat before.

NICK: Well, it's all right with me.

Analyzing Literature

1. What were some of the hardships that Washington's troops faced?
2. Summarize one argument Teague gives in favor of going home.
3. **Critical Thinking Comparing** How do Washington's reasons for fighting differ from Teague's?

Unit 3 The Nation Takes Shape

Viewing UNIT THEMES Celebrating the Nation

American artist John Lewis Krimmel painted this election celebration in 1815. This detail shows people of all ages enjoying parades and public debate in the streets of Philadelphia. By this time, Americans had developed strong feelings of pride in their young nation. ★ **Why do you think Americans at this time felt that an election was cause for celebration?**

Unit Theme Nationalism

In the years after winning independence and adopting a new Constitution, the United States grew and prospered. As the nation took shape, so did American nationalism. Nationalism is a feeling of loyalty and devotion to one's country.

Proud Americans sought to identify qualities that set the United States apart from older nations.

How did Americans of the time describe their feelings about their country? They can tell you in their own words.

★ ★

VIEWPOINTS ON AMERICAN NATIONALISM

❝Britain, whose children we are, and whose language we speak, should no longer be *our* standard.... Customs, habits, and language, as well as government, should be national. America should have her *own* distinct from all the world.❞

Noah Webster, scholar and dictionary writer (1789)

❝We have learned to love our country...because the sweat of our fathers' brows has subdued its soil;... because it embraces our fathers and mothers.❞

John Thornton Kirkland, Boston minister (1798)

❝Our country! In her [dealings] with foreign nations, may she always be in the right; but our country, right or wrong.❞

Stephen Decatur, naval hero (1816)

★ ★

Activity Writing to Learn Another word for nationalism is patriotism. Many things might stir patriotic feelings, including holidays like the Fourth of July, symbols like the flag, or songs like "The Star-Spangled Banner." List 5 or 6 other things that may stir patriotic feelings. Then, choose one of the items from your list. Write a paragraph describing what you think it represents.

Chapter 9

The New Republic Begins

1789–1800

In this chapter, you will learn about the early years of the United States. The new nation faced many decisions about how it would govern itself. Everything was a fresh issue, from what the President should be called to how the nation should pay its bills. The young republic also had to meet violent challenges inside its borders and on the high seas.

In these confusing times, leaders clashed over what policies to follow. Some wanted a stronger national government. Others felt the states should have more power. Before long, two political parties formed. Despite powerful feelings on both sides, the nation successfully elected its second President and moved into the 1800s.

Why Study History?

Again and again, as you study American history, you will find people arguing about something called "the tariff." Tariffs may not seem very exciting. However, they can directly affect how much we pay for the things we buy. To focus on a recent issue involving tariffs, see the *Why Study History?* feature, "The Debate Over Tariffs Continues," in this chapter.

American Events			
1789 George Washington becomes first President of the United States	**1791** Congress creates the Bank of the United States	**1793** Washington issues Neutrality Proclamation to keep the United States out of war	

| **1788** | **1790** | **1792** | **1794** |

World Events		
1789 World Event French Revolution begins	**1792 World Event** French assembly votes to end monarchy	

Symbols of a Proud New Nation

In the late 1700s, paper cutouts like this one were a popular form of artwork. This design shows an eagle holding a flag under the word LIBERTY— symbols of the new nation's patriotism. As President George Washington took office in 1789, Americans looked to the future with pride and hope. ★ **If you were an American in 1789, what hopes and worries might you have about the new government?**

1795
Jay's Treaty keeps
peace between the
United States and
Britain

1797
John Adams becomes
second President of the
United States

1798
Sedition Act
makes it a crime
to criticize the
government

1794   **1796**   **1798**   **1800**

 1794 World Event
Thaddeus Kosciusko
leads Polish uprising

1797 World Event
British sailors mutiny to
demand better conditions

Launching the New Government

As You Read

Explore These Questions

- How did George Washington's actions set an example for future Presidents?
- How did Alexander Hamilton plan to strengthen the nation's economy?
- Why did some people oppose Hamilton's economic plan?

Define

- inauguration
- precedent
- Cabinet
- national debt
- bond
- speculator
- tariff
- protective tariff

Identify

- Judiciary Act
- District of Columbia
- Bank of the United States
- Whiskey Rebellion

SETTING the Scene The new Congress met for the first time in the spring of 1789. Vice President John Adams brought up a curious question. How should people address the President?

For three weeks, members of Congress debated the issue. Some favored the simple title "President Washington." Others felt that it lacked dignity. Instead, they suggested titles such as "His Elective Highness" or "His Highness the President of the United States and Protector of the Rights of the Same."

Finally, Washington let Congress know he was content with "President of the United States." By choosing a simple title, Washington showed he was not interested in the kind of power that European monarchs had. In this decision, like many others, Washington set an example for later Presidents.

The New Government

George Washington was inaugurated in New York City on April 30, 1789. A President's **inauguration** is the ceremony at which the President officially takes the oath of office. A witness reported that the new President looked "grave, almost to sadness." Washington no doubt was feeling the awesome responsibility of his office. He knew that Americans were looking to him to make their new government work.

As the first President, Washington had no one to imitate. While the Constitution provided a framework for the new government, it did not explain how the President should govern from day to day. Washington knew he was setting an example for future generations. "There is scarcely any part of my conduct," he said, "which may not hereafter be drawn into precedent." A **precedent** (PREHS uh dehnt) is an act or decision that sets an example for others to follow.

Washington set one important precedent at the end of his second term. In 1796, he decided not to run for a third term. Not until 1940 did any President seek a third term.

The first Cabinet

The Constitution said little about how the executive branch should be organized. It was clear, however, that the President needed talented people to help him carry out his duties.

Connections With Civics

The President who finally broke Washington's two-term precedent was Franklin D. Roosevelt. In 1940, he ran for and won a third term. Four years later, Roosevelt was elected yet again. Today, the Twenty-Second Amendment to the Constitution prohibits any President from being elected more than twice.

Mug honoring President Washington's inauguration ➤

Viewing HISTORY **The First President**

George Washington traveled on horseback to his inauguration in New York City. Along the way, crowds gathered to cheer their new President. Here, women and children scatter flower petals in Washington's path. ★ **How can you tell this painter greatly admired Washington?**

In 1789, the first Congress created five executive departments. They were the departments of State, Treasury, and War and the offices of Attorney General and Postmaster General. The heads of these departments made up the President's **Cabinet.** Members of the Cabinet gave Washington advice and directed their departments.

Washington set a precedent by carefully choosing well-known leaders to serve in his Cabinet. The two most influential were the Secretary of State, Thomas Jefferson, and the Secretary of the Treasury, Alexander Hamilton.

The federal court system

The Constitution called for a Supreme Court. Congress, however, had to organize the federal court system. In 1789, Congress passed the **Judiciary Act.** It called for the Supreme Court to have one Chief Justice and five Associate Justices.* Washington named John Jay to serve as the first Chief Justice of the United States.

The Judiciary Act also set up a system of district courts and circuit courts across the nation. Decisions made in these lower courts could be appealed to the Supreme Court, the highest court in the land.

Battling the National Debt

As Secretary of the Treasury, Alexander Hamilton wanted to build a strong economy. He faced many major problems, however. Among the most pressing was the large national debt. The **national debt** is the total sum of money a government owes to others.

---

* Today, the Supreme Court has eight Associate Justices.

Biography Alexander Hamilton

Alexander Hamilton was born on the Caribbean island of Nevis in 1755. As a boy, he faced poverty, but he worked his way up in a local trading company. He later came to New York, served as an officer in the American Revolution, and became the first Secretary of the Treasury. This portrait was painted by John Trumbull, one of the most famous early American artists.
★ **How did Alexander Hamilton help strengthen the new nation?**

During the Revolution, both the national government and the individual states needed money to pay soldiers and buy supplies. They borrowed money from foreign countries and ordinary citizens.

Then, as now, governments borrowed money by issuing bonds. A **bond** is a certificate which promises to repay the money loaned plus interest on a certain date. For example, if a person pays $100 for a bond, the government agrees to pay back $100 plus interest in five or ten years.

By 1789, most southern states had paid off their debts from the Revolution. Other states and the federal government had not.

Hamilton insisted that all these debts be repaid. After all, he asked, who would lend money to the United States in the future if the country did not pay its old debts?

Hamilton's Plan

Hamilton developed a two-part plan to repay both the national and state debts. First, he wanted to buy up all the bonds issued by the national and state governments before 1789. He planned to sell new bonds to pay off those old debts. When the economy improved, the government would be able to pay off the new bonds. Second, he wanted the national government to pay off debts owed by the states.

Many people, including bankers and investors, welcomed Hamilton's plan. Others attacked it.

Madison leads the opposition

James Madison led the opposition to Hamilton's plan. Madison argued that the plan was unfair because it would reward speculators. A **speculator** is someone willing to invest in a risky venture in the hope of making a large profit.

During the Revolution, the government had paid soldiers and citizens who supplied goods with bonds. Many of these bondholders needed cash to survive. They sold their bonds to speculators. Speculators paid only 10 or 15 cents for bonds that had an original, or face, value of one dollar.

If the government repaid the bonds at face value, speculators stood to make great fortunes. Madison thought that speculators did not deserve to make such profits.

Hamilton disagreed. The United States had to repay its bonds in full, he said, in order to gain the trust and help of investors. The support of investors, he argued, was crucial for building the new nation's economy. After much debate, Hamilton convinced Congress to accept his plan of repaying the national debt.

As a southerner, James Madison also led the fight against the other part of Hamilton's plan. It called for the federal government to pay state debts. Many southern states had already paid their own debts in full. They thought other states should do the same. As a result, southerners bitterly opposed Hamilton's proposal.

Hamilton's compromise

To win support for his plan, Hamilton suggested a compromise. He knew that many southerners wanted to move the nation's capital to the South. He offered to persuade his northern friends to vote for a capital in the South if southerners supported the repayment of state debts.

Madison and other southerners accepted this compromise. In July 1790, Congress passed bills taking over state debts and providing for a new capital city.

The capital would not be part of any state. Instead, it would be built on land along the Potomac River between Virginia and Maryland. Congress called this area the **District of Columbia.** It is known today as Washington, D.C. Congress hoped that the new capital would be ready by 1800. Meanwhile, the nation's capital was moved from New York to Philadelphia.

Building Up the Economy

Hamilton's compromise with the South had resolved the problem of the national debt. Now he took steps to build up the new nation's economy.

A national bank

Hamilton called on Congress to set up a national bank. In 1791, Congress passed a bill creating the first **Bank of the United States.** The national government deposited the money it collected in taxes in the Bank. The Bank, in turn, issued paper money. The government used the paper money to make loans to farmers and businesses. By making loans to citizens, the Bank encouraged the growth of the economy.

The Bank also used the paper money to pay government bills. The new government had many expenses. It had to pay its employees, build the new capital, and keep up the army and navy.

Protecting American industry

Another part of Hamilton's economic program was designed to give American manu-

facturing a boost. He proposed that Congress pass a **tariff,** or tax, on all foreign goods brought into the country. Hamilton called for a very high tariff. He wanted to make imported goods more expensive to buy than goods made in the United States. Because such a tariff was meant to protect American industry from foreign competition, it was called a **protective tariff.**

In the North, where factories were growing, many people supported Hamilton's plan. Southern farmers, however, bought more imported goods than northerners did. They did not want a protective tariff that would make these goods more expensive.

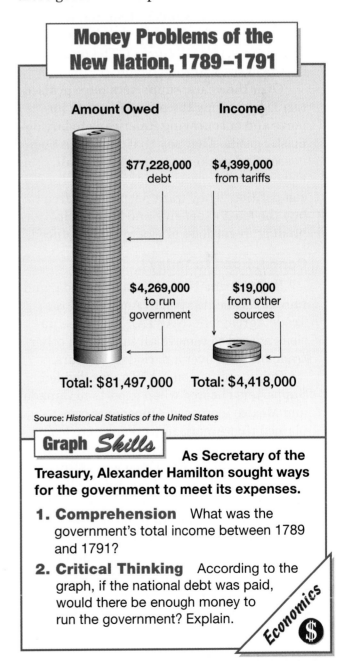

Money Problems of the New Nation, 1789–1791

Amount Owed

$77,228,000 debt

$4,269,000 to run government

Total: $81,497,000

Income

$4,399,000 from tariffs

$19,000 from other sources

Total: $4,418,000

Source: *Historical Statistics of the United States*

Graph Skills As Secretary of the Treasury, Alexander Hamilton sought ways for the government to meet its expenses.

1. **Comprehension** What was the government's total income between 1789 and 1791?

2. **Critical Thinking** According to the graph, if the national debt was paid, would there be enough money to run the government? Explain.

Economics $

Why Study History?

Because the Debate Over Tariffs Continues

★ ★

Historical Background

In the 1790s, Alexander Hamilton wanted protective tariffs placed on imports. Other American leaders disagreed. The national debate over tariffs had begun.

Over the years, supporters have praised tariffs for raising the price of foreign imports and encouraging Americans to buy domestic goods. They say that American businesses and workers prosper as a result. Opponents, however, feel that tariffs limit competition. They want people to be free to buy the least expensive and best-made product, regardless of where it is produced.

Connections to Today

By 1993, the United States, Canada, and Mexico formed the North American Free Trade Agreement (NAFTA). The three nations agreed to remove all tariffs and other trade barriers over a period of 15 years.

Public opinion on NAFTA was divided. Supporters cheered when exports to Canada and Mexico increased. Opponents complained that American workers were losing jobs as companies moved to Mexico where labor costs were lower. Opponents also charged that Mexico did not enforce laws banning child labor, ensuring safety in the workplace, and protecting the environment.

The opponents of NAFTA and similar agreements urged consumers to boycott, or not buy, goods made in countries with unfair or unsafe labor practices. In particular, they urged consumers to boycott foreign goods made by young children.

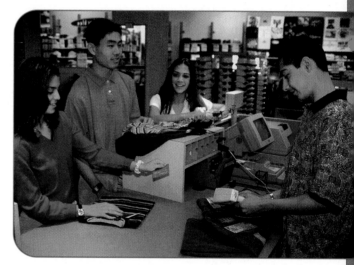

Tariffs can increase the cost of the goods you buy.

Connections to You

In one case, students in American schools made an impact. Manufacturers in Pakistan were using children to stitch soccer balls. In protest, American and European students threatened a boycott of soccer balls made in Pakistan. As a result, the manufacturers agreed to stop using child labor.

1. **Comprehension** **(a)** Explain one argument in favor of tariffs. **(b)** Explain one argument against tariffs.

2. **Critical Thinking** It can cost less to make some products in Mexico than in the United States. Why do you think this is so?

Debating Work with other students to stage a debate on NAFTA. One group will support the treaty. Another group will oppose it. Do additional research to find information supporting your position.

In the end, Congress did pass a tariff bill. However, its purpose was to raise money for operating the government, rather than protect American industries. For this reason, it was much lower than the protective tariff called for by Hamilton.

The Whiskey Rebellion

Congress also passed a bill that taxed all liquor made and sold in the United States. Hamilton wanted this tax to raise money for the Treasury. Instead, the whiskey tax led to a rebellion that tested the strength of the new government.

A hated tax

Like many other Americans, farmers in the backcountry grew corn. However, corn was bulky to haul over rough backcountry roads. Instead, farmers converted their corn into whiskey, which they could easily ship in barrels to markets in the East.

Backcountry farmers protested the whiskey tax. They compared it to the hated taxes Britain had forced on the colonies in the 1760s. Many farmers refused to pay the tax. A backcountry poet wrote:

66 Some chaps whom freedom's
   spirit warms
Are threatening hard to take up
   arms....
Their liberty they will maintain,
They fought for't, and they'll fight
   again. 99

In 1794, officials in western Pennsylvania tried to collect the tax. Farmers rebelled. Soon, thousands were marching through Pittsburgh. They sang Revolutionary songs and tarred and feathered tax officials.

A show of strength

Washington responded quickly to this challenge to authority. He called up the militia and sent them to Pennsylvania. When the rebels heard that 15,000 troops were marching against them, they scattered. Washington later pardoned the leaders of the rebellion.

The **Whiskey Rebellion** was a critical test of the strength of the new government. Washington had shown those who disagreed with the government that violence would not be tolerated. The President's quick response proved to Americans that their new government would act firmly in times of crisis.

★ Section 1 Review ★

Recall

1. **Identify** (a) Judiciary Act, (b) District of Columbia, (c) Bank of the United States, (d) Whiskey Rebellion.
2. **Define** (a) inauguration, (b) precedent, (c) Cabinet, (d) national debt, (e) bond, (f) speculator, (g) tariff, (h) protective tariff.

Comprehension

3. Describe one precedent that George Washington set for future governments of the United States.
4. (a) Why did Alexander Hamilton think it was important to pay off government bonds?

(b) Why did James Madison oppose Hamilton's repayment plan?
5. Describe two proposals Hamilton made to raise money for the new government.

Critical Thinking and Writing

6. **Linking Past and Present** By the late 1990s, the Cabinet included the heads of 13 separate departments. Why do you think the Cabinet has grown so much since Washington's time?
7. **Forecasting** What do you think might have happened if Washington had not taken strong action to put down the Whiskey Rebellion?

Activity **Acting a Scene** The year is 1789. Your family owns government bonds, but you are not sure whether the bonds will be repaid at full value. With a partner, act out a scene between two members of the family. Discuss whether you should hold onto the bonds or sell them to a speculator.

2 ★ A Policy of Neutrality

As You Read

Explore These Questions
- How did Americans react to the French Revolution?
- What policy did the United States adopt when war broke out in Europe?
- How did Washington's Farewell Address influence American foreign policy?

Define
- foreign policy

Identify
- French Revolution
- Neutrality Proclamation
- Jay's Treaty
- Farewell Address

SETTING the Scene Late in 1789, French ships arriving at American seaports brought startling news. On July 14, an angry mob in Paris, France, had destroyed the Bastille (bahs TEEL), a huge fort that was being used as a prison. The attack on the Bastille was one of several events that launched the **French Revolution**.

The French Revolution broke out a few years after Americans won independence. Like the Americans, the French fought for liberty and equality. As the French Revolution grew more violent, however, it ignited political quarrels that had been smoldering in the United States.

Revolution in France

The French had many reasons to rebel against their king, Louis XVI. Peasants and the middle class paid heavy taxes, while nobles paid none. Reformers called for a constitution to limit the power of the king. They also wanted a guarantee of rights like that in the American Constitution.

Americans support the revolution

At first, most Americans supported the French Revolution. Americans knew what it meant to struggle for liberty. Then, too, France had been the first ally of the United States in the war against Great Britain.

Many Americans wanted to rally behind the Marquis de Lafayette, a leading French reformer. They remembered that Lafayette had fought side by side with them in the American Revolution.

In the 1790s, however, the French Revolution entered a very violent stage. A radical group gained power. In 1793, they beheaded Louis XVI and his wife, Queen Marie Antoinette. During a "reign of terror," tens of thousands of French citizens were executed.

Violence divides American opinion

The violence in France divided Americans. Some, like Thomas Jefferson, continued to support the French. He condemned the killings of the king and queen. Still, he felt that the French had the right to use violence to win freedom.

Alexander Hamilton, John Adams, and others disagreed with Jefferson's view. They thought that the French Revolution was doomed to fail. One could no more create democracy through violence, claimed Adams, "than a snowball can exist in the streets of Philadelphia under a burning sun."

Remaining Neutral

The French Revolution shocked rulers and nobles across Europe. They feared the spread of revolutionary ideas to their own

The French Revolution

At the start of the French Revolution, famine gripped Paris. Thousands of angry women (above) marched on the palace of the king shouting, "Bread! Bread!" The statue at right honored the army of ragged peasants that rose up against long years of injustice. ★ **Why would the French expect Americans to support their revolution?**

lands. Britain, Spain, Prussia, Austria, and the Netherlands sent armies to overpower the revolutionaries in France. Europe was soon plunged into a war that continued on and off for more than 20 years.

A difficult decision

Faced with the war in Europe, Washington had to form a foreign policy for the nation. **Foreign policy** refers to the actions and stands that a nation takes in relation to other nations. An old treaty, signed during the American Revolution, allowed French ships to use American ports. As the war in Europe continued, the French wanted to use American ports to supply their ships and launch attacks on British ships.

"It is the sincere wish of United America," said the President, "to have nothing to do with...the squabbles of European nations." How could the United States honor its treaty with France and still remain neutral?

Divisions in the Cabinet

The issue of the treaty deepened divisions within Washington's Cabinet. Hamilton pointed out that the United States had signed the treaty with Louis XVI. Since the king was dead, he argued, the treaty was no longer valid. Jefferson, however, supported the French cause. He was suspicious of Hamilton, who wanted friendlier relations with Britain, the nation's old enemy.

After much debate, Washington issued the **Neutrality Proclamation** in April 1793. In it, he stated that the United States would not support either side in the war. It also forbade Americans to aid either Britain or France in any way.

Many viewed the Neutrality Proclamation as a defeat for Jefferson. Eventually, this and other conflicts with Hamilton caused Jefferson to leave the Cabinet.

An Unpopular Treaty

Declaring neutrality was easier than enforcing it. American merchants wanted to trade with both Britain and France. However, those warring nations ignored the rights of neutral ships. They seized American cargoes headed for each other's ports.

In 1793, the British captured more than 250 American ships trading in the French

West Indies. Americans clamored for war. Washington, however, knew that the United States was too weak to fight. He sent Chief Justice John Jay to Britain for talks.

Jay worked out a treaty. It called for Britain to pay damages for American ships seized in 1793. At the same time, Americans had to pay debts to British merchants, owed from before the Revolution. Britain agreed to give up forts it still held in the Ohio Valley. However, the treaty did nothing to protect the rights of neutral American ships.

George Washington retired to Mount Vernon, his Virginia home, where he died in 1799.

Jay's Treaty sparked a storm of protest. Many Americans felt they were giving up more than Britain was. After a furious debate, the Senate finally approved the treaty in 1795. Washington accepted the treaty because he wanted to avoid war.

Washington Retires

In 1796, George Washington published his **Farewell Address**. In it, he announced he would retire. He urged the United States to remain neutral in its relations with other countries:

> 66 Observe good faith and justice toward all nations.... Nothing is more essential than that permanent, [habitual hatred] against particular nations and passionate attachments for others should be excluded. 99

Washington warned Americans to avoid becoming involved in European affairs. " 'Tis our true policy to steer clear of permanent alliances with any portion of the foreign world," said the retiring President. Such alliances, he felt, would pull the United States into war. That advice guided American foreign policy for many years.

★ Section 2 Review ★

Recall

1. **Identify** (a) French Revolution, (b) Neutrality Proclamation, (c) Jay's Treaty, (d) Farewell Address.
2. **Define** foreign policy.

Comprehension

3. How did the revolution in France divide Americans?
4. Describe two actions Washington took to avoid war.
5. What advice did Washington give in his Farewell Address?

Critical Thinking and Writing

6. **Recognizing Points of View** Writing about the French Revolution, Thomas Jefferson said he was willing to see "half the earth devastated" in order to win the "liberty of the whole." (a) Restate Jefferson's main idea in your own words. (b) What does this statement tell you about Jefferson's values?
7. **Analyzing Information** How did geographic location help the United States to "steer clear of permanent alliances" with European nations for many years?

★ ★

Activity **Giving an Introduction** President Washington has chosen to deliver his Farewell Address in your school auditorium. You have been asked to introduce him. Prepare a two-minute introduction naming what you consider to be Washington's greatest achievements.

3 The Rise of Political Parties

★ ★

As You Read

Explore These Questions
- How did political differences lead to the rise of two political parties?
- What role did newspapers play in politics?
- How did the election of 1796 increase political tensions?

Define
- faction
- unconstitutional

Identify
- Democratic Republicans
- Federalists

SETTING the Scene When President Washington took office in 1789, the United States had no political parties. In fact, most American leaders opposed the very idea of forming parties. "If I could not go to heaven but with a party," said Thomas Jefferson, "I would not go at all."

Still, deep divisions began to form in the Cabinet and Congress. Jefferson described the unpleasant mood:

66 Men who have been [friends] all their lives cross streets to avoid meeting, and turn their heads another way, lest they should be obliged to touch their hats. 99

By the time Washington left office in 1789, there were two parties competing for power.

A Distrust of Political Parties

Americans had reason to distrust political parties. They had seen how **factions,** or opposing groups within parties, worked in Britain. British factions were made up of a few people who schemed to win favors from the government. Most were more interested in personal gain than in the public good.

Americans also saw political parties as a threat to national unity. They agreed with George Washington, who warned Americans that parties would lead to "jealousies and false alarms."

Despite the President's warning, parties grew up around two members of his Cabinet, Alexander Hamilton and Thomas Jefferson.

The two men differed in background, looks, and personality as well as in politics. Born in the West Indies, Hamilton had worked his way up from poverty. He dressed in fine clothes and spoke forcefully. Energetic, brilliant, and restless, Hamilton enjoyed political debate.

Jefferson was tall and lanky. Although he was a wealthy Virginia planter, he dressed and spoke informally. One senator recalled:

66 His clothes seem too small for him. He sits in a lounging manner, on one hip commonly, and with one of his shoulders elevated much above the other. His face has a sunny aspect. His whole figure has a loose, shackling air.... He spoke almost without ceasing. [His conversation] was loose and rambling; and yet he scattered information wherever he went. 99

Differing Views

Alexander Hamilton did not agree with Thomas Jefferson on many issues. At the root of their quarrels were different views about what was best for the young United States.

Manufacturing or farming

First, Hamilton and Jefferson disagreed about economic policy. Hamilton thought the United States should model itself on Britain. He felt the government should encourage

Viewing HISTORY Two Views of the Nation

Federalists and Republicans disagreed. Should the new nation build its future mainly on agriculture or on manufacturing? The farmer, above, and the ironworker, right, represent these two viewpoints.
★ **Which of these pictures represents Hamilton's view? Which picture represents Jefferson's view?**

manufacturing and trade. He also favored the growth of cities and the merchant class who helped make cities prosperous.

Jefferson believed that farmers, rather than merchants, were the backbone of the new nation. "Cultivators of the earth," he wrote, "are the most valuable citizens." He feared that a manufacturing economy would corrupt the United States by concentrating power in the hands of a small group of wealthy Americans.

Federal or state governments

Hamilton and Jefferson disagreed about the power of the federal government. Hamilton wanted the federal government to have greater power than state governments. A strong federal government, he argued, could encourage the growth of commerce. It would also have the power needed to restrain unruly mobs, such as the protesters who led the Whiskey Rebellion.

In contrast, Jefferson hoped to make the government as small as possible. Then, citizens would have the freedom to act as they

pleased. Jefferson feared that a strong federal government might take over powers that the Constitution gave to the states.

Strict or loose interpretation of the Constitution

These disagreements led the two leaders to clash over the Bank of the United States. Jefferson worried that a national bank would give too much power to the federal government and the wealthy investors who helped run it.

To oppose Hamilton's proposal, Jefferson argued that the law creating the bank was **unconstitutional,** that is, not permitted by the Constitution. Nowhere did the Constitution give Congress the power to create a Bank, he argued. Jefferson thought that any power not specifically given to the federal government belonged to the states.

Hamilton did not agree with Jefferson's strict interpretation of the Constitution. He preferred a looser interpretation. The Constitution gave Congress the power to make all laws "necessary and proper" to carry out

Skills

FOR LIFE

Critical Thinking

Managing Information

Communication

Maps, Charts, and Graphs

Outlining

How Will I Use This Skill?

In school and, later, at work, you may be asked to write a report or give a presentation. You will find the job easier if you prepare an outline. An outline helps you arrange information in logical order. In addition, when you speak in public, an outline can keep you from fumbling for words!

LEARN the Skill

Make an outline by following these four steps.

❶ Use the theme or topic as the title of your outline.

❷ Identify and list the main ideas in order. Label them with Roman numerals.

❸ Identify subtopics for each main idea. Label these with capital letters and list them under the main ideas.

❹ Identify details that support each subtopic. Label and list these with Arabic numerals as shown.

PRACTICE the Skill

The sample at right is a partial outline of the subsection Differing Views. Study the sample. Then, using the steps above, make an outline of the subsection Party Rivalry.

❶ Take notes as you read the subsection.

❷ Using your notes and the headings in the text, write down the main ideas.

❸ Using the topic sentences of the paragraphs in the text, identify the subtopics for your outline.

The Clash of Jefferson and Hamilton

I. Jefferson's Views
  A. Preferred farm economy
  B. Favored strict interpretation of Constitution
    1. Against Bank of United States
      a. Too much power to federal government
      b. Unconstitutional
    2. Favored state power
  C. Favored France in foreign policy
II. Hamilton's Views
  A. Supported manufacturing economy
  B. Favored loose interpretation of Constitution
    1. Planned Bank of United States
      a. Way to collect taxes
      b. Way to pay government bills
    2. Favored federal power
  C. Supported Britain in foreign policy

---

❹ Find and list supporting details from the text.

APPLY the Skill

Choose a topic that interests you. Make an outline for a short talk on this subject.

Federalists vs. Republicans

FEDERALISTS	REPUBLICANS
① Led by Alexander Hamilton	① Led by Thomas Jefferson
② Wealthy and well educated should lead nation	② People should have political power
③ Strong central government	③ Strong state governments
④ Emphasis on manufacturing, shipping, and trade	④ Emphasis on agriculture
⑤ Loose interpretation of Constitution	⑤ Strict interpretation of the Constitution
⑥ Pro-British	⑥ Pro-French
⑦ Favored national bank	⑦ Opposed national bank
⑧ Favored protective tariff	⑧ Opposed protective tariff

Graphic Organizer *Skills*

By the 1790s, there were two political parties in the United States—the Federalist party and the Republican party.

1. **Comprehension** Describe two ways the Republicans and Federalists differed on economic issues.
2. **Critical Thinking** "The average person is far too ignorant to make wise political decisions." Do you think a Republican or a Federalist would be more likely to agree with this statement? Explain.

Civics

its duties. Hamilton argued that the Bank was necessary for the government to collect taxes and pay its bills.

Britain or France

Finally, the two leaders clashed over foreign policy. Hamilton wanted to form close ties with Britain, an important trading partner. Jefferson favored France, the first ally of the United States and a nation struggling for its own liberty.

Party Rivalry

At first, Hamilton and Jefferson clashed in private. However, when Congress began to pass many of Hamilton's programs, Jefferson and James Madison decided to organize public support for their views.

Madison and Jefferson moved cautiously at first. In 1791, they went to New York, telling people that they were going to study its wildlife. In fact, Jefferson was interested in nature and did travel far into upstate New York. Their main purpose, though, was to meet with important New York politicians like Governor George Clinton and Aaron Burr, a strong critic of Hamilton. Jefferson asked Clinton and Burr to help defeat Hamilton's program by getting New Yorkers to vote for Jefferson supporters.

Republicans and Federalists

Soon, leaders in other states began organizing to support either Hamilton or Jefferson. Jefferson's supporters called themselves **Democratic Republicans,** often shortened to Republicans.[*] Republicans included small farmers, craftworkers, and some wealthy planters.

---

[*]Jefferson's Republican party was not the same as today's Republican party. In fact, his party later grew into the Democratic party.

Hamilton and his supporters were called **Federalists** because they wanted a strong federal government. Federalists drew most of their support from merchants and manufacturers in cities such as Boston and New York. They also gained the backing of some southern planters.

Newspapers take sides

In the late 1700s, the number of American newspapers more than doubled. This growth met a demand for information. A visitor from Europe noted with surprise that so many Americans could read:

66 The common people [in the United States] are on a footing, in point of literature with the middle ranks of Europe. They all read and write, and understand arithmetic; almost every little town now furnishes a circulating library. 99

As party rivalry grew, newspapers took sides. In the *Gazette of the United States*, publisher John Fenno printed articles in favor of Alexander Hamilton and the Federalists. Philip Freneau (frih NOH), a friend of Thomas Jefferson, started a rival paper, the *National Gazette*. Freneau vigorously supported Republicans.

Newspapers had great influence on public opinion. In stinging language, they raged against opponents. Often, articles mixed rumor and opinion with facts. Emotional attacks and counterattacks fanned the flames of party rivalry. Still, newspapers performed a needed service. They kept people informed and helped shape public opinion.

Election of 1796

Political parties played a major role in the election of George Washington's successor. In 1796, Republicans backed Thomas Jefferson for President and Aaron Burr for Vice President. Federalists supported John Adams for President and Thomas Pinckney for Vice President.

The election had an unexpected outcome, which created new tensions. Under the Constitution, the person with the most electoral votes became President. The person with the next highest total was made Vice President. John Adams, a Federalist, won office as President. The leader of the Republicans, Thomas Jefferson, came in second and became Vice President.

With the President and the Vice President from different parties, political tensions remained high. Future events would further increase the distrust between the two men. Meanwhile, John Adams took office in March 1797 as the second President of the United States.

★ Section 3 Review ★

Recall

1. **Identify** **(a)** Democratic Republicans, **(b)** Federalists.
2. **Define** **(a)** faction, **(b)** unconstitutional.

Comprehension

3. Describe two issues on which Thomas Jefferson and Alexander Hamilton disagreed.
4. How did newspapers contribute to the rivalry between political parties?

5. What role did parties play in the 1796 election?

Critical Thinking and Writing

6. **Drawing Conclusions** Why do you think political parties emerged even though most Americans opposed them?
7. **Ranking** Which of the disagreements between Jefferson and Hamilton do you think was the most serious? Explain.

★ ★

History AND YOU

Activity **Writing a Newspaper Headline** You are the publisher of either the *Gazette of the United States* or the *National Gazette*. Write three headlines about the election of 1796. Be sure your headlines express the point of view of your own newspaper.

The Second President

As You Read

Explore These Questions

- Why did many Americans favor war with France?
- Why did the Federalist party split in two?
- Why did the Alien and Sedition acts outrage many Americans?

Define

- immigrant
- sedition
- nullify

Identify

- XYZ Affair
- High Federalists
- Napoleon Bonaparte
- Alien and Sedition acts
- Kentucky and Virginia resolutions

SETTING the Scene Late in his life, John Adams looked back on his career with mixed feelings. He knew that leaders such as Washington and Jefferson were more widely admired than he was. Still, Adams wrote proudly of his life's work:

> 66 I have done more labor, run through more and greater dangers, and made greater sacrifices than any man...living or dead, in the service of my country. 99

At the same time, Adams found it hard to boast of his achievements. In the end, he concluded: "I am not, never was, and never shall be a great man."

Although he was not a popular hero, like Washington, Adams was an honest and able leader. As President, he tried to act in the best interests of the nation, even when his actions hurt him politically.

Conflict With France

No sooner did Adams take office than he faced a crisis with France. The French objected to Jay's Treaty because they felt that it favored Britain. In 1797, French ships began to seize American ships in the West Indies, as the British had done.

Once again, Americans called for war, this time against France. Adams tried to avoid war by sending diplomats to Paris to discuss the rights of neutral nations.

The XYZ Affair

France's foreign minister, Charles Maurice de Talleyrand, did not deal directly with the Americans. Instead, he sent three secret agents to offer the Americans a deal. Before Talleyrand would begin talks, the agents said, he wanted $250,000 for himself, as well as a loan to France of $10 million. "Not a sixpence!" replied one of the American diplomats angrily.

The diplomats informed Adams about the offer. Adams, in turn, told Congress. He did not reveal the names of the French agents, referring to them only as X, Y, and Z.

Many Americans were outraged when they heard about the **XYZ Affair** in 1798. They took up the slogan, "Millions for defense, but not one cent for tribute!" They were willing to spend money to defend their country, but they refused to pay a bribe to another nation.

Adams avoids war

Despite growing pressure, Adams refused to ask Congress to declare war on France. Still, he could not ignore French attacks on American ships. He moved to strengthen the navy. Shipyards built frigates—fast-sailing ships with many guns.

This show of strength helped convince Talleyrand to stop attacking American ships. He also promised Adams that if American ambassadors came to France, they would be treated with respect.

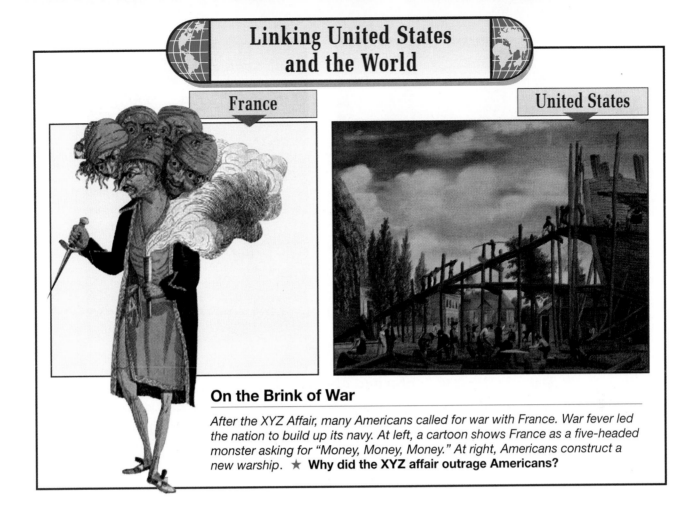

Linking United States and the World

France | United States

On the Brink of War

After the XYZ Affair, many Americans called for war with France. War fever led the nation to build up its navy. At left, a cartoon shows France as a five-headed monster asking for "Money, Money, Money." At right, Americans construct a new warship. ★ **Why did the XYZ affair outrage Americans?**

The Federalist Party Splits

Many Federalists, led by Hamilton, criticized Adams's actions. They hoped a war would weaken the Republicans, supporters of France. War would also force the United States to build up its military. A stronger army and navy would increase federal power, a major Federalist goal.

Although John Adams was a Federalist, he would not give in to Hamilton. Their disagreement created a split in the Federalist party. Hamilton and his supporters were called **High Federalists**.

Over Hamilton's opposition, Adams again sent diplomats to France. When they arrived, they found an ambitious young army officer, **Napoleon Bonaparte**, in charge. Napoleon did not have time for a war with the United States. He signed an agreement to stop seizing American ships.

Like Washington, Adams kept the nation out of war. His success, however, cost him the support of many Federalists.

Alien and Sedition Acts

During the crisis with France, Federalists pushed several laws through Congress. Passed in 1798, the laws were known as the **Alien and Sedition acts**.

The Alien Act allowed the President to expel any alien, or foreigner, thought to be dangerous to the country. Another law made it harder for immigrants to become citizens. An **immigrant** is a person who enters another country in order to settle there. Before, white immigrants could become citizens after living in the United States for 5 years. Under the new law, immigrants had to wait 14 years. This law was meant to keep new settlers, who often supported the Republicans, from voting.

Republican anger grew when Congress passed the Sedition Act. **Sedition** means stirring up rebellion against a government. Under this law, citizens could be fined or jailed if they criticized the government or its officials.

Locket given by John to Abigail Adams

Biography   John and Abigail Adams

Throughout 54 years of marriage, John Adams valued the advice and support of his wife, Abigail. A brilliant woman and fine writer, Abigail Adams supported greater rights for women. They were the first President and First Lady to live in the White House. Their son, John Quincy Adams, also became President. ★ **Why would it have been hard for Abigail Adams to pursue her own political career?**

Republicans protested that the Sedition Act violated the Constitution. After all, they argued, the First Amendment protected freedom of speech and freedom of the press. Jefferson warned that the new laws threatened American liberties:

❝ If this goes down, we shall immediately see attempted another act of Congress, declaring that the President shall continue in office during life, and after that other laws giving both the President and the Congress life terms in office. ❞

Under the Sedition Act, several Republican newspaper editors, and even members of Congress, were fined and jailed for expressing their opinions.

The Rights of States

Outraged, Jefferson urged the states to take strong action against the Alien and Sedition acts. He argued that the states had the right to **nullify,** or cancel, a law passed by the federal government. In this way, states could resist the power of the federal government.

With the help of Jefferson and Madison, Kentucky and Virginia passed resolutions in 1798 and 1799. The **Kentucky and Virginia resolutions** claimed that each state "has an equal right to judge for itself" whether a law is constitutional. If a state decides a law is unconstitutional, said the resolutions, it has the power to nullify that law within its borders.

Connections With Arts

The picture of Abigail Adams, above, is by Gilbert Stuart, one of the greatest American portrait painters. In fact, you may have a Gilbert Stuart painting in your pocket right now. His portrait of George Washington appears on the one dollar bill.

The Kentucky and Virginia resolutions raised a difficult question. Did a state have the right to decide on its own that a law was unconstitutional?

The question remained unanswered in Jefferson's lifetime. Before long, the Alien and Sedition acts were changed or dropped. Still, the issue of a state's right to nullify federal laws would come up again.

Election of 1800

By 1800, the cry for war against France was fading. As the election approached, the Republicans hoped to sweep the Federalists from office. Republicans focused on two issues. First, they attacked the Federalists for raising taxes to prepare for war. Second, they opposed the unpopular Alien and Sedition acts.

Republicans supported Thomas Jefferson for President and Aaron Burr for Vice President. Despite the bitter split in the Federalist party, John Adams was again named the Federalist candidate.

A deadlock

In the race for President, the Republicans won the popular vote. However, when the electoral college voted, Jefferson and Burr each received 73 votes. At the time, the electoral college did not vote separately for President and Vice President. Each Republican elector cast one vote for Jefferson and one vote for Burr.

Under the Constitution, if no candidate wins the electoral vote, the House of Representatives decides the election. The House vote, however, was also evenly split between Jefferson and Burr. After four days, and 36 votes, the tie was finally broken. The House chose Jefferson as President. Burr became Vice President.

Congress afterward passed the Twelfth Amendment. It required electors to vote separately for President and Vice President. The states ratified the amendment in 1804.

End of the Federalist era

The Republican victory set an important precedent for the nation. To this day, power continues to pass peacefully from one party to another.

After 1800, the Federalist party began to decline. Federalists won fewer seats in Congress. In 1804, the Federalist party was further weakened when their leader, Alexander Hamilton, was killed in a duel with Aaron Burr. Despite their decline, the Federalist party had helped shape the new nation. Republican Presidents eventually kept most of Hamilton's economic programs.

★ Section 4 Review ★

Recall

1. **Identify** (a) XYZ Affair, (b) High Federalists, (c) Napoleon Bonaparte, (d) Alien and Sedition acts, (e) Kentucky and Virginia resolutions.
2. **Define** (a) immigrant, (b) sedition, (c) nullify.

Comprehension

3. Why did many Americans want to declare war on France?
4. Why did John Adams lose the support of many Federalists?

5. (a) Why did Federalists favor the Alien and Sedition acts? (b) Why did Republicans oppose these laws?

Critical Thinking and Writing

6. **Applying Information** How did the Kentucky and Virginia resolutions reflect Jefferson's view of government?
7. **Analyzing Information** How did the Twelfth Amendment help prevent deadlocks like the one that took place in the election of 1800?

★ ★

Activity **Drawing a Political Cartoon** Suppose that the Sedition Act of 1798 were passed by Congress today. Draw a political cartoon expressing your opinion of the law.

Review and Activities

★ Sum It Up ★

Section 1   Launching the New Government
► George Washington set many precedents that determined how future Presidents would govern the nation.
► Alexander Hamilton formed a plan to improve the nation's finances.
► A rebellion against the national government quickly melted away when President Washington responded forcefully.

Section 2   A Policy of Neutrality
► Americans were sharply divided in their reaction to the French Revolution.
► Washington responded to war between Britain and France by declaring that the United States would remain neutral.

Section 3   The Rise of Political Parties
► Because of widely differing views on national issues, two major political parties soon formed in the new republic.
► Federalists supported a strong federal government, while Republicans opposed policies that made the national government too strong.

Section 4   The Second President
► Despite pressure, President John Adams avoided war with France.
► The unpopular Alien and Sedition acts led the states to consider ways to take power back from the federal government.
► In the election of 1800, power passed from the Federalists to the Republicans.

CD-ROM Review For additional review of the major ideas of Chapter 9, see *Guide to the Essentials of American History* or *Interactive Student Tutorial CD-ROM,* which contains interactive review activities, graphic organizers, and practice tests.

📖 Reviewing the Chapter

Define These Terms
Match each term with the correct definition.

Column 1
1. national debt
2. tariff
3. speculator
4. sedition
5. immigrant

Column 2
a. stirring up rebellion
b. type of tax
c. person who enters a country in order to settle there
d. someone who invests in a risky venture to make a profit
e. total a government owes

Explore the Main Ideas
1. Why did many southerners oppose Hamilton's plan to settle state debts?
2. How did Britain and France make Washington's neutrality policy difficult to enforce?
3. Describe the people who supported: **(a)** the Federalist party; **(b)** the Republican party.
4. How did President Adams avoid war?
5. How was the Sedition Act used to silence Republicans?

📖 Graph Activity

Look at the graph below and answer the following questions:
1. How many people served in the navy in 1798? **2.** What had happened to the navy by 1800?   **Critical Thinking** Why did the size of the navy change?

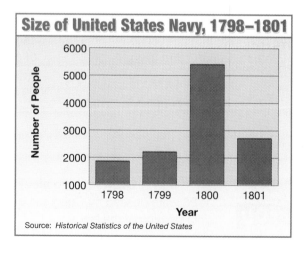

Size of United States Navy, 1798–1801

Source: *Historical Statistics of the United States*

Critical Thinking and Writing

1. **Exploring Unit Themes Nationalism**
How did each of the following strengthen the nation: **(a)** the presidency of Washington; **(b)** Hamilton's plan to pay off state debts; **(c)** Washington's response to the Whiskey Rebellion?

2. **Linking Past and Present** Washington urged the United States never to take sides in the world's wars. Do you think this policy would make sense in today's world? Explain.

3. **Defending a Position** Do you think the Constitution should be interpreted strictly or loosely? Give reasons for your position.

4. **Understanding Chronology** **(a)** Place the following events in chronological order: XYZ Affair; Neutrality Proclamation; French Revolution begins; Adams builds up American navy; Washington's Farewell Address. **(b)** Describe the relationship between two of these events.

Using Primary Sources

In its early years, Washington, D.C., was little more than a clearing in the wilderness. First Lady Abigail Adams described its location in a letter to a friend in 1800:

> **66** Woods are all you see, from Baltimore until you reach the city. . . . Here and there is a small [hut], without a glass window, [all alone] amongst the forests, through which you travel miles without seeing any human being. . . . But, surrounded with forests, can you believe that [fire]wood is not to be had, because people cannot be found to cut and cart it! **99**

Source: *Letters of Mrs. Adams,* edited by Charles Francis Adams, 1840.

Recognizing Points of View **(a)** Why was Abigail Adams unable to get firewood? **(b)** Why did she consider this surprising? **(c)** Do you think Abigail Adams approved of the new city? Explain.

ACTIVITY BANK

Interdisciplinary Activity

Exploring Economics Use library resources to locate information on our current national debt in newspapers or magazines. Prepare a three-minute presentation in which you explain what economic problems may arise because of the national debt.

Career Skills Activity

Reporters Early newspapers often mixed rumor and opinion with facts. Today, reporters have to keep facts and opinions apart. Practice this skill by writing a brief account of the election of 1796 as it might have appeared in a paper of the time. Then, write another account based only on facts.

Citizenship Activity

Researching Political Parties Learn about the political organizations in your area. Most groups will be glad to tell you about the rights and responsibilities of membership. Prepare a one-page data sheet covering at least two political parties. Describe their views and some of their recent or planned activities.

Internet Activity

Today, as in the 1790s, the United States has a special government bank. Use the Internet to find information about the Federal Reserve Bank. Then, write a reaction to the Federal Reserve Bank from the point of view of a Federalist or of a Democratic Republican.

EYEWITNESS Journal

You are a Federalist ship owner in 1797 or a Democratic Republican newspaper editor in 1798. In your EYEWITNESS JOURNAL, write an exciting account of how your life was affected by the events of your times.

Chapter 10

The Age of Jefferson
1801–1816

Republican Presidents in the early 1800s tried to serve the needs of ordinary Americans while limiting the role of government. During this time, events that affected France and Britain reached beyond their borders. As a result, the United States had the opportunity to double its size by purchasing the Louisiana territory from France. The young nation also faced war with Britain again. Although there was no clear winner in the war, many Americans became more proud of their growing nation.

Why Study History?

During the early 1800s, each branch of the new government was learning its responsibilities and limits. It was at this time that the power and importance of the Supreme Court began to emerge. To learn more about the powerful influence of the "highest court in the land," see this chapter's *Why Study History?* feature, "Supreme Court Decisions Affect You."

American Events			
1801 Thomas Jefferson becomes President	**1804** Lewis and Clark begin to explore Louisiana	**1807** Embargo Act bans trade with foreign nations	

| 1800 | 1802 | 1804 | 1806 | 1808 |

World Events

1803 World Event
France and Britain go to war

Lewis and Clark on the Lower Columbia

In 1803, President Thomas Jefferson doubled the size of the United States by purchasing the Louisiana territory. He sent Meriwether Lewis and William Clark to explore the land and establish friendship with Native Americans. In this painting by Charles M. Russell, Lewis (right) stands by the Native American Sacajawea as she addresses Chinook Indians. ★ **Do you think Native Americans welcomed Lewis and Clark? Explain.**

1811 ●
Harrison fights
Native Americans
at Tippecanoe

●**1812**
War begins between
United States and
Britain

●**1815**
Jackson defeats
British at New Orleans

1808	1810	1812	1814	1816

▲
1810 World Event
Simón Bolívar leads revolt
against Spanish rule in
South America

Republicans in Power

As You Read

Explore These Questions
- What were Jefferson's ideas about government?
- How did he reduce the power of government?
- Why was *Marbury* v. *Madison* important?

Define
- democratic
- laissez faire
- judicial review

Identify
- John Marshall
- *Marbury* v. *Madison*

SETTING the Scene When Thomas Jefferson became President of the United States in 1801, nearly nine out of ten Americans were farmers. This fact gave Jefferson confidence in the nation's future. Even though Jefferson came from a wealthy family, he believed in the importance of ordinary people, especially farmers. In a letter to James Madison, he expressed his faith in the American people:

66 Educate and inform the whole mass of the people. Enable them to see that it is their interest to preserve peace and order, and they will preserve them.... They are the only [ones to rely on] for the preservation of our liberty. 99

A More Democratic Style

As President, Jefferson tried to protect and expand the rights of ordinary citizens. He felt that the Federalists promoted the interests of the wealthy few, but neglected the needs of others. Jefferson was determined to make the government more democratic. **Democratic** means ensuring that all people have the same rights.

Jefferson's personal style matched his democratic beliefs. The new President preferred quiet dinners to the formal parties that Washington and Adams had given. He wore casual clothes and greeted people by shaking hands instead of bowing. With his informal manner, Jefferson showed that the President was an ordinary citizen.

Some Federalists worried about Jefferson's democratic beliefs. They knew that he supported the French Revolution and they feared that he might bring revolutionary change to the United States. They were also afraid that he might punish Federalists who had used the Alien and Sedition acts to jail Republicans.

In his inaugural address, Jefferson tried to quiet Federalists' fears. Though a minority, Federalists "possess their equal rights, which equal laws must protect," he told the nation. He called for an end to the political disputes of past years. "We are all Republicans, we are all Federalists," the President said. Jefferson was determined to unite the country, not divide it further.

Reduced Role of Government

Jefferson had no plan to punish Federalists. He did, however, want to change their policies. In his view, the Federalists had made the national government too large and too powerful. Jefferson wanted to reduce government power by cutting the federal budget and by reducing the federal debt.

Connections With Civics

When Jefferson became President in 1801, there were fewer than 1,000 federal employees. Today, the United States government employs more than 2 million people—not counting those in the military.

Jefferson believed in an idea known as laissez faire (lehs ay FAYR), from the French term for "let alone." According to laissez faire, government should play as small a role as possible in economic affairs. Laissez faire was very different from the Federalist idea of government. Alexander Hamilton, you recall, wanted government to promote trade and manufacturing.

President Jefferson tried to reduce the role of government in people's lives. He decreased the size of government departments and cut the federal budget. With the approval of Congress, he reduced the size of the army and navy. He also asked Congress to repeal the unpopular whiskey tax.

The Sedition Act expired the day before Jefferson took office. Jefferson hated the law, and he pardoned those who were in jail because of it. He also asked Congress to restore the law allowing foreign-born people to become citizens after only a five-year waiting period. Jefferson acted to change other Federalist policies as well.

Jefferson did not discard all Federalist programs, however. He kept the Bank of the United States, which he had once opposed. The federal government also continued to pay off state debts that it had taken over when Washington was President. In addition, Jefferson let many Federalists keep their government jobs.

A Stronger Supreme Court

The election of 1800 gave Republicans control of Congress. Federalists, however, remained powerful in the courts.

Several months passed between Jefferson's election and his inauguration on March 4, 1801. During that time, Federalists in the old Congress passed a law increasing the number of federal judges. President Adams then appointed Federalists to fill these new judicial positions.

One of the judges that Adams appointed was **John Marshall,** the Chief Justice of the Supreme Court. Like Jefferson, Marshall

Biography   Thomas Jefferson

Jefferson, author of the Declaration of Independence and third President of the United States, was a man of many talents. A skilled architect, he designed his own home, Monticello, in the classical style of ancient Greece and Rome. Jefferson felt that it was important for citizens in a democracy to be well educated. ★ **Why do you think Jefferson placed so much value on education?**

◄ Monticello, home of Thomas Jefferson

Why Study History?

Because Supreme Court Decisions Affect You

★ ★

Historical Background

In the early 1800s, the Supreme Court was not as respected as it is today. In fact, for a while, the justices met in the basement of the Capitol because the designers of Washington, D.C., had not provided a meeting place for the Court. However, under the strong leadership of Chief Justice John Marshall, the Supreme Court gained respect and power.

Connections to Today

Today, the Supreme Court is very important as the final authority on cases involving the Constitution. By exercising its power of judicial review (see page 269), the Supreme Court decides whether or not laws are constitutional. Supreme Court justices interpret the Constitution and define and limit our constitutional rights.

Connections to You

Supreme Court cases often involve young people like you. One recent example is the case of *Veronia School District* v. *Acton.*

In 1991, a seventh grader in Oregon wanted to join his school football team. The school required that he submit to a drug test. The student refused, and the school did not allow him to play on the team. The boy's parents sued, arguing that the school had violated the Fourth Amendment's protection against unreasonable searches. The case eventually went to the Supreme Court.

In a 6–3 decision, the Court agreed with the school. It ruled that schools can require athletes to undergo drug tests, just as they require physical examinations and vaccinations. The Court said that schools have a special responsibility to prevent drug abuse and to protect students' health.

This 1995 decision did not affect just one student in one school. The Court's ruling applied to student athletes across the nation. Indirectly, it also had an impact on other issues regarding the rights of students in American schools.

1. **Comprehension** **(a)** How did *Veronia School District* v. *Acton* involve the Constitution? **(b)** Why did the Supreme Court agree with the Oregon school's policy?

2. **Critical Thinking** How do you think the decision affected sports programs in other schools?

 Researching Use library or Internet sources to research a recent Supreme Court case. Report to the class on the issue, the Court's decision, and possible effects of the decision.

was a rich Virginia planter with a brilliant mind. Unlike Jefferson, however, Marshall was a Federalist. He wanted to make the federal government stronger.

The framers of the Constitution expected the courts to balance the powers of the President and Congress. However, John Marshall found the courts to be very weak. In his view, it was not clear what powers the federal courts had.

Marbury v. Madison

In 1803, Marshall decided a case that increased the power of the Supreme Court. The case involved William Marbury, another one of the judges appointed by Adams. Adams made the appointment on his last night as President.

The Republicans refused to accept this "midnight judge." They accused Federalists of using unfair tactics to keep control of the courts. Jefferson ordered Secretary of State James Madison not to deliver the official papers confirming Marbury's appointment.

Marbury sued Madison. According to the Judiciary Act of 1789, only the Supreme Court could decide a case that was brought against a federal official. Therefore, the case of *Marbury* v. *Madison* was tried before the Supreme Court.

An important precedent

In its decision, the Supreme Court ruled against Marbury. Chief Justice Marshall wrote the decision, stating that the Judiciary Act was unconstitutional. The Constitution, Marshall argued, did not give the Supreme Court the right to decide cases brought against federal officials. Therefore, Congress could not give the Court that power.

The Supreme Court's decision in *Marbury* v. *Madison* set an important precedent. It gave the Supreme Court the power to decide whether laws passed by Congress were constitutional and to reject laws that it considered to be unconstitutional. This power of the Court is called **judicial review**.

Jefferson was displeased that the decision gave more power to the Supreme Court. He felt that the decision upset the balance of power that existed among the three branches of government. Even so, the President and Congress accepted the right of the Court to overturn laws. Today, judicial review remains one of the most important powers of the Supreme Court.

★ Section 1 Review ★

Recall

1. **Identify** **(a)** John Marshall, **(b)** *Marbury* v. *Madison.*
2. **Define** **(a)** democratic, **(b)** laissez faire, **(c)** judicial review.

Comprehension

3. Explain how Jefferson's ideas on government differed from Federalist ideas.
4. Describe three steps Jefferson took to reduce the power of government.
5. **(a)** What precedent did *Marbury* v. *Madison* set?

(b) How did the precedent affect the balance of power in American government?

Critical Thinking and Writing

6. **Analyzing a Primary Source** "We are all Republicans, we are all Federalists." **(a)** What did Jefferson mean by these words? **(b)** Why did he need to make such a statement?
7. **Drawing Conclusions** Today, the federal government protects consumers by regulating the quality of certain goods. Would a laissez-faire economist agree with this policy? Why or why not?

★ ★

Activity **Writing a Letter** Welcome to the United States! You are a newly arrived immigrant from Europe. Write a letter to your friends in Europe describing your feelings about President Jefferson and the Republican government.

The Louisana Purchase

As You Read

Explore These Questions

- Why was control of the Mississippi River important to western farmers?
- How did the United States gain Louisiana?
- What did the Lewis and Clark expedition achieve?

Define

- expedition
- Continental Divide

Identify

- Pinckney Treaty
- Toussaint L'Ouverture
- Louisiana Purchase
- Lewis and Clark
- Sacajawea
- Zebulon Pike

◄ *William Clark's journal*

SETTING the Scene One day, President Jefferson received several packages. Inside, he found hides and skeletons of animals, horns of a mountain ram, and a tin box full of insects. There were also cages of live birds and squirrels, as well as gifts from the Mandan and Sioux Indians.

All of these packages were from Meriwether Lewis and William Clark. Jefferson had sent the two to explore the land west of the Mississippi River. Almost two years before, President Jefferson had purchased the territory for the United States. The packages confirmed his belief that the new lands were a valuable addition to the nation.

Control of the Mississippi

By 1800, almost one million Americans lived between the Appalachian Mountains and the Mississippi. Most were farmers.

With few roads west of the Appalachians, western farmers relied on the Mississippi to ship their wheat and corn. First, they sent their produce down the river to New Orleans. From there, oceangoing ships carried the produce to ports along the Atlantic coast.

Threats from Spain and France

Spain sometimes threatened to close the port of New Orleans to Americans. In 1795, President Washington sent Thomas Pinckney to find a way to keep the vital port open. In the **Pinckney Treaty**, Spain agreed to let

Americans ship their goods down the Mississippi and store them in New Orleans. The treaty also settled a dispute over the northern border of Spanish Florida.

For a time, Americans sent their goods to New Orleans without a problem. Then, however, Spain signed a treaty with Napoleon Bonaparte, the ruler of France. The treaty gave Louisiana back to France. President Jefferson was alarmed. Napoleon had already set out to conquer Europe. Jefferson feared that Napoleon might now try to build an empire in North America.

Revolt in Haiti

President Jefferson had good reason to worry. Napoleon wanted to grow food in Louisiana and ship it to French islands in the West Indies. However, events in Haiti soon ruined Napoleon's plan.

Haiti was the richest French colony in the Caribbean. There, enslaved Africans worked sugar plantations that made French planters wealthy. Inspired by the French Revolution, the African slaves in Haiti decided to fight for their liberty. **Toussaint L'Ouverture** (too SAN loo vehr TYOOR) led the revolt. By 1801, Toussaint and his followers had nearly forced the French out of Haiti.

Napoleon sent troops to retake Haiti. Although the French captured Toussaint, they did not regain control of the island. In 1804, Haitians declared their independence. Napoleon's dream of an empire in the Americas ended with the loss of Haiti.

Buying Louisiana

Meanwhile, President Jefferson decided to try to buy the city of New Orleans from Napoleon. Jefferson wanted to be sure that American farmers would always be able to ship their goods through the port. The President sent Robert Livingston and James Monroe to buy New Orleans and West Florida from the French. Jefferson said they could offer as much as $10 million.

A surprising deal

Livingston and Monroe negotiated with Talleyrand, the French foreign minister. At first, Talleyrand showed little interest in their offer. However, changing conditions in Haiti and in Europe were causing Napoleon to alter his plans for the future.

After losing Haiti, Napoleon had abandoned his plan for an empire in the Americas. He also needed money to pay for his very costly wars in Europe. Suddenly Talleyrand asked Livingston if the United States wanted to buy all of Louisiana, not just New Orleans.

Livingston and Monroe carefully debated the matter. They had no authority to buy all of Louisiana. However, they knew that Jefferson wanted control of the Mississippi. They agreed to pay the French $15 million for Louisiana. When he signed the treaty with France, Livingston proudly declared,

66 We have lived long, but this is the noblest work of our whole lives....From this day the United States take their place among the powers of the first rank. 99

Viewing HISTORY — A View of New Orleans

New Orleans, shown here in an 1803 painting by John L. Boqueta de Woiseri, grew prosperous by controlling trade on the Mississippi River. The city's strategic location near the Gulf of Mexico was one reason for the Louisiana Purchase.
★ **How does this 1803 painting show the prosperity of New Orleans?**

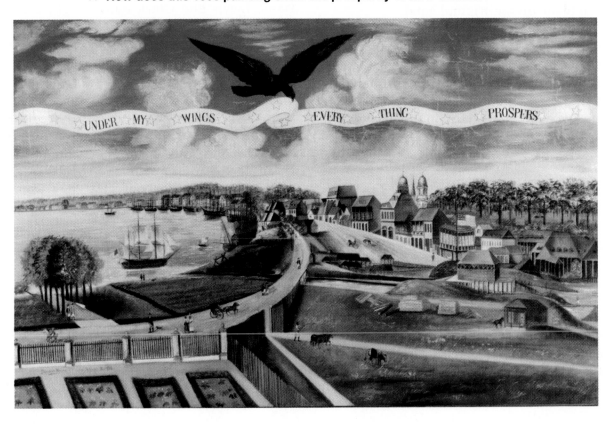

UNDER MY WINGS EVERY THING PROSPERS

Was the purchase constitutional?

Jefferson was pleased by the news from France, but he was not sure that he in fact had the constitutional power to purchase Louisiana. He had always insisted that the federal government had only those powers spelled out in the Constitution. The document said nothing about a President's power to buy land.

After giving it much thought, Jefferson decided that he did have the authority to buy Louisiana. The Constitution, he reasoned, allowed the President to make treaties. At his request, the Senate quickly approved a treaty making the **Louisiana Purchase.** In 1803, the United States took control of the vast lands west of the Mississippi.

Jefferson Plans an Expedition

The United States owned Louisiana now, but few Americans knew anything about the territory. In 1803, Congress provided money for a team of explorers to study the new lands. Jefferson chose Meriwether Lewis, his private secretary, to head the expedition. An expedition is a long journey or voyage of exploration. Lewis asked William Clark, another Virginian, to go with him. About 50 men made up the original band.

Jefferson gave Lewis and Clark careful instructions. He asked them to map a route to the Pacific Ocean. He also told them to study the climate, wildlife, and mineral resources of the new lands. The President requested a detailed report on the following:

> 66 Climate as characterized by the thermometer, by the proportion of rainy, cloudy, and clear days, by lightning, hail, snow, ice... by the winds prevailing at different seasons, the dates at which particular plants put forth or lose their flower, or leaf, times of appearance of particular birds, reptiles or insects. 99

Jefferson also instructed Lewis and Clark to learn about the Indian nations who lived in the Louisiana Purchase. For decades, these Native Americans had carried on a very busy trade with English, French, and Spanish merchants. Jefferson hoped that the Indians might trade with American merchants instead. Therefore, he urged Lewis and Clark to tell the Indians of "our wish to be neighborly, friendly, and useful to them."

The Lewis and Clark Expedition

In May 1804, **Lewis and Clark** started up the Missouri River from St. Louis. In time, their trip would take them to the Pacific Ocean. (Follow their route on the map on page 273.)

Across the plains

At first, the expedition's boats made slow progress against the Missouri's swift current. One night, the current tore away the riverbank where they were camping. The party had to scramble into the boats to avoid being swept downstream.

Lewis and Clark kept journals on their travels. They marveled at the broad, grassy plains that stretched "as far as the eye can reach." Everywhere, they saw "immense herds of buffalo, deer, elk, and antelopes."

As they traveled across the plains, the expedition met people of various Indian nations. Lewis and Clark had brought many gifts for Native Americans. They carried medals stamped with the United States seal. They also brought mirrors, beads, knives, blankets, and thousands of sewing needles and fishhooks.

During the first winter, Lewis and Clark stayed with the Mandans in present-day North Dakota. The explorers planned to continue up the Missouri in the spring. However, they worried about how they would cross the steep Rocky Mountains.

Connections With Science

Acting as botanist for the expedition, Meriwether Lewis collected and preserved many plants. He carefully dried and pressed each specimen. Of the more than 200 specimens Lewis brought back, 39 still remain at the Academy of Natural Sciences in Philadelphia.

Skills

FOR LIFE

Critical Thinking

Managing Information

Communication

Maps, Charts, and Graphs

Following Map Routes

How Will I Use This Skill?

You can use map routes to find your way through a school or office building. With a road map, you can chart a route from home to other places. You can also give directions to others.

LEARN the Skill

You can follow a map route by using the steps below.

❶ Identify the map's subject and symbols that indicate routes.

❷ Use the directional arrow that identifies N, S, E, and W to determine in what direction a route goes. Recognize other directions, such as northeast (NE), the direction between N and E. Other directions are southeast (SE), southwest (SW), and northwest (NW).

❸ Use the scale of miles to determine the distance of a route.

❹ Choose the map route you will follow and describe it in terms of direction and distance.

The Louisiana Purchase

OREGON COUNTRY (claimed by Great Britain, Russia, Spain, and the U.S.)

CANADA

Louisiana

Indiana Territory
St. Louis

Pikes Peak

SPANISH TERRITORY

Santa Fe

Mississippi Territory
Natchitoches

PACIFIC OCEAN

Key
Lewis and Clark 1804–1806
Pike 1805–1806
Pike 1806–1807

0   250   500 Miles
0   250 500 Kilometers

PRACTICE the Skill

Using the steps and the map above, answer the following questions.

❶ What does the map show? What symbols represent routes?

❷ In what general direction did Lewis and Clark travel from St. Louis?

❸ About how many miles did Lewis and Clark travel in order to reach the Pacific Ocean?

❹ Describe Pike's route from St. Louis to Natchitoches.

APPLY the Skill

Using a map of your community, describe the route that you follow to travel from home to school or to any other destination, such as a library or a park.

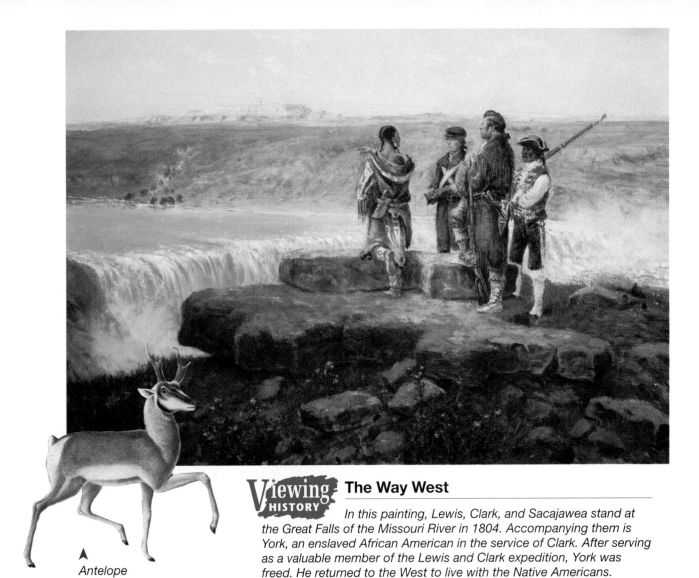

Antelope

Viewing HISTORY — **The Way West**

In this painting, Lewis, Clark, and Sacajawea stand at the Great Falls of the Missouri River in 1804. Accompanying them is York, an enslaved African American in the service of Clark. After serving as a valuable member of the Lewis and Clark expedition, York was freed. He returned to the West to live with the Native Americans.

★ **Why did Lewis and Clark include Sacajawea in the expedition?**

Over the Rockies

A Shoshone woman, **Sacajawea** (sahk uh juh WEE uh), was also staying with the Mandans that winter. The Shoshones (shoh SHOH neez) lived in the Rockies. Sacajawea and her French Canadian husband agreed to accompany Lewis and Clark and serve as translators.

In early spring, the party set out. In the foothills of the Rockies, the landscape and wildlife changed. Bighorn sheep ran along the high hills. The thorns of prickly pear cactus jabbed the explorers' moccasins. One day, a grizzly bear chased Lewis while he was exploring alone.

Sacajawea contributed greatly to the success of the expedition. She gathered wild vegetables and advised the men where to fish and hunt. She knew about the healing qualities of plants and herbs, so the expedition relied on her for medical help.

In the mountains, Sacajawea recognized the lands of her people. One day, Lewis met some Shoshone leaders and invited them back to camp. Sacajawea began to "dance and show every mark of the most extravagant joy." One of the men, she explained, was her brother. The Shoshone people supplied the expedition with food and horses. The Shoshones also advised Lewis and Clark about the best route to take over the Rockies.

In the Rocky Mountains, Lewis and Clark crossed the **Continental Divide.** A continental divide is a mountain ridge that separates river systems flowing toward opposite sides of a continent. In North America,

North Africa attacked vessels from Europe and the United States. The North African nations were called the **Barbary States.** To protect American ships, the United States paid a yearly tribute, or bribe, to the rulers of the Barbary States.

In the early 1800s, Tripoli, one of the Barbary States, demanded a larger bribe than usual. When President Jefferson refused to pay, Tripoli declared war on the United States. In response, Jefferson ordered the navy to blockade the port of Tripoli.

During the blockade, the American ship *Philadelphia* ran aground near Tripoli. Pirates boarded the ship and hauled the crew to prison. The pirates planned to use the *Philadelphia* to attack other ships.

Then, **Stephen Decatur,** a United States Navy officer, took action. Very late one night, Decatur and his crew quietly sailed a ship into Tripoli harbor. When they reached the captured American ship, they set it on fire so that the pirates could not use it.

In the meantime, American marines landed on the coast of North Africa. They then marched 500 miles (805 km) to launch a surprise attack on Tripoli. The war with Tripoli lasted until 1805. In the end, the ruler of Tripoli signed a treaty promising not to interfere with American ships.

American Neutrality Is Violated

During the early 1800s, American ships faced another problem. In 1803, Britain and France went to war again. At first, Americans profited from the war. British and French ships were too busy fighting to engage in trade. American merchants took advantage of the war to trade with both sides. As trade increased, American shipbuilders hurried to build new ships.

Of course, neither Britain nor France wanted the United States to sell supplies to its enemy. As in the 1790s, they ignored American claims of neutrality. Each nation tried to stop American trade with the other. Napoleon seized American ships bound for England, and the British stopped Yankee traders on their way to France. Between

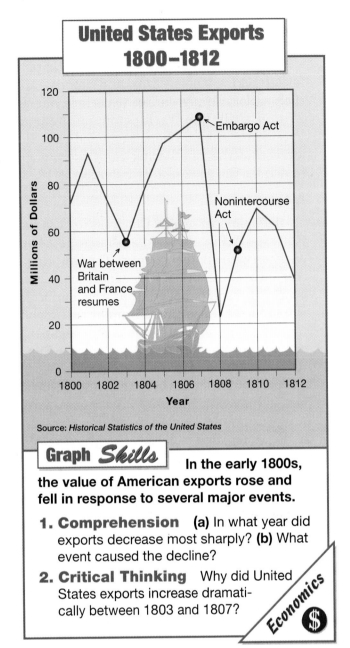

United States Exports 1800–1812

Millions of Dollars (y-axis: 0, 20, 40, 60, 80, 100, 120)

Year (x-axis: 1800, 1802, 1804, 1806, 1808, 1810, 1812)

Embargo Act

Nonintercourse Act

War between Britain and France resumes

Source: *Historical Statistics of the United States*

Graph Skills In the early 1800s, the value of American exports rose and fell in response to several major events.

1. **Comprehension** (a) In what year did exports decrease most sharply? (b) What event caused the decline?
2. **Critical Thinking** Why did United States exports increase dramatically between 1803 and 1807?

Economics $

1805 and 1807, hundreds of American ships were captured.

The British navy also seized American sailors and forced them to serve on British ships. This practice of forcing people into service, called **impressment,** was common in Britain. For centuries, impressment gangs had raided villages and forced young men to serve in the navy.

Because the British navy needed more men to fight France, British ships stopped and searched American vessels. British officers seized all British sailors serving on American ships. They also impressed thousands of American sailors.

Limits on Trade

Americans were furious with the British for attacking their ships and impressing their sailors. Many wanted to declare war on Britain. Still, like Washington and Adams, President Jefferson hoped to avoid war. He knew that the small American fleet was no match for the powerful British navy.

A total ban

Jefferson persuaded Congress to pass the Embargo Act in 1807. An embargo is a ban on trade with another country. The **Embargo Act** forbade Americans to export or import goods. Jefferson hoped that the embargo would hurt France and Britain by cutting off needed supplies. "Our trade is the most powerful weapon we can use in our defense," one Republican newspaper wrote.

The embargo hurt Britain and France, but it hurt the United States even more. Americans were unable to get imports such as sugar, tea, and molasses. Exports dropped from $108 million in 1807 to $22 million in 1808. American sailors had no work. Farmers could not ship wheat overseas. Docks in the South were piled high with cotton and tobacco. The Embargo Act hurt New England merchants most of all.

Merchants from New England and other parts of the country protested loudly against the embargo. Some went a step further and became smugglers. A smuggler is a person who violates trade laws by illegally sneaking goods into or out of a country.

To stop defiance of the law, President Jefferson began using the navy and federal troops to enforce the embargo. On the border between New York and Canada, smugglers fought back. Some engaged in skirmishes with federal troops. Others, disguised as Indians, fired on federal ships.

A limited ban

After more than a year, Jefferson admitted that the Embargo Act had failed. In 1809, Congress replaced it with the less severe **Nonintercourse Act**. It allowed Americans to carry on trade with all nations except Britain and France.

The embargo was the most unpopular measure of Jefferson's years in office. Still, the Republicans remained strong. In 1808, Jefferson followed the precedent set by Washington and refused to run for a third term. James Madison, his fellow Republican, easily won the presidential election. Madison hoped that Britain and France would soon agree to stop violating American neutrality.

★ Section 3 Review ★

Recall

1. **Identify** (a) Barbary States, (b) Stephen Decatur, (c) Embargo Act, (d) Nonintercourse Act.
2. **Define** (a) impressment, (b) embargo, (c) smuggler.

Comprehension

3. How did American merchants expand their trading operations in the 1780s and 1790s?
4. How did war in Europe affect American overseas trade?

5. (a) What was the purpose of the Embargo Act? (b) Why did it fail?

Critical Thinking and Writing

6. **Making Generalizations** How can war both benefit and hurt the economy of a neutral nation? Explain.
7. **Predicting Consequences** What do you think the United States will do if Britain and France continue to violate American neutrality after 1809?

Activity Drawing a Cartoon Suppose the United States were under a limited or total embargo today. Draw a cartoon showing how such an embargo might affect you.

The Road to War

Explore These Questions
- Why did the Prophet and Tecumseh unite Native Americans?
- How did fighting on the frontier lead to war with Britain?
- Why did War Hawks want war with Britain?

Define
- neutral
- nationalism

Identify
- Treaty of Greenville
- Tecumseh
- the Prophet
- William Henry Harrison
- Battle of Tippecanoe
- War Hawks
- Henry Clay

SETTING the Scene James Madison was a quiet, scholarly man. He had helped to write the Constitution and to pass the Bill of Rights. As President, he hoped to keep the United States out of war.

Many Americans, however, felt that Madison's approach was too timid. They argued that the United States must stand up to Native Americans and foreign countries. How could the nation grow if Native Americans stood in the way? How could the nation win respect if it allowed the British and French navies to seize American ships? The cost of war might be great, said one member of Congress. Yet, he continued, who would count in money "the slavery of our impressed seamen"?

This kind of talk aroused the nation. In the early 1800s, the United States went to war with several Native American nations. By 1812, many Americans were also calling for war with Britain.

Conflict With Native Americans

Thousands of white settlers had moved into the Northwest Territory in the 1790s. The large number of newcomers caused problems for Native Americans. The settlers ignored treaties the United States had signed with Indian nations of the region. They built farms on Indian lands. They hunted the animals that Indians depended on for food.

In the 1790s, U.S. infantry soldiers wore coats such as the one shown here.

Fighting often broke out between the Native Americans and settlers. Isolated acts of violence led to larger acts of revenge. As a result, both sides killed innocent people who had not taken part in acts of violence. In this way, warfare spread and minor conflicts grew into larger ones.

In 1791, the Miamis of Ohio joined with other Indian nations. Little Turtle, a skilled fighter, led the Miami nation. Armed with muskets and gunpowder supplied by the British, the Miamis drove white settlers from the area.

In 1794, President Washington sent General Anthony Wayne with a well-trained army into Miami territory. The Native American forces gathered at a place called Fallen Timbers. They thought that Wayne would have trouble fighting there because fallen trees covered the land. However, Wayne's army pushed through the tangle of logs and defeated the Indians.

In 1795, leaders of the Miamis and a number of other Indian nations signed the **Treaty of Greenville.** They gave up land that would later become part of Ohio. In return, they received $20,000 and the promise of more money if they kept the peace.

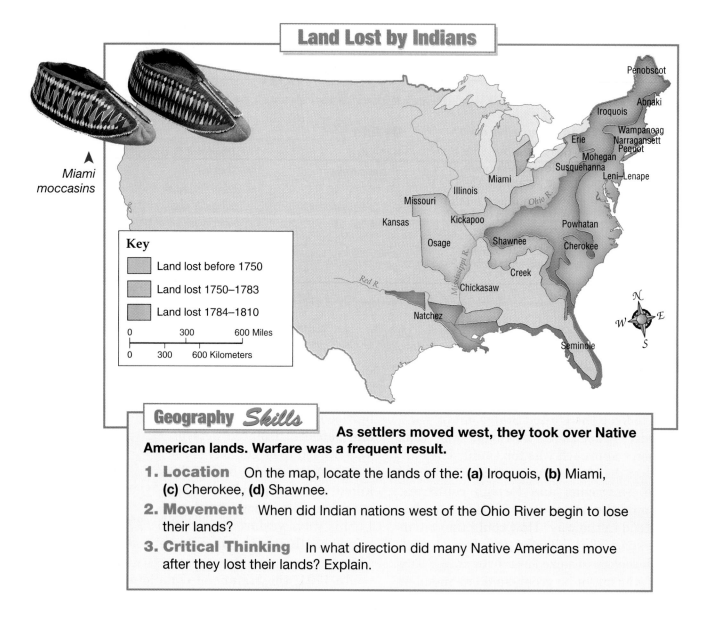

Land Lost by Indians

Penobscot
Abnaki
Iroquois
Wampanoag
Erie
Narragansett
Pequot
Mohegan
Susquehanna
Leni-Lenape
Miami
Illinois
Ohio R.
Missouri
Powhatan
Kansas
Kickapoo
Cherokee
Osage
Shawnee
Creek
Red R.
Mississippi R.
Chickasaw
Natchez
Seminole

Miami moccasins

Key

Land lost before 1750

Land lost 1750–1783

Land lost 1784–1810

0   300   600 Miles

0   300   600 Kilometers

Geography *Skills*

As settlers moved west, they took over Native American lands. Warfare was a frequent result.

1. **Location**   On the map, locate the lands of the: **(a)** Iroquois, **(b)** Miami, **(c)** Cherokee, **(d)** Shawnee.
2. **Movement**   When did Indian nations west of the Ohio River begin to lose their lands?
3. **Critical Thinking**   In what direction did many Native Americans move after they lost their lands? Explain.

Tecumseh's Confederation

Ohio joined the Union in 1803. By then, white settlers were pushing beyond Ohio into Indiana Territory. Many Native Americans grew angry. They wanted to keep settlers from taking more Indian land. Among those who felt this way were two Shawnee leaders: **Tecumseh** (tih KUHM suh) and his brother, called **the Prophet**.

Unity and the Old Ways

The Prophet said that he had journeyed to the spirit world. There, he learned the path that Indians must take if they were to live happily. Both the Prophet and Tecumseh said that white customs corrupted the Native American way of life. They said that many Indians depended on white trade goods, such as muskets, cloth, cooking pots, and whiskey. They believed that by returning to the old ways, Indians could gain the power to resist white invaders.

In 1808, the Prophet built a village for his followers along Tippecanoe Creek in Indiana Territory. Indians traveled from lands as far away as Missouri, Iowa, and Minnesota to hear his message. His teachings brought hope to many.

In the early 1800s, Tecumseh and the Prophet organized many Native American nations into a confederation, or league. The Prophet was the spiritual leader of the confederation and Tecumseh was its spokesperson. Tecumseh and the Prophet persuaded Native Americans to unite against white settlers:

> 66 The whites have driven us from the great salt water, forced us over the mountains....The way...to check and stop this evil is for all red men to unite in claiming a common equal right in the land. 99

Tecumseh also impressed white leaders. **William Henry Harrison,** governor of Indiana Territory, grudgingly admitted, "He is one of those uncommon geniuses which spring up occasionally to produce revolutions and overturn the established order of things."

Showdown at Tippecanoe

Rivalries among Native American nations kept Tecumseh from uniting all Indians east of the Mississippi River. Still, white settlers were alarmed at his success.

In 1811, Governor Harrison marched 1,000 soldiers against Tecumseh's town on the Tippecanoe Creek. The Prophet was in charge because Tecumseh was away organizing Indians in the South. The Prophet led a surprise night attack on Harrison's troops. Neither side won a clear victory in the battle that followed. Still, whites celebrated the **Battle of Tippecanoe** as a major victory.

Growing Conflict With Britain

The fighting with Native Americans caused relations between the United States and Britain to worsen. The British were supplying guns and ammunition to the Native Americans on the frontier. They were also encouraging Indians to attack United States' settlements.

Meanwhile, the United States and Britain also continued to disagree over trade. When the embargo against Britain and France was set to expire in 1810, the United States made a very daring offer. If either the British or French would stop seizing

 Biography **Tecumseh and the Prophet**

Tecumseh (left) and the Prophet (right) felt that no Indian nation could sell land unless all other Indian nations agreed. Tecumseh said, "Sell a country! Why not sell the air, the great sea, as well as the earth?" ★ **Why did Tecumseh and the Prophet dislike the Treaty of Greenville?**

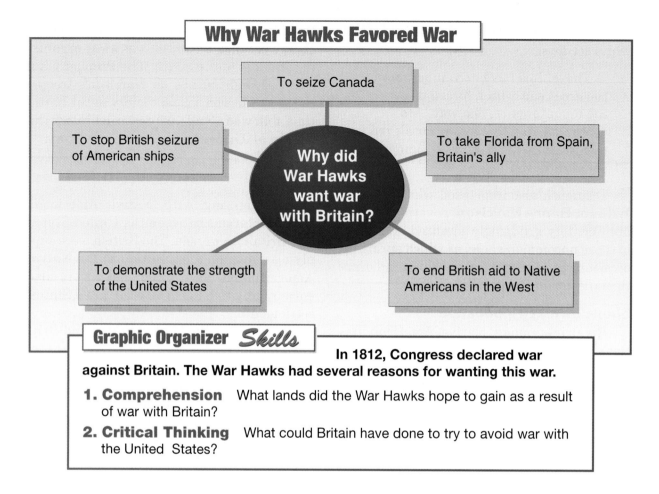

Why War Hawks Favored War

To seize Canada

To stop British seizure of American ships

Why did War Hawks want war with Britain?

To take Florida from Spain, Britain's ally

To demonstrate the strength of the United States

To end British aid to Native Americans in the West

Graphic Organizer *Skills*

In 1812, Congress declared war against Britain. The War Hawks had several reasons for wanting this war.

1. **Comprehension**   What lands did the War Hawks hope to gain as a result of war with Britain?

2. **Critical Thinking**   What could Britain have done to try to avoid war with the United States?

American ships, the United States would halt trade with the other nation.

Seizing the chance, Napoleon quickly announced that France would respect the United States' policy of staying **neutral,** or uninvolved in the war between Britain and France. As promised, the United States continued trade with France, but stopped all shipments to Britain.

The War Hawks

While President Madison did not want war, other Americans were not as cautious. Except in New England, where many merchants wanted to restore trade with Britain, anti-British feeling ran strong. Members of Congress from the South and the West called for war with Britain. They were known as **War Hawks**.

War Hawks had a strong sense of nationalism. **Nationalism** is pride in or devotion to one's country. War Hawks felt that Britain was treating the United States as if it were still a British colony. They were willing to fight a war to defend American rights.

Arguments for war

Henry Clay of Kentucky was the most outspoken War Hawk. Clay wanted war for two reasons. He wanted revenge on Britain for seizing American ships. He also wanted to conquer Canada. "The militia of Kentucky are alone [able] to place Montreal and Upper Canada at your feet," Clay boasted to Congress. Canadians, Clay believed, would be happy to leave the British empire and join the United States.

War Hawks saw other advantages of war with Britain. South of the United States, Florida belonged to Spain, Britain's ally. If Americans went to war with Britain, War Hawks said, the United States could seize Florida from Spain.

War Hawks had yet another reason to fight Britain. They pointed out that Britain was arming Native Americans on the frontier and encouraging them to attack settlers. The War Hawks felt that winning a war against Britain would bring lasting peace and safety to American settlers on the frontier.

Congress Declares War

In 1811, the United States and Britain drifted closer to war. To prevent Americans from trading with France, British warships blockaded some American ports. The British continued to board American ships and impress American seamen. In May 1811, near New York Harbor, a brief battle broke out between an American frigate and a British warship. The Americans crippled the British ship and left 32 British dead or wounded.

The War Hawks urged that Congress prepare for a war against Britain. One of the most radical and outspoken of the War Hawks was Felix Grundy, a Congressman from Tennessee. In December 1811, he gave a very emotional speech describing what he saw as the benefits of war:

> 66 This war...will have its advantages. We shall drive the British from our continent—they will no longer have an opportunity of intriguing with our Indian neighbors. 99

Grundy hoped that a war with Britain would achieve other more ambitious goals. Like most War Hawks, he dreamed of win-ning additional land for the United States. He closed his speech with these words: "I therefore feel anxious not only to add the Floridas to the South, but the Canadas to the North of this empire."

Others in Congress opposed the strong views of the War Hawks. John Randolph of Virginia warned that the people of the United States would "not submit to be taxed for this war of conquest and dominion." Representatives of New England were especially concerned. They feared that the British navy would attack New England seaports.

President Madison at last gave in to war fever. In June 1812, he asked Congress to declare war on Britain. The House voted 79 to 49 in favor of war. The Senate vote was 19 to 13. Americans soon discovered, however, that winning the war would not be as easy as declaring it.

Cannon used in the war against Britain ➤

★ Section 4 Review ★

Recall

1. **Locate**   Native American lands lost **(a)** from 1750 to 1783, **(b)** from 1784 to 1810.
2. **Identify**   **(a)** Treaty of Greenville, **(b)** Tecumseh, **(c)** the Prophet, **(d)** William Henry Harrison, **(e)** Battle of Tippecanoe, **(f)** War Hawks, **(g)** Henry Clay.
3. **Define**   **(a)** neutral, **(b)** nationalism.

Comprehension

4. Why was there conflict between Native Americans and white settlers?

5. How did the Battle of Tippecanoe help lead to war between Britain and the United States?
6. What did the War Hawks hope to gain from a war with Britain?

Critical Thinking and Writing

7. **Identifying Main Ideas**   What ideas did the Prophet and Tecumseh use to unite many Native Americans?
8. **Defending a Position**   In 1812, would you have favored or opposed war with Britain? Explain the reasons for your position.

★ ★

Activity   **Writing a Speech**   You are a Native American leader of the early 1800s. Write a speech explaining why you are against white settlement and what you think Native Americans can do to stop it. Deliver your speech to the class.

The War of 1812

As You Read

Explore These Questions
- How was the United States unready for war with Britain?
- What were the major turning points of the war in the West?
- What were the results of the war?

Identify
- Oliver Hazard Perry
- Battle of Lake Erie
- Andrew Jackson
- Battle of Horseshoe Bend
- Dolley Madison
- Battle of New Orleans
- Richard Allen
- Hartford Convention
- Treaty of Ghent

Many Americans welcomed the news of war with Britain. In some cities, they fired cannons and guns and danced in the streets. One New Jersey man wrote a song calling for a swift attack on Canada:

66 On to Quebec's embattled halls! Who will pause, when glory calls? Charge, soldiers, charge, its lofty walls. And storm its strong artillery. 99

Other Americans were less enthusiastic. New Englanders, especially, talked scornfully of "Mr. Madison's war." In fact, before the war ended, some New Englanders would threaten to leave the Union and make a separate peace with Britain.

Unready for War

The American declaration of war took the British by surprise. They were locked in a bitter struggle with Napoleon, and could not spare troops to fight the United States. As the war began, however, the United States faced difficulties of its own.

Because Jefferson believed in a small federal government and had reduced spending on defense, the United States was not ready for war. The navy had only 16 ships to fight against the huge British fleet. The army was small and ill equipped. Moreover, many of the officers knew little about the military. "The state of the Army," commented a member of Congress, "is enough to make any man

who has the smallest love of country wish to get rid of it."

Since there were few regular troops, the government relied on volunteers to fight the war. Congress voted to give them $124 and 360 acres of land for their service. The money was high pay at the time—equal to a year's salary for most workers.

Attracted by money and the chance to own their own farm, young men eagerly enlisted. They were poorly trained, however, and did not know how to be good soldiers. Many deserted after a few months.

Fighting at Sea

The British navy blockaded American ports to stop Americans from trading with other countries. The small American navy was unable to break the blockade. Still, several sea captains won stunning victories.

One famous battle took place early in the war, in August 1812. As he was sailing near Newfoundland, Isaac Hull, captain of the *Constitution*, spotted the British ship *Guerrière* (gai ree AIR). For nearly an hour, the two ships jockeyed for position.

At last, the guns of the *Constitution* roared into action. They tore holes in the sides of the *Guerrière* and shot off both masts. When the smoke cleared, Hull asked the British captain if he had "struck" his flag—that is, lowered his flag in surrender. "Well, I don't know," replied the stunned British captain. "Our mizzenmast is gone, our mainmast

The USS Constitution

The USS Constitution *became known as "Old Ironsides" because British cannonballs often bounced off her thick wooden hull. In 1905, the ship was docked in Boston and opened to the public. In 1997, the ship underwent major restoration. Today, the United States Navy invites you to come aboard and tour "Old Ironsides." In the nearby museum, you can relive history by commanding a ship, hoisting a sail, or firing a cannon.*

★ ***To learn more about this historic ship, write:*** *USS* Constitution *Museum, Charlestown Navy Yard, Charlestown, MA 02129.*

is gone. And, upon the whole, you may say we *have* struck our flag."

American sea captains won other victories at sea. These victories cheered Americans, but did little to win the war.

War in the West

One goal of the War Hawks was to conquer Canada. They were convinced that Canadians would welcome the chance to throw off British rule and join the United States. The United States planned to invade Canada at three different points: Detroit, the Niagara River, and Montreal.

Invasion of Canada

General William Hull moved American troops into Canada from Detroit. The Canadians had only a few untrained troops to ward off the invasion. However, they were led by a clever and skillful British leader, General Isaac Brock.

Brock paraded his soldiers in red coats to make it appear that experienced British troops were helping the Canadians. He also let a message with false information fall into American hands. It exaggerated the number of Indians who were fighting with the Canadians. Brock's scare tactics worked. Hull retreated from Canada.

Other attempts to invade Canada also failed. Americans were wrong in thinking that the Canadians would welcome them as liberators from British rule. Instead, the Canadians fought fiercely and forced the Americans into retreat.

Battle of Lake Erie

In 1813, the Americans set out to win control of Lake Erie. Captain **Oliver Hazard Perry** had no fleet, so he designed and built his own ships. In September 1813, he sailed his tiny fleet against the British.

During the **Battle of Lake Erie**, the British battered Perry's own ship and left it

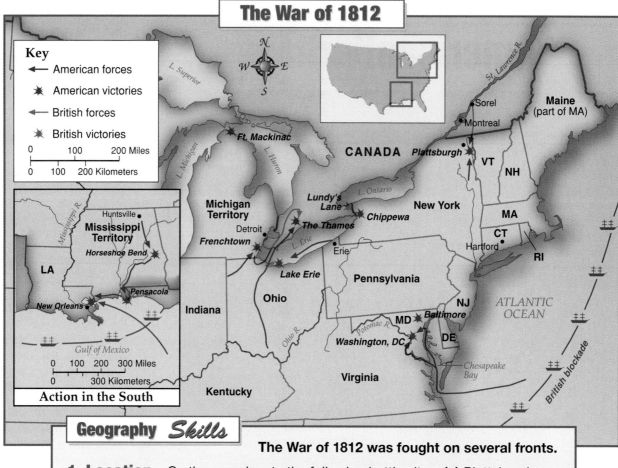

The War of 1812

Key
← American forces
✳ American victories
← British forces
✳ British victories

0 100 200 Miles
0 100 200 Kilometers

Action in the South

L. Superior

Ft. Mackinac

CANADA   Plattsburgh

Sorel

Montreal

St. Lawrence R.

Maine
(part of MA)

VT

NH

L. Michigan

L. Huron

Michigan
Territory

Detroit

Frenchtown

Lundy's
Lane

The Thames

L. Ontario

Chippewa

New York

MA

CT

Hartford

RI

L. Erie

Lake Erie

Erie

Pennsylvania

ATLANTIC
OCEAN

Indiana

Ohio

Ohio R.

NJ

MD   Baltimore

Washington, DC

DE

Potomac R.

Chesapeake
Bay

British blockade

Kentucky

Virginia

Mississippi R.

Huntsville

Mississippi
Territory

Horseshoe Bend

LA

Pensacola

New Orleans

Gulf of Mexico

0 100 200 300 Miles
0   300 Kilometers

Geography *Skills*

The War of 1812 was fought on several fronts.

1. **Location**   On the map, locate the following battle sites: **(a)** Plattsburgh, **(b)** Lake Erie, **(c)** The Thames, **(d)** Horseshoe Bend, **(e)** Washington, D.C., **(f)** Baltimore, **(g)** New Orleans.

2. **Movement**   Using the inset map, describe the route that American forces followed from Huntsville to New Orleans

3. **Critical Thinking**   How did the British blockade hurt the economy of the United States?

helpless. Perry took his flag down and rowed over to another American ship. There, he raised the colors again and continued to fight. Finally, the Americans won the battle. Captain Perry wrote his message of victory on the back of an envelope: "We have met the enemy and they are ours."

Native American losses

After losing control of Lake Erie, the British and their ally Tecumseh retreated from Detroit into Canada. General William Henry Harrison, veteran of Tippecanoe, pursued them. The Americans won a decisive victory at the Battle of the Thames. Tecumseh died in the fighting. Without Tecumseh's

leadership, the Indian confederation soon fell apart.

Still, the Creeks, Tecumseh's allies in the South, continued their fight against the settlers. **Andrew Jackson,** a Tennessee officer, took command of American troops in the Creek War. In 1814, with the help of the Cherokees, Jackson won a crushing victory at the **Battle of Horseshoe Bend.** The leader of the Creeks walked alone into Jackson's camp to surrender:

❝ I am in your power. Do unto me as you please.... If I had an army I would yet fight, and contend to the last.... But your people have destroyed my nation. ❞

For the time being, the fighting ended. Once again, Native Americans had to give up land to whites.

Final Battles

In 1814, Britain and its allies defeated France. With the war in Europe over, Britain could send more troops and ships against the United States.

The British burn Washington

In the summer of 1814, British ships sailed into Chesapeake Bay and landed an invasion force about 30 miles (48 km) from Washington, D.C. American troops met the British at Bladensburg, Maryland. President Madison himself watched the battle. To his dismay, the battle-hardened British quickly scattered the untrained Americans. The British met little further resistance as they continued their march to the capital.

In the White House, **Dolley Madison** waited for her husband to return. Hastily, she scrawled a note to her sister:

66 Will you believe it, my sister? We have had a battle or skirmish near Bladensburg and here I am still within sound of the cannon! Mr. Madison comes not. May God protect us. Two messengers covered with dust come bid me fly. But here I mean to wait for him. 99

Soon after, British troops marched into the capital. Dolley Madison gathered up important papers of the President and a portrait of George Washington. Then, she fled south. She was not there to see the British burn the White House and other buildings.

From Washington, the British marched north toward the city of Baltimore. The key to Baltimore's defense was Fort McHenry.

Linking Past and Present

Past

Present

The White House

After capturing Washington in August 1814, the British burned the White House. Margaret Smith, a resident of the city, recalled the sad scene: "Who would have thought that this mass so solid, so magnificent, so grand...[should] be thus irreparably destroyed." In fact, the White House was not destroyed. A torrential thunderstorm put out the flames and saved the structure. Today, the White House continues to serve as the official residence of Presidents of the United States. ★ **How do you think the burning of the White House affected American morale?**

In this engraving, Andrew Jackson stands atop the American defense works as he spurs his troops to victory. The Battle of New Orleans was the bloodiest engagement of the War of 1812. Neither side knew that the war had ended two weeks earlier. ★ **Why did it take so long for the news of war's end to reach New Orleans?**

From evening on September 13 until dawn on September 14, British rockets bombarded the harbor.

When the early morning fog lifted, the "broad stripes and bright stars" of the American flag still waved over Fort McHenry. The British withdrew. Francis Scott Key, who witnessed the battle, wrote a poem about the bombardment. Later, "The Star-Spangled Banner" was set to music and adopted as the national anthem of the United States.

Battle of New Orleans

In late 1814, the British prepared to attack New Orleans. From there, they hoped to sail up the Mississippi. However, Andrew Jackson was waiting for the British. Jackson had turned his frontier fighters into a strong army. He took Pensacola in Spanish Florida to keep the British from using it as a base. He then marched through Mobile and set up camp in New Orleans.

Jackson's force included thousands of frontiersmen. Many of them were expert riflemen. In addition, citizens of New Orleans joined the army to defend their city from the approaching British. Among the volunteers were hundreds of African Americans.

The American soldiers dug trenches to defend themselves. On January 8, 1815, the British attacked. Again and again, British soldiers marched toward the American trenches. More than 2,000 British fell under the deadly fire of American sharpshooters and cannons. Only seven Americans died.

All over the United States, Americans cheered the victory at the **Battle of New Orleans**. Andrew Jackson became a national hero. His fame did not dim even when Americans later learned that the battle could have been avoided. It took place two weeks after the United States and Britain had signed a treaty in Europe ending the war.

African Americans in the War

African Americans served alongside other Americans in the fight against the British. African American soldiers helped win the Battle of New Orleans. Following the British attacks on Washington and Baltimore, African American volunteers helped defend Philadelphia against a possible attack. Bishop **Richard Allen** and the Reverend Absalom Jones recruited more than 2,000 men to help build Philadelphia's fortifications. The state of New York, meanwhile, organized two regiments of black volunteers to serve in the army.

African Americans also served with distinction in the United States Navy. They helped win the Battle of Lake Erie as well as other naval battles. Commander Nathaniel Shaler praised one particular black sailor who was killed in battle: "When America has such [sailors], she has little to fear from the tyrants of the ocean."

Peace at Last

In the early 1800s, news took weeks to cross the Atlantic Ocean. By late 1814, Americans knew that peace talks had begun, but they did not know how they were progressing or how long they would last. As Jackson was preparing to fight the British at New Orleans, New Englanders were meeting to protest "Mr. Madison's war."

New Englanders protest

The British blockade had hurt New England's sea trade. Also, many New Englanders feared that the United States might win land in Florida and Canada. If new states were carved out of these lands, the South and the West would become more influential than New England.

Delegates from around New England met in Hartford, Connecticut, in December 1814. Most were Federalists. They disliked the Republican President and the war. The delegates to the **Hartford Convention** threatened to leave the Union if the war continued.

Then, while the delegates debated what to do, news of the peace treaty arrived. The Hartford Convention ended quickly. With the war over, the protest was meaningless.

"Nothing was settled"

The **Treaty of Ghent** was signed in the city of Ghent, Belgium, on December 24, 1814. John Quincy Adams, one of the Americans at Ghent, summed up the treaty in one sentence: "Nothing was adjusted, nothing was settled."

Britain and the United States agreed to restore prewar conditions. The treaty said nothing about impressment or neutrality. These issues had faded due to the end of the Napoleonic Wars in Europe. Other issues were settled later. In 1818, for example, the two nations settled a dispute over the border between Canada and the United States.

Looking back, some Americans felt that the War of 1812 had been a mistake. Others argued that Europe would now treat the young republic with more respect. The victories of heroes like Oliver Hazard Perry and Andrew Jackson gave Americans new pride in their country. As one Republican leader remarked, "The people are now more American. They feel and act more as a nation."

★ Section 5 Review ★

Recall

1. **Locate** (a) Lake Erie, (b) Detroit, (c) Chesapeake Bay, (d) Washington, D.C., (e) Baltimore, (f) New Orleans.
2. **Identify** (a) Oliver Hazard Perry, (b) Battle of Lake Erie, (c) Andrew Jackson, (d) Battle of Horseshoe Bend, (e) Dolley Madison, (f) Battle of New Orleans, (g) Richard Allen, (h) Hartford Convention, (i) Treaty of Ghent.

Comprehension

3. What military problems did the United States face as the War of 1812 began?

4. How did the death of Tecumseh affect the war in the West?
5. What were the results of the War of 1812?

Critical Thinking and Writing

6. **Understanding Causes and Effects** How do you think the War of 1812 helped Andrew Jackson to later become the President of the United States?
7. **Applying Information** Why did the results of the War of 1812 please some Americans, but disappoint others?

Activity **Writing a Song** Keep your head down! You are in the trenches at the Battle of New Orleans. Write a song describing what you see, hear, and feel as you help Andrew Jackson defeat the British and save New Orleans.

Review and Activities

★ Sum It Up ★

Section 1 Republicans in Power
▶ President Jefferson tried to help ordinary citizens and limit government power.
▶ The Supreme Court established its power to decide if laws are constitutional.

Section 2 The Louisiana Purchase
▶ In 1803, the United States bought the vast western territory of Louisiana from France.
▶ Lewis and Clark explored Louisiana and tried to establish friendly relations with Native Americans.

Section 3 New Threats From Overseas
▶ American trade increased but was threatened by France and Britain.
▶ The Embargo Act hurt the United States more than Britain and France.

Section 4 The Road to War
▶ Native Americans fought to preserve their lands and culture.
▶ War Hawks wanted war with Britain to protect American trade and to gain new lands.

Section 5 The War of 1812
▶ Though poorly prepared, American forces defeated the British in key battles.
▶ Not all Americans supported the war. For many, however, the war brought a new sense of national pride.

CD-ROM Review For additional review of the major ideas of Chapter 10, see *Guide to the Essentials of American History* or *Interactive Student Tutorial CD-ROM,* which contains interactive review activities, graphic organizers, and practice tests.

🗌 Reviewing the Chapter

Define These Terms
Match each term with the correct definition.

Column 1	Column 2
1. laissez faire	a. forcing people into naval service
2. judicial review	b. ban on trade with another country
3. impressment	c. government should play a very limited role in economic affairs
4. embargo	
5. nationalism	d. pride in one's country
	e. Supreme Court's power to decide if laws are constitutional

Explore the Main Ideas
1. Describe two of President Jefferson's ideas about the proper role of government.
2. Why did the United States buy Louisiana from France?
3. What were the goals of the Lewis and Clark expedition?
4. How did war between Britain and France affect the United States?
5. Why did many Native Americans unite under Tecumseh and the Prophet?
6. **(a)** Describe one major turning point in the War of 1812. **(b)** Explain one result of the war.

🗌 Geography Skills

Match the letters on the map with the following places:
1. Canada, 2. Battle of the Thames, 3. Battle of Horseshoe Bend, 4. Battle of New Orleans, 5. Baltimore, 6. British blockade.

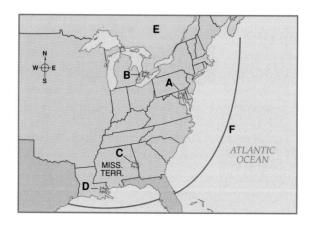

Critical Thinking and Writing

1. **Defending a Position** Do you agree or disagree with Jefferson's idea that federal power should be limited? Explain the reasons for your position.
2. **Understanding Chronology** How did a British-French war help lead to a British-American war?
3. **Solving Problems** Describe a treaty that might have satisfied both Native Americans and white settlers in the early 1800s.
4. **Exploring Unit Themes** **Nationalism** Describe two events or developments that caused many Americans to become more nationalistic during the Age of Jefferson.

Using Primary Sources

Soon after passage of the Embargo Act, President Jefferson received this letter from Jonathan Hall, a resident of New Hampshire:

> 66 Sir: I have respected your laws and your government for the United States of America and I wish to have you continue your laws and government and keep the embargo on till you see fit to take it off, though it is very trying to the people in this country about their debts.... I have a father and a mother and they can't take care of themselves and as times are I can't pay for their place so...I hope that...your [honor] will do a little for me, Jonathan Hall. 99

Source: *Jefferson Papers*. "Capt. Jonathan Hall to Jefferson." August 12, 1808.

Recognizing Points of View **(a)** Did Hall approve of the Embargo Act? **(b)** How did the embargo affect Hall? **(c)** Explain how the embargo might have caused this effect.

ACTIVITY BANK

Interdisciplinary Activity

Exploring Civics Create a chart comparing the different ideas of the Federalists and Republicans during the Age of Jefferson. Include categories such as ideas about democracy, economic policy, military policy, and foreign policy.

Career Skills Activity

Political Leaders Write a persuasive speech supporting or opposing war with Britain in 1812. The purpose of the speech is to persuade listeners to agree with your point of view. Deliver your speech to the class. Then, invite students to express their own views. If there is disagreement, you might wish to debate the issue.

Citizenship Activity

Creating a Poster "We are all Republicans, we are all Federalists," said President Jefferson. Create a poster describing and illustrating four goals you think all Americans should agree on, regardless of their political party.

Internet Activity

Use the Internet to find information about current or recent embargoes. In a written report, describe two of these modern embargoes and the reason for each. Explain whether or not each has been successful.

EYEWITNESS Journal

You are a War Hawk in Congress, or a Native American at the Battle of Horseshoe Bend, or a British soldier attacking Washington, D.C., or an American soldier at New Orleans. In your EYEWITNESS JOURNAL, record your participation in and feelings about the War of 1812.

Chapter 11

Industry and Growth

1790–1825

In the early 1800s, the United States changed rapidly. New technology caused a growth in industry. New factories sprang up along the nation's waterways, and with them new towns and cities. The nation increased in size, too, as settlers swarmed west along roads and rivers.

Change led to increased differences. Economic differences grew between the traditional farming society and the newer industrial society. Regional differences also grew between the North, South, and West. The nation's leaders struggled to strengthen and unify a rapidly expanding nation. They also faced the challenge of creating a bold new foreign policy, as neighboring nations in Latin America won independence.

Why Study *History?*

Today, we live in an era of rapid technological change. Our age is not the first time Americans have faced a revolution in technology. In the early 1800s, as today, new inventions changed forever the way people lived. To focus on this connection, see the *Why Study History?* feature, "Technology Continues to Change Our Lives," in this chapter.

American Events

1790 First American spinning mill opens

1793 Eli Whitney's cotton gin boosts textile industry

1806 Congress approves building the National Road

| 1785 | 1790 | 1795 | 1800 | 1805 |

World Events

1793 World Event China rejects British trade

1802 World Event Child labor law enacted in Britain

![Viewing History]

A New Age of Steamboats

Steam Ferry, St. Louis *by French artist Leon Pomarede is one of the earliest paintings of St. Louis, Missouri. It shows steam-powered ships puffing down the Mississippi toward the city. In the early 1800s, steamboats and other new means of transportation made it easier for settlers to travel to the West. At the same time, new technology changed how goods were produced and how people worked.*
★ **What advantages do you think steamboats might have had over earlier forms of travel?**

●1807
Fulton's
steamship makes
record-breaking trip

●1816
New tariff sparks
sectional dispute

●1823
Monroe Doctrine
warns Europe not
to recolonize the
Americas

| 1805 | 1810 | 1815 | 1820 | 1825 |

 1807 World Event
Gas street lighting
demonstrated in London

 1815 World Event
Napoleon defeated at
Waterloo

The Industrial Revolution

As You Read

Explore These Questions
- What were the effects of the Industrial Revolution?
- How did the Industrial Revolution come to the United States?
- What was life like in early factories?

Define
- spinning jenny
- capitalist
- factory system
- interchangeable parts
- urbanization

Identify
- Industrial Revolution
- Samuel Slater
- Moses Brown
- Francis Cabot Lowell
- Boston Associates
- "Lowell girls"
- Eli Whitney

 At dawn, the factory bell woke 11-year-old Lucy Larcom. Rising quickly, she ate her breakfast, and hurried to her job at a spinning mill in Lowell, Massachusetts. Years later, Larcom described her workplace:

66 I never cared much for machinery. The buzzing and hissing and whizzing of pulleys and rollers and spindles and flyers around me often grew tiresome.... I could look across the room and see girls moving backward and forward among the spinning frames, sometimes stooping, sometimes reaching up their arms, as their work required. 99

Factories and machinery were part of a revolution that reached the United States in the early 1800s. Unlike the American Revolution, this one had no battles or fixed dates. The new **Industrial Revolution** was a long, slow process which completely changed the way goods were produced.

The Industrial Revolution Begins

Before the 1800s, most people were farmers and most goods were produced by hand. As a result of the Industrial Revolution, this situation gradually began to change. Machines replaced hand tools. New sources of power, such as steam, replaced human and animal power. While most Americans continued to farm for a living, the economy began a gradual shift toward manufacturing.

New technology

The Industrial Revolution started in Britain in the mid-1700s. British inventors developed new technologies that transformed the textile industry.

Since early times, workers used spinning wheels to make thread. A spinning wheel, however, could spin only one thread at a time. In 1764, James Hargreaves developed the **spinning jenny,** a machine that could spin several threads at once. Later, Richard Arkwright invented a machine that could hold 100 spindles of thread. It was called the water frame because it required water power to turn its wheels.

Other inventions speeded up the process of weaving thread into cloth. In the 1780s, Edmund Cartwright built a loom powered by water. It allowed a worker to produce 200 times more cloth in a day than was possible before.

The factory system

New inventions led to a new method of production. Before the Industrial Revolution, most spinning and weaving took place in the home. Machines like the water frame, however, had to be housed in large mills near rivers. Water flowing downstream or over a waterfall turned a wheel that produced the power to run the machines.

To set up and operate a spinning mill required large amounts of capital, or money.

❶ *Wagons bring raw cotton to the mill to be spun into thread.*

❷ *Fast-moving water causes the water wheel to turn.*

❸ *The turning water wheel powers the mill's main shaft.*

❹ *The main shaft drives pulleys, which turn belts that drive the mill machinery.*

❺ *Carding machines comb the raw cotton fiber.*

❻ *Drawing machines pull the combed cotton fibers into ropelike strands.*

❼ *Spinning frames twist combed and drawn cotton strands into thread and wind them onto a bobbin.*

❽ *Wagons carry spun thread to weavers who use it to make cloth.*

Spinning Mill

New technology in the textile industry sparked the Industrial Revolution. As shown here, rapidly moving water turned a water wheel, like the one above. The wheel produced the power to run the machines. ★ **Would your town or community have been a suitable place for a spinning mill like this one? Why or why not?**

Main shaft of a spinning mill

Capitalists supplied this money. A **capitalist** is a person who invests in a business in order to make a profit. Capitalists built factories and hired workers to run the machines.

The new **factory system** brought workers and machinery together in one place to produce goods. Factory workers earned daily or weekly wages. They had to work a set number of hours each day.

A Revolution Crosses the Atlantic

Britain wanted to keep its new technology secret. It did not want rival nations to copy the new machines. The British Parliament passed a law forbidding anyone to take plans of Arkright's water frame out of the country. It also tried to prevent factory workers from leaving Britain.

Slater breaks the law

Samuel Slater soon showed that the law could not be enforced. Slater was a skilled mechanic in one of Arkwright's mills. When he heard that Americans were offering large rewards for plans of British factories, he decided to leave England.

In 1789, Slater boarded a ship bound for New York City. He knew that British officials searched the baggage of passengers sailing to the United States. To avoid getting caught, he memorized the design of the machines in Arkright's mill. He even used a false name when he traveled.

In New York, Slater learned that **Moses Brown,** a Quaker merchant, wanted to build a spinning mill in Rhode Island. Slater wrote confidently to Brown:

> 66 If I do not make as good yarn as they do in England, I will have nothing for my services, but will throw the whole of what I have attempted over the bridge. 99

Brown replied at once: "If thou canst do what thou sayest, I invite thee to come to Rhode Island."

The first American mill

In 1790, Slater and Brown opened their first mill in Pawtucket, Rhode Island. In the following years, Slater continued to work on improvements. His wife, Hannah Slater, also contributed to the success of the mill. She discovered how to make thread stronger so that it would not snap on the spindles.

The first American factory was a huge success. Before long, other American manufacturers began to build mills using Slater's ideas.

Lowell, Massachusetts: A Model Factory Town

The War of 1812 provided a boost to American industries. The British blockade cut Americans off from their supply of foreign goods. As a result, they had to produce more goods themselves.

Francis Cabot Lowell

During the war, **Francis Cabot Lowell,** a Boston merchant, found a way to improve on British textile mills. In Britain, one factory spun thread while a second factory wove it into cloth. Why not, Lowell wondered, combine spinning and weaving under one roof?

To finance his project, Lowell joined with several partners in 1813 to form the **Boston Associates.** They built a textile factory in Waltham, Massachusetts. The new mill had all the machines needed to turn raw cotton into finished cloth.

After Lowell's death, the Boston Associates took on a more ambitious project. They built an entire factory town and named it after him. In 1821, Lowell, Massachusetts, was a village of five farm families. By 1836, it boasted more than 10,000 people. Visitors to Lowell described it as a model community made up of "small wooden houses, painted white, with green blinds, very neat, very snug, very nicely carpeted."

"Lowell girls"

To work in their new mills, the Boston Associates hired young women from nearby farms. The **"Lowell girls,"** as they came to be called, usually worked for a few years in the mills before returning home to marry. Most sent their wages home to their families. Some saved part of their wages to help set up their own homes.

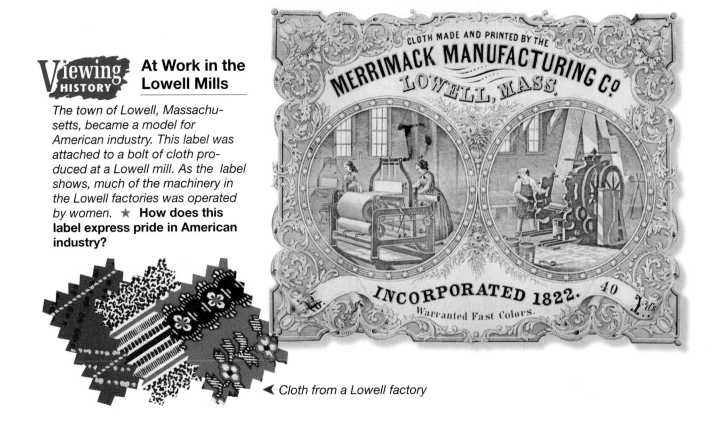

The town of Lowell, Massachusetts, became a model for American industry. This label was attached to a bolt of cloth produced at a Lowell mill. As the label shows, much of the machinery in the Lowell factories was operated by women. ★ **How does this label express pride in American industry?**

◀ *Cloth from a Lowell factory*

At first, parents hesitated to let their daughters work in the mills. To reassure parents, the Boston Associates built boarding houses for their workers. The company also built a church and made rules to protect the young women.

Factory work was often tedious and hard. However, many women valued the economic freedom they got from working in the mills. The *Lowell Offering*, a magazine by and for workers in the Lowell mills, printed a song that began:

❝ Despite of toil we all agree
Out of the mills, or in,
Dependent on others we ne'er will be
So long as we're able to spin. ❞

Impact on Daily Life

In Lowell and elsewhere, mill owners mostly hired women and children. They did this because they could pay women and children half of what they would have had to pay men.

Child labor

Boys and girls as young as seven years of age worked in factories. Small children were especially useful in textile mills because they could squeeze around the large machines to change spindles. "I can see myself now," recalled a woman who had worked in a mill as a child, "carrying in front of me a [spindle] bigger than I was."

Today, most Americans look upon child labor as cruel. Yet in the 1800s, farm children also worked hard from an early age. Most people did not see much difference between children working in a factory or on a farm. Often, a child's wages were needed to help support the family.

Long hours

Working hours in the mills were long—12 hours a day, 6 days a week. True, farmers also put in long hours. However, farmers worked shorter hours in winter. Mill workers, by contrast, worked nearly the same hours all year round.

In the early 1800s, conditions in American mills were generally much better than in most factories in Europe. As industries grew, however, competition increased and employers took less interest in the welfare of their workers. In later chapters, you will read how working conditions grew worse.

Why Study History?

Because Technology Continues to Change Our Lives

★ ★

Historical Background

Inventors like James Hargreaves and Richard Arkwright were not trying to change the world. They just wanted a better way to spin thread. (See page 294.) In the end, though, the Industrial Revolution changed forever how people worked, where they lived, and even how they spent their leisure time. Later inventions, such as the telephone and the automobile, have also transformed the world we live in.

Connections to Today

Not long before you were born, another revolution in technology began: the computer revolution. The earliest computers were not the kind you could have in your bedroom. One early model weighed 30 tons and filled an entire room!

Slowly, computers got smaller and spread out—to schools, businesses, hospitals, arcades, homes. Computers can help keep records, diagnose illnesses, or take people into outer space.

Connections to You

You already know some of the advantages of computers. You can research a report online and revise it on screen. You can enjoy a video game or create your own greeting cards. You can chat with people living in Sweden or Korea or Egypt.

Not every change is positive, though. Sitting at a computer screen for hours may cause severe headaches or hand injuries.

Some critics even fear that computers may lead to isolation. People can work, shop, and even make friends without leaving their homes. You may spend more time chatting with someone halfway around the world than going bowling with friends in your own neighborhood.

1. **Comprehension** **(a)** Name one result of the Industrial Revolution. **(b)** Name two results of the computer revolution.
2. **Critical Thinking** Do you think computers will lead to greater or less contact between people? Explain.

★ *Activity* **Making a Concept Web** Make a concept web to show some of the ways that computers affect you. Then, review your web and decide whether each effect is positive, negative, or both.

What point is this cartoon making about the impact of computers?

Changes in home life

The Industrial Revolution had a great impact on home life. On farms or in home workshops, families worked together as a unit. As the factory system spread, more family members left the home to earn a living.

These changes affected ideas about the role of women. In poorer families, women often had to go out to work. In wealthier families, husbands supported the family while women stayed at home. For many husbands, having a wife who stayed at home became a sign of a success.

Interchangeable Parts

Manufacturers benefited from the pioneering work of American inventor **Eli Whitney**. Earlier, skilled workers made goods by hand. For example, a gunsmith spent days making the barrel, stock, and trigger for a single musket. Because the parts were handmade, each musket differed a bit from the next. If a part broke, a gunsmith had to fashion a new part to fit that gun.

Whitney wanted to speed up gunmaking by having machines manufacture each part. Machine-made parts would all be alike—for example, one trigger would be identical to another. **Interchangeable parts** would save time and money.

Because the government bought many guns, Whitney went to Washington, D.C., to demonstrate his method. At first, officials laughed at his plan. Whitney paid them no attention. Carefully, he sorted parts for 10 muskets into separate piles. He then asked an official to choose one part from each pile. In minutes, the first musket was assembled. Whitney repeated the process until 10 muskets were complete.

The idea of interchangeable parts spread rapidly. Inventors designed machines to produce interchangeable parts for clocks, locks, and many other goods. With such machines, small workshops grew into factories.

Growing Cities

Since colonial times, cities played an important role in American life. The vast majority of people lived in rural areas. How-ever, farmers often sent crops to cities for sale or shipment. Cities were also centers of finance and manufacturing.

During the Industrial Revolution, many people left farms to work in factories. Older

Cause and Effect

Causes

- British ideas of a spinning mill and powerloom reach the United States
- War of 1812 prompts Americans to make their own goods
- Eli Whitney introduces the idea of interchangeable parts

The Industrial Revolution in the United States

Effects

- Factory system spreads
- Young women and children from nearby farms work in mills
- Growing cities face problems of fire, sewage, garbage, and disease

Effects Today

- United States becomes leader in industrialized world
- Oil is a highly valued natural resource

Graphic Organizer *Skills*

The Industrial Revolution brought with it many immediate and long-term changes.

1. **Comprehension**   What inventions and ideas contributed to the spread of the Industrial Revolution?
2. **Critical Thinking**   Do you think the impact of the Industrial Revolution was positive or negative? Give reasons.

Economics $

cities expanded rapidly, while new cities sprang up around factories. This movement of the population from farms to cities is called **urbanization**.

Urbanization was a steady but gradual process. In 1800, only 6 percent of the nation's population lived in urban areas. By 1850, the number had risen to 15 percent. Not until 1920 did more Americans live in cities than on farms.

By today's standards, these early cities were small. A person could walk from one end of any American city to the other in 30 minutes. Buildings were only a few stories tall. As the factory system spread, the nation's cities grew.

Hazards

Growing cities had many problems. Dirt and gravel streets turned into mudholes when it rained. Cities had no sewers, and people threw garbage into the streets. A visitor to New York reported:

66 The streets are filthy, and the stranger is not a little surprised to meet the hogs walking about in them, for the purpose of devouring the vegetables and trash thrown into the gutter. 99

In these dirty, crowded conditions, disease spread easily. Epidemics of yellow fever or cholera (KAHL er uh) raged through cities, killing hundreds.

Fire posed another threat to safety. If a sooty chimney caught fire, the flames quickly spread from one wooden house to the next. Rival volunteer companies often competed to get to a blaze first. Sometimes, they fought each other instead of the fire!

Attractions

Cities had attractions, too. Theaters, museums, and circuses created an air of excitement. In New York City, P. T. Barnum exhibited rare animals at his American Museum.

In rural areas, people depended on door-to-door peddlers for ready-made goods. In cities, people could shop in fine stores that sold the latest fashions from Europe. Some offered modern "ready-to-wear" clothing. One store in New York City advertised that "gentlemen can rely upon being as well fitted from the shelves as if their measures were taken."

Most women continued to sew their own clothes. However, they enjoyed visiting hat shops, china shops, shoe stores, and "fancy-goods" stores.

★ Section 1 Review ★

Recall

1. **Identify** (a) Industrial Revolution, (b) Samuel Slater, (c) Moses Brown, (d) Francis Cabot Lowell, (e) Boston Associates, (f) "Lowell girls," (g) Eli Whitney.
2. **Define** (a) spinning jenny, (b) capitalist, (c) factory system, (d) interchangeable parts, (e) urbanization.

Comprehension

3. Describe three ways the Industrial Revolution changed life.

4. How did industry move from Britain to the United States?
5. What were conditions like in the Lowell mills?

Critical Thinking and Writing

6. **Drawing Conclusions** Why were both inventors and capitalists needed to bring about the Industrial Revolution?
7. **Understanding Causes and Effects** How did the building of factories encourage the growth of cities?

★ ★

Activity **Writing a Letter** The time is 160 years ago. You are the same age you are now, but instead of being in school, you are working in the Lowell mills. Write a letter home describing how you feel about working in a factory to help support your family.

Moving Westward

As You Read

Explore These Questions
- How did settlers travel westward in the early 1800s?
- What steps did Americans take to improve roads?
- How did steamboats and canals affect transportation?

Define
- turnpike
- corduroy road
- canal

Identify
- Lancaster Turnpike
- National Road
- John Fitch
- Robert Fulton
- *Clermont*
- Henry Shreve
- Erie Canal
- DeWitt Clinton

 SETTING the Scene An Irish visitor to the United States described a stagecoach trip through Maryland:

66 The driver frequently had to call to the passengers in the stage, to lean out of the carriage first at one side, then at the other, to prevent it from oversetting in the deep ruts with which the road abounds: 'Now gentlemen, to the right,'... 'Now gentlemen, to the left,' and so on. 99

In the 1790s, travel was as difficult as it had been in colonial times. Most roads were mud tracks. River travel could be difficult, too, when boats had to push their way upstream against the current. As the young nation grew westward, Americans saw the need to improve transportation.

To the Mississippi

Settlers had been moving steadily westward since the 1600s. By the early 1800s, "the West" referred to the land between the Appalachians and the Mississippi.

In the early 1800s, the stream of pioneers turned into a flood. By 1820, so many people had moved west that the population in some of the original 13 states had actually declined!

Western routes

Settlers took a number of routes west. One well-traveled path was the Great Wagon Road across Pennsylvania. It dated back to colonial days. Some settlers continued south and west along the trail opened by Daniel Boone before the Revolution. Known as the Wilderness Road, it led through the Cumberland Gap into Kentucky. (See the map on page 303.)

Other settlers pushed west to Pittsburgh. There, they loaded their animals and wagons onto flatboats and journeyed down the Ohio River into Indiana, Kentucky, and Illinois. Flatboats were well suited to the shallow waters of the Ohio. Even when carrying heavy cargoes, these raftlike barges rode high in the water.

Pioneers from Georgia and South Carolina followed other trails west to Alabama and Mississippi. Enslaved African Americans

Many settlers headed west in covered wagons, such as this Conestoga wagon.

A Need for Better Roads

This painting, by a visitor from Russia, shows a stagecoach on its run between Philadelphia, Pennsylvania, and Trenton, New Jersey. Passengers traveling on rocky, muddy, unpaved roads could expect to be "crushed, shaken, thrown about...and bumped." ★ **What details in this painting suggest that these passengers were having a rough ride?**

helped to carve plantations in the rich, fertile soil of these territories.

People from New England, New York, and Pennsylvania pushed into the Northwest Territory. Some settlers traveled west from Albany, New York, along the Mohawk River and across the Appalachians. Some settlers then followed Indian trails around Lake Erie. Others sailed across the lake into Ohio.

New states

Before long, some western territories had populations large enough to apply for statehood. Between 1792 and 1819, eight states joined the Union: Kentucky (1792), Tennessee (1796), Ohio (1803), Louisiana (1812), Indiana (1816), Mississippi (1817), Illinois (1818), and Alabama (1819).

Better Roads

Settlers faced a difficult journey. Many roads were narrow trails, barely wide enough for a single wagon. One pioneer wrote of "rotten banks down which horses plunged" and streams that "almost drowned them." Tree stumps stuck up through the road and often broke the axles on the wagons of careless travelers. The nation badly needed better roads.

Turnpikes and bridges

In the United States, as in Europe, private companies built gravel and stone roads. To pay for these roads, the companies collected tolls from travelers. At various points along the road, a pike, or pole, blocked the road. After a wagon driver paid a toll, the pike keeper turned the pole aside to let the wagon pass. As a result, these toll roads were called **turnpikes.**

Probably the best road in the United States was the **Lancaster Turnpike.** Built in the 1790s by a private company, the road linked Philadelphia and Lancaster, Pennsylvania. Because the road was set on a bed of gravel, water drained off quickly. It was topped with smooth, flat stones.

In swampy areas, roads were made of logs. These roads were known as **corduroy roads** because the lines of logs looked like corduroy cloth. Corduroy roads kept wagons from sinking into the mud, but they made for a bumpy ride.

Bridges carried travelers across streams and rivers. Stone bridges were costly to build, but wooden ones rotted quickly. A clever Massachusetts carpenter designed a wooden bridge with a roof to protect it from the weather. Covered bridges lasted much longer than open ones.

The National Road

Some states set aside money to build or improve roads. In 1806, for the first time, Congress approved funds for a national road-building project. The **National Road** was to run from Cumberland, Maryland, to Wheeling, in western Virginia.

Work on the National Road began in 1811 and was completed in 1818. Later, the road was extended into Illinois. As each new section of road was built, settlers eagerly used it to drive their wagons west.

Steam Transport

Whenever possible, travelers and freight haulers used river transportation. Floating downstream on a flatboat was both faster and more comfortable than bumping along rutted roads. It also cost less.

Yet, river travel had its own problems. Moving upstream was difficult. People used paddles or long poles to push boats against the current. Sometimes, they hauled boats from the shore with ropes. Both methods were slow. A boat could travel downstream from Pittsburgh to New Orleans in about six weeks. The return trip upstream took at least 17 weeks!

Fitch and Fulton

A new invention, the steam engine, improved river travel. **John Fitch** improved on steam engines that had been built in Britain.

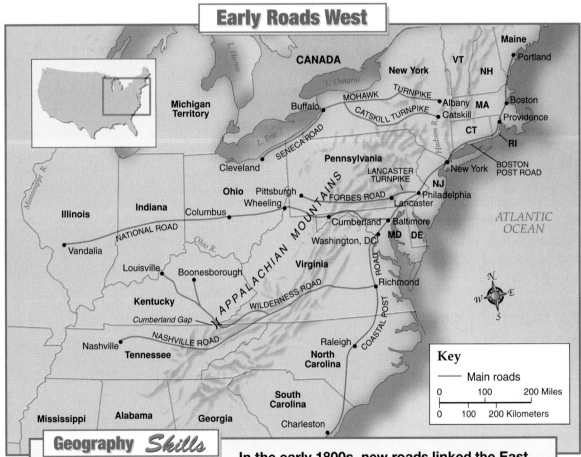

Early Roads West

Geography Skills
In the early 1800s, new roads linked the East to new settlements in the West.

1. **Location**   On the map, locate: **(a)** Appalachian Mountains, **(b)** Cumberland Gap, **(c)** Wilderness Road, **(d)** Lancaster Turnpike, **(e)** National Road.

2. **Movement**   What major roads would settlers use to travel from Boston, Massachussetts, to Nashville, Tennessee?

3. **Critical Thinking**   Based on this map, what effect do you think roadbuilding had on cities like Philadelphia, Baltimore, and Richmond?

Skills
FOR LIFE

| Critical Thinking | Managing Information | Communication | Maps, Charts, and Graphs |

Analyzing a Primary Source

How Will I Use This Skill?

A **primary source** is firsthand information about people and events. Historians use primary sources to learn about the past. You, too, use primary sources—when you watch an interview on television, or listen to two friends tell their sides of something that happened. Learning to analyze primary sources helps you determine the reliability of the information that you get.

LEARN the Skill

❶ Identify the source of the account. Decide if he or she has firsthand knowledge of the event.

❷ Determine which words indicate facts. Are there enough facts to make the speaker reliable?

❸ Recognize how emotions, points of view, and opinions affect the telling of the story.

❹ Judge how reliable the source is.

PRACTICE the Skill

Fanny Kemble, an English actress, visited the United States in the early 1800s. In her journal, she described a stagecoach ride with her father and some Americans. Read the excerpt, then answer the following questions:

❶ Explain why this journal is a primary source.

❷ (a) What facts does Kemble include about stagecoach travel? (b) What facts does she include about American rural life?

❸ What effect do you think Kemble's nationality and her discomfort may have had on her account?

❹ Would you consider this journal a reliable source of information? Explain.

> "Bones of me! what a road! Even my father's solid proportions…were jerked up to the roof and down again every three minutes. Our companions… laughed and talked [constantly], the young ladies, at the very top of their voices, and with the national nasal twang….The few cottages and farm-houses which we passed reminded me of similar dwellings in France and Ireland; yet the peasantry here have not the same excuse for disorder and [ruin] as either the Irish or French….The farms had the same desolate, untidy, untended look; the gates broken, the fences carelessly put up."

Excerpt from Journal by Frances Anne Kemble Butler

APPLY the Skill

Watch or read an interview given by an eye-witness to an event. Using the steps above, decide whether you think the interview is a reliable source of information.

The Erie Canal

The opening of the Erie Canal in 1825 launched an age of canal building. Today, at the Erie Canal Village in Rome, New York, you can relive life along the old Erie Canal. Here, passengers ride atop a canal boat, pulled along by a team of mules, just as they did 150 years ago. Riding up top could be risky, though. When the boatmen yelled "Low bridge!" passengers who did not duck could bump their heads.

★ **To learn more about this historic site, write:** Erie Canal Village, 5789 New London Road, Rome, NY 13440.

◄ Canal boat lantern

In 1787, he showed members of the Constitutional Convention how a steam engine could power a boat. He then opened a ferry service on the Delaware River. However, few people used the ferry, and Fitch went out of business.

Inventor **Robert Fulton** may have seen Fitch's steamboat in Philadelphia. In 1807, Fulton launched his own steamboat, the **Clermont,** on the Hudson River. On its first run, the *Clermont* carried passengers from New York City to Albany and back. The 300-mile (480-km) trip took just 62 hours—a record at the time.

The age of steamboats

Fulton's success ushered in the age of steamboats. Soon, steamboats were ferrying passengers up and down the Atlantic coast. More important, they revolutionized travel in the West. Besides carrying people, steamboats on the Mississippi, Ohio, and Missouri rivers gave farmers and merchants a cheap means of moving goods.

Because western rivers were shallow, **Henry Shreve** designed a flat-bottomed steamboat. It could carry heavy loads without getting stuck on sandbars.

Still, steamboat travel could be dangerous. Sparks from smokestacks could cause fires. As steamboat captains raced each other along the river, high-pressure boilers sometimes exploded. Between 1811 and 1851, 44 steamboats collided, 166 burned, and more than 200 exploded.

The Canal Boom

Steamboats and improved roads did not help western farmers get their goods directly to markets in the East. To meet this need, Americans dug canals. A canal is an artificial channel filled with water that allows boats to cross a stretch of land.

Major Canals

Geography Skills The success of the Erie Canal, completed in 1825, set off an age of canal building.

1. **Location** On the map, locate: **(a)** New York City, **(b)** Troy, **(c)** Buffalo, **(d)** Lake Erie, **(e)** Erie Canal.

2. **Movement** What two bodies of water were linked by the Illinois and Michigan Canal?

3. **Critical Thinking** Use the map to describe an all-water route from Evansville, Indiana, to New York City.

The earliest American canals were no more than a few miles long. Some provided routes around waterfalls on a river. Other canals linked a river to a nearby lake. By the early 1800s, however, Americans were building longer canals.

Building the Erie Canal

Some New Yorkers had a bold idea. They wanted to build a canal linking the Great Lakes with the Mohawk and Hudson rivers. The **Erie Canal** would let western farmers ship their goods to the port of New York. It would also bring business to towns along the route.

To many people, the idea of such a canal seemed farfetched. When Thomas Jefferson heard of the plan, he exclaimed:

❝ Why, sir, you talk of making a canal 350 miles through the wilderness—it is little short of madness to think of it at this day! ❞

New York governor **DeWitt Clinton** ignored such criticism. He persuaded state lawmakers to provide money for the Erie Canal. Scoffers referred to the project as "Clinton's Ditch."

Work on the Erie Canal began in 1817. At first, workers dug the waterway by hand. To speed up progress, inventors developed new equipment. One machine, a stump-puller, could pull out nearly 40 tree stumps a day. In two places, workers had to find ways to build stone bridges to carry the canal over other rivers along the way.

An instant success

By 1825, the immense job was finished. On opening day of the Erie Canal, a cannon fired a volley in Buffalo, New York. When the sound got to the next town along the route, it, too, fired a cannon. Town after town fired their cannons—all the way to New York City. The thunderous salute took 80 minutes to complete.

The Erie Canal was an instant success. It reduced travel time. The cost of shipping goods dropped to about 1/20 of what it was before the canal was built. The canal also helped to make New York City a center of commerce.

The success of the Erie Canal led other states to build canals. (See the map on the opposite page.) These canals created vital economic links between western farms and eastern cities.

Transportation Builds Prosperity

In 1831, a young Frenchman, Alexis de Tocqueville (TOHK vihl), made a nine-month tour of the United States. In his writings, Tocqueville described what he admired about the young nation. One of the things that impressed him most was the American transportation system.

"Of all the countries in the world," Tocqueville wrote, "America is that in which the spread of ideas and of human industry is most continual and most rapid." Tocqueville was amazed by "immense canals" and roads built in the middle of the wilderness. He also praised the American postal system:

> 66 In America one of the first things done in a new state is to make the post go there. In the forests of Michigan there is no cabin so isolated, no valley so wild but that letters and newspapers arrive at least once a week. 99

Tocqueville noted that Americans could easily ship goods from the western frontier to any part of the country. (By contrast, in his native France—a much smaller country—many large towns could not be reached by road at all!) Faster, easier transportation thus contributed to the growing prosperity of the United States.

★ Section 2 Review ★

Recall

1. **Locate** (a) Kentucky, (b) Tennessee, (c) Ohio, (d) Louisiana, (e) Indiana, (f) Mississippi, (g) Illinois, (h) Alabama.
2. **Identify** (a) Lancaster Turnpike, (b) National Road, (c) John Fitch, (d) Robert Fulton, (e) *Clermont,* (f) Henry Shreve, (g) Erie Canal, (h) DeWitt Clinton.
3. **Define** (a) turnpike, (b) corduroy road, (c) canal.

Comprehension

4. What means of transportation did settlers take to the West in the early 1800s?

5. **(a)** Why did the nation need better transportation in the early 1800s? **(b)** Describe two ways that travel improved.

Critical Thinking and Writing

6. **Linking Past and Present** Today, airplanes provide a faster means of travel than land transportation. Why do you think roads are still important to the nation?
7. **Identifying Alternatives** Examine the maps in this section. Then, describe two alternate ways a farmer might have shipped a cargo of grain from Cleveland, Ohio, to New York City.

Activity **Designing a Monument** You have been asked to design a monument honoring the two-hundredth anniversary of the Erie Canal. Draw a rough sketch of the monument, showing what design you would use. You may also include an inscription describing the importance of the canal.

Building National Unity

As You Read

Explore These Questions
- How did Congress try to strengthen the national economy?
- What were the goals of Henry Clay's American System?
- How did the Supreme Court strengthen national unity?

Define
- dumping
- sectionalism
- interstate commerce

Identify
- James Monroe
- John C. Calhoun
- Daniel Webster
- Henry Clay
- American System
- *McCulloch* v. *Maryland*
- *Gibbon* v. *Ogden*

 SETTING the Scene After his visit to the United States, Alexis de Tocqueville described what he saw as the character of the American people. He wrote:

66 The American...is less afraid than any other inhabitant of the globe to risk what he has gained in the hope of a better future.... There is not a country in the world where man more confidently takes charge of the future, or where he feels with more pride that he can fashion the universe to please himself. 99

Tocqueville echoed the confidence Americans felt in themselves. After the War of 1812, the country grew rapidly. New lands opened to settlers with improved transportation. New industries appeared. In Congress, a new generation of political leaders sought to direct this expansion.

An Era of Good Feelings

In 1816, the Republican candidate for President, **James Monroe**, easily defeated the Federalist, Rufus King. Once in office, Monroe spoke of creating a new sense of national unity.

Monroe was the last of three Presidents in a row to come from Virginia. He was also the last Revolutionary War officer to become President.

In 1817, Monroe made a goodwill tour of the country. Not since George Washington had a President made such a tour. In Boston, crowds cheered Monroe. Boston newspapers expressed surprise at this warm welcome for a Republican from Virginia. After all, Boston had been a Federalist stronghold. One newspaper wrote that the United States was entering an "Era of Good Feelings."

By the time Monroe ran for a second term in 1820, no candidate opposed him. The Federalist party had disappeared.

Three Sectional Leaders

While conflict between political parties declined, disputes between different sections of the nation sharpened. In Congress, three ambitious young men took center stage. All three played key roles in Congress for more than 30 years, as well as serving in other offices. Each represented a different section of the country.

Calhoun of the South

John C. Calhoun spoke for the South. He had grown up on a frontier farm in South Carolina. Later, he went to Yale College in Connecticut. Calhoun's immense energy and striking features earned him the nickname "young Hercules." His intense way of speaking sometimes made people uncomfortable in his presence.

Calhoun had supported the War of 1812. Like many southerners, though, he generally opposed policies that would strengthen the power of the federal government.

Webster of the North

Daniel Webster of New Hampshire was perhaps the most skillful public speaker of his time. With eyes flashing and shoulders thrown back, Webster was an impressive sight when he stood up to speak in Congress. An observer described him as a "great cannon loaded to the lips."

Like many New Englanders, Webster had opposed the War of 1812. He even refused to vote for taxes to pay for the war effort. After the war, he wanted the federal government to take a larger role in building the nation's economy.

Clay of the West

Henry Clay spoke for the West. You have already met Clay as a leader of the War Hawks who pushed for war against Britain in 1812.

Clay was born in Virginia. When he was 20, he traveled across the Cumberland Gap into Kentucky. As a young lawyer, he was once fined for brawling with an opponent. Usually, however, he charmed both friends and rivals. Supporters called him "Gallant Harry of the West." Like Webster, Clay strongly favored a more active role for the central government.

A New National Bank

After the War of 1812, leaders like Calhoun, Webster, and Clay had to deal with the nation's economic weakness. The problem was due in part to the lack of a national bank.

The charter for the Bank of the United States ran out in 1811. Without the Bank to lend money and regulate the nation's money supply, the economy suffered. State banks made loans and issued money. Often, they put too much money into circulation. With so much money available to spend, prices rose rapidly.

In the nation's early years, Republicans like Jefferson and Madison had opposed a national bank. By 1816, however, many Republicans believed that a bank was needed. They supported a law to charter the second Bank of the United States. By lending money and restoring order to the nation's money supply, the Bank helped American businesses grow.

Protection From Foreign Competition

Another economic problem facing the nation was foreign competition, especially from

CLAY

WEBSTER

CALHOUN

Viewing HISTORY **Three Sectional Leaders**

Henry Clay, left, was the first major political leader to emerge from the new states of the West. Along with Daniel Webster and John C. Calhoun, below, Clay played a major role in government for more than 30 years. ★ **What role did sectional politics play in the rise of Webster, Calhoun, and Clay?**

Effect of a Protective Tariff

In the United States

American-made cloth sells for $6 per roll

In Britain

British-made cloth sells for $5 per roll

Shipped to the United States

Add 25% tariff of $1.25 per roll

In the United States

British-made cloth sells for $6.25 per roll

Chart *Skills*

In 1816, Congress passed a protective tariff to help American factory owners.

1. **Comprehension** According to this chart, how much would 100 rolls of British cloth cost before the tariff? How much would they cost after the tariff?

2. **Critical Thinking** Why did southerners object to the tariff?

Economics $

Britain. In the early 1800s, the Embargo Act and then the War of 1812 kept most British goods out of the United States. In response, ambitious American business leaders like Francis Cabot Lowell set up their own mills and factories.

A flood of British goods

In 1815, British goods again poured into the United States. The British could make and sell goods more cheaply than Americans. Most British factories and machines were older and had already been paid for. By con-

trast, Americans still had to pay for building their new factories.

Sometimes, British manufacturers sold cloth in the United States for less than it cost to make. The practice of selling goods in another country at very low prices is today called **dumping.** Through dumping, British manufacturers hoped to put American rivals out of business.

Congress passes a protective tariff

Dumping caused dozens of New England businesses to fail. Angry owners asked Congress to place a protective tariff on all goods imported from Europe. As you recall, the purpose of a protective tariff is to protect a country's industries from foreign competition.

Congress responded by passing the Tariff of 1816. It greatly raised tariffs on imports. This increase made imported goods far more expensive than similar American-made goods. In 1818 and 1824, Congress passed even higher tariffs.

Higher tariffs led to angry protests, especially from southerners. Southerners had built few factories. As a result, they did not benefit from the tariff. Also, southerners bought many British goods. The new tariff drove up the price of British-made goods. Southerners complained that the tariff made northern manufacturers rich at the expense of the South.

Clay's American System

The bitter dispute over tariffs reflected the growth of sectionalism. **Sectionalism** is loyalty to one's state or section rather than to the nation as a whole. Americans identified themselves as southerners, northerners, or westerners. In Congress, representatives from different sections often clashed.

Henry Clay wanted to promote economic growth for all sections. He set out a program that became known as the **American System.** It called for high tariffs on imports, which would help northern factories. With wealth from industry, northerners would buy farm products from the West and the South. High tariffs would also reduce American dependence on foreign goods. Clay argued:

66 Every nation should . . . be able to feed and clothe and defend itself. If it rely upon a foreign supply that may be cut off . . . it cannot be independent. 99

Clay also urged Congress to use money from tariffs to build roads, bridges, and canals. A better transportation system, he believed, would make it easier and cheaper for farmers in the West and the South to ship goods to city markets.

Clay's American System never went fully into effect. Tariffs did remain high. However, Congress spent little on internal improvements. Southerners in particular disliked Clay's plan. The South had many fine rivers to transport goods. Many southerners opposed paying for roads and canals that brought them no direct benefits.

The Supreme Court Expands Federal Power

Under Chief Justice John Marshall, the Supreme Court strengthened the power of the federal government to promote economic growth. After Congress chartered the second Bank of the United States, Maryland tried to tax the bank in order to drive it out of the state. James McCulloch, the bank cashier, refused to pay the tax.

In the case of **McCulloch v. Maryland** (1819), the Court ruled that states had no right to interfere with federal institutions within their borders. "The power to tax involves the power to destroy," warned Marshall. The ruling strengthened federal power. It also allowed the National Bank to continue, which helped the economy to expand.

In another case, **Gibbon v. Ogden** (1824), the Supreme Court upheld the power of the federal government to regulate commerce. The Court struck down a New York law that tried to control steamboat travel between New York and New Jersey. The Court ruled that a state could only regulate trade within its own borders. Only the federal government had the power to regulate interstate commerce, or trade between different states. This decision helped the national economy by making it easier for the government to regulate trade.

★ Section 3 Review ★

Recall

1. **Identify** (a) James Monroe, (b) John C. Calhoun, (c) Daniel Webster, (d) Henry Clay, (e) American System, (f) *McCulloch* v. *Maryland*, (g) *Gibbon* v. *Ogden*.
2. **Define** (a) dumping, (b) sectionalism, (c) interstate commerce.

Comprehension

3. How did Congress try to solve each of the following problems: (a) the money supply, (b) foreign competition?
4. Describe Clay's program to promote economic growth.

5. Describe one way the Supreme Court upheld the authority of the federal government.

Critical Thinking and Writing

6. **Analyzing a Primary Source** In 1816, a member of Congress said, "I will buy where I can get [manufactured goods] cheapest. . . . It is unjust to aggravate the burdens of the people for the purpose of favoring the manufacturers." Do you think this speaker favored or opposed the Tariff of 1816? Explain.
7. **Drawing Conclusions** Based on your reading, do you think sectional differences were a serious threat to national unity? Give examples to support your conclusion.

★ ★

Activity Conducting an Interview You are a political reporter assigned to interview a Congressional leader around 1820. Choose either Clay, Calhoun, or Webster. List three or four questions you would ask about the issues facing the nation.

4 Latin America and the United States

★★

As You Read

Explore These Questions
- How did Latin American nations win independence?
- How did the United States gain Florida?
- What was the purpose of the Monroe Doctrine?

Define
- creole
- intervention

Identify
- Miguel Hidalgo
- Simón Bolívar
- José de San Martín
- "black Seminoles"
- John Quincy Adams
- Adams-Onís Treaty
- Monroe Doctrine

SETTING the Scene On a quiet Sunday in September 1810, the church bell rang in the Mexican village of Dolores. In the square, people found their priest, **Miguel Hidalgo** (mee GEHL ee DAHL goh), making a stirring speech. No one knows the exact words, but Mexicans remembered and passed along his message:

66 My children.... Will you be free? Will you recover the lands stolen 300 years ago from your forefathers by the hated Spaniards? We must act at once! 99

Thousands of Mexicans rallied to Father Hidalgo's call for freedom.

South of the United States, Spanish colonies in Latin America* fought wars for independence in the early 1800s. As new nations emerged, President Monroe formed a bold new foreign policy.

Revolution in Latin America

By 1810, many people in Spain's American colonies were eager for independence. They had many reasons for discontent. Most people, even wealthy creoles, had little or no say in government. **Creoles** were people born in Latin America to Spanish parents. Harsh laws ruled Indians and the poor. The French and American revolutions inspired colonists to seek self-rule.

Mexican independence

As you read, Miguel Hidalgo sounded the call for Mexican independence. Rebel forces won control of several provinces before Father Hidalgo was captured. In 1811, he was executed.

Another priest, José Morelos (hoh ZAY moh RAY lohs), took up the fight. Because he called for a program to give land to peasants, wealthy creoles opposed him. Before long, Morelos, too, was captured and killed by the Spanish.

Slowly, creoles began to support the revolution. In 1821, creole forces won control of Mexico. A few years later, Mexico became a republic with its own constitution.

The Liberator

In South America, too, a series of revolutions freed colonies from Spanish rule. The best-known revolutionary leader was **Simón Bolívar** (see MOHN boh LEE vahr). He became known as the Liberator for his role in the Latin American wars of independence.

Bolívar came from a wealthy creole family in Venezuela. As a young man, he took up the cause of Venezuelan independence. Bolívar promised, "I will never allow my hands to be idle, nor my soul to rest until I have broken the shackles which chain us to Spain."

Bolívar rose to become a leader of the rebel forces. In a bold move, he led an army

---

*Latin America refers to the region of the Western Hemisphere where Latin-based languages such as Spanish, French, and Portuguese are spoken. It includes Mexico, Central and South America, and the West Indies.

Biography   Simón Bolívar

As a young man, Simón Bolívar enjoyed a life of wealth and privilege. He studied the republican form of government of the United States. He also admired the military genius of Napoleon. Later, Bolívar's democratic ideals and military skills helped him free several South American nations from Spanish rule.

★ **Which nations did Bolívar help to liberate?**

Crown given to Bolívar by ➤
South American Indians

from Venezuela over the high Andes Mountains into Colombia. There, Bolívar took the Spanish forces by surprise and defeated them in 1819.

Soon after, Bolívar became president of the independent Republic of Great Colombia. It included the present-day nations of Venezuela, Colombia, Ecuador, and Panama.

Other new nations

Other independent nations emerged in Latin America. **José de San Martín** (san mahr TEEN) led Argentina to freedom in 1816. He then helped the people of Chile, Peru, and Ecuador win independence.

In 1821, the peoples of Central America declared independence from Spain. Two years later, they formed the United Provinces of Central America. It included the present-day nations of Nicaragua, Costa Rica, El Salvador, Honduras, and Guatemala. By 1825, Spain had lost all its colonies in Latin America except Puerto Rico and Cuba.

The Portuguese colony of Brazil won independence peacefully. Prince Pedro, son of the Portuguese king, ruled the colony. The king advised his son, "If Brazil demands independence, proclaim it yourself and put the crown on your own head." In 1822, Pedro became emperor of the new independent nation of Brazil.

The New Republics

Spain's former colonies modeled their constitutions on that of the United States. Yet their experience after independence was very different from that of their neighbor to the north.

Unlike the people of the 13 British colonies, the peoples of Latin America did not unite into a single country. In part, geography made unity difficult. Latin America covered a much larger area than the English colonies. Mountains like the high, rugged Andes acted as a barrier to travel and communication.

The new republics had a hard time setting up stable governments. Under Spanish rule, the colonists had little or no experience in self-government. Economic problems and deep divisions between social classes increased discontent. Powerful leaders took advantage of the turmoil to seize control. As a result, the new nations were often unable to achieve democratic rule.

Connections With Civics

Like the United States, new Latin American nations created national flags. Venezuela's flag of yellow, blue, and red symbolized the gold of the Americas separated from Spain by the blue ocean. Argentina's blue-white-blue flag was the same flag flown by pirates who attacked Spanish ports and ships along the coasts of South and Central America.

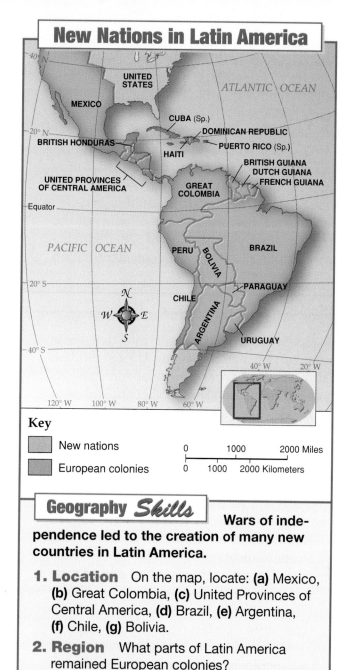

New Nations in Latin America

Key

New nations

European colonies

0   1000   2000 Miles

0   1000   2000 Kilometers

Geography *Skills*

Wars of independence led to the creation of many new countries in Latin America.

1. **Location** On the map, locate: **(a)** Mexico, **(b)** Great Colombia, **(c)** United Provinces of Central America, **(d)** Brazil, **(e)** Argentina, **(f)** Chile, **(g)** Bolivia.

2. **Region** What parts of Latin America remained European colonies?

3. **Critical Thinking** Use the world map in the Reference Section to identify the modern nations that were eventually carved out of the United Provinces of Central America.

The United States Gains Florida

Spain lost another one of its colonies, Florida—not to independence, but to the United States. Many Americans wanted to gain possession of Florida. As early as 1810, President Madison tried to claim West Florida for the United States.

Concern over Florida grew, especially among Southerners. Creek and Seminole Indians in Florida sometimes raided settlements in Georgia. Also, Florida was a refuge for many enslaved African Americans.

"Black Seminoles"

Since the 1700s, Spanish officials had protected slaves who fled from plantations in Georgia and South Carolina. Seminole Indians allowed African Americans to live near their villages. In return, these **"black Seminoles"** gave the Indians a share of the crops they raised every year. The black Seminoles adopted many Indian customs. In addition, some African Americans married Seminoles.

After the War of 1812, African Americans occupied a fort on the Apalachicola River. They invited runaway slaves to settle nearby. Soon, some 1,000 African Americans farmed on the banks of the Apalachicola, protected by the "Negro Fort."

American gunboats attack

General Andrew Jackson demanded that Spain demolish the Negro Fort. The Spanish governor refused. In 1816, Jackson's gunboats invaded Spanish territory and sailed up the Apalachicola.

Inside the Negro Fort, a force of free African Americans waited, cannons ready. They knew that the Americans had come to return them to slavery. After a spirited fight, the gunboats destroyed the fort. Black settlers along the Apalachicola were forced to flee. Many joined nearby Seminoles. Together, they continued to resist American raids into Florida.

Spain gives up Florida

In 1818, Jackson headed to Florida again with a force of over 3,000 soldiers. Spain protested, but it was busy fighting rebels in Latin America. It could not risk war with the United States.

In the end, Spain agreed to peace talks. Secretary of State **John Quincy Adams** worked out a treaty with Spain. In it, Spain agreed to give Florida to the United States in exchange for $5 million. The **Adams-Onís Treaty** took effect in 1821.

The Monroe Doctrine

Americans cheered as Latin American nations won independence. The actions of European powers, however, worried American officials. Prussia, France, Russia, and Austria seemed ready to help Spain regain its colonies in Latin America. In addition, Russia claimed lands on the Pacific coast of North America.

The British, too, were concerned about European nations meddling in the Western Hemisphere. They suggested issuing a joint statement with the United States. It would guarantee the freedom of the new nations.

Monroe decided to act independently of Britain. In a message to Congress in 1823, he made a bold foreign policy statement, known as the **Monroe Doctrine.** Monroe declared that the United States would not interfere in the affairs of European nations or colonies. At the same time, he warned European nations not to interfere with newly independent nations of Latin America:

66 The American continents . . . are henceforth not to be considered as subjects for future colonization by any European powers. . . . We should consider any attempt on their part to extend their system to any portion of this hemisphere as dangerous to our peace and safety. 99

The Monroe Doctrine also stated that the United States would oppose any attempt to build new colonies in the Americas. Monroe's message showed that the United States was determined to keep European powers out of the Western Hemisphere.

The United States did not have the military power to enforce the Monroe Doctrine. Britain, however, supported the statement. With its strong navy, it could stop Europeans from interfering in the Americas.

As the United States became stronger, the Monroe Doctrine grew in importance. On several occasions, the United States successfully challenged European **intervention,** or direct involvement, in Latin America. In the early 1900s, Presidents also used the Monroe Doctrine to justify sending troops to Caribbean nations. Thus, Monroe's bold statement helped shape United States foreign policy for more than 100 years.

★ Section 4 Review ★

Recall

1. **Locate** **(a)** Mexico, **(b)** Great Colombia, **(c)** Argentina, **(d)** United Provinces of Central America, **(e)** Brazil.
2. **Identify** **(a)** Miguel Hidalgo, **(b)** Simón Bolívar, **(c)** José de San Martín, **(d)** "black Seminoles," **(e)** John Quincy Adams, **(f)** Adams-Onís Treaty, **(g)** Monroe Doctrine.
3. **Define** **(a)** creole, **(b)** intervention.

Comprehension

4. **(a)** Why did Latin American nations seek independence in the early 1800s? **(b)** What problems did the new republics face?

5. Why did many Americans want to gain control of Florida?
6. Why did President Monroe issue the Monroe Doctrine?

Critical Thinking and Writing

7. **Making Inferences** How do you think the defenders of the Negro Fort in Florida might have inspired enslaved African Americans in the United States?
8. **Predicting Consequences** What do you think might have happened if Spain had sent an army to regain control of Mexico in the late 1820s?

Activity **Designing a Poster** Your school is participating in a "Know Your Neighbors" fair. The goal is to promote friendly relations with Latin American nations. Design a poster honoring how one neighboring nation gained independence.

★ Sum It Up ★

Section 1   The Industrial Revolution
▶ The Industrial Revolution spread to the United States from Britain in the late 1700s.
▶ Though factory work was hard, many people moved from farms to work in factories in cities and towns.

Section 2   Moving Westward
▶ Westward movement was so heavy that eight new states joined the nation between 1789 and 1819.
▶ Improved roads, steamboats, and canals reduced travel time and lowered the cost of moving goods and people.

Section 3   Building National Unity
▶ As disputes between different sections of the nation grew more intense, great sectional leaders emerged.
▶ Political leaders tried to use their power to make the United States stronger economically.

Section 4   Latin America and the United States
▶ In the early 1800s, almost all of Spain's Latin American colonies won their independence.
▶ The Monroe Doctrine stated that the United States would oppose European efforts to create new colonies in the Western Hemisphere.

For additional review of the major ideas of Chapter 11, see **Guide to the Essentials of American History** or **Interactive Student Tutorial CD-ROM,** which contains interactive review activities, graphic organizers, and practice tests.

🗖 Reviewing the Chapter

Define These Terms
Match each term with the correct definition.

Column 1
1. capitalist
2. urbanization
3. turnpike
4. canal
5. dumping

Column 2
a. channel that allows boats to cross a stretch of land
b. person who invests in a business to make a profit
c. practice of selling goods in another country at low prices
d. movement of populations from farms to cities
e. toll road

Explore the Main Ideas
1. Describe the factory system.
2. Why was river travel better than travel by road?
3. Identify the great leader who spoke for each of the three sections of the United States.
4. Why did Congress pass the Tariff of 1816?
5. What two important points did Monroe make in the Monroe Doctrine?

🗖 Geography Activity

Match the letters on the map with the following places:
1. Wheeling, Virginia, **2.** New York City, **3.** Cumberland Gap, **4.** Lancaster Turnpike, **5.** National Road, **6.** Erie Canal.
Interaction What obstacles did Americans overcome in building the Erie Canal?

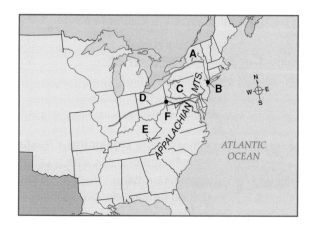

▣ Critical Thinking and Writing

1. **Understanding Chronology** **(a)** Did the War of 1812 begin before or after the formation of the Boston Associates? **(b)** How were these two events linked?

2. **Linking Past and Present** Do cities today have the same kinds of problems as cities in the early 1800s? Explain.

3. **Evaluating Information** What information do you have that suggests that "The Era of Good Feelings" did not last?

4. **Exploring Unit Themes** **Nationalism** Henry Clay has been called the "most nationalistic" of the great congressional leaders. What facts support this opinion?

▣ Using Primary Sources

Davy Crockett was a Tennessee settler who became a representative in Congress. He toured the city of Lowell in 1834 and gave this description:

> 66 The dinner bells were ringing, and the folks pouring out of the [work] houses like bees out of a gum [tree]. I looked at them as they passed, all well dressed, lively, genteel in their appearance.... I went in among the young girls, and talked with many of them. No one expressed herself as tired of her employment, or oppressed with work: all talked well, and looked healthy. 99

Source: *An Account of Col. Crockett's Tour to the North and Down East,* Davy Crockett, 1835.

Recognizing Points of View **(a)** What was the condition of the workers at Lowell, according to Crockett? **(b)** Why do you think a representative from Tennessee would have been interested in conditions at mills in Massachusetts?

ACTIVITY BANK

▶ Interdisciplinary Activity

Exploring the Arts With a partner, create a skit, dance, or song about the difficulties of travel in the early 1800s.

▶ Career Skills Activity

Engineers Draw a diagram or prepare a demonstration to show how early factories harnessed the force of water to create power to run machines.

▶ Citizenship Activity

Understanding Regional Politics Sectional politics is still an issue in the United States. Prepare a report in which you describe the needs of your own region. Consider such questions as: Does your region have special resource or energy needs? How do the needs of your region compare with the needs of other regions? What policies would benefit your region?

Internet Activity

Use the Internet to find sites dealing with the National Road, now called Route 40. Using your Web research, create a tourist map of the road showing the towns it passes through, nearby hotels and restaurants, and historic or interesting information about it.

Ⓔ YEWITNESS Journal

Take one of the following roles: a young woman working at the Lowell mills; a mayor of a frontier town; a settler living in the New York wilderness near the route of the Erie Canal; a black Seminole in Florida. In your EYEWITNESS JOURNAL, record three events that affected your life between 1800 and 1825.

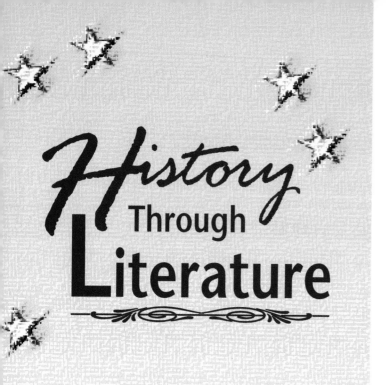

History Through Literature

Rip Van Winkle

by Washington Irving

Introduction

Washington Irving (1783–1859) was the first American to make a living as a popular writer. "Rip Van Winkle" is Irving's best-loved tale. The story is a humorous fantasy about a lazy farmer in a small New York village. One night in the early 1770s, Rip Van Winkle wanders up into the Catskill Mountains, falls asleep—and does not wake up for 20 years! In the selection below, Rip returns to his old village after his long nap.

Vocabulary

Before you read the selection, find the meaning of these words in a dictionary: **yore, assemblage, incomprehensible, metamorphosed, buff, disputatious, tranquillity, haranguing, vehemently.**

He had now entered the skirts of the village. A troop of strange children ran at his heels, hooting after him and pointing at his gray beard. The dogs, too, not one of which he recognized for an old acquaintance, barked at him as he passed. The very village was altered; it was larger and more populous. There were rows of houses which he had never seen before, and those which had been his familiar haunts had disappeared....

He now hurried forth and hastened to his old retreat, the village inn—but it too was gone. A large, rickety, wooden building stood in its place, with great gaping windows, some of them broken and mended with old hats and petticoats, and over the door was painted, "the Union Hotel, by Jonathan Doolittle." Instead of the great tree that used to shelter the quiet little Dutch town of yore, there now was reared a tall, naked pole, with something on the top that looked like a red nightcap,* and from it was fluttering a flag, on which was a singular assemblage of stars and stripes—all this was strange and incomprehensible. He recognized on the sign, however, the ruby face of King George...but even this was singularly metamorphosed. The red coat was changed for one of blue and buff, a sword was held in the hand instead of a scepter, the head was decorated with a cocked hat, and underneath was painted in large characters, GENERAL WASHINGTON.

There was, as usual, a crowd of folk about the door, but none that Rip recollected. The very character of the people seemed changed. There was a busy, bustling, disputatious tone about it, instead of the accustomed...drowsy tranquillity. He looked in vain for the sage Nicholas Vedder, with his broad face, double chin, and fair long pipe...or Van Bummel, the schoolmaster, doling forth the contents of an ancient newspaper. In place of these, a lean... fellow, with his pockets full of handbills, was haranguing vehemently about rights of citizens—elections—members of congress—liberty—Bunker's Hill—heroes of seventy-six—and other words, which were [strange] to the bewildered Van Winkle.

_____
*"Liberty poles" and "liberty caps" were popular symbols of both the American and French revolutions.

Painter John Quidor was a personal friend of Washington Irving. His painting, Return of Rip Van Winkle *(detail), shows Rip coming home to his village. Rip's long white beard and tattered clothing show the effects of his 20-year nap.*

★ **Identify two objects in this picture that confused Rip when he returned home. Why were they unfamiliar to him?**

The appearance of Rip, with his long, grizzled beard . . . and an army of women and children at his heels, soon attracted the attention of the tavern politicians. They crowded around him, eyeing him from head to foot with great curiosity. The orator bustled up to him and, drawing him partly aside, inquired "on which side he voted?" Rip stared in vacant stupidity. Another short but busy little fellow pulled him by the arm and, rising on tiptoe, inquired in his ear, "whether he was Federal or Democrat?" Rip was equally at a loss to comprehend the question. . . . "Alas! Gentlemen," cried Rip, somewhat dismayed, "I am a poor, quiet man, a native of this place, and a loyal subject of the king, God bless him!"

Here a general shout burst from the bystanders. "A tory! A tory! A spy! A refugee! Hustle him! Away with him!" It was with great difficulty that [a] self-important man in [a] cocked hat restored order; and . . . demanded again of the unknown culprit what he came there for and whom he was seeking. The poor man humbly assured him that he meant no harm, but merely came there in search of some of his neighbors, who used to keep about the tavern.

"Well—who are they? Name them."

Rip bethought himself a moment, and inquired . . . "Where's Brom Dutcher?"

"Oh, he went off to the army at the beginning of the war; some say he was killed at the storming of Stony Point—others say he was drowned in a squall at the foot of Antony's Nose. I don't know—he never came back again."

"Where's Van Bummel, the schoolmaster?"

"He went off to the wars, too, was a great militia general, and is now in congress."

Rip's heart died away at hearing of these sad changes in his home and friends, and finding himself thus alone in the world. Every answer puzzled him, too, by treating of such enormous lapses of time and of matter which he could not understand: war—congress—Stony Point. He had no courage to ask after any more friends, but cried out in despair, "Does nobody here know Rip Van Winkle?"

Analyzing Literature

1. Describe three changes Rip Van Winkle sees when he returns to his village.
2. Why does Rip get into trouble with the men gathered outside the tavern?
3. **Critical Thinking** **Making Inferences** According to the story, the very nature of the people seemed different to Rip. **(a)** How does Rip think the people changed? **(b)** What do you think may have caused this change?

Unit 4 The Nation Expands

Viewing UNIT THEMES

Wagon Trains to the West

William Henry Jackson, who later became a famous photographer, painted this dramatic scene. It shows long lines of wagons carrying settlers westward across Nebraska toward Oregon. In the mid-1800s, wagon trains like this carried thousands of American families from the East to newly acquired territories in the West. ★ **Based on this painting, jot down four words or phrases that you would use to describe a journey to the West by wagon train.**

Unit Theme **Expansion**

From 1820 to 1860, the United States grew in several ways. The most dramatic growth was in the size of the nation. It gained vast western territories, including California, Texas, Oregon, and New Mexico. For the first time, an American could travel by land from the Atlantic Ocean to the Pacific without leaving the country.

How did people of the time feel about westward expansion? They can tell you in their own words.

VIEWPOINTS ON WESTWARD EXPANSION

❝ Our population is rolling toward the shores of the Pacific....It will soon...reach the Rocky Mountains and be ready to pour into the Oregon territory. ❞
John C. Calhoun, South Carolina senator (1843)

❝ We traveled till 11 o'clock with the hope of finding water for the weary cattle. The sun was excessively oppressive. ❞
Susan Shelby Magoffin, New Mexico pioneer (1846)

❝ The white man comes and cuts down the trees, building houses and fences and the buffaloes get frightened and leave and never come back, and the Indians are left to starve. ❞
Muguara, Chief of the Penateka Comanche Indians (1840s)

Activity Writing to Learn Thousands of families left their homes in the East to make the long journey westward. What if your family was thinking of moving to another part of the country? List what you might gain by moving. Then, make another list of what you might lose. Use your lists to decide whether you want to move.

Chapter 12

Democracy in the Age of Jackson 1824–1840

In this chapter, you will learn that the Age of Jackson was a time of expanding democracy and political conflict. As more and more white males gained the right to vote, two political parties, the Whigs and Democrats, competed for their support. Nominating conventions and heated election campaigns became part of American politics. Not all, however, shared in democracy's growth. Women, Native Americans, African Americans, and others had to wait for political and social equality.

Why Study History?

Soon, you will have a right and a responsibility of all American citizens—voting. Learning more about how politics worked in past elections may help you make wise voting decisions in the future. To learn more about politics and your right to vote, see this chapter's *Why Study History?* feature, "You Will Choose Our Nation's Leaders."

American Events

1820s
Right to vote extended to most white men

1828
Andrew Jackson is elected President

1830
Indian Removal Act forces Native Americans to move west of the Mississippi

1824　1826　1828　1830　1832

World Events

 1824 World Event
Simón Bolívar becomes president of Peru

 1829 World Event
Swiss adopt universal male suffrage

Viewing HISTORY **Election Day**

The Age of Jackson was a time of expanding democracy. During the 1820s and 1830s, more and more Americans gained the right to vote. In his painting County Election, *George Caleb Bingham shows that Election Day was a time for voting, socializing, and celebrating.* ★ **How does this painting suggest that women were not allowed to participate fully in American democracy?**

1832
President Jackson vetoes charter of the Bank of the United States

1835
Seminole War begins

1840
William Henry Harrison is elected President

1832   1834   1836   1838   1840

1832 World Event
Reform Act doubles number of eligible voters in Britain

1837 World Event
Canadian colonists revolt, demanding democratic reform

A New Era in Politics

As You Read

Explore These Questions
- Why was John Quincy Adams an unpopular President?
- How did voting rights change in the 1820s and 1830s?
- How did political parties become more democratic?

Define
- majority
- suffrage
- caucus
- nominating convention

Identify
- John Quincy Adams
- Whigs
- Democrats
- Alexis de Tocqueville

SETTING the Scene Harry Ward, a New England teacher, made a visit to Cincinnati, Ohio, during the 1824 presidential election campaign. Writing to a friend, he described how Ohioans felt about Andrew Jackson, who was running for President. "Strange! Wild! Infatuated! All for Jackson!" he observed.

On election day, more people voted for Andrew Jackson than for any of the other candidates. Oddly enough, Jackson did not become President that year.

The Disputed Election of 1824

There were four candidates for President in 1824. All four were members of the old Republican party. However, each had support in different parts of the country. **John Quincy Adams** was strong in New England. Henry Clay and Andrew Jackson had support in the West. William Crawford was favored in the South but became too ill to campaign.

The candidates

John Quincy Adams of Massachusetts was the son of Abigail and John Adams, the second President. The younger Adams was a graduate of Harvard University. He had served as Secretary of State and had helped end the War of 1812. People admired Adams for his intelligence and high morals. Adams, however, was uncomfortable campaigning among the common people.

Henry Clay, by contrast, was charming. A Kentuckian, Clay was a shrewd politician who had become Speaker of the House of Representatives. In Congress, Clay was a skillful negotiator. He worked out several important compromises. Despite his abilities, Clay was less popular than the other candidate from the West, Andrew Jackson.

Most Americans knew Andrew Jackson for his military victories in the War of 1812. He was the "Hero of New Orleans." Though he was a landowner and a slave owner, many saw him as a man of the people. Jackson was born in a log cabin and his parents were poor farmers. He was admired by small farmers and others who felt left out of the growing economy in the United States.

The "corrupt bargain"

No clear winner emerged from the election of 1824. Jackson won the popular vote, but no candidate won a **majority,** or more than half, of the electoral votes. As a result, the House of Representatives had to choose the President from among the top three candidates. Because he finished fourth, Clay was out of the running. As Speaker of the House, though, he was able to influence the results.

Clay urged members of the House to vote for Adams. After Adams became President, he made Clay his Secretary of State. Jackson and his backers were furious. They accused Adams and Clay of making a "corrupt bargain" and stealing the election from Jackson. As Jackson was riding home to Tennessee, he met an old friend. "Well, General," said the friend, "we did all we could for you here, but the rascals at Washington cheated you out of it."

"Indeed, my old friend," replied Jackson, "there was *cheating* and *corruption,* and *bribery,* too." In fact, such charges were not true. The election had been decided as the Constitution stated. Still, the anger of Jackson and his supporters seriously hampered President Adams's efforts to unify the nation.

An Unpopular President

Adams knew that the election had angered many Americans. To "bring the whole people together," he pushed for a program of economic growth through internal improvements. His plan backfired, however, and opposition to him grew.

Promoting economic growth

Similar to Alexander Hamilton and Henry Clay, Adams thought that the federal government should promote economic growth. He called for the government to pay for new roads and canals. These internal improvements would help farmers to transport goods to market.

Adams also favored projects to promote the arts and the sciences, as governments in Europe did. He suggested building a national university and an observatory from which astronomers could study the stars.

Most Americans objected to spending money on such programs. They feared that the federal government would become too powerful. Congress approved money for a national road and some canals, but turned down most of Adams's other programs.

A bitter campaign

In 1828, Adams faced an uphill battle for reelection. This time, Andrew Jackson was Adams's only opponent.

The campaign was a bitter contest. Jackson supporters renewed charges that Adams had made a "corrupt bargain" after the 1824 election. They attacked Adams as an aristocrat, or member of the upper class. Adams

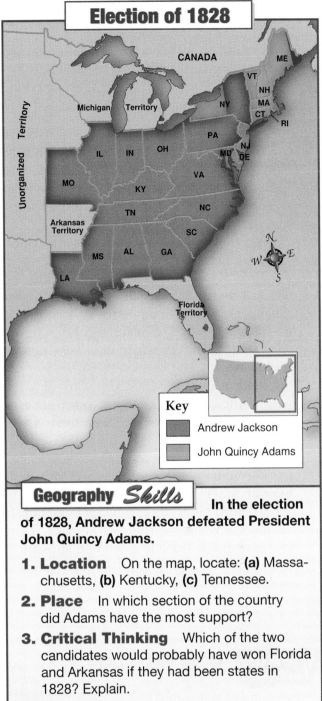

Election of 1828

Geography Skills In the election of 1828, Andrew Jackson defeated President John Quincy Adams.

1. **Location** On the map, locate: **(a)** Massachusetts, **(b)** Kentucky, **(c)** Tennessee.
2. **Place** In which section of the country did Adams have the most support?
3. **Critical Thinking** Which of the two candidates would probably have won Florida and Arkansas if they had been states in 1828? Explain.

supporters replied with similar attacks. They called Jackson a dangerous "military chieftain." If Jackson became President, they warned, he could become a dictator like Napoleon Bonaparte of France.

Jackson won the election easily. His supporters cheered the outcome as a victory for common people. By common people, they meant farmers in the West and South and city workers in the East.

More Voters

During the 1820s, more people gained **suffrage,** or the right to vote. Others, however, were denied full participation in the growing democracy.

Expanding suffrage

The United States was growing rapidly. New states were joining the Union and there were many new voters. Many of them lived in western states between the Appalachians and the Mississippi.

In the West, many frontier people began life poor, but prospered through hard work. As a result, westerners commonly believed that it was possible to achieve success by being honest and working hard. This democratic spirit was reflected in suffrage laws. In the western states, any white man over age 21 could vote.

Reformers in the East also worked to expand suffrage. By the 1830s, most eastern states dropped the requirement that voters own land. In this way, many craftsworkers and shopkeepers won the right to vote.

Throughout the country, growing numbers of Americans exercised their right to vote. Before 1828, the turnout of eligible voters was never more than 27 percent. That low percentage rose to nearly 58 percent in the election of 1828. By 1840, voter turnout was nearly 80 percent.

Limits on suffrage

Despite the growing democratic spirit, many Americans did not have the right to vote. They included women, Native Americans, and most African Americans. Slaves had no political rights.

In fact, as more white men were winning suffrage, free African Americans were losing it. In the early years of the nation, most northern states had allowed free African American men to vote. In the 1820s, many of these states took away that right. By 1830, only a few New England states permitted African American men to vote on equal terms with white men. In New York, African American men had to own property in order to vote. White men did not.

New Political Practices

By 1820, the disappearance of the Federalist party temporarily ended party differences. In the 1830s, new political parties took shape. They grew out of the conflict between John Quincy Adams and Andrew Jackson.

Two new parties

People who supported Adams and his programs for national growth called themselves National Republicans. In 1834, they became known as **Whigs.** Whigs wanted the federal government to spur the economy. Whigs included eastern business people, some south-

Viewing HISTORY **Limits on Suffrage**

The watercolor painting Two Women by Eunice Pinney shows two women engaged in conversation. During the Age of Jackson, women could not vote in a single state. Most men of the time thought that women should take care of household responsibilities.
★ **How do you think women were able to influence the outcome of elections?**

Past

Present

The People and the Presidency

In 1829, President Jackson held a party at the White House to celebrate his inauguration. Cheerful guests helped themselves to slices of a huge cheese. Today, Presidents invite Americans into their home for tours or special events. One example is the Easter egg roll, held each year on the White House lawn. ★ **Why did some people criticize Jackson for opening the White House to the common people?**

ern planters, and former Federalists. Jackson and his supporters called themselves **Democrats.** Today's Democratic party traces its roots to Andrew Jackson's time. Democrats included frontier farmers, as well as factory workers in the East.

New ways to choose candidates

The two new political parties developed more democratic ways to choose candidates for President. In the past, powerful members of each party held a **caucus,** or private meeting. There, they chose their candidate. Critics called the caucus system undemocratic because only a few powerful people were able to take part in it.

In the 1830s, each party began to hold a **nominating convention,** where delegates from all the states chose the party's candidate for President. Nominating conventions gave people a more direct voice in choosing future leaders. Party leaders might still dom-

inate a particular convention, but the nominating process was becoming subject to the will of the people. Today, the major political parties still hold conventions.

Growing Spirit of Equality

The spirit of democracy affected American ideas about social classes. Most Americans did not feel that the rich deserved special respect. "Does a man become wiser, stronger or more virtuous and patriotic because he has a fine house?" asked a Democrat.

Wealthy European visitors to the United States were surprised that American servants expected to be treated as equals. Others were amazed that butlers and maids refused to be summoned with bells, as in Europe. **Alexis de Tocqueville** (tohk VEEL), a visitor from France, became especially well known for his observations on American democracy.

Alexis de Tocqueville

In 1831, Alexis de Tocqueville arrived in the United States. The French government had sent him to study the American prison system. Over a period of several months, Tocqueville toured much of the United States. He observed much more than prisons. He observed a society that was becoming more and more democratic.

After his return to France, Tocqueville recorded his experiences and observations in a book titled *Democracy in America*. In it, he admired the American democratic spirit and its goals of equality and freedom.

66 Although the revolution that is taking place in the social condition, laws, ideas, and feelings of men is still far from coming to an end, yet its results are already incomparably greater than anything which has taken place in the world before. 99

Jacksonian democracy

Andrew Jackson's inauguration in 1829 reflected the spirit of Jacksonian democracy. As Jackson traveled to Washington, large crowds cheered him along the way. For the first time, thousands of ordinary people flooded the capital to watch the President take the oath of office.

After Jackson was sworn in, the crowd followed the new President to a reception at the White House. The appearance and behavior of the "common people" shocked an onlooker:

66 A rabble, a mob, of boys, negros, women, children, scrambling, fighting, romping. What a pity, what a pity! No arrangements had been made, no police officers on duty, and the whole house had been [filled] by the rabble mob. 99

The President, he continued, was "almost suffocated and torn to pieces by the people in their eagerness to shake hands."

Jackson's critics said the scene showed that "King Mob" was ruling the nation. Amos Kendall, a loyal Jackson supporter, viewed the inauguration celebration in a more positive way: "It was a proud day for the people. General Jackson is *their own* President."

★ Section 1 Review ★

Recall

1. **Locate** (a) Massachusetts, (b) Kentucky, (c) Tennessee.
2. **Identify** (a) John Quincy Adams, (b) Whigs, (c) Democrats, (d) Alexis de Tocqueville.
3. **Define** (a) majority, (b) suffrage, (c) caucus, (d) nominating convention.

Comprehension

4. Why did voters not reelect John Quincy Adams to the Presidency in 1828?
5. (a) How did suffrage expand in the 1820s and 1830s? (b) What Americans were denied suffrage?

6. How were nominating conventions more democratic than the caucus system?

Critical Thinking and Writing

7. **Applying Information** Based on what you learned about the election of 1824, if no candidate won a majority of electoral votes in the next presidential election, how would the President be chosen?
8. **Defending a Position** Do you agree or disagree with John Quincy Adams's position that the government should spend money to support the arts and sciences? Explain the reasons for your position.

Activity **Writing an Advertisement** Suffrage has expanded greatly since the Age of Jackson. Still, many Americans do not exercise their right to vote. Write a radio or television advertisement urging people to get out and vote next Election Day.

Jackson in the White House

As You Read

Explore These Questions
- What qualities helped Jackson succeed?
- Why did Jackson replace many office-holders?
- Why did Jackson fight against the Bank of the United States?

Define
- spoils system
- pet bank

Identify
- Old Hickory
- kitchen cabinet
- Nicholas Biddle

SETTING the Scene During the 1828 election campaign, many stories about Andrew Jackson spread. Like the one that follows, they often showed Jackson's courage and determination.

Years before he ran for President, Jackson was a judge in Tennessee. One day, a disorderly lawbreaker, Russell Bean, refused to appear before the court. The story tells how Jackson strutted out of the courthouse. "Surrender, you infernal villain," he roared, "or I'll blow you through." Bean looked into Jackson's blazing eyes and quietly surrendered. The iron will that made Russell Bean surrender also made Jackson a powerful President.

Andrew Jackson

Like many who admired him, Jackson was born in a log cabin on the frontier. His parents had left Ireland to settle on the Carolina frontier. Both died before Jackson was 15. Young Andrew had to grow up quickly.

A tough fighter

Like many other boys who grew up on the frontier, young Andrew Jackson was a determined fighter. Even though he had a slight

A young Andrew Jackson

build, he was strong and determined. A friend who wrestled with him recalled, "I could throw him three times out of four, but he would never stay throwed."

Jackson showed his toughness during the American Revolution. At age 13, he joined the Patriots but was captured by the British. When a British officer ordered the young prisoner to clean his boots, Jackson refused. The officer took a sword and slashed the boy's hand and face. The memory of that attack stayed with Jackson for the rest of his life.

A self-made man

After the Revolution, Jackson studied law in North Carolina. Later, he moved to Tennessee and set up a successful law practice. He became very wealthy by buying and selling land in Georgia and Alabama. While still in his twenties, he was elected to Congress.

Jackson won national fame for his achievements during the War of 1812. He commanded the American forces to a major victory over the British at the Battle of New Orleans. He also defeated the Creek Indians and forced them to give up vast amounts of land in Georgia and Alabama.

A man of many qualities

Andrew Jackson was a man of many qualities. He had led a violent and adventurous life. He was no stranger to brawls, gambling, and duels. He was quick to lose his temper and he dealt with his enemies harshly.

Jackson's supporters admired his ability to inspire and lead others. They considered him a man of his word and a champion of the common people. The soldiers who served under Jackson called him **Old Hickory.** To them, he was as tough as the wood of a hickory tree.

To the Creek Indians, however, Jackson was an enemy who showed no mercy. After defeating them, Jackson had threatened to kill their leaders if they did not give up lands that earlier treaties had guaranteed them. As a result, the Creeks had no affection for Jackson. Their name for him was Sharp Knife.

The Spoils System

In 1828, President Jackson knew that Americans wanted change. "The people expected reform," he said. "This was the cry from Maine to Louisiana."

Reward for victory

After taking office, Jackson fired many government employees. He replaced them with his own supporters. Most other Presidents had done the same, but Jackson did it on a larger scale.

Critics accused Jackson of rewarding Democrats who had helped elect him instead of choosing qualified men. Jackson replied that he was serving democracy by letting more citizens take part in government. He felt that ordinary Americans could fill government jobs. "The duties of all public officers are ...so plain and simple that men of intelligence may readily qualify themselves for their performance," he said.

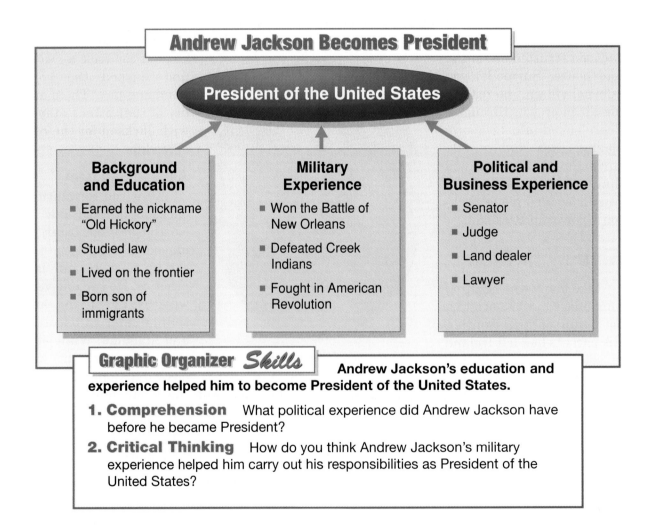

Andrew Jackson Becomes President

President of the United States

Background and Education
- Earned the nickname "Old Hickory"
- Studied law
- Lived on the frontier
- Born son of immigrants

Military Experience
- Won the Battle of New Orleans
- Defeated Creek Indians
- Fought in American Revolution

Political and Business Experience
- Senator
- Judge
- Land dealer
- Lawyer

Graphic Organizer *Skills* Andrew Jackson's education and experience helped him to become President of the United States.

1. **Comprehension** What political experience did Andrew Jackson have before he became President?
2. **Critical Thinking** How do you think Andrew Jackson's military experience helped him carry out his responsibilities as President of the United States?

A Kitchen Cabinet Dispute

President Jackson often asked for advice from an unofficial group of advisers. This cartoon presents one artist's view of Jackson's "kitchen cabinet." ★ **What was the cartoonist's opinion of the kitchen cabinet? Explain.**

A Jackson supporter explained the system another way. "To the victor belong the spoils," he declared. Spoils are profits or benefits. From then on, the practice of rewarding supporters with government jobs became known as the **spoils system.**

The kitchen cabinet

Jackson rewarded a number of his supporters with Cabinet jobs. Only Secretary of State Martin Van Buren was truly qualified for his position.

As a result, Jackson seldom met with his official Cabinet. Instead, he relied on a group of unofficial advisers. They included Democratic leaders and newspaper editors. These men had a good sense of the nation's mood. Because Jackson met with them in the White House kitchen, the group became known as the **kitchen cabinet.**

The Bank War

President Jackson waged war on the Bank of the United States. Like many westerners, he thought that it was too powerful.

Mr. Biddle's bank

From the first, the Bank of the United States had been a subject of dispute. (See page 247.) The Bank had great power because it controlled loans made by state banks. When the Bank's directors thought that state banks were making too many loans, they limited the amount these banks could lend. The cutbacks angered farmers and merchants who borrowed money to buy land or finance new businesses.

President Jackson and other leading Democrats saw the Bank as undemocratic. Although Congress had created the Bank, it was run by private bankers. Jackson condemned these men as agents of "special privilege" who grew rich with public funds. He especially disliked **Nicholas Biddle,** president of the Bank since 1823.

Biddle came from a wealthy Philadelphia family. He was well qualified to run the bank, but he was also arrogant and vain. Jackson felt that Biddle used the Bank to benefit only the rich. He also resented Biddle's influence over certain members of Congress.

$ Connections With Economics

Today, the Federal Reserve Board supervises a national system of banks and has much influence over the economy. It can tighten the money supply and reduce inflation by raising interest rates. By lowering interest rates on loans, it can encourage economic growth.

The war begins

Biddle and other Whigs worried that the President might try to destroy the Bank. Two Whig senators, Henry Clay and Daniel Webster, thought of a way to save the Bank and defeat Jackson at the same time.

The Bank's charter was not due for renewal by Congress until 1836. However, Clay and Webster wanted to make the Bank an issue in the 1832 election. They persuaded Biddle to apply for renewal early.

The Whigs believed that most Americans supported the Bank of the United States. If Jackson vetoed the bill to renew the charter, they felt sure that he would anger voters and lose the election. Clay pushed the charter renewal bill through Congress in 1832. Jackson was sick in bed when he heard that Congress had renewed the Bank's charter. "The Bank...is trying to kill me," Jackson fumed, "but I will kill it!"

Jackson's veto

In an angry message to Congress, Jackson vetoed the Bank bill. He gave two reasons for his veto. First, he declared the Bank unconstitutional, even though the Supreme Court had ruled in the Bank's favor. Jackson believed that only states, not the federal government, had the right to charter banks. Second, Jackson felt that the Bank helped aristocrats at the expense of the common people. He warned:

66 When the laws undertake...to make the rich richer and the potent more powerful, the humble members of society—the farmers, mechanics, and laborers—...have a right to complain of the injustice of their government. 99

As planned, the Whigs made the Bank a major issue in the election of 1832. They chose Henry Clay as their candidate to run against Andrew Jackson. When the votes were counted, Jackson won a stunning election victory. The common people had supported Jackson and rejected the Bank of the United States.

The Bank closes

Without a new charter, the Bank would have to close in 1836. Jackson refused to wait. He ordered Secretary of the Treasury Roger Taney to stop putting government money in the Bank. Instead, Taney deposited federal money in state banks. They became known as **pet banks** because Taney and his friends controlled many of them.

The loss of federal money crippled the Bank of the United States. Its closing in 1836 contributed to an economic crisis.

★ Section 2 Review ★

Recall

1. **Identify** (a) Old Hickory, (b) kitchen cabinet, (c) Nicholas Biddle.
2. **Define** (a) spoils system, (b) pet bank.

Comprehension

3. How did Andrew Jackson's education and experience help prepare him for the Presidency of the United States?
4. Why did critics object to the spoils system?

5. Why did many farmers and merchants dislike the Bank of the United States?

Critical Thinking and Writing

6. **Understanding Causes and Effects** How did the spoils system lead to the creation of the kitchen cabinet?
7. **Analyzing Information** What do you think the Creeks were saying about Jackson when they called him Sharp Knife?

Activity **Writing a Script** Write the script for a television drama in which Andrew Jackson and Nicholas Biddle discuss the Bank of the United States and pet banks.

3 ★ Struggles Over States' Rights

As You Read

Explore These Questions
- How did John C. Calhoun and Daniel Webster disagree on states' rights?
- How did Jackson deal with the Nullification Crisis?
- Why did Native Americans of the Southeast have to leave their lands?

Define
- nullification
- states' rights
- secede

Identify
- Tariff of Abominations
- Nullification Crisis
- Sequoyah
- Indian Removal Act
- Trail of Tears
- Osceola
- Seminole War

SETTING the Scene As President, Andrew Jackson had to deal with a tariff crisis that threatened to split the nation. He also played a major role in deciding the future of many Native Americans. At the heart of both cases was a question that challenged the nation. Did states or the federal government have greater authority?

A Crisis Over Tariffs

In 1828, Congress passed the highest tariff in the nation's history. Southerners called it the **Tariff of Abominations.** An abomination is something that is hated.

Just like earlier tariffs, the new law protected manufacturers from foreign competition. Most manufacturers lived in the North. Southern planters, however, were hurt by the tariff. They sold their cotton in Europe and bought European goods in return. The high tariff meant that southerners had to pay more for these imports.

Calhoun vs. Webster

A leader in the South's fight against the tariff was Vice President John C. Calhoun. He used an argument that Thomas Jefferson had made in the Kentucky and Virginia resolutions. (See page 260.) Like Jefferson, Calhoun claimed that a state

A tariff collector used this stencil to mark goods.

had the right to nullify, or cancel, a federal law that it considered to be unconstitutional. This idea is called **nullification.**

Calhoun supported **states' rights,** the right of states to limit the power of the federal government. He argued that the states had final authority because the states had created the national government.

Daniel Webster disagreed. In 1830, he made a speech in the Senate attacking the idea of nullification. The Constitution, he said, united the American people, not just the states. If states had the right to nullify federal laws, the nation would fall apart. Webster ended his speech with stirring words: "Liberty and Union, now and forever, one and inseparable."

Calhoun resigns

Southerners and westerners strongly supported states' rights. They expected Jackson, who had been born in the South and lived in the West, to support their view.

The President's position soon became clear. Jackson and Calhoun attended a political dinner in 1830. Several guests made toasts in favor of states' rights. Finally, Jackson rose. The room fell silent. Old Hickory

Skills

FOR LIFE

| Critical Thinking | Managing Information | Communication | Maps, Charts, and Graphs |

Reaching a Compromise

How Will I Use This Skill?

When individuals or groups disagree, they can solve the problem and avoid conflict by reaching a compromise. In a compromise, the opposing sides give up some of their demands in order to forge an agreement that both can accept. Knowing how to reach a compromise will help you settle disagreements, solve problems, and get along with others.

LEARN the Skill

You can reach a compromise by following these four steps:

❶ Understand the positions of the opposing sides.

❷ Recognize the probable effects of not reaching compromise.

❸ Determine what each side might give up or concede in order to reach an agreement.

❹ Negotiate a deal by discussing the conflicting issues and offering possible concessions. Compromise is reached when an agreement is acceptable to both sides.

PRACTICE the Skill

Using the steps above, review the compromise concerning the Tariff of Abominations and the Nullification Crisis in this section.

❶ Explain the positions of northern manufacturers and southern planters on the two issues.

❷ What did each side threaten to do if a compromise was not reached?

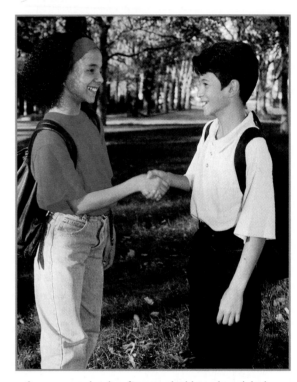

A compromise is often sealed by a handshake.

❸ What did each side give up in order to reach an agreement?

❹ With a partner, reenact a negotiation as it might have occurred between representatives of the North and South.

APPLY the Skill

Working with a partner, role-play a dispute that might occur today between an employer and an employee. Identify various issues that they might disagree on. Then, apply what you have learned in order to reach a compromise.

raised his glass, looked straight at the Vice President, and proclaimed, "Our Federal Union—it must be preserved!"

The drama continued. Calhoun raised his glass and answered the President's challenge: "The Union—next to our liberty, most dear." To him, the liberty of a state was more important than the Union.

Because Calhoun strongly disagreed with Jackson, he resigned from the office of Vice President. He was then elected senator from South Carolina. The debate over states' rights would rage for years.

The Nullification Crisis

Anger against the tariff increased in the South. In 1832, Congress passed a new tariff that lowered the rate slightly. South Carolina was not satisfied. It passed the Nullification Act, declaring the new tariff illegal. It also threatened to **secede,** or withdraw, from the Union if challenged.

Jackson was furious. He knew that nullification could lead to civil war. In private, he raged:

> 66 If one drop of blood be shed there in defiance of the laws of the United States, I will hang the first man of them I can get my hands on to the first tree I can find. 99

Publicly the President supported a lower compromise tariff proposed by Henry Clay. Jackson also asked Congress to pass the Force Bill. It allowed him to use the army, if necessary, to enforce the tariff.

Faced with Jackson's firm stand, no other state chose to support South Carolina. Calhoun supported the compromise tariff that Clay had proposed. South Carolina repealed the Nullification Act and the **Nullification Crisis** passed. However, sectional tensions between the North and South would increase in the years ahead.

Tragedy for Native Americans

Jackson took a firm stand on another key issue. It affected the fate of Native Americans. Since the early colonial era, white settlers had forced Native Americans off their

Biography Sequoyah

Sequoyah adapted Greek, Hebrew, and English letters to create the 86 symbols of his Cherokee alphabet. The Cherokees used Sequoyah's alphabet to write a constitution. ★ **Why would the lack of a written language be a disadvantage to a society?**

land. Indian leaders like Pontiac and Tecumseh had failed to stop the invasion of white settlers.

Indian nations in the Southeast

The Creek, Choctaw, Chickasaw, Cherokee, and Seminole nations lived in the Southeast. Many hoped to live in peace with their white neighbors. Their fertile land, however, was ideal for growing cotton. Settlers wanted the land for themselves.

Like earlier Presidents, Jackson sided with the white settlers. At his urging, the government set aside lands beyond the Mississippi River and then persuaded or forced Indians to move there. Jackson believed that this policy would provide land for white settlers as well as protect Native Americans from destruction.

Few Indians wanted to move. Some, like the Cherokee nation, had adopted customs of

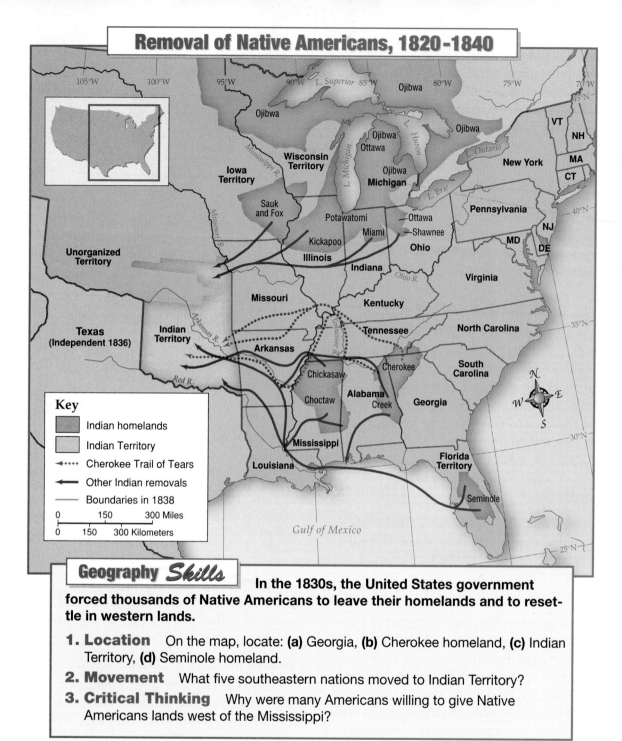

Removal of Native Americans, 1820-1840

Key
- Indian homelands
- Indian Territory
- Cherokee Trail of Tears
- Other Indian removals
- Boundaries in 1838

0   150   300 Miles
0   150   300 Kilometers

Geography Skills In the 1830s, the United States government forced thousands of Native Americans to leave their homelands and to resettle in western lands.

1. **Location** On the map, locate: **(a)** Georgia, **(b)** Cherokee homeland, **(c)** Indian Territory, **(d)** Seminole homeland.
2. **Movement** What five southeastern nations moved to Indian Territory?
3. **Critical Thinking** Why were many Americans willing to give Native Americans lands west of the Mississippi?

white settlers. The Cherokees lived in farming villages. They had a constitution that set up a republican form of government.

In 1821, **Sequoyah** (sih KWOI uh) created a written alphabet for his people. Using Sequoyah's letters, Cherokee children learned to read and write. The Cherokees also published a newspaper.

A legal battle

In 1828, Georgia claimed the right to make laws for the Cherokee nation. The Cherokees went to court to defend their rights. They pointed to treaties with the federal government that protected their rights and property. The Cherokee case reached the Supreme Court. In the 1832 case of *Worcester v. Georgia,* Chief Justice John Marshall ruled in favor of the Cherokees. The Court declared Georgia's action unconstitutional and stated that Native Americans were protected by the United States Constitution.

However, President Jackson refused to enforce the Court's decision. In the Nullification Crisis, Jackson defended the power of the federal government. In the Cherokee case, he backed states' rights. He said that the federal government could not stop Georgia from extending its authority over Cherokee lands. "John Marshall has made his decision," Jackson reportedly said. "Now let him enforce it."

Forced to Leave

In 1830, Jackson supporters in Congress pushed through the **Indian Removal Act.** It forced many Native Americans to move west of the Mississippi. Whites did not mind turning this land over to Indians because they thought the region was a vast desert. During the 1830s, thousands of southeastern Indians were driven from their homes and forced to march to Indian Territory, west of the Mississippi.

A tragic march

In 1838, the United States Army drove more than 15,000 Cherokees westward to a land they had never seen. The Cherokees trekked hundreds of miles over a period of several months. They had little food or shelter. Thousands perished during the march, mostly children and the elderly. In all, about one fourth of the Indians died.

The Cherokees' long, sorrowful journey west became known as the **Trail of Tears.** An eyewitness described the suffering:

66 The Cherokees are nearly all prisoners. They had been dragged from their homes and encamped at the forts and military places, all over the nation. In Georgia especially, multitudes were allowed no time to take anything with them except the clothes they had on. 99

The Seminoles resist

In Florida, the Seminole Indians resisted removal. Led by Chief **Osceola** (ahs ee OH luh), they fought the United States Army. The **Seminole War** lasted from 1835 to 1842. It was the costliest war waged by the government to gain Indian lands. More than 1,500 soldiers died in the war and about 20 million dollars were spent in the war effort.

In the end, the Seminoles were defeated. The government forced the Seminole leaders and most of their people to leave Florida. By 1844, only a few thousand Native Americans remained east of the Mississippi River.

★ Section 3 Review ★

Recall

1. **Locate** (a) South Carolina, (b) Georgia, (c) Cherokee homeland, (d) Indian Territory, (e) Seminole homeland.
2. **Identify** (a) Tariff of Abominations, (b) Nullification Crisis, (c) Sequoyah, (d) Indian Removal Act, (e) Trail of Tears, (f) Osceola, (g) Seminole War.
3. **Define** (a) nullification, (b) states' rights, (c) secede.

Comprehension

4. Why did northerners and southerners disagree on the tariff issue?

5. How did Andrew Jackson respond to South Carolina's Nullification Act?
6. Why did Jackson support the policy of using force to move Native Americans beyond the Mississippi River?

Critical Thinking and Writing

7. **Forecasting** What do you think might have happened if other southern states supported South Carolina in the Nullification Crisis?
8. **Drawing Conclusions** Why do you think Andrew Jackson supported states' rights in the Cherokee case but not in the Nullification Crisis?

Activity **Writing a Protest Letter** You are a Cherokee on the Trail of Tears. Write a protest letter to President Jackson explaining why you consider his policy of Indian removal to be unjust.

4 The Presidency After Jackson

★ ★

As You Read

Explore These Questions
- What economic problems did Martin Van Buren face?
- How did Whigs and Democrats compete for the Presidency in 1840?
- Why did John Tyler have little success as President?

Define
- speculator
- depression
- laissez faire
- mudslinging

Identify
- Martin Van Buren
- Panic of 1837
- William Henry Harrison
- John Tyler

SETTING the Scene Andrew Jackson retired from office after two terms. Americans then elected **Martin Van Buren** to the Presidency. Van Buren had served as Vice President during Jackson's second term.

As Van Buren took the oath of office in March 1837, Jackson stood at his side. Onlookers watched the outgoing President, not Van Buren. As Old Hickory left the platform, a rousing cheer rose from the crowd. In that moment, the people expressed their loyalty and respect for Andrew Jackson, the "Hero of New Orleans."

Van Buren and Hard Times

Martin Van Buren was very different from Andrew Jackson. He was a politician, not a war hero. Davy Crockett, a Congressman from Tennessee, once described Van Buren as "an artful, cunning, intriguing, selfish, speculating lawyer." As President, however, Van Buren needed more than sharp political instincts.

The Panic of 1837

Two months after taking office, Van Buren faced the worst economic crisis the nation had known. It was called the **Panic of 1837.** The panic had several causes. During the 1830s, the government sold millions of acres of public land in the West. Farmers bought some land, but **speculators** bought even more, hoping that their risky investment would earn them huge profits. To pay for the land, speculators borrowed money from state banks. After the Bank of the United States closed, the state banks could lend money without limit.

To meet the demand for loans, state banks printed more and more paper money. Often, the paper money was not backed by gold or silver. Paper money had value only if people trusted the banks that issued it.

Before leaving office, Jackson had grown alarmed at the wild speculation in land. To slow it down, he ordered that anyone buying public land had to pay for it with gold or silver. Speculators and others rushed to state banks to exchange their paper money for gold and silver. Many banks did not have enough gold and silver and had to close.

Economic depression

The panic worsened when cotton prices went down because of an oversupply. Cotton planters often borrowed money, which they repaid when they sold their crop. Low cotton prices meant that planters could not repay their loans. As a result, more banks failed.

The nation plunged into a deep economic **depression,** a period when business declines and many people lose their jobs. The depression lasted three years. In the worst days, 90 percent of the nation's factories were closed. Thousands of people were out of work. In some cities, hungry crowds broke into warehouses and stole food.

Van Buren's response

It was easy for people to blame President Van Buren for the country's economic depression. Van Buren took little action because he believed in **laissez faire**—the idea that government should play as small a role as possible in the nation's economic affairs. "The less the government interferes with private pursuits," he said, "the better for the general prosperity."

Van Buren's limited actions did little to help the economy. He tried to set up a more stable banking system. He also cut back on government expenses. For example, when he entertained visitors at the White House, they were served simple dinners. Still, the depression wore on. As a result, criticism of Van Buren increased.

Campaigns of 1840

Even though Van Buren had lost support, the Democrats chose him to run for reelection in 1840. The Whigs, learning from the Democrats, chose a candidate who would appeal to the common people. He was **William Henry Harrison** of Ohio. Harrison was known as the hero of the Battle of Tippecanoe. (See page 281.) To run for Vice President, the Whigs chose John Tyler.

Log cabin campaign

Most Americans knew very little about Harrison's stand on the issues. To appeal to voters, the Whigs focused on his war record. "Tippecanoe and Tyler too" became their campaign slogan.

The Whigs created an image for Harrison as a "man of the people." They presented him as a humble farmer who had been born in a log cabin. Harrison was actually a wealthy, educated man who lived in a large mansion. Still, the Whigs made the log cabin their campaign symbol. In a typical Whig cartoon, Harrison stands outside a log cabin, greeting Van Buren and his aides:

> 66 Gentlemen,... If you will accept the [simple food] of a log cabin, with a western farmer's cheer, you are welcome. I have no champagne but can give you a mug of good cider, with some ham and eggs, and good clean beds. I am a plain backwoodsman. I have cleared some land, killed some Indians, and made the Red Coats fly in my time. 99

A new sort of politics

The campaigns of 1840 reflected a new sort of politics. Harrison traveled across the land, making speeches and greeting voters. Both parties competed for votes with rallies, banquets, and entertainment. Ordinary citizens participated by giving speeches and singing campaign songs like this one:

> 66 The times are bad, and want curing;
> They are getting past all enduring:
> So let's turn out Martin Van Buren
> And put in old Tippecanoe! 99

Viewing HISTORY **Log Cabin Campaign**

Harrison's log cabin symbol swept the nation in 1840. Marchers in parades often carried miniature cabins such as the one shown here. The cabin was attached to a pole and raised aloft for all to see. ★ **Why was the log cabin image appealing to many voters?**

Why Study History?

Because You Will Choose Our Nation's Leaders

★ ★

Historical Background

In the political campaigns of 1840, Democrats and Whigs showed little concern for the key issues of the day. Instead, they organized parades, chanted slogans, offered free cider, and participated in name-calling. Candidates also used newspapers, posters, and even whisky jugs to carry their political messages. In 1840, the Whigs' log cabin campaign was a success and William Henry Harrison was elected President. (See page 339.)

Connections to Today

When election day draws near today, politicians flood the radio, television, Internet, and various other media with campaign sound bites. Like politicians of the 1840s, some candidates try to avoid the issues. Some candidates may even use questionable or inappropriate campaign tactics to win votes.

Responsible voters are familiar with the workings of political campaigns. They make their voting decisions based on a clear understanding of the candidates' past performance and stand on the issues. They want to vote for the most qualified candidate. Other voters, however, may be swayed more by clever campaign tactics and political advertisements.

Connections to You

Right now, you may participate in school elections. In a few years, you will have the right and responsibility of voting for our nation's leaders. You will help to choose leaders of your nation, state, and community. Politicians of today, like those of the 1840s, will sometimes use aggressive campaign tactics to try to win your vote. Learning about politics during the Age of Jackson and during other eras of American history can help you to become a knowledgeable and responsible voter.

1. Comprehension
(a) What campaign tactics did the Whigs use in the election of 1840?
(b) What role does advertising play in political campaigns today?

2. Critical Thinking
How can you learn more about a candidate's past performance and stand on major issues?

★Activity **Interviewing** Write several questions to help you learn how people make their voting decisions. Then, use your questions to interview people you know who voted in a recent election. Keep a written or taped record of their responses. What conclusions can you draw from your interviews?

Along the campaign trail, Whigs organized colorful parades in both small towns and big cities. At every stop, they served plenty of free cider. The log cabin symbol appeared on banners, quilts, and even packages of shaving soap.

Name-calling, half-truths, and lies

In their campaigns, both Whigs and Democrats engaged in mudslinging, or the use of insults to attack an opponent's reputation. They used name-calling, half-truths, and lies to win votes.

The Whigs attacked the President. One newspaper falsely reported that Van Buren spent thousands of dollars to install a bathtub in the White House. They blamed "Martin Van Ruin" for the depression. Daniel Webster charged that the Democrats had replaced "Old Hickory" Jackson with "Slippery Elm" Van Buren.

The Democrats responded with their own attacks and name-calling. They revealed that "Granny Harrison, the Petticoat General," had resigned from the army before the War of 1812 ended. They accused "General Mum" of not speaking on the issues. "Should Harrison be elected?" they asked voters. "Read his name spelled backwards," they advised. "No sirrah."

Whigs in the White House

Harrison won the election of 1840 easily. As a result, a Whig was in the White House for the first time in 12 years. "We have taught them how to conquer us!" complained one Democrat.

The Whigs had a clear-cut program. They wanted to create a new Bank of the United States and improve roads and canals. Also, they wanted a high tariff.

However, Whig hopes soon crashed. Just weeks after taking office, President Harrison died of pneumonia. **John Tyler** became the first Vice President to succeed a President who died in office.

President Tyler failed to live up to Whig expectations. A former Democrat, he opposed some Whig plans for developing the economy. When the Whigs in Congress passed a bill to recharter the Bank of the United States, Tyler vetoed it.

In response, most of Tyler's Cabinet resigned and the Whigs threw Tyler out of their party. Democrats welcomed the squabbling. "Tyler is heartily despised by everyone," reported an observer. "He has no influence at all." With few friends in either the Whig or Democratic party, Tyler could do little during his term in office.

★ **Section 4 Review** ★

Recall

1. **Identify** (a) Martin Van Buren, (b) Panic of 1837, (c) William Henry Harrison, (d) John Tyler.
2. **Define** (a) speculator, (b) depression, (c) laissez faire, (d) mudslinging.

Comprehension

3. Describe the economic depression that occurred after the Panic of 1837.
4. Describe some of the campaign tactics Democrats and Whigs used in the election of 1840.

5. Why did the Whigs throw President Tyler out of their party?

Critical Thinking and Writing

6. **Solving Problems** What do you think President Van Buren could have done to ease the economic crisis of the 1830s?
7. **Comparing** How do campaign tactics of today compare with those of 1840?

Activity Researching If you had money in a bank that failed today, would you lose your money just as people did in the 1830s? To find the answer, conduct research on the Federal Deposit Insurance Corporation, also known as the FDIC.

Review and Activities

★ Sum It Up ★

Section 1 A New Era in Politics
▶ The 1828 election of Andrew Jackson for President was seen as a victory for the common people.
▶ In the 1820s, democracy expanded as more and more white males gained the right to vote.
▶ Women and African Americans did not share in the growth of democracy.

Section 2 Jackson in the White House
▶ Jackson rewarded his supporters with government jobs and relied on the advice of his unofficial kitchen cabinet.
▶ Jackson fought against the national bank, which he saw as a tool of the wealthy.

Section 3 Struggles Over States' Rights
▶ In his second term, Jackson used compromise and strong leadership to end a crisis over tariffs and states' rights.
▶ Jackson's Indian removal policy forced thousands of Native Americans to leave their homelands and move west.

Section 4 The Presidency After Jackson
▶ The Panic of 1837 brought an economic depression that caused President Van Buren to lose popular support.
▶ In 1840, Whigs used new political campaign tactics to get William Henry Harrison elected President.

CD-ROM Review

For additional review of the major ideas of Chapter 12, see *Guide to the Essentials of American History* or *Interactive Student Tutorial CD-ROM,* which contains interactive review activities, graphic organizers, and practice tests.

▢ Reviewing the Chapter

Define These Terms
Match each term with the correct definition.

Column 1
1. suffrage
2. caucus
3. nominating convention
4. spoils system
5. kitchen cabinet

Column 2
a. private meeting to choose candidates
b. right to vote
c. practice of rewarding supporters with government jobs
d. meeting where state delegates choose candidates
e. Jackson's group of unofficial advisers

Explore the Main Ideas
1. Why were there more voters in 1828 than in 1824?
2. What role did each of the following play in the struggle over the Bank: **(a)** Nicholas Biddle, **(b)** Henry Clay, **(c)** Andrew Jackson.
3. Why did South Carolina want to nullify the tariffs of 1828 and 1832?
4. Describe President Jackson's Indian removal policy.
5. What were the causes of the Panic of 1837?

▢ Geography Activity

Match the letters on the map with the following places:
1. Indian Territory, **2.** Chickasaw, **3.** Choctaw, **4.** Creek, **5.** Cherokee, **6.** Seminole. **Place** Why did settlers want Cherokee lands in the Southeast?

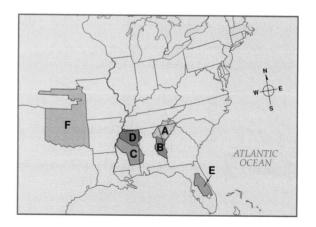

Critical Thinking and Writing

1. **Defending a Position** Do you think more Americans should have supported John Quincy Adams's plans to promote economic growth? Why or why not?
2. **Understanding Chronology** Place these events in chronological order: **(a)** Jackson becomes President, **(b)** the Cherokees are ordered off their land, **(c)** the Seminole War begins.
3. **Linking Past and Present** How are today's political tactics similar to those of the Jackson era? How are the tactics different?
4. **Exploring Unit Themes** **Expansion** We often think of the Age of Jackson as a time of expanding democracy. In what ways did American democracy expand during the Age of Jackson?

Using Primary Sources

President Jackson wanted to move all Native Americans west of the Mississippi River. In 1835, when it seemed that the Seminoles would resist, Jackson wrote a forceful letter to them.

> **My Children—**
> I am sorry to have heard that you have been listening to bad counsel....I have ordered a large military force to be sent among you....If you listen to the voice of friendship and truth, you will go quietly and voluntarily. But should you listen to the bad birds that are always flying about you and refuse to move, I have then directed the commanding officer to remove you by force. This will be done. I pray the Great Spirit, therefore, to incline you to do what is right.
>
> Your friend,
> A. Jackson

Source: "President Andrew Jackson's Letter to the Seminoles" in *History of the Indian Wars,* ed. Henry Trumbull, 1841.

Recognizing Points of View (a) How did President Jackson suggest that he was a friend of the Seminoles? **(b)** How do you think the Seminoles felt about Jackson after reading this letter?

ACTIVITY BANK

▶ Interdisciplinary Activity

Exploring Economics Review the Tariff of Abominations. Then do research to learn about the North American Free Trade Agreement of the 1990s. In an oral report, explain the differences between these two national economic policies.

▶ Career Skills Activity

Artists Select an issue or incident related to Andrew Jackson's presidency. Then create a political cartoon based on your selection. Remember that political cartoonists represent a point of view by using various symbols. Be prepared to explain your cartoon and its symbolism.

▶ Citizenship Activity

Running a Food Drive Thousands of Cherokees died of starvation on the Trail of Tears. Today, in many communities, some people do not have enough food to eat. Form a student group to plan and run a food drive. Work with a charitable organization to deliver food to those in need.

Internet Activity

Search the Internet to find sites dealing with Cherokee culture and history. Continue exploring until you find Cherokee viewpoints on the Indian Removal and the Trail of Tears. Use the Cherokee viewpoints to write a poem about how people suffered on the Trail of Tears.

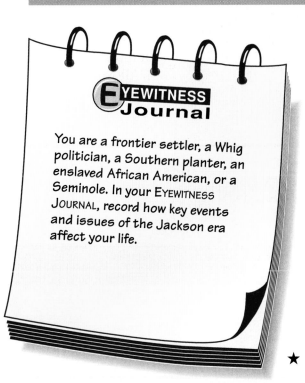

EYEWITNESS Journal

You are a frontier settler, a Whig politician, a Southern planter, an enslaved African American, or a Seminole. In your EYEWITNESS JOURNAL, record how key events and issues of the Jackson era affect your life.

Chapter 13 Westward Expansion

1820–1860

By the mid-1800s, Americans began to dream of extending their territory to the Pacific Ocean. In this chapter, you will see how that dream came true.

First, the United States secured the Pacific Northwest by signing a treaty with Britain. Next, after American settlers declared independence from Mexico, the United States brought Texas into the Union. Americans then won California and the Southwest by fighting a war with Mexico. As settlers poured into the Southwest, a new culture developed that blended American, Mexican, and Indian cultures.

Why Study *History?*

Every year, millions of Americans visit historic memorials, from battlefields to the homes of famous people. To many Texans, for example, the best-loved historic site is a San Antonio mission called the Alamo. Why do so many Americans work to preserve the places where history happened? To explore this question, see this chapter's *Why Study History?* feature, "History Is All Around You."

American Events

●1821
First white American traders arrive in Santa Fe, New Mexico

●1836
Republic of Texas is formed

1820	1825	1830	1835	1840

World Events

1833 World Event
Santa Anna comes to power in Mexico

West Side Main Plaza San Antonio Texas 1849   WGMSamuel

Viewing HISTORY

A Growing Texas City

This painting by William G. Samuel shows a street in San Antonio, Texas, in 1849. Texas had joined the Union a few years before, after winning independence from Mexico. In the mid-1800s, the United States gained vast western territories, including Texas, California, Oregon, and New Mexico. As a result, the nation stretched from the Atlantic Ocean to the Pacific. ★ **How does this painting show the Mexican roots of the Southwest?**

1845 James K. Polk becomes President

1846 Americans in northern California declare independence from Mexico

1859 Oregon is admitted to the Union

| 1840 | 1845 | 1850 | 1855 | 1860 |

 1840 World Event
Britain recognizes Texas as an independent nation

 1854 World Event
Japan and United States sign trade agreement

Oregon Country

As You Read

Explore These Questions
- How did rival claims to Oregon Country develop?
- How did fur trappers and missionaries help open up the Far West?
- What hardships did settlers face?

Define
- mountain man
- rendezvous

Identify
- John Jacob Astor
- James Beckwourth
- Marie Dorion
- Marcus and Narcissa Whitman

 In 1851, Horace Greeley, a New York newspaper editor, published an article titled "To Aspiring Young Men." In it, Greeley offered the following advice:

“ If you have no family or friends to aid you, . . . turn your face to the great West and there build up your home and fortune. ”

The public soon came to know Greeley's message as a simple, four-word phrase: "Go West, young man." His advice exactly suited the spirit of the times. Thousands of young men—and women—rallied to the cry "Westward Ho!"

The Lure of Oregon

By the 1820s, white settlers had occupied much of the land between the Appalachians and the Mississippi River. Families in search of good farmland continued to move west. Few, however, settled on the Great Plains between the Mississippi and the Rockies. Instead, they went onward to lands in the Far West.

Americans first heard about the area known as Oregon Country in the early 1800s. Oregon Country was the huge area beyond the Rocky Mountains. Today, this land includes Oregon, Washington, Idaho, and parts of Wyoming, Montana, and Canada.

The varied geography of Oregon Country attracted both farmers and trappers. Along the Pacific coast, the soil is fertile. Temperatures are mild all year round and rainfall is plentiful. Early white settlers found fine farmland in the Willamette River valley and the lowlands around Puget Sound.

Farther inland, dense forests covered a coastal mountain range. Beaver and other fur-bearing animals roamed these forests, as well as the Rocky Mountains on the eastern boundary. As a result, trappers flocked to Oregon Country.

Between the coastal mountains and the Rockies is a high plateau. This intermountain region is much drier than the coast and has some desert areas. This region of Oregon had little to attract early settlers.

Competing Claims

In the early 1800s, four countries had claims to Oregon. These countries were the United States, Great Britain, Spain, and Russia. Of course, several Native American groups had lived in Oregon for thousands of years. The land rightfully belonged to them. However, the United States and competing European nations gave little thought to Indian rights.

The United States based its claim to Oregon on several expeditions to the area. For example, Lewis and Clark had journeyed through the area in 1805 and 1806.

The British claim to Oregon dated back to a visit by the English explorer Sir Francis Drake in 1579. Also, Fort Vancouver, built by the British, was the only permanent outpost in Oregon Country.

In 1818, the United States and Britain reached an agreement. The two countries would occupy Oregon jointly. Citizens of each nation would have equal rights in Oregon. Spain and Russia had few settlers in the area and agreed to drop their claims.

Fur Trappers in the Far West

At first, the few Europeans or Americans who traveled to Oregon Country were mostly fur traders. Since furs could be sold at tremendous profits in China, merchants from New England stopped along the Oregon coast before crossing the Pacific. In fact, so many Yankee traders came to Oregon that, in some areas, the Indian name for a white man was "Boston."

Only a few hardy trappers actually settled in Oregon. These adventurous men hiked through Oregon's vast forests, trapping animals and living off the land. They were known as **mountain men.**

Mountain men won admiration as rugged individualists, people who follow their own independent course in life. Even their colorful appearance set them apart from ordinary society. They wore shirts and trousers made of animal hides and decorated with porcupine quills. Their hair reached to their shoulders. Pistols and tomahawks hung from their belts.

Lives filled with danger

Mountain men could make a small fortune trapping beaver in Rocky Mountain streams. They led dangerous lives, however. The long, cold mountain winters demanded special survival skills. In the thick forests, trappers had to be on the lookout for attacks by bears, wildcats, or other animals.

During the harsh winters, game was scarce. Facing starvation, trappers would eat almost anything. "I have held my hands in an anthill until they were covered with ants, then greedily licked them off," one mountain man recalled.

Trappers often spent winters in Native American villages. They learned many trapping skills from Indians. Many mountain men married Indian women who taught the newcomers how to find their way and survive in the mountains.

Relations with Native Americans were not always friendly, however. Indians, like the Blackfeet, sometimes attacked mountain men who trapped on Indian hunting grounds without permission.

Trading furs

During the fall and spring, mountain men tended their traps. Then in July, they

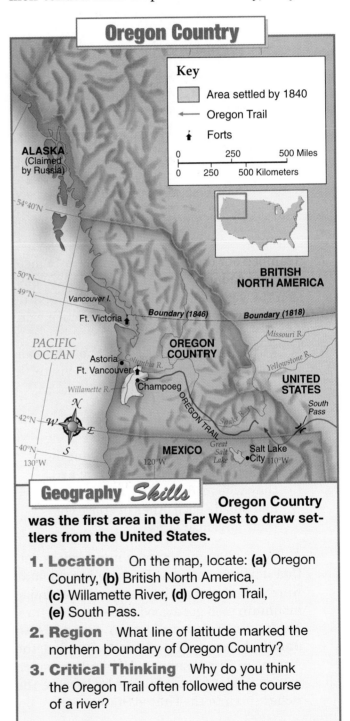

Oregon Country

Key
- ▢ Area settled by 1840
- ← Oregon Trail
- ⚑ Forts

0   250   500 Miles
0   250   500 Kilometers

ALASKA (Claimed by Russia)

54°40'N

50°N
49°N   Vancouver I.
Ft. Victoria

PACIFIC OCEAN
Astoria
Ft. Vancouver
Willamette R.
Champoeg

42°N

40°N
130°W   120°W   MEXICO   Great Salt Lake

Boundary (1846)   Boundary (1818)

BRITISH NORTH AMERICA

Missouri R.

OREGON COUNTRY

Columbia R.

Yellowstone R.

UNITED STATES

South Pass

Snake R.

Salt Lake City   110°W

Geography Skills   **Oregon Country was the first area in the Far West to draw settlers from the United States.**

1. **Location**   On the map, locate: **(a)** Oregon Country, **(b)** British North America, **(c)** Willamette River, **(d)** Oregon Trail, **(e)** South Pass.

2. **Region**   What line of latitude marked the northern boundary of Oregon Country?

3. **Critical Thinking**   Why do you think the Oregon Trail often followed the course of a river?

Viewing HISTORY The Fur Trade

Alfred Miller painted this watercolor, Fort Laramie, *in 1837. Located in present-day Wyoming, Fort Laramie was originally built as a fur-trading post. Once a year, mountain men and Indian trappers gathered at trading posts like this one to sell their furs and have fun.* ★ **How did Native Americans help fur trappers?**

tramped out of the wilderness, ready to meet the fur traders. They headed to a place chosen the year before, called the **rendezvous** (RAHN day voo). Rendezvous is a French word meaning get-together.

For trappers, the first day of the rendezvous was a time to have fun. A visitor to one rendezvous captured the excitement:

66 [They] engaged in contests of skill at running, jumping, wrestling, shooting with the rifle, and running horses.... They sang, they laughed, they whooped; they tried to out-brag and out-lie each other in stories of their adventures. 99

Soon, though, trappers and traders settled down to bargain. Because beaver hats were in demand in the East and in Europe, mountain men got a good price for their furs. Trading companies did even better. **John Jacob Astor,** a New Yorker, founded the American Fur Company. He made so much money in the fur trade that he became the richest man in the United States.

By the late 1830s, the fur trade was dying out. Trappers had killed so many beavers that the animals had grown scarce. Also, beaver hats went out of style. Even so, the mountain men's skills were still in demand. Some began leading settlers across the rugged trails into Oregon.

Exploring New Lands

In their search for furs, mountain men explored much new territory in the West. They followed Indian trails across the Rockies and through mountain passes. Later, they showed these trails to settlers moving west.

Jedediah Smith led white settlers across the Rockies through South Pass, in present-day Wyoming. Manuel Lisa, a Spanish American fur trader, led a trip up the Missouri River in 1807. He founded Fort Manuel, the first outpost on the upper Missouri.

James Beckwourth, an African American, headed west from Virginia to escape slavery. He was accepted as a chief by the Crow Indians. As a guide, Beckwourth discovered a mountain pass through the

Sierra Nevadas that later became a major route to California.

At least one mountain "man" was a woman. **Marie Dorion,** an Iowa Indian, first went to Oregon with fur traders in 1811. She won fame for her survival skills.

Missionaries in Oregon

The first white Americans to build permanent homes in Oregon Country were missionaries. Among them were **Marcus and Narcissa Whitman.** The couple married in 1836 and set out for Oregon, where they planned to convert local Native Americans to Christianity.

The Whitmans built their mission near the Columbia River and began to work with Cayuse (KI oos) Indians. They set up a mission school. Soon, other missionaries and settlers joined the Whitmans. As more settlers arrived and took over Cayuse lands, conflicts arose. Even worse, the newcomers brought diseases that often killed the Indians.

In 1847, tragedy struck. An outbreak of measles among the settlers spread to the Cayuses. Many Cayuse children died. Blaming the settlers, a band of angry Indians attacked the mission, killing the Whitmans and 12 others.

Wagon Trains West

Despite the killing of the Whitmans, other bold pioneers set out on the long trek to Oregon. Missionaries sent back glowing reports about the land. Farmers back East marveled at tales of wheat that grew taller than a man and turnips five feet around. Stories like these touched off an outbreak of "Oregon fever."

Oregon fever spread quickly. Soon, pioneers clogged the trails west. Beginning in 1843, wagon trains left every spring for Oregon. They followed a route called the Oregon Trail. (See the map on page 347.)

Families planning to go west met at Independence, Missouri, in the early spring. When enough families had gathered, they formed a wagon train. Each group elected leaders to make decisions along the way.

The Oregon-bound pioneers hurried to leave Independence in May. Timing was important. Travelers had to reach Oregon by early October, before snow began to fall in the mountains. This meant that pioneers had to cover 2,000 miles (3,200 km) on foot in five months!

Life on the trail

Once on the trail, pioneer families woke to a bugle blast at dawn. Each person had a job to do. Young girls helped their mothers prepare breakfast. Men and boys harnessed the horses and oxen. By 6 A.M., the cry of "Wagons Ho!" rang out across the plains.

*B*iography Narcissa Whitman

Narcissa Prentiss married Marcus Whitman in 1836. They then set out on a seven-month journey to Oregon. When they finally reached the Columbia River valley, she wrote, "The beauty of this extensive valley at the hour of twilight was enchanting and [turned] my mind from the fatigue under which I was laboring."
★ **Why did Narcissa Whitman journey to Oregon?**

China trunk brought to ➤ Oregon by eastern pioneers

Wagon trains stopped for a brief meal at noon. Then it was back on the trail until 6 or 7 P.M. At night, wagons were drawn up in a circle to keep the cattle from wandering.

Most pioneer families set out on the journey west with a lot of heavy gear. When it came time to cross rivers and scale mountains, however, many possessions were left behind to lighten the load. One traveler found the Oregon Trail littered with objects such as "blacksmiths' anvils, ploughs, large grindstones, baking ovens, kegs, barrels, harness [and] clothing."

The long trek west held many dangers. During spring rains, travelers risked their lives floating wagons across swollen rivers. In summer, they faced blistering heat on the treeless plains. Early snowstorms often blocked passes through the mountains.

The biggest threat was sickness. Cholera and other diseases could wipe out whole wagon trains. Because the travelers lived so close together, germs spread quickly.

Trading with Native Americans

As they moved west toward the Rockies, pioneers often saw Indians. The Indians seldom attacked the whites trespassing on their land. A guidebook published in 1845 warned that pioneers had more to fear from their own guns than from Indians: "We very frequently hear of emigrants being killed from the accidental discharge of firearms; but we very seldom hear of their being killed by Indians."

Many Native Americans traded with the wagon trains. Hungry pioneers were grateful for food the Indians sold. A traveler noted:

66 Whenever we camp near any Indian village, we are no sooner stopped than a whole crowd may be seen coming galloping into our camp. The [women] do all the swapping. 99

Oregon at last!

Despite the many hardships, more than 50,000 people reached Oregon between 1840 and 1860. Their wagon wheels cut so deeply into the plains that the ruts can still be seen today.

By the 1840s, Americans greatly outnumbered the British in parts of Oregon. As you have read, the two nations agreed to occupy Oregon jointly in 1818. Now, many Americans began to feel that Oregon should belong to the United States alone.

★ Section 1 Review ★

Recall

1. **Locate** (a) Oregon Country, (b) Willamette River, (c) South Pass, (d) Oregon Trail.
2. **Identify** (a) John Jacob Astor, (b) James Beckwourth, (c) Marie Dorion, (d) Marcus and Narcissa Whitman.
3. **Define** (a) mountain man, (b) rendezvous.

Comprehension

4. How did the United States and Britain settle their claims to Oregon Country?
5. (a) Why did mountain men first go to Oregon? (b) How did they contribute to later settlement?

6. (a) Why did settlers flock to Oregon after the 1840s? (b) Describe two difficulties along the way.

Critical Thinking and Writing

7. **Linking Past and Present** (a) What qualities helped the mountain men survive in the wilderness? (b) Do you think such qualities are still important today? Explain.
8. **Analyzing Ideas** Economists talk about the "law of supply and demand." It states that when people want a product that is hard to get, the price goes up. How does the Oregon fur trade illustrate the idea of supply and demand?

Activity **Writing a Letter to the Editor** You are one of the young people Horace Greeley told to "go West." You took his advice. Now, write him a letter and tell him what it was like traveling to the West!

Texas Wins Independence

Explore
These Questions
- Why did many Americans settle in Texas?
- How did Texas become an independent nation?
- What challenges did the new Republic of Texas face?

Define
- siege
- annex

Identify
- Stephen Austin
- Antonio López de Santa Anna
- Tejanos
- Sam Houston
- Alamo
- William Travis
- Battle of San Jacinto
- Lone Star Republic

SETTING the Scene In late 1835, the word spread: Americans in Texas had rebelled against Mexico! Joseph Barnard, a young doctor, recalled:

66 I was at Chicago, Illinois, practicing medicine, when the news of the Texan revolt from Mexico reached our ears.... They were in arms for a cause that I had always been taught to consider sacred,... Republican principles and popular institutions. 99

Along with hundreds of other Americans, Dr. Barnard made his way to Texas. Their fight led to the creation of a new nation.

Americans in Mexican Texas

Since the early 1800s, American farmers, especially from the South, had looked eagerly at the vast region called Texas. At the time, Texas was part of the Spanish colony of Mexico.

At first, Spain refused to let Americans move into the region. Then in 1821, Spain gave Moses Austin a land grant in Texas. Austin died before he could set up a colony. His son Stephen took over the project.

This seal from Mexican Texas shows an eagle, serpent, and cactus—symbols of Mexico.

Meanwhile, Mexico won its independence from Spain. The new nation let **Stephen Austin** lead settlers into Texas. Only about 4,000 Mexicans lived there. Mexico hoped that the Americans would help develop the area and control Indian attacks.

Mexico gave each settler a large grant of land. In 1821, Austin and 300 families moved to Texas. Many of these newcomers were slaveowners who brought their slaves with them. Under Austin's leadership, the colony grew rapidly. By 1830, about 20,000 Americans had resettled in Texas.

Conflict With Mexico

In return for land, Austin and the original settlers agreed to become citizens of Mexico and worship in the Roman Catholic Church. However, later American settlers felt no loyalty to Mexico. They spoke only a few words of Spanish. Also, most of the Americans were Protestants. Conflict soon erupted with the Mexican government.

Mexico enforces its laws

In 1830, Mexico forbade any more Americans to move to Texas. Mexico feared that the Americans wanted to make Texas part of

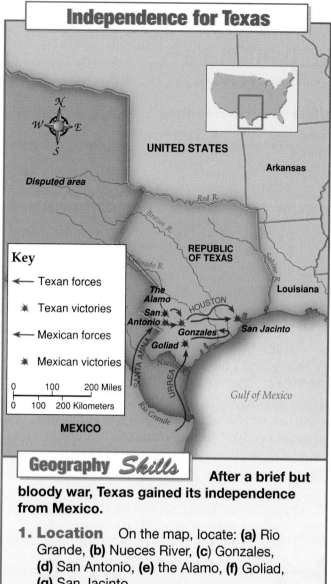

Independence for Texas

Key

← Texan forces

✳ Texan victories

← Mexican forces

✳ Mexican victories

0   100   200 Miles

0   100   200 Kilometers

Geography *Skills*

After a brief but bloody war, Texas gained its independence from Mexico.

1. **Location** On the map, locate: **(a)** Rio Grande, **(b)** Nueces River, **(c)** Gonzales, **(d)** San Antonio, **(e)** the Alamo, **(f)** Goliad, **(g)** San Jacinto.

2. **Movement** **(a)** Where did Santa Anna's army first fight the Texans? **(b)** Describe the movement of Mexican and Texan forces after the Alamo.

3. **Critical Thinking** Refer to the map of the United States in the Reference Section. How do the boundaries of the Republic of Texas compare with the boundaries of Texas?

laws and the Mexican troops who came north to enforce them.

In 1833, General **Antonio López de Santa Anna** came to power in Mexico. Two years later, he threw out the Mexican constitution. Rumors spread that Santa Anna intended to drive all Americans out of Texas.

Texans take action

Texans felt that the time had come for action. In this, they had the support of many **Tejanos** (teh HAH nohs), Mexicans who lived in Texas. Tejanos did not necessarily want independence from Mexico. However, they did want to be rid of Santa Anna, who ruled as a military dictator.

In October 1835, Texans in the town of Gonzales (gahn ZAH lehs) clashed with Mexican troops. The Texans forced the Mexicans to withdraw. Inspired by the victory, Stephen Austin vowed to "see Texas forever free from Mexican domination." Two months later, Texans stormed and took San Antonio. Determined to stamp out the rebellion, Santa Anna marched north with a large army.

While Santa Anna assembled his troops, Texans declared independence on March 2, 1836. They set up a new nation called the Republic of Texas and appointed **Sam Houston** commander of the army. Volunteers of many nationalities, as well as African Americans and Tejanos, joined the fight for Texan independence from Mexico.

Siege at the Alamo

By the time Santa Anna arrived in San Antonio, many of the Texans who had taken the city had drifted away. Fewer than 200 Texans remained as defenders.

In spite of the tremendous odds against them, the Texans refused to give up. Instead, they retired to an old Spanish mission called the **Alamo.**

Against tremendous odds

Texans who gathered in the Alamo in the winter of 1835–1836 were poorly equipped for a battle. Supplies of ammunition and medicine were low. Food consisted of some beef and corn, and access to water was limited. Worst of all, there were only about 150

the United States. Mexico had some reason for this fear. The United States had already tried twice to buy Texas.

Mexico also decided to make Texans obey Mexican laws that they had ignored for years. One was the law requiring Texans to worship in the Catholic Church. Another law banned slavery in Texas. Texans resented the

Why Study History?

Because History Is All Around You

★ ★

Historical Background

Did you know that we almost lost the Alamo? After 1836, it was used as an army supply depot, a warehouse, and a general store. For a time, its neighbors included a beer garden and a meat market. In 1903, there was even talk that it might be turned into a hotel.

Then, the Daughters of the Republic of Texas stepped in. They urged the state government to save the Alamo from destruction. Adina De Zavala gained public attention by barricading herself inside the old mission. In 1905, the state of Texas entrusted the Alamo to the Daughters of the Republic.

The Alamo

Connections to Today

Each year, thousands of tourists visit the Alamo. They walk the same ground where Texans fought for independence.

Throughout the nation, government and citizens work to save and restore important historic sites. Federal laws protect a variety of places, including ruins of Native American towns, homes of famous Americans, and even old factories. The National Trust for Historic Preservation, a nonprofit educational group, helps people to acquire and preserve historic properties.

Today, ordinary people are restoring and living in historic buildings. Some have transformed old train stations, schools, or factories into restaurants, shops, or apartment buildings. Several cities have revitalized old run-down neighborhoods and warehouse districts. These historic areas attract new businesses and residents.

Connections to You

History is all around you. It is there for you to visit and explore. Check out the *National Register of Historic Places* in your local library. It lists thousands of places and structures that have played a role in your nation's history. To find out how you can help preserve American history, contact your local historical society or the National Trust for Historic Preservation.

1. **Comprehension**   What have ordinary citizens and local government done to save important historic sites?
2. **Critical Thinking**   How can visiting an historic site be more interesting and informative than reading about it?

 Visiting an Historic Site Visit a nearby historic site. In a brief presentation, explain the site's importance and describe how it has been preserved and restored.

▲ Republic of Texas flag

Viewing HISTORY Winning Texas Independence

Sam Houston was wounded in the leg during the Battle of San Jacinto. Despite tremendous pain and a boot full of blood, Houston fought on to victory. This painting shows Houston accepting the surrender of Mexican commander Santa Anna.
★ **Why was San Jacinto a turning point in Texas history?**

Texans to defend the Alamo against 6,000 Mexican troops!

Young **William Travis** commanded the Texans inside the mission. Among the volunteers were the famous frontiersmen Jim Bowie and Davy Crockett. Several Tejano families, two Texan women, and two young male slaves were also present.

"Victory or Death!"

On February 23, 1836, Mexican troops began a siege of the Alamo. In a siege, enemy forces try to capture a city or fort, usually by surrounding and bombarding it. The Texan defenders fought bravely. Still, Travis knew that unless he received help, he and his troops were doomed. He sent a messenger through the Mexican lines with a letter addressed "to the People of Texas and all the Americans in the World":

> 66 The enemy have demanded a surrender. . . . I have answered the demand with a cannon shot and our flag still waves proudly from the walls.
> *I shall never surrender or retreat.*
> I call on you in the name of Liberty, of patriotism, and of everything dear to the American character to come to our aid with all dispatch. . . . *Victory or Death!* 99

Travis also sent scouts to seek additional soldiers and provisions. About 40 men were able to sneak through enemy lines and join the fighters in the Alamo. However, no large force ever arrived.

For 12 days, the defenders held off Mexican bombardment. Then, at dawn on March 6, Mexican cannon fire broke through the Alamo walls. Thousands of Mexican soldiers poured into the mission. When the bodies were counted, 183 Texans and almost 1,500 Mexicans lay dead. The Texan survivors, including Davy Crockett, were executed.

Connections With Geography

Santa Anna crossed the Rio Grande on February 16, 1836, in the middle of a harsh Texas winter. Many of the army's cattle died from the brutal cold and inadequate grazing land. For the final thirty days before reaching the Alamo, soldiers ate only eight ounces of corn cake per day.

Texan Independence

The fall of the Alamo set off cries for revenge. The fury of the Texans grew even stronger three weeks later, when Mexican forces killed several hundred Texan soldiers at Goliad after they had surrendered. Volunteers flooded into Sam Houston's army. Men from the United States also raced south to help the Texan cause.

On April 21, 1836, Houston decided that the moment had come to attack. Santa Anna was camped with his army near the San Jacinto (jah SEEN toh) River. With cries of "Remember the Alamo!" the Texans charged the surprised Mexicans.

The **Battle of San Jacinto** lasted only 18 minutes. Although they were outnumbered, Texans killed 630 Mexicans and captured 700 more. The following day, Texans captured Santa Anna himself. They forced the general to sign a treaty granting Texas its independence.

The Lone Star Republic

In battle, Texans had carried a flag with a single white star. After winning independence, they nicknamed their nation the **Lone Star Republic.** They drew up a constitution based on the Constitution of the United States and elected Sam Houston as their president.

The new country faced several problems. First, Mexico refused to accept the treaty signed by Santa Anna. Mexicans still claimed Texas as part of their country. Second, Texas was nearly bankrupt. Most Texans thought that the best way to solve both problems was for Texas to become part of the United States.

In the United States, Americans were divided about whether to **annex**, or add on, Texas. Most white southerners were in favor of the idea. Many northerners, however, were against it. At issue was slavery.

In the 1830s, antislavery feelings were growing in the North. Because many Texans owned slaves, northerners did not want to allow Texas to join the Union. President Andrew Jackson also worried that annexing Texas would lead to war with Mexico. As a result, Congress refused to annex Texas.

Over the next 10 years, the Lone Star Republic prospered under Houston's leadership. During the Panic of 1837, thousands of Americans moved to Texas to find land and start businesses. Settlers from Germany and Switzerland also swelled the population. By the 1840s, there were about 140,000 people in Texas, including many Mexicans and African Americans.

★ Section 2 Review ★

Recall
1. **Locate** (a) Mexico, (b) Gonzales, (c) Goliad, (d) Republic of Texas.
2. **Identify** (a) Stephen Austin, (b) Antonio López de Santa Anna, (c) Tejanos, (d) Sam Houston, (e) Alamo, (f) William Travis, (g) Battle of San Jacinto, (h) Lone Star Republic.
3. **Define** (a) siege, (b) annex.

Comprehension
4. Why did Mexico encourage Americans to move to Texas?

5. **(a)** Why did Texans seek independence from Mexico? **(b)** How did they finally achieve their goal?
6. Why did northerners and southerners disagree about annexing Texas?

Critical Thinking and Writing
7. **Drawing Conclusions** Why was the fall of the Alamo both a defeat and a victory for Texans?
8. **Solving Problems** Why do you think many Texans believed that annexation by the United States would help them solve their problems?

Activity **Writing an Appeal** You are trapped in the Alamo with the rebel Texans and Tejanos. Write an appeal to people in the United States to come help you—make it quick!

3 California and the Southwest

Explore These Questions

- What brought the first white settlers to New Mexico?
- What was life like for Native Americans in California?
- Why did Americans want to expand to the Pacific Ocean?

Identify

- New Mexico Territory
- William Becknell
- Santa Fe Trail
- Junípero Serra
- Manifest Destiny
- James K. Polk

As You Read

In 1819, John Quincy Adams made a bold claim. The world, he said, would have to accept the fact that the United States would one day possess all of North America:

66 From the time we became an independent nation, it was as much a law of nature that this would become our claim as that the Mississippi should flow to the sea. 99

By the 1840s, many Americans agreed. They, too, believed that it was the mission of the United States to expand all the way to the Pacific Ocean. Americans began to look with interest to the vast, rich lands of California and the Southwest.

New Mexico Territory

The entire Southwest belonged to Mexico in the 1840s. This huge region was called **New Mexico Territory.** It included most of the present-day states of Arizona and New Mexico, all of Nevada and Utah, and parts of Colorado.

Much of the Southwest is hot and dry. In some areas, thick grasses grow. There are also desert and mountain areas. Before the Spanish arrived, Zuñi Indians irrigated and farmed the land. Other Native Americans, such as the Apaches, lived by hunting.

A Spanish explorer, Juan de Oñate, had claimed the territory of New Mexico for Spain in 1598. In the early 1600s, the Spanish built Santa Fe as the capital of the territory. Under the Spanish, Santa Fe grew into a busy trading town. However, Spain refused to let Americans settle in New Mexico. Only after Mexico won its independence in 1821 were Americans welcome in Santa Fe.

William Becknell, a merchant and adventurer, was the first American to head for Santa Fe. In 1821, Becknell led a group of traders from Franklin, Missouri, across the plains. When they reached Santa Fe, they found Mexicans eager to buy their cloth and other goods. Other Americans soon followed Becknell's route. It became known as the **Santa Fe Trail.** (See the map on page 366.)

Early Years in California

California, too, belonged to Mexico in the early 1840s. Spain had claimed the region 65 years before English colonists settled in Jamestown. In the years that followed, Spanish and Native American cultures shaped life in California.

Land and climate

California is a land of dramatic contrasts. Two tall mountain ranges slice through the region. One range hugs the coast. The other sits inland on the border of Nevada and Arizona. Between these two ranges is California's fertile Central Valley.

Northern California receives plenty of rain. In the south, though, water is scarce and much of the land is desert. California enjoys mild temperatures all year, except for areas high in the mountains.

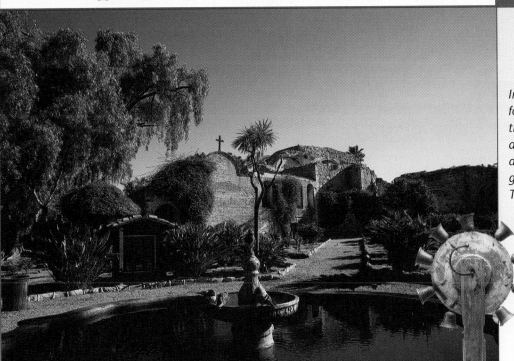

Mission San Juan Capistrano

In 1776, Father Junípero Serra founded Mission San Juan Capistrano in southern California. Today, you can still walk among its adobe walls, enjoy its peaceful gardens, and listen to its old bells. These mission bells told the priests and Native Americans who lived there when to wake up, when to eat, when to pray, when to work, and when to go to bed.

★ **To learn more about this historic site, write:** *Mission San Juan Capistrano, P.O. Box 697, San Juan Capistrano, CA 92693.*

◀ *Mission bells*

A string of missions

As you have read, Spanish soldiers and priests built the first European settlements in California. In 1769, Captain Gaspar de Portolá led a group of soldiers and missionaries up the Pacific coast. The chief missionary was Father **Junípero Serra** (hoo NEE peh roh SEHR rah). Father Serra built his first mission at San Diego. He went on to build eight others.

Eventually, there were 21 Spanish missions along the California coast. Each mission claimed the surrounding land and soon was able to take care of all its own needs. Spanish soldiers built forts near the missions. The missions supplied meat, grain, and other foods to the forts.

Mission life for Native Americans

California Indians lived in small, scattered groups rather than large, organized nations. As a result, they were not able to offer much organized resistance to soldiers who forced them to work for the missions.

Native Americans herded sheep and cattle and raised crops for the missions. In return, they lived at the missions and learned about the Roman Catholic religion. Many Spanish missionaries were truly concerned with converting the Indians to Christianity. However, mission life was hard. Thousands of Native Americans died from overwork and diseases.

Sometimes, Indians did resist mission life. Many were baptized as Christians but continued to follow their traditional beliefs. Others simply ran away. Still, most continued to live and labor at the missions.

After Mexico won its independence, conditions for Native Americans in California grew even worse. The new Mexican government offered mission land to ranchers. On some ranches, Indians faced cruel mistreatment. If they tried to run away, the ranchers hunted them down. An American observer reported that California Indians lived in a state "even more degrading, and more oppressive than that of our slaves in the South."

Skills
FOR LIFE

| Critical Thinking | Managing Information | Communication | Maps, Charts, and Graphs |

Distinguishing Fact From Opinion

How Will I Use This Skill?

A fact is a statement that can be observed or proven. An opinion is a judgment that reflects a person's beliefs or feelings. To get a true picture of events, even in everyday conversation, you must be able to distinguish between facts and personal opinions.

LEARN the Skill

To tell fact from opinion, follow these steps:

❶ Identify facts. Look at each phrase or sentence and ask, "Can this be observed or proven?"

❷ Identify words that express the writer's opinion. Some opinions are clearly indicated with phrases like "I think," or "In my opinion." Others are not so easy to identify. Watch for words that express or inspire emotion.

❸ Decide whether the facts can support the writer's opinions. (Remember, this does not mean that you must *agree* with the opinion.)

PRACTICE the Skill

The excerpt to the right is from an 1846 newspaper article urging the United States to gain possession of California.

❶ List three facts that are included in this article. What makes them facts?

❷ (a) What words show that the first sentence is an opinion? (b) Identify two other opinions expressed in this excerpt.

❸ How do the facts presented by the writer support his opinion about gaining California? Give two examples.

We do regard it as extremely desirable that California—a part, at least, of the province known by that name—should become the property of the United States. Lower California, embracing the long, narrow peninsula between the Gulf and the Pacific, stretching from the 21° to 33° latitude, a distance of about 800 miles, is universally represented by travelers as sterile and hopelessly desolate. It consists, indeed, of a chain of volcanic, treeless, barren mountains of rock, broken only by still more dreary plains of sand. It may well, therefore, be left to Mexico.

The remaining part of Upper California—that which lies nearest the Pacific coast—is not only by far the best portion of the province but one of the most beautiful regions on the face of the earth. Among the highlands which enclose this valley are vast forests filled with the loftiest and finest cedars and pines in the world, with every variety of soil, freshwater lakes, and every element of unbounded agricultural wealth, except a good climate.

Source:
Adapted from the *American Review*,
January 1846.

APPLY the Skill

Choose an article in your local newspaper that includes opinions. Circle facts and underline opinions. Write a paragraph stating whether you think the facts in the article support the opinion.

These harsh conditions had a deadly effect. From 1770 to 1850, the Native American population of California declined from about 310,000 to 100,000.

Expansion: A Right and a Duty

As late as the mid-1840s, only about 700 people from the United States lived in California. Every year, however, more and more Americans began to look toward the West. The United States government even tried to buy California from Mexico several times. Officials were especially interested in gaining the fine ports at San Francisco and San Diego.

The nation's destiny

Many Americans saw the culture and the democratic government of the United States as the best in the world. They believed that the United States had the right and the duty to spread its rule all the way to the Pacific Ocean.

In the 1840s, a newspaper in New York coined a phrase for this belief. The phrase was **Manifest Destiny.** Manifest means clear or obvious. Destiny means something that is sure to happen. Americans who believed in Manifest Destiny thought that the United States was clearly meant to expand to the Pacific.

Manifest Destiny had another side, too. Many Americans believed that they were superior to Native Americans and Mexicans. For these Americans, racism justified taking over lands belonging to Indians and Mexicans.

Election of 1844

Manifest Destiny played an important part in the election of 1844. The Whigs nominated Henry Clay for President. Clay was a famous and respected national leader. The Democrats chose a little-known candidate, **James K. Polk**.

Voters soon came to know Polk as the candidate who favored expansion. Polk demanded that Texas and Oregon be added to the United States. Clay, on the other hand, opposed the annexation of Texas.

The Democrats made Oregon a special campaign issue. As you read, Britain and the United States held Oregon jointly. Polk demanded the whole region all the way to its northern border at latitude 54°40′N. "Fifty-four forty or fight!" became the Democrats' campaign cry. On election day, Americans showed their support for expansion by choosing Polk as President.

★ Section 3 Review ★

Recall

1. **Locate** (a) Sante Fe, (b) Santa Fe Trail, (c) California, (d) San Diego, (e) San Francisco.
2. **Identify** (a) New Mexico Territory, (b) William Becknell, (c) Santa Fe Trail, (d) Junípero Serra, (e) Manifest Destiny, (f) James K. Polk.

Comprehension

3. Describe how American settlers first went to New Mexico.
4. How did mission life affect Native Americans?
5. How did belief in Manifest Destiny affect the election of 1844?

Critical Thinking and Writing

6. **Making Inferences** How do you think missionaries justified forcing Indians to live and work on missions?
7. **Analyzing Ideas** "The irresistible army of [American settlers] has begun to pour down upon [California], armed with the plough and the rifle, and marking its trail with schools and colleges, courts and representative halls, mills and meetinghouses." What does this quotation show you about people's belief in the idea of Manifest Destiny?

Activity **Drawing a Political Cartoon** Draw a political cartoon from the point of view of Native Americans about conditions on California missions or ranches before 1845.

4

War With Mexico

As You Read

Explore These Questions
- How did the United States gain Oregon?
- What were the causes and results of the Mexican War?
- How did cultures blend in the new American territories?

Define
- cede

Identify
- Zachary Taylor
- Mexican War
- Winfield Scott
- Stephen Kearny
- Bear Flag Republic
- John C. Frémont
- Chapultepec
- Mexican Cession
- Gadsden Purchase

 SETTING the Scene American troops marched off to war with Mexico in 1846. Many Americans were eager to fight. Soldiers proudly sang new words to the popular tune "Yankee Doodle":

> 66 They attacked our men upon our land,
> And crossed our river too, sir.
> Now show them all with sword in hand
> What yankee boys can do, sir. 99

Not all Americans supported the war against Mexico. Some even accused President Polk of provoking the war himself in order to win Texas.

The bloody Mexican War lasted 20 months. In the end, it helped the United States achieve its dream of Manifest Destiny.

Dividing Oregon

James K. Polk took office in March 1845. Acting on his campaign promise, he moved to gain control of Oregon. War with Britain threatened.

Polk did not really want a war with Britain. In 1846, he agreed to a compromise. Oregon was divided at latitude 49°N. Britain got the lands north of the line, and the United States got the lands south of the line. The United States named its portion the Oregon Territory. Later, the states of Oregon

(1859), Washington (1889), and Idaho (1890) were carved out of the Oregon Territory.

Annexing Texas

Texas proved a more dangerous problem. As you read, the United States at first refused to annex Texas. In 1844, Sam Houston, president of Texas, signed a treaty of annexation with the United States. The Senate again refused to ratify the treaty. Senators feared that annexing Texas would cause a war with Mexico.

Sam Houston would not give up. To persuade the Americans to annex Texas, he pretended that Texas might become an ally of Britain. Houston's trick worked. Americans did not want Europe's greatest power to gain a foothold on their western border. In 1845, Congress passed a joint resolution admitting Texas to the Union.

Sam Houston

Conflict With Mexico

The annexation of Texas made Mexicans furious. They had never accepted the independence of Texas. They also were concerned that the example set by Texas would encourage Americans in California and New Mexico to rebel.

At the same time, Americans resented Mexico. President Polk offered to pay Mexico $30 million for California and New Mexico. However, Mexico strongly opposed any further loss of territory and refused the offer. Many Americans felt that Mexico stood in the way of Manifest Destiny.

The war begins

A border dispute finally sparked war. The United States claimed that the southern border of Texas was the Rio Grande. Mexico argued that it was the Nueces (noo AY says) River, some 200 miles (320 km) to the north. Both nations claimed the land between the two rivers.

In January 1846, Polk ordered General **Zachary Taylor** to cross the Nueces River and set up posts in the disputed area along the Rio Grande. (See the map below.) Polk knew that the move might lead to war. In April 1846, Mexican troops crossed the Rio

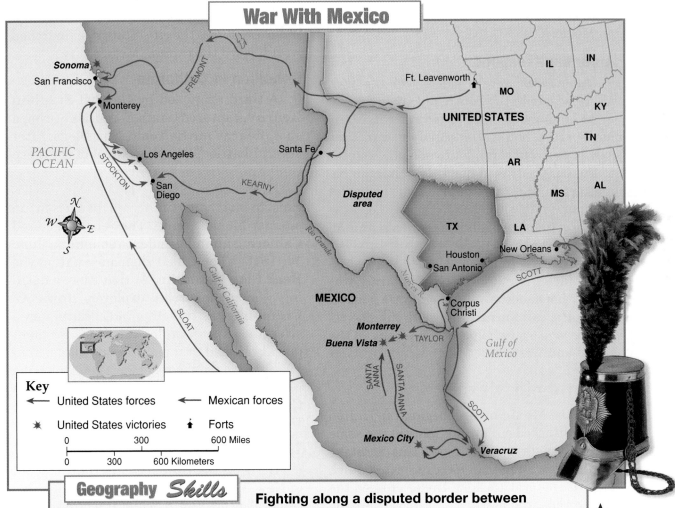

War With Mexico

Key
← United States forces ← Mexican forces
✳ United States victories ♦ Forts

0   300   600 Miles
0   300   600 Kilometers

Cap of a United States soldier in the Mexican War

Geography Skills Fighting along a disputed border between Texas and Mexico triggered the Mexican War.

1. Location On the map, locate: **(a)** Rio Grande, **(b)** Nueces River, **(c)** Buena Vista, **(d)** Veracruz, **(e)** Mexico City.

2. Movement Describe the movements of each of the following American commanders: **(a)** Winfield Scott, **(b)** Stephen Kearny, **(c)** John Frémont.

3. Critical Thinking Based on the map, was sea power important to the United States in the Mexican War? Explain.

Grande and fought briefly with the Americans. Soldiers on both sides were killed.

President Polk was already considering going to war with Mexico. When he heard about the fighting at the Rio Grande, he asked Congress to issue a declaration of war. Polk told Congress:

> 66 Mexico has passed the boundary of the United States, has invaded our territory, and shed American blood upon American soil. 99

Not everyone supported Polk's request. Abraham Lincoln, a young Whig Congressman, disputed Polk's claim that the fighting actually took place "upon American soil." Still, at Polk's urging, Congress declared war on Mexico.

Americans respond

Americans were divided over the war. Many people in the South and West wanted more land and so were eager to fight. Many northerners, however, opposed the war. They saw it as a southern plot to add slave states to the Union. "Fresh markets of human beings are to be established," claimed Charles Sumner, a Massachusetts opponent of slavery. "Further opportunities for this hateful traffic are to be opened."

Still, many Americans joined the war effort. Since the nation's standing army was small, thousands of volunteers were needed. When the call for recruits went out, the response was overwhelming, especially in the South and West.

Fighting in Mexico

As the **Mexican War** began, the United States attacked on several fronts at the same time. President Polk hoped this strategy would allow American forces to win a quick victory. General Zachary Taylor crossed the Rio Grande into northern Mexico. There, he won several battles against the Mexican army. In February 1847, Taylor met Santa Anna at the Battle of Buena Vista. The Mexican troops greatly outnumbered the American forces, but the Americans were better armed and led. After fierce fighting, Santa Anna retreated. A major in Taylor's army later recalled feeding wounded Mexican soldiers after the battle:

> 66 We collected the wounded, who were suffering awfully from hunger and thirst as well as their wounds, and sent them to hospitals in town.... When coffee and biscuit were placed before them, they showed even in their famished state some signs of surprise and gratitude. This was the greatest victory of all, a victory unstained by blood.... 99

Meanwhile, General **Winfield Scott** had landed another American army at the Mexican port of Veracruz. After a long battle, the Americans took the city. Scott then marched west toward the capital, Mexico City.

Rebellion in California

A third army, led by General **Stephen Kearny**, captured Santa Fe without firing a shot. Kearny hurried on to San Diego. After several battles, he took control of southern California early in 1847.

Even before hearing of the war, Americans in northern California had risen up against Mexican rule. The rebels declared California an independent republic on June 14, 1846. They called their new nation the **Bear Flag Republic.** At that time, a dashing young American explorer, **John C. Frémont,** was traveling in California on a scientific expedition for the army. Frémont quickly rushed to support the rebellion. Taking command of the rebel forces, he drove the Mexican governor's troops out of northern California. Frémont later joined forces with United States troops.

The final battle

By 1847, the United States controlled all of New Mexico and California. Meanwhile, General Scott had reached the outskirts of Mexico City.

Before they could take the Mexican capital, Scott's troops faced a fierce battle. Mexican soldiers made a heroic last stand at **Chapultepec** (chah POOL tuh pehk), a fort just outside Mexico City. Like the Texans who died at the Alamo, the Mexicans at Cha-

Growth of the United States to 1853

(Ceded by Britain, 1818)

CANADA

OREGON COUNTRY
(Agreement with Britain, 1846)

LOUISIANA PURCHASE
(Purchased from France, 1803)

THE UNITED STATES, 1783

ORIGINAL 13 STATES

MEXICAN CESSION
(Treaty of Guadalupe-Hidalgo, 1848)

PACIFIC OCEAN

ATLANTIC OCEAN

TEXAS ANNEXATION
(Annexed by Congress, 1845)

GADSDEN PURCHASE
(Purchased from Mexico, 1853)

FLORIDA
(Ceded by Spain, 1819)

MEXICO

Gulf of Mexico

Key

Present-day state boundaries

0   400   800 Miles

0   400   800 Kilometers

N W E S

Geography Skills

By 1848, the United States stretched all the way from the Atlantic Ocean to the Pacific Ocean.

1. **Location** On the map, locate: **(a)** Mexican Cession, **(b)** Gadsden Purchase, **(c)** Oregon Country.

2. **Region** Which of the territories shown on this map did the United States purchase from other nations?

3. **Critical Thinking** Refer to the map of the United States in the Reference Section. **(a)** Is your home state included on the map above? **(b)** If so, when and how did it become part of the United States?

---

pultepec fought to the last man. Today, Mexicans honor these young soldiers as heroes.

Achieving Manifest Destiny

With their capital in American hands, the Mexican government had no choice but to make peace. In 1848, Mexico signed the Treaty of Guadalupe-Hidalgo (gwah duh LOOP ay-ih DAHL goh). The treaty forced Mexico to **cede,** or give, all of California and New Mexico to the United States. These lands were called the **Mexican Cession.** (See the map above.)

In return, the United States paid Mexico $15 million. Americans also agreed to respect the rights of Spanish-speaking people in the Mexican Cession.

A few years after the end of the Mexican War, the United States completed its expansion across the continent. In 1853, it agreed to pay Mexico $10 million for a strip of land in present-day Arizona and New Mexico. The Americans needed this land to complete the building of a railroad. The land was called the **Gadsden Purchase.** The dream of Manifest Destiny was now complete.

A Mix of Cultures in the Southwest

English-speaking settlers poured into the Southwest. They brought their own culture with them, including their ideas about democratic government. The newcomers also learned a great deal from the older residents of the region. Mexican Americans taught the newcomers how to mine silver and irrigate the soil for growing crops. Many Spanish and Native American words—such as stampede, buffalo, tortilla, soda, and tornado—became part of the English language.

The new settlers often treated Mexican Americans and Native Americans poorly. The earlier residents struggled to protect their traditions and rights. However, when Mexican Americans went to court to de-fend their property, judges rarely upheld their claims. The family of Mariano Guadalupe Vallejo (vah YAY hoh) had lived in California for decades before the English-speaking settlers arrived. Vallejo, a wealthy landowner, noted how some new settlers were able to gain control of much of the land:

Many Mexican homes in the Southwest contained religious statuettes like this one.

66 In their dealings with the rancheros, [Americans] took advantage of laws which they understood, but which were new to the Spaniards. 99

At the same time, Americans in the Southwest kept some Mexican laws. One of these laws said that a husband and wife owned property together. In the rest of the United States, married women could not own any property. Another Mexican law said that landowners could not cut off water to their neighbors. This law was important in the Southwest, where water was scarce.

★ Section 4 Review ★

Recall

1. **Locate** (a) Rio Grande, (b) Nueces River, (c) Buena Vista, (d) Veracruz, (e) Mexico City.
2. **Identify** (a) Zachary Taylor, (b) Mexican War, (c) Winfield Scott, (d) Stephen Kearny, (e) Bear Flag Republic, (f) John C. Frémont, (g) Chapultepec, (h) Mexican Cession, (i) Gadsden Purchase.
3. **Define** cede.

Comprehension

4. How did President Polk avoid war with Britain over Oregon?
5. (a) What event sparked the beginning of the Mexican War? (b) What were the final results of the war?
6. (a) Name two things that English-speaking settlers learned from Mexican Americans in the Southwest. (b) Name one tradition that settlers brought with them.

Critical Thinking and Writing

7. **Identifying Alternatives** Do you think the United States could have avoided going to war with Mexico in 1846? Explain.
8. **Recognizing Points of View** Frederick Douglass, an African American who fought to end slavery, wrote of the Mexican War that Americans "ought [to] blush and hang our heads for shame." (a) Why do you think Douglass opposed the war? (b) Who might have agreed with his statement? Who might have disagreed?

★ ★

Activity **Roleplaying** With your classmates, choose among the following roles: a citizen of Mexico; a white American living in Texas; a Mexican living in Texas; an American Californian; a northerner; a southerner; President Polk. Hold a debate about whether the United States should go to war with Mexico.

5 ★ A Rush to the West

As You Read

Explore These Questions
- How did the Mormons settle Utah?
- How did the discovery of gold affect life in California?
- Why did California have a diverse population?

Define
- forty-niner
- vigilante

Identify
- Mormons
- Joseph Smith
- Brigham Young
- Sutter's Mill

SETTING the Scene In 1848, exciting news reached Toishan, a district in southern China. Mountains of gold had been discovered across the Pacific Ocean, in a place called California. It was there just for the digging!

The penalty for trying to leave China was harsh and sure—a swift beheading. Still, tens of thousands of Chinese risked the executioner's axe to cross the Pacific. Like other prospectors from Europe to Boston to South America, they were eager to join the California Gold Rush.

Gold was not the only thing that attracted settlers to the West in the mid-1800s. California, New Mexico, Oregon, and Texas were all now part of the United States. Restless pioneers, always eager to try something new, headed into these lands to build homes and a new way of life.

A Refuge for the Mormons

The largest group of settlers to move into the Mexican Cession were the **Mormons.** Mormons belonged to the Church of Jesus Christ of Latter-day Saints. The church was founded by **Joseph Smith** in 1830. Smith, a farmer who lived in upstate New York, attracted many followers.

Troubles with neighbors

Smith was an energetic and popular man. His teachings, however, angered many non-Mormons. For example, Mormons at first be-lieved that property should be owned in common. Smith also said that a man could have more than one wife. Angry neighbors forced the Mormons to leave New York for Ohio. From Ohio, they were forced to move to Missouri, and from there to Illinois. In the 1840s, the Mormons built a community called Nauvoo on the banks of the Mississippi River in Illinois.

Before long, the Mormons again clashed with their neighbors. In 1844, an angry mob killed Joseph Smith. The Mormons chose **Brigham Young** as their new leader.

Brigham Young realized that the Mormons needed to find a home where they would be safe. He had read about a valley between the Rocky Mountains and the Great Salt Lake in Utah. Young decided that the isolated valley would make a good home for the Mormons.

A difficult journey

To move 15,000 men, women, and children from Illinois to Utah in the 1840s was an awesome challenge. Relying on religious faith and careful planning, Brigham Young achieved his goal.

In 1847, Young led an advance party into the Great Salt Lake valley. Wave after wave of Mormons followed. For the next few years, Mormon wagon trains struggled across the plains and over the Rockies to Utah. When they ran short of wagons and oxen, thousands made the long trip pulling their gear in handcarts.

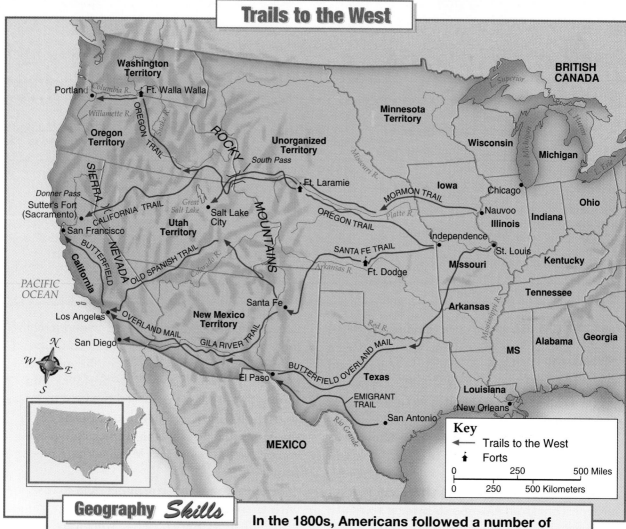

Trails to the West

Geography Skills

In the 1800s, Americans followed a number of different trails to the West. Mountain passes allowed settlers to cross the Rockies and Sierra Nevada.

1. **Location** On the map, locate: **(a)** Santa Fe, **(b)** Santa Fe Trail, **(c)** Sierra Nevada, **(d)** Rocky Mountains, **(e)** San Diego, **(f)** San Francisco, **(g)** Salt Lake City.
2. **Movement** Which trails ended in cities in California?
3. **Critical Thinking** **(a)** What would be the best route for a pioneer family to take from Independence, Missouri, to Sutter's Fort, California? **(b)** What mountains would they have to cross? **(c)** In which town might they seek shelter along the way?

Prospering in the desert

In Utah, the Mormons had to survive in a harsh desert climate. Still, Young was convinced that, for the Mormons, Utah was Zion, or the promised land:

> **❝** We will raise our wheat, build our houses, fence our farms, plant our vineyards and orchards, and produce everything that will make our bodies comfortable and happy and in this manner we intend to build up Zion on the earth. **❞**

To meet his goals, Young planned an irrigation system to bring water to farms. He also drew up plans for a large city, called Salt Lake City, to be built in the desert.

The Mormon settlement in Utah grew quickly. Like other whites, Mormons took over thousands of acres of Native American land, usually paying nothing for it.

Congress recognized Brigham Young as governor of the Utah Territory in 1850. Trouble later broke out when non-Mormons moved to the area. In the end, peace was restored, and Utah became a state in 1896.

California Gold Rush

While the Mormons trekked to Utah, thousands of other Americans were racing to California. These adventurous men and women all had a single objective: Gold!

Sutter's Mill

In 1848, John Sutter was building a sawmill on the American River, north of Sacramento, California. James Marshall was in charge of the job. On the morning of January 24, Marshall set out to inspect a ditch his crew was digging. He later told a friend what he saw that day:

> ❝ It was a clear, cold morning; I shall never forget that morning. As I was taking my usual walk, . . . my eye was caught with the glimpse of something shining in the bottom of the ditch. There was about a foot of water running then. I reached my hand down and picked it up; it made my heart thump, for I was certain it was gold. ❞

In a few days, word of the gold strike at **Sutter's Mill** spread to San Francisco. Carpenters threw down their saws. Bakers left bread in their ovens. Schools emptied as teachers and students joined the rush to the gold fields.

From San Francisco, the news spread across the United States and to the rest of the world. Thousands of Americans caught gold fever. People from Europe, China, Australia, and South America joined the rush as well. More than 80,000 people made the long journey to California in 1849. They became known as **forty-niners.**

In the gold fields

The first miners needed little skill. Because the gold was near the surface of the Earth, they could dig it out with knives. Later, the miners found a better way. They loaded sand and gravel from the riverbed into a washing pan. Then, they held the pan under water and swirled it gently. The water washed away lighter gravel, leaving the heavier gold in the pan. This process was known as "panning for gold."

Cause and Effect

Causes

- Oregon has fertile land
- Texas is ideal for raising cattle and growing cotton
- Many Americans believe in Manifest Destiny
- Mormons seek a safe home
- Gold is discovered in California

Westward Movement

Effects

- Texas wins war for independence
- United States annexes Texas
- Britain and United States divide Oregon
- United States defeats Mexico in war
- Cotton Kingdom spreads

Effects Today

- United States stretches from sea to sea
- California and Texas are the most populous states
- Mexican American culture enriches the United States

Graphic Organizer *Skills*

Westward movement increased at a tremendous rate in the mid-1800s.

1. **Comprehension** List two attractions that drew Americans to the West.
2. **Critical Thinking** According to this chart, was Manifest Destiny successful? Explain.

Economics $

Only a few miners actually struck it rich. Most went broke trying to make their fortunes. Still, although many miners left the gold fields, they stayed in California.

China

United States

From China to the Golden Mountain

Some 25,000 Chinese left their ordered society for the rough-and-tumble world of the California gold fields. Few struck it rich, but their knowledge of farming helped the territory prosper. At left, Chinese peasants tend a rice field. At right, Chinese miners work at a gold claim. ★ **What qualities did the Chinese and other forty-niners need to succeed?**

Women joined the gold rush. Some staked claims and mined for gold. Others took advantage of economic opportunities in the mining camps. Women ran boarding houses, took in laundry, sewed, and ran bakeries.

A new state

The Gold Rush changed life in California. Almost overnight, San Francisco grew from a sleepy town to a bustling city.

Greed led some forty-niners to become criminals. Murders and robberies plagued many mining camps. To fight crime, miners formed vigilance committees. **Vigilantes**

(vihj uh LAN teez), self-appointed law enforcers, dealt out punishment even though they had no legal power to do so. Sometimes an accused criminal was lynched, that is, hanged without a legal trial.

Californians realized they needed a government to stop the lawlessness. In 1849, they drafted a state constitution. They then asked to be admitted to the Union. Their request caused an uproar in the United States. Americans wondered whether the new state would allow slavery. As you will read, after a heated debate, California was admitted to the Union in 1850 as a free state.

California's Unique Culture

Most mining camps in California included a mix of peoples. A visitor to a mining town might meet runaway slaves from the South, Native Americans, and New Englanders. There were also people from Hawaii, China, Peru, Chile, France, Germany, Italy, Ireland, and Australia.

Connections With Arts

The California Gold Rush provided the background for the still-popular folk song "My Darling Clementine." The song begins: "In a canyon, in a cavern / Excavating for a mine / Lived a miner, forty-niner / And his daughter Clementine."

Most of the miners, however, were white Americans. During the wild days of the Gold Rush, they often ignored the rights of other Californians.

Mexican Americans and Indians

California included many Mexicans and Native Americans who had lived there long before the Gold Rush. In many instances, Mexican Americans lost land they had owned for generations. Still, they fought to preserve the customs of their people. José Carrillo (cah REE yoh) was from one of the oldest families in California. In part through his efforts, the state's first constitution was written in both Spanish and English.

Indians fared worst of all. Many Native Americans were driven off their lands and later died of starvation or diseases. Others were murdered. In 1850, about 100,000 Indians lived in California. By the 1870s, there were only 17,000 Indians left in the state.

Chinese Americans

Attracted by the tales of a "mountain of gold," thousands of Chinese began arriving in California in 1848. Because California needed workers, the Chinese were welcomed at first. When the Chinese staked claims in the gold fields, however, white miners often drove them off.

Discrimination against Chinese Americans and, later, other Asians would continue in California for many decades. Still, many Chinese Americans stayed in California and helped the state to grow. They farmed, irrigated, and reclaimed vast stretches of land.

African Americans

Free blacks, too, rushed to the California gold fields hoping to strike it rich. Some did become wealthy. By the 1850s, in fact, California had the richest African American population of any state. Yet African Americans were also denied certain rights. For example, California law denied blacks and other minorities the right to testify against whites in court. After a long struggle, blacks gained this right in 1863.

In spite of these problems, California thrived and grew. Settlers continued to arrive in the state. By 1860, it had 100,000 citizens. The mix of peoples in California gave it a unique culture.

★ Section 5 Review ★

Recall

1. **Locate** (a) Nauvoo, (b) Salt Lake City, (c) Sacramento, (d) San Francisco.
2. **Identify** (a) Mormons, (b) Joseph Smith, (c) Brigham Young, (d) Sutter's Mill.
3. **Define** (a) forty-niner, (b) vigilante.

Comprehension

4. Why did Brigham Young lead the Mormons to Utah?
5. Describe two effects of the Gold Rush on California.
6. Explain the problems that each of the following faced in California: **(a)** Mexican Americans, **(b)** Native Americans, **(c)** Chinese Americans, **(d)** African Americans.

Critical Thinking and Writing

7. **Comparing** Compare the settling of Utah with the settling of California. How were they similar? How were they different?
8. **Linking Past and Present** In the 1990s, almost 30 percent of immigrants to the United States settled in California. The largest group were from Asia. **(a)** Why do you think California still attracts many immigrants? **(b)** Why do so many Asian immigrants come to California?

★ ★

History AND YOU

Activity **Writing a Speech** There's trouble ahead! You and your friend went to California in the Gold Rush. Now, vigilantes are accusing your friend of a crime he didn't commit—stealing a horse. Write a speech in which you declare his innocence and call upon the vigilantes to wait until your friend can receive a legal trial.

Chapter **13** $\bigstar$ **Review** and **Activities**

★ Sum It Up ★

Section 1   Oregon Country
▶ The first white people to live in Oregon Country were hardy fur trappers.
▶ Settlers traveling by wagon train braved great dangers to reach Oregon Country.

Section 2   Texas Wins Independence
▶ Americans living in Texas, as well as Tejanos, rebelled against the Mexican government in 1835.
▶ After winning several battles, Texans set up an independent republic.

Section 3   California and the Southwest
▶ In the early years of white settlement, California was dotted with Spanish missions, forts, and ranches.
▶ In the 1840s, many Americans came to believe that the United States was destined to expand to the Pacific.

Section 4   War With Mexico
▶ The United States made Texas a part of the Union, and then went to war with Mexico in a border dispute.
▶ After defeating Mexico, the United States gained the Southwest and California.

Section 5   A Rush to the West
▶ Seeking religious freedom, the Mormons built a community in the Utah desert.
▶ A gold rush in California drew many newcomers to that region.

CD-ROM Review For additional review of the major ideas of Chapter 13, see **Guide to the Essentials of American History** or **Interactive Student Tutorial CD-ROM,** which contains interactive review activities, graphic organizers, and practice tests.

▢ Reviewing the Chapter

Define These Terms
Match each term with the correct definition.

Column 1	Column 2
1. rendezvous	a. get-together for trappers
2. annex	b. person who joined the California Gold Rush
3. cede	c. to give something up
4. forty-niner	d. to add something on
5. vigilante	e. self-appointed law enforcer

Explore the Main Ideas
1. Describe the way of life of the mountain men in Oregon Country.
2. How did Texans force Santa Anna to grant them independence?
3. What role did the Catholic Church play in the settlement of California?
4. Describe one cause and one effect of the Mexican War.
5. Name the groups that made up the mixed culture of California in the mid-1800s.

▢ Geography Activity

Match the letters on the map with the following places:
1. Louisiana Purchase, **2.** Gadsden Purchase, **3.** Oregon Country, **4.** Florida, **5.** The United States in 1783, **6.** Texas Annexation, **7.** Mexican Cession.   **Location** At what latitude did the United States and Britain agree to divide Oregon?

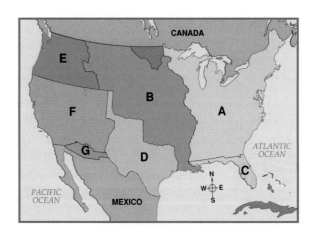

Critical Thinking and Writing

1. **Linking Past and Present** If you were Horace Greeley today, what advice would you give to young people seeking opportunity?

2. **Understanding Chronology** **(a)** List the following events in their correct order: Mexican War; annexation of Texas; founding of the Lone Star Republic; Battle of San Jacinto; Treaty of Guadalupe-Hidalgo. **(b)** Why was it unlikely that the United States would go to war with Mexico *before* Texas joined the Union?

3. **Understanding Causes and Effects** **(a)** What was the immediate cause of the war with Mexico? **(b)** Identify two long-range causes.

4. **Exploring Unit Themes** **Expansion** **(a)** Describe the idea of Manifest Destiny. **(b)** Explain how the nation achieved this goal. **(c)** What do you think were some of the positive and negative effects of Manifest Destiny?

Using Primary Sources

In a letter written in 1844, Henry Clay explained his thoughts about the annexation of Texas:

> 66 Annexation and war with Mexico are identical. Now, for one, I certainly am not willing to involve this country in a foreign war for the object of acquiring Texas. I know there are those who regard such a war... as a trifling affair, on account of the weakness of Mexico.... But I do not look upon it thus lightly. I regard all wars as great calamities, to be avoided, if possible, and honorable peace as the wisest and truest policy of this country. 99

Source: *National Intelligencer*, April, 17, 1844.

Recognizing Points of View **(a)** What did Clay predict would happen if the United States annexed Texas? **(b)** Why did he oppose the idea? **(c)** How do you think Sam Houston would have responded to Clay's letter?

ACTIVITY BANK

Interdisciplinary Activity

Exploring Science Working with a partner, give a presentation on how a geologic feature of the West influenced history. For example, you might choose the Rio Grande, the Great Salt Lake, the Rocky Mountains, the Central Valley of California, or the gold in California.

Career Skills Activity

City Planner You are a city official of San Francisco in 1849. You know that thousands of people will be moving to your city over the next few years. Write a report in which you propose a plan for growth.

Citizenship Activity

Exploring Immigration Like Californians, most Americans today are immigrants or descended from immigrants. Do you know when any of your ancestors first came to this country? If so, prepare a chart tracing your ancestors back to the first people in your family to come to the United States.

Internet Activity

Use the Internet to find sites dealing with the early history of the Mormons. Take notes on what you find and use them to compose a two-paragraph report on early Mormon history.

EYEWITNESS Journal

You are a mountain man or a missionary in Oregon; an American or Tejano in Texas; an American or Mexican in California; a Mormon in Utah; or a forty-niner. In your EYEWITNESS JOURNAL, describe your participation in whatever was, for you, the single most important event of the years 1820–1860.

Chapter 14

The Worlds of North and South 1820–1860

As the 1800s progressed, the North and the South continued to develop differently. In many ways, the two regions were like separate worlds. The North based its economy largely on industry. The South, meanwhile, developed an agricultural system that relied primarily on cotton. The industry of the North depended on paid workers. These workers struggled to make a living and endured hard working conditions. Still, they were free. In contrast, cotton production in the South depended on the labor of enslaved African Americans. These enslaved people had no rights or freedoms.

Why Study History?

In the mid-1800s, many Americans could trace their roots to one of the British Isles, to Spain, or to a particular region of Africa. New immigrants were arriving from Germany, Ireland, and other European nations. Americans of all backgrounds were proud of their rich heritage. To learn about cultural influences that helped to shape several styles of American music, see this chapter's *Why Study History?* feature, "Music Is Part of Our Culture."

American Events	**1820s** Skilled workers begin to organize unions	**1830s** Railroads allow goods to be shipped quickly and cheaply

1820	1825	1830	1835	1840

World Events

1829 World Event
Steam-powered locomotive travels 30 miles per hour in England

Viewing HISTORY · **Different Worlds**

By the mid-1800s, the North and South had different economies. The North developed a variety of industries based on the labor of free workers. The South depended largely on agriculture and the labor of enslaved African Americans. A typical southern scene appears in William Aiken Walker's painting Plantation Economy in the Old South, *shown above.* ★ **What other economic differences between North and South do the pictures above suggest?**

1840s
Cotton boom in South leads to spread of slavery

1844
Morse receives patent for telegraph

1850s
Millions of Irish and German immigrants settle in the United States

| 1840 | 1845 | 1850 | 1855 | 1860 |

1840 World Event
World Anti-Slavery Convention held in Great Britain

1848 World Event
Revolutions in Germany

Industry in the North

★ ★

As You Read

Explore These Questions
- How did new inventions change manufacturing and farming in the North?
- How did new means of communication and transportation benefit business?
- How did steam power help industry grow?

Define
- telegraph
- locomotive
- clipper ship

Identify
- Elias Howe
- John Deere
- Cyrus McCormick
- Samuel F. B. Morse
- John Griffiths

Elias Howe sewing machine

SETTING the Scene In 1834, a young French engineer, Michel Chevalier, toured the North. He was most impressed by the burst of industry there—the textile factories, shipyards, and iron mills. He wrote:

> 66 Everywhere is heard the noise of hammers, of spindles, of bells calling the hands to their work, or dismissing them from their tasks.... It is the peaceful hum of an industrious population, whose movements are regulated like clockwork. 99

Northern industry grew steadily in the mid-1800s. Most northerners still lived on farms. However, more and more of the northern economy centered on manufacturing and trade.

New Machines

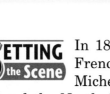

The 1800s brought a flood of new inventions in the North. "In Massachusetts and Connecticut," a European visitor exclaimed, "there is not a laborer who has not invented a machine or a tool."

In 1846, **Elias Howe** patented a sewing machine. A few years later, Isaac Singer improved on Howe's machine. Soon, clothing makers bought hundreds of the new sewing machines. Workers could now make dozens of shirts in the time it took a tailor to sew one by hand.

Some new inventions made work easier for farmers. **John Deere** invented a lightweight steel plow. Earlier plows made of heavy iron or wood had to be pulled by slow-moving oxen. A horse could pull a steel plow through a field more quickly.

In 1847, **Cyrus McCormick** opened a factory in Chicago that produced mechanical reapers. The reaper was a horse-drawn machine that mowed wheat and other grains. McCormick's reaper could do the work of five people using hand tools.

The reaper and the steel plow helped farmers raise more grain with fewer hands. As a result, thousands of farm workers left the countryside. Some went west to start farms of their own. Others found jobs in new factories in northern cities.

$ Connections With Economics

Cyrus McCormick used a new business practice to help struggling farmers buy a reaper. He let farmers put some money down and pay the rest in installments. This practice is known as the installment plan or buying on credit.

The Telegraph

In 1844, **Samuel F. B. Morse** received a patent for a "talking wire," or telegraph. The **telegraph** was a device that sent electrical signals along a wire. The signals were based on a code of dots, dashes, and spaces. Later, this system of dots and dashes became known as the Morse code.

Congress gave Morse funds to run wire from Washington, D.C., to Baltimore. On May 24, 1844, Morse set up his telegraph in the Supreme Court chamber in Washington. As a crowd of onlookers watched, Morse tapped out a short message: "What hath God wrought!" A few seconds later, the operator in Baltimore tapped back the same message. The telegraph worked!

Morse's invention was an instant success. Telegraph companies sprang up everywhere. Thousands of miles of wire soon stretched across the country. As a result of the telegraph, news could now travel long distances in a matter of minutes.

The telegraph helped many businesses to thrive. Merchants and farmers could have quick access to information about supply, demand, and prices of goods in different areas of the country. For example, western farmers might learn of a wheat shortage in New York and ship their grain east to meet the demand.

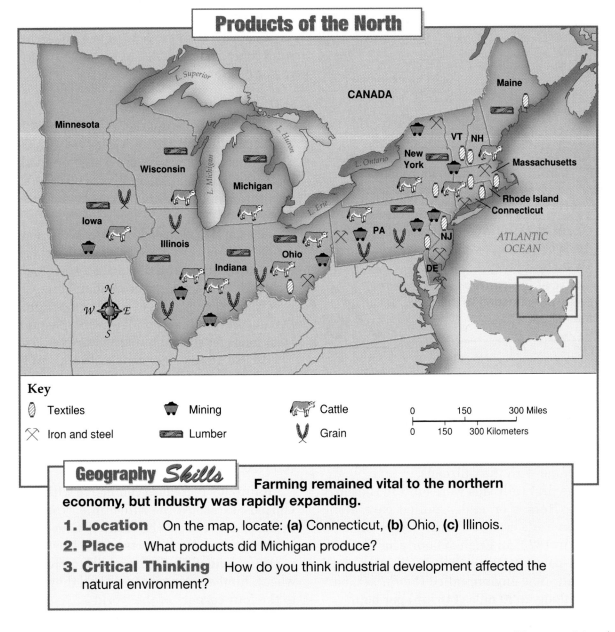

Products of the North

Key

- Textiles
- Iron and steel
- Mining
- Lumber
- Cattle
- Grain

0   150   300 Miles
0   150   300 Kilometers

Geography Skills   Farming remained vital to the northern economy, but industry was rapidly expanding.

1. **Location**   On the map, locate: **(a)** Connecticut, **(b)** Ohio, **(c)** Illinois.
2. **Place**   What products did Michigan produce?
3. **Critical Thinking**   How do you think industrial development affected the natural environment?

Growth of Railroads

Thousands of Miles of Track

35
30
25
20
15
10
5
0

1840 1845 1850 1855 1860

Year

Source: *Historical Statistics of the United States*

Graph *Skills*

Between 1840 and 1860, railroad construction increased greatly. More railroad lines were built in the North than in the South.

1. **Comprehension** Approximately how many miles of track were laid between 1855 and 1860?
2. **Critical Thinking** What raw materials were needed to build and run the railroads?

Economics $

The First Railroads

Improved transportation also boosted the economy. Americans continued to build new roads and canals. The greatest change, however, came with the railroads.

The first railroads were built in the early 1800s. Horses or mules pulled cars along wooden rails covered with strips of iron. Then, in 1829, an English family developed a steam-powered **locomotive** engine to pull rail cars. The engine, called the *Rocket,* barreled along at 30 miles (48 km) per hour.

Early difficulties

In the United States, there was some initial opposition to railroads. Farmers did not want railroads running through their fields. Teamsters who moved freight on horse-drawn wagons feared that they would lose their jobs. Likewise, people who invested in canals worried that competition from the railroads might cause them to lose their investments. Some states protected the canals by placing limits on railroads. One such limit was that railroads could carry freight only when canals were frozen.

Another problem for the railroads was concern over reliability and safety. Early steam locomotives often broke down. Soft roadbeds and weak bridges contributed to accidents. Locomotives were extremely noisy and belched thick black smoke from their smokestacks. Hot embers from smokestacks sometimes burned holes in passengers' clothing or set nearby buildings on fire.

A railroad boom

Despite these problems, promoters believed in the future of train travel. One boasted that the railroads were "unrivaled for speed, cleanliness, civility of officers and servants, and admirable accommodations of every kind."

Gradually, railroad builders overcame problems and removed obstacles. Engineers learned to build sturdier bridges and solid roadbeds. They replaced wooden rails with iron rails. Such improvements made railroad travel safer and faster. Meanwhile, legal restrictions on railroad building were removed.

By the 1850s, railroads crisscrossed the nation. The major lines were concentrated in the North and West. New York, Chicago, and Cincinnati became major rail centers. The South had much less track than the North.

Yankee Clippers

Railroads increased commerce within the United States. At the same time, trade also increased between the United States and other nations. At seaports in the Northeast, captains loaded their ships with cotton, fur, wheat, lumber, and tobacco. Then they sailed to the four corners of the world.

Speed was the key to successful trade at sea. In 1845, an American named **John Griffiths** launched the *Rainbow,* the first of the **clipper ships.** These sleek vessels had tall masts and huge sails that caught every gust of wind. Their narrow hulls clipped swiftly through the water.

In the 1840s, American clipper ships broke every speed record. One clipper sped from New York to Hong Kong in 81 days, flying past older ships that took five months to reach China. The speed of the clippers helped the United States win a large share of the world's sea trade in the 1840s and 1850s.

The golden age of the clipper ship was brief. In the 1850s, Britain launched the first oceangoing iron steamships. These sturdy vessels carried more cargo and traveled even faster than clippers.

The Northern Economy Expands

By the 1830s, factories began to use steam power instead of water power. Machines that were driven by steam were powerful and cheap to run. Also, factories that used steam power could be built almost anywhere, not just along the banks of swift-flowing rivers. As a result, American industry expanded rapidly.

At the same time, new machines made it possible to produce more goods at a lower cost. These more affordable goods attracted eager buyers. Families no longer had to make clothing and other goods in their homes. Instead, they could buy factory-made products.

Railroads allowed factory owners to transport large amounts of raw materials and finished goods cheaply and quickly. Also, as railroads stretched across the nation, they linked distant towns with cities and factories. These towns became new markets for factory goods.

The growth of railroads also affected northern farming. Railroads brought cheap grain and other foods from the West to New England. New England farmers could not compete with this new source of cheap foods. Many left their farms to find new jobs as factory workers, store clerks, and sailors. More and more, New Englanders turned to manufacturing and trade.

★ Section 1 Review ★

Recall

1. **Identify** **(a)** Elias Howe, **(b)** John Deere, **(c)** Cyrus McCormick, **(d)** Samuel F. B. Morse, **(e)** John Griffiths.
2. **Define** **(a)** telegraph, **(b)** locomotive, **(c)** clipper ship.

Comprehension

3. What new inventions made work easier for farmers?
4. Explain how each of the following helped industry grow: **(a)** telegraph, **(b)** railroads, **(c)** clipper ships.

5. How did steam power and new machines change northern industry?

Critical Thinking and Writing

6. **Linking Past and Present** What technology of today helps businesses in the same way that the telegraph helped businesses in the 1800s?
7. **Understanding Causes and Effects** How did the building of railroads cause many New Englanders to abandon farming?

Activity **Creating an Advertisement** It is the mid-1800s and you are working at an advertising agency. Create an advertisement poster urging people to buy or use one of the new inventions of the period. Use both words and pictures to make your advertisement persuasive.

Life in the North

As You Read

Explore These Questions

- What conditions caused northern workers to organize?
- Why did many Europeans move to the United States in the mid-1800s?
- What was life like for African Americans in the North?

Define

- artisan
- trade union
- strike
- famine
- nativist
- discrimination

Identify

- Sarah Bagley
- Know-Nothing party
- Henry Boyd
- Macon Allen
- John Russworm

SETTING the Scene Alzina Parsons never forgot her thirteenth birthday. The day began as usual, with work in the local spinning mill. Suddenly, Alzina cried out. She had caught her hand in the spinning machine, badly mangling her fingers. The foreman summoned the factory doctor. He cut off one of the injured fingers and sent the girl back to work.

In the early 1800s, such an incident probably would not have happened. Factory work was hard, but mill owners treated workers like human beings. By the 1840s, however, there was an oversupply of workers. Many factory owners now treated workers like machines.

Factory Conditions Worsen

Factories of the 1840s and 1850s were very different from the mills of the early 1800s. The factories were larger, and they used steam-powered machines. More laborers worked longer hours for lower wages. Workers lived in dark, dingy houses in the shadow of the factory.

Families in factories

As the need for workers increased, entire families labored in factories. In some cases, a family agreed to work for one year. If even one family member broke the contract, the entire family might be fired.

The factory day began when a whistle sounded at 4 A.M. Father, mother, and children dressed in the dark and headed off to work. At 7:30 A.M. and at noon, the whistle sounded again to announce breakfast and lunch breaks. The workday did not end until 7:30 P.M., when a final whistle sent the workers home.

Hazards at work

During their long day, factory workers faced discomfort and danger. Few factories had windows or heating systems. In summer, the heat and humidity inside the factory were stifling. In winter, the extreme cold chilled workers' bones and contributed to frequent sickness.

Factory machines had no safety devices, and accidents were common. Owners ignored the hazards. There were no laws regulating factory conditions. Injured workers often lost their jobs.

In 1855, a visitor to a textile mill in Fall River, Massachusetts, asked the manager of the mill how he treated his workers. In his reply, the manager was harsh but honest. He described his feelings about the workers.

66 I regard people just as I regard my machinery. So long as they can do my work for what I choose to pay them, I keep them, getting out of them all I can. 99

Workers Join Together

Poor working conditions and low wages led workers to organize. The first to do so were **artisans.** Artisans are workers who have learned a trade, such as carpentry or shoemaking.

Trade unions and strikes

In the 1820s and 1830s, artisans in each trade united to form **trade unions.** The unions called for a shorter workday, higher wages, and better working conditions. Sometimes, unions went on strike to gain their demands. In a **strike,** union workers refuse to do their jobs.

At the time, strikes were illegal in many parts of the United States. Strikers faced fines or jail sentences. Employers often fired strike leaders.

Progress for artisans

Slowly, however, workers made progress. In 1840, President Van Buren approved a 10-hour workday for government employees. Other workers pressed their demands until they won the same hours as government workers. Workers celebrated another victory in 1842 when a Massachusetts court declared that they had the right to strike.

Artisans won better pay because factory owners needed their skills. Unskilled workers, however, were unable to bargain for better wages. Unskilled workers held jobs that required little or no training. Because these workers were easy to replace, employers did not listen to their demands.

Women Workers Organize

The success of trade unions encouraged other workers to organize. Workers in New England textile mills especially were eager to protest cuts in wages and unfair work rules. Many of these workers were women.

Women workers faced special problems. First, they had always earned less money than men did. Second, most union leaders did not want women in their ranks. Like many people at the time, they believed that women should not work outside the home. In fact, the goal of many unions was to raise men's wages so that their wives could leave their factory jobs.

Viewing HISTORY   **Working in a Factory**

Factory employees faced crowded and dangerous working conditions. Many were injured on the job. The workers in this scene are making McCormick reapers. ★ **What kinds of accidents could occur in a factory such as this?**

▼ *A worker's lunch pail*

Skills

FOR LIFE

| Critical Thinking | Managing Information | Communication | Maps, Charts, and Graphs |

Teaching Others

How Will I Use This Skill?

You already use it. You may teach others how to do school work, how to make something, how to play a sport, or how to use a computer program. In the future, you may teach job skills to co-workers. If you become a parent, you will teach your child. We are all teachers.

LEARN the Skill

You can teach others by following these four steps:

❶ Make sure you know the material you will teach.

❷ Prepare a teaching plan that is interesting, informative, and at the proper level of difficulty.

❸ Present your lesson. Encourage your students to participate and to ask questions.

❹ Check that your students have learned the material and reteach if necessary.

PRACTICE the Skill

Using the steps above, teach some classmates about the immigrants who came to the United States in the mid-1800s.

❶ Study and take notes on the material in this section under the heading Millions of New Americans.

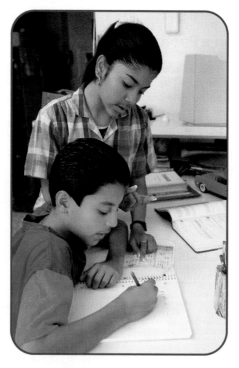

Teaching and learning

❷ Prepare the teaching plan that you will use for your lesson. You might make an outline or chart or write a skit. You might use additional books or videotapes.

❸ Present your lesson. Keep your students involved! Ask interesting questions and encourage your students to participate.

❹ Provide a quiz or activity to check for student understanding. If your students did not learn the lesson well enough, use a different method and try again.

APPLY the Skill

You can apply this skill by volunteering to tutor a classmate or younger student who is having difficulty with reading, mathematics, or another school subject. You might also teach a friend about a hobby or game that interests you.

Despite these problems, women workers organized. They staged several strikes at Lowell, Massachusetts, in the 1830s. In the 1840s, **Sarah Bagley** organized the Lowell Female Labor Reform Association. The group petitioned the state legislature for a 10-hour workday.

Millions of New Americans

By the late 1840s, many factory workers in the North were immigrants. An immigrant is a person who enters a new country in order to settle there. In the 1840s and 1850s, about 4 million immigrants arrived in the United States.

From Ireland and Germany

In the 1840s, a disease destroyed the potato crop across Europe. The loss of the crop caused a famine, or severe food shortage, especially in Ireland. Between 1845 and 1860, over 1.5 million Irish fled to the United States.

Most Irish immigrants were too poor to buy farmland. They settled in the cities where their ships landed. In New York and Boston, thousands of Irish crowded into poor neighborhoods.

In the 1850s, nearly one million German immigrants arrived in the United States. In 1848, revolutions had broken out in several parts of Germany. The rebels fought for democratic reforms. When the revolts failed, thousands had to flee.

Many other German immigrants came to the United States simply to make a better life for themselves.

Enriching the nation

Immigrants supplied much of the labor that helped the nation's economy to grow. Many Irish immigrants worked in northern factories because they did not have enough money to buy farmland. Other Irish workers helped build the canals and railroads that were crisscrossing the nation.

Immigrants from Germany often had enough money to move west and buy good farmland. Many of them were artisans and merchants. Towns of the Midwest often had German grocers, butchers, and bakers.

A Reaction Against Immigrants

Not everyone welcomed the flood of immigrants. One group of Americans, called nativists, wanted to preserve the country for native-born, white citizens. Using the slogan "Americans must rule America," they called for laws to limit immigration. They also wanted to keep immigrants from voting until they had lived in the United States for 21 years. At the time, newcomers could vote after only 5 years in the country.

Some nativists protested that newcomers "stole" jobs from native-born Americans by working for lower pay. Others blamed immigrants for crime in the growing cities. Still others mistrusted Irish and German newcomers because many of them were Catholics. Until the 1840s, the majority of immigrants from Europe were Protestants.

In the 1850s, nativists formed a new political party. It was known as the **Know-Nothing party** because members answered, "I know nothing," when asked about the party. Many meetings and rituals of the party were kept secret. In 1856, the Know-Nothing candidate for President won 21 percent of the popular vote. Soon after, however, the party died out. Still, many Americans continued to blame the nation's problems on immigrants.

African Americans in the North

During the nation's early years, slavery was legal in the North. By the early 1800s, however, all the northern states had outlawed slavery. As a result, thousands of free African Americans lived in the North.

Denied equal rights

Free African Americans in the North faced discrimination. Discrimination is a policy or an attitude that denies equal rights to certain groups of people. As one writer pointed out, African Americans were denied "the ballot-box, the jury box, the halls of the legislature, the army, the public lands, the school, and the church."

Biography John Jones

In the 1840s, John Jones ran a profitable tailoring business in Chicago. He helped runaway slaves and opposed Illinois laws that discriminated against African Americans. In the 1870s, he would help to integrate Chicago's public schools.

★ **What obstacles did Jones probably have to overcome?**

Even skilled African Americans had trouble finding good jobs. One black carpenter was turned away by every furniture maker in Cincinnati. At last, a shop owner hired him. However, when he entered the shop, the other carpenters dropped their tools. Either he must leave or they would, they declared. Similar experiences occurred throughout the North.

Some success

Despite the obstacles in their way, some African Americans achieved notable success in business. William Whipper grew wealthy as the owner of a lumber yard in Pennsylvania. He devoted much of his time and money to help bring an end to slavery. **Henry Boyd** operated a profitable furniture company in Cincinnati.

African Americans made strides in other areas as well. Henry Blair invented a corn planter and a cotton seed planter. In 1845, **Macon Allen** became the first African American licensed to practice law in the United States. After graduating from Bowdoin College in Maine, **John Russworm** became one of the editors of *Freedom's Journal*, the first African American newspaper.

★ Section 2 Review ★

Recall

1. **Identify** (a) Sarah Bagley, (b) Know-Nothing party, (c) Henry Boyd, (d) Macon Allen, (e) John Russworm.
2. **Define** (a) artisan, (b) trade union, (c) strike, (d) famine, (e) nativist, (f) discrimination.

Comprehension

3. How did working conditions in factories worsen in the 1840s and 1850s?
4. In the mid-1800s, why did so many immigrants to the United States come from Ireland and Germany?

5. How did discrimination affect free African Americans in the North?

Critical Thinking and Writing

6. **Making Inferences** Who do you think were the strongest supporters of laws that made strikes illegal? Explain.
7. **Recognizing Points of View** Make a graphic organizer that identifies the reasons for the nativist point of view.

Activity **Writing a Petition** You are a female mill worker of the 1840s. You are unhappy about the harsh working conditions in the mills. Write a petition to the state legislature listing your complaints and asking for better working conditions.

3 Cotton Kingdom in the South

As You Read

Explore These Questions
- Why did cotton planters begin to move westward?
- How did the cotton gin affect slavery in the South?
- Why did the South have less industry than the North?

Identify
- Eli Whitney
- Cotton Kingdom
- William Gregg

Cotton gin

SETTING the Scene In 1827, an Englishman, Basil Hall, traveled through much of the South aboard a riverboat. He complained that the southerners he met were interested in only one thing—cotton:

> 66 All day and almost all night long, the captain, pilot, crew and passengers were talking of nothing else; and sometimes our ears were so wearied with the sound of cotton! cotton! cotton! that we gladly hailed fresh...company in hopes of some change—but alas!...'What's cotton at?' was the first eager inquiry. 99

Cotton became even more important to the South in the years after Hall's visit. Even though southerners grew other crops, cotton was the region's leading export. Cotton plantations—and the slave system on which they depended—shaped the way of life in the South.

Cotton Gin, Cotton Boom

The Industrial Revolution greatly increased the demand for southern cotton. Textile mills in the North and in Britain needed more and more cotton to make cloth. At first, southern planters could not meet the demand. They could grow plenty of cotton because the South's soil and climate were ideal. However, removing the seeds from the cotton by hand was a slow process. Planters needed a better way to clean cotton.

Eli Whitney's invention

In 1793, **Eli Whitney**, a young Connecticut schoolteacher, was traveling to Georgia. He was going to be a tutor on a plantation. When Whitney learned of the planters' problem, he decided to build a machine to clean cotton.

In only 10 days, Whitney came up with a model. His cotton engine, or gin, had two rollers with thin wire teeth. When cotton was swept between the rollers, the teeth separated the seeds from the fibers. (See Linking History and Technology on page 384.)

The cotton gin was simple, but its effects were enormous. A worker using a gin could do the work of 50 people cleaning cotton by hand. Because of the gin, planters could now grow cotton at a huge profit.

Connections With Science

Technology thieves stole Eli Whitney's first cotton gin. Before Whitney could build another, someone filed a patent for a machine that copied his invention. To receive the profits that were due to him, Whitney went to court. He filed more than 50 lawsuits.

❶ Cotton bolls, made up of fiber and seeds, are fed into the cotton gin. The red arrows show the path of the cotton through the gin.

❷ As the handle is turned, the cylinder and brushes rotate.

❸ Wire teeth catch the cotton bolls and pull them through narrow wire slots.

❹ The seeds are too large to pass through the slots. They fall to the bottom of the gin.

❺ Rotating brushes pull cleaned cotton fiber from the wire teeth and sweep it out of the gin.

The Cotton Gin

The cotton gin separated unwanted seeds from cotton fiber. With the help of a gin, a worker was able to process as much as 50 pounds of cotton in a single day. As a result, cotton production became a very profitable business.
★ **How did the gin separate the seeds from the fiber?**

▲ *A cotton boll*

Cotton Kingdom and slavery

The cotton gin led to a boom in cotton production. In 1792, planters grew only 6,000 bales of cotton a year. By 1850, the figure was over 2 million bales.

Planters soon learned that soil wore out if planted with cotton year after year. They needed new land to cultivate. After the War of 1812, cotton planters began to move west.

By the 1850s, there were cotton plantations extending in a wide band from South Carolina through Alabama and Mississippi to Texas. (See the map on page 386.) This area of the South became known as the **Cotton Kingdom**.

Tragically, as the Cotton Kingdom spread, so did slavery. Even though cotton could now be cleaned by machine, it still had to be planted and picked by hand. The result was a cruel cycle. The work of slaves brought profits to planters. Planters used the profits to buy more land and more slaves.

An Agricultural Economy

Cotton was the South's most profitable cash crop. However, the best conditions for growing cotton could be found mostly in the southernmost portion of the South. In other areas of the South, rice, sugar cane, and tobacco were major crops. In addition, Southerners raised much of the nation's livestock.

Rice was an important crop along the coasts of South Carolina and Georgia. Sugar cane was important in Louisiana and Texas. Growing rice and sugar cane required expensive irrigation and drainage systems. Cane growers also needed costly machinery to grind their harvest. Small-scale farmers could not afford such expensive equipment, however. As a result, the plantation system dominated areas of sugar and rice production just as it did areas of cotton production.

Tobacco had been an export of the South since 1619, and it continued to be planted in Virginia, North Carolina, and Kentucky. However, in the early 1800s, the large tobacco plantations of colonial days had given way to small tobacco farms. On these farms, a few field hands tended five or six acres of tobacco.

In addition to the major cash crops of cotton, rice, sugar, and tobacco, the South also led the nation in livestock production. Southern livestock owners profited from hogs, oxen, horses, mules, and beef cattle. Much of this livestock was raised in areas that were unsuitable for growing crops, such as the pine woods of North Carolina.

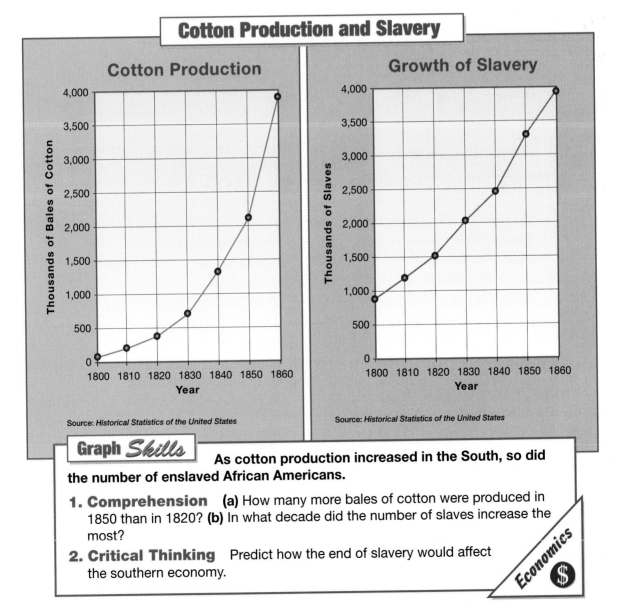

Cotton Production and Slavery

Source: *Historical Statistics of the United States*

Graph Skills As cotton production increased in the South, so did the number of enslaved African Americans.

1. **Comprehension** (a) How many more bales of cotton were produced in 1850 than in 1820? (b) In what decade did the number of slaves increase the most?

2. **Critical Thinking** Predict how the end of slavery would affect the southern economy.

Economics $

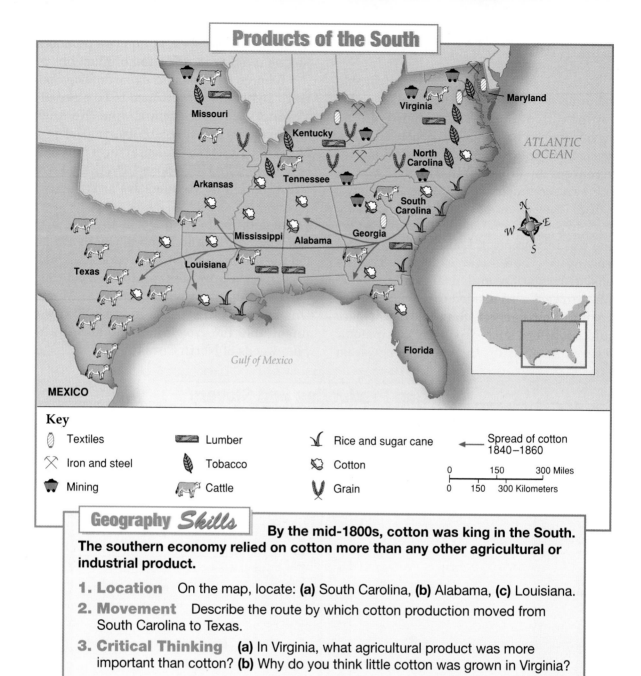

Products of the South

Key

Textiles	Lumber	Rice and sugar cane
Iron and steel	Tobacco	Cotton
Mining	Cattle	Grain

← Spread of cotton 1840–1860

0   150   300 Miles
0   150   300 Kilometers

Geography Skills   **By the mid-1800s, cotton was king in the South. The southern economy relied on cotton more than any other agricultural or industrial product.**

1. **Location**   On the map, locate: **(a)** South Carolina, **(b)** Alabama, **(c)** Louisiana.
2. **Movement**   Describe the route by which cotton production moved from South Carolina to Texas.
3. **Critical Thinking**   **(a)** In Virginia, what agricultural product was more important than cotton? **(b)** Why do you think little cotton was grown in Virginia?

Limited Industry

Some southerners wanted to encourage the growth of industry in the South. **William Gregg**, for example, modeled his cotton mill in South Carolina on the mills in Lowell, Massachusetts. Gregg built houses and gardens for his workers and schools for their children.

The South also developed a few other successful industries. In Richmond, Virginia, for example, the Tredegar Iron Works turned out railroad equipment, machinery, tools, and cannons. Flour milling was another important southern industry.

Even so, the South lagged behind the North in manufacturing. Rich planters invested their money in land and slaves rather than in factories.

Also, slavery reduced the need for southern industry. In the North, most people had enough money to buy factory goods. In the South, however, millions of slaves could not buy anything. As a result, the demand for goods in the South was not as great as in the North. This hurt southern industry.

Economically Dependent

Many southerners ordered goods from northern and European manufacturers. This advertisement appeared in the mail-order catalog of a store located in Milledgeville, Illinois. ★ **Why were there so few factories in the South?**

Economically Dependent

With little industry of its own, the South came to depend more and more on the North and on Europe. Southern planters often borrowed money from northern banks in order to expand their plantations. They also purchased much of their furniture, farm tools, and machines from northern or European factories.

Many southerners resented this situation. One southerner described a burial to show how the South depended on the North for many goods in the 1850s:

❝ The grave was dug through solid marble, but the marble headstone came from Vermont. It was in a pine wilderness but the pine coffin came from Cincinnati. An iron mountain overshadowed it but the coffin nails and the screws and the shovel came from Pittsburgh. . . . A hickory grove grew nearby, but the pick and shovel handles came from New York. . . . That country, so rich in underdeveloped resources, furnished nothing for the funeral except the corpse and the hole in the ground. ❞

Still, most southerners were proud of the booming cotton industry in their region. As long as cotton remained king, southerners believed, they could look to the future with confidence.

★ Section 3 Review ★

Recall

1. **Locate** (a) South Carolina, (b) Alabama, (c) Mississippi, (d) Texas.
2. **Identify** (a) Eli Whitney, (b) Cotton Kingdom, (c) William Gregg.

Comprehension

3. Why did the Cotton Kingdom spread westward?
4. How did the cotton gin cause slavery to expand in the South?

5. Why did the South not develop as much industry as the North?

Critical Thinking and Writing

6. **Predicting Consequences** How might the southern economy have developed differently if the cotton gin had never been invented?
7. **Analyzing Primary Sources** Review the quotation that appears at the end of the section. Is the southerner praising or criticizing the economy of the South? Explain.

Activity **Linking Past and Present** The cotton gin had a major impact on the South's way of life. In a chart, list some modern inventions, describe what they do, and explain how they are changing the way you live today.

4 Life in the South

As You Read

Explore These Questions
- What five groups made up society in the South?
- How did African Americans suffer under slavery?
- How did African Americans struggle against slavery?

Define
- slave code
- extended family

Identify
- "cottonocracy"
- Norbert Rillieux
- Henry Blair
- Denmark Vesey
- Nat Turner

SETTING the Scene 66 I was born in 1844.... First [thing] I remember was my ma and us [children] being sold off the [auction] block to Mistress Payne. When I was...too little to work in the field, I stayed at the big house most of the time and helped Mistress Payne feed the chickens, make scarecrows to keep the hawks away and put wood on the fires. After I got big enough to hoe, I went to the field same as the other[s]. 99

In this excerpt, Jack Payne recalls his life as an enslaved person in Texas. Payne was only one of millions of African Americans throughout the South who suffered the anguish of slavery. Toiling from dawn till dusk, they had neither freedom nor rights.

White Southerners

The Old South is often pictured as a land of vast plantations worked by hundreds of slaves. Such grand estates did exist in the South. However, most white southerners were not rich planters. In fact, most whites owned no slaves at all.

The "cottonocracy"

A planter was someone who owned at least 20 slaves. In 1860, only one white southerner in 30 belonged to a planter family. An even smaller number—less than 1 percent—owned 50 or more slaves. These wealthy families were called the **"cottonocracy"** because they made huge amounts of money from cotton. Though few in number, their views and way of life dominated the South.

The richest planters built elegant homes and filled them with expensive furniture from Europe. They entertained lavishly. They tried to dress and behave like European nobility.

Planters had responsibilities, too. Because of their wealth and influence, many planters became political leaders. They devoted many hours to local, state, and national politics. Planters hired overseers to run day-to-day affairs on their plantations and to manage the work of slaves.

Small farmers

About 75 percent of southern whites were small farmers. These "plain folk" owned the

Connections With Arts

In later years, both literature and film gave a false view of plantation life. Writers and film producers focused on the "gentility" of the planters and largely ignored the injustices of slavery. The most successful of these fictional works is the 1939 film *Gone With the Wind.* Based on Margaret Mitchell's novel, the film won 10 Academy Awards, including Best Picture.

AmericanHeritage
M A G A Z I N E

HISTORY HAPPENED HERE

Rosedown Plantation

Rosedown Plantation, built in 1835, is located in St. Francisville, Louisiana. It was owned by the wealthy cotton planter, Daniel Turnbull, and his wife Martha. The Turnbulls filled their mansion with beautiful furniture and art from Europe. They surrounded their home with avenues of trees and formal gardens. Today, visitors can tour Rosedown, its gardens, and its many outbuildings. You can even stay overnight and recall the luxurious lifestyle of the southern aristocracy.

★ ***To learn more about this historic site, write:*** *Rosedown Plantation, 12501 Highway 10, St. Francisville, LA 70775.*

Original bedroom furniture at Rosedown

land they farmed. They might also own one or two slaves. Unlike planters, plain folk worked with their slaves in the fields.

Among small farmers, helping each other was an important duty. "People who lived miles apart counted themselves as neighbors," wrote a farmer in Mississippi. "And in case of sorrow or sickness, there was no limit to the service neighbors provided."

Poor whites

Lower on the social ladder was a small group of poor whites. They did not own the land they farmed. Instead, they rented it, often paying the owner with part of their crop. Many barely made a living.

Poor whites often lived in the hilly, wooded areas of the South. They planted crops such as corn, potatoes, and other vegetables. They also herded cattle and pigs. Poor whites had hard lives, but they enjoyed rights denied to all African Americans, enslaved or free.

African American Southerners

Both free and enslaved African Americans lived in the South. Although free under the law, free African Americans faced harsh discrimination. Enslaved African Americans had no rights at all.

Free African Americans

Most free African Americans were descendants of slaves freed during and after the American Revolution. Others had bought their freedom. In 1860, over 200,000 free blacks lived in the South. Most lived in Maryland and Delaware, where slavery was

Chapter 14 ★ **389**

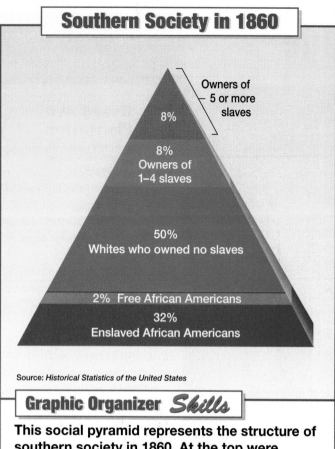

Southern Society in 1860

- 8% — Owners of 5 or more slaves
- 8% Owners of 1–4 slaves
- 50% Whites who owned no slaves
- 2% Free African Americans
- 32% Enslaved African Americans

Source: *Historical Statistics of the United States*

Graphic Organizer *Skills*

This social pyramid represents the structure of southern society in 1860. At the top were wealthy and powerful planters. At the bottom were millions of enslaved African Americans.

1. **Comprehension** Which group in southern society was most numerous?

2. **Critical Thinking** Many white southerners owned no slaves but still supported the institution of slavery. Why do you think they did so?

in decline. Others lived in cities such as New Orleans, Richmond, and Charleston.

Slave owners did not like free African Americans living in the South. They feared that free African Americans set a bad example, encouraging slaves to rebel. Also, slave owners justified slavery by claiming that African Americans could not take care of themselves. Free African American workers proved this idea wrong.

To discourage free African Americans, southern states passed laws that made life even harder for them. Free African Americans were not allowed to vote or travel. In some southern states, they either had to move out of the state or allow themselves to be enslaved.

Despite these limits, free African Americans made valuable contributions to southern life. For example, **Norbert Rillieux** (RIHL yoo) invented a machine that revolutionized the way sugar was made. Another inventor, **Henry Blair,** patented a seed planter.

Enslaved African Americans

By 1860, enslaved African Americans made up one third of the South's population. Most worked as field hands on cotton plantations. Both men and women cleared new land and planted and harvested crops. Children helped by pulling weeds, collecting wood, and carrying water to the field hands. By the time they were teenagers, they too worked between 12 and 14 hours a day.

On large plantations, some African Americans became skilled workers, such as carpenters and blacksmiths. A few worked in cities and lived almost as if they were free. Their earnings, however, belonged to their owners.

Life Without Freedom

The life of enslaved African Americans was determined by strict laws and the practices of individual slave owners. Conditions varied from plantation to plantation. Some owners made sure their slaves had clean cabins, decent food, and warm clothes. Other planters spent as little as possible on their slaves.

Slave codes

Southern states passed laws known as **slave codes** to keep slaves from either running away or rebelling. Under the codes, enslaved African Americans were forbidden to gather in groups of more than three. They could not leave their owner's land without a written pass. They were not allowed to own guns.

Slave codes also made it a crime for slaves to learn how to read and write. Owners hoped that this law would make it hard for African Americans to escape slavery. They reasoned that uneducated runaway slaves would not be able to use maps or read train schedules. They would not be able to find their way north.

Why Study History?

Because Music Is Part of Our Culture

★ ★

Historical Background

From the colonial era on, southerners of diverse backgrounds shared their music with one another. As a result, a variety of rich musical traditions developed in the American South.

African Americans built on the musical heritage of their ancestral homelands. One common technique was the "call and response" in which a soloist sang a line and the group responded. African American music stressed varied rhythms and improvisation, the spontaneous creation of new lyrics and melodies. In the 1800s, these qualities were typical of African American work songs, religious songs, and folk songs.

The early musical traditions of most white southerners were rooted in the tunes and melodies of the British Isles. German, Mexican, Cajun, and other traditions also enriched Southern folk music. The sounds of fiddles and banjos often celebrated house raisings, harvest feasts, and other major events.

Connections to Today

Several American music styles of today are firmly rooted in the South. Blues, jazz, and gospel music emerged from the traditions of African American southerners. Country music and rock-and-roll developed from the folk music of both white and black southerners. In fact, most early rock performers of the 1950s came from the South.

Connections to You

The sounds of jazz, country, and rock are all around you. The next time you pop in your favorite CD, consider the roots of the music

▲ Gospel singers

▲ Country music singer

you hear. When you watch a television show, note its theme music. When you go to the movies, listen to the soundtrack. You will discover that American music owes much to the rich and diverse traditions of the American South.

1. **Comprehension**   What music styles of today can be traced to traditions in the American South?
2. **Critical Thinking**   Why do you think jazz and blues music developed in the South rather than in the North?

 Planning a Documentary
Research the history of a music style discussed here. Then, outline a television documentary on that style. List the topics and pictures that will appear in your documentary.

Viewing History — African American Community

The painting Plantation Burial *by John Antrobus is unusual for providing a realistic portrait of life on a southern plantation. The central figures are African Americans. To the left, a white couple keeps a respectful distance from the religious ceremony.* ★ **What role did religion play in the life of enslaved African Americans?**

Some laws were meant to protect slaves, but only from the worst forms of abuse. However, enslaved African Americans did not have the right to testify in court. As a result, they were not able to bring charges against owners who abused them.

Enslaved African Americans had only one real protection against mistreatment. Owners looked on their slaves as valuable property. Most slave owners wanted to keep this human property healthy and productive.

Hard work

Even the kindest owners insisted that their slaves work long, hard days. Slaves worked from "can see to can't see," or from dawn to dusk, up to 16 hours a day. Frederick Douglass, who escaped slavery, recalled his life under one harsh master:

❝ We were worked in all weathers. It was never too hot or too cold; it could never rain, blow, hail, or snow too hard for us to work in the field. Work, work, work.... The longest days were too short for him and the shortest nights too long for him. ❞

Some owners and overseers whipped slaves to get a full day's work. However, the worst part of slavery was not the beatings. It was the complete loss of freedom.

Family life

It was hard for enslaved African Americans to keep their families together. Southern laws did not recognize slave marriages or slave families. As a result, owners could sell a husband and wife to different buyers. Children were often taken from their parents and sold.

On large plantations, many enslaved families did manage to stay together. For those African Americans, the family was a source of strength, pride, and love. Grandparents, parents, children, aunts, uncles, and cousins formed a close-knit group. This idea of an **extended family** had its roots in Africa.

Enslaved African Americans preserved other traditions as well. Parents taught their children traditional African stories and songs. They used folk tales to pass on African history and moral beliefs.

Religion offers hope

By the 1800s, many enslaved African Americans were devout Christians. Planters often allowed white ministers to preach to their slaves. African Americans also had their own preachers and beliefs.

Religion helped African Americans cope with the harshness of slave life. Bible stories about how the ancient Hebrews had escaped from slavery inspired many spiritual songs. As they worked in the fields, slaves sang about a coming day of freedom. One spiritual, "Go Down, Moses," includes these lines:

❝ We need not always weep and
    moan,
  Let my people go.
And wear these slavery chains
    forlorn,
  Let my people go. ❞

Resistance Against Slavery

Enslaved African Americans struck back against the system that denied them both freedom and wages. Some broke tools, destroyed crops, and stole food.

Many enslaved African Americans tried to escape to the North. Because the journey was long and dangerous, very few made it to freedom. Every county had slave patrols and sheriffs ready to question an unknown black person.

A few African Americans used violence to resist the brutal slave system. **Denmark Vesey**, a free African American, planned a revolt in 1822. Vesey was betrayed before the revolt began. He and 35 other people were executed.

In 1831, an African American preacher named **Nat Turner** led a major revolt. Turner led his followers through Virginia, killing more than 57 whites. Terrified whites hunted the countryside for Turner. They killed many innocent African Americans before catching and hanging him.

Nat Turner's revolt increased southern fears of an uprising of enslaved African Americans. Revolts were rare, however. Since whites were cautious and well armed, a revolt by African Americans had almost no chance of success.

★ Section 4 Review ★

Recall

1. **Identify** **(a)** "cottonocracy," **(b)** Norbert Rillieux, **(c)** Henry Blair, **(d)** Denmark Vesey, **(e)** Nat Turner.
2. **Define** **(a)** slave code, **(b)** extended family.

Comprehension

3. How did the "cottonocracy" dominate economics and politics in the South?
4. Describe three ways that African Americans suffered under slavery.

5. How did African Americans struggle against the slave system?

Critical Thinking and Writing

6. **Applying Information** How were successful free African Americans a threat to the slave system?
7. **Making Decisions** If you had been an enslaved African American, would you have decided to live under slavery, to try to escape, or to rebel? Explain the reasons for your decision.

★ ★

Activity **Writing a Speech** You are an enslaved African American living in the South in the 1850s. Write a speech encouraging people to resist slavery and explaining ways in which they can do it.

★ Sum It Up ★

Section 1 Industry in the North
▶ During the mid-1800s, new inventions helped industry grow in the North.
▶ Railroads linked the Northeast with Chicago and other midwestern cities.
▶ With produce coming in from western farms, agriculture declined in the Northeast.

Section 2 Life in the North
▶ Northern factory workers endured long hours, dangerous conditions, and low pay.
▶ As millions of immigrants arrived in the United States, nativist fears grew.
▶ Free African Americans faced discrimination. Still, some became very successful.

Section 3 Cotton Kingdom in the South
▶ Due to the invention of the cotton gin, growing cotton became very profitable.
▶ As the Cotton Kingdom spread from the Atlantic coast to Texas, so did slavery.
▶ As planters invested in land and slaves, the South developed an agricultural economy rather than an industrial one.

Section 4 Life in the South
▶ Southern society consisted of rich planters, small farmers, poor whites, and free and enslaved African Americans.
▶ Enslaved people lacked freedoms and rights and were forced to work for no pay.
▶ Some enslaved African Americans resisted slavery by rebelling or running away.

 CD-ROM Review For additional review of the major ideas of Chapter 14, see **Guide to the Essentials of American History** or **Interactive Student Tutorial CD-ROM,** which contains interactive review activities, graphic organizers, and practice tests.

🔲 Reviewing the Chapter

Define These Terms

Match each term with the correct definition.

Column 1
1. clipper
2. nativist
3. discrimination
4. skilled worker

Column 2
a. a policy or attitude that denies equal rights to certain groups
b. a swift ship with tall masts, huge sails, and a narrow hull
c. a person who has learned a trade
d. someone who favors native-born citizens

Explore the Main Ideas

1. Describe three developments that caused the North's economy to expand.
2. **(a)** Why did workers form unions in the early and mid-1800s? **(b)** Describe two reasons for immigration to the United States in the 1840s and 1850s.
3. How did the cotton gin change life in the South?
4. Describe two ways that slaves resisted slavery.
5. What were two key differences between the North's economy and the South's economy?

🔲 Graph Activity

Use the graph below to answer the following questions: **1.** In what year did Irish immigration to the United States double? **2.** How many Irish immigrants came to the United States in 1851? **Critical Thinking** Why did increasing immigration alarm some Americans?

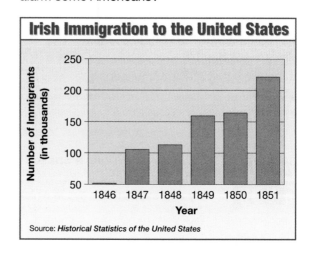

Irish Immigration to the United States

Number of Immigrants (in thousands)

Year

Source: *Historical Statistics of the United States*

Critical Thinking and Writing

1. **Using Chronology** Place these events in chronological order: **(a)** over 1.5 million Irish enter the United States, **(b)** the Know-Nothing party forms, **(c)** famine breaks out in Ireland.

2. **Ranking** In your opinion, what two inventions had the greatest impact on American life in the early and mid-1800s? Explain.

3. **Making Decisions** If you were directing a nation's economy, would you develop agriculture more than industry or industry more than agriculture? Explain.

4. **Exploring Unit Themes** **Expansion** **(a)** Why did slavery spread west during the early 1800s? **(b)** How did economic differences between the North and South grow?

Using Primary Sources

Solomon Northrup was a free African American until he was kidnapped and sold as a slave in 1845. For the next twelve years, he worked on a cotton plantation in Louisiana. Below, he describes the start of a typical workday.

> ❝ [My bed]...was a plank twelve inches wide and ten feet long. My pillow was a stick of wood. The bedding was a coarse blanket.... The cabin is constructed of logs, without floor or window.... In stormy weather, the rain drives through [spaces between the logs].... An hour before daylight the horn is blown. Then the slaves arouse, prepare their breakfast...and hurry to the field again. It is an offense invariably followed by a flogging, to be found at the quarters after daybreak. ❞

Source: *Twelve Years a Slave* by Solomon Northrup, 1853.

Recognizing Points of View **(a)** How does Northrup show his home to be uncomfortable? **(b)** How does he feel about the start of each day? Explain.

ACTIVITY BANK

Interdisciplinary Activity

Exploring Science It is fairly easy to make a telegraph. In your school or local library, find a science book with information on how to build one. Working with other students, create your own telegraph and transmit a message using Morse code.

Career Skills Activity

Musicians Learn a spiritual sung by enslaved people in the South in the 1800s. Possible songs are "Go Down, Moses," "Deep River," and "Swing Low, Sweet Chariot." Perform the spiritual for the class and then explain the meaning of the song.

Citizenship Activity

Protecting Religious Freedom Nativists of the mid-1800s discriminated against Catholics even though Americans are guaranteed religious freedom. Create a poster encouraging citizens to respect the religious beliefs of all Americans.

Internet Activity

Use the Internet to find primary sources on enslaved African Americans in the 1800s. Use the information you find to write a short story about a typical day in the life of an enslaved African American.

EYEWITNESS Journal

In the early 1800s, you are a northern manufacturer or farmer, or a southern planter or enslaved person. In your EYEWITNESS JOURNAL, describe how new inventions are changing your life.

Chapter 15

An Era of Reform

1820–1860

In the mid-1800s, dedicated reformers sought to better American society. Many of these reformers acted out of political ideals. They wanted the nation to live up to its promise of "liberty and equality for all." Religious feeling also spurred many reformers.

Reform took many directions. Two of the most sweeping goals were equal rights for women and the abolition of slavery. Reformers often faced opposition, criticism, and even threats. Yet, they continued to struggle and slowly gained support. In this chapter, you will read about the individuals who contributed to this era of reform.

Why Study History?

Today, as in the 1800s, the reforming impulse is strong in the United States. Americans still work to correct many types of social problems. To learn more about one reform movement that has attracted many Americans, young and old, see the *Why Study History?* feature, "The Fight Against Alcohol Abuse Continues," in this chapter.

American Events			
1826 James Fenimore Cooper publishes *The Last of the Mohicans*		**1831** William Lloyd Garrison begins antislavery newspaper	**1837** Horace Mann begins educational reforms in Massachusetts

1820	1825	1830	1835	1840

World Events

 1822 World Event
Liberia is established in Western Africa

 1837 World Event
First kindergarten opens in Germany

Spirit of Religion

This painted tray honors Lemuel Haynes, a famous African American preacher. From the nation's earliest years, religion was a powerful influence in the United States. In the early 1800s, a religious revival movement fed a new spirit of reform. ★ **Why would religious feelings lead some people to try to find ways to improve society?**

1848●
Women's Rights
Convention is held
at Seneca Falls

●1851
Maine bans the
sale of alcohol

| 1840 | 1845 | 1850 | 1855 | 1860 |

 1843 World Event
Charles Dickens publishes
A Christmas Carol

 1848 World Event
First women's college in
Great Britain opens

The Spirit of Reform

Explore These Questions
- What were the political and religious roots of reform?
- What goals did social reformers pursue?
- How did Americans improve public education in the mid-1800s?

Define
- social reform
- predestination
- revival
- penal system
- temperance movement

Identify
- Second Great Awakening
- Charles Grandison Finney
- Dorothea Dix
- Horace Mann
- Prudence Crandall
- Thomas Gallaudet
- Samuel Gridley Howe
- Laura Bridgman

As You Read

SETTING the Scene In 1840, New England philosopher Ralph Waldo Emerson wrote about Americans' growing passion for improving society:

66 We are all a little wild here with numberless projects for social reform. But what is man born for but to be a Reformer...a restorer of truth and good? 99

Many idealistic Americans shared Emerson's beliefs. Between 1820 and 1860, a wide variety of reform movements sprang up to cure the nation's ills.

The Reforming Impulse

Social reform is an organized attempt to improve what is unjust or imperfect in society. The reforming impulse had both political and religious roots. The political roots went back to the ideals of liberty and equality expressed in the Declaration of Independence. The religious reform involved new teachings about salvation and the individual.

Political ideals

The election of Andrew Jackson in 1828 unleashed a wave of democratic change in the nation. More people could vote and take part in government than ever before.

Still, some critics argued that "Jacksonian democracy" was far from democratic. Many said that a true democracy would not allow slavery. Others questioned why women had fewer rights than men. Reformers hoped that by changing such injustices, they might move the nation closer to its political ideals.

A new religious movement

Many early American Protestants believed that God decided in advance which people would gain salvation in heaven. This idea is known as **predestination.** Belief in predestination led many people to think that society could not be changed. In fact, they felt it was sinful to want to improve the world.

In the early 1800s, a dynamic religious movement, known as the **Second Great Awakening,** swept the nation. Its leaders stressed free will rather than predestination. They taught that individuals could choose by their own actions to save their own souls.

Throughout the nation, preachers held huge outdoor meetings. The goal of these **revivals** was to stir religious feelings. Revivals often lasted for days and attracted thousands of people. A witness described the excitement of a revival in Kentucky:

66 The vast sea of human beings seemed to be agitated as if by storm. I counted seven ministers all preaching at once....Some of the people were singing, others praying, some crying for mercy. 99

Deeply affected, converts vowed to reform their lives.

One of the leaders of the Second Great Awakening was a Presbyterian minister named **Charles Grandison Finney.** A powerful speaker, Finney wrote articles giving tips on effective preaching. He also taught that individual salvation was the first step toward improving society. He told followers that their goal was "the complete reformation of the whole world." Through teachings like these, the Second Great Awakening encouraged the growing spirit of reform.

Helping the Mentally Ill

Some reformers turned their attention to what one minister called the "outsiders" in society—criminals and the mentally ill. One of the most vigorous of these reformers was a Boston schoolteacher named **Dorothea Dix.**

One day in 1841, Dix visited a jail for women near Boston. She was shocked to discover that some of the prisoners had committed no crime. These women were in jail because they were mentally ill.

The jailer locked the mentally ill prisoners in small, dark, unheated cells. The women were half frozen. Dix demanded to know why these women were treated so cruelly. The jailer replied that "lunatics" did not feel the cold.

That moment changed Dix's life forever. During the next 18 months, Dix visited every jail, poorhouse, and hospital in Massachusetts. Her report shocked state legislators:

66 I proceed, gentlemen, briefly to call your attention to the present state of Insane Persons confined . . . in cages, closets, cellars, stalls, pens! Chained, naked, beaten with rods, and lashed into obedience. 99

Eventually, legislators agreed to fund a new mental hospital. Dix then went on to inspect jails in states as far away as Louisiana and Illinois. In nearly every state, her reports persuaded legislatures to treat the mentally ill as patients, not criminals.

Reforming Prisons

Dix also joined others in trying to reform the **penal system,** or system of prisons.

Biography **Dorothea Dix**

Dorothea Dix was shocked by the sight of "harmless lunatics" shackled in dark cells. When she was told that "nothing" could be done, Dix replied, "I know no such word." Largely through her efforts, more than 15 states established special hospitals for the care of the mentally ill by 1860. ★ **How did Dix go about achieving reform?**

Prisons were at the time fairly new to the United States. In colonial days, states generally imposed the death penalty for serious offenses. People who committed minor offenses received some form of physical punishment, such as a public whipping.

In the early 1800s, imprisonment gradually replaced physical punishment. In the early prisons, men, women, and children were often crammed together in cold, damp rooms. When food supplies were low, prisoners might go hungry—unless they had money to buy meals from jailers. Some jailers even made extra money selling rum to prisoners.

Five out of six people in northern jails were in jail because they could not pay their debts. While behind bars, debtors had no way to earn money to pay back their debts.

Why Study History?

Because the Fight Against Alcohol Abuse Continues

★ ★

Historical Background

Americans in the early 1800s consumed more alcohol per person than at any other time in American history. Some American reformers grew concerned about the impact of alcohol on society. The temperance movement that began in the 1820s hoped to end alcohol abuse.

In the late 1800s, the temperance movement grew. Groups like the Women's Christian Temperance Union attracted many followers. Finally, in 1919, the states ratified the Eighteenth Amendment, prohibiting the production and sale of alcoholic drinks. However, law enforcement officials found it nearly impossible to enforce Prohibition. It was repealed in 1933 by the Twenty-first Amendment.

Connections to Today

Reformers now focus on the problems of underage and excessive drinking. Today, the legal drinking age in every state is 21 years. A variety of organizations and programs exist to help people who suffer from alcoholism. Still, as many as 40 million Americans are problem drinkers—people whose drinking causes harm to themselves or their family and friends.

One of the most destructive forms of alcohol abuse is drinking and driving. In the early 1990s, more than 25,000 Americans died each year in accidents involving drunk drivers. Young people were often the victims. In fact, alcohol-related accidents were the number-one killer of teenagers.

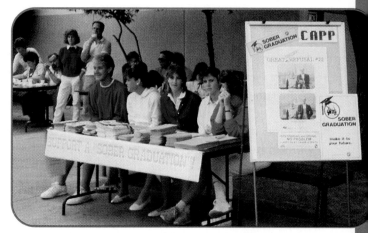

Students organize to warn about the dangers of alcohol.

Connections to You

If you or someone you know has a problem with alcohol, there are several things you can do. You can seek support from your parents or other family members. You can get information from school counselors or a family physician. Also, your school may participate in the Students Against Drunk Driving (SADD) program. Students who belong to SADD promise to call their parents if they cannot get a safe ride with a sober driver.

1. **Comprehension** Name and describe the two constitutional amendments related to the use of alcohol in the United States.

2. **Critical Thinking** Why do you think some people make the irresponsible decision to drink and drive?

 Making a Poster Construct a poster that warns people about the dangers of underage drinking, excessive drinking, or drinking and driving.

As a result, many debtors remained in prison for years.

Dorothea Dix and others called for changes in the penal system. Some states built prisons with only one or two inmates to a cell. Cruel punishments were banned, and people convicted of minor crimes received shorter sentences. Slowly, states stopped treating debtors as criminals.

Battling "Demon Rum"

Alcohol abuse was widespread in the early 1800s. At political rallies, weddings, and funerals, men, women, and sometimes even children drank heavily. Men could buy whiskey in candy stores or barber shops as easily as at taverns.

During the late 1820s, reformers began the **temperance movement,** a campaign against alcohol abuse. Women often took a leading role in the temperance movement. They knew that "demon rum" could lead to wife beating, child abuse, and the breakup of families.

Some temperance groups urged people to drink less. Others sought to wipe out all drinking of alcohol. They won a major victory in the 1850s, when Maine banned the sale of alcohol. Eight other states passed "Maine laws." Although most states later repealed the laws, temperance crusaders pressed on. They gained new strength in the late 1800s.

Improving Education

In 1816, Thomas Jefferson wrote, "If a nation expects to be ignorant and free, it expects what never was and never will be."

$ Connections With Economics

The temperance movement got a lot of support from factory owners. They thought workers would be more productive if they did not drink. Today, many businesses pay for programs to combat alcohol and drug abuse among their employees. In what ways do you think drug or alcohol abuse can hurt the economy?

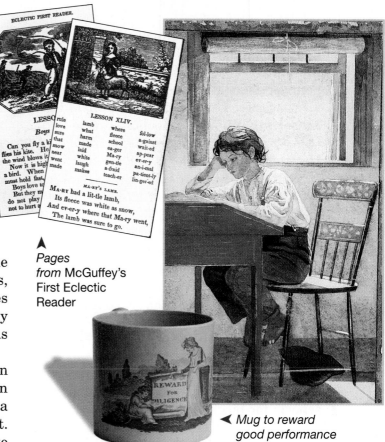

▲ Pages from McGuffey's First Eclectic Reader

◀ Mug to reward good performance

Viewing HISTORY   A Better Education

The painting Homework *by Winslow Homer shows an elementary school student of the mid-1800s. This boy may be reading a lesson from one of William McGuffey's* Eclectic Readers. *First published in 1836, McGuffey's popular textbooks used rhymes and stories to teach spelling, grammar, and good behavior.* ★ **What methods are used today to teach children to read?**

He knew that a republic needed educated citizens. As more men won the right to vote, reformers acted to improve education.

Before the 1820s, few American children attended school. Public schools were rare. Those that did exist were usually old and run-down. Teachers were poorly trained and ill paid. Students of all ages crowded together in a single room.

Growth of public schools

New York State took the lead in improving public education. In the 1820s, the state ordered every town to build a grade school. Before long, other northern states required towns to support public schools.

In Massachusetts, **Horace Mann** led the fight for better schools. Mann became head of the state board of education in 1837. He hounded legislators to provide more money for education. Under his leadership, Massachusetts built new schools, extended the school year, and raised teacher pay. The state also opened three colleges to train teachers.

Reformers in other states urged their legislatures to follow the lead of Massachusetts and New York. By the 1850s, most northern states had set up free tax-supported elementary schools. Schools in the South improved more slowly. In both the North and South, schooling usually ended in the eighth grade. There were few public high schools.

Education for African Americans

In most areas, African Americans had little chance to attend school. A few cities, like Boston and New York, set up separate schools for black students. However, these schools received less money than schools for white students did.

Some attempts to educate African Americans met with great hostility. In the 1830s, **Prudence Crandall,** a Connecticut Quaker, began a school for African American girls. The community was outraged. Crandall continued to teach even when rocks crashed through the classroom window. She was jailed three times. Finally, a band of men broke in one night and destroyed the school.

Despite such obstacles, some free African Americans attended private colleges such as Harvard, Dartmouth, and Oberlin. In the 1850s, several colleges for African Americans opened in the North. The first was Lincoln University, in Pennsylvania.

Meeting special needs

Some reformers took steps to improve education for people with disabilities. In 1817, **Thomas Gallaudet** (gal uh DEHT) set up a school for the deaf in Hartford, Connecticut.

A few years later, **Samuel Gridley Howe** became director of the first American school for blind students. Howe created a system of raised letters that allowed blind students to read with their fingers. One of Howe's pupils, **Laura Bridgman,** was the first deaf and blind student to receive a formal education. She later assisted Howe in teaching other blind students.

★ Section 1 Review ★

Recall

1. **Identify** (a) Second Great Awakening, (b) Charles Grandison Finney, (c) Dorothea Dix, (d) Horace Mann, (e) Prudence Crandall, (f) Thomas Gallaudet, (g) Samuel Gridley Howe, (h) Laura Bridgman.
2. **Define** (a) social reform, (b) predestination, (c) revival, (d) penal system, (e) temperance movement.

Comprehension

3. Describe two reasons the reforming spirit grew in the mid-1800s.

4. What were the goals of (a) prison reformers, and (b) leaders of the temperance movement?
5. What improvements were made in public education after the 1820s?

Critical Thinking and Writing

6. **Linking Past and Present** Do churches and religious leaders still take an active role in promoting social reform today? Give examples.
7. **Understanding Causes and Effects** How would lack of educational opportunities for African Americans contribute to prejudice against them?

Activity **Acting a Scene** The year is 1843. You are a legislator. You are unwilling to raise taxes to improve conditions for prisoners while tax money is needed to improve conditions for law-abiding citizens. With a partner, act out a scene between you and Dorothea Dix. For each argument for prison reform given by Dix, present an opposing argument.

The Fight Against Slavery

As You Read

Explore These Questions
- How did reformers try to end slavery?
- How did the underground railroad work?
- How did Americans react to the antislavery movement?

Define
- abolitionist
- underground railroad

Identify
- American Colonization Society
- David Walker
- Maria Stewart
- Frederick Douglass
- William Lloyd Garrison
- Angelina and Sarah Grimké
- Harriet Tubman

SETTING the Scene In 1848, a group of reformers met to listen to a minister named Henry Highland Garnet. Garnet had once escaped slavery himself. He told the crowd:

This medallion was a popular emblem of the antislavery movement.

66 America is my home, my country. . . . I mourn because the accursed shade of slavery rest[s] upon it. I love my country's flag, and I hope that soon it will be cleansed of its stains, and be hailed by all nations as the emblem of freedom and independence. 99

A growing number of Americans—black and white—spoke out against slavery. Only by ending slavery, they believed, could the United States become truly democratic.

Roots of the Antislavery Movement

In the Declaration of Independence, Thomas Jefferson wrote that "all men are created equal." Yet, many white Americans, including Jefferson, did not think the statement applied to enslaved African Americans. In the 1800s, many reformers disagreed.

Religious beliefs led some Americans to speak out against slavery. Since colonial times, Quakers had said that it was a sin for one human being to own another. They preached that all men and women were equal in the eyes of God. Later, ministers like Charles Grandison Finney called on other Christians to join a crusade to stamp out slavery.

In the North, slavery came to an early end. By 1804, all states from Pennsylvania to New England had promised to free their slaves. Still, there were only 50,000 slaves in the North in 1800, compared to nearly one million in the South.

A Colony in Africa

Some Americans proposed to end slavery by setting up an independent colony in Africa for freed slaves. Supporters of colonization founded the **American Colonization Society** in 1817. Five years later, President Monroe helped the society found the nation of Liberia in western Africa. The name Liberia comes from the Latin word for free.

Many white southerners supported the colonization movement because it did not call for an end to slavery. The society promised to pay slave owners who freed their slaves.

Some African Americans also favored colonization. They felt they would never have equal rights in the United States. Most African Americans, however, opposed the movement. Nearly all, enslaved or free, were born in the United States. They wanted to stay in their homeland. In the end, only a few thousand Americans settled in Liberia.

Biography

William Lloyd Garrison

To William Lloyd Garrison, slavery was a disease that threatened the whole nation. He once even burned a copy of the Constitution because the document permitted slavery. Garrison refused to back down even after a mob in Boston almost killed him. ★ **How did Garrison spread his antislavery message?**

▲ *Garrison's vow*

A Call to End Slavery

Supporters of colonization did not attack slavery directly. Another group of Americans, known as **abolitionists,** wanted to end slavery in the United States completely.

Some abolitionists favored a gradual end to slavery. They expected slavery to die out if it were kept out of the western territories. Other abolitionists demanded that slavery end everywhere, at once.

African American abolitionists

African Americans played an important part in the abolitionist movement. Some tried to end slavery through lawsuits and petitions. James Forten and other wealthy African Americans gave generously to antislavery efforts. In the 1820s, Samuel Cornish and John Russwurm set up an abolitionist newspaper, *Freedom's Journal.* They hoped to turn public opinion against slavery by printing stories about the brutal treatment of enslaved African Americans.

David Walker called for stronger measures. In 1829, he published *Appeal to the Colored Citizens of the World.* He encouraged enslaved African Americans to free themselves by any means necessary. Walker's friend **Maria Stewart** also spoke out against slavery. Stewart was the first American woman to make public political speeches.

Douglass speaks out

The best known African American abolitionist was **Frederick Douglass.** Douglass was born into slavery in Maryland. As a child, he defied the slave codes and taught himself to read.

In 1838, Douglass escaped and made his way to Boston. One day at an antislavery meeting, he felt a powerful urge to speak. Rising to his feet, he talked about the sorrows of slavery and the meaning of freedom. The audience was moved to tears. Soon, Douglass was lecturing across the United States and Britain. In 1847, he began publishing an antislavery newspaper, the *North Star.*

Garrison and *The Liberator*

The most outspoken white abolitionist was a fiery, young man named **William Lloyd Garrison.** Garrison launched his antislavery paper, *The Liberator,* in 1831. In it, he proclaimed that slavery was an evil to be ended immediately. On the very first page of the first issue, Garrison revealed his commitment:

> ❝ I will be as harsh as truth, and as uncompromising as justice...I am in earnest...I will not excuse—I will not retreat a single inch—and I WILL BE HEARD. ❞

A year later, Garrison helped to found the New England Anti-Slavery Society. Members included Theodore Weld, a young minister connected with Charles Grandison Finney. Weld brought the energy of a religious revival to antislavery meetings.

The Grimké sisters

Women also played an important role in the abolitionist cause. **Angelina and Sarah Grimké** were the daughters of a wealthy slaveholder in South Carolina. They came to hate slavery and moved to Philadelphia to work for abolition. Their lectures drew large crowds.

Some people, including other abolitionists, objected to women speaking out in public. Sarah Grimké replied that "whatsoever it is morally right for a man to do, it is morally right for a woman to do." As you will see, this belief led the Grimkés and others to crusade for women's rights.

The Underground Railroad

Some abolitionists, black and white, risked prison and death to help African Americans escape slavery. These bold men and women formed the underground railroad. It was not a real railroad, but a network of abolitionists who secretly helped slaves reach freedom in the North or Canada.

"Conductors" guided runaways to "stations" where they could spend the night. Some stations were homes of abolitionists. Others were churches, or even caves. Conductors sometimes hid runaways under loads of hay in wagons with false bottoms.

One daring conductor, **Harriet Tubman,** had escaped slavery herself. Risking her freedom and her life, Tubman returned to the South 19 times. She led more than 300 slaves, including her parents, to freedom.

Admirers called Tubman the "Black Moses," after the ancient Hebrew leader who

Viewing History — Conductor on the Underground Railroad

"There was one of two things I had a right to," declared Harriet Tubman, "liberty or death. If I could not have the one, I would have the other." After escaping slavery, Tubman became a fearless conductor on the underground railroad. Here, Tubman (left) poses with some of the hundreds of people she led to freedom.
★ **Why was Tubman called the "Black Moses"?**

Skills FOR LIFE

| Critical Thinking | Managing Information | Communication | Maps, Charts, and Graphs |

Analyzing Visual Evidence

How Will I Use This Skill?
Today, newspapers and television present us with a world full of images. A photograph of a bombing victim or a sketch of a courtroom can have a powerful impact. Still, artists and photographers can be influenced by their own viewpoints. We must analyze visual evidence to determine the reliability of what we see.

LEARN the Skill
❶ Identify the subject matter of the drawing, painting, or photograph.

❷ Note the details of the picture. Pay attention to facial expressions, actions, objects, and clothing.

❸ What is the artist's point of view? How does the artist use details to stir sympathy or anger?

❹ Determine the reliability of the visual evidence. Is it an accurate picture of what is shown? What may have been left out?

PRACTICE the Skill
The painting at right depicts a scene of the underground railroad. Look at the picture and answer the following questions.

❶ (a) Where do you think this scene is taking place? (b) Who are the two people in the center of the picture? (c) Describe what is happening in this scene.

❷ (a) What is the man holding in his right hand? What does this tell you about him? (b) What does the expression on the woman's face tell you about her? (c) Why is there a hay wagon in the background?

❸ Do you think the artist was sympathetic toward the underground railroad? How can you tell?

❹ Based on your reading, do you think this picture is reliable? Explain.

APPLY the Skill
Analyze a news photograph that had an emotional impact on you. List the details of the photograph that added to the emotional effect.

led the Israelites out of slavery in Egypt. Slave owners offered a $40,000 reward for Tubman's capture.

Reaction in the North

Abolitionists like Douglass and Garrison made enemies in both the North and the South. Northern mill owners, bankers, and merchants depended on cotton from the South. They saw attacks on slavery as a threat to their livelihood. Some northern workers also opposed abolition. They feared that African Americans might come north and take their jobs by working for low pay.

In New York and other northern cities, mobs sometimes broke up antislavery meetings or attacked homes of abolitionists. At times, the attacks backfired and won support for the abolitionists. One night, a Boston mob dragged William Lloyd Garrison through the streets at the end of a rope. A witness wrote, "I am an abolitionist from this very moment."

Reaction in the South

Not all white southerners favored slavery. Some bravely spoke out against it. Others, such as the Grimké sisters, moved north rather than live in a slaveholding state.

Most white southerners, however, were disturbed by the growing abolitionist movement. They accused abolitionists of preaching violence. Many southerners blamed Nat Turner's revolt on William Lloyd Garrison. (See page 383.) Garrison had founded *The Liberator* in 1831, only a few months before Turner's rebellion. David Walker's call for a slave revolt seemed to confirm the worst fears of southerners.

Many slave owners reacted to the abolitionist crusade by defending slavery even more. One slave owner wrote that if slaves were treated well, they would "love their master and serve him...faithfully." Other owners argued that slaves were better off than northern workers who labored long hours in dusty, airless factories.

Even some southerners who owned no slaves defended slavery. To them, slavery was essential to the southern economy. Many southerners believed northern support for the antislavery movement was greater than it really was. They began to fear that northerners wanted to destroy their way of life.

★ Section 2 Review ★

Recall

1. **Locate** Liberia.
2. **Identify** (a) American Colonization Society, (b) David Walker, (c) Maria Stewart, (d) Frederick Douglass, (e) William Lloyd Garrison, (f) Angelina and Sarah Grimké, (g) Harriet Tubman.
3. **Define** (a) abolitionist, (b) underground railroad.

Comprehension

4. Choose two abolitionists. Describe how each contributed to the antislavery movement.

5. (a) Why did some northerners oppose abolition? (b) Describe two effects of the abolitionist movement in the South.

Critical Thinking and Writing

6. **Drawing Conclusions** Why do you think slavery ended more easily in the North than in the South?
7. **Defending a Position** (a) Why do you think some abolitionists favored a gradual end to slavery? (b) How do you think William Lloyd Garrison or Frederick Douglass would have replied?

★ ★

Activity **Writing a Letter** You are a conductor on the underground railroad. You have a cousin in New Jersey whom you need to hide runaway slaves. Write a letter to the cousin describing who will be coming, what signals they will use to gain entry, and how they can be helped. (You might want to disguise your message in case it gets into the wrong hands.)

3 Struggle for Women's Rights

As You Read

Explore These Questions
- What rights did women lack in the early 1800s?
- What were the goals of the Seneca Falls Convention?
- How did opportunities for women improve in the mid-1800s?

Define
- women's rights movement

Identify
- Sojourner Truth
- Lucretia Mott
- Elizabeth Cady Stanton
- Seneca Falls Convention
- Susan B. Anthony
- Emma Willard
- Mary Lyon
- Elizabeth Blackwell

 SETTING the Scene As you have read, Sarah and Angelina Grimké became powerful speakers against slavery. However, the boldness of their activities shocked many people. Some New England ministers even scolded the sisters in a newspaper. "When [a woman] assumes the place and tone of a man as a public reformer," they wrote, "her character becomes unnatural."

Unmoved by such criticism, Angelina Grimké asked, "What then can woman do for the slave, when she herself is under the feet of man and shamed into silence?" More determined than ever, the Grimkés continued their crusade. Now, however, they had a second topic to lecture about—women's rights.

Seeking Equal Rights

Women had few political or legal rights in the mid-1800s. They could not vote or hold office. When a woman married, her husband became owner of all her property. If a woman worked outside the home, her wages belonged to her husband. A husband also had the right to hit his wife as long as he did not seriously injure her.

Many women, like the Grimkés, had joined the abolitionist movement. As these women worked to end slavery, they became aware that they lacked full social and political rights themselves. Both black and white abolitionists joined the struggle for women's rights.

Truth speaks out

One of the most effective women's rights leaders was born into slavery in New York. Her original name was Isabella Baumfree. After gaining her freedom, she came to believe that God wanted her to crusade against slavery. Vowing to sojourn, or travel, across the land speaking the truth, Baumfree took the name **Sojourner Truth.**

Truth was a spellbinding speaker. Her exact words were rarely written down. However, her powerful message spread by word of mouth. According to one witness, Truth ridiculed the idea that women were inferior to men by nature:

> ❝ I have as much muscle as any man, and can do as much work as any man. I have plowed and reaped and husked and chopped and mowed, and can any man do more than that? ❞

Connections With Science

In the mid-1800s, women wore tightly laced corsets to make the waist as tiny as possible. Doctors warned that these "tightlacers" caused fainting, squeezed the internal organs, and could even crush the rib cage. Instead, reformers supported a looser, trouserlike garment known as bloomers.

Mott and Stanton

Other abolitionists also turned to the cause of women's rights. The two most influential were Lucretia Mott and Elizabeth Cady Stanton.

Lucretia Mott was a Quaker and the mother of five children. A quiet speaker, she won the respect of many listeners with her persuasive logic. Mott also used her organizing skills to set up petition drives across the North.

Elizabeth Cady Stanton was the daughter of a New York judge. As a child, she was an excellent student as well as an athlete. However, her father gave his gifted daughter little encouragement. Stanton later remarked that her "father would have felt a proper pride had I been a man." In addition, clerks in her father's law office used to tease her by reading laws that denied basic rights to women. Such experiences made her a lifelong foe of inequality.

In 1840, Stanton and Mott joined a group of Americans at a World Antislavery Convention in London. However, convention officials refused to let women take an active part in the proceedings. Female delegates were even forced to sit behind a curtain, hidden from view. After returning home, Mott and Stanton took up the cause of women's rights with new energy.

A Historic Meeting

While they were still in London, Mott and Stanton decided to hold a convention to draw attention to the problems women faced. "The men...had [shown] a great need for some education on that question," Stanton later recalled.

Eight years later, in 1848, in Seneca Falls, New York, the meeting finally took place. About 200 women and 40 men attended the **Seneca Falls Convention.**

 iography   **Elizabeth Cady Stanton and Sojourner Truth**

Elizabeth Cady Stanton (left) was born into a well-to-do, middle-class family and raised her own children in comfort. Sojourner Truth (right) was born into slavery and saw at least one of her children sold. Despite their vastly different backgrounds, the two women became allies in the fight for women's rights. ★ **Both Truth and Stanton were abolitionists. How was abolition linked to the movement for women's rights?**

The Spirit of Reform

Reform Movements

Social Reform
- Humane treatment for mentally ill
- Prison reform
- Temperance movement against alcohol
- Improvements in education

Antislavery Movement
- End of slavery in the North
- Establishment of Liberia
- Abolitionist speeches, books, and newspapers
- Underground railroad

Women's Rights Movement
- Seneca Falls Convention
- Schools for women
- New legal rights in some states
- New work opportunities

Graphic Organizer Skills The spirit of reform of the 1800s motivated some people to try to improve American society.

1. **Comprehension** What were two types of social reform addressed by reformers in the mid-1800s?
2. **Critical Thinking** What did the reforms shown in this graphic organizer have in common?

Civics

"Women are created equal"

At the meeting, leaders of the women's rights movement presented a Declaration of Sentiments. Modeled on the Declaration of Independence, it proclaimed, "We hold these truths to be self-evident: that all men and women are created equal."

The women and men at Seneca Falls voted for resolutions that demanded equality for women at work, at school, and in church. Only one resolution met any opposition at the convention. It demanded that women be allowed to vote. Even the bold women at Seneca Falls hesitated to take this step. In the end, the resolution narrowly passed.

A long struggle

The Seneca Falls Convention marked the start of an organized campaign for equal rights, or **women's rights movement.** Other leaders took up the struggle. **Susan B. Anthony** built a close-working partnership with Elizabeth Cady Stanton. While Stanton usually had to stay at home with her seven children, Anthony was free to travel across the country. Anthony was a tireless speaker. Even when audiences heckled her and threw eggs, she always finished her speech.

In the years after 1848, women worked for change in many areas. They won additional legal rights in some states. For example, New York passed laws allowing married women to keep their own property and wages. Still, many men and women opposed the women's rights movement. The struggle for equal rights would last many years.

New Opportunities

In the early 1800s, women from poor families had little hope of learning even to read. Middle-class girls who went to school learned dancing and drawing rather than science or mathematics. After all, people argued, women were expected to care for their families. Why did they need an education?

The women at Seneca Falls believed that education was a key to equality. Elizabeth Cady Stanton said:

66 The girl must be allowed to romp and play, climb, skate, and swim. Her clothes must be more like those of the boy—strong, loose-fitting garments, thick boots.... Like the boy, she must be taught to look forward to a life of self-dependence and to prepare herself early for some trade profession. 99

The American Medical Women's Association gives this annual medal in honor of Elizabeth Blackwell.

Schools for women

Reformers worked to improve education for women. **Emma Willard** opened a high school for girls in Troy, New York. Here, young women studied "men's" subjects, such as mathematics and physics.

Mary Lyon opened Mount Holyoke Female Seminary in Massachusetts in 1837. She did not call the school a college because many people thought it was wrong for women to attend college. In fact, Mount Holyoke was the first women's college in the United States.

New careers

At about this time, a few men's colleges began to admit women. As their education improved, women found jobs teaching, especially in grade schools.

A few women entered fields such as medicine. **Elizabeth Blackwell** attended medical school at Geneva College in New York. To the surprise of school officials, she graduated first in her class. Women had provided medical care since colonial times, but Blackwell was the first woman in the United States to earn a medical degree. She later set up the nation's first medical school for women.

Women made their mark in other fields as well. Maria Mitchell became a noted astronomer. In the 1850s, Antoinette Blackwell was the first American woman to be ordained as a minister. She also campaigned for abolitionism, temperance, and women's right to vote.

★ Section 3 Review ★

Recall

1. **Identify** (a) Sojourner Truth, (b) Lucretia Mott, (c) Elizabeth Cady Stanton, (d) Seneca Falls Convention, (e) Susan B. Anthony, (f) Emma Willard, (g) Mary Lyon, (h) Elizabeth Blackwell.
2. **Define** women's rights movement.

Comprehension

3. Describe three ways that laws discriminated against women in the early 1800s.
4. What resolutions did the delegates at Seneca Falls make?

5. (a) What type of education did most women receive in the mid-1800s? (b) How did reformers change women's education?

Critical Thinking and Writing

6. **Understanding Causes and Effects** How was the women's rights movement a long-term effect of the antislavery movement?
7. **Predicting Consequences** How do you think the growth of educational opportunities affected the future of the women's rights movement?

★ ★

Activity **Designing a T-shirt** It is four weeks before the Seneca Falls Convention. You have been asked to create a T-shirt for all the attendees. Draw a clever and attractive design that expresses the feelings and demands of the women's rights movement.

American Literature and Art

As You Read

Explore These Questions
- What themes did American novelists and poets explore?
- What ideas did Emerson and Thoreau express?
- How did American painters create their own styles?

Define
- transcendentalism

Identify
- Washington Irving
- James Fenimore Cooper
- Ralph Waldo Emerson
- Henry David Thoreau
- Walt Whitman
- Emily Dickinson
- Hudson River School

 SETTING the Scene In 1820, a Scottish minister named Sydney Smith blasted what he saw as a lack of culture in the United States:

> ❝ In the four quarters of the globe, who reads an American book? Or goes to an American play? Or looks at an American picture or statue? What does the world yet owe to Americans? ❞

Even as Smith wrote these words, American writers and artists were breaking free of European traditions. These men and women created a voice and a vision that were truly American.

American Storytellers

Until the early 1800s, most American writers depended on Europe for their ideas and inspiration. In the 1820s, however, a new crop of writers began to write stories with American themes.

Two early writers

One of the most popular American writers was **Washington Irving,** a New Yorker. Irving first became known for *The Sketch Book,* a collection of tales published in 1820. Two of the best-loved tales are "Rip Van Winkle" and "The Legend of Sleepy Hollow." (See page 318.)

Irving's stories gave Americans a sense of the richness of their past. His appeal went beyond the United States, however. Irving was the first American writer to also enjoy fame in Europe.

James Fenimore Cooper also published novels set in the past. In *The Deerslayer* and *The Last of the Mohicans,* Cooper created the character Natty Bumppo, a heroic model of a strong, silent, solitary frontiersman. The novels also gave an idealized view of relations between whites and Native Americans on the frontier. The stories were so exciting, however, that few readers cared if they were true to life.

Later writers

Nathaniel Hawthorne drew on the history of Puritan New England to create his novels and short stories. Hawthorne was fascinated by Puritan notions of sin and guilt. His best-known novel, *The Scarlet Letter,* was published in 1850.

In 1851, Herman Melville published *Moby-Dick.* The novel tells the story of Ahab, the crazed captain of a whaling ship. Ahab vows revenge against the white whale that years earlier bit off his leg. *Moby-Dick* had only limited success when it was first published. Today, however, critics rank it among the finest American novels.

Edgar Allan Poe became famous for his many tales of horror. His short story "The Tell-Tale Heart" tells of a murderer, driven mad by guilt, who imagines he can hear his victim's heartbeat. Poe is also called the "father of the detective story" for his mystery stories, such as "The Murders in the Rue Morgue."

William Wells Brown published *Clotel,* a novel about slave life, in 1853. Brown was the first African American to earn his living as a writer.

Women writers

Many best-selling novels of the period were written by women. Some novels told about young women who gained wealth and happiness through honesty and self-sacrifice. Others showed the hardships faced by widows and orphans.

Few of these novels are read today. However, writers like Catherine Sedgwick and Fanny Fern earned far more than Hawthorne or Melville. Hawthorne complained about the success of a "mob of scribbling women."

The "Inner Light"

In New England, a small group of writers and thinkers, known as Transcendentalists,

emerged. **Transcendentalism** was the belief that the most important truths in life transcended, or went beyond, human reason. Transcendentalists stressed emotions over reason. They believed that each individual had control over his or her life. This belief influenced many transcendentalists to support social reform.

One Transcendentalist, Margaret Fuller, wrote *Woman in the Nineteenth Century.* The book strongly influenced the movement for women's rights.

Emerson

The leading Transcendentalist was **Ralph Waldo Emerson.** Emerson was the most popular essayist and lecturer of his day. Audiences flocked to hear him talk on subjects such as self-reliance and character. Emerson believed that the human spirit was reflected in nature. Civilization might provide material wealth, he said, but nature held higher values that came from God.

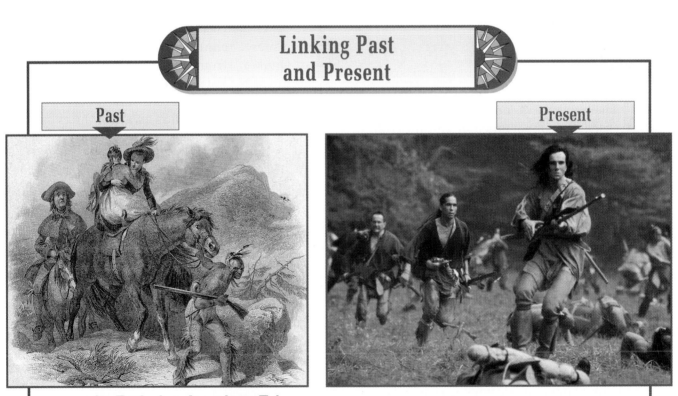

Linking Past and Present

Past

Present

An Enduring American Tale

In 1826, James Fenimore Cooper's frontier tale The Last of the Mohicans *(left) was a bestseller. In 1992, a film version of Cooper's novel (right) was one of the year's most popular movies. The works of other early American writers, such as Hawthorne and Melville, have also been turned into movies or television miniseries.* ★ **Why do you think modern audiences would still enjoy a movie version of *The Last of the Mohicans?***

Thomas Cole wrote that "it is of the greatest importance for a painter always to have his mind upon Nature." In paintings like Kaaterskill Falls, *left, Cole captured the beauty and power of New York's Hudson River valley.*
★ **What kinds of emotion might a painting like this stir?**

In his essays and lectures, Emerson stressed the importance of the individual. Each person, Emerson said, has an "inner light." He urged people to use this inner light to guide their lives and improve society.

Thoreau

Henry David Thoreau (thuh ROW), Emerson's friend and neighbor, believed that the growth of industry and the rise of cities were ruining the nation. He urged people to live as simply as possible. In *Walden,* his best-known work, Thoreau describes spending a year alone in a cabin on Walden Pond in Massachusetts.

Like Emerson, Thoreau believed that each individual must decide what is right or wrong. He wrote:

> 66 If a man does not keep pace with his companions, perhaps it is because he hears a different drummer. Let him step to the music he hears. 99

Thoreau's "different drummer" told him that slavery was wrong. He was a fierce abolitionist and served as a conductor on the underground railroad.

Poetic Voices

Henry Wadsworth Longfellow was the favorite poet of Americans in the mid-1800s. Longfellow based many poems on events from the past. "Paul Revere's Ride" honored the Revolutionary War hero. "The Song of Hiawatha" idealized Native American life.

Other poets spoke out on social issues. John Greenleaf Whittier, a Quaker from Massachusetts, and Frances Watkins Harper, an African American woman from Maryland, used their pens to make readers aware of the evils of slavery.

Walt Whitman published only one book of poems, *Leaves of Grass.* However, he added to it over a period of 27 years. Whitman had great faith in the common people. His poetry celebrated democracy and the diverse people who made the nation great. He wrote proudly of being part of a "Nation of many nations":

Connections With Civics

In his essay *Civil Disobedience,* Thoreau argued that people had a right to disobey unjust laws if their consciences demanded it. He once went to jail for refusing to pay taxes to support the Mexican War, which he felt promoted slavery. Thoreau's ideas on nonviolent protest later influenced Mohandas Gandhi and Martin Luther King, Jr.

> 66 A Southerner soon as a
>   Northerner...
> At home on the hills of Vermont or
>   in the woods of Maine, or the
>   Texan ranch,
> Comrade of Californians, comrade of
>   free North-Westerners....
> Of every hue and caste am I, of
>   every rank and religion,
> A farmer, mechanic, artist, gentle-
>   man, sailor, quaker,
> Prisoner, fancy-man, rowdy, lawyer,
>   physician, priest. 99

Today, critics consider **Emily Dickinson** one of the nation's greatest poets. Yet, only seven of her more than 1,700 poems were published in her lifetime. A shy woman who rarely left her home, Dickinson called her poetry "my letter to the world / That never wrote to me."

American Painters

Before the 1800s, most American painters studied in Europe. In 1772, Benjamin West of Philadelphia was appointed historical painter to King George III. Many American painters journeyed to London to study with West, including Charles Willson Peale and Gilbert Stuart. Both Peale and Stuart painted famous portraits of George Washington.

By the mid-1800s, American artists began to develop their own style. The first group to do so became known as the **Hudson River School** because they painted landscapes of New York's Hudson River region. Two of the best-known painters of the Hudson River School were Thomas Cole and Asher B. Durand. African American artist Robert S. Duncanson also reflected the style of the Hudson River School.

Other American artists painted scenes of hardworking country people. George Caleb Bingham was inspired by his native Missouri. His paintings show frontier life along the rivers that feed the great Mississippi.

Several painters tried to capture the culture of Native Americans on canvas. George Catlin and Alfred Jacob Miller traveled to the Far West. Their paintings record the daily life of Indians on the Great Plains and in the Rockies.

★ Section 4 Review ★

Recall

1. **Identify** (a) Washington Irving, (b) James Fenimore Cooper, (c) Ralph Waldo Emerson, (d) Henry David Thoreau, (e) Walt Whitman, (f) Emily Dickinson, (g) Hudson River School.
2. **Define** Transcendentalism.

Comprehension

3. Describe the subjects explored by each of the following writers: (a) Nathaniel Hawthorne, (b) Edgar Allan Poe, (c) William Wells Brown, (d) Henry Wadsworth Longfellow.
4. What did Emerson and Thoreau think about the importance of the individual?

5. (a) Where did early American painters get their inspiration? (b) How did this situation change in the mid-1800s?

Critical Thinking and Writing

6. **Drawing Conclusions** Why do you think writers and artists did not develop a unique American style until the mid-1800s?
7. **Linking Past and Present** (a) What do you think Walt Whitman meant when he called the United States a "Nation of many nations"? (b) Do you think these words can still be used to describe the nation today? Explain.

Activity Creating a Chart Henry David Thoreau is returning to look at today's society. He will spend a week in your community. Make a two-column chart. In the left column, list things, places, and activities he will probably criticize. On the right, list things, places, and activities he will appreciate.

Review and Activities

★ Sum It Up ★

Section 1   The Spirit of Reform
▶ Political and religious ideals encouraged a spirit of reform.
▶ Reformers worked for many goals, including temperance, improved education, and better treatment for the mentally ill.

Section 2   The Fight Against Slavery
▶ Abolitionists fought to end slavery in many ways, including publishing newspapers, lecturing, and helping runaway slaves escape on the underground railroad.
▶ Slavery was defended by northerners who depended on cotton for their livelihood and by Southerners who felt their economy depended on slavery.

Section 3   Struggle for Women's Rights
▶ Many women joined the struggle for women's rights after fighting for abolition of slavery.
▶ The Seneca Falls Convention in 1848 marked the beginning of an organized women's rights movement.

Section 4   American Literature and Art
▶ In the 1820s, American writers began to explore American themes in their stories and poems.
▶ American artists gradually broke away from European models and developed their own styles.

CD-ROM Review For additional review of the major ideas of Chapter 15, see *Guide to the Essentials of American History* or *Interactive Student Tutorial CD-ROM,* which contains interactive review activities, graphic organizers, and practice tests.

☐ Reviewing the Chapter

Define These Terms
Match each term with the correct definition.

Column 1
1. revival
2. temperance movement
3. abolitionist
4. underground railroad
5. penal system

Column 2
a. system of prisons
b. network of people who helped runaway slaves reach freedom
c. campaign against drinking
d. person who wanted to end slavery
e. huge outdoor religious meeting

Explore the Main Ideas
1. What were two goals of the Second Great Awakening?
2. What goals did Dorothea Dix pursue?
3. Why was Harriet Tubman called the "Black Moses"?
4. Why did supporters of the women's rights movement seek better education for women?
5. Name two writers in the 1800s who wrote about American experiences.

☐ Graph Activity

Look at the graph below and answer the following questions:
1. About how many students were enrolled in American schools in 1840? In 1860? **2.** How much did school enrollment increase between 1850 and 1870? **Critical Thinking** Based on what you have read, why did school enrollment increase steadily in the mid-1800s?

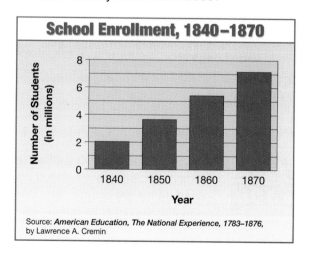

School Enrollment, 1840–1870

Source: *American Education, The National Experience, 1783–1876,* by Lawrence A. Cremin

📇 Critical Thinking and Writing

1. **Linking Past and Present** **(a)** How did reformers in the 1800s try to gain public support? **(b)** What methods do people use to win public support today?

2. **Analyzing Ideas** In his *Appeal to the Colored Citizens of the World,* David Walker wrote that "all men are created equal; that they are endowed by their Creator with certain inalienable rights." **(a)** From which document did Walker borrow this idea? **(b)** What point do you think he was making by including these words?

3. **Ranking** In the mid-1800s, women like Sojourner Truth, the Grimké sisters, Lucretia Mott, and Elizabeth Cady Stanton organized to fight for abolition and women's rights. Make a list of the demands of these women. Then rank the demands from most important to least important. Give reasons for this ranking.

4. **Exploring Unit Themes** **Expansion** How do you think westward expansion increased concerns about slavery?

📇 Using Primary Sources

Frederick Douglass denounced the slave trade in the South:

> ❝ Fellow citizens, this murderous traffic is, today, in active operation in this boasted republic. I see the bleeding footsteps; I hear the doleful wail of [chained] humanity on the way to the slave markets where the victims are to be sold like horse, sheep, and swine.... My soul sickens at the sight. ❞

Source: Frederick Douglass, speech to New York abolitionist society, 1852.

Recognizing Points of View **(a)** What words did Douglass use to stir up anger against the slave trade? **(b)** What did he mean when he called the United States a "boasted republic"? **(c)** How did Douglass's background make him an effective speaker on the subject of slavery?

ACTIVITY BANK

▶ Interdisciplinary Activity

Exploring the Arts Do research on one of the American painters discussed in this chapter. Then, prepare a guidebook for a museum exhibit of that painter's work. Include a brief biographical note and descriptions of two or three paintings.

▶ Career Skills Activity

Musicians Write and perform a marching song to be used at one of the following events: a temperance rally; an abolitionist meeting; the Seneca Falls Convention. You may work alone or with a group.

▶ Citizenship Activity

Creating a Campaign Today, as in the past, communities are concerned with making sure all students get a good education. Plan a campaign designed to encourage students to stay in school. Your campaign may include posters, speeches, or other public events.

➤ Internet Activity

Use the Internet to find information on any five of the following women: Antoinette Blackwell, Emily Blackwell, Amelia Bloomer, Myra Bradwell, Margaret Fuller, Matilda Joslyn Gage, Maria Mitchell, Lucy Stone. Write a one-sentence summary of the contribution each woman made to the women's rights movement.

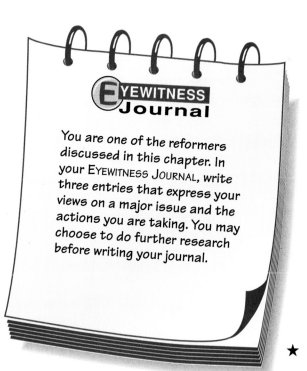

EYEWITNESS Journal

You are one of the reformers discussed in this chapter. In your EYEWITNESS JOURNAL, write three entries that express your views on a major issue and the actions you are taking. You may choose to do further research before writing your journal.

Nightjohn

by Gary Paulsen

Introduction

Nightjohn, set in the 1850s, is told by Sarny, a 12-year-old slave on a southern plantation. When John comes to live there, Sarny's life is changed forever. John had escaped to the North. Yet, he came back— to teach others to read. As this excerpt begins, Sarny is talking to John late at night in the slave quarters. She is deciding whether to let John teach her some letters.

I knew about reading. It was something that the people in the white house did from paper. They could read words on paper. But we weren't allowed to be reading. We weren't allowed to understand or read nothing but once I saw some funny lines on the side of a feed sack. It said:

100 lbs.

I wrote them down in the dirt with a stick and mammy gave me a smack on the back of the head that like to drove me into the ground.

"Don't you take to that, take to writing," she said.

"I wasn't doing it. I was just copying something I saw on a feed sack."

"Don't. They catch you doing that and they'll think you're learning to read. You learn to read and they'll whip you.... Or cut your thumb off. Stay away from writing and reading."

So I did. But I remembered how it had looked, the drawings on the sack and in the dirt, and it still puzzled me....

[Sarny then speaks to John.]
"You saying you can read?"
He nodded.
"I give you something to read, you can read it? Just like that?"
"I can."...
"Way it works," he said, "is you got to learn all the letters and numbers before you can learn to read. You got to learn the alphabet."
"Alphabet?"
He nodded. "There be lots of letters, and each one means something different. You got to learn each one."
...Then he made a drawing with his thumb.

A

"Tonight we just do *A*." He sat back on his heels and pointed. "There it be."...
"What does it mean?"
"It means *A*—just like I said. It's the first letter in the alphabet. And when you see it you make a sound like this: *ayyy,* or *ahhhh.*"

Learning to Read—In Secret

This illustration from the novel Nightjohn *shows John teaching Sarny to read. By the mid-1800s, many southern states had made it illegal for enslaved African Americans to learn to read and write. Yet many slaves risked severe punishment to learn anyway.*

★ **Why do you think enslaved African Americans valued education so highly?**

"That's reading? To make that sound?" He nodded. "When you see that letter on paper or a sack or in the dirt you make one of those sounds. That's reading."

"Well, that ain't hard at all."

He laughed. That same low roll. Made me think of thunder long ways off, moving in a summer sky. "There's more to it. Other letters. But that's it."

"Why they be cutting our thumbs off if we learn to read—if that's all it is?"

"'Cause to know things, for us to know things, is bad for them. We get to wanting and when we get to wanting it's bad for them. They thinks we want what they got.... That's why they don't want us reading." He sighed. "I got to rest now. They run me ten miles in a day and worked me into the ground. I need some sleep."

He moved back to the corner and settled down and I curled up to mammy in amongst the young ones again.

A, I thought, *ayyy, ahhhh.* There it is. I be reading.

"Hey there in the corner," I whispered.

"What?"

"What's your name?"

"I be John."

"I be Sarny."

"Go to sleep, Sarny."

But I didn't. I snuggled into mammy and pulled a couple of the young ones in for heat and kept my eyes open so I wouldn't sleep and thought:

A.

Analyzing Literature

1. Why did Sarny's mother tell her to stay away from reading and writing?

2. According to John, why did the slave owners want to keep the slaves from learning to read and write?

3. **Critical Thinking Making Inferences** Based on this excerpt, what are some of John's qualities? How can you tell?

Viewing UNIT THEMES ── **War Divides the Nation**

In 1861, conflict between the North and the South erupted into war. Winslow Homer, one of the country's greatest artists, painted Prisoners From the Front. *It shows a northern officer (right) inspecting captured southern troops (left). The opposing soldiers look on each other with pride and hostility.* ★ **Based on what you have learned in earlier units, identify two differences between the North and South.**

Unit Theme **Sectionalism**

Sectionalism is loyalty to a state or region rather than to the country as a whole. From colonial days, Americans felt strong loyalties to the regions where they lived. By the mid-1800s, several issues increased sectional differences between the North and South. The most dramatic of these issues was slavery. Extreme sectionalism eventually led to war.

How did people of the time feel about sectional divisions? They can tell you in their own words.

★ ★

VIEWPOINTS ON SECTIONAL DIVISIONS

❝ We have always been taught to look upon the people of New England as a selfish, cunning set of fellows. ❞

Davy Crockett, Tennessee member of Congress (1835)

❝ I have heard something said about allegiance to the South. I know no South, no North, no East, no West, to which I owe any allegiance…. The Union, sir, is my country. ❞

Henry Clay, senator from Kentucky (1848)

❝ Union! I can more easily conceive of the Lion and Lambs lying down together, than of a union of the North and South. ❞

Sarah Chase, Massachusetts teacher in the South (1866)

★ ★

Activity **Writing to Learn** Today, the United States is often divided into these geographic regions: the Northeast; the Midatlantic; the Southeast; the Midwest; the Rocky Mountain states; the Southwest; the Pacific Coast states. List three features, other than location, that make the region you live in special. Then, write a paragraph explaining whether you feel more loyal to your region or to the United States as a whole.

Chapter 16

A Dividing Nation

1820–1861

Between 1820 and 1861, the nation grew increasingly divided as it struggled to answer difficult questions concerning slavery. Should slavery be allowed to spread to the West? Should slavery be abolished throughout the nation? For a time, northerners and southerners settled their differences through compromises. Gradually, however, violence became more and more common. In 1860, voters elected Abraham Lincoln, a member of the antislavery Republican party, to be the next President of the United States. In response, southern states withdrew from the Union. The North and the South then prepared for war.

Why Study History?

Many consider Abraham Lincoln to be one of the greatest leaders in American history. Some call him an American hero. Frequently, therefore, he is held as a role model for others to imitate. Could Lincoln be a role model for you? To answer this question, see this chapter's *Why Study History?* feature, "Heroes of the Past Can Be Models for Today."

American Events

1820
Missouri Compromise allows slavery in some western territories

1850
Fugitive Slave Law requires citizens to help catch runaway slaves

1852
Uncle Tom's Cabin increases support for abolitionism

1820 | 1848 | 1850 | 1852 | 1854

World Events

 1833 World Event
Slavery is abolished in British empire

 1850 World Event
Taiping Rebellion begins civil war in China

Viewing HISTORY | **From Slavery to Freedom**

In the painting On to Liberty *by Theodor Kaufmann, fugitive slave families try to reach the North and freedom. In the 1850s, many northerners protested against a law requiring all citizens to help return runaway slaves. Disagreement over slavery heightened the growing division between North and South.* ★ **How do you think enslaved African Americans felt as they tried to escape to the North?**

●**1854**
Kansas-Nebraska Act
leads to violence

●**1857**
Supreme Court
says Congress
cannot outlaw
slavery in territories

1861 ●
Abraham Lincoln
becomes
President

| 1854 | 1856 | 1858 | 1860 | 1862 |

▲
 1857 World Event
New constitution in
Mexico prohibits slavery

The Slavery Issue in the West

As You Read

Explore These Questions
- What were the various views on slavery in the West?
- What was the goal of the Free Soil party?
- What were the results of the Compromise of 1850?

Define
- sectionalism
- popular sovereignty
- secede
- fugitive
- civil war

Identify
- Missouri Compromise
- Wilmot Proviso
- Free Soil party
- Zachary Taylor
- Stephen Douglas
- Compromise of 1850
- Fugitive Slave Law of 1850

 SETTING the Scene In 1820, Thomas Jefferson was in his seventies. The former President had vowed "never to write, talk, or even think of politics." Still, he voiced alarm when he heard about a fierce debate going on in Congress:

❝ In the gloomiest moment of the revolutionary war, I never had any [fears] equal to what I feel from this source.... We have a wolf by the ears, and we can neither hold him nor safely let him go. ❞

Jefferson feared that the "wolf," or the issue of slavery, would tear the North and South apart. He was correct. As settlers continued to move west, tension over slavery worsened. Again and again, Congress faced an agonizing decision. Should it prohibit slavery in the territories and later admit them to the Union as free states? Or should it permit slavery in the territories and later admit them as slave states?

The Missouri Compromise

When Missouri asked to join the Union as a slave state, a crisis erupted. The admission of Missouri would upset the balance of power in the Senate. In 1819, there were 11 free states and 11 slave states. (See the graph on page 427.) Missouri's admission would give the South a majority in the Senate. Determined not to lose power, northerners opposed letting Missouri enter as a slave state.

The argument over Missouri lasted many months. Finally, Senator Henry Clay proposed a compromise. During the long debate, Maine had also applied for statehood. Clay suggested admitting Missouri as a slave state and Maine as a free state. His plan, called the **Missouri Compromise,** kept the number of slave and free states equal.

As part of the Missouri Compromise, Congress drew an imaginary line across the southern border of Missouri at latitude 36° 30′ N. Slavery was permitted in the part of the Louisiana Purchase south of that line. It was banned north of the line. The only exception to this was Missouri. (See the map on page 431.)

New Western Lands

The Missouri Compromise applied only to the Louisiana Purchase. In 1848, the Mexican War added a vast stretch of western land to the United States. (See the map on page 363.) Once again, the question of slavery in the territories arose.

The Wilmot Proviso

Many northerners feared that the South would extend slavery into the West. David Wilmot, a Congressman from Pennsylvania, called for a law to ban slavery in any lands won from Mexico. Southern leaders angrily opposed the **Wilmot Proviso.** They said that Congress had no right to ban slavery in the western territories.

United States

Russia

Forced Labor

In the painting at left, enslaved African Americans await the results of a slave auction. At the same time in Russia, millions of workers were serfs. Serfs were bound to the land and had to work for wealthy nobles. One Russian observer sadly reported "of men and women torn from their families and their villages, and sold...of children taken from their parents and sold to cruel masters." ★ **How was slavery in the United States similar to serfdom in Russia?**

In 1846, the House passed the Wilmot Proviso, but the Senate defeated it. As a result, Americans continued to argue about slavery in the West even while their army fought in Mexico.

Opposing views

The Mexican War strengthened feelings of sectionalism in the North and South. Sectionalism is loyalty to a state or section, rather than to the country as a whole. Many southerners were united by their support for slavery. They saw the North as a growing threat to their way of life. Many northerners saw the South as a foreign country, where American rights and liberties did not exist.

As the debate over slavery heated up, people found it hard not to take sides. Northern abolitionists demanded that slavery be banned throughout the country. They insisted that slavery was morally wrong. By the late 1840s, many northerners agreed.

Southern slaveholders thought that slavery should be allowed in any territory. They also demanded that slaves who escaped to the North be returned to them. Even white southerners who did not own slaves generally agreed with these ideas.

Between these two extreme views were more moderate positions. Some moderates argued that the Missouri Compromise line should be extended across the Mexican Cession to the Pacific Ocean. Any new state north of the line would be a free state. Any new state south of the line could allow slavery.

$ Connections With Economics

In response to the Wilmot Proviso, some southern states proposed cutting off all trade with the North. Another economic threat was that southerners would stop payments on debts owed to northern banks and businesses.

Other moderates supported the idea of **popular sovereignty,** or control by the people. In other words, voters in a new territory would decide for themselves whether or not to allow slavery in the territory. Slaves, of course, could not vote.

The Free Soil Party

The debate over slavery led to the birth of a new political party. By 1848, many northerners in both the Democratic party and the Whig party opposed the spread of slavery. However, the leaders of both parties refused to take a stand on the question. They did not want to give up their chance of winning votes in the South. Some also feared that the slavery issue would split the nation.

In 1848, antislavery members of both parties met in Buffalo, New York. There, they founded the **Free Soil party.** Their slogan was "Free soil, free speech, free labor, and free men." The main goal of the Free Soil party was to keep slavery out of the western territories. Only a few Free Soilers were abolitionists who wanted to end slavery in the South.

In the 1848 presidential campaign, Free Soilers named former President Martin Van Buren as their candidate. Democrats chose Lewis Cass of Michigan. The Whigs selected **Zachary Taylor,** a hero of the Mexican War.

For the first time, slavery was an important election issue. Van Buren called for a ban on slavery in the Mexican Cession. Cass supported popular sovereignty. Because Taylor was a slave owner from Louisiana, many southern voters assumed that he supported slavery.

Zachary Taylor won the election, but Van Buren took 10 percent of the popular vote. Thirteen other Free Soil candidates won seats in Congress. The success of the new Free Soil party showed that slavery had become a national issue.

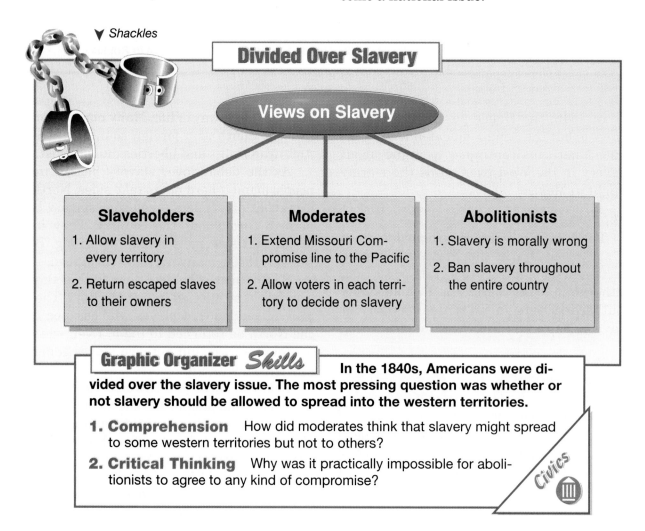

▼ *Shackles*

Divided Over Slavery

Views on Slavery

Slaveholders
1. Allow slavery in every territory
2. Return escaped slaves to their owners

Moderates
1. Extend Missouri Compromise line to the Pacific
2. Allow voters in each territory to decide on slavery

Abolitionists
1. Slavery is morally wrong
2. Ban slavery throughout the entire country

Graphic Organizer *Skills*

In the 1840s, Americans were divided over the slavery issue. The most pressing question was whether or not slavery should be allowed to spread into the western territories.

1. Comprehension   How did moderates think that slavery might spread to some western territories but not to others?

2. Critical Thinking   Why was it practically impossible for abolitionists to agree to any kind of compromise?

Civics

Need for a New Compromise

For a time after the Missouri Compromise, both slave and free states entered the Union peacefully. However, when California requested admission to the Union as a free state in 1850, the balance of power in the Senate was once again threatened. (See the graph to the right.)

California's impact

In 1849, there were 15 slave states and 15 free states in the nation. If California entered the union as a free state, the balance of power would be broken. Furthermore, it seemed quite possible that Oregon, Utah, and New Mexico might also join the Union as free states.

Many Southerners feared that the South would be hopelessly outvoted in the Senate. Some even suggested that southern states might want to **secede,** or remove themselves, from the United States. Northern congressmen, meanwhile, argued that California should enter the Union as a free state because most of the territory lay north of the Missouri Compromise line.

As Congress tried to reach a new compromise, tempers raged. One frightening incident involved Senators Thomas Hart Benton of Missouri and Henry Foote of Mississippi. Benton supported California's entry as a free state even though he himself was a slave owner. He denounced Foote for opposing California's admission. In response, Foote rose angrily from his seat and aimed a pistol at Benton. As other senators watched in horror, Benton roared, "Let him fire. Stand out of the way and let the assassin fire!"

No blood was shed in the Senate that day. However, it was clear that the nation faced a crisis. Many in Congress looked to Senator Henry Clay for a solution.

Clay vs. Calhoun

Clay had won the nickname "the Great Compromiser" for working out the Missouri Compromise. Now, nearly 30 years later, the 73-year-old Clay was frail and ill. Still, he pleaded for the North and South to reach an agreement. If they failed to do so, Clay warned, the nation could break apart.

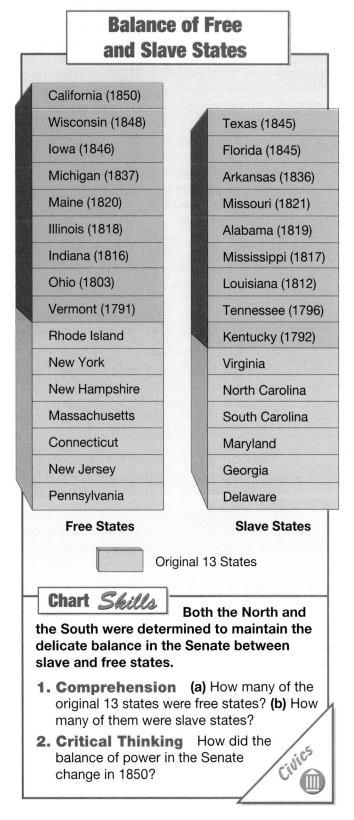

Balance of Free and Slave States

Free States	Slave States
California (1850)	
Wisconsin (1848)	Texas (1845)
Iowa (1846)	Florida (1845)
Michigan (1837)	Arkansas (1836)
Maine (1820)	Missouri (1821)
Illinois (1818)	Alabama (1819)
Indiana (1816)	Mississippi (1817)
Ohio (1803)	Louisiana (1812)
Vermont (1791)	Tennessee (1796)
Rhode Island	Kentucky (1792)
New York	Virginia
New Hampshire	North Carolina
Massachusetts	South Carolina
Connecticut	Maryland
New Jersey	Georgia
Pennsylvania	Delaware

☐ Original 13 States

Chart Skills   Both the North and the South were determined to maintain the delicate balance in the Senate between slave and free states.

1. **Comprehension** (a) How many of the original 13 states were free states? (b) How many of them were slave states?

2. **Critical Thinking** How did the balance of power in the Senate change in 1850?

Civics

Senator John C. Calhoun of South Carolina prepared the South's reply to Clay. Calhoun was dying of tuberculosis and could not speak loudly enough to address the Senate. He stared defiantly at his northern foes while Senator James Mason of Virginia read his speech.

Viewing HISTORY

Protest!

In 1854, a Boston court ordered that fugitive slaves Anthony Burns and Thomas Sims be returned to their owners in the South. Public outcry against the decision was so great that United States marines and artillery were sent into Boston. Angry protesters lined the streets as the two were led to the ship that would return them to slavery.

★ **Do you think the court made the right decision in this case? Explain.**

Calhoun refused to compromise. He insisted that slavery be allowed in the western territories. Calhoun also demanded that **fugitive,** or runaway, slaves be returned to their owners in the South. He wanted northerners to admit that southern slaveholders had the right to reclaim their "property."

If the North would not agree to the South's demands, Calhoun told the Senate, "let the states . . . agree to part in peace. If you are unwilling that we should part in peace, tell us so, and we shall know what to do." Everyone knew what Calhoun meant. If an agreement could not be reached, the South would secede from the Union.

Webster calls for unity

Daniel Webster of Massachusetts spoke next. He supported Clay's plea to save the Union. Webster stated his position clearly:

66 I speak today not as a Massachusetts man, nor as a northern man, but as an American. . . . I speak today for the preservation of the Union. . . . There can be no such thing as a peaceable secession. Peaceable secession is an utter impossibility. 99

Webster feared that the states could not separate without a **civil war.** A civil war is a war between people of the same country.

Like many northerners, Webster viewed slavery as evil. Disunion, however, he believed was worse. To save the Union, Webster was willing to compromise with the South. He would support its demand that northerners be required to return fugitive slaves.

Compromise of 1850

In 1850, as the debate raged, Calhoun died. His last words reportedly were "The South! The South! God knows what will become of her!" President Taylor also died in 1850. The new President was Millard Fillmore. Unlike Taylor, he supported Clay's compromise plan. An agreement finally seemed possible.

Henry Clay gave more than 70 speeches in favor of a compromise. At last, however, he became too sick to continue. **Stephen Douglas,** an energetic senator from Illinois, took up the fight for him. Douglas tirelessly guided each part of Clay's plan, called the **Compromise of 1850,** through Congress.

The Compromise of 1850 had five parts. First, it allowed California to enter the Union as a free state. Second, it divided the rest of the Mexican Cession into the territories of New Mexico and Utah. Voters in each would decide the slavery question according to popular sovereignty. Third, it ended the slave trade in Washington, D.C., the nation's capital. Congress, however, declared that it had no power to ban slave trade between slave states. Fourth, it included a strict fugitive slave law. Fifth, it settled a border dispute between Texas and New Mexico.

Fugitive Slave Law of 1850

Most northerners had ignored the Fugitive Slave Law of 1793. As a result, fugitive slaves often lived as free citizens in northern cities. The **Fugitive Slave Law of 1850** was harder to ignore. It required all citizens to help catch runaway slaves. People who let fugitives escape could be fined $1,000 and jailed for six months.

The new law also set up special courts to handle the cases of runaways. Judges received $10 for sending an accused runaway to the South. They received only $5 for setting someone free. Lured by the extra money, some judges sent African Americans to the South whether or not they were runaways.

The Fugitive Slave Law enraged antislavery northerners. By forcing them to catch runaways, the law made northerners feel they were part of the slave system. In several northern cities, crowds tried to rescue fugitive slaves from their captors.

Martin R. Delany, an African American newspaper editor, spoke for many northerners, black and white:

66 My house is my castle. . . . If any man approaches that house in search of a slave—I care not who he may be, whether constable or sheriff, magistrate or even judge of the Supreme Court . . . if he crosses the threshold of my door, and I do not lay him a lifeless corpse at my feet, I hope the grave may refuse my body a resting place. 99

The North and South had reached a compromise. Still, tensions remained because neither side got everything that it wanted. The new Fugitive Slave Law was especially hard for northerners to accept. Each time the law was enforced, it convinced more northerners that slavery was evil.

★ Section 1 Review ★

Recall

1. **Locate** (a) Missouri, (b) Maine, (c) Missouri Compromise Line, (d) California, (e) New Mexico Territory, (f) Utah Territory.
2. **Identify** (a) Missouri Compromise, (b) Wilmot Proviso, (c) Free Soil party, (d) Zachary Taylor, (e) Stephen Douglas, (f) Compromise of 1850, (g) Fugitive Slave Law of 1850.
3. **Define** (a) sectionalism, (b) popular sovereignty, (c) secede, (d) fugitive, (e) civil war.

Comprehension

4. Describe three different views on the issue of slavery in the West.

5. Why did some people leave the Whig and Democratic parties and create the Free Soil party?
6. Explain the five parts of the Compromise of 1850.

Critical Thinking and Writing

7. **Analyzing Ideas** Why might the goals of the Free Soil party have pleased some northerners but not others?
8. **Analyzing Visual Evidence** Based on your understanding of the painting on page 428, how did the Compromise of 1850 create new conflict over the slavery issue?

Activity **Making a Decision** You are a northerner of the 1850s. There is a knock at your door. It's a fugitive slave! Will you help the runaway or will you turn the person in to the authorities? Write a brief statement explaining the reasons for your decision.

The Crisis Turns Violent

As You Read

Explore These Questions
- How did *Uncle Tom's Cabin* affect attitudes toward slavery?
- Why did a civil war break out in Kansas?
- How did the Dred Scott decision divide the nation?

Define
- repeal
- guerrilla warfare
- lawsuit

Identify
- Harriet Beecher Stowe
- *Uncle Tom's Cabin*
- Kansas-Nebraska Act
- Franklin Pierce
- Border Ruffians
- John Brown
- Bleeding Kansas
- Charles Sumner
- Dred Scott decision

 SETTING the Scene In the mid-1850s, proslavery and antislavery forces battled for control of the territory of Kansas. An observer described election day in one Kansas district in 1855:

66 On the morning of the election, before the polls were opened, some 300 or 400 Missourians and others were collected in the yard...where the election was to be held, armed with bowie-knives, revolvers, and clubs. They said they came to vote, and whip the...Yankees, and would vote without being sworn. Some said they came to have a fight, and wanted one. 99

Hearing of events in Kansas, Abraham Lincoln, then a young lawyer in Illinois, predicted that "the contest will come to blows, and bloodshed." Once again, the issue of slavery in the territories divided the nation.

An Antislavery Bestseller

An event in 1852 added to the growing antislavery mood of the North. That year, **Harriet Beecher Stowe** published a novel called ***Uncle Tom's Cabin.*** Stowe wrote the novel to show the evils of slavery and the injustice of the Fugitive Slave Law. She had originally published the story as a serial in an abolitionist newspaper.

A powerful story

Stowe told the story of Uncle Tom, an enslaved African American noted for his kindness and his devotion to his religion. Tom is bought by Simon Legree, a cruel planter who treats his slaves brutally. In the end, Uncle Tom refuses to obey Legree's order to whip another slave. Legree then whips Uncle Tom to death.

Uncle Tom's Cabin had wide appeal in the North. The first 5,000 copies that were printed sold out in two days. In its first year, Stowe's novel sold 300,000 copies. The book was also published in many different languages. Soon, a play based on the novel appeared in cities not only in the North but around the world.

Nationwide reaction

Although *Uncle Tom's Cabin* was popular in the North, southerners objected to the book. They claimed that it did not give a true picture of slave life. Indeed, Stowe had seen little of slavery firsthand.

Even so, the book helped to change the way northerners felt about slavery. No longer could they ignore slavery as a political problem for Congress to settle. They now saw the slavery issue as a moral problem facing every American. For this reason, *Uncle Tom's Cabin* was one of the most important books in American history.

Kansas-Nebraska Act

Americans had hoped that the Compromise of 1850 would end debate over slavery in the West. In 1854, however, the issue of slavery in the territories surfaced yet again.

In January 1854, Senator Stephen Douglas introduced a bill to set up a government for the Nebraska Territory. This territory stretched from Texas north to Canada, and from Missouri west to the Rockies.

Douglas knew that white southerners did not want to add another free state to the Union. He proposed that the Nebraska Territory be divided into two territories, Kansas and Nebraska. (See the map below.) The settlers living in each territory would decide the issue of slavery by popular sovereignty. Douglas's bill was known as the **Kansas-Nebraska Act.**

Support for the act

The Kansas-Nebraska Act seemed fair to many people. After all, the Compromise of 1850 had applied popular sovereignty in New Mexico and Utah.

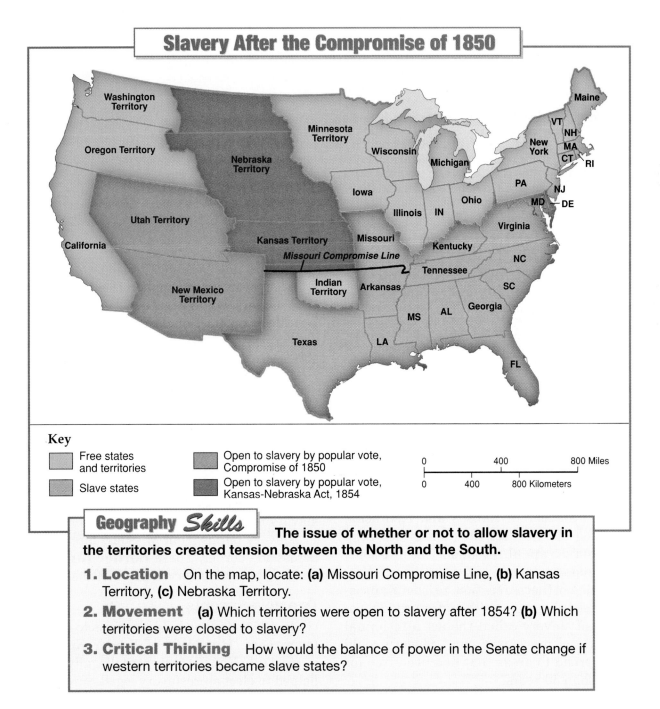

Slavery After the Compromise of 1850

Key
- Free states and territories
- Slave states
- Open to slavery by popular vote, Compromise of 1850
- Open to slavery by popular vote, Kansas-Nebraska Act, 1854

0   400   800 Miles
0   400   800 Kilometers

Geography *Skills*
The issue of whether or not to allow slavery in the territories created tension between the North and the South.

1. **Location** On the map, locate: **(a)** Missouri Compromise Line, **(b)** Kansas Territory, **(c)** Nebraska Territory.
2. **Movement** **(a)** Which territories were open to slavery after 1854? **(b)** Which territories were closed to slavery?
3. **Critical Thinking** How would the balance of power in the Senate change if western territories became slave states?

Viewing History

Bleeding Kansas

In 1856, a bloody civil war broke out in Kansas. Proslavery and antislavery forces fought for control of the territory. The battle depicted here took place at Hickory Point, 25 miles north of Lawrence. ★ **How was the violence in Kansas related to the Kansas-Nebraska Act?**

Abolitionist's saber ▶

Southern leaders especially supported the Kansas-Nebraska Act. They were sure that slave owners from neighboring Missouri would move across the border into Kansas. In time, they hoped, Kansas would become a slave state.

President **Franklin Pierce,** a Democrat elected in 1852, also supported the bill. With the President's help, Douglas pushed the Kansas-Nebraska Act through Congress. He did not realize it at the time, but he had lit a fire under a powder keg.

Northern outrage

Other people were unhappy with the new law. The Missouri Compromise had already banned slavery in Kansas and Nebraska, they insisted. In effect, the Kansas-Nebraska Act would repeal, or undo, the Missouri Compromise.

The northern reaction to the Kansas-Nebraska Act was swift and angry. Opponents of slavery called the act a "criminal betrayal of precious rights." Slavery could now spread to areas that had been free for more than 30 years.

Bleeding Kansas

Kansas now became a testing ground for popular sovereignty. Stephen Douglas hoped that settlers would decide the slavery issue peacefully on election day. Instead, proslavery and antislavery forces sent settlers to Kansas to fight for control of the territory.

Most of the new arrivals were farmers from neighboring states. Their main interest in moving to Kansas was to acquire cheap land. Few of these settlers owned slaves. At the same time, abolitionists brought in more than 1,000 settlers from New England.

Proslavery settlers moved into Kansas as well. They wanted to make sure that antislavery forces did not overrun the territory. Proslavery bands from Missouri often rode across the border. These **Border Ruffians** battled the antislavery forces in Kansas.

Two governments

In 1855, Kansas held elections to choose lawmakers. Hundreds of Border Ruffians crossed into Kansas and voted illegally. They helped to elect a proslavery legislature.

The new legislature quickly passed laws to support slavery. One law said that people could be put to death for helping slaves escape. Another made speaking out against slavery a crime punishable by two years of hard labor.

Antislavery settlers refused to accept these laws. They elected their own governor and legislature. With two rival governments, Kansas was in chaos. Armed gangs roamed the land looking for trouble.

A bloody battleground

In 1856, a band of proslavery men raided the town of Lawrence, an antislavery stronghold. The attackers destroyed homes and smashed the press of a Free Soil newspaper.

John Brown, an abolitionist, decided to strike back. Brown had moved to Kansas to help make it a free state. He claimed that God had sent him to punish supporters of slavery.

Brown rode with his four sons and two other men to the town of Pottawatomie (paht uh WAHT uh mee) Creek. In the middle of the night, they dragged five proslavery settlers from their beds and murdered them.

The killings at Pottawatomie Creek led to more violence. Both sides fought fiercely and engaged in **guerrilla warfare,** or the use of hit-and-run tactics. By late 1856, more than 200 people had been killed. Newspapers called the territory **Bleeding Kansas.**

Violence in the Senate

Even before John Brown's attack, the battle over Kansas had spilled into the Senate. **Charles Sumner** of Massachusetts was the leading abolitionist senator. In one speech, the sharp-tongued Sumner denounced the proslavery legislature of Kansas. He then viciously criticized his southern foes, singling out Andrew Butler, an elderly senator from South Carolina.

Butler was not in the Senate on the day Sumner spoke. A few days later, however, Butler's nephew, Congressman Preston Brooks, marched into the Senate chamber. Using a heavy cane, Brooks beat Sumner until he fell down, bloody and unconscious, to the floor.

Many southerners felt that Sumner got what he deserved for his verbal abuse of another senator. Hundreds of people sent canes to Brooks to show their support. To northerners, however, the brutal act was just more evidence that slavery led to violence.

The Dred Scott Case

With Congress in an uproar, many Americans looked to the Supreme Court to settle the slavery issue and restore peace. In 1857, the Court ruled on a case involving a slave named Dred Scott. Instead of bringing harmony, however, the Court's decision further divided North and South.

Dred Scott had lived for many years in Missouri. Later, he moved with his owner to Illinois and then to the Wisconsin Territory,

Biography   Dred Scott

Dred Scott filed a lawsuit for his freedom. He argued that he should be a free man because he had lived in a free territory. The Supreme Court, however, ruled that he had no right to sue because he was property and not a citizen. After the decision, Scott's new owner granted freedom to Scott and his family. Just one year later, Scott died of consumption. ★ **How did the Dred Scott decision overturn the Missouri Compromise?**

where slavery was not allowed. After they returned to Missouri, Scott's owner died. Antislavery lawyers helped Scott to file a **lawsuit,** a legal case brought by a person or group against another to settle a dispute between them. Scott's lawyers argued that since Scott had lived in a free territory, he was a free man.

The Supreme Court's decision

In time, the case reached the Supreme Court. The Court's decision startled Americans who opposed slavery. The Court ruled that Scott could not file a lawsuit because, as an enslaved person, he was not a citizen. Also, the Court clearly stated that slaves were property.

The Court's ruling did not stop there. Instead, the Justices went on to make a sweeping decision about the larger issue of slavery in the territories. According to the Court, Congress did not have the power to outlaw slavery in any territory. The Court's ruling meant that the Missouri Compromise was unconstitutional.

The nation reacts

White southerners rejoiced at the **Dred Scott decision.** It meant that slavery was legal in all the territories. This was just what white southerners had been demanding for years.

African Americans responded angrily to the Dred Scott decision. In the North, many held public meetings to condemn the ruling. At a meeting in Philadelphia, a speaker hoped that the Dred Scott decision would lead more whites to "join with us in our efforts to recover the long lost boon of freedom."

White northerners were also shocked by the ruling. Many had hoped that slavery would eventually die out if it were restricted to the South. Now, however, slavery could spread throughout the West. Even northerners who disliked abolitionists felt that the Dred Scott ruling was wrong. A newspaper in Cincinnati declared, "We are now one great...slaveholding community." In New England, another newspaper asked, "Where will it all end?"

★ Section 2 Review ★

Recall

1. **Locate** (a) Kansas Territory, (b) Nebraska Territory.
2. **Define** (a) repeal, (b) guerrilla warfare, (c) lawsuit.
3. **Identify** (a) Harriet Beecher Stowe, (b) *Uncle Tom's Cabin,* (c) Kansas-Nebraska Act, (d) Franklin Pierce, (e) Border Ruffians, (f) John Brown, (g) Bleeding Kansas, (h) Charles Sumner, (i) Dred Scott decision.

Comprehension

4. (a) How did *Uncle Tom's Cabin* portray slavery? (b) How did the book affect people's attitudes toward slavery?
5. How did the Kansas-Nebraska Act lead to violence in Kansas?

6. Explain how each of the following reacted to the Dred Scott decision: (a) white southerners, (b) African Americans, (c) white northerners.

Critical Thinking and Writing

7. **Analyzing Primary Sources** After the Kansas-Nebraska Act was passed, Stephen Douglas stated, "The struggle for freedom was forever banished from the halls of Congress to the western plains." (a) What did Douglas mean? (b) Do you agree or disagree with his statement? Explain.

8. **Comparing** Compare Harriet Beecher Stowe's and John Brown's contributions to the abolitionist movement.

Activity **Writing a Protest Letter** You are outraged by the Dred Scott decision! Write a protest letter to the justices of the Supreme Court explaining why you think their decision in this case was wrong.

3 ★ A New Party Challenges Slavery

As You Read

Explore These Questions
- Why did the Republican party come into being in the mid-1850s?
- What were Abraham Lincoln's views on slavery?
- How did northerners and southerners respond differently to the raid on Harpers Ferry?

Define
- arsenal
- martyr

Identify
- Republican party
- John C. Frémont
- James Buchanan
- Abraham Lincoln

SETTING the Scene In the mid-1850s, people who opposed slavery in the territories needed a new political voice. Neither Whigs nor Democrats would take a strong stand against slavery. "We have submitted to slavery long enough," an Ohio Democrat declared.

Free Soilers, northern Democrats, and antislavery Whigs met in towns and cities across the North. In 1854, a group gathered in Michigan to form the **Republican party.** The new party grew quickly. By 1856, it was ready to challenge the older parties for power.

The Republican Party

In the 1850s, the main goal of the Republican party was to keep slavery out of the western territories. A few Republicans were abolitionists. They hoped to end slavery in the South as well. Most Republicans, however, wanted only to stop the spread of slavery.

In 1856, Republicans selected **John C. Frémont** to run for President. Frémont was a frontiersman who had fought for California's independence. (See page 362.) He had little political experience, but he opposed the spread of slavery.

John C. Frémont

Frémont's main opponent was Democrat **James Buchanan** of Pennsylvania. He had served as a senator and as Secretary of State. Many Democrats considered Buchanan to be a "compromise" candidate because he was a "northern man with southern principles." They hoped that he would attract voters in both the North and the South.

Buchanan won the election with support from a large majority of southerners and many northerners. Still, the Republicans made a strong showing in the election. Without the support of a single southern state, Frémont won one third of the popular vote. Southerners worried that their influence in the national government was fading.

Abe Lincoln of Illinois

The next test for the Republican party came in 1858 in the state of Illinois. **Abraham Lincoln,** a Republican, challenged Democrat Stephen Douglas for his seat in the Senate. The election captured the attention of the whole nation. The race was important because most Americans thought that Douglas would run for President in 1860.

In this painting, Stephen Douglas sits to Lincoln's right during a debate held at Charleston, Illinois, in September 1858. Thousands of people attended the Lincoln-Douglas debates. ★ **What was the most important issue discussed in the debates?**

A self-starter from Kentucky

Abraham Lincoln was born in the back-country of Kentucky. Like many frontier people, his parents moved often to find better land. The family lived in Indiana and later in Illinois. As a child, Lincoln spent only a year in school. Still, he taught himself to read and spent many hours reading by firelight.

After Lincoln left home, he opened a store in Illinois. There, he studied law on his own and launched a career in politics. After spending eight years in the state legislature, Lincoln served one term in Congress. Bitterly opposed to the Kansas-Nebraska Act, he decided to run for the Senate in 1858.

"Just folks"

When the race began, Lincoln was not a national figure. Still, people in Illinois knew him well and liked him. To them, he was "just folks"—someone who enjoyed picnics, wrestling contests, and all their other favorite pastimes.

People also admired his honesty and wit. His plainspoken manner made him a good speaker. Even so, a listener once complained that he could not understand one of Lincoln's speeches. "There are always some fleas a dog can't reach" was Lincoln's reply.

Lincoln-Douglas Debates

During the Senate campaign, Lincoln challenged Douglas to a series of debates. Douglas was not eager to accept, but he did. During the campaign, the two debated seven times. Slavery was the important issue.

Views on slavery

Douglas wanted to settle the slavery question by popular sovereignty. He disliked slavery, but he thought that people in the territories should be able to vote "down or up" for it.

Lincoln, like nearly all whites of his day, did not believe in "perfect equality" between blacks and whites. He did, however, believe that slavery was a "moral, social, and political wrong." He believed that blacks were entitled to the rights named in the Declaration of Independence—"life, liberty, and the pursuit of happiness."

Since slavery was wrong, said Lincoln, Douglas and other Americans should not treat it as an unimportant question to be voted "down or up." Lincoln was totally opposed to slavery in the territories. Still, he was not an abolitionist. He had no wish to interfere with slavery in the states where it already existed.

Lincoln believed that the nation could not survive if it remained divided by slavery. On June 16, 1858, Lincoln spoke in a crowded hall in Springfield, Illinois:

66 A house divided against itself cannot stand. I believe this government cannot endure permanently half slave and half free. I do not expect the Union to be dissolved—I do not expect the house to fall—but I do expect it will cease to be divided. It will become all one thing, or all the other. 99

Why Study History?

Because Heroes of the Past Can Be Models for Today

★ ★

Historical Background

Many consider Abraham Lincoln one of the truly heroic figures in American history. Through education and hard work, "Honest Abe" rose from humble beginnings to national leadership. As President, he would lead the nation through the horrors of a civil war and help bring an end to slavery.

Lincoln Memorial

Connections to Today

Today, we still honor Lincoln. Each year, we remember him on Presidents' Day. His image is on the money we use every day. In addition, thousands of people show their respect by visiting the Lincoln Memorial in Washington, D.C.

Admirers of Lincoln consider him a model for others to imitate. They point to his easygoing manner, keen wit, high sense of morality, and ability to make wise decisions in tough situations.

Connections to You

Do you think Lincoln is an American hero? Should you look to him as a role model? To help you decide, read the following excerpts from Lincoln's conversations, speeches, and writings.

"I have no other [ambition] so great as that of being truly esteemed of my fellow men, by rendering myself worthy of their esteem."—June 13, 1836

"The better part of one's life consists in his friendships."
—May 19, 1849

"Let us have faith that Right makes Might, and in that faith, let us to the end, dare to do our duty."
—February 27, 1860

"I want every man to have a chance—and I believe a black man is entitled to it— in which he can better his condition."—March 6, 1860

"The people's will, constitutionally expressed, is the ultimate law for all."—October 19, 1864

"Whenever I hear anyone arguing for slavery, I feel a strong impulse to see it tried on him personally."
—March 17, 1865

1. Comprehension How do Americans show their respect for Abraham Lincoln today?

2. Critical Thinking **(a)** Which quotation deals most directly with the idea of racial equality? **(b)** What was Lincoln's position on equality?

 Writing an Essay Do you consider Lincoln an American hero and role model? Develop your answer in a brief essay, using the quotations above to describe some of Lincoln's ideas and values.

A leader emerges

Week after week, both men spoke nearly every day to large crowds. Newspapers reprinted their campaign speeches. The more northerners read Lincoln's speeches, the more they thought about the injustice of slavery.

In the end, Douglas won the election by a slim margin. However, Lincoln was a winner, too. He was now known throughout the country. Two years later, the two rivals would again meet face to face—both seeking the office of President.

John Brown's Raid

In the meantime, more bloodshed pushed the North and South farther apart. In 1859, John Brown carried his antislavery campaign from Kansas to the East. He led a group of followers, including five African Americans, to Harpers Ferry, Virginia.

There, Brown planned to raid a federal **arsenal,** or gun warehouse. He thought that enslaved African Americans would flock to him at the arsenal. He would then give them weapons and lead them in a revolt.

Sentenced to death

Brown quickly gained control of the arsenal. No slave uprising took place, however. Instead, troops led by Robert E. Lee killed 10 of the raiders and captured Brown.

Most people, in both the North and the South, thought that Brown's plan to lead a slave revolt was insane. After all, there were not many enslaved African Americans in Harpers Ferry. At his trial, however, Brown seemed perfectly sane. He sat quietly as the court found him guilty of murder and treason and sentenced him to death.

Hero or villain?

Brown became a hero to many northerners. Some considered him a **martyr** because he was willing to give up his life for his beliefs. On the morning he was hanged, church bells rang solemnly throughout the North. In years to come, New Englanders would sing a popular song: "John Brown's body lies a mold'ring in the grave, but his soul is marching on."

To white southerners, the northern response to John Brown's death was outrageous. People were singing the praises of a man who had tried to lead a slave revolt! Many southerners became convinced that the North wanted to destroy slavery—and the South along with it. The nation was poised for a violent clash.

★ Section 3 Review ★

Recall

1. **Identify** **(a)** Republican party, **(b)** John C. Frémont, **(c)** James Buchanan, **(d)** Abraham Lincoln.
2. **Define** **(a)** arsenal, **(b)** martyr.

Comprehension

3. What was the main goal of the Republican party?
4. How did Abraham Lincoln's opinions on slavery differ from those of Stephen Douglas?

5. **(a)** How did Northerners respond to John Brown's execution? **(b)** How did Southerners respond?

Critical Thinking and Writing

6. **Identifying Main Ideas**   Reread the subsection on page 436 called Just folks. State the main idea of this subsection.
7. **Analyzing Ideas**   Lincoln said the nation could not "endure permanently half slave and half free." Do you agree that slavery was too great an issue to allow differences among the states? Explain.

Activity   **Writing Headlines** You are a journalist in the 1850s. Choose three events discussed in Section 3. Write two headlines for each event—one for a northern newspaper, the other for a southern newspaper.

4 The Nation Splits in Two

As You Read

Explore These Questions
- Why was Abraham Lincoln able to win the election of 1860?
- How did the South react to Lincoln's election victory?
- What events led to the outbreak of the Civil War?

Identify
- John Breckinridge
- John Bell
- John Crittenden
- Confederate States of America
- Jefferson Davis
- Fort Sumter

Republican campaign banner

SETTING the Scene In May 1860, thousands of people swarmed into Chicago for the Republican national convention. They filled the city's 42 hotels. When beds ran out, they slept on billiard tables. All were there to find out one thing. Who would win the Republican nomination for President—William Seward of New York or Abraham Lincoln of Illinois?

On the third day of the convention, a delegate rushed to the roof of the hall. There, a man stood waiting next to a cannon. "Fire the salute," ordered the delegate. "Old Abe is nominated!"

As the cannon fired, crowds surrounding the hall burst into cheers. Amid the celebration, a delegate from Kentucky struck a somber note. "Gentlemen, we are on the brink of a great civil war."

The Election of 1860

The Democrats held their convention in Charleston, South Carolina. Southerners wanted the party to support slavery in the territories. However, Northern Democrats refused to do so.

In the end, the party split in two. Northern Democrats chose Stephen Douglas to run for President. Southern Democrats picked **John Breckinridge** of Kentucky.

Some Americans tried to heal the split between North and South by forming a new party. The Constitutional Union party chose **John Bell** of Tennessee, a Whig, to run for President. Bell was a moderate who wanted to keep the Union together. He got support only in a few southern states that were still trying to find a compromise.

Senator Douglas was sure that Lincoln would win the election. However, he believed that Democrats "must try to save the Union." He pleaded with southern voters to stay with the Union, no matter who was elected.

When the votes were counted, Lincoln had carried the North and won the election. Southern votes did not affect the outcome at all. Lincoln's name was not even on the ballot in 10 southern states. Northerners outnumbered southerners and outvoted them.

The Union Is Broken

Lincoln's election brought a strong reaction in the South. A South Carolina woman described how the news was received:

    66 The excitement was very great. Everybody was talking at the same time. One...more moved than the others, stood up saying...'The die is cast—No more vain regrets—Sad forebodings are useless. The stake is life or death—'...No doubt of it. 99

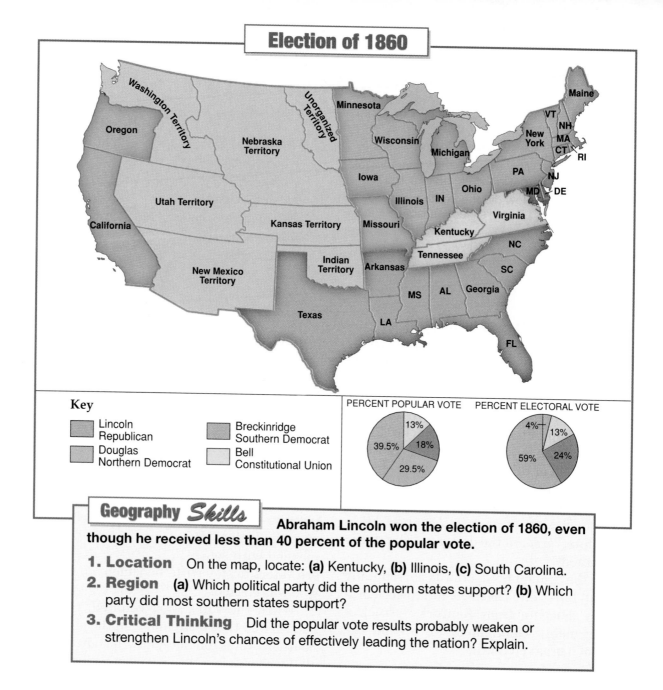

Election of 1860

Key

- Lincoln Republican
- Douglas Northern Democrat
- Breckinridge Southern Democrat
- Bell Constitutional Union

PERCENT POPULAR VOTE

13% | 18% | 29.5% | 39.5%

PERCENT ELECTORAL VOTE

4% | 13% | 24% | 59%

Geography Skills

Abraham Lincoln won the election of 1860, even though he received less than 40 percent of the popular vote.

1. **Location** On the map, locate: **(a)** Kentucky, **(b)** Illinois, **(c)** South Carolina.
2. **Region** **(a)** Which political party did the northern states support? **(b)** Which party did most southern states support?
3. **Critical Thinking** Did the popular vote results probably weaken or strengthen Lincoln's chances of effectively leading the nation? Explain.

To many southerners, Lincoln's election meant that the South no longer had a voice in national government. They believed that the President and Congress were now set against their interests—especially slavery. Even before the election, South Carolina's governor had written to other southern governors. If Lincoln won, he wrote, it would be their duty to leave the Union.

Secession

Senator **John Crittenden** of Kentucky made a last effort to save the Union. In December 1860, he introduced a bill to extend the Missouri Compromise line to the Pacific. He also suggested adding an "unamendable" amendment to the Constitution to forever guarantee the right to hold slaves in states south of the compromise line.

The compromise bill received little support. Slavery in the West was no longer the issue. Many southerners believed that the North had put an abolitionist in the White House. They felt that secession was their only choice. Most Republicans also refused to compromise. They were unwilling to surrender what they had won in the national election.

Skills FOR LIFE

| Critical Thinking | Managing Information | Communication | Maps, Charts, and Graphs |

Comparing Points of View

How Will I Use This Skill?

When two or more people describe the same event, their descriptions of the event often differ. That is because each person's point of view is subjective, or influenced by personal experiences and feelings. By comparing different sources, you can learn objective information, or facts, as well as subjective points of view regarding those facts.

LEARN the Skill

You can compare points of view by following the steps below.

❶ Identify the author of each source. Consider how each report might be affected by the author's point of view.

❷ Find objective information common to two or more sources.

❸ Identify subjective statements that reflect the author's point of view.

❹ Draw conclusions about the historical event and different points of view on it.

PRACTICE the Skill

The newspaper articles above give different viewpoints on Abraham Lincoln's victory in the election of 1860. Compare the two viewpoints by answering the following questions.

❶ (a) Which source is a southern newspa-

Bullying the Free States

November 19, 1860
The New York Tribune

Abraham Lincoln has been designated for next President of this Republic by the popular vote of nearly every Free State, and the ruling politicians of the Slave States are not pleased with the selection. We can fancy their feelings, as we felt much the same when they put a most undesired President upon us four years ago. Moreover, we…advise them to do as we did—Bear it with fortitude, and hope to do better next time.

Devotion to the Union Is Treason to the South

November 19, 1860
Oxford Mississippi Mercury

We have at last reached that point in our history when it is necessary for the South to withdraw from the Union....

[A] powerful sectional majority are now about to seize upon the Government...to destroy the institution of Slavery....We cannot stand still and quietly see the Government pass into the hands of such an infamous crew.

South Carolina,...Georgia, Mississippi, Alabama, Louisiana, Texas, and Arkansas, will soon be united as brothers to defend each other from the inroads of the fanatics of the North.

---

per? (b) Which source is a northern newspaper? (c) Why would you expect the two to have different opinions about Lincoln?

❷ What factual information do you find in both articles?

❸ How do the two articles describe the election result differently?

❹ (a) Why did the election cause conflict between North and South? (b) What did the *Tribune* think the South should do? (c) What did the *Mercury* recommend?

APPLY the Skill

In two or more newspapers or news magazines, find different points of view on some issue or event. Use the steps you have learned to compare the various viewpoints.

HISTORY HAPPENED HERE

Fort Sumter

The Civil War began in 1861 when Confederate forces bombarded and captured Fort Sumter in Charleston Harbor, South Carolina. Later in the war, Union gunships reduced Sumter to rubble. The fort was rebuilt, and it remained part of the seacoast defenses until 1947. Today, Fort Sumter is a national monument. Tour boats to the fort leave regularly from downtown Charleston.

★ **To learn more about this historic site, write:** Fort Sumter National Monument, Sullivan's Island, SC 29482.

◄ Union flag from Fort Sumter

The first state to secede was South Carolina. On December 20, 1860, delegates to a convention in Charleston voted for secession. "The state of South Carolina has resumed her position among the nations of the world," the delegates proudly declared. By late February, 1861, Alabama, Florida, Georgia, Louisiana, Mississippi, and Texas had seceded.

The Confederacy

The seven states that had seceded held a convention in Montgomery, Alabama. There, the southern states formed a new nation, the **Confederate States of America.** To lead the new country, they named **Jefferson Davis** of Mississippi as the first president of the Confederacy.

Most southerners believed that they had every right to secede. After all, the Declaration of Independence said that "it is the right of the people to alter or to abolish" a government that denies the rights of its citizens. Lincoln, they believed, would deny white southerners their right to own slaves.

Lincoln Speaks to the Nation

When Abraham Lincoln took office on March 4, 1861, he faced a national crisis. Crowds gathered in Washington, D.C., to hear him take the presidential oath of office. In his Inaugural Address, the new President assured Americans of both the North and the South that he had two goals. He hoped to maintain the Union and avoid war.

On the first goal, preserving the Union, Lincoln would not compromise. Secession of states from the Union, he said, was unconstitutional. Lincoln believed that his duty as

🏛 Connections With Civics

Texas voters chose secession, but Governor Sam Houston refused to swear allegiance to the new Confederacy. He was replaced by a new governor. Houston sadly warned his fellow Texans that the North would "move with the steady momentum and perseverance of a mighty avalanche; and…overwhelm the South."

President was clear. He would take strong action to preserve national union.

> 66 In view of the Constitution and the law, the Union is unbroken;...I will take care...that the laws of the Union be faithfully executed in all the States. 99

At the same time, however, Lincoln tried to reassure the South. He promised that there would not be war with the South unless southern states started it:

> 66 We are not enemies, but friends. We must not be enemies. Though passion may have strained, it must not break our bonds of affection. 99

Civil War

The Confederacy, however, had already started seizing federal forts in the South. It felt that the forts were a threat because the United States was now a "foreign power."

Lincoln's difficult decision

President Lincoln faced a difficult decision. Should he let the Confederates take over federal property? If he did, he would seem to be admitting that states had the right to leave the Union. On the other hand, if he sent troops to hold the forts, he might start a civil war. He might also lose the support of the eight slave states that had not seceded from the Union.

In April, the Confederacy forced Lincoln to make up his mind. By then, Confederate troops controlled nearly all forts, post offices, and other federal buildings in the South. The Union held only three forts off the Florida coast and Fort Sumter in South Carolina. **Fort Sumter** was important to the Confederacy because it guarded Charleston Harbor.

Bombardment of Fort Sumter

President Lincoln learned that food supplies at Fort Sumter were running low. He notified the governor of South Carolina that he was going to ship food to the fort. Lincoln promised not to send troops or weapons.

The Confederates could not leave the fort in Union hands, however. On April 11, 1861, they asked for Fort Sumter's surrender.

Major Robert Anderson, the Union commander, refused to give in. Confederate guns then opened fire. Anderson and his troops quickly ran out of ammunition. On April 13, Anderson surrendered the fort.

When Confederate troops shelled Fort Sumter, people in Charleston had gathered on their rooftops to watch. To many, it was like a fireworks display. No one knew that the fireworks marked the beginning of a civil war that would last four terrible years.

★ Section 4 Review ★

Recall

1. **Identify** **(a)** John Breckinridge, **(b)** John Bell, **(c)** John Crittenden, **(d)** Confederate States of America, **(e)** Jefferson Davis, **(f)** Fort Sumter.

Comprehension

2. Why were there two Democratic candidates for President in 1860?
3. Why did many southerners feel that secession was necessary after Lincoln won the Presidency in 1860?
4. How did the Civil War begin at Fort Sumter in 1861?

Critical Thinking and Writing

5. **Making Inferences** How do you think the split in the Democratic party helped Lincoln win the election of 1860?
6. **Solving Problems** Write a compromise plan that tries to save the Union in 1861. Your plan should offer advantages to both the North and the South.

★ ★

Activity **Writing Slogans** You are a famous political campaign manager of the mid-1800s. Write a campaign slogan for each of the four candidates in the presidential election of 1860.

Review and Activities

★ Sum It Up ★

Section 1 The Slavery Issue in the West
▶ Americans disagreed on whether slavery should be allowed in the western territories.
▶ The new Free Soil party wanted to limit the spread of slavery.
▶ The Compromise of 1850 settled the issue for a time, but the new Fugitive Slave Law angered many.

Section 2 The Crisis Turns Violent
▶ The novel *Uncle Tom's Cabin* turned many northerners against slavery.
▶ After the Kansas-Nebraska Act of 1854, proslavery and antislavery settlers battled for control of Kansas.
▶ In the Dred Scott case, the Supreme Court ruled that Congress could not outlaw slavery in any territory.

Section 3 A New Party Challenges Slavery
▶ The Republican party wanted to keep slavery out of the western territories.
▶ Abraham Lincoln emerged as a leader of the Republican party.
▶ John Brown's raid on Harpers Ferry brought the nation to the brink of war.

Section 4 The Nation Splits in Two
▶ Abraham Lincoln won the presidential election of 1860.
▶ Southern states seceded from the Union and formed a new nation.
▶ A civil war broke out between the North and the South.

CD-ROM Review For additional review of the major ideas of Chapter 16, see *Guide to the Essentials of American History* or *Interactive Student Tutorial CD-ROM,* which contains interactive review activities, graphic organizers, and practice tests.

📖 Reviewing the Chapter

Define These Terms
Match each term with the correct definition.

Column 1	Column 2
1. sectionalism	**a.** a law to ban slavery in any lands won from Mexico
2. fugitive	**b.** a runaway
3. civil war	**c.** a gun warehouse
4. arsenal	**d.** a war between people of the same country
5. Wilmot Proviso	**e.** loyalty to a part of a nation rather than the whole

Explore the Main Ideas
1. What were the four parts of the Compromise of 1850?
2. Why was Kansas referred to as Bleeding Kansas in the 1850s?
3. What effect did the Dred Scott decision have on the Missouri Compromise?
4. What groups combined to form the new Republican party?
5. Why did South Carolina secede from the Union in 1860?

📖 Geography Activity

Match the letters on the map with the following places:
1. Missouri, **2.** Maine, **3.** California, **4.** Kansas Territory, **5.** Nebraska Territory, **6.** New Mexico Territory, **7.** Utah Territory. **Region** Which area listed above was admitted to the Union as a free state in 1850?

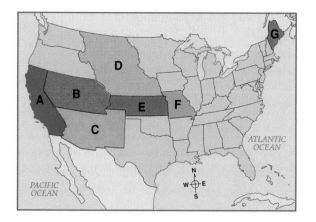

☐ Critical Thinking and Writing

1. **Understanding Chronology**   Place the following events in chronological order: **(a)** Kansas-Nebraska Act, **(b)** Compromise of 1850, **(c)** Lincoln becomes President, **(d)** Dred Scott decision.

2. **Understanding Cause and Effect**   **(a)** What caused the Democratic party to split in 1860? **(b)** How did the split affect the election of 1860?

3. **Identifying Alternatives**   Describe one alternative to secession that the slave states could have chosen.

4. **Exploring Unit Themes**   **Sectionalism** The 1860 Republican convention was held in Illinois, then considered a western state. How did this help bring victory for Lincoln in the national election?

☐ Using Primary Sources

In 1860, Abraham Lincoln was elected to succeed James Buchanan as President. As his term of office came to an end, President Buchanan offered his thoughts on the possibility of secession and civil war:

> 66 Our Union rests upon public opinion, and can never be cemented by the blood of its citizens shed in civil war. If it cannot live in the affections of the people, it must one day perish. Congress may possess many means of preserving it by [compromise], but the sword was not placed in their hand to preserve it by force. 99

Source: *The Rise and Fall of the Confederate Government* by Jefferson Davis, 1881.

Recognizing Points of View   **(a)** Was Buchanan in favor of a war to prevent southern states from leaving the Union? Explain. **(b)** Do you agree or disagree with Buchanan? Defend your position.

ACTIVITY BANK

▶ Interdisciplinary Activity

Exploring the Arts   In a painting, drawing, collage, sculpture, or other form of art, express the reaction of the North or the South to one event described in this chapter. Display your work to the class. Ask other students to identify the event and point of view that your art work reflects.

▶ Career Skills Activity

Lawyer   Choose the role of prosecutor or defense lawyer at the trial of John Brown. Depending on the role you have chosen, write a speech declaring Brown to be either guilty or not guilty. Present your speech to the class and ask them to reach a verdict.

▶ Citizenship Activity

Reaching a Compromise   Find an issue in your community that is the subject of heated debate between two groups. Then brainstorm solutions to the problem that will offer something to both sides. Type up your suggestions and offer them to a neutral party who might be able to mediate between the two groups.

Internet Activity   Use the Internet to find sites dealing with Abraham Lincoln. Use your research to write a biography or a character sketch. Use as many quotations as possible. Make a bibliography by writing down the title, author, and address of each Web site that you use.

EYEWITNESS Journal

You are an African American or white American living in the North or the South between 1820 and 1861. In your EYEWITNESS JOURNAL, describe your reaction to the important events of these years: 1820, 1850, 1859, 1860, 1861.

The Civil War

1861–1865

For more than four years, Americans fought Americans in the Civil War. The South wanted to exist as an independent nation. The North wanted to force the South back into the Union. The war was also linked closely to the question of slavery. President Lincoln made this clear when he issued the Emancipation Proclamation.

Throughout the North and the South, both soldiers and civilians experienced much suffering. The Union's armies struggled in the early years of the war. However, the North's superior resources wore heavily on the South. By the end of 1863, the South was in retreat. In 1865, the South surrendered and the Civil War came to an end.

Why Study History?

During the Civil War, millions of northerners and southerners served their nation well. Their efforts, as both soldiers and civilians, affected the course of the war. To see an example of how one person can affect the course of history, see this chapter's *Why Study History?* feature, "One Person Can Make a Difference." The feature focuses on the achievements of Clara Barton.

American Events			
1861 Civil War begins with attack on Fort Sumter	**1862** Union gunboats capture New Orleans and Memphis	**1863** Abraham Lincoln issues Emancipation Proclamation	

1861   **1862**   **1863**

World Events		
1861 World Event Russian czar frees serfs	**1862 World Event** Britain refuses to recognize the Confederacy	

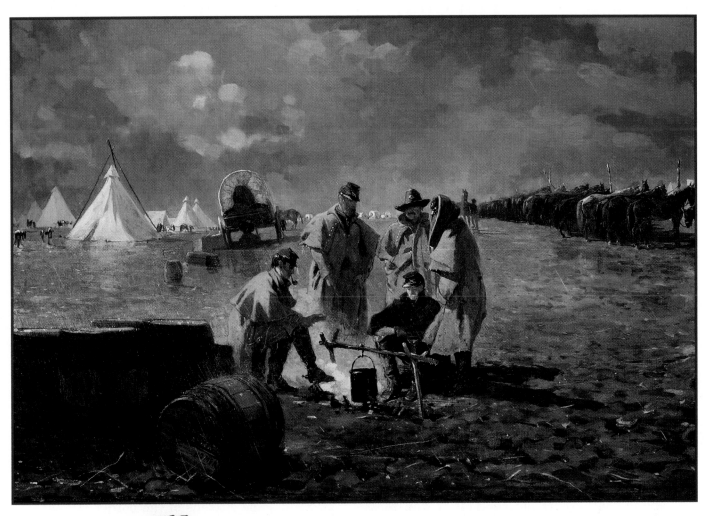

Viewing HISTORY

The Soldiers of the Civil War

In A Rainy Day in Camp *by Winslow Homer, Civil War soldiers find time to gather around a campfire. It is estimated that more than 2,500,000 men served as soldiers in the Civil War. Over 600,000 of them died—more than in any other American war.* ★ **What emotions do you think soldiers felt on the eve of a battle? Explain.**

●**1863**
Battle of Gettysburg
ends Confederate
drive into the North

●**1864**
General Grant
becomes
commander of
Union army

●**1865**
General Lee
surrenders at
Appomattox
Courthouse

1863   **1864**   **1865**

 1863 World Event
First Red Cross
societies established
in Europe

The Conflict Takes Shape

As You Read

Explore These Questions
- What strengths and weaknesses did the Confederacy have?
- What strengths and weaknesses did the Union have?
- What special qualities did Presidents Abraham Lincoln and Jefferson Davis possess?

Define
- racism
- martial law

Identify
- border states
- Robert E. Lee

Confederate canteen

SETTING the Scene In April 1861, President Abraham Lincoln called for 75,000 volunteers to serve as soldiers for 90 days in a campaign against the South. The response was overwhelming. Throughout the North, crowds cheered the Stars and Stripes and booed the southern "traitors."

Southerners were just as enthusiastic for the war. They rallied to the Stars and Bars, as they called the new Confederate flag. Volunteers flooded into the Confederate army.

With flags held high, both northerners and southerners marched off to war. Most felt certain that a single, gallant battle would bring a quick end to the conflict. Few suspected that the Civil War would last four terrible years and be the most destructive war in the nation's history.

A Nation Divided

As the war began, each side was convinced that its cause was just. Southerners believed that they had the right to leave the Union. In fact, they called the conflict the War for Southern Independence. Southerners wanted independence so that they could keep their traditional way of life—including the institution of slavery.

Northerners, meanwhile, believed that they had to fight to save the Union. At the outset of the war, abolishing slavery was not an official goal of the North. In fact, many northerners, guided by feelings of racism, approved of slavery. **Racism** is the belief that one race is superior to another.

In April 1861, eight slave states were still in the Union. They had to make the difficult decision of which side to join. Virginia,* North Carolina, Tennessee, and Arkansas joined the Confederacy. The four **border states** of Delaware, Kentucky, Missouri, and Maryland remained in the Union. (See the map on page 449.)

Still, some citizens of the border states supported the South. For example, in April 1861, pro-Confederate mobs attacked Union troops in Baltimore, Maryland. In response, President Lincoln declared **martial law**, or rule by the army instead of the elected government. Many people who sided with the South were arrested.

Strengths and Weaknesses

Both sides in the conflict had strengths and weaknesses as the war began. The South had the strong advantage of fighting a defensive war. It was up to the North to go on the offensive, to attack and defeat the South. If the North did not move its forces into the South, the Confederacy would remain a separate country.

---

*Many people in western Virginia supported the Union. When Virginia seceded, westerners formed their own government. West Virginia became a state of the Union in 1863.

The South

Southerners believed that they were fighting a war for independence, similar to the American Revolution. Defending their homeland and their way of life gave them a strong reason to fight bravely. "Our men must prevail in combat," one Confederate said, "or they will lose their property, country, freedom—in short, everything."

Also, many southerners had skills that made them good soldiers. Hunting was an important part of southern life. From an early age, boys learned to ride horses and use guns. Wealthy young men often went to military school. Before the Civil War, many of the best officers in the United States Army were from the South.

The South, however, had serious economic weaknesses. (See the chart on page 450.) It had few factories to produce weapons and other vital supplies. It also had few railroads to move troops and supplies. The railroads that it did have often did not connect to one another. The South also had political problems. The Confederate constitution favored states' rights and limited the authority

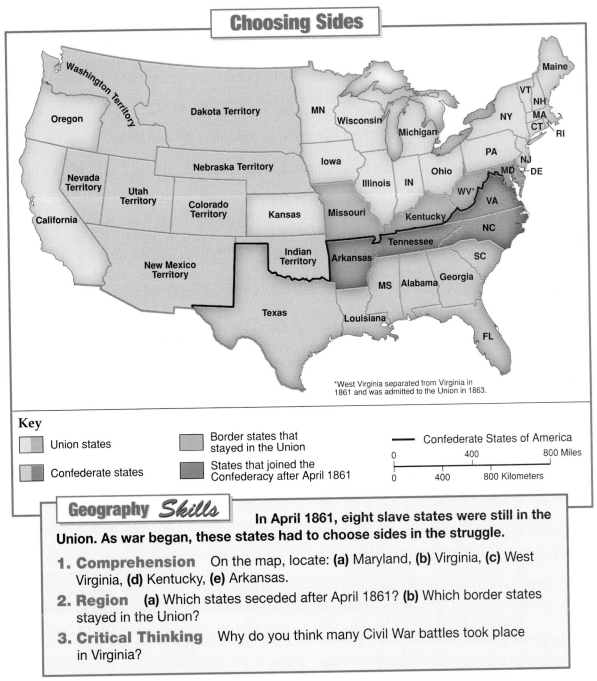

Choosing Sides

*West Virginia separated from Virginia in 1861 and was admitted to the Union in 1863.

Key

Union states

Confederate states

Border states that stayed in the Union

States that joined the Confederacy after April 1861

——— Confederate States of America

0   400   800 Miles

0   400   800 Kilometers

Geography Skills

In April 1861, eight slave states were still in the Union. As war began, these states had to choose sides in the struggle.

1. **Comprehension** On the map, locate: **(a)** Maryland, **(b)** Virginia, **(c)** West Virginia, **(d)** Kentucky, **(e)** Arkansas.
2. **Region** **(a)** Which states seceded after April 1861? **(b)** Which border states stayed in the Union?
3. **Critical Thinking** Why do you think many Civil War battles took place in Virginia?

Resources of the North and South, 1861

Resources	North		South	
	Number	Percent of Total	Number	Percent of Total
Farmland	105,835 acres	65%	56,832 acres	35%
Railroad Track	21,847 miles	71%	8,947 miles	29%
Value of Manufactured Goods	$1,794,417,000	92%	$155,552,000	8%
Factories	119,500	85%	20,600	15%
Workers in Industry	1,198,000	92%	111,000	8%
Population	22,340,000	63%	9,103,000 (3,954,000 slaves)	37%

Source: *Historical Statistics of the United States*

Chart *Skills*   As the Civil War began, the North enjoyed a number of economic advantages over the South. These advantages affected the war's outcome.

1. **Comprehension** (a) How many acres of farmland did each side have? (b) What percentage of the nation's factories did the South have?

2. **Critical Thinking** (a) Which side had more railroad track? (b) How do you think this advantage affected the war?

Economics $

of the central government. As a result, it was often difficult for the Confederate government to get things done. On one occasion, for example, the governor of Georgia insisted that only Georgia officers be in command of Georgia troops.

Finally, the South had a small population. Only about 9 million people lived in the Confederacy, compared with 22 million in the Union. More than one third of the southern population were enslaved African Americans. As a result, the South did not have enough people to serve as soldiers and to support the war effort.

The North

The North had almost four times as many free citizens as the South. Thus, it had a large source of volunteers. It also had many people to grow food and to work in factories making supplies.

Industry was the North's greatest resource. Before the war, northern factories made more than 90 percent of the nation's manufactured goods. These factories quickly began making supplies for the Union army.

The North also had more than 70 percent of the nation's rail lines, which it used to transport both troops and supplies.

The North also benefited from a strong navy and a large fleet of trading ships. With few warships and only a small merchant fleet, the South was unable to compete with the North at sea.

Despite these advantages, the North faced a difficult military challenge. To bring the South back into the Union, northern soldiers had to conquer a huge area. Instead of defending their homes, they were invading unfamiliar land. As Union armies invaded the South, their lines of supply would be much longer than those of the Confederates and thus more open to attack.

Wartime Leaders

Leadership was a very important factor in the Civil War. President Jefferson Davis of the Confederacy, President Abraham Lincoln of the Union, and military leaders on both sides played key roles in determining the war's outcome.

Skills

FOR LIFE

Critical Thinking

Managing Information

Communication

Maps, Charts, and Graphs

Keeping Files

How Will I Use This Skill?

A file system is a method for organizing and storing information, usually in a cabinet or on a computer disk. By keeping files, you can save and retrieve information quickly and easily. In school, this skill is useful for research projects. At home, a file system can help organize recipes, coupons, or documents and bills. Finally, you will probably use a file system in your future job or career.

Recipe file

LEARN the Skill

❶ Set up and name various file sections. For example, a recipe file would need separate sections for appetizers, entrees, and desserts.

❷ Create and label file folders for each section of the file. For example, a dessert section of a recipe file might need one folder for pies and another for cakes.

❸ Create or collect the information or material that will be filed.

❹ File the informtion or material in the appropriate folders.

PRACTICE the Skill

Read the subsection titled Strengths and Weaknesses on pages 448–450. Use the following steps to file information on the North and South.

❶ Create a file system with two sections. Label one section The South. What should you label the other section?

❷ For each of the two sections, create a file folder labeled Economy. Create and name two other file folders for each section. (You will have a total of six folders.)

❸ For each of the two sections, record two or three facts to go into the Economy file folders. Write each fact on a separate sheet of paper. Place each sheet of paper in the appropriate folder.

❹ In the same way, record and file other facts about the North and South.

APPLY the Skill

Create a file system for discount grocery coupons. You might start by making a section for dairy products that includes a folder for yogurt, another for cheese, and a third for butter. Offer your completed file system to someone who uses discount coupons.

President Jefferson Davis

Many people thought Davis was a stronger leader than Lincoln. Davis had attended the United States Military Academy at West Point. He had served as an officer in the Mexican War. Later, he served as Secretary of War. He was widely respected for his honesty and courage.

Davis, however, did not like to turn over to others the details of military planning. When he made a decision, according to his wife, he "could not understand any other man coming to a different conclusion." As a result, Davis spent much time arguing with his advisers.

President Abraham Lincoln

At first, some northerners had doubts about Abraham Lincoln's ability to lead. He had little experience in national politics or military matters. In time, however, Lincoln proved to be a patient but strong leader and a fine war planner.

Day by day, Lincoln gained the respect of those around him. Many especially liked his sense of humor. They noted that Lincoln even accepted criticism with a smile. When Secretary of War Edwin Stanton called Lincoln a fool, Lincoln commented, "Did Stanton say I was a fool? Then I must be one, for Stanton is generally right and he always says what he means."

Military leaders

As the war began, army officers in the South had to make a choice. They could stay in the Union army and fight against their home states, or they could join the Confederate forces.

Robert E. Lee faced this dilemma when his home state of Virginia seceded. President Lincoln asked Lee to command the Union army. Lee refused. He explained in a letter to a friend:

> 66 I cannot raise my hand against my birthplace, my home, my children. I should like, above all things, that our difficulties might be peaceably arranged.... What ever may be the result of the contest, I foresee that the country will have to pass through a terrible ordeal. 99

Later, **Robert E. Lee** became commander of the Confederate army. In fact, many of the best officers served for the Confederacy. As a result, President Lincoln had trouble finding generals to match those of the South.

★ Section 1 Review ★

Recall

1. **Locate** (a) West Virginia, (b) Delaware, (c) Kentucky, (d) Missouri, (e) Maryland.
2. **Identify** (a) border states, (b) Robert E. Lee.
3. **Define** (a) racism, (b) martial law.

Comprehension

4. Describe two advantages that the South had over the North at the start of the Civil War.
5. Describe two advantages that the North had over the South at the start of the Civil War.

6. Explain one strength and one weakness of each of the following leaders: (a) President Abraham Lincoln, (b) President Jefferson Davis.

Critical Thinking and Writing

7. **Identifying Alternatives** List arguments for and against a border state's staying in the Union in 1861.
8. **Analyzing Ideas** Jefferson Davis said this of the Confederacy: "All we ask is to be left alone." (a) What do you think Davis meant? (b) Why was the Union unwilling to agree to Davis's wish?

Activity **Making a Decision** You are the captain of your hometown school basketball team. A rival school's coach has offered you a scholarship if you will play for them. Write the coach a letter informing him of your decision and the reasons for your decision. As you write your letter, keep in mind Robert E. Lee's difficult choice at the start of the Civil War.

A Long, Difficult Struggle

As You Read

Explore These Questions
- What were the military plans of each side?
- Which of its military goals did the Union achieve?
- Why did the Union fail to win major battles in the East?

Identify
- Stonewall Jackson
- Battle of Bull Run
- George McClellan
- *Merrimack*
- *Monitor*
- Battle of Antietam
- Battle of Fredericksburg
- Battle of Chancellorsville
- Ulysses S. Grant
- Battle of Shiloh

Union infantry drum

SETTING the Scene In the summer of 1861, the armies of the North and the South marched off to war with flags flying and crowds cheering. Each side expected a quick victory. However, the reality of war soon shattered this dream. Abner Small, a volunteer from Maine, described a scene that would be repeated again and again:

> 66 I saw…the dead and hurt men lying limp on the ground. From somewhere across the field a battery [heavy guns] pounded us. We wavered, and rallied, and fired blindly; and men fell writhing. 99

It soon became clear that there would be no quick, easy end to the war. Leaders on both sides began to plan for a long, difficult struggle.

Strategies for Victory

The North and South had different strategies for victory. The Union planned to use its naval power to cripple the South's economy. At the same time, Union armies would invade southern territory. The South, meanwhile, planned to defend itself until the North lost the will to fight.

Union plans

First, the Union planned to use its navy to blockade southern ports. This would cut off the South's supply of manufactured goods by halting its trade with Europe.

In the East, Union generals wanted to seize Richmond, Virginia, the Confederate capital. They thought that they might end the war quickly by capturing the Confederate government.

In the West, the Union planned to seize control of the Mississippi River. This would prevent the South from using the river to supply its troops. It would also separate Arkansas, Texas, and Louisiana from the rest of the Confederacy.

Confederate plans

The South's strategy was simpler: The Confederate army would fight a defensive war until northerners tired of the fighting. If the war became unpopular in the North, President Lincoln would have to stop the war and recognize the South's independence.

The Confederacy counted on European money and supplies to help fight the war. Southern cotton was important to the textile mills of England and other countries. Southerners were confident that Europeans would quickly recognize the Confederacy as an

The Civil War in the East, 1861–1863

Key

← Union troops

← Confederate troops

✱ Union victories

✱ Confederate victories

0   50   100 Miles

0   50   100 Kilometers

Geography *Skills*

Early in the war, Union armies were unsuccessful in their attempt to capture Richmond, the Confederate capital.

1. **Location** On the map, locate: **(a)** Washington, DC, **(b)** Richmond, **(c)** Bull Run, **(d)** Chancellorsville, **(e)** Potomac River.

2. **Movement** Describe the route that General McClellan took when he tried to capture Richmond in 1862.

3. **Critical Thinking** Do you think the Confederacy made a wise decision in locating its capital at Richmond? Explain.

independent nation and continue to buy southern cotton for their factories.

Forward to Richmond!

"Forward to Richmond! Forward to Richmond!" Every day for more than a month, the influential *New York Tribune* blazed this "Nation's War Cry" across its front page. Re-

sponding to popular pressure for a quick victory, President Lincoln ordered the attack.

Battle of Bull Run

In July 1861, Union troops set out from Washington, D.C., for Richmond, about 100 miles (160 km) away. They met with Confederate soldiers soon after they left. The battle that followed took place near a small stream called Bull Run, in Virginia.

July 21, 1861, was a lovely summer day. Hundreds of Washingtonians rode out to watch their army crush the Confederates. Many carried picnic baskets. In a holiday mood, they spread out on a grassy hilltop overlooking Bull Run and awaited the battle.

The spectators, however, were shocked. Southern troops did not turn and run as expected. Inspired by the example of General Thomas Jackson, they held their ground. A Confederate officer remarked that Jackson stood his ground "like a stone wall." From that day on, the general was known as **"Stonewall" Jackson.**

In the end, it was Union troops who panicked and ran. A congressman who witnessed the retreat reported,

> ❝ Off they went... across fields, toward the woods, anywhere, everywhere, to escape.... To enable them better to run, they threw away their blankets, knapsacks, canteens, and finally muskets, cartridge-boxes, and everything else. ❞

The Confederates did not pursue the fleeing Union army. Had they done so, they might even have captured Washington, D.C. Instead, they remained behind to gather the gear thrown away by the Union troops.

The **Battle of Bull Run** showed both the Union and the Confederacy that their soldiers needed training. It also showed that the war would be long and bloody.

Caution, delay, and retreat

After the shocking disaster at Bull Run, President Lincoln appointed General **George McClellan** as commander of the Union army of the East, known as the Army of the Potomac. McClellan, a superb

Biography

Robert E. Lee and Stonewall Jackson

Robert E. Lee (left) was perhaps the greatest general of the Civil War. Earlier, he had served admirably in the Mexican War and as superintendent of the United States Military Academy. Stonewall Jackson (right) was one of Lee's most skillful generals. Jackson's clever tactics and swift troop movements contributed to many victories.
★ **How did Jackson earn the nickname of "Stonewall" Jackson?**

organizer, transformed inexperienced recruits into an army of trained soldiers prepared for battle.

McClellan, however, was very cautious. He delayed leading his troops into battle. Newspapers reported "all quiet along the Potomac" so often that the phrase became a national joke. Finally, President Lincoln lost patience. "If McClellan is not using the army," the President snapped, "I should like to borrow it."

Finally, in March 1862, McClellan was ready to move. He and most of his troops left Washington by steamboat and sailed down the Potomac River for Richmond. The rest of the army stayed in Washington.

Landing south of Richmond, McClellan began inching slowly toward the Confederate capital. General Robert E. Lee launched a series of brilliant counterattacks. Lee also sent General Stonewall Jackson north to threaten Washington. Lincoln was thus prevented from sending the rest of the Union army to help McClellan. Cautious as usual, McClellan abandoned the attack and retreated. Once again, there was a lull in the war in the East.

Naval Action

Early in the war, Union ships blockaded southern ports. At first, some small, fast ships slipped through the blockade. These "blockade runners" brought everything from matches to guns into the Confederacy.

In time, however, the blockade became more effective. Trade through southern ports dropped by more than 90 percent. The South desperately needed a way to break the Union blockade. One method it tried was the ironclad ship.

At the start of the war, the Union abandoned a warship named the ***Merrimack*** near Portsmouth, Virginia. Confederates covered the ship with iron plates 4 inches (10.2 cm) thick and sent it into battle against the Union navy. On March 8, 1862, the *Merrimack* sank one Union ship, drove another aground, and forced a third to surrender. The Union vessels' cannonballs bounced harmlessly off the *Merrimack's* metal skin.

The Union countered with its own ironclads. One of these, the ***Monitor,*** battled the *Merrimack* in the waters off Hampton Roads, Virginia. The Confederate ship had more firepower, but the *Monitor* maneuvered more easily. In the end, neither ship seriously damaged the other, and both withdrew.

Ironclad ships changed naval warfare. Both sides rushed to build more of them. However, the South never mounted a serious attack against the Union navy. The Union blockade held throughout the war.

The 11-inch guns were large compared with the Merrimack's.

Revolving gun turret

Iron plates protected the Monitor from enemy fire and from ramming by enemy ships.

Boiler room

Boilers

Turret gears and machinery

Engine room

Main engine

Rudder

Propeller

Antietam

In September 1862, General Lee took the offensive and marched his troops north into Maryland. He believed that a southern victory on northern soil would be a great blow to northern morale.

Luck was against Lee, however. A Confederate messenger lost Lee's battle plans. Two Union soldiers found them and turned them over to General McClellan.

Even with Lee's battle plan before him, however, McClellan was slow to act. After waiting a few days, he finally attacked Lee's main force at Antietam (an TEE tuhm) on September 17. In the day-long battle that fol-

lowed, more than 23,000 Union and Confederate soldiers were killed or wounded.

On the night of September 18, Lee ordered his troops to slip back into Virginia. The Confederates breathed a sigh of relief when they saw that McClellan was not pursuing them.

Neither side was a clear winner at the **Battle of Antietam.** The North was able to claim victory, though, because Lee had ordered his forces to withdraw. As a result, northern morale increased. Still, President Lincoln was keenly disappointed. The Union army had suffered huge numbers of dead and wounded. Furthermore, General McClellan had failed to follow up his victory by pursuing

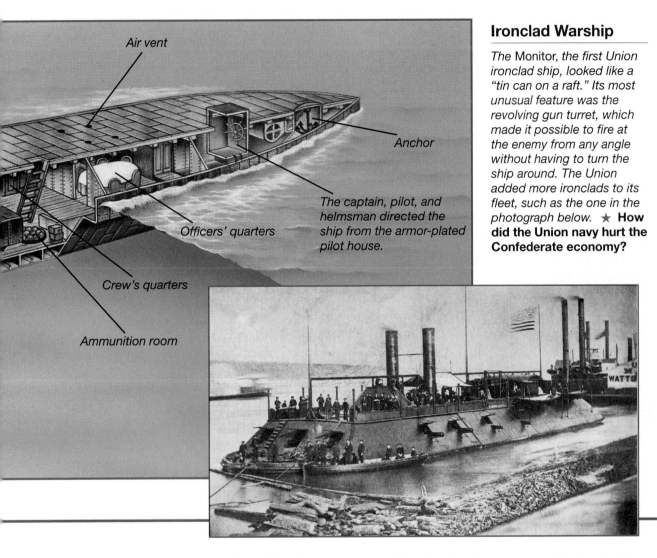

Air vent

Officers' quarters

Crew's quarters

Ammunition room

Anchor

The captain, pilot, and helmsman directed the ship from the armor-plated pilot house.

Ironclad Warship

The Monitor, *the first Union ironclad ship, looked like a "tin can on a raft." Its most unusual feature was the revolving gun turret, which made it possible to fire at the enemy from any angle without having to turn the ship around. The Union added more ironclads to its fleet, such as the one in the photograph below.* ★ **How did the Union navy hurt the Confederate economy?**

the Confederates. In November, Lincoln appointed General Ambrose Burnside to replace McClellan as commander of the Army of the Potomac.

Confederate Victories

Two stunning victories for the Confederacy came in late 1862 and 1863. (See the map on page 454.) General Robert E. Lee won by outsmarting the Union generals who fought against him.

Fredericksburg

In December 1862, Union forces set out once again toward Richmond. This time, they were led by General Ambrose Burnside.

Meeting Lee's army outside Fredericksburg, Virginia, Burnside ordered his troops to attack. Lee pulled back and left the town to Burnside. The Confederates dug in at the crest of a treeless hill above Fredericksburg. There, in a strong defensive position, they waited for the Union attack.

As the Union soldiers advanced, Confederate guns mowed them down by the thousands. Six times Burnside ordered his men to charge. Six times the rebels drove them back. "We forgot they were fighting us," one southerner wrote, "and cheer after cheer at their fearlessness went up along our lines." The **Battle of Fredericksburg** was one of the Union's worst defeats.

Chancellorsville

In May 1863, Lee, aided by Stonewall Jackson, again outwitted the Union army. This time, the battle took place on thickly wooded ground near Chancellorsville, Virginia. Lee and Jackson defeated the Union troops in three days.

Although the South won the **Battle of Chancellorsville,** it paid a high price for the victory. At the end of one day, nervous Confederate sentries fired at what they thought was an approaching Union soldier. The "Union soldier" was General Stonewall Jackson. Jackson died as a result of his injuries several days later.

The War in the West

While Union forces struggled in the East, those in the West met with success. As you have read, the Union strategy was to seize control of the Mississippi River. General **Ulysses S. Grant** began moving toward that goal. (See the map on page 470.) In February 1862, Grant attacked and captured Fort Henry and Fort Donelson in Tennessee. These Confederate forts guarded two important tributaries of the Mississippi.

Grant now pushed south to Shiloh, a village on the Tennessee River. At Shiloh, on April 6, he was surprised by Confederate forces. The Confederates won the first day of the **Battle of Shiloh.** They drove the Union troops back toward the river.

Grant now showed the toughness and determination that would enable him to win many battles in the future. "Retreat?" he replied to his doubting officers after that first day. "No. I propose to attack at daylight and whip them."

With the aid of reinforcements, Grant was able to win his victory and beat back the Confederates. However, the Battle of Shiloh was one of the bloodiest encounters of the Civil War. More Americans were killed or wounded at Shiloh than in the American Revolution, the War of 1812, and the Mexican War combined.

While Grant was fighting at Shiloh, the Union navy moved to gain control of the Mississippi River. In April 1862, Union gunboats captured New Orleans. Other ships seized Memphis, Tennessee. By capturing these two cities, the Union controlled both ends of the Mississippi. No longer could the South use the river as a supply line.

★ Section 2 Review ★

Recall
1. **Locate** (a) Richmond, (b) Washington, D.C., (c) Potomac River, (d) Fort Henry, (e) Fort Donelson, (f) New Orleans, (g) Memphis.
2. **Identify** (a) Stonewall Jackson, (b) Battle of Bull Run, (c) George McClellan, (d) *Merrimack,* (e) *Monitor,* (f) Battle of Antietam, (g) Battle of Fredericksburg, (h) Battle of Chancellorsville, (i) Ulysses S. Grant, (j) Battle of Shiloh.

Comprehension
3. (a) Describe the North's three-part plan for defeating the South. (b) Which part of the plan did the North achieve first?

4. Why was President Lincoln unhappy with General McClellan's performance as commander of the Union armies?

5. How did the loss of New Orleans and Memphis affect the South?

Critical Thinking and Writing
6. **Analyzing Primary Sources** In response to Stonewall Jackson's death, General Lee said, "I have lost my right arm." What did Lee mean by this statement?

7. **Analyzing Visual Evidence** Study the ironclad ships on pages 456-457. Explain how such ships were superior to wooden sailing ships.

Activity **Making a Map** You are the chief cartographer for the Union army. Your assignment is to make a map illustrating the Union's three-part plan for defeating the South.

3

A Promise of Freedom

★ ★

Explore These Questions
- Why did Lincoln issue the Emancipation Proclamation?
- What were the effects of the Proclamation?
- How did African Americans contribute to the Union war effort?

Define
- emancipate
- discrimination

Identify
- Emancipation Proclamation
- 54th Massachusetts Regiment
- Fort Wagner

As You Read

Antislavery potholders

SETTING the Scene At first, the Civil War was not a war against slavery. Yet wherever Union troops went, enslaved African Americans eagerly rushed to them, expecting to be freed. Most were sorely disappointed. Union officers often held these runaways until their masters arrived to take them back to slavery.

Some northerners began to raise questions. Was slavery not the root of the conflict between North and South? Were tens of thousands of men dying so that a slaveholding South would come back into the Union? Questions like these led Northerners to wonder what the real aim of the war should be.

Lincoln Was Cautious

The Civil War began as a war to restore the Union, not to end the institution of slavery. President Lincoln made this clear in the following statement.

66 If I could save the Union without freeing any slave, I would do it; and if I could save it by freeing all the slaves, I would do it; and if I could do it by freeing some and leaving others alone, I would also do that. 99

Lincoln had a reason for handling the slavery issue cautiously. As you have read, four slave states remained in the Union. The President did not want to do anything that might cause these states to shift their loyalty

to the Confederacy. The resources of the border states might allow the South to turn the tide of the war.

The Emancipation Proclamation

By mid-1862, however, Lincoln came to believe that he could save the Union only by broadening the goals of the war. He decided to **emancipate,** or free, enslaved African Americans living in the Confederacy. In the four loyal slave states, however, slaves would not be freed. Nor would slaves be freed in Confederate lands that had already been captured by the Union, such as the city of New Orleans.

Motives and timing

Lincoln had practical reasons for his emancipation plan. At the start of the Civil War, more than 3 million enslaved people labored for the Confederacy. They helped grow the food that fed Confederate soldiers. They also worked in iron and lead mines that were vital to the South's war effort. Some served as nurses and cooks for the army. Lincoln knew that emancipation would weaken the Confederacy's ability to carry on the war.

However, Lincoln did not want to anger slave owners in the Union. Also, he knew that many northerners opposed freedom for

Freedom proclaimed

On September 22, 1862, five days after the Union victory at Antietam, Lincoln issued a preliminary proclamation. It warned that on January 1, 1863, anyone held as a slave in a state still in rebellion against the United States would be emancipated.

Then, on January 1, 1863, Lincoln issued the formal Emancipation Proclamation. The **Emancipation Proclamation** declared:

> 66 On the 1st day of January, in the year of our Lord 1863, all persons held as slaves within any state or...part of a state [whose] people...shall then be in rebellion against the United States, shall be then, thenceforward, and forever free. 99

Impact of the Proclamation

Because the rebelling states were not under Union control, no slaves actually gained their freedom on January 1, 1863. Nevertheless, as a result of the Emancipation Proclamation, the purpose of the war changed. Now, Union troops were fighting to end slavery as well as to save the Union.

The opponents of slavery greeted the proclamation with joy. In Boston, African American abolitionist Frederick Douglass witnessed one of the many emotional celebrations that took place:

> 66 The effect of this announcement was startling...and the scene was wild and grand....My old friend Rue, a Negro preacher,...expressed the heartfelt emotion of the hour, when he led all voices in the anthem, 'Sound the loud timbrel o'er Egypt's dark sea, Jehovah hath triumphed, his people are free!' 99

Viewing HISTORY — The Emancipation Proclamation

The Emancipation Proclamation meant that Union troops were now fighting to end slavery. Lincoln's action, however, did not please all northerners. Opposition to the preliminary proclamation contributed to Republican party losses in the Congressional elections of 1862.

★ **How does this poster make use of symbolism?**

enslaved African Americans. Lincoln therefore hoped to introduce the idea of emancipation slowly, by limiting it to territory controlled by the Confederacy.

The President had another very important motive, too. As you read in Chapter 16, Lincoln believed that slavery was wrong. When he felt that he could act to free slaves without threatening the Union, he did so.

Lincoln was concerned about the timing of his announcement. The war was not going well for the Union. He did not want Americans to think he was freeing slaves as a desperate effort to save a losing cause. He waited for a victory to announce his plan.

Connections With Arts

Many northerners greeted the Emancipation Proclamation with music and song. At Boston's Music Hall, people celebrated with performances of Mendelssohn's *Hymn of Praise,* and Handel's *Hallelujah Chorus.*

The Proclamation won the Union the sympathy of people in Europe, especially workers. As a result, it became less likely that Britain or any other European country would come to the aid of the South.

African Americans Help

When the war began, thousands of free blacks volunteered to fight for the Union. At first, federal law forbade African Americans to serve as soldiers. When Congress repealed that law in 1862, however, both free African Americans and escaped slaves enlisted in the Union army.

In the Union army

The army assigned these volunteers to all-black units, commanded by white officers. At first, the black troops served only as laborers. They performed noncombat duties such as building roads and guarding supplies. Black troops received only half the pay of white soldiers.

African American soldiers protested against this policy of **discrimination** that denied them the same rights and treatment as other soldiers. Gradually, conditions changed. By 1863, African American troops were fighting in major battles against the Confederates. In 1864, the United States War Department announced that all soldiers would receive equal pay. By the end of the war, about 200,000 African Americans had fought for the Union. Nearly 40,000 lost their lives.

Acts of bravery

One of the most famous African American units in the Union army was the **54th Massachusetts Regiment.** The 54th accepted African Americans from all across the

Viewing HISTORY Assault on Fort Wagner

In this painting by Tom Lovell, African American soldiers of the 54th Massachussetts Regiment charge against Confederate troops at Fort Wagner. Nearly half the regiment died in the failed attack, including the regiment's commander, Colonel Robert Gould Shaw. ★ **Why do you think the Union army was reluctant to appoint African American officers?**

North. Frederick Douglass helped recruit troops for the regiment, and two of his sons served in it.

On July 18, 1863, the 54th Massachusetts Regiment led an attack on **Fort Wagner** near Charleston. Under heavy fire, troops fought their way into the fort before being forced to withdraw. In the desperate fighting, almost half the regiment, including its young commander, Robert Shaw, were killed.

The courage of the 54th Massachusetts and other regiments helped to win respect for African American soldiers. Sergeant William Carney of the 54th Massachusetts was awarded the Congressional Medal of Honor for acts of bravery. He was the first of 16 African American soldiers to be so honored during the Civil War. In a letter to President Lincoln, Secretary of War Stanton praised African American soldiers.

❝ [They] have proved themselves among the bravest of the brave, performing deeds of daring and shedding their blood with a heroism unsurpassed by soldiers of any race. ❞

Behind Confederate lines

In the South, despite the Emancipation Proclamation, African Americans still had to work as slaves on plantations. However, many enslaved African Americans slowed down their work. Others refused to work at all or to submit to punishment. In so doing, they knew they were helping to weaken the South's war effort. They knew that when victorious Union troops arrived in their area, they would be free.

Throughout the South, thousands of enslaved African Americans also took direct action to free themselves. Whenever a Union army appeared in an area, the slaves from all around would flee their former masters. They crossed over to the Union lines and to freedom. By the end of the war, about one fourth of the enslaved population in the South had escaped to freedom.

The former slaves helped Union armies achieve victory in a variety of ways. They used their knowledge of the local terrain to serve as guides and spies. Many more enlisted in African American regiments of the Union army.

★ Section 3 Review ★

Recall

1. **Identify** (a) Emancipation Proclamation, (b) 54th Massachusetts Regiment, (c) Fort Wagner.

2. **Define** (a) emancipate, (b) discrimination.

Comprehension

3. (a) Why was President Lincoln cautious about making emancipation a goal of the war? (b) Why did he finally decide to issue the Emancipation Proclamation?

4. Why were no slaves actually freed when the Proclamation was issued?

5. (a) How did the 54th Massachussetts Regiment's attack on Fort Wagner affect public opinion about enslaved African American soldiers?

(b) How did African Americans help to weaken the Confederacy?

Critical Thinking and Writing

6. **Drawing Conclusions** What did the Union army's policy toward all-black regiments reveal about northern attitudes toward African Americans? Explain.

7. **Analyzing Primary Sources** In 1861, Frederick Douglass said, "This is no time to fight with one hand when both hands are needed. This is no time to fight with only your white hand, and allow your black hand to remain tied!" (a) What did Douglass mean by this statement? (b) Did the United States Congress agree with Douglass? Explain.

Activity **Writing a Poem** A monument is being built to honor the courageous African American soldiers of the Civil War. Write a poem to be engraved on the monument, mentioning some of the facts you have learned in this section.

Hardships of War

★ ★

As You Read

Explore These Questions
- What was life like for soldiers in the Civil War?
- How did women contribute to the war effort?
- What problems did each side face during the war?

Define
- civilians
- draft
- habeas corpus
- income tax
- inflation
- profiteer

Identify
- Copperheads
- Loreta Janeta Velazquez
- Rose Greenhow
- Dorothea Dix
- Clara Barton
- Sojourner Truth
- Sally Tompkins

SETTING the Scene The Civil War caused hardships not only for soldiers but for people at home as well. Southerners, especially, suffered from the war, because most of the fighting took place in the South.

On both sides, **civilians,** or people who were not in the army, worked on farms and labored in factories to support the war effort. They used their mules to move troops and supplies. They tended the wounded. As their hardships increased, so did opposition to the war.

The Hard Life of Soldiers

On both sides, most soldiers were under age 21. However, war quickly turned gentle boys into tough men. Soldiers drilled and marched for long hours. They slept on the ground even in rain and snow. In combat, boys of 18 learned to stand firm as cannon blasts shook the earth and bullets whizzed past their ears.

New technology added to the horror of war. Cone-shaped bullets, which made rifles twice as accurate, replaced round musket balls. New cannons could hurl exploding shells several miles. The new weapons had deadly results. In most battles, one fourth or more of the soldiers were killed or wounded.

Sick and wounded soldiers faced other horrors. Medical care on the battlefield was crude. Surgeons routinely cut off injured

▲ *Confederate cap*

▲ *Union cap*

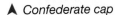

arms and legs. Minor wounds often became infected. With no medicines to fight infection, thousands of wounded died. Diseases like pneumonia and malaria killed more men than guns or cannons did.

On both sides, prisoners of war faced horrifying conditions. At Andersonville, a prison camp in Georgia, more than one Union prisoner out of three died of disease or starvation. One prisoner wrote:

> 66 There is no such thing as delicacy here.... In the middle of last night I was awakened by being kicked by a dying man. He was soon dead. I got up and moved the body off a few feet, and went to sleep to dream of the hideous sights. 99

Discontent in the North

Some northerners opposed using force to keep the South in the Union. Supporters of the war called these people **Copperheads,** after the poisonous snake. Other northerners supported the war but opposed the way Lincoln was conducting it. In some northern cities, this opposition led to riots.

Viewing HISTORY **The Faces of War**

Confederate soldiers wore gray uniforms and were sometimes called Johnny Rebs. Union soldiers wore blue and were called Billy Yanks. During the Civil War, about 1 of every 10 soldiers deserted from service. ★ **Why do you think desertion rates were high in both armies?**

The draft law

As the war dragged on, public support dwindled. Soon, not enough men were volunteering to serve in the Union army. The government took action.

In 1863, Congress passed a **draft** law. It required all able-bodied males between the ages of 20 and 45 to serve in the military if they were called.

Under the law, a man could avoid the draft by paying the government $300 or by hiring someone to serve in his place. This angered many people. They began to see the Civil War as "a rich man's war and a poor man's fight."

Riots in the cities

Opposition to the draft law led to riots in several northern cities. The draft law had gone into effect soon after Lincoln issued the Emancipation Proclamation. As a result, some northerners believed that they were being forced to fight to end slavery. This idea angered some white workers, especially recent immigrants in the cities. Like many other northerners, some of these immigrants held racist beliefs. They also feared that free African Americans would be employed at jobs that they needed, too.

The worst riot took place in New York City during July 1863. For four days, white workers attacked free blacks. Rioters also attacked rich New Yorkers who had paid to avoid serving in the army. At least 74 people were killed during the riot.

President Lincoln moved to stop the riots and other "disloyal practices." Several times, he denied **habeas corpus** (HAY bee uhs KOR puhs), the right to have charges filed or a hearing before being jailed. Lincoln defended his actions by saying that the Constitution gave him the right to deny people their rights "when in the cases of rebellion or invasion, the public safety may require it."

Problems in the South

President Davis, meanwhile, struggled to create a strong federal government for the Confederacy. Many southerners were strong supporters of states' rights. They resisted paying taxes to a central government. At one point, Georgia threatened to secede from the Confederacy!

Like the North, the South had to pass a draft law to fill its army. However, men who owned or supervised more than 20 slaves did not have to serve in the army. Southern farmers who owned few or no slaves resented this law.

Near war's end, the South no longer had enough white men to fill the ranks. Robert E. Lee urged that enslaved African Americans be allowed to serve as soldiers. Desperate, the Confederate congress finally agreed. However, the war ended before any enslaved people put on Confederate uniforms.

Why Study History?

Because One Person Can Make a Difference

★ ★

Historical Background

In the early days of the Civil War, Clara Barton and other women provided medical care to wounded soldiers. However, the government required women to stay far from battle. As a result, many soldiers received treatment too late and died of their wounds. Barton therefore sought permission to work directly on the fields of battle.

After some initial refusals, the government gave in. Through the remainder of the war, Clara Barton served as a battlefield nurse. Because of her courageous efforts, she became known as the "Angel of the Battlefield."

Connections to Today

After the Civil War, Barton continued to make a difference. In Europe, she worked with the International Red Cross, an organization that aided victims of war. In 1881, after returning to the United States, she founded the American Red Cross. This new organization served both victims of war and victims of natural disaster.

Today, disaster relief remains a primary service of the Red Cross. The Red Cross helps people recover from natural disasters such as fires, floods, and hurricanes. It provides victims with medical assistance, food, clothing, and shelter.

The American Red Cross provides other services as well. It helps homeless people and seniors in need. It supervises donations of blood and other organs. It also provides instruction in a variety of safety programs.

Connections to You

Like Clara Barton, you too can make a difference. You can learn about first aid and safety procedures in a Red Cross educational course. Courses include first aid, water safety, fire prevention, and even babysitting. Some local Red Cross chapters invite teens to serve as volunteers. You might also organize or participate in a drive to help raise funds for the Red Cross. Red Cross disaster relief services are provided free of charge because of contributions made by caring Americans.

▲ Clara Barton

▲ Red Cross book

1. **Comprehension** How does the American Red Cross help victims of disaster?

2. **Critical Thinking** At the start of the Civil War, why do you think government officials allowed men, but not women, to aid wounded soldiers on the field of battle?

 Making an Advertisement Create an advertisement that seeks public support for the Red Cross by informing people about the many services the Red Cross provides.

Nursing the Wounded

In this Civil War scene, painted by Allyn Cox in 1974, women are nursing the wounded in the rotunda of the Capitol building. During the war, many public buildings served as temporary hospitals. The painting decorates a corridor of the Capitol today.
★ **How else did women help in the war effort?**

The Northern Economy

The Civil War cost far more than any earlier war. The Union had to use several strategies to raise money. In some ways, though, war helped the North's economy.

Taxation and inflation

In 1861, to pay for the war, Congress established the nation's first **income tax** on people's earnings. In addition, the Union issued bonds worth millions of dollars. Still, taxes and bonds did not raise enough money. To get the funds it needed, the North printed more than $400 million in paper money.

As the money supply increased, each dollar was worth less. In response, businesses charged more for their goods. The North was experiencing **inflation,** a rise in prices and a decrease in the value of money. During the war, prices for goods nearly doubled in the North.

Economic benefits

In some ways, the war helped the North's economy. Because many farmers went off to fight, more machines were used to plant and harvest crops. As a result, farm production actually went up during the war.

The wartime demand for clothing, shoes, guns, and other goods helped many northern industries. Some manufacturers made fortunes by profiteering. **Profiteers** charged excessive prices for goods the government desperately needed for the war.

The Southern Economy

For the South, war brought economic ruin. The South had to struggle with the cost of the war, the loss of the cotton trade, and severe shortages brought on by the Union blockade.

The economy suffers

To raise money, the Confederacy imposed an income tax and a tax-in-kind. The tax-in-kind required farmers to turn over one tenth of their crops to the government. The government took crops because it knew that southern farmers had little money.

Like the North, the South printed paper money. It printed so much, in fact, that wild inflation set in. By 1865, one Confederate dollar was worth only two cents in gold.

The war did serious damage to the cotton trade, the South's main source of income. Early in the war, President Davis halted cotton shipments to Britain. He hoped that Britain would side with the South in order to get cotton. The tactic backfired. Britain simply bought more cotton from Egypt and

$ Connections *With* Economics

As inflation in the South worsened, it became more and more difficult to feed and clothe a family. Near the end of the war, a barrel of flour cost $1,000 and a pair of shoes cost $400.

India. Davis succeeded only in cutting the South's income.

Effects of the blockade

The Union blockade created severe shortages in the South. Confederate armies sometimes had to wait weeks for supplies of food and clothing. Guns and ammunition were also in short supply. With few factories of its own, the South bought many of its weapons in Europe. However, the blockade cut off most deliveries from Europe.

For civilians, the blockade brought food shortages. Even the wealthy went hungry. "I had a little piece of bread and a little molasses today for my dinner," wrote plantation mistress Mary Chesnut in her diary. By 1865, there was widespread famine in the Confederacy.

Women at War

Women of both the North and South played vital roles during the war. As men left for the battlefields, women took jobs in industry, in teaching, and on farms.

Women and the military

Women's aid societies helped supply the troops with food, bedding, clothing, and medicine. Throughout the North, women held fairs and other fund-raising events to pay for the supplies. They succeeded in raising millions of dollars.

A few women disguised themselves so they could serve as soldiers. **Loreta Janeta Velazquez,** for example, fought for the South at Bull Run and Shiloh. Other women worked as spies. **Rose Greenhow** gathered information for the South while entertaining Union leaders in her Washington, D.C., home. She was caught, convicted of treason, and exiled.

Nursing the wounded

Women on both sides worked as nurses. Doctors were unwilling at first to permit even trained nurses to work in military hospitals. When wounded men began to swamp army hospitals, however, this attitude soon changed.

Dorothea Dix, famous for her work reforming prisons and mental hospitals, became superintendent of nurses for the Union army. **Clara Barton** earned fame as a Civil War nurse. She later founded the American Red Cross. **Sojourner Truth,** the African American antislavery leader, worked in Union hospitals and in camps for freed slaves. In the South, **Sally Tompkins** set up a hospital in Richmond, Virginia.

★ Section 4 Review ★

Recall

1. **Identify** (a) Copperheads, (b) Loreta Janeta Velazquez, (c) Rose Greenhow, (d) Dorothea Dix, (e) Clara Barton, (f) Sojourner Truth, (g) Sally Tompkins.
2. **Define** (a) civilians, (b) draft, (c) habeas corpus, (d) income tax, (e) inflation, (f) profiteer.

Comprehension

3. Describe three hardships faced by soldiers during the Civil War.

4. Describe three ways women contributed to the war effort.
5. How did the Union blockade affect the South?

Critical Thinking and Writing

6. **Linking Past and Present** (a) What advances in technology made Civil War battles deadly? (b) In what ways would a war today be even more deadly?
7. **Defending a Position** What facts support the charge that the Civil War was "a rich man's war and a poor man's fight"?

Activity **Making a Chart** You are the graphic illustrator for an economics magazine. Create a flowchart or cause-and-effect chart to illustrate how the high cost of the Civil War led to high inflation.

5

The War Ends

As You Read

Explore These Questions
- What was the significance of the Union victories at Vicksburg and Gettysburg?
- What ideals did Lincoln express in the Gettysburg Address?
- How did Union generals use a new type of war to defeat the Confederacy?

Define
- siege
- total war

Identify
- Battle of Gettysburg
- Gettysburg Address
- Ulysses S. Grant
- Philip Sheridan
- William Tecumseh Sherman

SETTING the Scene As you have read, Confederate armies won major battles at Fredericksburg in December 1862 and at Chancellorsville in May 1863. These were gloomy days for the North.

Then, in July 1863, the tide of war turned against the South. In the West, the Union extended its control of the Mississippi River and cut the South in two. At the Battle of Gettysburg, in Pennsylvania, both Union and Confederate forces suffered terrible losses. However, as President Davis later explained, "Theirs could be repaired, ours could not."

The following year, President Lincoln would appoint Ulysses S. Grant commander in chief of the Union army. In Grant, Lincoln had found the general who could lead the Union to victory.

The Fall of Vicksburg

After capturing New Orleans and Memphis, the Union controlled both ends of the Mississippi River. Still, the North could not safely use the river because Confederates held Vicksburg, Mississippi. Vicksburg sat on a cliff high above the river. Cannons there could shell boats traveling between New Orleans and Memphis.

Early in 1863, Grant's forces tried again and again to seize Vicksburg. The Confederates held out bravely. At last, Grant devised a brilliant plan. Marching his troops inland, he launched a surprise attack on Jackson, Mississippi. Then, he turned west and attacked Vicksburg from the rear. (See the map on page 470.)

For over six weeks, Grant's forces lay siege to Vicksburg. A **siege** is a military blockade of an enemy town or position in order to force it to surrender. Day after day, the Union soldiers pushed their lines closer to the town. Union artillery and gunboats on the Mississippi bombarded the besieged soldiers and inhabitants. As their food supplies ran out, the southerners began to use mules and rats as food. Finally, on July 4, 1863, the Confederates surrendered Vicksburg.

On July 9, Union forces also captured Port Hudson, Louisiana. The entire Mississippi was now under Union control. The Confederacy was split into two parts. Texas, Arkansas, and Louisiana were cut off from the rest of the Confederacy.

Union Victory at Gettysburg

In the East, after his victory at Chancellorsville, General Lee moved his army north into Pennsylvania. He hoped to take the Yankees by surprise. If he was successful, Lee planned to then swing south and capture Washington, D.C.

American Heritage
M A G A Z I N E

Vicksburg National Military Park

You can learn about the siege of Vicksburg, Mississippi, by touring the actual battle site. The park includes a museum, miles of defensive earthworks, and more than 125 cannons. You can even walk the deck of a Union ironclad gunboat, raised from the Mississippi River in the 1960s. Throughout the park, numerous monuments honor the soldiers who fought and died for control of this small Mississippi River town.

★ **To learn more about this historic site, write:** *Vicksburg National Military Park, 3201 Clay Street, Vicksburg, MS 39180.*

◄ Ohio regiment monument

On June 30, 1863, a Union force under General George C. Meade met part of Lee's army at the small town of Gettysburg, Pennsylvania. Both sides quickly sent in reinforcements. The three-day Battle of Gettysburg that followed was one of the most important battles of the Civil War.

At the start of the battle, the Confederates drove the Union forces out of Gettysburg. The Yankees took up strong positions on Cemetery Ridge, overlooking the town. On July 2, a Confederate attack failed with heavy casualties. Nevertheless, Lee decided to launch another attack. On July 3, he ordered General George Pickett to lead 15,000 men in a daring charge against the center of the Union line. To reach the Yankees, Pickett's men had to cross an open field and run up a steep slope.

Pickett gave the order to charge and the Union guns opened fire. Row after row of soldiers fell to the ground, bleeding. Still, the Confederate troops continued to rush forward against a rain of bullets and shells. Few were able to reach the Union lines. A Union soldier described the fighting at the crest of the ridge:

❝ Men fire into each other's faces not five feet apart. There are bayonet thrusts, saber strokes, pistol shots, men going down on their hands and knees... gulping blood, falling, legless, armless, headless. ❞

Pickett's charge failed. As the survivors limped back, Lee rode among them. "It's all my fault," he admitted humbly. Lee had no choice but to retreat. After their defeat at the **Battle of Gettysburg,** the Confederates would never again invade the North.

The Union victories at Vicksburg and Gettysburg marked the turning point of the Civil War. On July 4, 1863, northerners had good reason to celebrate.

The Gettysburg Address

The Battle of Gettysburg left more than 40,000 dead or wounded. When the soldiers who died there were buried, their graves stretched as far as the eye could see. On November 19, 1863, northerners held a ceremony to dedicate this cemetery.

President Lincoln attended the ceremony, but he was not the main speaker. At the time, his popularity was quite low. Lincoln sat with his hands folded as another speaker talked for two hours. When it was his turn, the President rose and spoke for about three minutes.

In his **Gettysburg Address,** Lincoln said that the Civil War was a test of whether or not a democratic nation could survive. He reminded Americans that their nation was founded on the belief that "all men are created equal." Looking out at the thousands of graves, Lincoln told the audience:

66 We here highly resolve that these dead shall not have died in vain—that this nation, under God, shall have a new birth of freedom—and that government of the people, by the people, for the people, shall not perish from the earth. 99

Union Advances in the South

As the Civil War dragged on, Union armies advanced deeper and deeper into the South. General Sherman marched his troops through Georgia and the Carolinas.

Geography Skills

1. **Location** On the map, locate: **(a)** Vicksburg, **(b)** Atlanta, **(c)** Savannah.
2. **Place** What three Confederate states were cut off from the rest of the Confederacy after Union forces gained control of the Mississippi River?
3. **Critical Thinking** Based on the map, why would the South be hurt more than the North—no matter who won the war?

Few people listened to Lincoln that day. Newspapers gave his speech little attention. Later generations, however, have honored Lincoln's brief address as a profound statement of American ideals.

The Union Wages Total War

For three years, Lincoln had searched for a general who could lead the Union to victory. More and more, he thought of **Ulysses S. Grant.** After capturing Vicksburg, Grant continued to win battles in the West. In 1864, Lincoln appointed him commander of the Union forces.

Some questioned the choice, but President Lincoln felt that "Unconditional Surrender" Grant was the general who would lead the Union to victory. "I can't spare this man," Lincoln said. "He fights."

Grant and other Union generals began to wage total war against the South. In total war, civilians as well as soldiers are affected. The Union army waged total war by destroying food and equipment that might be useful to the enemy. Civilians in the South suffered the same hardships as soldiers.

Sheridan in the Shenandoah

Grant had a plan for ending the war. He wanted to destroy the South's ability to fight. Grant sent General **Philip Sheridan** and his cavalry into the rich farmland of Virginia's Shenandoah Valley. He instructed Sheridan:

> ❝ Leave nothing to invite the enemy to return. Destroy whatever cannot be consumed. Let the valley be left so that crows flying over it will have to carry their rations along with them. ❞

Sheridan obeyed. In the summer and fall of 1864, he marched through the valley, destroying farms and livestock.

Sherman's march to the sea

Grant also ordered General **William Tecumseh Sherman** to capture Atlanta, Georgia, and then march to the Atlantic coast. Like Sheridan, Sherman had orders to destroy everything useful to the South.

Cause and Effect

Causes

- Issue of slavery in the territories divides the North and South
- Abolitionists want slavery to end
- South fears it will lose power in the national government
- Southern states secede after Lincoln's election
- Confederates bombard Fort Sumter

The Civil War

Effects

- Lincoln issues the Emancipation Proclamation
- Northern economy booms
- South loses its cotton trade with Britain
- Total war destroys the South's economy
- Hundreds of thousands of Americans killed

Effects Today

- Sectionalism is less of a force in American life and politics
- African Americans have equal protection under the Constitution
- Millions of Americans visit Civil War battlefields each year

Graphic Organizer *Skills*

The Civil War was a major turning point in the history of the United States.

1. **Comprehension** How did the war affect the northern and southern economies differently?
2. **Critical Thinking** Describe another cause or effect that could be added to this chart.

Sherman's troops captured Atlanta in September 1864. They burned the city in November. Then Sherman began his "march to the sea."

Sherman's troops ripped up railroad tracks, built bonfires from the ties, then heated and twisted the rails. They killed livestock and tore up fields. They burned barns, homes, and factories.

Lincoln Is Reelected

In 1864, Lincoln ran for reelection. At first, his defeat seemed, in his own words, "extremely probable." Before the capture of Atlanta, Union chances for victory looked bleak. Lincoln knew that many northerners were unhappy with his handling of the war. He thought that this might cost him the election.

The Democrats nominated General George McClellan to oppose Lincoln. Although he had commanded the Union army, McClellan was more willing than Lincoln to compromise with the South. If peace could be achieved, he was ready to restore slavery.

When Sherman took Atlanta in September, the North rallied around Lincoln. Sheridan's smashing victories in the Shenandoah Valley in October further increased Lincoln's popular support. In the election in November, the vote was close, but Lincoln remained President.

In his second Inaugural Address, Lincoln looked forward to the coming of peace:

66 With malice toward none, with charity for all . . . let us strive . . . to bind up the nation's wounds . . . to do all which may achieve a just and a lasting peace among ourselves and with all nations. 99

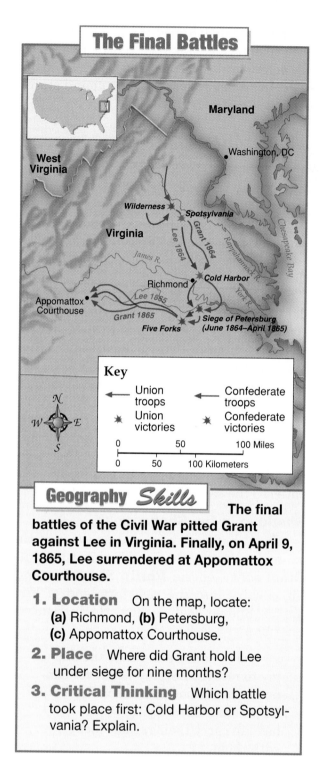

The Final Battles

Geography Skills   The final battles of the Civil War pitted Grant against Lee in Virginia. Finally, on April 9, 1865, Lee surrendered at Appomattox Courthouse.

1. **Location**   On the map, locate:
   (a) Richmond, (b) Petersburg,
   (c) Appomattox Courthouse.
2. **Place**   Where did Grant hold Lee under siege for nine months?
3. **Critical Thinking**   Which battle took place first: Cold Harbor or Spotsylvania? Explain.

The War Ends

Grant had begun a drive to capture Richmond in May 1864. Throughout the spring and summer, he and Lee fought a series of costly battles.

Northerners read with horror that Grant had lost 60,000 dead and wounded in a single month at the battles of the Wilderness, Spotsylvania, and Cold Harbor. Still, Grant pressed on. He knew that the Union could replace men and supplies. The South could not.

Lee dug in at Petersburg, near Richmond. Here, Grant kept Lee under siege for nine months. At last, with a fresh supply of troops, Grant took Petersburg on April 2, 1865. The same day, Richmond fell.

General Lee surrenders to General Grant at Appomattox Courthouse.

Lee and his army withdrew to a small Virginia town called Appomattox Courthouse. There, a week later, they were trapped by Union troops. Lee knew that his men would be slaughtered if he kept fighting. On April 9, 1865, Lee surrendered.

At Appomattox Courthouse, Grant offered generous terms of surrender to the defeated Confederate army. Soldiers were required to turn over their rifles, but officers were allowed to keep their pistols. Soldiers who had horses could keep them. Grant knew that southerners would need the animals for spring plowing.

As the Confederates surrendered, Union soldiers began to cheer. Grant ordered them to be silent. "The war is over," he said. "The rebels are our countrymen again."

Effects of the War

More than 360,000 Union soldiers and 250,000 Confederate soldiers lost their lives in the Civil War. No war has ever resulted in more American deaths. As a result, feelings of bitterness remained among both northerners and southerners.

Southerners had special reasons to view the North with resentment. They had lost their struggle for independence. Their way of life had been forcibly changed. Union armies had destroyed much of their land. In addition, many southerners feared that the North would seek revenge against the South after the war.

Finally, the Civil War was a major turning point in American history. The Union was secure. States' rights had suffered a terrible blow. As a result, the power of the federal government grew. The war also brought freedom to millions of African Americans. Still, a long and difficult struggle for equality lay ahead.

★ Section 5 Review ★

Recall

1. **Locate** (a) Vicksburg, (b) Port Hudson, (c) Gettysburg, (d) Atlanta, (e) Petersburg, (f) Appomattox Courthouse.
2. **Identify** (a) Battle of Gettysburg, (b) Gettysburg Address, (c) Ulysses S. Grant, (d) Philip Sheridan, (e) William Tecumseh Sherman.
3. **Define** (a) siege, (b) total war.

Comprehension

4. Why did the Union victories at Vicksburg and Gettysburg mark a turning point in the war?

5. What ideals did Lincoln express in his Gettysburg Address and Second Inaugural Address?
6. How did Sheridan and Sherman use total war to destroy the South's ability to fight?

Critical Thinking and Writing

7. **Predicting Consequences** If Sherman and Sheridan had not won victories just before the election of 1864, how might the election and the war have turned out differently?
8. **Defending a Position** Some people have condemned Grant's decision to wage total war. Do you agree or disagree with this position? Explain.

★ ★

Activity **Writing a Speech** It is a sad day for the South. You are a member of the Confederate Congress and you have just heard of Lee's surrender. Write a speech in which you reflect on the hardships of the war and offer hope for the future.

★ Sum It Up ★

Section 1   The Conflict Takes Shape
▶ The Union's advantages included a greater population and superior industrial resources.
▶ The Confederacy's advantages included better military leaders and its position of defending the homeland.

Section 2   A Long, Difficult Struggle
▶ The Union navy blockaded southern ports. Union armies tried to take Richmond and the Mississippi Valley.
▶ The Confederates won major battles in the East. Union armies were more successful in the West.

Section 3   A Promise of Freedom
▶ The Emancipation Proclamation made the end of slavery a goal of the war.
▶ African Americans worked, fought, and died in the effort to preserve the Union and end slavery.

Section 4   Hardships of War
▶ Both men and women suffered hardships in their efforts to win the war.
▶ During the war, the Union and Confederacy both struggled with political and economic problems.

Section 5   The War Ends
▶ The North waged total war deep into the South, disrupting civilian lives and inflicting great losses.
▶ Lee surrendered his army at Appomattox Courthouse, Virginia, on April 9, 1865.

For additional review of the major ideas of Chapter 17, see *Guide to the Essentials of American History* or *Interactive Student Tutorial CD-ROM*, which contains interactive review activities, graphic organizers, and practice tests.

🗍 Reviewing the Chapter

Define These Terms
Match each term with the correct definition.

Column 1
1. emancipate
2. martial law
3. draft
4. profiteers
5. inflation

Column 2
a. rule by the army
b. set free
c. people who overcharge for desperately needed goods
d. a rise in prices
e. a law requiring people to serve in the military

Explore the Main Ideas
1. What advantages did the United States have over the Confederate States?
2. Why were Confederate armies in the East often victorious in the early years of the war?
3. What were the results of the Emancipation Proclamation?
4. How did women support the war effort?
5. Explain how total war affected the South.

🗍 Chart Activity

Use the chart below to answer the following questions:
1. How many members of Company D were captured and imprisoned by the Union? **2.** How many soldiers were in Company D at the start of the war?   **Critical Thinking** Why do you think so many soldiers died from disease?

Seventh Virginia Infantry, Company D	
Original members	122
Killed in battle or died of wounds	17
Died of disease	14
Discharged	29
Transferred	6
Prisoners of war	27
On leave, hospitalized, or at home	8
Deserted	12
Surrendered at Appomattox	9

Source: David E. Johnston, *The Story of a Confederate Boy in the Civil War*

☐ Critical Thinking and Writing

1. **Understanding Chronology** For each pair of events that follow, select the event that happened first: **(a)** Battle of Bull Run, Battle of Gettysburg; **(b)** fall of Richmond, Emancipation Proclamation; **(c)** Sherman's march to the sea, fall of Vicksburg.

2. **Linking Past and Present** How do you think Americans would react today if a general lost 60,000 soldiers in one month as General Grant once did? Explain your answer.

3. **Identifying Alternatives** Should African American men have volunteered to serve in the Union army in 1862? Explain two reasons for volunteering and two reasons for not volunteering.

4. **Exploring Unit Themes Sectionalism** Do you think sectional differences and conflicts continued even after the end of the Civil War? Explain the reasons for your answer.

☐ Using Primary Sources

Confederate General John B. Gordon described how his troops felt at Appomattox Courthouse as General Lee was about to surrender:

> ❝ The men cried like children. Worn, starved, and bleeding as they were, they had rather have died than have surrendered.... But I could not permit it.... That these men should have wept at surrendering so unequal a fight, at being taken out of this constant [bloodshed] and storm, at being sent back to their families...was [proof of bravery] and patriotism that might set an example. ❞

Source: *Reminiscences of the Civil War* by John B. Gordon, 1903.

Recognizing Points of View (a) Why did General Gordon's troops cry? **(b)** How did Gordon feel about the behavior of the soldiers? **(c)** How do you think Confederate veterans felt about northern soldiers occupying southern lands after the war?

ACTIVITY BANK

▶ Interdisciplinary Activity

Exploring Science Research and prepare a report on medical care during the Civil War. Include information on battlefield hospitals, common diseases, and people who cared for the sick and wounded.

▶ Career Skills Activity

Cartographer Choose a Civil War battle and make a map showing the positions and movements of troops in the battle. Do research to find the information you need.

▶ Citizenship Activity

Writing a Speech In the late 1860s, Memorial Day emerged as a day to honor soldiers who had died in the Civil War. Today, the holiday honors those whose lives were sacrificed in all American wars. Write a brief speech explaining why it is important to honor those who have died in American wars.

▶ Internet Activity

On the Internet, find sites dealing with the Civil War. Choose a specific Civil War topic and prepare a five-minute presentation to give to the class. Possible topics include: a specific battle, a particular military or political leader, or the poetry and music of the Civil War.

EYEWITNESS Journal

Assume the role of an enslaved African American living in the Confederacy or an enslaved African American living in the Union. In your EYEWITNESS JOURNAL, describe your thoughts and feelings on January 1, 1863, the day the Emancipation Proclamation took effect.

The Reconstruction Era

1864–1877

After the Civil War, rebuilding the ruined South was a tremendous job. Just as troubling was the task of bringing the former Confederate states back into the Union. Should southerners who had fought against the United States government be welcomed back or treated harshly? How could the nation protect the newly won rights of freed African Americans?

During a period called Reconstruction, North and South slowly reunited. At the same time, the economy of the South slowly recovered, and African Americans in the South gained several important rights and freedoms. However, in the years following Reconstruction, many of these rights were lost.

Why Study History?

During Reconstruction and after, many African Americans became victims of violence. Groups like the Ku Klux Klan used terror to prevent black citizens from voting. Today, Americans continue to battle "hate crimes" and encourage tolerance, or acceptance of all people. To focus on this connection, see the *Why Study History?* feature in this chapter, "Tolerance Begins With You."

American Events

1865
Abraham Lincoln is assassinated

1867
Reconstruction Act imposes strict measures on southern states

1868
House of Representatives votes to impeach President Johnson

1864	1866	1868	1870

World Events

1864 World Event
Maximillian becomes Emperor of Mexico

1867 World Event
Dominion of Canada is formed

Viewing HISTORY | **Reunion Begins**

This painting by Dennis Malone Carter shows Abraham Lincoln arriving in Richmond, Virginia. The President visited the captured Confederate capital during the final days of the Civil War. The painting shows Lincoln receiving a hero's welcome. In fact, though, many Richmond residents resented the visit by the leader of the victorious North. The reunion of the nation would not be easy. ★ **Predict two problems that the nation would face as the North and South reunited.**

●**1870**
Fifteenth Amendment guarantees voting rights for African American men

●**1872**
Congress pardons former Confederate officials

1877 ●
Rutherford B. Hayes becomes President; Reconstruction ends

1870 **1872** **1874** **1876**

1870 World Event
Italy is unified

1873 World Event
Abolition of slave markets in Zanzibar

First Steps to Reunion

As You Read

Explore These Questions
- What hardships did the South face after the Civil War?
- What was President Lincoln's plan for reuniting the nation?
- Why did Congress oppose President Johnson's Reconstruction plan?

Define
- freedmen
- amnesty

Identify
- Reconstruction
- Ten Percent Plan
- Wade-Davis Bill
- Freedmen's Bureau
- John Wilkes Booth
- Andrew Johnson
- Thirteenth Amendment

 At the end of the Civil War, the future looked bleak to many southerners. Susan Dabney Smedes described how her father, once a wealthy planter, coped with life after the war:

66 My father had come home to a house stripped of nearly every article of furniture and to a plantation stripped of the means of cultivating any but a small proportion of it. A few mules and one cow were all that were left of the stock.... When he was 70 years of age, he decided to grow a garden. He had never performed manual labor, but he now applied himself to learn to hoe as a way of supplying his family with vegetables. 99

The South faced staggering problems after the war. Southern cities and farmlands lay in ruins, and a whole way of life had ended. All southerners—rich and poor, black and white—faced a long, uphill struggle to rebuild their lives.

Postwar Problems

After four years of war, both northerners and southerners had to adjust to a changed world. The adjustment was far more difficult in the South.

The victorious North

Despite their victory, the North faced some economic problems after the Civil War.

Some 800,000 returning Union soldiers needed jobs. Yet the government was canceling its war orders. Factories were laying off workers, not hiring them. Still, the North's economic disruption was only temporary. Boom times quickly returned.

The North lost more soldiers in the war than the South did. However, except for the battles of Gettysburg and Antietam, no fighting had taken place on northern soil. Northern farms and cities were hardly touched. One returning Union soldier remarked, "It seemed...as if I had been away only a day or two, and had just taken up...where I had left off."

The defeated South

Confederate soldiers had little chance of taking up where they left off. In some areas, every house, barn, and bridge had been destroyed. "The fine houses have fallen to decay or been burnt down," reported one witness, "the grounds neglected and grown over with weeds." Two thirds of the South's railroad tracks had been turned into twisted heaps of scrap. The cities of Columbia, Richmond, and Atlanta had been leveled.

The war wrecked the South's financial system. After the war, Confederate money was worthless. People who lent money to the Confederacy were never repaid. Many southern banks closed, and depositors lost their savings.

Southern society was changed forever by the war. No longer were there white owners and black slaves. Now, almost four million **freedmen**—men and women who had been slaves—lived in the South. Most had no land, no jobs, and no education. Under slavery, they had been forbidden to own property and to learn to read and write. What would become of them?

Early Plans for Reconstruction

Even before the war ended, President Lincoln worried about rebuilding the South. He wanted to make it fairly easy for southerners to rejoin the Union. The sooner the nation was reunited, Lincoln believed, the faster the South would be able to rebuild.

As early as 1863, Lincoln outlined a Reconstruction plan. **Reconstruction** refers to the rebuilding of the South after the Civil War. Under Lincoln's **Ten Percent Plan,** a southern state could form a new government after 10 percent of its voters swore an oath of loyalty to the United States. Once it was formed, the new government had to abolish

slavery. Voters could then elect members of Congress and take part in the national government once again.

Lincoln's plan also offered **amnesty,** or a government pardon, to Confederates who swore loyalty to the Union. Amnesty would not apply to former leaders of the Confederacy, however.

Many Republicans in Congress felt that Lincoln's plan was too generous toward the South. In 1864, they passed the **Wade-Davis Bill,** a rival plan for Reconstruction. It required a majority of white men in each southern state to swear loyalty to the Union. It also denied the right to vote or hold office to anyone who had volunteered to fight for the Confederacy.

The Freedmen's Bureau

Lincoln refused to sign the Wade-Davis Bill because he felt it was too harsh. Congress and the President did agree on one proposal, however. One month before Lee

Linking Past and Present

Past

Present

Ruin and Revival

If you visit the city of Richmond, Virginia, today, you will see an attractive, modern city. You would not guess that, at one time, the city was largely in ruins. Rebuilding its cities and farms was one of the first tasks facing the South after the Civil War. ★ **Why was Richmond so badly damaged in the Civil War?**

Both old and young were eager to learn. Grandparents and grandchildren sat side by side in the classroom. One bureau agent in South Carolina observed that freedmen "will starve themselves, and go without clothes, in order to send their children to school." Charlotte Forten, an African American woman from Philadelphia, came south as a volunteer teacher. She wrote of her students:

> 66 I never before saw children so eager to learn....It is wonderful how a people who have been so long crushed to the earth...can have so great a desire for knowledge, and such a capacity for attaining it. 99

The Freedmen's Bureau laid the foundation for the South's public school system. It set up more than 4,300 grade schools. It also created colleges for African American students, including Howard, Morehouse, and Fisk. Many graduates of these schools became teachers themselves. By the 1870s, African Americans were teaching in grade schools throughout the South.

Lincoln Is Assassinated

President Lincoln hoped to persuade Congress to accept his Reconstruction plan. However, he never got the chance.

On April 14, 1865, just five days after Lee's surrender, the President attended a play at Ford's Theater in Washington, D.C. As Lincoln watched the play, **John Wilkes Booth,** a popular actor from the South, crept into the President's box and shot Lincoln in the head. Within a few hours, the President was dead. Booth was later caught and killed in a barn outside the city.

Biography Charlotte Forten

Charlotte Forten came from a wealthy Philadelphia family. A strong abolitionist, she devoted her life to helping other African Americans improve their lives through education. When she was 25, she helped set up a school on the Sea Islands off South Carolina. Later, she helped recruit other teachers for the Freedmen's Bureau. ★ **Why do you think education was so important to freedmen?**

surrendered, Congress passed a bill creating the **Freedmen's Bureau.** Lincoln signed it.

The Freedmen's Bureau gave food and clothing to former slaves. It also tried to find jobs for freedmen. The bureau helped poor whites as well. It provided medical care for more than one million people. One former Confederate was amazed to see "a Government which was lately fighting us with fire, and sword, and shell, now generously feeding our poor and distressed."

One of the bureau's most important tasks was to set up schools for freed slaves in the South. By 1869, about 300,000 African Americans attended bureau schools. Most of the teachers were volunteers, often women, from the North.

Connections With Arts

Walt Whitman's famous poem "O Captain! My Captain!" expresses his grief at the death of Lincoln. It begins, "O Captain! my Captain! our fearful trip is done, / The ship has weather'd every rack, the prize we sought is won." You can find this and other Civil War poems in Whitman's collection *Leaves of Grass*.

The nation plunged into grief. Millions who had been celebrating the war's end now mourned Lincoln's death. "Now he belongs to the ages," commented Secretary of War Edwin Stanton.

A New President

Vice President **Andrew Johnson** became President when Lincoln died. Johnson had served as governor of Tennessee and had represented that state in Congress. When Tennessee seceded, Johnson had remained loyal to the Union.

At first, many Republicans in Congress were pleased when Johnson became President. They believed that he would support a strict Reconstruction plan. As it turned out, Johnson's plan was much milder than expected.

Johnson called for a majority of voters in each southern state to pledge loyalty to the United States. He also demanded that each state ratify the **Thirteenth Amendment,** which banned slavery throughout the nation. (As you have read, Lincoln's Emancipation Proclamation did not free slaves in states that remained loyal to the Union.) Congress

Playbill from Ford's Theater on the night Lincoln was shot

had approved the Thirteenth Amendment in January 1865.

Rebellion in Congress

The southern states quickly met Johnson's conditions. As a result, the President approved their new state governments in late 1865. Voters in the South then elected representatives to Congress. Many of those elected had held office in the Confederacy. For example, Alexander Stephens, the former vice president of the Confederacy, was elected senator from Georgia.

Republicans in Congress were outraged. The men who had led the South out of the Union were being elected to the House and Senate. Also, no southern state allowed African Americans to vote.

When Congress met in December 1865, Republicans refused to let southern representatives take their seats. Instead, they set up a Joint Committee on Reconstruction to draw up a new plan for the South. The stage was set for a showdown between Congress and the President.

★ Section 1 Review ★

Recall

1. **Identify** **(a)** Reconstruction, **(b)** Ten Percent Plan, **(c)** Wade-Davis Bill, **(d)** Freedmen's Bureau, **(e)** John Wilkes Booth, **(f)** Andrew Johnson, **(g)** Thirteenth Amendment.
2. **Define** **(a)** freedmen, **(b)** amnesty.

Comprehension

3. Describe two problems the South faced after the Civil War.
4. **(a)** What was President Lincoln's Reconstruction plan? **(b)** How did it differ from the Wade-Davis Bill?

5. **(a)** What was President Johnson's plan for readmitting the former Confederate states to the Union? **(b)** How did Republicans in Congress react to Johnson's plan?

Critical Thinking and Writing

6. **Analyzing Information** The North lost more soldiers in the Civil War than the South did. Why was it easier for the North to recover from the war?
7. **Ranking** **(a)** What services did the Freedmen's Bureau provide? **(b)** Which do you think was most important? Explain.

Activity **Writing a Poem** President Lincoln has been shot! Taking the viewpoint of a northerner or southerner, write a poem about the death of Lincoln. If you like, you may set your poem to music.

Radical Reconstruction

Explore These Questions

- What were the goals of the Radical Republicans?
- Why did Congress try to remove President Johnson from office?
- What were the Fourteenth and Fifteenth Amendments?

Define
- black codes
- radical
- impeach

Identify
- Radical Republicans
- Thaddeus Stevens
- Charles Sumner
- Fourteenth Amendment
- Radical Reconstruction
- Reconstruction Act
- Fifteenth Amendment

 In the spring of 1866, disturbing reports trickled into Congress. In some southern cities, peddlers were openly selling Confederate flags. Throughout the South, people sang a new song, "I'm a good old rebel / And I don't want no pardon for anything I done."

These reports confirmed what many Republicans had suspected. "The rebellion has not ended," declared one angry Republican. "It has only changed its weapons!"

Black Codes

After the war, most southern states had promptly ratified the Thirteenth Amendment, which banned slavery. At the same time, however, Southern legislatures passed **black codes,** laws that severely limited the rights of freedmen.

Black codes forbade African Americans to vote, own guns, or serve on juries. In some states, African Americans were permitted to work only as servants or farm laborers. In others, the codes required freedmen to sign contracts for a year's work. Those without contracts could be arrested and sentenced to work on a plantation.

Black codes did give African Americans some rights they did not have before the Civil War. For example, the codes permitted African Americans to marry legally and to own some kinds of property. Still, the codes were clearly meant to keep freedmen from gaining political or economic power.

The North Reacts

Republicans were angered by the black codes, as well as by the election of former Confederate leaders to Congress. The Joint Committee on Reconstruction sent the President a report accusing the South of trying to "preserve slavery in its original form as much and as long as possible." When Johnson ignored the report, members of Congress vowed to take Reconstruction out of the President's hands.

Those who led the opposition to President Johnson were called **Radical Republicans,** or Radicals. A **radical** wants to make drastic changes in society. **Thaddeus Stevens** of Pennsylvania led the Radicals in the House. **Charles Sumner** of Massachusetts was the chief Radical Republican in the Senate.

Radicals had two main goals. First, they wanted to break the power of wealthy planters who had long ruled the South. Radicals blamed these "aristocrats" for the Civil War. Second, Radicals wanted to ensure that freedmen received the right to vote.

Radical Republicans did not control Congress. To accomplish their goals, they needed the support of moderate Republicans, the largest group in Congress. Moderates and Radicals disagreed on many issues. However, they shared a strong political motive for endorsing strict treatment of the South. Most southerners were Democrats. With southerners barred from Congress, Republicans easily controlled both houses.

The President vs. Congress

The conflict between the President and Congress came to a head in 1866. In April, Congress passed the Civil Rights Act, giving citizenship to African Americans. Congress hoped to combat the black codes and secure basic rights for African Americans. When Johnson vetoed the bill, Congress overrode the veto.

The Fourteenth Amendment

Congressional Republicans worried that the Supreme Court might declare the Civil Rights Act unconstitutional. In the Dred Scott decision of 1857, the Court had ruled that African Americans were not citizens. Hoping to avoid a similar ruling, Republicans proposed the Fourteenth Amendment.

The **Fourteenth Amendment** granted citizenship to all persons born in the United States. This included nearly all African Americans. It also guaranteed all citizens "equal protection of the laws" and declared that no state could "deprive any person of life, liberty, or property without due process of law." This provision made it illegal for states to discriminate against an individual on unreasonable grounds, such as skin color.

The Fourteenth Amendment also provided that any state that denied African Americans the right to vote would have its representation in Congress reduced. Republicans believed that freedmen would be able to defend their rights if they could vote.

With the Fourteenth Amendment, Republicans hoped to secure basic political rights for African Americans in the South. In fact, the nation had far to go before all Americans achieved equality. Over the next 100 years, citizens would seek to obtain their rights by asking the courts to enforce the Fourteenth Amendment.

Election of 1866

President Johnson urged the former Confederate states to reject the Fourteenth Amendment. He also decided to make the amendment an issue in the November 1866 congressional elections. Traveling through the North, the President called on voters to reject the Radical Republicans.

FAMILY RECORD

BEFORE THE WAR — AND — SINCE THE WAR.

Viewing HISTORY **New Rights for Freedmen**

Under the black codes, former slaves gained some new rights, such as the right to marry legally. Forms like this one helped freedmen keep their marriage and family records. ★ **Why were family records so valuable to freedmen?**

In many towns, audiences heckled the President. One heckler shouted that Johnson should hang Jefferson Davis. Losing his temper, Johnson yelled back, "Why not hang Thad Stevens?" Many northerners criticized Johnson for acting in an undignified manner.

In July, white mobs in New Orleans, Louisiana, killed 34 African Americans. This convinced many northerners that stronger measures were needed to protect freedmen.

In the end, the election results were a disaster for Johnson. Republicans won majorities in both houses of Congress. They also won every northern governorship and majorities in every northern state legislature.

The Radical Program

In 1867, Republicans in Congress prepared to take charge of Reconstruction. The period that followed is often called **Radical Reconstruction.** With huge majorities in

Rival Plans for Reconstruction

Plan	Ten Percent Plan	Wade-Davis Bill	Johnson Plan	Reconstruction Act
Proposed by	President Abraham Lincoln (1863)	Republicans in Congress (1864)	President Andrew Johnson (1865)	Radical Republicans (1867)
Conditions for former Confederate states to rejoin Union	■ 10 percent of voters must swear loyalty to Union ■ Must abolish slavery	■ Majority of white men must swear loyalty ■ Former Confederate volunteers cannot vote or hold office	■ Majority of white men must swear loyalty ■ Must ratify Thirteenth Amendment ■ Former Confederate officials may vote and hold office	■ Must disband state governments ■ Must write new constitutions ■ Must ratify Fourteenth Amendment ■ African American men must be allowed to vote

Graphic Organizer *Skills*   In the early years of Reconstruction, federal leaders debated several plans for readmitting southern states.

1. **Comprehension** (a) Identify one similarity between the Wade-Davis Bill and President Johnson's plan. (b) Identify one difference.
2. **Critical Thinking** If Lincoln had lived, do you think he would have supported the 1867 Reconstruction Act? Explain.

Civics

both the House and the Senate, Congress could easily override a presidential veto.

First Reconstruction Act

In March 1867, Congress passed the first **Reconstruction Act** over Johnson's veto. The Reconstruction Act threw out the southern state governments that had refused to ratify the Fourteenth Amendment—all the former Confederate states except Tennessee. The act also divided the South into five military districts under army control.

The Reconstruction Act required the former Confederate states to write new constitutions and to ratify the Fourteenth Amendment before rejoining the Union. Most important, the act stated that African Americans must be allowed to vote in all southern states.

Further Republican victories

Once the new constitutions were in place, the reconstructed states held elections to set up new state governments. To show their disgust with Radical Reconstruction policies, many white southerners stayed away from the polls. Freedmen, on the other hand, proudly turned out to exercise their new right to vote. As a result, Republicans gained control of all of the new southern state governments.

Congress passed several more Reconstruction acts. Each time, the Republicans easily overrode Johnson's veto.

Johnson Is Impeached

It was Johnson's duty, as President, to enforce the new Reconstruction laws. However, many Republicans feared he would not do so. Republicans in Congress decided to remove the President from office.

On February 24, 1868, the House of Representatives voted to impeach President Johnson. To **impeach** means to bring formal charges of wrongdoing against an elected official. According to the Constitution, the House can impeach the President only for "high crimes and misdemeanors." The Senate tries the case. The President is removed from office only if found guilty by two thirds of the senators.

During Johnson's trial, it became clear that he was not guilty of high crimes and misdemeanors. Even Charles Sumner, the President's bitter foe, admitted that the charges were "political in character."

Despite intense pressure, seven Republican senators refused to vote for conviction. The Constitution, they believed, did not allow a President to be removed from office simply because he disagreed with Congress. In the end, the Senate vote was 35 for and 19 against impeachment—one vote short of the two-thirds majority needed to remove the President from office. Johnson served out the few remaining months of his term.

A New President

In 1868, Republicans nominated General Ulysses S. Grant as their candidate for President. Grant was the Union's greatest hero in the Civil War.

By election day, most of the southern states had rejoined the Union. As Congress demanded, the new southern governments allowed African Americans to vote. About 500,000 blacks went to the polls in the 1868 election. Nearly all cast their votes for Grant. He easily defeated his opponent, Horatio Seymour.

The Fifteenth Amendment

In 1869, Republicans in Congress proposed another amendment to the Constitution. The **Fifteenth Amendment** forbade any state to deny African Americans the right to vote because of their race.

Many Republicans had moral reasons for supporting the Fifteenth Amendment. They remembered the great sacrifices that were made by African American soldiers in the Civil War. They also felt it was wrong to let African Americans vote in the South but not in the North.

Some Republicans also supported the Fifteenth Amendment for political reasons. African American votes had brought Republicans victory in the South. If African Americans could also vote in the North, they would help Republicans to win elections there, too.

The Fifteenth Amendment was ratified in 1870. At last, all African American men over age 21 had the right to vote.

★ Section 2 Review ★

Recall

1. **Identify** (a) Radical Republicans, (b) Thaddeus Stevens, (c) Charles Sumner, (d) Fourteenth Amendment, (e) Radical Reconstruction, (f) Reconstruction Act, (g) Fifteenth Amendment.
2. **Define** (a) black codes, (b) radical, (c) impeach.

Comprehension

3. Describe the Reconstruction plan enacted by Congress in 1867.
4. (a) Why did Congress impeach President Johnson? (b) What was the result?

5. Describe the goals of: (a) the Fourteenth Amendment; (b) the Fifteenth Amendment.

Critical Thinking and Writing

6. **Defending a Position** (a) Compare Johnson's plan for Reconstruction with the Radical Reconstruction plan. (b) Which plan would you have supported? Defend your position.
7. **Analyzing Ideas** A senator who voted against the removal of President Johnson later said that he did not vote in favor of Johnson but in favor of the presidency. What do you think he meant?

Activity **Writing a Speech** Write a speech from the point of view of a radical or moderate Republican. Present your position on Reconstruction and give reasons for your opinion.

3 ★ Changes in the South

As You Read

Explore These Questions
- What groups dominated southern politics during Reconstruction?
- What did Reconstruction governments do to rebuild the South?
- Why did many southerners sink into a cycle of poverty?

Define
- scalawag
- carpetbagger
- sharecropper

Identify
- Hiram Revels
- Blanche K. Bruce
- Conservatives
- Ku Klux Klan

SETTING the Scene By 1867, life in the South had changed dramatically. African Americans were free to work for themselves, to vote, and to run for office. In Alabama, a political convention of freedmen drew up this ringing declaration:

66 We claim exactly the same rights, privileges and immunities as are enjoyed by white men. We ask nothing more and will be content with nothing less. 99

Before the Civil War, a small group of rich planters controlled southern politics. During Reconstruction, however, new groups dominated state governments in the South. They tried to reshape southern politics. At the same time, others were taking strong action to reverse the gains made by African Americans.

New Forces in Southern Politics

The state governments created during Radical Reconstruction were different from any governments the South had known before. The old leaders had lost much of their influence. Three groups stepped in to replace them. These new groups were white southerners who supported the Republicans, northerners who moved south after the war, and African Americans.

Scalawags

Some white southerners supported the new Republican governments. Many were business people who had opposed secession in 1860. They wanted to forget the war and get on with rebuilding the South.

Many whites in the South felt that any southerner who helped the Republicans was a traitor. They called white southern Republicans **scalawags,** a word used for small, scruffy horses.

Carpetbaggers

Northerners who came south after the war were another important force. To white southerners, the new arrivals from the North were **carpetbaggers**—fortune hunters hoping to profit from the South's misery. Southerners claimed that these northerners were in such a hurry they had time only to fling a few clothes into cheap suitcases, or carpetbags.

In fact, northerners went south for a number of reasons. A few were fortune hunters who hoped to profit as the South was being rebuilt. Many more, however, were Union soldiers who had grown to love the South's rich land. Others, both white and

To many southerners, the carpetbag became a hated symbol of Reconstruction.

During Reconstruction, several African Americans won election to Congress. Here, Robert Brown Elliott of South Carolina stands in the House of Representatives to argue for a civil rights bill. Words from his speech appear on the banner above. "What you give to one class, you must give to all. What you deny to one class, you shall deny to all." ★ **Summarize Elliott's main point in your own words.**

black, were teachers, ministers, and reformers who sincerely wanted to improve the lives of the freedmen.

African Americans

Freedmen and other African Americans were the third major new group in southern politics. Before the war, African Americans had no voice in southern government. During Reconstruction, they not only voted in large numbers, but they also ran for and were elected to public office in the South.

African Americans became sheriffs, mayors, and legislators in the new state and local governments. Between 1869 and 1880, 16 African Americans were elected to Congress.

Two African Americans, both representing Mississippi, served in the Senate. **Hiram Revels,** a clergyman and teacher, became the nation's first black senator in 1870. He completed the unfinished term of former Confederate president Jefferson Davis. In 1874, **Blanche K. Bruce** became the first African American to serve a full term in the Senate. Born into slavery, Bruce escaped to freedom when the Civil War began and later served as a country sheriff.

Freedmen had less political influence than many whites claimed, however. Only in South Carolina did African Americans win a majority in one house of the state legislature. No state elected a black governor.

Conservatives Resist

From the start, most prominent white southerners resisted Reconstruction. These **Conservatives** wanted the South to change as little as possible. They were willing to let African Americans vote and hold a few offices. Still, they were determined that real power would remain in the hands of whites.

A few wealthy planters tried to force African Americans back onto plantations. Many small farmers and laborers wanted the government to take action against the millions of freedmen who now competed with them for land and power.

Most of these white southerners were Democrats. They declared war on anyone who cooperated with the Republicans. "This is a white man's country," they cried, "and white men must govern it."

Spreading terror

White southerners formed secret societies to help them regain power. The most dangerous was the **Ku Klux Klan,** or KKK. The Klan worked to keep blacks and white Republicans out of office.

Spreading Terror

Wearing white hoods, the Ku Klux Klan used terror and violence to keep African Americans from voting. Famous cartoonist Thomas Nast attacked the Klan and other secret societies.

★ **Identify two Klan actions shown in the cartoon. Why do you think Nast labeled his cartoon "WORSE THAN SLAVERY"?**

Ku Klux Klan hood ➤

Dressed in white robes and hoods to hide their identity, Klansmen rode at night to the homes of African American voters, shouting threats and burning wooden crosses. When threats did not work, the Klan turned to violence. Klan members murdered hundreds of African Americans and their white allies.

Congress responds

Many moderate southerners condemned the violence of the Klan. Yet they could do little to stop the Klan's reign of terror. Freedmen turned to the federal government for help. In Kentucky, African American voters wrote to Congress:

> 66 We believe you are not familiar with the Ku Klux Klan's riding nightly over the country spreading terror wherever they go by robbing, whipping, and killing our people without provocation. 99

Congress tried to end Klan violence. In 1870, Congress made it a crime to use force to keep people from voting. As a result, Klan activities decreased. Yet the threat of violence lingered. Some African Americans continued to vote and hold office despite the risk. Many others were frightened away from the ballot box.

The Task of Rebuilding

Despite political problems, Reconstruction governments tried to rebuild the South. They built public schools for both black and white children. Many states gave women the right to own property. In addition, Reconstruction governments rebuilt railroads, telegraph lines, bridges, and roads. Between 1865 and 1879, the South put down 7,000 miles of railroad track.

Rebuilding cost money. Before the war, southerners paid very low taxes. Reconstruction governments raised taxes sharply. This created discontent among many southern whites.

Southerners were further angered by widespread corruption in the Reconstruction governments. One state legislature, for example, voted $1,000 to cover a member's bet on a horse race. Other items billed to the state included hams, perfume, and a coffin.

Corruption was not limited to the South. After the Civil War, dishonesty plagued northern governments as well. In fact, most southern officeholders served their states honestly.

A Cycle of Poverty

In the first months after the war, freedmen left the plantations on which they had

$ Connections With Economics

While the Ku Klux Klan carried out its program of violence, others used economic weapons to intimidate African Americans. Planters refused to rent land to blacks. Employers refused to hire them, and storekeepers denied them credit. What effect do you think such pressures had?

| Critical Thinking | Managing Information | Communication | Maps, Charts, and Graphs |

Interpreting a Political Cartoon

How Will I Use This Skill?

Almost every newspaper today includes political cartoons. Cartoonists comment on current events through both visual imagery and words. Their pictures often use symbols and exaggeration to make their point. Learning to analyze cartoons can help you better understand views on current issues.

LEARN the Skill

❶ Identify the characters and symbols used in the cartoon. Remember that a symbol is an object that represents something beyond itself. The eagle, for example, is often used as a symbol for the United States.

❷ Note details in the drawing. Are some details larger or smaller than normal? Are any facial features or actions in the cartoon exaggerated?

❸ Analyze the relationship between the pictures and any words in the cartoon.

❹ Identify the cartoonist's point of view. Try to identify policies or actions that the cartoonist wants readers to support.

PRACTICE the Skill

The cartoon on the right appeared in a northern newspaper in the 1870s. Use the steps above to analyze the cartoon.

❶ The figure at the top of the cartoon is President Grant. Explain what these other symbols represent: (a) the woman; (b) the soldiers; (c) the carpetbag.

❷ (a) Note the size of the details in this

drawing. Are any larger than normal? Why? (b) What do Grant's facial expression and the position of his arms suggest about his attitude toward the South?

❸ (a) What words are written on the paper sticking out of the carpetbag? What do they mean? (b) What is the woman doing? (c) Is her task easy or difficult?

❹ (a) How do you think this cartoonist felt about Radical Reconstruction? Explain. (b) What policy do you think the cartoonist would want his readers to support?

APPLY the Skill

Find a current political cartoon in the editorial section of a newspaper. Using the skills you have learned in this section, write a paragraph explaining the cartoon.

lived and worked. They found few opportunities, however.

"Nothing but freedom"

Some Radical Republicans talked about giving each freedman "40 acres and a mule." Thaddeus Stevens suggested breaking up big plantations and distributing the land. Most Americans opposed the plan, however. In the end, former slaves received—in the words of a freedman—"nothing but freedom."

Through hard work or good luck, some freedmen were able to become landowners. Most, however, had little choice but to return to where they had lived in slavery.

Sharecropping

Some large planters had held onto their land and wealth through the war. Now, they had land but no slaves to work it. During Reconstruction, many freedmen and poor whites went to work on the large plantations. These **sharecroppers** farmed the land, using seed, fertilizer, and tools provided by the planters. In return, the planters got a share of the crop at harvest time. Sharecroppers hoped to have their own land one day. Mean-

while, they were lucky to have enough food for themselves and their families.

Even farmers who owned land faced hard times. Each spring, the farmers received supplies on credit. In the fall, they had to repay what they had borrowed. Often, the harvest did not cover the debt. Unable to pay, many farmers lost their land and became sharecroppers themselves. Many southerners became locked in a cycle of poverty.

Sharecroppers growing cotton behind their cabin

★ Section 3 Review ★

Recall

1. **Identify** **(a)** Hiram Revels, **(b)** Blanche K. Bruce, **(c)** Conservatives, **(d)** Ku Klux Klan.
2. **Define** **(a)** scalawag, **(b)** carpetbagger, **(c)** sharecropper.

Comprehension

3. **(a)** What role did freedmen play in Reconstruction governments? **(b)** How was this different from the role of African Americans before the Civil War?
4. **(a)** What were two accomplishments of Reconstruction governments? **(b)** What were two problems?

5. Why did many freedmen and poor whites become sharecroppers?

Critical Thinking and Writing

6. **Understanding Causes and Effects** During Reconstruction, freedmen proved that, given the chance, they could do the same jobs as whites. Do you think this made southern Conservatives more willing or less willing to accept African Americans as equals? Explain.
7. **Linking Past and Present** Many southerners were angered by high taxes imposed by Reconstruction governments. **(a)** How do voters today feel about paying high taxes? **(b)** Do you think some services should be provided even if they require high taxes? Explain.

★ ★

Activity   **Drawing a Political Cartoon**   Draw a political cartoon expressing your opinion about scalawags, carpetbaggers, the Ku Klux Klan, or another aspect of Reconstruction in the South.

Reconstruction Ends

As You Read

Explore These Questions
- Why did Reconstruction end?
- How did the southern economy expand after Reconstruction?
- How did African Americans in the South lose rights?

Define
- poll tax
- literacy test
- grandfather clause
- segregation
- lynching

Identify
- Rutherford B. Hayes
- Henry Grady
- James Duke
- Jim Crow laws
- *Plessy* v. *Ferguson*

SETTING the Scene In 1876, millions of Americans visited a great Centennial Exposition held in Philadelphia. The fair celebrated the first hundred years of the United States. Visitors gazed at the latest wonders of modern industry—the elevator, the telephone, a giant steam engine.

As Americans looked to the future, they lost interest in Reconstruction. By the late 1870s, white Conservatives had regained control of the South.

Radicals in Decline

By the 1870s, Radical Republicans were losing power in Congress. Many northerners grew weary of trying to reform the South. It was time to forget the Civil War, they believed, and let southerners run their own governments—even if that meant African Americans might lose their rights.

Republicans were also hurt by disclosure of widespread corruption in the government of President Grant. The President had appointed many friends to office. Some used their position to steal large sums of money from the government. Grant won reelection in 1872, but many northerners had lost faith in Republican leaders and their policies.

Congress reflected the new mood of the North. In May 1872, it passed the Amnesty Act, which restored the right to vote to nearly all white southerners. As expected, they voted solidly Democratic. At the same time, southern whites terrorized African Americans who tried to vote.

White Conservatives were firmly in control once more. One by one, the Republican governments in the South fell. By 1876, only three southern states—Louisiana, South Carolina, and Florida—were still controlled by Republicans.

Election of 1876

The end of Reconstruction came with the election of 1876. The Democrats nominated Samuel Tilden, governor of New York, for President. Tilden was known for fighting corruption. The Republican candidate was **Rutherford B. Hayes,** governor of Ohio. Like Tilden, Hayes vowed to fight dishonesty in government.

Tilden won 250,000 more popular votes than Hayes. However, Tilden had only 184 electoral votes—one vote short of the number needed to win. Twenty other votes were in dispute. The outcome of the election hung on these votes. All but one of the disputed votes came from Florida, Louisiana, and South Carolina—the three southern states still controlled by Republicans.

As inauguration day drew near, the nation still had no one to swear in as President. Congress set up a special commission to settle the crisis. A majority of the commission members were Republicans. The commission decided to give all the disputed electoral votes to Hayes.

Southern Democrats could have fought the election of Hayes. Hayes, however, had privately agreed to end Reconstruction. Once in office, he removed all remaining federal troops from South Carolina, Louisiana, and Florida. Reconstruction was over.

Industry and the "New South"

During Reconstruction, the South made some progress toward rebuilding its economy. Cotton production, long the basis of the South's economy, slowly recovered. By 1880, planters were growing as much cotton as they had in 1860.

After Reconstruction, a new generation of southern leaders worked to expand the economy. **Henry Grady,** editor of the *Atlanta* *Constitution,* made stirring speeches calling for the growth of a "New South." Grady argued that the South should use its vast natural resources to build up its own industry, instead of depending on the North.

Agricultural industries

Southerners agreed that the best way to begin industrializing was to process the region's agricultural goods. Investors built textile mills to turn cotton into cloth. By 1880, the entire South was still producing fewer textiles than Massachusetts. In the next decade, though, more and more communities started building textile mills.

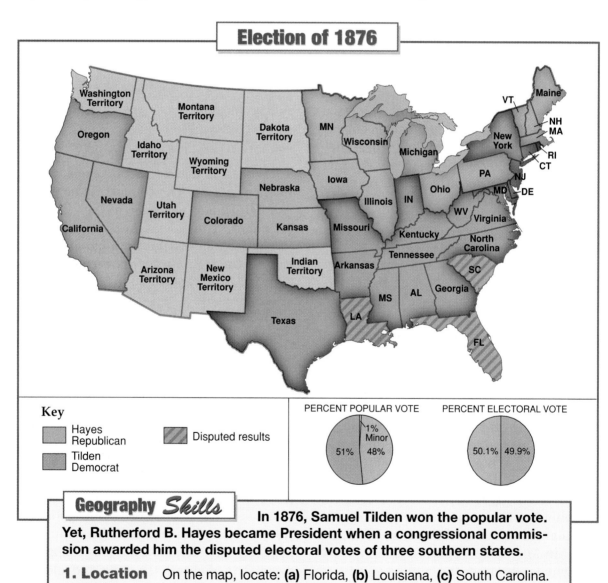

Election of 1876

Key
- Hayes Republican
- Tilden Democrat
- Disputed results

PERCENT POPULAR VOTE
51% | 48% | 1% Minor

PERCENT ELECTORAL VOTE
50.1% | 49.9%

Geography Skills In 1876, Samuel Tilden won the popular vote. Yet, Rutherford B. Hayes became President when a congressional commission awarded him the disputed electoral votes of three southern states.

1. Location On the map, locate: **(a)** Florida, **(b)** Louisiana, **(c)** South Carolina.

2. Movement Which candidate carried the undisputed southern vote?

3. Critical Thinking Based on the map, do you think the Civil War ended sectionalism in the United States? Explain.

The tobacco industry also grew rapidly. In North Carolina, **James Duke** used new machinery to revolutionize production of tobacco products. In 1890, he bought out several competitors to form the American Tobacco Company. Duke eventually controlled 90 percent of the nation's tobacco industry.

New industries

The South also tapped its mineral resources. Local deposits of iron ore and coal, as well as low wages for workers, made steel production cheaper in Alabama than in Pennsylvania. Oil refineries developed in Louisiana and Texas. Other states became leading producers of coal, copper, granite, and marble.

By the 1890s, many northern forests had been cut down. The southern yellow pine was competing with the northwestern white pine as a lumber source. Some southern factories began to make cypress shingles and hardwood furniture.

A visitor from New England described what he found on a visit to the South in 1887:

> 66 We find a South wide awake with business, excited and even astonished at the development of its own immense resources in metals, marbles, coal, timber, fertilizers, eagerly laying lines of communication, rapidly opening mines, building furnaces, foundries, and all sorts of shops for utilizing the native riches. 99

By 1900, the South had developed a more balanced economy. Still, it failed to keep up with even more rapid growth in the North and the West.

Restricting the Rights of African Americans

The years after Reconstruction brought prosperity to some southerners. For African Americans, though, the end of Reconstruction had tragic effects.

With the North out of southern affairs, white Conservatives tightened their grip on southern governments. Some groups continued to use violence to keep African Ameri-

Viewing **HISTORY**   **Rise of the New South**

From Darkness to Light *by Grant Hamilton shows the New South rising from the ruins of war. Hamilton created this picture for one of several industrial expositions held in Atlanta, Georgia, in the late 1800s.* ★ **According to this picture, what products helped the southern economy grow?**

cans from voting. Southern states also found new ways to keep African Americans from exercising their rights.

Voting restrictions

In the 1880s, many southern states began passing new laws that restricted the right to vote. **Poll taxes** required voters to pay a fee each time they voted. As a result, poor freedmen could rarely afford to vote. **Literacy tests** required voters to read and explain a section of the Constitution. Since most freedmen had little education, such tests kept them away from the polls.

Many poor southern whites also could not pass the literacy test. To increase the number of eligible white voters, states passed **grandfather clauses.** If a voter's father or grandfather had been eligible to vote on January 1, 1867, the voter did not have to take

Why Study History?

Because Tolerance Begins With You

Historical Background

During and after Reconstruction, hate groups like the Ku Klux Klan used violence and terror to keep African Americans from voting or holding any political office. Angry mobs set fire to African American homes, churches, and schools. They even lynched people. Often, these tactics worked. Yet many whites and African Americans continued to speak out against injustice.

Artist Jim Osborn created this painting to encourage respect and tolerance.

Connections to Today

Discrimination and hate crimes have not been limited to African Americans in the South in the 1800s. Almost every group in this nation has suffered the pain of senseless hatred. People feel the sting of prejudice for many reasons: religion, race, economic status, age, or physical or mental abilities.

Acts of prejudice continue today. In recent years, Jewish cemeteries have been vandalized. African American churches have been burned. Asian American stores have been covered in racist graffiti. Mexican American or Arab American businesses have been attacked. In some areas, police have set up special "hate crime" units to investigate actions such as these.

Connections to You

Tolerance begins with you. You can fight prejudice by respecting and appreciating people's differences. Everyone in your class has different talents and experiences. You can get to know your classmates for who they are, rather than on the basis of what you think you know about them. You will find that you have much in common with students who seem different.

Many schools provide opportunities for you to increase your ability to get along with others. Human relations clubs promote understanding of diverse groups. Peer-mediation programs can teach you how to deal with anger and conflict. By keeping an open mind and educating yourself, you can help end discrimination and prejudice.

1. **Comprehension** **(a)** What tactics did hate groups use against African Americans in the South? **(b)** Identify two kinds of discrimination some people face today.

2. **Critical Thinking** How do prejudice and discrimination begin?

 Making a Poster Make a list of three things that you could do to promote tolerance. Create a poster illustrating one of them.

a literacy test. Since no African Americans in the South could vote before 1868, grandfather clauses were a way to ensure that only white men could vote.

Racial segregation

Southern blacks lost more than the right to vote. After 1877, segregation became the law of the South. **Segregation** means separating people of different races in public places. Southern states passed laws that separated blacks and whites in schools, restaurants, theaters, trains, streetcars, playgrounds, hospitals, and even cemeteries. **Jim Crow laws,** as they were known, trapped southern blacks in a hopeless situation. In 1885, the Louisiana novelist George Washington Cable described segregation as:

> 66 . . . a system of oppression so rank that nothing could make it seem small except the fact that [African Americans] had already been ground under it for a century and a half. 99

African Americans brought lawsuits to challenge segregation. In 1896, in the case of **Plessy v. Ferguson,** the Supreme Court ruled that segregation was legal so long as facilities for blacks and whites were equal. In fact, facilities were rarely equal. For example, southern states spent much less on schools for blacks than for whites.

Violence

When Reconstruction ended, groups like the Ku Klux Klan declined. However, violent acts against African Americans continued. During the 1890s, almost 200 Americans were lynched each year. **Lynching** is the illegal seizure and execution of someone by a mob. Four out of five lynchings took place in the South, and the majority of the victims were African American.

Some lynching victims were accused of crimes. Others were simply considered troublemakers. Victims—including some women and children—were hanged, shot, or burned to death, often after painful torture. Members of lynch mobs rarely faced punishment. By the late 1800s, some reformers began to speak out against lynching.

Results of Reconstruction

Reconstruction was a time of both success and failure. Southerners faced hard times. Still, the South gained a public education system and expanded its rail lines.

As a result of Reconstruction, all African Americans became citizens for the first time. These rights eroded after Reconstruction ended. However, the laws passed during Reconstruction, such as the Fourteenth Amendment, became the basis of the civil rights movement almost 100 years later.

★ Section 4 Review ★

Recall

1. **Identify** (a) Rutherford B. Hayes, (b) Henry Grady, (c) James Duke, (d) Jim Crow laws, (e) *Plessy* v. *Ferguson.*
2. **Define** (a) poll tax, (b) literacy test, (c) grandfather clause, (d) segregation, (e) lynching.

Comprehension

3. Why did Radical Republicans' power decline?
4. How did the economy of the South change?

5. Describe two ways that African Americans lost their rights after Reconstruction ended.

Critical Thinking and Writing

6. **Evaluating Information** Do you think that Reconstruction was successful? Explain.
7. **Predicting Consequences** How do you think *Plessy* v. *Ferguson* affected later efforts to achieve equality for African Americans?

Activity **Acting a Scene** With a partner, act out a scene of an African American man trying to vote in the South in the late 1880s. Begin by considering how you might feel if you knew that you had the right to vote, yet someone was able to prevent you from voting.

Review and Activities

★ Sum It Up ★

Section 1   First Steps to Reunion
▶ After the Civil War, the South faced the task of repairing tremendous destruction.
▶ The Freedmen's Bureau helped newly freed African Americans learn to read, and provided food and clothing to the needy.
▶ Presidents Lincoln and Johnson recommended mild plans for Reconstruction, but Congress refused to accept either one.

Section 2   Radical Reconstruction
▶ Radical Republicans wanted to break the power of rich planters in the South and make sure that freedmen could vote.
▶ Congress tried and failed to remove President Johnson from office.
▶ Republicans proposed the Fourteenth and Fifteenth amendments to ensure the civil rights of African Americans.

Section 3   Changes in the South
▶ Southern Republicans, whites from the North, and freed African Americans played important roles in southern governments.
▶ Landless black and white sharecroppers became locked in a cycle of poverty.

Section 4   Reconstruction Ends
▶ Reconstruction ended after presidential candidate Rutherford B. Hayes made a private deal with southern politicians.
▶ After Reconstruction, a new industrial economy began to emerge in the South.
▶ Southern whites passed new laws to deny African Americans equal rights.

CD-ROM **Review** For additional review of the major ideas of Chapter 18, see *Guide to the Essentials of American History* or *Interactive Student Tutorial CD-ROM,* which contains interactive review activities, graphic organizers, and practice tests.

🗔 Reviewing the Chapter

Define These Terms
Match each term with the correct definition.

Column 1	Column 2
1. freedman	**a.** laws that severely limited the rights of freedmen
2. black codes	
3. scalawag	**b.** tax required before someone could vote
4. poll tax	
5. segregation	**c.** white southern Republican
	d. former slave
	e. separating people of different races in public places

Explore the Main Ideas
1. Describe the condition of the South after the war.
2. How did Republicans in Congress gain control of Reconstruction?
3. Give two reasons why Republicans supported the Fifteenth Amendment.
4. Describe the economic recovery of the South after the Civil War.
5. Why did most Americans lose interest in Reconstruction in the 1870s?
6. What was the purpose of Jim Crow laws?

🗔 Geography Activity

Match the letters on the map with the following places:
1. South Carolina, **2.** Florida, **3.** Louisiana, **4.** Ohio, **5.** New York.   **Region** Which southern states were under Republican control in 1876?

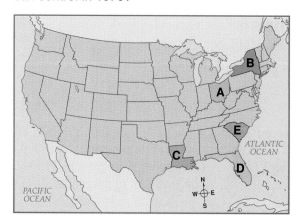

Critical Thinking and Writing

1. **Understanding Chronology** **(a)** Put the following in the order in which they were first proposed: the Reconstruction Acts; the Wade-Davis Bill; the Ten Percent Plan; Jim Crow laws. **(b)** Why did Lincoln have so little influence on Reconstruction?

2. **Exploring Unit Themes** **Sectionalism** Briefly state your own plan for repairing the bitter feelings between North and South.

3. **Analyzing Ideas** Most people call groups such as the Ku Klux Klan "un-American." Explain the reasons for this belief.

4. **Predicting Consequences** After the Civil War, the United States entered a period of industrial growth that made it the richest nation in the world. How do you think the South's experiences during Reconstruction affected its share in this industrial boom?

Using Primary Sources

Born into slavery, Booker T. Washington became a leading educator. Here, he describes one of the problems that came with emancipation:

> **❝** Was it any wonder that within a few hours the wild rejoicing ceased and a feeling of deep gloom seemed to pervade the slave quarters? To some it seemed that, now that they were in actual possession of it, freedom was a more serious thing than they expected to find it. Some of the slaves were seventy or eighty years old; their best days were gone. They had no strength with which to earn a living in a strange place and among strange people, even if they had been sure where to find a new place of abode. **❞**

Source: *Up From Slavery,* Booker T. Washington, 1901.

Recognizing Points of View **(a)** What caused the "wild rejoicing" Washington mentions? **(b)** Why did the rejoicing end so quickly? **(c)** Why do you think many African Americans were unprepared for the realities of freedom?

ACTIVITY BANK

▶ Interdisciplinary Activity

Connections With Arts Review the goals of the Freedmen's Bureau. Then create a poster advertising the Bureau's work and encouraging volunteers to participate.

▶ Career Skills Activity

Playwrights and Actors Find out more about the events and issues leading up to the trial of President Andrew Johnson. Then prepare a skit in which you act out Johnson's trial in the United States Senate.

▶ Citizenship Activity

Understanding the Constitution Study the text of the Fourteenth and Fifteenth amendments printed in the Reference Section. Create a graphic organizer for each amendment. Include the main ideas of each amendment and show how it affects the daily lives of Americans today. You may illustrate your work with original drawings or clippings.

Internet Activity

Use the Internet to find primary sources on Reconstruction. Then use the primary source to create a newspaper interview with the person who wrote the material you have found. Create questions that are answered by quotations taken from the primary source.

EYEWITNESS Journal

You are a freedman, a Radical Republican, a Conservative southern planter, or a northerner who went south during Reconstruction. In your EYEWITNESS JOURNAL, describe your reaction to three important events of the Reconstruction era.

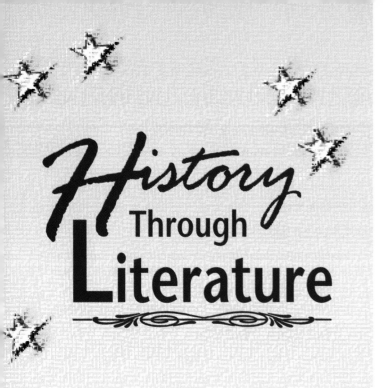

History Through Literature

The Red Badge of Courage

Stephen Crane

Introduction

Stephen Crane was born six years after the Civil War ended. He spent many hours reading about the war and talking to veterans. In 1895, he published his great Civil War novel, *The Red Badge of Courage*. It tells the story of Henry Fleming, a young volunteer in the Union Army. The following passage describes Henry's departure from home and his early days in the army.

Vocabulary

Before you read the selection, find the meaning of these words in a dictionary: **doggedly, shirking, monotonous, province, pickets, philosophical, reflectively, reproached, infantile, assurance.**

W hen [Henry] had stood in the doorway with his soldier's clothes on his back, and with the light of excitement and expectancy in his eyes almost defeating the glow of regret for the home bonds, he had seen two tears leaving their trails on his mother's scarred cheeks.

Still, she had disappointed him by saying nothing whatever about returning with his shield or on it.* He had privately primed himself for a beautiful scene. He had prepared certain sentences which he thought could be used with touching effect. But her words destroyed his plans. She had doggedly peeled potatoes and addressed him as follows: "You watch out, Henry, an' take good care of yerself in this here fighting business —you watch out, an' take good care of yerself. Don't go a-thinkin' you can lick the hull rebel army at the start, because yeh can't. Yer jest one little feller amongst a hull lot of others, and yeh've got to keep quiet an' do what they tell yeh. I know how you are, Henry.

"I've knet yeh eight pair of socks, Henry, and I've put in all yer best shirts, because I want my boy to be jest as warm and comf'able as anybody in the army. Whenever they get holes in 'em, I want yeh to send 'em rightaway back to me, so's I kin dern 'em.

"An' allus be careful an' choose yer comp'ny. There's lots of bad men in the army, Henry. The army makes 'em wild, and they like nothing better than the job of leading off a young feller like you, as ain't never been away from home much and has allus had a mother, an' a-learning 'em to drink and swear. Keep clear of them folks, Henry....

"I don't know what else to tell yeh, Henry, excepting that yeh must never do no shirking, child, on my account. If so be a time comes when yeh have to be kilt or do a mean thing, why, Henry, don't think of anything 'cept what's right, because there's many a woman has to bear up 'ginst sech things these times, and the Lord'll take keer of us all.

"Don' forget about the socks and the shirts, child; and I've put a cup of blackberry jam with yer bundle, because I know yeh like it

---

* The Spartan people of ancient Greece carried home their dead warriors on their shields.

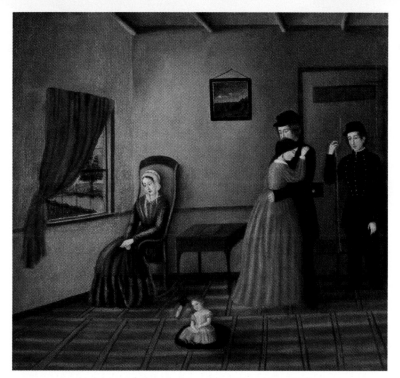

This anonymous painting, Off to the Front, 1861, *is owned by the museum of the United States Military Academy at West Point, New York. It shows a young soldier saying goodbye to his family in the first year of the Civil War. Scenes like this were common in homes throughout the North and South.* ★ **Choose one of the people in this painting. What do you think are that person's thoughts and feelings?**

above all things. Good-by, Henry. Watch out, and be a good boy."

He had, of course, been impatient under the ordeal of this speech. It had not been quite what he expected, and he had borne it with an air of irritation. He departed feeling vague relief.

Still, when he had looked back from the gate, he had seen his mother kneeling among the potato parings. Her brown face, upraised, was stained with tears, and her spare form was quivering. He bowed his head and went on, feeling suddenly ashamed. . . .

After complicated journeyings with many pauses, there had come months of monotonous life in a camp. He had had the belief that real war was a series of death struggles with small time in between for sleep and meals; but since his regiment had come to the field the army had done little but sit still and try to keep warm. . . .

He had grown to regard himself merely as a part of a vast blue demonstration. His province was to look out, as far as he could, for his personal comfort. For recreation he could twiddle his thumbs and speculate on the thoughts which must agitate the minds of the generals. Also, he was drilled and drilled and reviewed, and drilled and drilled and reviewed.

The only foes he had seen were some pickets along the river bank. They were a sun-tanned, philosophical lot, who sometimes shot reflectively at the blue pickets. When reproached for this afterward, they usually expressed sorrow, and swore by their gods that the guns had exploded without their permission. The youth, on guard duty one night, conversed across the stream with one of them. He was a slightly ragged man, who spat skillfully between his shoes and possessed a great fund of bland and infantile assurance. The youth liked him personally.

"Yank," the other had informed him, "yer a right dum good feller." This sentiment, floating to him upon the still air, had made him temporarily regret war.

Analyzing Literature

1. What advice did Henry's mother give him?
2. How was a soldier's life different than what Henry expected?
3. **Making Generalizations**   What does Henry's experience with the enemy picket suggest about the special problems of fighting a civil war?

Epilogue

Linking Past to Present

1877–Present

After the Civil War, the United States enjoyed tremendous growth. Technology and new business practices helped the economy to soar. Despite periods of hard times, the United States became the most prosperous nation in the world. In addition, by the 1940s, the United States was a world superpower.

The nation also saw tremendous social and political changes. Immigrants helped build a rich cultural diversity. African Americans waged a long struggle to win back their constitutional rights. Women won their right to vote, as well as greater opportunities in other areas. Reformers sought to put more power in the hands of voters. As a result, more Americans enjoy the rights of citizenship today than ever before.

Why Study *History?*

You have learned a lot about American history this year. By studying our nation's past you can become an informed, responsible citizen. There are many other things you can learn from the past. As historian Gerda Lerner noted, "Human beings have always used history in order to find their direction toward the future: to repeat the past or depart from it."

American Events

●1880s
Immigration from Southern and Eastern Europe increases

●1913
Henry Ford introduces assembly line

●1929
Great Depression begins

1875   **1910**   **1945**

World Events

1893 World Event
New Zealand gives vote to women

1914 World Event
World War I begins in Europe

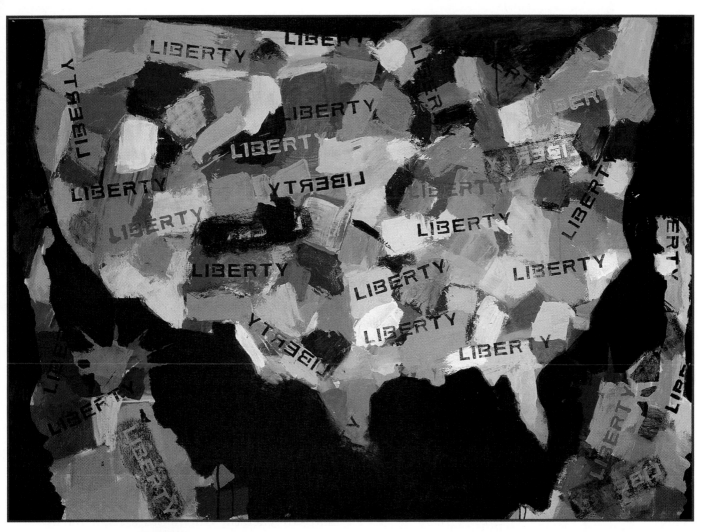

Viewing History · A Land of Liberty

Since the nation's beginning, millions of people have come to the United States seeking freedom and opportunity. One of these immigrants was the Taiwanese-born artist Tsing-fang Chen. In his 1986 painting Liberty States, *Chen uses familiar images to stress the continuing importance of liberty to the American nation.*

★ **What do the figures in the lower left and right corners represent?**

1945
World War II ends;
Cold War begins

1965
Congress passes
Voting Rights Act

1993
United States
signs North
American Free
Trade Agreement

1945 **1980** **Present**

1950 World Event
North Korean troops
invade South Korea

1991 World Event
Soviet Union breaks up

A Diverse Nation

As You Read

Explore These Questions
- Why have immigrants come to the United States from all parts of the world?
- How did the growth of cities change American culture?
- How have advances in communication transformed American life?

Define
- quota system
- illegal alien
- amnesty
- jazz

Identify
- Sunbelt
- Louis Armstrong
- Elvis Presley
- Neil Armstrong

SETTING the Scene In 1884, Rosa Cristoforo left her village in Italy to join her husband in "l'America." After two weeks on a cramped steamship, she finally caught sight of land:

66 America! The country where everyone could find work! Where wages were so high no one had to go hungry! Where all men were free and equal and where even the poor could own land! But now we were so near it seemed too much to believe. 99

Millions of immigrants flocked to the United States after the Civil War. Most came from Eastern and Southern Europe. Latin Americans and Asians came, too. All left homelands that offered them little hope for a better future. The United States, they heard, was a land of opportunity.

Today, as in the past, immigrants continue to add to the diversity of the United States. Such diversity has brought its share of challenges. At the same time, diversity has been a major source of pride and strength for Americans.

A Tide of Immigration

Between 1866 and 1915, more than 25 million immigrants entered the United States. Most of these "new immigrants" were far different from earlier groups.

"New immigrants"

Most early European immigrants were Protestants who came from Northern or Western Europe. The new immigrants, however, came from countries in Southern and Eastern Europe, such as Italy, Poland, or Russia. Many were Catholics. Others were Jews fleeing persecution in Eastern Europe. Besides Europeans, immigrants from Asia and Latin America also arrived.

The new immigrants endured great hardships to reach the United States. Spurred by dreams of a better life, they left their homes and families. Many suffered a long, rough voyage across the Atlantic or Pacific. On the return journey, cattle and cargo filled the same spaces that had held the immigrants.

Most European immigrants arrived at Ellis Island, near the Statue of Liberty in New York Harbor. After 1900, the city of Galveston, Texas, took many immigrants that Ellis Island could not handle. On the West Coast, immigrants from China, Japan, and Korea entered through San Francisco, California, as well as Seattle, Washington, and Oahu, Hawaii. From Mexico,

Phrase book for Chinese immigrants

ENGLISH-CHINESE PHRASEOLOGY.

汝有乜貨物出賣
What goods have you for sale?

樣樣都有
I have all kinds.

我想買条好褲
I want to get a pair of your best pants.

汝爱乜價銀
What do you ask for them?

汝能減少吟
Can you take less for them?

不能先生
I can not, sir.

families traveled north to El Paso and Laredo in Texas.

Facing discrimination

Like the Irish and Germans who arrived in the 1840s and 1850s, the new immigrants faced discrimination. Their religious beliefs, customs, and languages seemed strange to many Americans. Congress responded to anti-immigrant feeling by passing laws to restrict immigration. An 1882 law excluded Chinese immigrants. In the 1920s, another law set up a **quota system,** allowing only a set number of people from each country to enter the United States each year. The quota system favored immigrants from Northern Europe, especially Britain.

Despite the new restrictions, people from all over the world still dreamed of coming to the United States. They, too, wanted to share in the American dream of freedom and economic opportunity.

Recent newcomers

In 1965, Congress ended the quota system. In the years that followed, many immigrants arrived from Latin American nations, especially Mexico and Cuba. By 2000, Latin Americans were becoming the largest ethnic minority in the United States.

The number of immigrants from Asia rose sharply as well. Most were Filipinos, Chinese, and Koreans. During and after the Vietnam War, many Vietnamese and Cambodians also sought new homes in the United States. Today, Asian Americans are the nation's fastest-growing ethnic group.

In the 1980s, about 6 million immigrants entered the United States legally. Another 3 to 5 million were **illegal aliens,** people who enter the nation without permission. In 1986, Congress took steps to control illegal immigration. It did, however, grant an **amnesty,** or pardon, to illegal aliens who had arrived before 1982. Despite the legislation, illegal aliens continued to enter the country. In 1994, Congress passed a law that allowed local police to arrest illegal immigrants. It also nearly doubled the number of officials who patrol certain of the nation's borders.

At the same time, legal immigration has continued to rise. By 1995, legal immigrants were applying for American citizenship in record numbers.

Each wave of immigrants has enriched American life. Over the years, immigrants have helped to build railroads, subways, and factories. They have worked on farms, built skyscrapers, and started new businesses. Their songs, stories, foods, and customs have helped to make American culture richer.

The Rise of Cities

The growth of cities also changed American life. At the end of Reconstruction, less

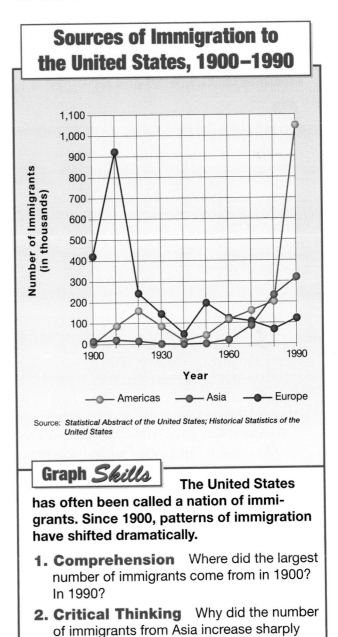

Sources of Immigration to the United States, 1900–1990

Source: *Statistical Abstract of the United States; Historical Statistics of the United States*

Graph Skills The United States has often been called a nation of immigrants. Since 1900, patterns of immigration have shifted dramatically.

1. **Comprehension** Where did the largest number of immigrants come from in 1900? In 1990?

2. **Critical Thinking** Why did the number of immigrants from Asia increase sharply after the 1960s?

Biography — Louis Armstrong

Louis "Satchmo" Armstrong was one of the brilliant young musicians who helped create jazz. Armstrong learned to play the trumpet in a New Orleans orphanage. After coming to Chicago in 1922, he quickly became the most popular jazz musician of his day. Armstrong often experimented with a simple melody, allowing his listeners to hear many different sides of it. ★ **What were the origins of jazz?**

than one quarter of all Americans lived in cities. Between 1880 and 1900, the number of people living in cities doubled. By 1920, a majority of Americans made their homes in cities or suburbs. By 1990, nearly 80 percent of all Americans lived in metropolitan areas.

The move to the cities changed American culture. City newspapers printed more interesting—and sometimes more sensational—news stories. Huge department stores offered a wide range of goods. Subways and trolleys whisked people from one side of town to the other. Cities offered a wide variety of recreation, from theaters to professional sports.

During the 1970s and 1980s, older cities of the Northeast and Midwest lost population. Many people were moving to the **Sunbelt,** the states of the Southeast and Southwest. Many went in search of jobs. The sunny climate with mild winters also was an attraction. By 1990, the 30 fastest-growing urban areas in the nation were all in the South and the West.

A Rich Musical Heritage

The richness of American life has always been expressed in music. Since colonial times, folk songs have been popular. Some were the ballads of Irish and Scottish immigrants. Some were spirituals sung in slave quarters. Others were banjo tunes from the gold fields of California.

As the United States changed, so did its music. In the early 1900s, a new kind of music, called jazz, was heard in the South. **Jazz** combined West African rhythms, African American work songs and spirituals, and European harmonies. African American musicians like **Louis Armstrong** helped develop jazz into a unique American musical form that is still popular around the world.

In the 1950s, another sound swept the nation—rock 'n' roll. Artists like Chuck Berry, Little Richard, and Bill Haley used drums and electric guitars to create music with a strong, lively beat. **Elvis Presley** captured the attention of millions of young Americans. Across the nation, teenagers dressed like him, bought his records, and nicknamed him "the King."

Over the past 50 years, popular music has taken many forms. Americans of all ages and backgrounds have enjoyed country and western, rhythm and blues, heavy metal, new wave, jazz, and rap. Superstars like Pearl Jam, Garth Brooks, Queen Latifah, and Madonna have sold millions of recordings.

Mass Communication

Advances in communication have transformed American life since the late 1800s. Radio, motion pictures, and television all have brought Americans closer together.

During the 1920s, radio stations began to broadcast across the nation. They brought news, sports, and entertainment into American homes. Today, new media such as computers and television have replaced radio as the major information and entertainment source. Still, thanks to advanced technology, tiny radios the size of a credit card have become a standard feature of American life.

Motion pictures revolutionized American culture as well. The first movie theaters opened in the early 1900s. Until 1927, movies were silent—that is, they had no sound track. Audiences read subtitles to follow the plot. Today, movies feature not only sound but computer-generated special effects that both startle and scare.

Television became popular in the late 1940s. By the 1950s, millions of Americans were buying television sets. Today, almost every home has at least one TV, and television—for better or worse—has become a major influence in American life. In the 1980s, cable television greatly increased the number of television channels and the variety of programs available. Cable channels offer programs for country-and-western music fans, home shoppers, and comedy lovers. Channels like Univision (UNI), which broadcasts in Spanish, serve a variety of specific audiences.

Radio, movies, and television allow Americans to share experiences. They also help to shape public opinion. For example, many Americans make voting decisions after watching candidates debate on television.

Technology

In July 1969, American astronaut **Neil Armstrong** became the first person to walk on the moon. "That's one small step for a man, one giant leap for mankind," he declared as he stepped onto the moon's surface. The moon landing was only one example of advanced American technology following World War II. Much of this technological progress can be traced to development of the electronic computer.

The first electronic computers were built in the 1940s. Since then, the computer revolution has affected every aspect of American life. Businesses use computers to print documents or send bills. Students use computers to research and write papers. Without computers, our complex government could not function as efficiently.

Some people have expressed concern about the spread of computers. Computers keep records of nearly everything we do, from banking to visiting the doctor. People could abuse this information and threaten our privacy. Others, however, argue that computer technology has helped to spread information among diverse people and increased communication around the world.

★ Section 1 Review ★

Recall

1. **Identify** (a) Sunbelt, (b) Louis Armstrong, (c) Elvis Presley, (d) Neil Armstrong.
2. **Define** (a) quota system, (b) illegal alien, (c) amnesty, (d) jazz.

Comprehension

3. (a) How did Congress respond to anti-immigrant feeling in the 1920s? (b) What changes did Congress make in the immigration laws in 1965?
4. Describe the growth of cities from the time of Reconstruction to today.

5. What new forms of communication developed in the 1900s?

Critical Thinking and Writing

6. **Predicting Consequences** (a) Where did most immigrants come from in the late 1800s? (b) Where do most immigrants come from today? (c) How might this change affect the nation's culture in the future?
7. **Making Inferences** How do mass media such as movies and television bring Americans closer together?

Activity **Writing a Handbook** You are an immigrant to the United States, either 100 years ago or today. Write at least one page for a handbook for future immigrants from your country. Tell them what problems they should expect to have and how they can overcome those problems.

A Changing Economy

2

As You Read

Explore These Questions

- How did the growth of railroads change the nation?
- What new ways of doing business developed in the late 1800s?
- How is the United States linked with other nations in today's global economy?

Define

- transcontinental railroad
- reservation
- assembly line
- corporation
- stock
- monopoly
- conglomerate
- service industry
- trade deficit

Identify

- Thomas Alva Edison
- Henry Ford
- Orville and Wilbur Wright
- North American Free Trade Agreement

SETTING the Scene At the end of the Civil War, train travel usually meant discomfort and delay. Journeys were long, and passengers had no place to eat or sleep. Often, they had to wait for hours while workers fixed a derailed car or switched locomotives.

Within 20 years, American railroads had been transformed. In 1882, a British tourist boasted about his "scamper through America" on a train outfitted with luxurious sleeping cars and serving a breakfast of hot breads, eggs, sausage, oysters, and trout.

Most important, the improved railroads benefited business. Able to move goods cheaply and easily, they linked the distant sections of the nation and opened every corner to settlement and industry.

Growth of the Railroads

After 1865, railroads expanded quickly. Rail service became more efficient, and the cost of shipping freight by rail dropped sharply.

In 1869, workers completed the first railroad that stretched across the continent from coast to coast. In the next 25 years, four more **transcontinental railroads** spanned the nation. These railroads opened up the West to settlement by miners, cattle ranchers, and farmers.

As settlers moved into the Great Plains and the Far West, they clashed with Native Americans living there. In a series of wars, the United States Army defeated the Indians. The government forced Indians to move onto **reservations**—limited areas set aside for Native Americans. For Plains Indians, this marked the end of their traditional way of life.

The expanding rail system gave a giant boost to industry. Railroad construction created a huge demand for coal, iron, steel, and lumber. Also, the railroads opened up new markets in towns and villages across the nation. New businesses sprang up where rail lines crossed.

An Age of Invention

From 1860 to 1890, the United States patent office issued more than half a million patents for new inventions. These inventions helped industry to grow and become more efficient. They also made daily life easier for many Americans.

For industry, one of the most important innovations was a new way to make steel. The Bessemer process, as it was called, was developed in the 1850s. It enabled steelmakers to make high-grade steel much more cheaply than before. The new steel found many uses. Long-lasting steel rails replaced rust-prone iron rails on the nation's rail-

American Heritage
MAGAZINE

The Henry Ford Museum

Not far from his Detroit auto plant, Henry Ford built a place to display "every household article, every kind of vehicle, every sort of tool." Today, at the Henry Ford Museum, you can explore the world's largest transportation collection, from canoes to giant locomotives to classic cars. You can also see devices you might have had in your home 100 years ago.

★ *To learn more about this historic site, write: Henry Ford Museum, P.O. Box 1970, Dearborn, MI 48121.*

Early American washing machine ➤

roads. Steel girders supported skyscrapers, or buildings of 20 stories or more. Many everyday items, such as nails, screws, needles, and pins, also began to be made of steel.

During the late 1800s, **Thomas Alva Edison** pioneered a new approach to invention. He set up the first modern research laboratory, where teams of experts worked together to develop inventions. Hundreds of new products came out of Edison's laboratory, including the phonograph, the motion picture camera, and the electric light bulb. Today, huge research laboratories run by American companies produce thousands of inventions every year.

Edison also developed the electric power plant. Soon, American streets, businesses, and homes were lit by electric lights.

A Transportation Revolution

In the 1900s, Americans were introduced to two new means of transportation—the au-

tomobile and the airplane. In time, the car and the plane transformed the world.

Automobiles

In 1900, only 4,000 "horseless carriages" chugged along the nation's dirt roads. Then, in 1913, automaker **Henry Ford** introduced the **assembly line.** In this method of production, workers are stationed in one place as products edge along on a moving belt. The assembly line made it possible for workers to put together many cars quickly and cheaply. Ford explained:

❝ The way to make automobiles is to make one automobile like another automobile…just as one pin is like another pin when it comes from a pin factory. ❞

Because of the assembly line, Ford could sell his cars at lower prices that more people could afford. By 1920, more than 9 million cars were on the roads. By the mid-1990s, that number had skyrocketed to more than 140 million.

Airplanes

In 1903, two bicycle mechanics, **Orville and Wilbur Wright,** made the first successful airplane flight. The first passenger airline in the United States began service in 1914. Airplanes were also used during World War I (1914–1918).

After the war, planes moved more and more mail, freight, and passengers. During World War II (1939–1945), scientists developed jet engines. Today, jets traveling at hundreds of miles per hour carry goods and people to all parts of the world.

New Business Methods

Before the Civil War, most businesses were small. They usually sold their products in their own or neighboring villages or towns. After the war, increased demand for products caused businesses to grow.

Growth of corporations

During the late 1800s, businesses developed new ways to run more efficiently. Many businesses became corporations, or businesses owned by investors. A corporation sells stock, or shares in the business, to investors. The corporation can use the money invested by stockholders to build new factories or buy new machines.

Still, the rapid growth of industry caused problems. In many industries, companies became large enough to force almost all competitors out of business. A company that gains control over the business in a certain industry is known as a monopoly. Monopolies dominated steel, oil, and sugar production, as well as other industries.

Government regulation

Reformers in the early 1900s fought against the abuses of monopolies. They called for government regulation of industry. Many monopolies were broken up under Presidents Theodore Roosevelt, William Howard Taft, and Woodrow Wilson.

Today, government regulations are intended to prevent any company from gaining a monopoly. Still, many modern companies are far larger than the monopolies of the late 1800s. Often, a single corporation owns a large number of smaller companies in different fields. These giant corporations are known as conglomerates. A single conglomerate may own a bus company, a cosmetics company, a toy company, and a football team.

The Labor Force

The rise of large corporations changed the American workplace. Many factories were dangerous places to work. In steel

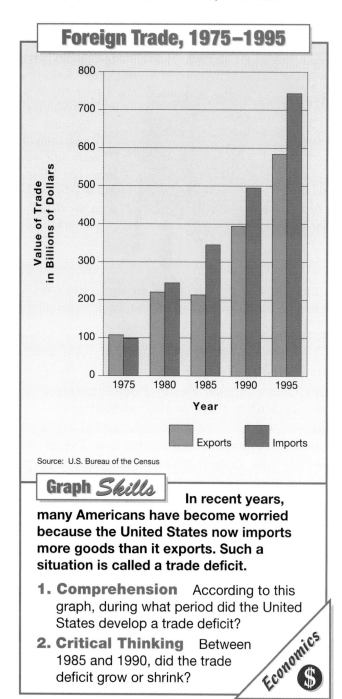

Foreign Trade, 1975–1995

Value of Trade in Billions of Dollars

Year

Exports   Imports

Source: U.S. Bureau of the Census

Graph Skills   In recent years, many Americans have become worried because the United States now imports more goods than it exports. Such a situation is called a trade deficit.

1. **Comprehension**   According to this graph, during what period did the United States develop a trade deficit?
2. **Critical Thinking**   Between 1985 and 1990, did the trade deficit grow or shrink?

Economics $

mills, for example, workers stood only inches away from vats of hissing, molten steel.

Unions gain strength

To protect themselves against poor working conditions and long hours, some workers joined together in labor unions. At first, labor unions faced opposition from both factory owners and the public. In the late 1800s, the police or the army often arrested strikers.

Slowly, however, unions won acceptance. In 1935, Congress passed a law making it legal for unions to bargain with factory owners. By 1940, there were 9 million union workers. Large labor unions became an accepted part of American business.

A shifting job market

Today, the workplace is changing once more. In some industries, computers direct the operation of labor-saving robots. Skilled workers program the computers and maintain the equipment. In other industries, workers face hazards from newly developed materials. Often, the long-range health effects of new products are not known for many years.

More people today are working in **service industries,** businesses in which workers provide a service rather than produce goods.

Service industries range from banking and education to recreation and transportation.

Foreign Competition

In the 1900s, the United States developed a healthy foreign trade. It exported far more goods than it imported. By the 1980s, however, American industries faced greater competition from other countries in Asia and Europe. Foreign competition caused a trade deficit for the United States. A **trade deficit** occurs when a nation buys more goods and services from foreign countries than it sells to them.

American industries have taken steps to meet foreign competition. Many have improved their plants and products. Some have asked the government to limit foreign imports by imposing tariffs.

Today, industries across the world are linked in a global economy. Many nations have signed trade agreements that allow them to compete more fairly. In 1993, for example, the United States, Canada, and Mexico ratified the **North American Free Trade Agreement,** or NAFTA. NAFTA reduced or eliminated many tariffs among the three countries.

★ Section 2 Review ★

Recall

1. **Identify** **(a)** Thomas Alva Edison, **(b)** Henry Ford, **(c)** Orville and Wilbur Wright, **(d)** North American Free Trade Agreement.

2. **Define** **(a)** transcontinental railroad, **(b)** reservation, **(c)** assembly line, **(d)** corporation, **(e)** stock, **(f)** monopoly, **(g)** conglomerate, **(h)** service industry, **(i)** trade deficit.

Comprehension

3. List three ways that the railroads changed the United States.

4. **(a)** Why did businesses form corporations in the late 1800s? **(b)** What problems resulted?

5. What steps is the United States taking to meet foreign competition today?

Critical Thinking and Writing

6. **Ranking** List five inventions that you have read about in this section. Then, rank the inventions in order of importance. Explain your ranking.

7. **Making a Generalization** Make a generalization about a trend in American business or labor since the late 1800s. List two facts to support your generalization.

★ ★

Activity **Playing a Role** Choose one of the inventions mentioned in this section. In a brief skit, play the role of a person seeing the invention for the first time.

3   A Changing Government

Explore These Questions

- How did women and minorities win the full rights of citizenship?
- How did the role of government increase as a result of the Great Depression?
- Why do some people want to limit the power of the government?

Define

- integration
- civil disobedience
- suffragist
- initiative
- referendum
- recall
- primary

Identify

- civil rights movement
- Martin Luther King, Jr.
- Voting Rights Act of 1965
- Nineteenth Amendment
- Sandra Day O'Connor
- Progressives
- Great Depression
- Franklin Roosevelt
- New Deal
- Ronald Reagan

SETTING the Scene In 1916, President Woodrow Wilson was giving his annual State of the Union message to Congress. Suddenly, six women leaned over the balcony above and unrolled a yellow banner. Its bold letters read, "Mr. President, what will you do for woman suffrage?"

Wilson smiled faintly and continued his speech. A doorkeeper ran angrily up the aisle and pulled the banner down. Still, the women had made their point. Newspapers across the nation carried the story. Before long, Wilson gave his support to the campaign to give women the vote.

Woman suffrage was only one political issue that occupied the nation after the Civil War. From the late 1800s on, many citizens have worked to broaden rights for individuals and reform government in other ways.

Rights for All

Today, all American citizens over age 18 have the right to vote. In 1860, however, only white men age 21 or over could vote. For the nation's women and minorities, winning the full rights of citizenship has been a long, hard struggle.

Rights for African Americans

In 1870, the Fifteenth Amendment gave black men the right to vote. After Reconstruc-

tion, however, southern states passed laws that made it difficult or impossible for African Americans to vote. Also, as you read, Jim Crow laws segregated blacks and whites.

In the North, too, African Americans faced discrimination. Landlords in white neighborhoods refused to rent them homes. Hotels and restaurants would not serve them. Employers hired them for only the lowest-paying jobs.

Thousands of African Americans fought in World War I and World War II, serving in all-black regiments. Finally, in 1948, President Harry Truman ordered the **integration,** or bringing together, of blacks and whites in the military.

In the 1950s and 1960s, African Americans and their white supporters began new campaigns for equal treatment under the law. Their efforts became known as the **civil rights movement.** Civil rights workers won a major victory in 1954, when the Supreme Court outlawed segregation in schools.

A Baptist minister, **Martin Luther King, Jr.,** emerged as the main leader of the civil rights movement. He led his followers in acts of **civil disobedience,** or nonviolent protest and refusal to obey laws that are seen as unjust. King told his followers:

66 If we protest courageously, and yet with dignity and Christian love,

when the future history books are written, somebody will have to say, 'There lived a race of people, of black people, of people who had the moral courage to stand up for their rights.' **99**

In response to the civil rights movement, Congress passed laws to help end segregation and discrimination. The **Voting Rights Act of 1965** protected African Americans who registered to vote. In 1964, only 35 percent of African Americans in the South were registered. By the 1990s, about 7,500 African Americans held elected office in the United States. They included more than 330 mayors and 26 members of Congress.

Citizenship for Asian immigrants

From its earliest days, the United States welcomed immigrants from other lands and provided that they could become citizens after a certain number of years. A law passed in 1790, however, restricted the right of citizenship to "white" immigrants.

As a result of this law, Asian immigrants were denied full participation in American life. Unlike other immigrants, they could not become citizens and vote. In states that allowed only citizens to own property, Asian immigrants could not own farms, businesses, or even their own homes.

In the 1920s, Takao Ozawa, a Japanese immigrant who had lived in the United States more than 20 years, challenged the law. However, the Supreme Court ruled against him. Finally, in 1952, Congress allowed Asian immigrants to become citizens.

Women's rights

As you read, the Seneca Falls Convention in 1848 passed a resolution demanding suffrage for women. (See page 410.) During the late 1800s and early 1900s, **suffragists** campaigned to win women's right to vote. One

Linking United States and the World

India

United States

Civil Disobedience

Mohandas Gandhi (left) used nonviolent resistance to help free India from British rule. Gandhi and his followers refused to obey unjust laws. When arrested, they submitted peacefully. American civil rights leader Martin Luther King, Jr., adopted Gandhi's idea of civil disobedience. At right, King leads a peaceful protest march. ★ **Why do you think Gandhi and King were willing to be arrested?**

Viewing HISTORY — Women Demand the Vote

To win the vote, suffragists staged parades across the country. These women, along with their children, are marching down a New York City street in 1912.
★ **Why do you think these marchers carried American flags?**

▲
Window banner from 1915

suffragist told of her efforts during a train trip through Kansas:

> 66 About a dozen passengers were in the caboose...and we held a meeting and discussion which lasted about 45 minutes. Upon reaching Osborne at three o'clock I found about 100 people assembled for an auction sale in the middle of the street.... The temptation to hold a meeting overcame fatigue. I jumped into an automobile nearby and had a most interested crowd until the auctioneer came. 99

By 1919, women in many states could vote in state and local elections. Finally, in 1920, the states ratified the **Nineteenth Amendment.** It guaranteed the right to vote for women in all states.

After the 1960s, women won greater civil and economic rights. Federal laws made it illegal to favor men over women in hiring or wages. Women also made gains in politics. In 1981, **Sandra Day O'Connor** became the first woman to sit on the Supreme Court. In 1997, Madeleine Albright became the first woman to serve as Secretary of State.

Lowering the voting age

In March 1971, Congress passed the Twenty-sixth Amendment. It guaranteed the right to vote to citizens age 18 or older.

At the time the amendment was submitted, 18-year-olds were allowed to fight and die in the Vietnam War but were not allowed to vote. The amendment won strong support, and it was ratified in less than four months.

Connections With Arts

In 1997, the Lilith Fair toured the United States. A series of concerts celebrated women's achievements in music. Performers ranged from Sheryl Crow and Tracy Chapman to country singers Emmylou Harris and Mary Chapin Carpenter. The tour also raised money for various charities, including shelters for abused women.

A Growing Role for Voters

American voters have won wider powers. In some states, citizens can introduce a bill in the state legislature by collecting signatures on a petition. This process is called an **initiative.** In a **referendum,** people can vote directly on a bill. In some states, voters also have the power to remove a person from office in a **recall** election.

The initiative, referendum, and recall were ideas first supported by reformers in the early 1900s. These reformers were called **Progressives.** Progressives also supported primary elections and direct election of senators. In a **primary,** voters from each political party decide who will be their party's candidate in the general election. The creation of primaries meant that political bosses could no longer hand-pick candidates.

The Constitution originally called for senators to be chosen by state legislatures. The Seventeenth Amendment, ratified in 1913, gave voters in each state the right to elect two senators directly.

A More Active Federal Government

As the nation has expanded, the role of the federal government has grown. Often, the government has used its power to help or protect Americans.

Regulating business

In the late 1800s, the growth of industry created large monopolies. Wealthy business leaders sometimes used their influence unfairly to gain favors from the government.

Reformers called on Congress to regulate large businesses and protect ordinary workers and citizens. Congress created the Interstate Commerce Commission, or ICC, in 1887. The ICC investigated complaints and took some big companies to court.

The Great Depression

During the 1900s, the government became increasingly involved in the lives of Americans. One of the major turning points came during the **Great Depression,** which lasted from 1919 to 1941. It was the worst economic crisis in the nation's history. Millions of Americans lost their jobs, farms, or homes.

At the height of the depression, in 1933, **Franklin Roosevelt** became President. Roosevelt reassured suffering Americans:

❝ This great nation will endure as it has endured, will revive and will prosper. So, first of all, let me assert my firm belief that the only thing we have to fear is fear itself—nameless, unreasoning, unjustified terror which

Biography — Franklin and Eleanor Roosevelt

Franklin D. Roosevelt (FDR) was the only person elected President four times. To combat the effects of the Great Depression, FDR greatly expanded the role of the federal government in the economy. His wife, Eleanor, played an active role in her husband's administration. She used her position as First Lady to speak out on issues ranging from conditions in coal mines, to women's rights, to justice for African Americans. ★ **During the depression, President Roosevelt told Americans that "the only thing we have to fear is fear itself." What do you think he meant?**

paralyzes needed efforts to convert retreat into advance. "

With the help of Congress, Roosevelt set up many new programs to relieve the suffering of the unemployed. Under Roosevelt's program, known as the **New Deal,** the government also put unemployed people to work on projects such as building dams, schools, and parks.

One major program of the New Deal was Social Security. It set up a system of pensions for older people. It also set up a system of unemployment insurance and gave states money to support dependent children and people with disabilities. The Social Security system remains in effect today.

Debating the role of government

Following the trend begun during the New Deal, the federal government continued to expand its role in American life. The government passed laws that protected con-

▲ 1980 Ronald Reagan campaign button

sumers from harmful foods and medicines. It inspected shops and factories to ensure that they were safe for workers. In the 1970s, concerns about the environment led Congress to pass laws cleaning up polluted rivers and smog-filled air.

By the 1980s and 1990s, some Americans began to worry about the high costs of government programs. They worried, too, that the federal government had too much power. In 1980, Americans elected **Ronald Reagan** as President. "Government is not the solution to our problem," Reagan said, "government is the problem." Reagan promised to cut taxes and spending. He also sought to reduce government regulation, which he said kept businesses from growing. In the 1990s, President Bill Clinton, a middle-of-the-road Democrat, worked with the Republican Congress to cut federal spending while continuing to protect the neediest citizens.

★ Section 3 Review ★

Recall

1. **Identify** (a) civil rights movement, (b) Martin Luther King, Jr., (c) Voting Rights Act of 1965, (d) Nineteenth Amendment, (e) Sandra Day O'Connor, (f) Progressives, (g) Great Depression, (h) Franklin Roosevelt, (i) New Deal, (j) Ronald Reagan.

2. **Define** (a) integration, (b) civil disobedience, (c) suffragist, (d) initiative, (e) referendum, (f) recall, (g) primary.

Comprehension

3. List one advance in civil rights won by each of the following during the 1900s: (a) African Americans, (b) Asians, (c) women.

4. (a) What steps did Franklin Roosevelt take to relieve the Great Depression? (b) How did the trend toward big government continue after the New Deal?

5. Why do many Americans today want to reduce the size of the federal government?

Critical Thinking and Writing

6. **Making a Generalization** Make a generalization about the expansion of civil rights in the United States during the past 100 years. Give three examples to support your generalization.

7. **Linking Past and Present** (a) Describe three ways in which the federal government directly affects your life today. (b) Do you think you are better off or worse off as a result? Explain.

* *

Activity **Writing a Speech** You are a leader of one of the civil rights movements described in this section. Write a speech to inspire other Americans to support your cause.

4 Becoming a World Power

As You Read

Explore These Questions
- Why did the United States become more involved in world affairs?
- What was the Cold War?
- What role does the United States play in the world today?

Define
- imperialism
- annex
- totalitarian state

Identify
- Spanish-American War
- Theodore Roosevelt
- World War I
- Adolf Hitler
- World War II
- Joseph Stalin
- Cold War
- United Nations
- Vietnam War

SETTING the Scene In 1858, Cyrus Field completed the laying of an underwater telegraph cable across the Atlantic Ocean. The cable carried a few messages between England and the United States and then snapped. Field tried again, with an improved cable, in 1866. This time, he succeeded.

In the years after the Civil War, Field's transatlantic cable connected the United States to Europe. At the same time, new oceangoing steamers and improved railroads cut travel times on land and sea. As technology shrank distances between nations, the United States became more involved in world affairs.

Growing Involvement in World Affairs

During its first 100 years, the United States paid relatively little attention to political events in other countries. Washington, Jefferson, and other early Presidents believed that the young nation would be better able to grow and prosper if it did not become entangled in foreign affairs.

Foreign trade

Despite this policy of isolation from the political affairs of other countries, the United States conducted a lively foreign trade. Europe was the most important market. After the Civil War, trade with Asia and Latin America also grew.

In the 1870s, European nations entered an age of imperialism. **Imperialism** is the control by powerful countries of weaker countries or regions. France, Britain, Germany, and other powers colonized the lands of Africa and Asia. They built great empires that increased their power and wealth.

Americans could not ignore Europe's race for colonies. The United States had become a world leader in industry and agriculture. It needed new markets for its goods. In Congress, Senator Albert Beveridge of Indiana urged the United States to look abroad, especially to Asia:

> 66 Our largest trade henceforth must be with Asia. The Pacific is our ocean.... China is our natural customer.... That statesman commits a crime against American trade... who fails to put America where she may command that trade. 99

New territories

In 1898, the United States **annexed,** or added, Hawaii, a chain of islands in the Pacific Ocean. With a safe harbor in Hawaii, the United States could more easily open and protect markets in Asia.

The **Spanish-American War** of 1898 added other territory to the United States. The war broke out as a result of a dispute over Spain's rule of Cuba. American troops quickly defeated the Spanish. Under the peace treaty, Spain gave the islands of Puerto Rico in the Caribbean, and Guam and the Philippines in the Pacific, to the United States.

Relations With Latin America

The United States also took a more active role in Latin America. In 1901, **Theodore Roosevelt** became President. Roosevelt favored direct action. His motto was "Speak softly, but carry a big stick." By this, he meant that the United States would strive for peace but use force when necessary.

Roosevelt often used the "big stick" in Latin America. For example, Roosevelt wanted to build a canal connecting the Atlantic and Pacific oceans. When Colombia refused to sell the land for the canal, Roosevelt arranged for citizens of Colombia to revolt against the government. The rebels created a new country, Panama. Panama then quickly

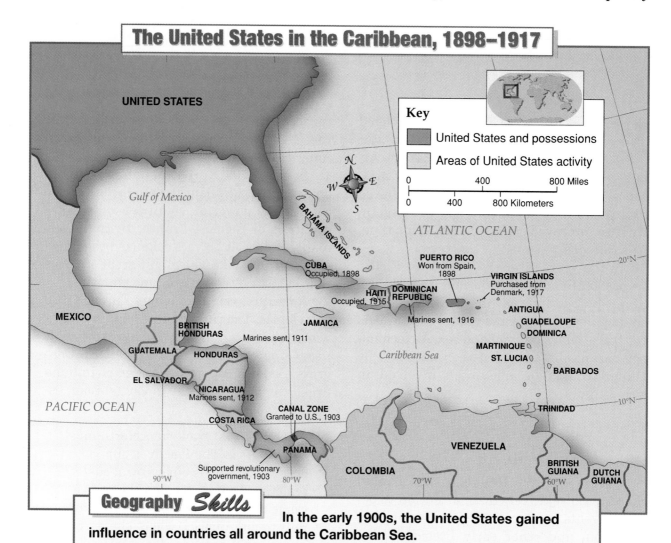

The United States in the Caribbean, 1898–1917

Key
- United States and possessions
- Areas of United States activity

0   400   800 Miles
0   400   800 Kilometers

Geography Skills In the early 1900s, the United States gained influence in countries all around the Caribbean Sea.

1. **Location** On the map, locate: **(a)** Colombia, **(b)** Panama, **(c)** Dominican Republic, **(d)** Haiti, **(e)** Honduras, **(f)** Puerto Rico.

2. **Region** What areas shown on the map were governed directly by the United States?

3. **Critical Thinking** Look at the chart on page 618. Which territories shown on this map still belong to the United States?

agreed to let the United States build the Panama Canal.

For most of the 1900s, the United States continued to intervene in Latin America to protect its interests there. President Taft, for example, sent troops into Nicaragua and Honduras. President Wilson intervened in the Dominican Republic and Haiti. President Reagan ordered troops to invade Grenada. President Clinton sent troops to Haiti to oversee elections there.

Over the years, Americans have debated the "big stick" policy. Opponents argue that the United States has made enemies by intervening in the internal affairs of weaker nations. Supporters respond that the United States has a duty to maintain peace and order in Latin America.

Two World Wars

In 1914, **World War I** broke out in Europe. At first, President Woodrow Wilson declared American neutrality. Then, in 1917, the United States entered the war on the side of the Allies—Britain, France, and 22 other nations. The war ended in 1918 with an Allied victory. Afterward, Wilson tried to get the United States to join a League of Nations to prevent future wars. However, Congress refused. Now that the war was over, many Americans sought once more to avoid involvement in foreign affairs.

In the 1930s, the nations of Europe again moved toward war. In Germany, dictator **Adolf Hitler** set up a **totalitarian state,** in which a single party controls the government and every aspect of people's lives. In 1939,

war broke out when Hitler invaded neighboring Poland. Italy and Japan sided with Hitler, forming the Axis powers. They fought against the Allies, which included Britain, France, and the Soviet Union.

Again, the United States tried to remain neutral. On December 7, 1941, however, the Japanese launched a surprise attack on Pearl Harbor in Hawaii. Congress quickly declared war on Japan. Days later, Italy and Germany declared war on the United States.

World War II cost millions of lives. The Allies defeated Germany and Italy in April 1945. The war against Japan did not end until August 1945, when American planes dropped atomic bombs on the Japanese cities of Hiroshima and Nagasaki.

The Cold War

After World War II, the United States became concerned about the expanding power of the Soviet Union. The two nations had been allies during the war. Now, however, the Soviets, under **Joseph Stalin,** were setting up communist governments in the countries in Eastern Europe. To contain Soviet influence, the United States and the nations of Western Europe formed the North Atlantic Treaty Organization, or NATO.

Rivalry between the United States and the Soviet Union never erupted into direct armed conflict. With each side pointing nuclear missiles at the other, the prospect of a shooting war was too frightening. Instead, the two superpowers entered a long period of tension and rivalry known as the **Cold War.**

Twice, the United States became involved in regional wars to contain communist expansion. Between 1950 and 1953, American troops battled to turn back an invasion of South Korea by communist North Korea. In the Korean War, Americans fought under the command of the **United Nations,** an international peacekeeping organization set up in 1945.

In the 1960s and 1970s, American soldiers fought against communist rebels in Vietnam. The government argued that, if Vietnam fell to communism, neighboring nations would be threatened. Many Americans, especially young people, protested the war.

Connections With Civics

To honor the dead of World War I, the United States dedicated the Tomb of the Unknown Soldier. In 1921, the body of an unidentified American soldier was brought from an unmarked grave in France to a military cemetery in Arlington, Virginia. Above his grave, a marble monument bears the inscription: "Here rests in honored glory an American soldier known but to God."

Viewing History — Honoring American Veterans

Americans honor those men and women who served in the nation's military. At left, members of the Veterans of Foreign Wars salute a Veterans Day parade in Texas. At right, people visit the Vietnam Veterans Memorial in Washington, D.C. The memorial, designed by Maya Lin, is inscribed with the names of more than 58,000 Americans killed or missing in the Vietnam War. ★ **How does your community honor veterans?**

They said that the conflict was a civil war and that it did not threaten American security. In the early 1970s, American troops finally returned home. More than 57,000 Americans had lost their lives in the **Vietnam War.**

After 1985, superpower tensions eased as Premier Mikhail Gorbachev (mee kah EEL gor buh CHAWF) launched economic and democratic reforms in the Soviet Union. In 1989, countries in Eastern Europe rejected their communist governments. Two years later, the Soviet Union itself broke up. The Cold War was over.

Working for Peace

As the Cold War faded, conflicts in many areas of the globe still threatened the peace. During the 1990s, the United States worked with many nations in an effort to create a more stable, more democratic world.

Presidents George Bush and Bill Clinton used United States influence to help bring stability to war-torn regions such as Bosnia in Eastern Europe. In 1992, American forces led a United Nations mission to Somalia in eastern Africa. The troops helped distribute food during a famine caused by civil war. Two years later, American troops joined a UN mission to Haiti. They forced out military dictators and restored an elected president to the Caribbean island.

The United States also took an active role in the Middle East. The United States supported the peace process between Israel and its Arab neighbors. In 1991, American troops joined a UN force to drive Iraqi invaders out of Kuwait.

The United States also used diplomacy to bring about peace. In Northern Ireland, long-standing disputes between Protestants and Catholics had resulted in thousands of deaths. President Clinton sent former Senator George Mitchell to Ireland for peace talks. Mitchell's negotiations helped produce a peace agreement in April 1998.

The Last Superpower

With the Soviet Union gone, the United States became the world's remaining superpower. Some Americans hoped the country would take the opportunity to reduce its role in world affairs. "In the post-Cold War world, we will no longer require our people to carry an unfair burden for the rest of humanity," said Representative Dana Rohrabacher of California.

Others argued that the nation had a responsibility to use its power when needed. "The U.S. must lead, period," declared Newt Gingrich, the Speaker of the House of Representatives. President Bill Clinton told a meeting of foreign policy experts:

66 If we are going to be strong at home and lead abroad, we have to overcome a dangerous and growing temptation in our own land to focus solely on the problems we face here in America. The new isolationists must not be allowed to pull America out of the game. 99

The Future of a Free People

In this book, you have read about the many individuals, groups, and cultures who helped create the United States. The progress of the republic was never easy. In 1776, the problems facing the United States seemed so great that many believed the new nation would not survive.

What does the future hold? Since 1877, the United States has become a superpower and a model for democratic nations everywhere. It can continue as one only if every American works to preserve the values of life, liberty, and the pursuit of happiness. Your generation holds the power to shape the nation's future.

★ Section 4 Review ★

Recall

1. **Locate** (a) Hawaii, (b) Puerto Rico, (c) Philippines, (d) Panama, (e) Vietnam.

2. **Identify** (a) Spanish-American War, (b) Theodore Roosevelt, (c) World War I, (d) Adolf Hitler, (e) World War II, (f) Joseph Stalin, (g) Cold War, (h) United Nations, (i) Vietnam War.

3. **Define** (a) imperialism, (b) annex, (c) totalitarian state.

Comprehension

4. Why did the United States become more involved in world affairs in the late 1800s?

5. Why did the United States distrust the Soviet Union after World War II?

6. Give two examples of how the United States used its power to promote democracy and stability after the end of the Cold War.

Critical Thinking and Writing

7. **Making Generalizations** Make a generalization about the role of the United States in world affairs since the late 1800s. Give three examples to support your generalization.

8. **Understanding Alternatives** Review the subsection The Last Superpower, above. (a) What alternatives are suggested for the United States in the post–Cold War era? (b) Which alternative would you support? Explain.

Activity Interviewing Interview someone in your own family or community who served overseas. Think of at least five questions to ask about that person's experiences in the military.

Epilogue

Review and Activities

★ Sum It Up ★

Section 1   A Diverse Nation

▶ Today, as in the past, immigrants from many nations contribute to the rich culture of the United States.

▶ Since the 1800s, the majority of the population has shifted from farms to cities and suburbs.

▶ Mass communication has brought many different people closer together.

Section 2   A Changing Economy

▶ New inventions and business practices sparked tremendous economic growth.

▶ Today, the United States must compete with many nations in a global economy.

Section 3   A Changing Government

▶ In the 1900s, women and minorities have fought to secure their full rights under the Constitution.

▶ The role of the federal government expanded, especially after the Great Depression.

▶ Today, many Americans want to reduce the size and cost of the government.

Section 4   Becoming a World Power

▶ The United States has steadily become more involved in world affairs.

▶ During the Cold War, the United States entered a long rivalry with the Soviet Union.

▶ Today, Americans debate whether the United States should take a leading role in the affairs of other nations.

For additional review of the major ideas of the Epilogue, see *Guide to the Essentials of American History* or *Interactive Student Tutorial CD-ROM,* which contains interactive review activities, graphic organizers, and practice tests.

🗂 Reviewing the Chapter

Define These Terms

Match each term with the correct definition.

Column 1
1. corporation
2. monopoly
3. civil disobedience
4. referendum
5. imperialism

Column 2
a. system where people vote directly on a law
b. business owned by investors
c. control of weaker nations by a stronger nation
d. nonviolent protest
e. company that gains control of a certain industry

Explore the Main Ideas

1. How did the "new immigrant" of the late 1800s and early 1900s differ from earlier immigrants?
2. How did railroads spur industrial growth?
3. How did the United States develop a trade deficit?
4. Describe two victories of the civil rights movement.
5. What policy did the United States follow toward Latin America?

🗂 Geography Activity

Match the letters on the map with the following places:
1. United States, **2.** Puerto Rico, **3.** Canal Zone, **4.** Cuba, **5.** Nicaragua, **6.** Dominican Republic.   **Region** Which of the above lands became a United States territory as a result of the Spanish-American War?

520 ★ Epilogue

▣ Critical Thinking and Writing

1. **Linking Past and Present** **(a)** Why did many immigrants come to the United States in the late 1800s and early 1900s? **(b)** Do immigrants today come for the same reasons? Explain.

2. **Using Chronology** **(a)** Place the following forms of transportation in their order of invention: airplane; automobile; railroad. **(b)** What advantages did the later forms have?

3. **Analyzing Ideas** Why do you think many people feel it is important for citizens to oppose discrimination even when it does not affect them directly?

4. **Ranking** What would you consider the three most important events described in this chapter? Give reasons for your choices.

▣ Using Primary Sources

In 1996, President Bill Clinton addressed a group of American business leaders:

❝ Every day all you have to do is pick up the paper or watch the evening news to see that differences among people—racial, ethnic, religious, and other differences—are tearing the heart out of societies... all around the world. In America we're turning all those differences to our advantage. And I think more and more we're getting comfortable with the fact that we are more than ever still a nation of immigrants. ❞

Source: M2 PressWIRE, October 1, 1996.

Recognizing Points of View **(a)** According to Clinton, how do differences among people affect many places in the world? **(b)** How does he say the United States differs from these other places?

ACTIVITY BANK

▶ Interdisciplinary Activity

Exploring the Arts Do research on the early days of jazz or rock 'n' roll. Then, prepare a five-minute presentation on a pioneering musician such as Louis Armstrong, or Elvis Presley. Include a recording.

▶ Career Skills Activity

Architects Find out more about the layout and the buildings of a city in the late 1800s. Then, create a model of a city of the period. Include skyscrapers, tenements, stores, theaters, parks, and other features of the city.

▶ Citizenship Activity

Learning About Democracy Does your state allow initiatives or referendums? If so, find out about some recent examples. Working with other class members, prepare for a debate or a panel discussion on one of these issues.

Internet Activity
Use the Internet to find a Web site for a national or local news agency, newspaper, or television station. Report on what kinds of news you can get from that site, and how you can use that site to keep informed about current and future issues.

EYEWITNESS Journal

You are yourself, a young student attending an American school right now. In your EYEWITNESS JOURNAL, describe three events of the past 25 years that have had the biggest impact on your life. You may write as if you had the ability to go back in time to witness these events.

Viewpoints: Source Readings in American History

Historical Documents, Literature, and Eyewitness Accounts

Unit 1 — Early Heritage of the Americas

★ 1–1 ★ The Mountains of California

Eyewitness Account

Introduction In the late 1800s, Scottish-born naturalist John Muir walked across much of the United States, describing each region. Through his efforts, the government established Yosemite and Sequoia national parks. In 1892, Muir founded the Sierra Club, an organization dedicated to the conservation of American forest lands. This excerpt is from Muir's 1894 book, *The Mountains of California*.

Vocabulary Before you read the selection, find the meanings of these words in a dictionary: **reposing, luminous, celestial, ineffably, adamant, composite, inaccessible.**

★ ★ ★ ★ ★ ★ ★ ★ ★ ★

Making your way through the mazes of the Coast Range to the summit of any of the inner peaks or passes opposite San Francisco, in the clear springtime, the grandest and most telling of all California landscapes is outspread before you. At your feet lies the great Central Valley glowing golden in the sunshine, extending north and south farther than the eye can reach, one smooth, flowery, lake-like bed of fertile soil. Along its eastern margin rises the mighty Sierra, miles in height, reposing like a smooth, cumulous cloud in the sunny sky, and so gloriously colored, and so luminous, it seems to be not clothed with light, but wholly composed of it, like the wall of some celestial city. Along the top, and extending a good way down, you

see a pale, pearl gray belt of snow; and below it a belt of blue and dark purple, marking the extension of the forests; and along the base of the range a broad belt of rose purple and yellow, where lie the miner's goldfields and the foot-hill gardens. All these colored belts blending smoothly make a wall of light ineffably fine, and as beautiful as a rainbow, yet firm as adamant.

When I first enjoyed this superb view, one glowing April day, from the summit of the Pacheco Pass, the Central Valley, but little trampled or plowed as yet, was one furred, rich sheet of golden composite, and the luminous wall of the mountains shone in all its glory. Then it seemed to me the Sierra should be called not the Nevada, or Snowy Range, but the Range of Light. And after ten years spent in the heart of it, rejoicing and wondering, bathing in its glorious floods of light, seeing the sunbursts of morning among the ivy peaks, the noonday radiance on the trees and rocks and snow, the flush of the alpenglow, and a thousand dashing waterfalls with their marvelous abundance of irised spray, it still seems to me above all others the Range of Light, the most divinely beautiful of all the mountain-chains I have ever seen.

The Sierra is about 500 miles long, 70 miles wide, and from 7,000 to nearly 15,000 feet high. In general views no mark of man is visible on it, nor anything to suggest the rich-

Viewing HISTORY

Yosemite Valley

During the late 1800s, German-born Albert Bierstadt traveled from New York City to the Pacific Ocean. His landscapes, like this one of the Sierra Nevada, show the huge, empty spaces and great beauty of the American west. ★ **What feelings did Bierstadt try to suggest in this painting? How can you tell?**

Albert Bierstadt, Landscape

ness of the life it cherishes, or the depth and grandeur of its sculpture. None of its magnificent forest-crowned ridges rises much above the general level to publish its wealth. No great valley or lake is seen, or river, or group of well-marked features of any kind, standing out in distinct pictures. Even the summit-peaks, so clear and high in the sky, seem comparatively smooth and featureless. Nevertheless, glaciers are still at work in the shadows of the peaks, and thousands of lakes and meadows shine and bloom beneath them, and the whole range is furrowed with canyons to a depth of from 2,000 to 5,000 feet, in which once flowed majestic glaciers, and in which now flow and sing a band of beautiful rivers.

Though of such stupendous depth, these famous canyons are not raw, gloomy, jagged-walled gorges, savage and inaccessible. With rough passages here and there they still make delightful pathways for the mountaineer, conducting from the fertile lowlands to the highest icy fountains, as a kind of mountain streets full of charming life and light, graded and sculptured by the ancient glaciers, and presenting, throughout all their courses, a rich variety of novel and attractive scenery, the most attractive that has yet been discovered in the mountain-ranges of the world.

Source: *The Mountains of California,* John Muir, 1894.

Analyzing Primary Sources

1. What first impressed Muir about the Sierra Nevada?
   A. the light
   B. the height of the mountains
   C. the destruction of the land
   D. the mild weather

2. Muir recommends the range to
   F. farmers.
   G. gold miners.
   H. mountain climbers.
   J. painters.

3. **Critical Thinking Recognizing Points of View** What do you think was the main reason that Muir wrote this description?

Historical Critique

Why is Muir's description of the Sierra Nevada an authentic historical document? What facts does Muir include here that could not have come from his own personal observations?

Introduction   Katharine Lee Bates was an English professor at Wellesley College in Massachusetts. She wrote many poems and children's books during her long career. However, she is best known for writing the words to "America the Beautiful." Bates wrote the hymn in 1893 and revised it in 1911. Over the years, many people have suggested that this song should become the national anthem of the United States.

Vocabulary   Before you read the selection, find the meanings of these words in a dictionary: **amber, strife, alabaster.**

★ ★ ★ ★ ★ ★ ★ ★ ★

O beautiful for spacious skies,
For amber waves of grain,
For purple mountain majesties
Above the fruited plain!
America! America!
God shed His grace on thee
And crown thy good with brotherhood
From sea to shining sea!

O beautiful for pilgrim feet,
Whose stern, impassioned stress
A thoroughfare for freedom beat
Across the wilderness!

America! America!
God mend thine every flaw,
Confirm thy soul in self-control,
Thy liberty in law!

O beautiful for heroes proved
In liberating strife,
Who more than self their country loved,
And mercy more than life!
America! America!
May God thy gold refine,
Till all success be nobleness
And every gain divine!

O beautiful for patriot dream
That sees beyond the years
Thine alabaster cities gleam
Undimmed by human tears!
America! America!
God shed his grace on thee,
And crown thy good with brotherhood
From sea to shining sea!

Source: *America the Beautiful and Other Poems,* Katharine Lee Bates, 1911.

Viewing HISTORY **Amber Waves of Grain**

This landscape by photographer Adam Jones suggests the "amber waves of grain" described in the song "America the Beautiful." ★ **In what region of the United States might this scene be located? Explain your answer.**

Analyzing Literature

1. What is the main topic of the song?
   - **A.** the founding of the United States
   - **B.** farm life
   - **C.** city life
   - **D.** American scenery

2. To what "heroes" does the song refer?
   - **F.** Pilgrims
   - **G.** soldiers
   - **H.** explorers
   - **J.** farmers

3. **Critical Thinking   Synthesizing Information** Briefly list the historical events that the author mentions in the song.

Historical Critique

Patriotic songs are meant to stir feelings of pride in one's country. How does the first verse of "America the Beautiful" encourage feelings of pride?

★ Chapter 2 ★ The First Americans

★ 2–1 ★ The Spider Woman

Introduction   Weaving is an important part of Navajo culture. The following folk tale tells how Navajo women learned to weave. The Kisani woman, the main character, has been rejected by society because she is considered ugly. She comes upon the Spider Woman sitting in a cave.

Vocabulary   Before you read the selection, find the meanings of these words in a dictionary: **abode, hogan, loom.**

★ ★ ★ ★ ★ ★ ★ ★ ★

The Kisani woman climbed down . . . into the abode of the Spider Woman who was weaving something. "Come down and sit here beside me and watch what I do, my grandchild," the old woman said. And the Kisani woman did as she asked.

The Spider Woman was using a stick about a foot long with a hole in one end like a needle, and with this she passed the thread in and out, making a blanket. "What is this that you do, grandmother?" the Kisani girl asked.

"It is a blanket I weave," the old woman replied.

"Does it have a name, my grandmother?"

"I will name it Black Design Blanket." And this became the Black Design Blanket, the first blanket of the Navajo. . . . Then Spider Woman told the girl the sun was low and it would soon be dark. . . .

"It is late and I must be leaving," the girl said.

"Please. Spend the night with me, my grandchild." This the Kisani woman agreed to and began to settle for the night. . . .

Spider Woman made some dumplings out of grass seeds and fed the girl and the next morning started weaving another blanket. She worked so fast that she finished it that day. It was square and as long as her arm and she named this new blanket Pretty Design Blanket. The girl watched her all day and stayed there a second night, and the following morning the Spider Woman started still another blanket. She finished this blanket, which she called White Striped Blanket, that day, and on the fourth morning she began another. This was a "Beautiful Design Skirt" such as Yeibichai dancers and Snake dancers wear, and was white with figures in black.

The next morning the Kisani girl went back to the hogan where she had been

Blanket weaving was a valued tradition among the Navajo people of the Southwest. Designs varied from village to village and were handed down from one generation to the next. The blanket shown here was woven in the late 1800s. ★ **Why are Navajo blankets prized today?**

staying and asked the Navajos for some cotton in three colors—yellow, black, and white. After the cotton had been given to her, she put up a loom, but not like the Spider Woman's loom. She put it up the way Navajo women do now and began a blanket. Her blanket was about half done when another Kisani woman came in and looked at the loom and the design. The girl had made a picture of a bird on both sides of the blanket.

"Where did you learn to do that?" the Kisani woman asked. "I did this on my own thought," answered the girl. "It is called a Black Design Blanket."

She finished it in one day, and the next morning she put up her loom again and asked for more cotton to weave. She made a Beautiful Design Skirt the same day. It was finished when two Kisani men came to see what she was doing and asked to see the blankets she had made. One examined the Beautiful Design Blanket very carefully. The second man observed the Black Design weaving. They then returned to their homes and made looms, copying the designs they had learned. And this is why it is the Kisani men who are known for their beautiful weaving.

The girl only made two blankets and then went back to Spider Woman's house. Spider Woman was now weaving a wicker water jar and after that she wove a big carrying basket such as Navajo women used to carry on their backs. The Kisani girl learned to make the basket and then the water jar. "When I went back," she told Spider Woman, "I showed the people how to make blankets like yours. Now I will go back and make carrying baskets and water jars."

"That is good," said Spider Woman. "I am glad you have taught them. But whenever you make a blanket, you must leave a hole in the middle the way I do. For if you do not, your weaving thoughts will be trapped within the cotton and not only will it bring you bad luck, but it will drive you mad."

The girl went back to her hogan and made a carrying basket and a water jar.

"Where do you learn all these things?" The People asked.

"I just guessed it out," she said.

The Navajo women watched her, and soon they were all making carrying baskets and then they learned to make water jars and blankets too, just like those of the Spider Woman. Unlike the Kisani men, it is the Navajo women who kept on with their blanket weaving. And they always left the spider-hole in the center of a spider web. That keeps them from getting "blanket sickness" of the mind from keeping the weaving patterns inside their heads. Navajo women almost never draw their blanket patterns down but keep them inside as Spider Woman did.

And that's true, even today.

Source: *Sweet Salt: Navajo Folk Tales and Mythology,* edited by Raymond Friday Locke, 1990.

Analyzing Literature

1. What distinguishes a blanket woven by a Navajo?
   A. It contains three different colors.
   B. It is made on a loom.
   C. It contains a picture of the sun.
   D. It has a hole in the middle.

2. What is Kisani's obligation to the Spider Woman?
   F. to sell the Spider Woman's blankets
   G. to learn to weave much faster
   H. to take care of the Spider Woman
   J. to teach others how to weave

3. **Critical Thinking   Making Generalizations** What role do you think folk tales play in a society?

Historical Critique

This tale was first told in the Navajo language. Also, like many folk tales, it was passed on orally for generations before being written down. How might these two facts affect the authenticity of this version of the story?

★ 2–2 ★   ## A Descripton of Montezuma

Eyewitness Account

Introduction   Bernal Díaz del Castillo was one of the Spanish soldiers who conquered the Aztec empire in the 1500s. He later settled in Guatemala and wrote his memoirs. In this passage, Díaz describes a visit to the Aztec emperor Montezuma.

Vocabulary   Before you read the selection, find the meanings of these words in a dictionary: **proportioned, sparse, fragrant, idol, lavishly, frothy, cacao, stewards, provisioners.**

★ ★ ★ ★ ★ ★ ★ ★ ★

The great Montezuma was about 40 years old, of good height, well proportioned, and slender; he was not very dark but the color natural for an Indian. He did not wear his hair long, only long enough to cover his ears. He had few whiskers, dark and well set and sparse. His face was a little long, but pleasant, while his eyes were attractive, and he showed in his person and in his glance both affection and, when necessary, seriousness. He was most clean, bathing every day, in the afternoon. . . .

There were more than 200 of his main guards in rooms close to his own—not so that they could all talk with him, but only a few at a time. When they went to speak with him, they had to take off their rich clothes and put on others of little value, but they had to be clean. They had to enter barefoot and with their eyes down, and not look at his face. They had to bow three times and say, "Lord, my lord, my great lord," as soon as they reached his presence; and after they told him what they had come for, he attended to them with a few words. They did not turn their backs on him when they left, but kept their faces and eyes directed toward the floor near his feet while they backed from the room.

Let us leave this and return to the way things were served at mealtime. If it was cold, they made a large fire of coals of a wood that did not smoke. The scent of its bark was very fragrant, and so that it would not give off more heat than was wanted, they put in front of it a kind of screen worked in gold and with figures of idols. He [Montezuma] sat at a low stool, soft and rich. The table was also low, and made in the same design as the seats. . . . Four very beautiful and clean women brought water for the hands in things like deep basins called *xicales*. Below, to catch the water, they put a different kind of dish, and they brought him towels while two other women brought him tortillas.

When he began to eat, they placed in front of him a kind of screen of wood lavishly

Montezuma, Emperor of the Aztecs

This oil painting by a later artist gives a fanciful portrait of the last Aztec emperor, Montezuma. From descriptions and sketches of Aztec life, the artist shows how feathers and gold were used as armor and decoration. ★ **How does this portrait suggest that Montezuma was a great leader?**

painted with gold, so he could not be seen eating. The four women stood aside, and at his sides sat four elderly great chiefs, with whom Montezuma spoke from time to time and asked questions. As a great favor he would give to each of them a plate of what he thought was best. It was said that these elders were close relatives, counselors, and judges....

After Montezuma had eaten, all the guards and the house servants had their meal, and it seems to me that they took out more than a thousand plates of food and more than two thousand pitchers of frothy cacao and a countless quantity of fruit. With his women and servants and tortilla makers and cacao makers, how much must it have cost him? Then there were the stewards and the treasurers, the provisioners and the wine cellarers, and those who had charge of the houses where maize was kept. If I tried to tell about each thing by itself, there would be so much to write about that I wouldn't know where to begin. We were astonished at the organization and the quantities of everything.

Source: *The Bernal Díaz Chronicles,* translated by Albert Idel, 1956.

Analyzing Primary Sources

1. What was Díaz describing in the passage above?
   A. differences between the Spanish and Aztecs
   B. Montezuma's great power and majesty
   C. the beauty of Aztec women
   D. Montezuma's appearance and eating habits

2. What aspect of Aztec life did Díaz emphasize in this description?
   F. the cleanliness of the Aztec emperor
   G. Aztec religious practices
   H. Montezuma's warlike appearance
   J. the abundance of gold and silver

3. **Critical Thinking   Recognizing Points of View**   Based on this excerpt, how did Díaz view Montezuma? Explain.

Historical Critique

Why is Bernal Díaz's memoir a historical document? How might its accuracy be limited?

★ Chapter 3 ★ A Meeting of Different Worlds

★ 3–1 ★ Two Descriptions of the Middle Passage

Eyewitness Account

Introduction Enslaved Africans were packed onto ships and brought to the Americas on a route known as the Middle Passage. The following two excerpts are the views and observations of men who witnessed it firsthand. John Newton was a former slave ship captain who later became a minister. Dr. Falconbridge was a surgeon who served on a slave ship during the time of the African slave trade.

Vocabulary Before you read the selection, find the meaning of this word in a dictionary: **ensued.**

★ ★ ★ ★ ★ ★ ★ ★ ★

The Reverend John Newton:
The cargo of a vessel of a hundred tons or a little more is calculated to purchase from 220 to 250 slaves. Their lodging rooms below the deck which are three (for the men, the boys, and the women) besides a place for the sick, are sometimes more than five feet high and sometimes less; and this height is divided toward the middle for the slaves lie in two rows, one above the other, on each side of the ship, close to each other like books upon a shelf. I have known them so close that the shelf would not easily contain one more.

The poor creatures, thus cramped, are likewise in irons for the most part which makes it difficult for them to turn or move or attempt to rise or to lie down without hurting themselves or each other.

Dr. Falconbridge:
Some wet and blowing weather. . . having occasioned the port-holes to be shut and the grating to be covered,. . . fever among the Negroes ensued. While they were in this situation, I frequently went down among them till at length their rooms became so extremely hot as to be only bearable for a very short time. . . . The climate was too warm to admit the wearing of any clothing but a shirt and that I had pulled off before I went down; notwithstanding which, by only continuing among them for about a quarter of an hour, I was so overcome with the heat, stench and foul air that I nearly fainted; and it was only with assistance that I could get on deck. The consequence was that I soon after fell sick of the same disorder from which I did not recover for several months.

Source: *Black Cargoes: A History of the Atlantic Slave Trade 1518–1865,* Daniel P. Mannix, 1962.

Viewing HISTORY **On Board a Slave Ship**

An English officer painted this rare eyewitness picture of a slave ship. Yet it gives only a limited picture of the brutal conditions endured by enslaved Africans. Slave ship captains often crammed people into their cargo holds, knowing that many would die during the Middle Passage. ★ **Why was the death rate so high during the Middle Passage?**

Analyzing Primary Sources

1. What is the main subject of Dr. Falconbridge's account?
   - **A.** bad weather
   - **B.** living conditions on the ship
   - **C.** his illness
   - **D.** the ship's captain

2. According to Captain Newton, what was one of his main jobs as the captain of a slave ship?
   - **F.** to provide a safe and comfortable passage
   - **G.** to load the slave ship to maximum capacity
   - **H.** to keep the crew and passengers healthy
   - **J.** to avoid bad weather

3. **Critical Thinking   Recognizing Points of View** Do you think that Dr. Falconbridge and Captain Newton have similar points of view about conditions aboard slave ships?

Historical Critique

Both of these reports, as well as the painting on page 531, are by officers who worked on slave ships. Why do you think there are fewer eyewitness accounts from enslaved Africans on the Middle Passage? What kind of information would an African witness have been able to give that Newton and Falconbridge could not?

★ 3–2 ★   ## The Mayflower Compact

Historical Document
★★★★★★

Introduction Before the *Mayflower* anchored off the coast of what is now Cape Cod, Massachusetts, the 41 male passengers on board the ship signed a binding agreement. The 1620 document established a basis for self-government of their new colony, Plymouth. This agreement, known as the Mayflower Compact, is often considered one of the key documents in American history. Since women had no political rights, the women aboard the *Mayflower* were not asked to sign the document.

Vocabulary Before you read the selection, find the meanings of these words in a dictionary: **sovereign, covenant.**

★ ★ ★ ★ ★ ★ ★ ★ ★

In the name of God Amen, We whose names are underwritten, the loyal subjects of the dread sovereign Lord King James by the grace of God, of Great Britain, France, and Ireland king, defender of the faith, etc.

 Pilgrims Go to Church

This painting shows Pilgrim families going to church. It was painted in the 1800s, many years after the Mayflower Compact. Faith in God and study of the Bible were central to Pilgrim life.
★ **What does the fact that the men are carrying weapons suggest about the lives of the Pilgrims?**

Having undertaken for the glory of God, and advancements of the Christian faith and honor of our King and country, a voyage to plant the first colony in the northern parts of Virginia, do by these presents solemnly and mutually in the presence of God, and one of another, covenant and combine ourselves together into a civil body politic; for our better ordering and preservation and furtherance of the ends afore said; and by virtue hereof to enact, constitute, and frame such just and equal laws, ordinances, acts, constitutions, and offices, from time to time, as shall be thought most meet and convenient for the general good of the colony: unto which we promise all due submission and obedience.

In witness whereof we have here under subscribed our names at Cape Cod the 11 of November, in the year the reign of our sovereign Lord King James of England, France, and Ireland, the eighteenth and of Scotland the fifty-fourth Anno Domini 1620.

Source: *The American Reader: Words That Moved a Nation,* edited by Diane Ravitch, 1990.

Analyzing Primary Sources

1. What was the purpose of the Mayflower Compact?
   A. to elect church members
   B. to write a new constitution
   C. to establish a governing body
   D. to honor the English king

2. Where was the document signed?
   F. England
   G. France
   H. Cape Cod
   J. Virginia

3. **Critical Thinking   Linking Past and Present** How are the ideas in the Mayflower Compact reflected in the form of government that exists in the United States today?

Historical Critique

Pilgrim men signed the Mayflower Compact while they were still on board ship. What can the document tell us about the government of the Plymouth colony after they landed? What can it not tell us?

★ Chapter 4 ★ *The 13 English Colonies*

★ 4–1 ★ *Attracting Settlers to the Carolinas*

Historical Document

Introduction In 1663, King Charles II of England gave eight loyal friends a huge tract of land in North America known as Carolina. These eight Lord Proprietors, as they were called, were eager to attract settlers who would make their land profitable. In 1666, the Lord Proprietors published a pamphlet called *A Brief Description of the Province of Carolina.* The excerpts that follow are taken from this pamphlet.

Vocabulary Before you read the selection, find the meanings of these words in a dictionary: **spacious, magnitude, fowls, thrive, exceedingly, swineherd, sturgeon, plaice, industrious, ingenious, partake, felicities, livelihood, abrogate, subsistence, dowry, civil.**

★ ★ ★ ★ ★ ★ ★ ★ ★

Carolina is a fair and spacious province on the continent of America. . . . The land is of diverse sorts as in all countries of the world. That which lies near the sea is sandy and barren, but bears many tall trees, which make good timber for several uses; and this sandy ground is by experienced men thought

Viewing HISTORY — Growing Indigo

Early on, indigo plants were introduced to South Carolina and became a successful crop. Indigo produced a blue dye that English manufacturers used in their textiles. This sketch shows a South Carolina indigo plantation in 1773. ★ **How did crops like indigo help colonies to prosper?**

to be one cause of the healthfulness of the place. But up the river about twenty or thirty mile[s], where they have made a town, called Charles Town, there is plenty of as rich ground as any in the world. . . . The woods are stored with deer and wild turkeys, of a great magnitude, weighing many times above 50 lb. a piece, and of a more pleasant taste than in England, being in their proper climate; other sorts of beasts in the woods that are good for food, and also fowls, whose names are not known to them.

This is what they found naturally upon the place; but they have brought with them most sorts of seeds and roots of the Barbados [in the West Indies] which thrive [in] the most temperate clime . . . and they have potatoes, and the other roots and herbs of Barbados, and New England, what they could afford. They have indigo, tobacco, very good, and cotton wool; lime trees, orange, lemon, and other fruit trees they brought, thrive exceedingly. They have two crops of Indian corn in one year, and great increase every crop. Apples, pears, and other English fruit grow there out of the planted kernels.

The marshes and meadows are very large, from 1,500 to 3,000 acres and upwards, and are excellent food for cattle, and will bear any grant being prepared . . . some cattle, both great and small, will live well all the winter, and keep their fat without fodder: hogs find so much mast and other food in the woods that they want no other care than a swineherd to keep them from running wild. The meadows are very proper for rice, rapeseed, linseed, etc., and may many of them be made to overflow at pleasure with a small charge.

Here are as brave rivers as any in the world, stored with great abundance of sturgeon, salmon, bass, plaice, trout, and Spanish mackerel, with many other most pleasant sorts of fish, both flat and round, for which the English tongue has no name. Also, in the little winter they have, abundance of wild geese, ducks, teals, widgeons, and many other pleasant fowl. And (as it is said before) the rivers are very deep and navigable above 100 miles up; also there are wholesome springs and rivulets.

Last of all, the air comes to be considered, which is not the least considerable to the well being of a plantation, for without a wholesome air all other considerations avail nothing. And this is it which makes this place so desirable, being seated in the glorious light of heaven brings many advantages, and His convenient distance secures them from the inconvenience of His scorching beams. . . .

If, therefore, any industrious and ingenious persons shall be willing to partake of the felicities of this country, let them embrace the first opportunity, that they may obtain the greater advantages. . . .

The chief of the privileges are as follows:

First, there is full and free liberty of conscience granted to all, so that no man is to be molested or called in question for matters of religious concern; but everyone to be obedient to the civil government, worshipping God after their own way.

Second, there is freedom from custom for all wine, silk, raisins, currants, oil, olives, and almonds that shall be raised in the province for seven years. . . .

Third, every freeman and freewoman that transport themselves and servants by the 25th of March next, being 1667, shall have for himself, wife, children, and menservants, for each 100 acres of land for him and his heirs forever, and for every womanservant and slave, 50 acres. . . .

Fourth, every manservant at the expiration of their time, is to have of the country 100 acres of land to him and his heirs forever, paying only 1/2D. per acre, per annum, and the women 50 acres of land on the same conditions; their masters also are to allow them two suits of apparel and tools such as he is best able to work with, according to the custom of the country.

Fifth, they are to have a governor and council appointed from among themselves to see the laws of the Assembly put in due execution; but the governor is to rule but three years, and then learn to obey; also he has no power to lay any tax or make or abrogate any law without the consent of the colony in their Assembly.

Sixth, they are to choose annually from among themselves a certain number of men, according to their divisions, which constitute the General Assembly with the governor and his council, and have the sole power of making laws and laying taxes for the common good when need shall require. . . .

Such as are here [in England] tormented with much care how to get worth to gain a livelihood, or that with their labor can hardly get a comfortable subsistence, shall do well to go to this place [Carolina], where any man whatever that is but willing to take moderate pains may be assured of a most comfortable subsistence, and be in a way to raise his fortunes far beyond what he could ever hope for in England. . . .

If any maid or single woman have a desire to go over, they will think themselves in the Golden Age, when men paid a dowry for their wives; for if they be but civil, and under fifty years of age, some honest man or other will purchase them for their wives.

Source: *Historical Collections of South Carolina,* edited by B. R. Carrol, 1836.

Analyzing Primary Sources

1. What idea does this section of the pamphlet emphasize?
   A. need for settlers
   B. healthy air
   C. abundant resources
   D. warm climate

2. What do the proprietors promise settlers?
   F. freedom of religion
   G. freedom of speech
   H. no taxes
   J. all of the above

3. **Critical Thinking Making Inferences**
   (a) For what purpose was this pamphlet issued? (b) Do you think people in England in the 1660s would have found the land described in the pamphlet appealing? Explain.

Historical Critique

In 1660s, Europeans knew nothing about South Carolina so they had to rely on pamphlets like these. Why do you think people might have believed what the pamphlet said? Do you think it gives an accurate account of South Carolina? What subjects does it not include? Why?

Introduction This excerpt from Benjamin Franklin's autobiography describes his early education and his apprenticeship to his brother James, a printer. Franklin also writes about the role printers played in bringing attention to colonial opposition to British rule.

Vocabulary Before you read the selection, find the meanings of these words in a dictionary: **tithe, censured, admonishing, satire, contrivance.**

★ ★ ★ ★ ★ ★ ★ ★ ★

I was put to the grammar-school at eight years of age, my father intending to devote me, as the tithe of his sons, to the service of the Church. My early readiness in learning to read (which must have been very early, as I do not remember when I could not read), and the opinion of all his friends, that I should certainly make a good scholar, encouraged him in this purpose of his. . . . But my father, in the mean time, from the view of the expense of a college education, which having so large a family he could not well afford . . . took me from the grammar-school, and sent me to a school for writing and arithmetic. . . . At ten years old I was taken home to assist my

father in his business, which was that of a tallow-chandler and soapboiler. . . . Accordingly, I was employed in cutting wick for the candles, filling the dipping mold and the molds for cast candles, attending the shop, going of errands etc. . . .

From a child I was fond of reading, and all the little money that came into my hands was ever laid out in books. . . .

This bookish inclination at length determined my father to make me a printer, though he had already one son (James) of that profession. In 1717 my brother James returned from England with a press and letters to set up his business in Boston. I liked it much better than that of my father, but still had a hankering for the sea. To prevent the apprehended effect of such an inclination, my father was impatient to have me bound to my brother. I stood out some time, but at last was persuaded, and signed the indenture when I was yet but twelve years old. I was to serve as an apprentice till I was twenty-one years of age, only I was to be allowed journeyman's wages during the last year. In a little time I made great proficiency in the business, and became a useful hand to my brother.

Viewing HISTORY **Ben Franklin, Printer**

In 1723, young Ben Franklin left Boston for Philadelphia. Through hard work, he turned The Pennsylvania Gazette *into a successful newspaper. The* Gazette *allowed Franklin to share his ideas with a large audience.* ★ **How might Franklin's early experiences have helped him make *The Pennsylvania Gazette* prosper?**

Though a brother, he considered himself as my master, and me as his apprentice, and accordingly, expected the same services from me as he would from another, while I thought he demeaned me too much in some he required of me, who from a brother expected more indulgence. Our disputes were often brought before our father, and I fancy I was either generally in the right, or else a better pleader, because the judgment was generally in my favor. But my brother was passionate, and had often beaten me, which I took extremely amiss; and, thinking my apprenticeship very tedious, I was continually wishing for some opportunity of shortening it, which at length offered in a manner unexpected.

One of the pieces in our newspaper on some political point, which I have now forgotten, gave offense to the Assembly, He [James] was taken up, censured, and imprisoned for a month, by the speaker's warrant, I suppose, because he would not discover [reveal] his author. I too was taken up and examined before the council; but, though I did not give them any satisfaction, they contented themselves with admonishing me, and dismissed me, considering me, perhaps, as an apprentice, who was bound to keep his master's secrets.

During my brother's confinement, which I resented a good deal, notwithstanding our private differences, I had the management of the paper; and I made bold to give our rulers some rubs in it, which my brother took very kindly, while others began to consider me in an unfavorable light, as a young genius that had a turn for libeling and satire. My brother's discharge was accompanied with an order of the House (a very odd one), that "James Franklin should no longer print the paper called the New England Courant."

There was a consultation held in our printing-house among his friends, what he should do in this case. Some proposed to evade the order by changing the name of the paper; but my brother, seeing inconveniences in that, it was finally concluded on as a better way, to let it be printed for the future under the name of BENJAMIN FRANKLIN; and to avoid the censure of the Assembly, that might fall on him as still printing it by his apprentice, the contrivance was that my old indenture should be returned to me, with full discharge on the back of it, to be shown on occasion, but to secure to him the benefit of my service, I was to sign new indentures for the remainder of the term, which were to be kept private. A very flimsy scheme it was; however, it was immediately executed, and the paper went on accordingly, under my name for several months.

Source: *Autobiography of Benjamin Franklin,* edited by John Bigelow, 1868.

Analyzing Primary Sources

1. Why did his father decide Benjamin Franklin should become a printer?
   A. He liked books.
   B. He did not do well in school.
   C. His brother was a printer.
   D. He had a large family.

2. Why was James Franklin censured?
   F. He published an offensive political statement.
   G. He refused to pay his taxes.
   H. He beat his brother.
   J. He permitted Benjamin Franklin to run his newspaper.

3. **Critical Thinking** **Recognizing Points of View** Based on this excerpt, how do you think Benjamin Franklin viewed the British?

Historical Critique

Benjamin Franklin wrote his autobiography when he was around 50 years old. How does an autobiography differ from a diary as a source of historical information?

Unit 2

A Nation Is Born

★ Chapter 5 ★ The Road to Revolution

★ 5–1 ★ Exploring the Ohio Valley

Eyewitness Account

Introduction After the French and Indian War, Britain sent George Croghan to explore the Illinois Territory, part of the region Britain had won from France. Croghan could negotiate with Indians in the area because he knew several Indian languages. The excerpts below are taken from Croghan's journal for 1765.

Vocabulary Before you read the selection, find the meanings of these words in a dictionary: **prospect, dispatched, hoisted, embroiled, breadth, subsistence, clemency.**

★ ★ ★ ★ ★ ★ ★ ★ ★

May 15, 1765. I set off from Fort Pitt with two batteaux [boats] and encamped at Chartier's Island, in the Ohio, three miles below Fort Pitt.

16th. Being joined by deputies of the Seneca, [Shawnee], and Delawares that were to accompany me, we set off at 7 o'clock in the morning.... About a mile below the mouth of the Beaver Creek we passed an old settlement of the Delawares, where the French, in 1756, built a town for that nation. On the north side of the river some of the stone chimneys are yet remaining....

17th. At 6 o'clock in the morning we embarked, and were delighted with the prospect of a fine open country on each side of the river as we passed down. We came to a place called the Two Creeks, about 15 miles from Yellow Creek, where we put to shore; here the Seneca have a village on a high bank, on the north side of the river; the chief of this village offered me his service to go with me to the Illinois, which I could not refuse for fear of giving him offense, although I had a sufficient number of deputies with me already....

20th. At 6 in the morning we embarked in our boats, and proceeded down to the mouth of the Hochocken or Bottle River.... From here I dispatched an Indian to the Plains of Scioto with a letter to the French traders from the Illinois residing there, amongst the [Shawnees], requiring them to come and join me at the mouth of Scioto, in order to proceed with me to their own country, and take the oaths of allegiance to His Britannic Majesty, as they were now become his subjects....

[June] 6th. We arrived at the mouth of the Ouabache [Wabash]... The mouth of this river is about 200 yards wide, and in its course runs through one of the finest countries in the world, the lands being exceedingly rich, and well watered....

9th. An hour before day we set out on our march; passed through thick woods, some highlands, and small savannas, badly watered. Traveled this day about 30 miles.

10th. We set out very early in the morning, and marched through a high country, extremely well timbered.... The remainder of this day we traveled through fine rich bottom, overgrown with reeds, which make the best pasture in the world.... Here is great plenty of wild game of all kinds....

Map of the Ohio River Valley

Fur traders, soldiers, and explorers like George Croghan supplied the information for maps like this one of the Ohio River valley. This early map also shows the southern shore of Lake Erie. ★ **Why did colonists and the British want accurate maps of the Ohio River valley?**

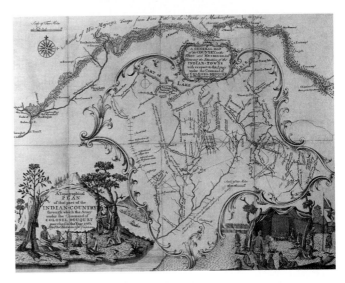

August 1. Within a mile of the Twightwee village, I was met by the chiefs of that nation, who received us very kindly. The most part of these Indians knew me, and conducted me to their village, where they immediately hoisted an English flag that I had formerly given them at Fort Pitt. The next day they held a council, after which they gave me up all the English prisoners they had, then made several speeches, in all which they expressed the great pleasure it gave them, to see the unhappy differences which embroiled the several nations in a war with their brethren, the English, were now so near a happy conclusion, and that peace was established in their country.

17th. In the morning we arrived at the fort, which is a large stockade enclosing about eighty houses; it stands close on the north side of the river, on a high bank, commands a very pleasant prospect for nine miles above and nine miles below the fort; the country is thick settled with French; their plantations are generally laid out about three or four acres in breadth on the river, and eighty acres in depth; the soil is good, producing plenty of grain. All the people here are generally poor wretches, and consist of three or four hundred French families, a lazy idle people, depending chiefly on the [Indians] for their subsistence; though the land, with little labor, produces plenty of grain, they scarcely raise as much as will supply their wants....

In the last Indian war the most part of the French were concerned in it (although the whole settlement had taken the oath of allegiance to His Britannic Majesty); they have, therefore, great reason to be thankful to the English clemency in not bringing them to deserved punishment.

Source: *A History of the Commonwealth of Kentucky,* Mann Butler, 1834.

Analyzing Primary Sources

1. Who accompanied Croghan?
   A. soldiers
   B. settlers
   C. Indians
   D. mapmakers
2. Croghan wants the French traders to
   F. guide him down the river.
   G. take an oath of loyalty to England.
   H. sell him furs.
   J. sign a peace treaty.

3. **Critical Thinking   Recognizing Points of View** Based on these excerpts, how did Croghan view the Indians he met on his travels?

Historical Critique

What is Croghan's attitude toward the French people he meets? How do you think recent events may have affected his attitude?

Introduction   In 1773, the Tea Act placed a new tax on tea sold in the colonies. The song "Revolutionary Tea," written by an anonymous colonist, reveals how many colonists felt about not only the Tea Act but about their relationship with far-away Britain.

Vocabulary   Before you read the selection, find the meanings of these words in a dictionary: **pence, quoth, conveyed, steeped.**

★ ★ ★ ★ ★ ★ ★ ★ ★

There was an old lady lived over the sea.
And she was an Island Queen;
Her daughter lived off in a new country,
With an ocean of water between.
The old lady's pockets were full of gold,
But never contented was she,
So she called on her daughter to pay her
    a tax
Of three pence a pound on her tea,
Of three pence a pound on her tea.

"Now mother, dear mother," the daughter
    replied,
"I shan't do the thing that you ax;
I'm willing to pay a fair price for the tea,
But never the three penny tax."
"You shall," quoth the mother, and red-
    dened with rage,
"For you're my own daughter, you see,
And sure 'tis quite proper the daughter
    should pay
Her mother a tax on her tea,
Her mother a tax on her tea."

And so the old lady her servant called up,
And packed off a budget of tea,
And eager for three pence a pound, she
    put in
Enough for a large family.
She ordered her servants to bring home
    the tax,
Declaring her child should obey,
Or old as she was, and almost woman
    grown,
She'd half whip her life away,
She'd half whip her life away.

The tea was conveyed to the daughter's
    door,
All down by the ocean's side;
And the bouncing girl poured out every
    pound
In the dark and boiling tide.
And then she called out to the Island
    Queen,
"Oh, mother, dear mother," quoth she,
"Your tea you may have when 'tis steeped
    enough,
But never a tax from me.
But never a tax from me."

Source: *Father Kemp's Old Folks Concert Music.*

Viewing **Colonial Tea Urn**
HISTORY

Wealthy colonists took pride in owning silver tea servers. This elegant urn was made in England by a famous silversmith in 1774. It was a wedding present for John P. Custis, son of Martha Washington by her first husband. ★ **Why might colonists want tea services made in England rather than ones made in the colonies?**

Analyzing Literature

1. What is the main point of "Revolutionary Tea"?
   A. The colonists will remain loyal to Britain.
   B. The British and the American colonists both love tea.
   C. The American colonists are like disobedient children.
   D. Colonists resent the tax on tea.

2. The "old lady" represents
   F. Massachusetts.
   G. colonial tea merchants.
   H. Britain.
   J. redcoats in Boston.

3. **Critical Thinking   Synthesizing Information (a)** What historical event does the last verse of the song describe? **(b)** From whose point of view does it present this event?

Historical Critique

Protest songs like "Revolutionary Tea" expressed the feelings of people at the time. What feeling does the song express? Why do you think colonists might have sung this song and not joined other protests?

★ Chapter 6 ★ *The American Revolution*

★ 6–1 ★   *Common Sense*

Introduction   In January 1776, patriot Thomas Paine published a pamphlet called *Common Sense.* In the following passage from that pamphlet, Paine presents several arguments for the 13 colonies to declare their independence from Britain. He also discusses the advantages of representative government.

Vocabulary   Before you read the selection, find the meanings of these words in a dictionary: **venture, duplicity, unalterable, concord, posterity, expedience.**

★ ★ ★ ★ ★ ★ ★ ★ ★

Another reason why the present time is preferable to all others, is, that the fewer our numbers are, the more land there is yet unoccupied, which instead of being lavished by the k___ on his worthless dependents, may be hereafter applied, not only to the discharge of the present debt, but to the constant support of government. No nation under heaven hath such an advantage as this.

The infant state of the colonies, as it is called, so far from being against, is an argument in favor of independence. We are sufficiently numerous, and were we more so, we might be less united. It is a matter worthy of observation, that the more a country is peopled, the smaller their armies are. In military numbers, the ancients far exceeded the moderns: and the reason is evident, for trade being the consequence of population, men become too much absorbed thereby to attend to anything else. Commerce diminishes the spirit, both of patriotism and military defense. And history sufficiently informs us, that the bravest achievements were always accomplished in the non-age of a nation. With the increase of commerce, England has lost its spirit. The city of London, notwithstanding its numbers, submits to continued insults with the patience of a coward. The more men have to lose, the less willing are they to venture. The rich are in general slaves to fear, and submit to courtly power with the trembling duplicity of a spaniel.

In this picture by John McRae, Patriots raise a liberty pole, symbol of freedom. Women, men, and children join to show their support for independence from Great Britain. ★ **Do you think Thomas Paine's writings encouraged scenes like this? Explain.**

Youth is the seed time of good habits, as well in nations as in individuals. It might be difficult, if not impossible, to form the continent into one government half a century hence. The vast variety of interests, occasioned by an increase in trade and population, would create confusion. Colony would be against colony. Each being able might scorn each other's assistance: and while the proud and foolish gloried in their little distinctions, the wise would lament that the union had not been formed before. Wherefore, the *present time* is the *true time* for establishing it. The intimacy which is contracted in infancy, and the friendship which is formed in misfortune, are, of all others, the most lasting and unalterable. Our present union is marked with both these characters: we are young, and we have been distressed; but our concord hath withstood our troubles, and fixes a memorable era for posterity to glory in.

The present time, likewise, is that peculiar time, which never happens to a nation but once, [that is] the time of forming itself into a government. Most nations have let slip this opportunity, and by that means have been compelled to receive laws from their conquerors, instead of making laws for themselves. First, they had a king, and then a form of government; whereas, the articles or charter for government should be formed first, and men delegated to execute them afterward: but from the errors of other nations, let us learn wisdom, and lay hold of the present opportunity—to begin government at the right end....

In a former page I likewise mentioned the necessity of a large and equal representation; and there is no political matter which more deserves our attention. A small number of electors, or a small number of representatives, are equally dangerous. But if the number of representatives be not only small, but unequal, the danger is increased....

Immediate necessity makes many things convenient, which if continued would grow into oppressions. Expedience and right are different things. When the calamities of America required a consultation, there was no method so ready, or at that time so proper, as to appoint persons from the several Houses of Assembly for that purpose and the wisdom with which they have proceeded hath preserved this continent from ruin. But as it is more than probable that we shall never be without a Congress, every well wisher to good order, must own, that the mode for choosing members of that body, deserves consideration. And I put it as a question to those who make a study of mankind, whether representation and election is not too great a power for one and the same body of men to possess?

When we are planning for posterity, we ought to remember that virtue is not hereditary.

Source: *Common Sense,* Thomas Paine, edited by Isaac Kramnick, 1982.

Analyzing Primary Sources

1. According to Paine, what is one reason to declare independence?
   A. The population of the country is small.
   B. Trade is flourishing.
   C. There is a well-trained military.
   D. Americans have diverse interests.

2. In Paine's view, what is the first step in forming a government?
   F. to write a constitution
   G. to pass laws
   H. to raise taxes
   J. to elect representatives

3. **Critical Thinking   Making Inferences**
   To support what particular cause did Thomas Paine write this document?

Historical Critique

Common Sense was read and discussed throughout the 13 colonies. In evaluating a historical document, why is it important to know how popular and influential the document was?

★ 6–2 ★   **Letters on Independence**

Introduction   John Adams and his wife, Abigail, corresponded through lengthy letters during John's many trips away from home. An avid letter writer, Abigail wrote to her family and friends about her life, including her observations of the political scene. She supported women's rights and opposed slavery. On March 31, 1776, Abigail Adams wrote to her husband while the Continental Congress discussed declaring independence. On April 14, John Adams responded to his wife's concerns.

Vocabulary   Before you read the selection, find the meanings of these words in a dictionary: **tyrants, foment, impunity, despotism, oligarchy, ochlocracy.**

★ ★ ★ ★ ★ ★ ★ ★ ★

Abigail to John
   .... I long to hear that you have declared an independency—and by the way in the new code of laws which I suppose it will be neces-

sary for you to make I desire you would remember the ladies, and be more generous and favorable to them than your ancestors. Do not put such unlimited power into the hands of the husbands. Remember all men would be tyrants if they could. If particular care and attention is not paid to the ladies we are determined to foment a rebellion, and will not hold ourselves bound by any laws in which we have no voice, or representation.

That your sex are naturally tyrannical is a truth so thoroughly established as to admit of no dispute, but such of you as wish to be happy willingly give up the harsh title of master for the more tender and endearing one of friend. Why then, not put it out of the power of the vicious and the lawless to use with cruelty and indignity with impunity? Men of sense of all ages abhor those customs which treat us only as the vassals of your sex. Regard us then as beings placed by providence under your protection and in imitation

In colonial times, most well-bred New England women learned to stitch samplers. Mary Richardson stitched this sampler in 1783, when she was 11 years old. ★ **Besides teaching embroidery, how did samplers help educate girls?**

of the supreme being make use of that power only for our happiness.

John to Abigail
.... As to your extraordinary code of laws, I cannot but laugh. We have been told that our struggle has loosened the bands of government everywhere. That children and apprentices were disobedient—that schools and colleges were grown turbulent.... But your letter was the first intimation that another tribe more numerous and powerful than all the rest were grown discontented. This is rather too coarse a compliment but you are so saucy, I won't blot it out.

Depend upon it, we know better than to repeal our masculine systems. Although they are in full force, you know they are little more than theory. We dare not exert our power in its full latitude. We are obliged to go fair, and softly, and in practice you know we are the subjects. We have only the name of masters, and rather than give up this, which would completely subject us to the despotism of the petticoat, I hope General Washington, and all our brave heroes would fight. I am sure every good politician would plot, as long as he would against despotism, empire, monarchy, aristocracy, oligarchy, or ochlocracy. A fine story indeed. I begin to think the ministry as deep as they are wicked.... At last they have stimulated the [ladies] to demand new privileges and threaten to rebel.

Source: *The American Reader: Words That Moved a Nation,* edited by Diane Ravitch, 1990.

Analyzing Primary Sources

1. In her letter, Abigail Adams asks her husband, John, to make sure that the new government
   A. declares independence.
   B. treats women fairly.
   C. ends slavery.
   D. puts power in the hands of husbands.

2. What does John Adams say about the relationship between men and women in society?
   F. Men and women are equal under the law.
   G. Men rule over women as tyrants.
   H. Men are usually ruled over by women.
   J. Men should protect women.

3. **Critical Thinking   Recognizing Points of View** How did John Adams reply to his wife's request? What does his response indicate about his thinking?

Historical Critique

Abigail and John Adams wrote hundreds of letters to each other. Would reading more of their letters help you to evaluate the ones printed above? Explain.

★ 7–1 ★ Delegates to the Constitutional Convention

Eyewitness Account

Introduction William Pierce of Georgia, one of the delegates to the Constitutional Convention in 1787, wrote character sketches of some of the other delegates. His sketches include information about the age, occupation, war record, and political experience of the men who wrote the United States Constitution.

Vocabulary Before you read the selection, find the meanings of these words in a dictionary: **integrity, perseverance, mercantile, cant, embellish.**

★ ★ ★ ★ ★ ★ ★ ★ ★

Viewing HISTORY **The Liberty Bell**

The Liberty Bell hung in Philadelphia long before the Revolution. Written on it are words from the Bible: "Proclaim liberty throughout the land. . . ." In the 1800s, the Liberty Bell became an honored symbol of the United States. Because of a crack in the bell, it was no longer rung. ★ **Why is Philadelphia a suitable place for the Liberty Bell?**

Mr. Gerry's character is marked for integrity and perseverance. He is a hesitating and laborious speaker: possesses a great degree of confidence and goes extensively into all subjects that he speaks on, without respect to elegance or flower of diction. He is connected and sometimes clear in his arguments, conceives well, and cherishes as his first virtue, a love for his country. Mr. Gerry is very much of a gentlemen in his principles and manners. He has been engaged in the mercantile line and is a man of property. He is about 37 years of age. . . .

Mr. Sherman exhibits the oddest shaped character I ever remember to have met with. He is awkward, [expressionless], and unaccountably strange in his manner. But in his train of thinking there is something regular, deep, and comprehensive; yet the oddity of his address, the vulgarisms that accompany his public speaking, and that strange New England cant which runs through his public as well as his private speaking make everything that is connected with him grotesque and laughable. And yet he deserves infinite praise,—no man has a better heart or a clearer head. If he cannot embellish he can furnish thoughts that are wise and useful. He is an able politician, and extremely artful in accomplishing any particular object. It is

remarked that he seldom fails. I am told that he sits on the bench in Connecticut, and is very correct in the discharge of his judicial functions. . . . He is about 60. . . .

Colonel Hamilton is deservedly celebrated for his talents. He is a practitioner of the law, and reputed to be a finished scholar. . . . Hamilton requires time to think. He inquires into every part of his subject with the searchings of philosophy, and when he comes forward he comes highly charged with interesting matter, there is no skimming over the surface of a subject with him, he must sink to the bottom to see what foundation it rests on. . . . He is about 33 years old, of small stature, and lean. . . .

Mr. Lansing is a practicing attorney at Albany, and mayor of that [city]. He has a hesitation in his speech, that will prevent his being an orator of any eminence. His legal knowledge I am told is not extensive, nor his education a good one. He is however a man of good sense, plain in his manners, and sincere in his friendships. He is about 32 years of age.

Mr. Patterson is one of those kind of men whose powers break in upon you, and create wonder and astonishment. He is a man of great modesty, with looks that bespeak talents of no great extent, but he is a classic, a lawyer, and an orator; and of a disposition so favorable to his advancement that everyone seemed ready to exalt him with their praises. He is very happy in the choice of time and manner of engaging in a debate, and never speaks but when he understands his subject well. This gentleman is about 34 years of age, of a very low stature....

Dr. Franklin is well known to be the greatest philosopher of the present age; all the operations of nature he seems to understand—the very heavens obey him, and the clouds yield up their lightning to be imprisoned in his rod. But what claim he has to the politician, posterity must determine.... He is 82 years old, and possesses an activity of mind equal to a youth of 25 years of age....

Robert Morris... [although] not learned, yet he is as great as those who are. I am told that when he speaks in the assembly of Pennsylvania, that he bears down all before him. What could have been his reason for not speaking in the convention I know not—but he never once spoke on any point. This gentleman is about 50 years old.

Source: *The Records of the Federal Convention of 1787,* edited by Max Farrand, 1911.

Analyzing Primary Sources

1. Pierce describes Dr. Benjamin Franklin as a
   A. great philosopher.
   B. man of great modesty.
   C. great politician.
   D. great speaker.

2. Which one of the following men is not a lawyer?
   F. Colonel Hamilton
   G. Mr. Gerry
   H. Mr. Patterson
   J. Mr. Lansing

3. **Critical Thinking   Recognizing Points of View** Based on this excerpt, how did William Pierce view these delegates to the Constitutional Convention?

Historical Critique

What information might help you decide if William Pierce's opinions of his fellow delegates are reliable?

★ 7–2 ★   The Federalist Papers

Introduction In 1787, three early American leaders—Alexander Hamilton, James Madison, and John Jay—published a series of essays titled *The Federalist.* The purpose of these essays was to persuade people in the separate states to support the new federal Constitution. Today, the collected essays are known as *The Federalist Papers.* The first passage below is from The *Federalist, Number 1,* written by Hamilton. It introduces the series. The second excerpt is from *The Federalist, Number 10,* written by Madison.

In it, Madison discusses what he sees as the many advantages of the proposed system of government.

Vocabulary Before you read the selection, find the meanings of these words in a dictionary: **unequivocal, inefficiency, inducements, philanthropy, solicitude, formidable, diminution, emolument, aggrandize, faction, candid.**

★ ★ ★ ★ ★ ★ ★ ★ ★

iewing HISTORY — Celebrating Ratification

When the Constitution was ratified, celebrations and parades were common throughout the nation. This parade in New York City featured a float representing the "ship of state." ★ **Why do you think the name *Hamilton* is included on the float?**

Number 1 (Hamilton)

After an unequivocal experience of the inefficiency of the subsisting federal government, you are called upon to deliberate on a new Constitution for the United States of America. The subject speaks its own importance; comprehending in its consequences nothing less than the existence of the UNION, the safety and welfare of the parts of which it is composed, the fate of an empire in many respects the most interesting in the world. It has been frequently remarked that it seems to have been reserved to the people of this country, by their conduct and example, to decide the important question, whether societies of men are really capable or not of establishing good government from reflection and choice, or whether they are forever destined to depend for their political constitutions on accident and force. If there be any truth in the remark, the crisis at which we are arrived may with propriety be regarded as the era in which that decision is to be made; and a wrong election of the part we shall act may, in this view, deserve to be considered as the general misfortune of mankind.

This idea will add the inducements of philanthropy to those of patriotism, to heighten the solicitude which all considerate and good men must feel for the event. Happy will it be if our choice should be directed by a judicious estimate of our true interests, unperplexed and unbiased by considerations not connected with the public good. But this is a thing more ardently to be wished than seriously to be expected. The plan offered to our deliberations affects too many particular interests, innovates upon too many local institutions, not to involve in its discussion a variety of objects foreign to its merits, and of views, passions, and prejudices little favorable to the discovery of truth.

Among the most formidable of the obstacles which the new Constitution will have to encounter may readily be distinguished the obvious interest of a certain class of men in every state to resist all changes which may hazard a diminution of the power, emolument, and consequence of the offices they hold under the state establishments; and the perverted ambitions of another class of men, who will either hope to aggrandize themselves by the confusions of their country, or will flatter themselves with fairer prospects of elevation from the subdivision of the empire into several partial confederacies than from its union under one government.

Number 10 (Madison)

Among the numerous advantages promised by a well constructed union, none deserves to be more accurately developed than its tendency to break and control the violence of faction.... The instability, injustice, and confusion introduced into the public councils have, in truth, been the mortal diseases under which popular governments have everywhere perished.... The valuable improvements made by the American Constitution on the popular models, both ancient and modern, cannot certainly be too much admired; but it would be an unwarranted partiality to contend that they have as effectually obviated the danger on this side, as was wished and expected. Complaints are everywhere heard from our most considerate and virtuous citizens, equally the friends of public and private faith and of public and personal liberty, that our governments are too unstable, that the public good is disregarded in the conflicts of rival parties, and that measures are too often decided, not according to the rules of justice and the rights of the minor party, but by the superior force of an interested and overbearing majority.... It will be found, indeed, on a candid review of our situation, that some of the distresses under which we labor have been erroneously charged on the operation of our governments; but it will be found, at the same time, that other causes will not alone account for many of our heaviest misfortunes. . . . These must be chiefly, if not wholly, effects of the unsteadiness and injustice with which a factious spirit has tainted our public administrations.

Source: *Words That Made American History,* Volume 1, edited by Richard N. Current, 1972.

Analyzing Primary Sources

1. What is the main subject of *The Federalist*?
   A. the American Revolution
   B. the Constitution
   C. the Declaration of Independence
   D. the Articles of Confederation

2. What does Madison say is the main problem in forming a new government?
   F. conflicts between different people
   G. holding elections
   H. passing new laws
   J. choosing a good President

3. **Critical Thinking   Comparing** How does Madison's view of government compare with Hamilton's?

Historical Critique

People often try to win support by attacking their opponents. Give one example of how Hamilton attacks the Antifederalists.

★ Chapter 8 ★ The Constitution at Work

★ 8–1 ★ *The Magna Carta*

Historical Document

Introduction   On June 15, 1215, King John of England made peace with rebellious barons by agreeing to sign the Magna Carta, or Great Charter. The Magna Carta ensured the barons' rights and limited the king's power. The historic document established the principle that even the king has to obey the law of the land. The Magna Carta became the basis for democratic government in England. Later, in 1787, American leaders used many of the principles found in the Magna Carta when they wrote the Constitution of the United States.

Vocabulary Before you read the selection, find the meanings of these words in a dictionary: **inviolate, compelled, bailiffs, assessment, abbots, counsel, constable, credible, dispossessed, peers.**

★ ★ ★ ★ ★ ★ ★ ★ ★

John, by the grace of God, king of England, lord of Ireland, duke of Normandy and Aquitaine, count of Anjou to the archbishops, bishops, abbots, earls, barons, justiciars, foresters, sheriffs, reeves, servants, and all his bailiffs and his faithful people greeting. . . .

1. In the first place we have granted to God and by this our present charter confirmed for us and our heirs forever that the English church shall be free, and shall hold its rights entire, and her liberties inviolate. . . . We have granted moreover to all free men of our kingdom for us and our heirs forever all the liberties written below, to be held by them and their heirs from us and our heirs forever. . . .

8. No widow shall be compelled to marry, so long as she prefers to live without a husband; provided always that she gives security not to marry without our consent, if she holds of us,* or without the consent of the lord of whom she holds, if she holds of another. . . .

14. And for holding a common council of the kingdom concerning the assessment of an aid [tax] . . . we shall cause to be summoned the archbishops, bishops, abbots, earls, and greater barons . . . we shall cause to be summoned by our sheriffs and bailiffs all others who hold of us in chief, for a fixed date . . . and at a fixed place; and in all letters of such summons we will specify the reason of the summons. And when the summons has thus been made, the business shall proceed on the day appointed, according to the counsel of such as are present, although not all who were summoned have come. . . .

30. No sheriff or bailiff of ours, or other person, shall take the horses or carts of any freeman for transport duty, against the will of the said freeman.

31. Neither we nor our bailiffs shall take, for our castles or for any other work of ours, wood which is not ours, against the will of the owner of that wood. . . .

38. No bailiff for the future shall, upon his own unsupported complaint, put anyone to his "law," without credible witness brought for this purpose.

---

*To "hold of" meant to live on land granted by the king or by another lord.

 The British Parliament Meets

This print shows the House of Commons meeting in London in the 1700s. The British parliamentary tradition was a major influence on the government of the United States. ★ **What branch of the American government is similar to Parliament?**

39. No free man shall be taken, or imprisoned, or dispossessed, or outlawed, or banished, or in any way destroyed, except by the legal judgment of his peers or by the law of the land.

40. To no one will we sell, to no one will we deny, or delay, right or justice.

Source: *Readings in European History,* Volume 1, edited by James Harvey Robinson, 1904.

Analyzing Primary Sources

1. What is the purpose of the Magna Carta?
   A. to give more rights to the king
   B. to write a new constitution
   C. to ensure the rights of nobles
   D. to give more land for the people

2. What part of the United States legal system is based on article 39?
   F. freedom of religion
   G. trial by jury
   H. election of representatives
   J. freedom of speech

3. **Critical Thinking   Drawing Conclusions** Why do you think the Magna Carta is considered one of the key documents of American democracy?

Historical Critique

The Magna Carta was originally written in Latin and has been translated into English. Why is it important to know whether a document has been translated?

★ 8–2 ★   *The Volunteer Spirit: Three Views*

Eyewitness Account

Introduction   The Peace Corps program, started in 1961 by President John Kennedy, gives young people the opportunity to live in another country and teach skills to others. The first two passages below are from Peace Corps volunteers (PCVs) in the Philippines and in Paraguay. In the third account, a fish farmer in Thailand tells how Peace Corps volunteers helped him.

Vocabulary   Before you read the selection, find the meanings of these words in a dictionary: **illiteracy, materialistic, atypical.**

★ ★ ★ ★ ★ ★ ★ ★ ★

Dennis Drake:

My first introduction to the [Peace] Corps was via a television advertisement that ran under the slogan, "The toughest job you'll ever love." Perhaps it was partly the slogan that got me thinking about joining or just the chance to change my life and help people at the same time. Really a simplistic view but maybe common thinking for more than just a few volunteers. Just imagine a person thinking he can actually do something about world hunger, poverty, illiteracy, or disease. Those are not "just" problems, but problems the size of mountains, yet the average Peace Corps volunteer believes he can do his part by chipping away at those mountains . . . one person at a time.

Kathleen Maria Sloop:

At the time I received my assignment from Washington, I had just been promoted to a great position as a market analyst in the bank at which I was working. I was a recent college graduate, so it was hard to give up all the things I had recently acquired, like a car, a good job, a nice house that I was sharing with two roommates whom I loved. But, I also knew that I'd learn more as a PCV, and I'd be "richer" as a person, if I lived and ate and shared with people who needed my help and friendship. I saw I was easily slipping into the easy, yet sometimes empty, materialistic life we Americans lead. I wanted to do something that would remind me for the rest of my life that Americans' lifestyles are atypical, not the norm in the world. It was hard to give up the convenience and comfort of the U.S., and I won't say there haven't been times when I wished I could blink and be home again, but I've also never regretted making the decision I did to serve.

Mr. Prakong:

Volunteers have helped me a lot in two different ways: first, with their labor, helping me to run the farm—just proving that they are willing to "get their feet wet" alongside me. They dress in jeans, they put on "farmer pants," sometimes they get diseases or infections, but that's the way they work. The other way they help is that volunteers know something about how to raise fish, the different species, what [food] they need. I never knew anything like that before volunteers came. They taught me induced fish spawning techniques, they helped me build signs on the road to market my fish. . . . If I had to rely on government administrations, I would be starving by now. They work from the top down, they are eager to show off their technical expertise, but they don't know the faces of the people they want to instruct. Peace Corps volunteers work from the bottom up. They have the theory, but they are not afraid to get their feet wet, to work one-on-one with the farmers.

Working this way with Volunteers, a very close relationship develops. I am the "older

Viewing HISTORY **A Peace Corps Volunteer in Costa Rica**

This Peace Corps worker is helping students in a school in the Central American nation of Costa Rica. Volunteers do many different kinds of jobs, both in the United States and overseas. ★ **Why do you think many Americans volunteer their time and energy to help other people?**

brother," the Volunteer is the "younger brother or sister." We suffer the same problems together, we sit together, we eat together—sometimes don't eat together if there's no food—joke together. We are family. I cried when the last Volunteer left. I will cry when Ron Rice (my Volunteer coworker) leaves.

Source: *Who Cares? Millions Do: A Book About Altruism,* Milton Meltzer, 1994.

Analyzing Primary Sources

1. Where do most Peace Corps volunteers work?
   A. in Washington, D.C.
   B. on fish farms
   C. in foreign countries
   D. in Thailand

2. According to Mr. Prakong, what did Peace Corps volunteers teach him?
   F. how to read
   G. fish farming methods
   H. how to stop infections
   J. television advertising

3. **Critical Thinking** **Comparing** Based on this excerpt, what was Mr. Prakong's view of the Peace Corps volunteers?

Historical Critique

Author Milton Meltzer collected these three accounts for a book titled *Who Cares? Millions Do: A Book About Altruism.* (Altruism is unselfish concern for others.) Do you think Meltzer wanted to present a positive or negative view of the Peace Corps? How might this have influenced what he included in his book?

Unit 3 The Nation Takes Shape

★ 9–1 ★ **A Description of George Washington**

Eyewitness Account

Introduction Thomas Jefferson, author of the Declaration of Independence, knew all the chief leaders of the Revolution and the new republic. He himself served as third President of the United States. He also wrote on many subjects ranging from philosophy, religion, and science to education and farming. As he grew older, he was often asked about leaders of the Revolutionary era. This excerpt is from a letter Jefferson wrote to Dr. Walter Jones, who had asked about George Washington.

Vocabulary Before you read the selection, find the meanings of these words in a dictionary: **delineate, acute, judiciously, prudence, colloquial, mediocrity, copiousness, fluency, indifferent, constellation, worthies.**

★ ★ ★ ★ ★ ★ ★ ★ ★

I think I knew General Washington intimately and thoroughly; and were I called on to delineate his character, it should be in terms like these.

His mind was great and powerful, without being of the very first order; his penetration [keenness of mind] strong, though not so acute as that of a Newton, Bacon, or Locke; and as far as he saw, no judgment was ever sounder. It was slow in operation, being little aided by invention or imagination, but sure in conclusion. Hence the common remark of his officers, of the advantage he derived [gained] from councils of war, where hearing all suggestions, he selected whatever was best; and certainly no General ever planned

Viewing HISTORY Honoring Washington

An admirer said that George Washington was "first in war, first in peace, first in the hearts of his countrymen." This banner honors the first President. ★ **What symbols of the United States can you identify on this banner?**

his battles more judiciously. But if deranged [upset] during the course of the action, if any member of his plan was dislocated by sudden circumstances, he was slow in readjustment.

The consequence was, that he often failed in the field, and rarely against an enemy in station, as in Boston and York.

He was incapable of fear, meeting personal dangers with the calmest unconcern. Perhaps the strongest feature in his character was prudence, never acting until every circumstance, every consideration, was maturely weighed; refraining if he saw a doubt, but, when once decided, going through with his purpose, whatever obstacles opposed....

His heart was not warm in its affections; but he exactly calculated every man's value, and gave him a solid esteem proportioned to it. His person, you know, was fine, his stature exactly what one would wish, his deportment [bearing] easy, erect and noble; the best horseman of his age, and the most graceful figure that could be seen on horseback. Although in the circle of his friends, where he might be unreserved with safety, he took a free share in conversation, his colloquial talents were not above mediocrity, possessing neither copiousness of ideas, nor fluency of words. In public, when called on for a sudden opinion, he was unready, short and embarrassed. Yet he wrote readily, rather diffusely [wordily], in an easy and correct style....

On the whole, his character was, in its mass, perfect, in nothing bad, in a few points indifferent; and it may truly be said, that never did nature and fortune combine more perfectly to make a man great, and to place him in the same constellation with whatever worthies have merited from man an everlasting remembrance.

Source: *The Complete Jefferson,* edited by Saul K. Padover, 1943.

Analyzing Primary Sources

1. What was Jefferson mainly describing in this passage?
  A. General Washington's greatest victories
  B. the first President's political ideas
  C. George Washington's character
  D. his long friendship with George Washington

2. In Jefferson's view, what was one of Washington's greatest strengths?
  F. his speaking ability
  G. his imagination
  H. his careful judgment
  J. his warmth

3. Critical Thinking   Recognizing Points of View Based on this excerpt, does Jefferson think Washington's strengths outweigh his weaknesses? Explain your answer.

Historical Critique

Would you consider Thomas Jefferson to be a reliable source of information about George Washington? Why or why not?

★ 9–2 ★   *Farewell Address*

Introduction   In 1796, after serving two terms as President, George Washington wrote his famous Farewell Address. In it, he announced that he would not seek a third term. As he retired from public service, the outgoing President gave his views on the best policies for the young republic to follow. As the nation's first President, he knew firsthand the great issues of the day. He was especially concerned about the rise of political parties and the danger of the nation becoming involved in European wars. Washington's advice about foreign policy influenced future Presidents for more than a century. The following excerpt is from Washington's Farewell Address.

Vocabulary   Before you read the selection, find the meanings of these words in a dictionary: **apprise, baneful, enfeeble, agitate, animosity, foment, facilitate access, enjoin, magnanimous, benevolence, provocation, maxim.**

★ ★ ★ ★ ★ ★ ★ ★ ★

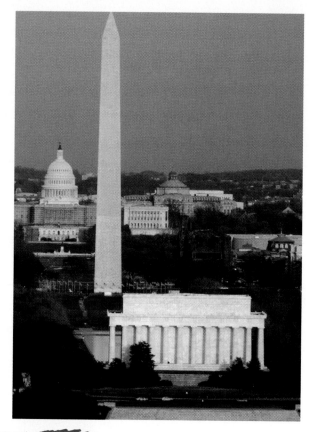

Viewing History

The Nation's Capital

When George Washington left office in 1797, the new nation's new capital city was still in the planning stages. As a result, Washington was the only President never to live in Washington, D.C. This photograph shows Washington today. The tall white tower is the Washington Monument. ★ **How was the location for the nation's capital chosen?**

FRIENDS AND FELLOW-CITIZENS:

The period for a new election of a citizen, to administer the executive government of the United States, being not far distant . . . , it appears to me proper, . . . that I should now apprise you of the resolution I have formed to decline being considered among the number of those out of whom a choice is to be made. . . .

I have already intimated [suggested] to you the danger of parties in the State, with particular reference to the founding of them on geographical discriminations [bases]. Let me now take a more comprehensive view, and warn you in the most solemn manner against the baneful effects of the spirit of party, generally. . . .

It serves always to distract the public councils and enfeeble the public administra-tion. It agitates the community with ill-founded jealousies and false alarms, kindles the animosity of one part against another, fo-ments occasionally riot and insurrection. It opens the door to foreign influence and cor-ruption, which find a facilitated access to the government itself through the channels of party passions. Thus the policy and the will of one country, are subjected to the policy and will of another. . . .

Observe good faith and justice toward all nations. Cultivate peace and harmony with all. Religion and morality enjoin this conduct and can it be that good policy does not equally enjoin it? It will be worthy of a free, enlight-ened, and at no distant period, a great nation, to give to mankind the magnanimous and too novel example of a people always guided by an exalted justice and benevolence. . . .

The great rule of conduct for us in regard to foreign nations is, in extending our com-mercial relations to have with them as little political connection as possible. So far as we have already formed engagements let them be fulfilled, with perfect good faith. Here let us stop.

Europe has a set of primary interests which to us have none, or a very remote rela-tion. Hence she must be engaged in frequent controversies, the causes of which are essen-tially foreign to our concerns. . . .

Our detached and distant situation in-vites and enables us to pursue a different course. If we remain one people, under an ef-ficient government, the period is not far off when we may defy material injury from ex-ternal [outside] annoyance; when we may take such an attitude as will cause the neu-trality we may at any time resolve upon to be scrupulously [carefully] respected; when belligerent [warring] nations, under the impossibility of making acquisitions upon us, will not lightly hazard [risk] the giving us provocation; when we may choose peace or war, as our interest, guided by justice, shall counsel. . . .

It is our true policy to steer clear of per-manent alliances with any portion of the for-eign world, so far, I mean as we are now at liberty to do it; for let me not be understood as capable of patronizing [supporting] infidelity [unfaithfulness] to existing engagements. I hold the maxim no less applicable to public than to private affairs that honesty is always the best policy. I repeat, therefore, let those engagements be observed in their genuine sense. But in my opinion it is unnecessary and would be unwise to extend them.

Taking care always to keep ourselves by suitable establishments on a respectable defensive posture, we may safely trust to temporary alliances for extraordinary emergencies.

Source: *A Documentary History of the United States,* edited by Richard D. Heffner, 1952.

Analyzing Primary Sources

1. What was Washington's view of political parties?
   A. They cost too much money.
   B. They caused dangerous divisions within the nation.
   C. They resulted in the rise of monarchs.
   D. They weakened the system of checks and balances.

2. What advice about foreign policy did Washington give?
   F. Seek trade but avoid other links with Europe.
   G. Have no contact with European countries.
   H. Cancel all treaties with European countries.
   J. Build up a strong army and navy.

3. **Critical Thinking   Understanding Cause and Effect** How does Washington think the United States should behave toward other nations? Why does he give that advice?

Historical Critique

Washington himself belonged to no political party. Do you think that fact increases or decreases the effectiveness of what he has to say about parties?

★ Chapter 10 ★ The Age of Jefferson

★ 10–1 ★   Traveling With Lewis and Clark

Eyewitness Account ★ ★ ★ ★ ★ ★

Introduction   A Shoshone woman named Sacajawea, her husband, and her baby son Pomp accompanied Lewis and Clark on their expedition across the Louisiana Territory. As a child Sacajawea had been kidnapped from her village by the Minnetarees, a rival Native American group. She was adopted by a Minnetaree family and lived in their village. Sacajawea met Lewis and Clark when they camped at the Minnetaree village. Years later, Sacajawea told her life story to James Willard Schultz. This passage is from Schultz's book *Bird Woman.* In this passage, Sacajawea refers to Lewis and Clark as Long Knife and Red Hair.

Vocabulary   Before you read the selection, find the meaning of this word in a dictionary: **abandon.**

★ ★ ★ ★ ★ ★ ★ ★ ★

Upon my man's return to the fort the boats were all loaded. We had two large ones and six small ones, and we abandoned the fort and headed up river. At the same time that we started, Long Knife and Red Hair sent their very large boat down the river in charge of some of their men. It was loaded with many skins, bones, and other

Viewing HISTORY Wildlife of the American West

Thomas Jefferson asked Lewis and Clark to explore lands west of the Mississippi. The President also asked them to send back information on the animal life they found. Clark sketched this bird and salmon in his journal. ★ **If you were sending an expedition into an unfamiliar land, what kind of information would you ask for?**

things, presents for the great chief of the whites. Counting in my son, we were thirty-three people in our eight boats. I was given a place in one of the two large ones.

As we went on and on up the river, sometimes making a long distance between the rising and the setting of the sun, I was, at times, I believe, happier than I had ever been in my life, for each day's travel brought me so much nearer my people whom I so much longed to see. Then at other times, whenever I thought of what was before us, I would become very unhappy. I would say to myself that we could not possibly survive the dangers we should be sure to encounter along the way. I may as well say it: my good, kind white chiefs were not cautious; they were too brave, too sure of themselves. From the very start they and their men would foolishly risk their lives by attacking all the mankilling

bears that came in sight of us. At night they would build great fires and would be sure to attract to us any wandering war party that might be in the country. After we passed the mouth of the Yellowstone and entered the country of the Blackfeet, I begged my chiefs to be more cautious. I asked them to stop always a short time before dark and build little cooking-fires, and then, after our meal, to put out the fires, and then go on until dark and make camp in the darkness. But they only laughed at me and answered: "We have good guns and know how to use them."

I often said to myself: "Strange are these white men! Strange their ways! They have a certain thing to do, to make a trail to the west to the Everywhere-Salt-Water. Why, then, are we not on horseback and traveling fast and far each day? Here we are in boats, heavily loaded with all kinds of useless things, and when the wind is bad or the water swift, we make but little distance between sun and sun! We could have all got all the horses that we needed from the Earth House tribes, and had we done that, we should long since have arrived at the mountains. Yes, right now I should probably be talking with my own people!"

And those medicine packages of theirs, packages big and little piled all around me in the boat in which I rode, how my chiefs valued them! One day a sudden hard wind struck our sail and the boat began to tip and fill with water. More and more it filled, and the men in it and those on the shore went almost crazy with fear. But I was not afraid. Why should I be when I knew that I could cast off my robe and swim ashore with my little son? More and more water poured into the boat and the medicine packages began to float out of it. I seized them one by one as they were going, and kept seizing them and holding them, and when, at last, we reached the shore, my good white chiefs acted as though I had done a wonderful thing in saving their packages; it seemed as though they could not thank me enough for what I had done. Thinking about it, after it was all over, and when the things had been spread out to dry, I said to myself: "Although I cannot understand them, these little instruments of shining steel and these writings on thin white paper must be powerful medicine. Hereafter, whenever we run into danger, I shall, after my son, have my first thought for their safety, and so please my kind white chiefs."

After leaving the mouth of Little River, or, as my white chiefs named it, Milk River, we went up through a part of the Big River Valley that I had not seen. . . . When we arrived at the mouth of the stream my white chiefs named the Musselshell, some of the men went up it during the afternoon, and, returning, told of a stream coming into it from the plain on the right. My chiefs then told me that it should have my name, as they called it, Sah-ka-já-we-ah.

I asked my man to tell them that I wished they would give it my right name, Bo-í-naiv, Grass Woman.

Source: *Bird Woman*, James Willard Schultz, 1918.

Analyzing Primary Sources

1. Whom did Sacajawea help?
   A. Lewis and Clark
   B. the Blackfeet
   C. the Minnetaree
   D. the Mandan

2. In this excerpt, what transportation did the expedition use?
   F. mules
   G. wagons
   H. boats
   J. horses

3. **Critical Thinking Recognizing Points of View** Why do you think that Sacajawea found the ways of Lewis and Clark strange?

Historical Critique

Sacajawea told her life story to a writer, who did not publish it until 1918. Identify two factors that might affect the reliability of the published account.

★ 10–2 ★ *The Pioneers*

Introduction James Fenimore Cooper wrote action-filled adventure stories that were very popular. The central character in five of his novels is a wilderness hunter named Natty Bumppo, or Leather-stocking, who lives between the Indian and white worlds. Bumppo has learned the forest skills of the Indians. This selection is from *The Pioneers.* In this scene, Leather-stocking realizes that the wilderness is fast falling to settlers.

Vocabulary Before you read the selection, find the meanings of these words in a dictionary: **species, sapling, gaunt, vain, prodigious, profusion, uneasy, sentiments, indignant.**

★ ★ ★ ★ ★ ★ ★ ★ ★

If the heavens were alive with pigeons, the whole village seemed equally in motion, with men, women, and children. Every species of fire-arms, from the French duck-ing-gun, with a barrel near six feet in length, to the common horseman's pistol, was to be seen in the hands of the men and boys; while bows and arrows, some made of the simple stick of a walnut sapling, and others in a rude [simple] imitation of the ancient cross-bows, were carried by many of the latter. . . .

Amongst the sportsmen was the tall, gaunt form of Leather-stocking, walking over the field, with his rifle hanging on his arm, his dogs at his heels; the latter now scenting the dead or wounded birds, that were beginning to tumble from the flocks, and then crouching under the legs of their master, as if they participated in his feelings, at this wasteful and unsportsmanlike execution.

The reports of the fire-arms became rapid, whole volleys rising from the plain, as flocks of more than ordinary numbers darted over the opening, shadowing the field, like a cloud; and then the light smoke of a single piece would issue from among the leafless bushes on the mountain, as death was hurled on the retreat of the affrighted birds, who were rising from a volley, in a vain effort to escape. Arrows, and missiles of every kind, were in the midst of the flocks; and so numerous were the birds, and so low did they take their flight, that even long poles, in the hands of those on the sides of the mountain, were used to strike them to the earth....

So prodigious was the number of birds, that the scattering fire of the guns, with the hurling of missiles, and the cries of the boys, had no other effect than to break off small flocks from the immense masses that continued to dart along the valley, as if the whole of the feathered tribe were pouring through one pass. None pretended to collect the game, which lay scattered over the fields in such profusion, as to cover the very ground with the fluttering victims.

Leather-stocking was a silent, but uneasy spectator of all these proceedings [events], but was able to keep his sentiments to himself until he saw the introduction of the swivel [cannon] into the sports.

"This comes of settling a country!" he said—"here have I known the pigeons to fly for forty long years, and, till you made your clearings, there was nobody to skear [scare] or to hurt them. I loved to see them come into the woods, for they were company to a body; hurting nothing; being, as it was, as harmless as a garter-snake. But now it gives me sore thoughts when I hear the frighty things whizzing through the air, for I know it's only a motion to bring out all the brats in the village. Well! the Lord won't see the waste of his creaters for nothing, and right will be done to the pigeons, as well as others, by-and-by...."

Among the sportsmen was Billy Kirby, who, armed with an old musket, was loading, and, without even looking into the air, was firing, and shouting as his victims fell even on his own person. He heard the speech of Natty, and took upon himself to reply—

"What! old Leather-stocking," he cried, "grumbling at the loss of a few pigeons! If you had to sow your wheat twice, and three times, as I have done, you wouldn't be so massy-fully [mercifully] feeling'd to'wards the divils.—Hurrah, boys! scatter the feathers. This is better than shooting at a turkey's head and neck, old fellow."

"It's better for you, maybe, Billy Kirby," replied the indignant old hunter, "and all them that don't know how to put a ball down a rifle-barrel, or how to bring it up ag'in with a true aim; but it's wicked to be shooting into flocks in this wastey manner; and none do it, who know how to knock over a single bird. If a body has a craving for pigeon's flesh, why! it's made the same as all other creater's, for man's eating, but not to kill twenty and eat one."

Source: *The Pioneers*, James Fenimore Cooper, 1823.

 Settling the Wilderness

As they moved westward, settlers had to hack homes out of thick forests. This engraving shows a group of pioneers in the Ohio Valley. Even the smallest child had to work in order for the family to survive. ★ **Based on this picture, identify two reasons settlers chopped down many trees in the frontier forests.**

Analyzing Literature

1. Why did Natty Bumppo object to the killing of the pigeons?
   - A. He disliked the sound of gunfire.
   - B. He felt that eating pigeons was sinful.
   - C. He thought the killing was wasteful.
   - D. He was afraid people would get shot.

2. Why did the settlers shoot the pigeons?
   - F. to sell the feathers
   - G. to protect their wheat fields
   - H. to show off their hunting skills
   - J. to frighten the Indians

3. **Critical Thinking Linking Past and Present** How is Natty Bumppo's conflict with the settlers similar to that between environmentalists and developers today?

Historical Critique

Fiction writers often express their views through the mouths of their characters. Which character do you think expresses Cooper's view: Leather-stocking or Kirby? Give reasons for your answer.

★ Chapter 11 ★ Industry and Growth

★ 11–1 ★ Working in the Lowell Mills

Eyewitness Account ★★★★★

Introduction In 1898, Harriet Hanson Robinson published a book, *Loom and Spindle,* which tells of her experiences working in the Lowell, Massachusetts, textile mills in the 1830s. In the following passage, Robinson describes life in Lowell, and tells about the first strike there.

Vocabulary Before you read the selection, find the meaning of these words in a dictionary: **modes, incendiary, consternation, ardent, irresolute, accede.**

★ ★ ★ ★ ★ ★ ★ ★ ★

In 1831 Lowell was little more than a factory village. Several corporations were started, and the cotton-mills belonging to them were building. Help was in great demand; and stories were told all over the country of the new factory town, and the high wages that were offered to all classes of work-people—stories that reached the ears of mechanics' and farmers' sons, and gave new life to lonely and dependent women in distant towns and farmhouses. Into this Yankee El Dorado,* these needy people began to

*El Dorado refers to a place rich in opportunity to become wealthy.

pour by the various modes of travel known to those slow old days. The stagecoach and the canal boat came everyday, always filled with new recruits for this army of useful people. The mechanic and machinist came, each with his home-made chest of tools, and oftentimes his wife and little ones. The widow came with her little flock and her scanty housekeeping goods to open a boarding-house or variety store, and so provided a home for her fatherless children. Many farmers' daughters came to earn money to complete their wedding outfit, or buy the bride's share of housekeeping articles....

One of the first strikes of cotton factory operatives that ever took place in this country was that in Lowell, in October 1836. When it was announced that the wages were to be cut down, great indignation was felt, and it was decided to strike, *en masse.* This was done. The mills were shut down, and the girls went in procession from their several corporations to the "grove" on Chapel Hill, and listened to "incendiary" speeches from early labor reformers.

One of the girls stood on a pump, and gave vent to the feelings of her companions

The textile mills in Lowell, Massachusetts, employed mostly young, unmarried women. These "Lowell girls" published their own magazine, the Lowell Offering. ★ **What view of life in a factory town does this magazine cover suggest? Explain.**

in a neat speech, declaring that it was their duty to resist all attempts at cutting down the wages. This was the first time a woman had spoken in public in Lowell, and the event caused surprise and consternation among her audience.

Cutting down the wages was not their only grievance, nor the only cause of the strike. Hitherto the corporations had paid twenty-five cents a week towards the board of each operative, and now it was their purpose to have the girls pay the sum; and this, in addition to the cut in wages, would make a difference of at least one dollar a week....

My own recollection of this first strike (or "turn out" as it was called) is very vivid. I worked in a lower room, where I had heard the proposed strike fully, if not vehemently, discussed; I had been an ardent listener to what was said against this attempt at "oppression" on the part of the corporation, and naturally I took sides with the strikers. When the day came on which the girls were to turn out, those in the upper rooms started first, and so many of them left that our mill was at once shut down. Then, when the girls in my room stood irresolute, uncertain what to do, asking each other, "Would you?" or "Shall we turn out?" and not one of them having the courage to lead off, I, who began to think they would not go out, after all their talk, became impatient, and started on ahead, saying, with childish bravado, "I don't care what you do, I am going to turn out, whether any one else does or not"; and I marched out, and was followed by the others....

It is hardly necessary to say that so far as results were concerned this strike did no good. The dissatisfaction of the operatives subsided, or burned itself out, and though the authorities did not accede to their demands, the majority returned to their work, and the corporation went on cutting down the wages.

Source: *Loom and Spindle,* Harriet Hanson Robinson, 1898.

Analyzing Primary Sources

1. Why did the mill workers go on strike?
   A. Children had been hired to work in the mills.
   B. Factory owners wanted them to work longer hours.
   C. Some workers had been fired.
   D. Wages were going to be cut.

2. This passage is mainly about
   F. transportation in Lowell.
   G. working in a cottonmill.
   H. women's rights.
   J. child labor.

3. **Critical Thinking   Recognizing Points of View** How did the author view the cotton-mill workers?

Historical Critique

How much of what Robinson reports did she witness herself? How much did she learn from other sources?

Introduction   In his State of the Union message to Congress in December 1823, James Monroe issued a warning to European powers not to try to extend their influence in the Western Hemisphere. His warning, which has come to be known as the Monroe Doctrine, had immediate implications. At the time, Russia threatened to encroach in the far Northwest, Great Britain showed some interest in acquiring Cuba, and it was thought that the Quadruple Alliance* wanted to help Spain recover its lost American colonies. The following passage includes relevant excerpts from the Monroe Doctrine.

Vocabulary   Before you read the selection, find the meaning of these words in a dictionary: **amicable, acceded, solicitude, comport, felicity, candor, de facto, eminently.**

★ ★ ★ ★ ★ ★ ★ ★ ★

Annual Message

December 2, 1823

Fellow-citizens of the Senate and House of Representatives:

...At the proposal of the Russian Imperial Government, made through the minister of the Emperor residing here, a full power and instructions have been transmitted to the ministers of the United States at St. Petersburg to arrange by amicable negotiations the respective rights and interests of the two nations on the northwest coast of this continent. A similar proposal had been made by His Imperial Majesty to the government of Great Britain, which had likewise been acceded to. The government of the United States has been desirous, by this friendly proceeding, of manifesting the great value which they have invariably attached to the friendship of the Emperor and their solicitude to cultivate the best understanding with his government. In the discussions to which this interest has given rise and in the arrangements by which they may terminate, the occasion has been judged proper for asserting, as a principle in which the rights and interests of the United States are involved, that the American continents, by the free and independent condition which they have assumed and maintain, are henceforth not considered as subject for future colonization by any European powers....

The citizens of the United States cherish sentiments the most friendly in favor of the liberty and happiness of their fellow men on that side of the Atlantic. In the wars of the European powers in matters relating to themselves we have never taken any part, nor does it comport with our policy so to do. It is only when our rights are invaded or seriously menaced that we resent injuries or make preparations for our defense. With the movements in this hemisphere we are of necessity more immediately connected, and by causes which must be obvious to all enlightened and impartial observers. The political system of the allied powers is essentially different in this respect from that of America. This difference proceeds from that which exists in their respective governments; and to the defense of our own, which has been achieved by the loss of so much blood and treasure, and matured by the wisdom of their most enlightened citizens, and under which we have enjoyed unexampled felicity, this whole nation is devoted. We owe it, therefore, to candor and to the amicable relations existing between the United States and those powers to declare that we should consider any attempt on their part to extend their system to any portion of this hemisphere as dangerous to our peace and safety. With the existing colonies or dependencies of any European power we shall not interfere. But with the governments who have declared their independence and maintained it, and whose independence we have, on great consideration and on just principles, acknowledged, we could not view any interposition for the purpose of oppressing them or

---
* The Quadruple Alliance was a group of European nations that worked together to achieve their goals. It included Britain, Austria, Prussia, and—later—France.

This painting uses symbols to celebrate Mexico's struggle for independence. Father Miguel Hidalgo, left, places a victory wreath on the head of a woman representing Mexico. The growth of new nations in Latin America led President James Monroe to issue the Monroe Doctrine. ★ **What do you think the man in the lower left represents?**

controlling in any other manner their destiny, by any European power in any other light than as the manifestation of an unfriendly disposition toward the United States....

Our policy in regard to Europe, which was adopted at an early stage of the wars which have so long agitated that quarter of the globe, nevertheless remains the same, which is, not to interfere in the internal concerns of any of its powers; to consider the government *de facto* as the legitimate government for us; to cultivate friendly relations by a frank, firm, and manly policy, meeting in all instances the just claims of every power, submitting to injuries from none. But in regard to those continents circumstances are eminently and conspicuously different. It

is impossible that the allied powers should extend their political system to any portion of either continent without endangering our peace and happiness; nor can anyone believe that our southern brethren, if left to themselves, would adopt it of their own accord. It is equally impossible, therefore, that we should behold such interposition in any form with indifference. If we look to the comparative strength and resources of Spain and those new governments, and their distances from each other, it must be obvious that she can never subdue them. It is still the true policy of the United States to leave the parties to themselves, in the hope that other powers will pursue the same course.

Source: *Words That Made American History,* Volume 1, Richard N. Current, 1972.

Analyzing Primary Sources

1. What is the main point of the Monroe Doctrine?

  A. It recognizes the independent nations in Latin America.

  B. It warns Europe against further colonization in the Americas.

  C. It permits Russia to settle in the Northwest.

  D. It warns Spain against invading Portugal.

2. What policy does the Monroe Doctrine apply to the wars in Europe?

  F. not to interfere in them

  G. to send aid when asked

  H. to help negotiate a peace treaty

  J. not to colonize European countries

3. Critical Thinking   Evaluating Information Why did the United States issue the Monroe Doctrine?

Historical Critique

Monroe addressed this speech to "Fellow-citizens of the Senate and House of Representatives." What other audience did he intend his message to reach?

Unit 4

The Nation Expands

★ 12–1 ★ Against Nullification

Historical Document

Introduction In 1830, Senator Robert Y. Hayne of South Carolina, representing the southern states, spoke in the Senate in support of states' rights and nullification. Senator Daniel Webster of Massachusetts then replied to Hayne. His dramatic speech, given over two days, became famous throughout the nation. The following excerpt is from Webster's reply to Hayne.

Vocabulary Before you read the selection, find the meanings of these words in a dictionary: **sovereign, construe, interpolated, conscientiously, vigilantly.**

★ ★ ★ ★ ★ ★ ★ ★ ★

If anything be found in the national Constitution...which ought not be in it, the people know how to get rid of it. If any construction is established unacceptable to them, so as to become practically a part of the Constitution, they will amend it, at their own sovereign pleasure. But while the people choose to maintain it as it is, while they are satisfied with it, and refuse to change it, who has given, or who can give, to the state legislatures a right to alter it, either by interference, construction, or otherwise? Gentlemen do not seem to recollect that the people have any power to do anything for themselves. They imagine there is no safety for them, any longer than they are under the close guardianship of the state legislatures....

The people of the United States have at no time, in no way, directly or indirectly, authorized any state legislature to construe or interpret *their* high instrument of government; much less to interfere, by their own power, to arrest its course and operation.

Viewing History **Two Nationalist Leaders**

Massachusetts sculptor Thomas Ball created these bronze statuettes of Henry Clay (left) and Daniel Webster (right) in the 1850s. Ball greatly admired Clay and Webster for their efforts to preserve the union. ★ **What impression of Daniel Webster do you get from Ball's sculpture and from Webster's speech?**

If, sir, the people in these respects had done otherwise than they have done, their Constitution could neither have been preserved, nor would it have been worthy preserving. And if its plain provisions shall now be disregarded, and these new doctrines interpolated in it, it will become as feeble and helpless a being as its enemies, whether early or more recent, could possibly desire. It will exist in every state but as a poor dependent on state permission....

But, sir, although there are fears, there are hopes also. The people have preserved this, their own chosen Constitution, for forty years, and have seen their happiness, prosperity, and renown grow with its growth, and strengthen with its strength. They are now, generally, strongly, attached to it. Overthrown by direct assault, it cannot be; evaded, undermined, *nullified,* it will not be, if we, and those who shall succeed us here, as agents and representatives of the people, shall conscientiously and vigilantly discharge the two great branches of our public trust, faithfully to preserve, and wisely to administer it....

While the Union lasts, we have high, exciting, gratifying prospects spread out before us, for us and our children....Liberty *and* Union, now and forever, one and inseparable!

Source: *American Reader: Words That Moved a Nation,* edited by Diane Ravitch, 1990.

Analyzing Primary Sources

1. According to Webster, the liberty of the American people is safeguarded by
   A. Congress.
   B. the Constitution.
   C. state legislatures.
   D. prosperity.

2. In his speech, Webster is supporting
   F. states' rights.
   G. the War of 1812.
   H. preservation of the Union.
   J. succession.

3. **Critical Thinking   Identifying Main Ideas** What are the main ideas in Webster's speech?

Historical Critique

In their speeches, politicians often use emotional appeals to rally support for a particular cause. How do Webster's final words appeal to his listeners' emotions? How do you think he used his voice to increase the effect of his words?

★ 12–2 ★   *The Cherokee Removal*

Introduction   The Indian Removal Act forced the Cherokee, the Creek, the Chickasaw, and the Choctaw to resettle west of the Mississippi. When it came time for the Cherokees to leave their homes in 1838, many resisted. Evan Jones, a Baptist missionary, worked among the Cherokee in North Carolina and joined them on their westward march. The following excerpt is from a series of letters written by Jones.

Vocabulary   Before you read the selection, find the meanings of these words in the dictionary: **plunderers, wretches, agitation, consoling, disposition, perpetrated, manifests.**

★ ★ ★ ★ ★ ★ ★ ★ ★

Camp Hetzel, Near Cleveland, June 16

The Cherokees are nearly all prisoners. They have been dragged from their houses, and encamped at the forts and military posts, all over the nation. In Georgia, especially, multitudes were allowed no time to take anything with them, except the clothes they had on. Well-furnished houses were a prey to plunderers, who, like hungry wolves, follow in the train of the captors. These wretches rifle the houses, and strip the helpless, unoffending owners of all they have on earth.... The property of many has been taken, and sold before their eyes for almost nothing—the sellers and buyers, in many cases, being combined to cheat the poor Indians.... The poor captive, in a state of distressing agitation, his weeping wife almost frantic with terror, surrounded by a group of crying, terrified children, without a friend to speak a consoling word, is in a poor condition to make a good disposition of his property and is in most cases stripped of the whole, at one blow. Many of the Cherokees, who, a few days ago, were in comfortable circumstances, are now victims of abject poverty. Some, who have been allowed to return home, under passport, to inquire after their property, have found their cattle, horses, swine, farming tools, and house furniture all gone. And this is not a description of extreme cases. It is altogether a faint representation of the work which has been perpetrated on the unoffending, unarmed, and unresisting Cherokees....

It is due to justice to say, that, at this station (and I learn the same is true of some others), the officer in command treats his prisoners with great respect and indulgence. But fault rests somewhere. They are prisoners, without a crime to justify the fact....

July 10 and July 11

The work of war in time of peace, is commenced in the Georgia part of the Cherokee nation, and is carried on, in most cases, in the most unfeeling and brutal manner; no regard being paid to the orders of the commanding General, in regard to humane treatment of the Indians. I have heard of only one officer in Georgia (I hope there are

Viewing HISTORY — Along the Trail of Tears

Robert Liudneux painted this view of Cherokee families traveling west on the Trail of Tears. Blue-coated soldiers force Cherokee families to move to Indian Territory. Some families carry their belongings in wagons, but many others must make the journey on foot. ★ **How does the painting suggest the hardships the Cherokees faced?**

more), who manifests anything like humanity, in his treatment of this persecuted people....

The work of capturing being completed, and about 3,000 sent off, the General had agreed to suspend the further transportation of the captives till the first of September. This arrangement, though but a small favor, diffused universal joy through the camps of the prisoners....

On our way, we met a detachment of 1,300 prisoners. As I took some of them by hand, the tears gushed from their eyes. Their hearts, however, were cheered to see us, and to hear a word of consolation. Many members of the church were among them. At Fort Butler, we found a company of 300, just arrived from the mountains, on their way to the general depot, at the agency. Several of our members were among these also.

Source: *The Cherokee Removal: A Brief History With Documents,* edited by Theda Perdue and Michael Green, 1995.

Analyzing Primary Sources

1. Where were the Cherokees living when Jones wrote these letters?
    A. in Georgia
    B. in California
    C. in Texas
    D. in Ohio

2. Where were the Cherokees being taken?
    F. to their homes
    G. to reservations
    H. to forts and military posts
    J. to Cleveland

3. **Critical Thinking   Recognizing Points of View** Based on the excerpt, how did Evan Jones view the United States Army's treatment of the Cherokees?

Historical Critique
Did Evan Jones directly witness everything he describes in his letters? Explain.

★ Chapter 13 ★ Westward Expansion

★ 13–1 ★   Death Comes for the Archbishop

Introduction Many of the novels of Willa Cather focus on pioneer life on the Great Plains. In *Death Comes for the Archbishop,* however, her setting is the American Southwest during the 1850s. The book's main character, Bishop Jean Latour, journeys with his Native American guide, Jacinto, through Arizona and New Mexico. In the following selection, Latour and Jacinto camp for the night during a journey to a distant mission.

Vocabulary Before you read the selection, find the meanings of these words in a dictionary: **firmament, proposition, vehement.**

★ ★ ★ ★ ★ ★ ★ ★ ★

Jacinto got firewood and good water from the Lagunas, and they made their camp in a pleasant spot on the rocks north of the village. As the sun dropped low, the light brought the white church and the yellow adobe houses up into relief from the flat ledges. Behind their camp, not far away, lay a group of great mesas. The Bishop asked Jacinto if he knew the name of the one nearest them.

"No, I do not know any name," he shook his head. "I know Indian name," he added, as if, for once, he were thinking aloud.

"And what is the Indian name?"

"The Laguna Indians call Snow-Bird mountain." He spoke somewhat unwillingly.

"That is very nice," said the Bishop musingly. "Yes, that is a pretty name...."

The Bishop sat drinking his coffee slowly out of the tin cup, keeping the pot near the embers. The sun had set now, the yellow rocks were turning grey, down in the pueblo the light of the cook fires made red patches of the glassless windows, and the smell of [pine] smoke came softly through the still air.

The whole western sky was the color of golden ashes, with here and there a flush of red on the lip of a little cloud. High above the horizon the evening-star flickered like a lamp just lit, and close beside it was another star of constant light, much smaller....

The two companions sat, each thinking his own thoughts as night closed in about them; a blue night set with stars, the bulk of the solitary mesas cutting into the firmament. The Bishop seldom questioned Jacinto about his thoughts or beliefs. He didn't think it polite, and he believed it to be useless. There was no way he could transfer his own memories of European civilization into the Indian mind, and he was quite willing to believe that behind Jacinto there was a long tradition, a store of experience, which no language could translate to him. A chill came with the darkness. Father Latour put on his old fur-lined cloak, and Jacinto, loosening the blanket tied about his loins, drew it up over his head and shoulders.

"Many stars," he said presently. "What do you think about the stars, Padre?"

"The wise men tell us they are worlds like ours, Jacinto...."

"I think not," [Jacinto] said in the tone of one who has considered a proposition fairly and rejected it. "I think they are leaders— great spirits."

"Perhaps they are," said the Bishop with a sigh. "Whatever they are, they are great. Let us say *Our Father*, and go to sleep, my boy."

Kneeling on either side of the embers they repeated the prayer together and then

Viewing History

A Mission in California

An unknown California artist painted Oriana Day, Mission Francisco Solano de Sonoma *in the mid-1800s. It shows Native Americans at a mission in northern California. Throughout the Southwest, the Spanish had forced many Indians into missions.* ★ **Study the picture. What seems to be the main building of the mission? Where on the mission grounds did Indians live?**

rolled up in their blankets. The Bishop went to sleep thinking with satisfaction that he was beginning to have some sort of human companionship with his Indian boy. One called the young Indians "boys," perhaps because there was something youthful and elastic in their bodies. Certainly about their behavior there was nothing boyish in the American sense, nor even in the European sense. Jacinto was never, by any chance, [naive]; he was never taken by surprise. One felt that his training, whatever it had been, had prepared him to meet any situation which might confront him. He was as much at home in the Bishop's study as in his own pueblo—and he was never too much at home anywhere. Father Latour felt he had gone a good way toward gaining his guide's friendship, though he did not know how.

The truth was, Jacinto liked the Bishop's way of meeting people; thought he had the right tone with Padre Gallegos, the right tone with Padre Jesus, and that he had good manners with the Indians. In his experience, white people, when they addressed Indians, always put on a false face. There were many kinds of false faces; Father Vaillant's, for example, was kindly but too vehement. The Bishop put on none at all. He stood straight and turned to the Governor of Laguna, and his face underwent no change. Jacinto thought this remarkable.

Source: *Death Comes for the Archbishop,* Willa Cather, 1927.

Analyzing Literature

1. The bishop rarely asked Jacinto about his thoughts and beliefs because
   A. he did not care about Indian beliefs.
   B. he knew Jacinto did not want to talk about his beliefs.
   C. he knew Jacinto did not speak English well.
   D. he did not think Europeans and Indians could fully understand each other.

2. Jacinto came to trust the bishop because the bishop
   F. taught Jacinto how to pray.
   G. always told the truth.

H. was familiar with the countryside.
J. never put on a false face.

3. **Critical Thinking   Comparing**
   (a) Compare the bishop's and Jacinto's beliefs concerning the stars. **(b)** What did each man think of the other's belief?

Historical Critique

Willa Cather wrote *Death Comes for the Archbishop* in the 1920s—more than 70 years after the novel takes place. What kinds of historical sources could she have used to help her write her novel?

★ 13–2 ★   Trapped in the Sierra Nevada

Eyewitness Account

Introduction   In 1846, a group of settlers started over the Sierra Nevada on their way to California. They were caught by an early winter snowstorm in what is now called Donner Pass. Of the 79 people in the party, only 45 survived. The following is an excerpt from the diary of H. H. Bancroft about the rescue of the trapped Donner party.

Vocabulary   Before you read the selection, find the meanings of these words in a dictionary: **emigrants, intervals, famine, provision, repletion, imperatively.**

★ ★ ★ ★ ★ ★ ★ ★ ★

Foster had told us that we should find the emigrants at or near Truckee Lake, (since called Donner Lake) and in the direction of this we journeyed. Of course we had no guide, and most of our journey was through a dense pine forest, but the lofty peak which overlooks the lake was in sight at intervals, and this and the judgment of our two leaders were our sole means of direction....When we started from the fort, Capt. Sutter assured us that we should be followed by other parties as soon as the necessary preparations could be made. For the guidance of those who might follow us and as a signal to any of the emigrants who might be straggling about in the mountains as well as for our own direction on our return trip, we set fire to every dead pine on or near our trail....

At sunset of the 16th day we crossed Truckee Lake on the ice and came to the spot where we had been told we should find the emigrants. We looked all around but no living thing except ourselves was in sight and we thought that all must have perished. We raised a loud hello and then we saw a woman emerge from a hole in the snow. As we approached her several others made their appearance in like manner coming out of the snow. They were gaunt with famine and I never can forget the horrible, ghastly sight they presented. The first woman spoke in a hollow voice very much agitated and said, "Are you men from California or do you come from heaven?"

They had been without food except a few work oxen since the first fall of snow, about 3 weeks. They had gathered up the bones of the slaughtered cattle and boiled them to extract the grease and had roasted some of the hides which formed the roofs of their cabins. We gave them food very sparingly and retired for the night having some one on guard until morning to keep close watch on our provision to prevent the starving emigrants from eating them, which they would have done until they died of repletion.

When these emigrants had first been stopped by snow they had built small cabins using skins of the slaughtered oxen for roofs. Storms nearly continuous had caused the snow to fall to the depth of 18 feet so that the tops of their cabins were far beneath the surface....

The morning after our arrival John P. Rhoads and Tucker started for another camp distant 8 miles east, where were the Donner family, to distribute what provisions could be spared and to bring along such of the party as had sufficient strength to walk. They returned bringing four girls and two boys of the Donner family and some others.

The next morning we started on our return trip accompanied by 21 emigrants mostly women and children. John Rhoads carried a child in his arms which died the second night. On the third day, an emigrant named John Denton, exhausted by starvation and totally snow-blind, gave out. He tried to keep up a hopeful and cheerful appearance, but we knew he could not live much longer. We made a platform of saplings, built a fire on it, cut some boughs

Viewing History   A Snowy Mountain Pass

The journey to California was long and difficult. Travelers had to navigate narrow passes through the Rocky Mountains and the Sierra Nevada before reaching their destination. This photograph shows Carson Pass in the Sierra Nevada. ★ **If you were a settler heading west in the 1840s, what emotions might you have on seeing this view?**

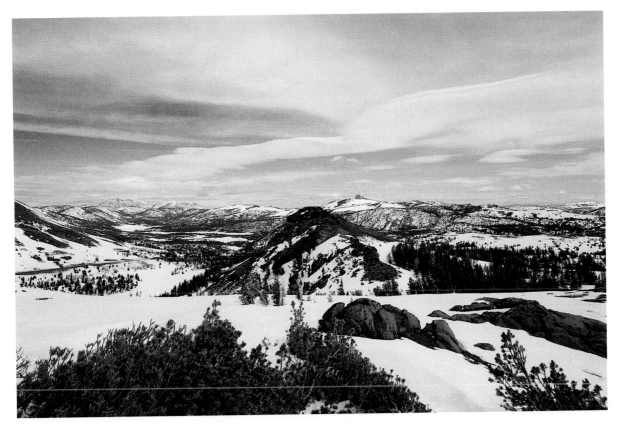

for him to sit upon and left him. This was imperatively necessary. The party who followed in our trail from California found his dead body a few days after we had left him, partially eaten by wolves.

Source: *Overland in 1846: Diaries and Letters of the California-Oregon Trail,* edited by Dale Morgan, 1993.

Analyzing Primary Sources

1. At what location were the Donner party survivors found?
   A. California
   B. a pine forest
   C. Truckee Lake
   D. Sutter's fort

2. How were the Donner party stranded?
   F. They lost their way.
   G. Their wagons broke down.
   H. There was an early winter snowstorm.
   J. They ran out of food.

3. **Critical Thinking   Recognizing Points of View** Based on the excerpt, how do you think H. H. Bancroft viewed the Donner party survivors?

Historical Critique
What information in this selection was Bancroft able to give as an eyewitness? What information did he have to get from members of the Donner party?

★ Chapter 14 ★ The Worlds of North and South

★ 14–1 ★   Three Views of Irish Immigration

Eyewitness Account

Introduction   Under British rule, most farmland in Ireland was used to grow wheat and oats for sale outside of Ireland. Irish peasants depended on the potato for nourishment. Then, in 1845, disease destroyed the potato crop. To escape starvation, thousands of poor Irish families emigrated to the United States. In the first letter below, a young woman in Ireland describes the famine to her parents in Quebec, Canada. The second and third letters were written by new immigrants in New York to their villages back home.

Vocabulary   Before you read the selection, find the meanings of these words in a dictionary: **scourge, endeavor, steward, inconceivable, quarries.**

★ ★ ★ ★ ★ ★ ★ ★ ★

Mary Rush:
Ardnaglass, Ireland
September 6, 1846

Dear Father and Mother,
   Pen cannot dictate the poverty of this country at present. The potato crop is quite done away all over Ireland. There is nothing expected here, only an immediate famine. If you knew what danger we and our fellow countrymen are suffering, if you were ever so much distressed, you would take us out of this poverty isle. We can only say, the scourge of God fell down on Ireland, in taking away the potatoes, they being the only support of the people. So, dear father and mother, if you don't endeavor to take us out of it, it will be the first news you will hear by some friend of me and my little family to be lost by hunger, and there are thousands dread they will share the same fate. So, I conclude with my blessings to you both....
   For God's sake take us out of poverty, and don't let us die with the hunger.

Poverty in Ireland

Even before famine struck, many Irish peasants lived in desperate poverty. They had to pay high rents to absentee English landlords, who often evicted tenants at will. This print from the later 1800s shows an Irish family thrown off their land with just a few meager possessions. ★ **Why do you think the United States attracted so many Irish immigrants?**

★ ★ ★ ★ ★ ★ ★ ★

Daniel Guiney:
Buffalo, New York
August 9, 1850

Dear Mother and Brothers,

We mean to let you know our situation at present. We arrived here at five o'clock in the afternoon of yesterday, fourteen of us together, where we were received with the greatest kindness and respectability by Matthew Leary and Denis Danihy. When we came to the house we could not state to you how we were treated. We had potatoes, meat, butter, bread, and tea for dinner. . . .

Dear friends, if you were to see old Denis Danihy, he never was in as good health and looks better than he ever did at home. . . . If you were to see Denis Reen when Daniel Danihy dressed him with clothes suitable for this country, you would think him to be a boss or steward, so that we have scarcely words to state to you how happy we felt at present. And as to the girls that used to be trotting on the bogs at home, to hear them talk English would be of great astonishment to you. Mary Keefe got two dresses, one from Mary Danihy and the other from Biddy Matt.

★ ★ ★ ★ ★ ★ ★ ★

William Dever:
New York, New York
September 14, 1848

My dear Uncle and Brothers,

It's inconceivable the thousands that land here every week from all the old countries flying from tyranny and oppression. Wealthy farmers with their whole families are coming here and purchasing farms, some the best land in the whole world. Germans, French, Hollanders are doing this on a large scale.

But most of the Irish come out poor, unable to purchase farms. They work digging quarries, carrying brick and mortar in scorching sun up to the fourth stories of houses, in winter nothing to do, all their money spent. They are despised and kicked about. Many write home they are happy and wealthy, when they are of that class above mentioned. I heard friends of a young man in this city enquiring if John...was not a banker here, as he wrote home that he was so and persuaded all his relatives to come join him. But what was he, think you? He was sweeper of the office of the bank. They were astonished when told so. And thousands are just like him.

Source: *Out of Ireland: The Story of Irish Emigration to America*, Kerby Miller and Paul Wagner, 1994.

Analyzing Primary Sources

1. Why did Mary Rush send a letter to her parents?
   A. She wanted to leave Ireland.
   B. She wanted to tell them about life in the United States.
   C. She wanted to tell them the latest news from the village.
   D. She wanted them to send her money.

2. According to William Dever, unlike German immigrants, the Irish
   F. were not good farmers.
   G. were treated with great kindness.
   H. could not afford to buy land.
   J. worked in the banking business.

3. **Critical Thinking Recognizing Points of View** Explain how you think each of the following might have reacted if they had read Daniel Guiney's letter: **(a)** Mary Rush; **(b)** William Dever.

Historical Critique

How does Dever's letter show why we cannot always take primary sources at face value?

★ 14–2 ★ *The Fires of Jubilee*

Introduction In 1831, Nat Turner led a group of slaves on an uprising across Southampton County, Virginia. More than 50 white people were killed. Modern writer Stephen B. Oates wrote a dramatic account of this rebellion in *The Fires of Jubilee: Nat Turner's Fierce Rebellion.* The following excerpt describes the reaction of the white community after the rebellion.

Vocabulary Before you read the selection, find the meanings of these words in a dictionary: **pummeled, insurgents, disaffection, dire, commencement, couriers, communiqués, ascertain.**

★ ★ ★ ★ ★ ★ ★ ★ ★

In September, new alarms pummeled upper North Carolina. A man from Murfreesboro, having attended a slave trial in Virginia's Sussex County, reported back that the Southampton insurgents had expected armed slave resistance "from distant neighborhoods," including the large plantations on the Roanoke. Yes, the fellow cried, testimony in the Sussex trial "proved" that a concerted uprising was to have taken place in Virginia and upper North Carolina, where Negro preachers had been spreading disaffection, and that "dire and extensive would have been the slaughter but for a mistake in the day of commencement." The plan, the man said, called for the larger rebellion to begin on the last Sunday in August. But he contended that the Southampton rebels mistook August 21 as the target Sunday, all the while their North Carolina allies were waiting for August 28!

Though no such plan had existed, the report traumatized whites in the northeastern tier of counties, especially in neighborhoods with heavy slave concentrations. Couriers rode for Raleigh to beg for muskets and ammunition. Militia outfits mustered along the Roanoke, chased after imaginary insurgents and...imprisoned...still more innocent blacks. Phantom slave columns marched out

Viewing HISTORY

Picking Cotton

The economy of the South depended on cotton, and cotton depended on slavery. This woodcut shows enslaved African Americans picking, baling, and ginning cotton on a plantation.

★ **Compare this picture to the reading. How do they give different pictures of slave life?**

BALING COTTON.

GINNING COTTON BY ST

of the Dismal Swamp, only to vanish when militia units rushed out to fight them.

In mid-September came the most shattering alarm of all: couriers reported that a full-scale rebellion had blazed up in southeastern North Carolina, in Duplin and Sampson counties.... Such communiqués were completely false, but frantic whites were now reacting to their own shadows. Militia commanders alerted their troops and sent off exaggerated reports to the governor, which gathered additional frills as express riders bore them to the capital. Meanwhile, mass hysteria gripped the town of Wilmington down near the Atlantic Ocean....

But no slave army appeared. Out of blind vengeance, whites turned on the local Negro population and ... forced five hapless blacks into confessing that, yes, they were to meet insurgents from Sampson County....

Raleigh too was in turmoil, as a succession of express riders burst into the city with doomsday reports: slave rebels had allegedly set much of eastern North Carolina afire....

In all the excitement, a few people managed to keep their heads. On September 16, the Raleigh *Star* corrected its initial reports and denied the disturbing news now "circulating through the country." A few days later the Raleigh *Register* admitted that its own account of insurrections in North Carolina had been "highly exaggerated." The storm had passed now, the paper declared, so that it was possible to ascertain the truth. While slaves in the southeastern part of the state had undoubtedly "talked about insurrection," none in fact had transpired.

Source: *The Fires of Jubilee: Nat Turner's Fierce Rebellion,* Stephen B. Oates, 1975.

Analyzing Literature

1. What alarmed the white community ?
    - **A.** the verdict in a slave trial
    - **B.** the burning of Raleigh
    - **C.** the presence of militia in the towns
    - **D.** talk of a slave rebellion

2. Newspapers in Raleigh
    - **F.** supported a slave revolt.
    - **G.** called for an end to slavery.
    - **H.** ignored rumors of a slave revolt.
    - **J.** corrected their earlier reports.

3. **Critical Thinking Distinguishing Fact From Opinion** **(a)** On what information did the people in North Carolina base their belief that slaves were about to rebel? **(b)** What facts in the selection contradict those beliefs?

Historical Critique

How can you tell that Stephen B. Oates did historical research before writing his book?

Introduction   Frederick Douglass escaped from slavery in 1838 and later became a leading abolitionist. From the money he earned writing and lecturing, Douglass was able to buy his freedom. In 1845, Douglass wrote *Narrative of the Life of Frederick Douglass.* In the following excerpt, Douglass explains why learning to read and write was so important to him.

Vocabulary   Before you read the selection, find the meanings of these words in a dictionary: **blighting, impudent, tranquil, irresponsible, commenced, revelation, perplexing.**

★ ★ ★ ★ ★ ★ ★ ★ ★

My new mistress proved to be all she appeared when I first met her at the door—a woman of the kindest heart and finest feelings. She had never had a slave under her control previously to myself, and prior to her marriage she had been dependent upon her own industry for a living. She was by trade a weaver; and by constant application to her business, she had been in a good degree preserved from the blighting and dehumanizing effects of slavery. I was utterly astonished at her goodness.... She did not deem it impudent or unmannerly for a slave to look her in the face. The meanest slave was put fully at ease in her presence, and none left without feeling better for having seen her. Her face was made of heavenly smiles, and her voice of tranquil music.

But, alas! this kind heart had but a short time to remain such. The fatal poison of irresponsible power was already in her hands, and soon commenced its infernal work. That

Viewing HISTORY **Frederick Douglass Speaks Out**

In 1845, Frederick Douglass published his Narrative. *The same year, a song celebrating his escape appeared in the North. The photograph (far left) was taken in 1848, the year after Douglass started his antislavery newspaper, the* North Star. ★ **"Expose slavery and it dies,"** **said Frederick Douglass. How did his actions reflect this belief?**

cheerful eye, under the influence of slavery, soon became red with rage....

Very soon after I went to live with Mr. and Mrs. Auld, she very kindly commenced to teach me the A, B, C. After I had learned this, she assisted me in learning to spell words of three or four letters. Just at this point of my progress, Mr. Auld found out what was going on, and at once forbade Mrs. Auld to instruct me further, telling her, among other things, that it was unlawful, as well as unsafe, to teach a slave to read. To use his own words, further, he said, "If...you teach that nigger (speaking of myself) how to read, there would be no keeping him. It would forever unfit him to be a slave. He would at once become unmanageable, and of no value to his master. As to himself, it could do him no good, but a great deal of harm. It would make him discontented and unhappy." These words sank deep into my heart, stirred up sentiments within that lay slumbering, and called into existence an entirely new train of thought. It was a new and special revelation, explaining dark and mysterious things, with which my youthful understanding had struggled, but struggled in vain. I now understood what had been to me a most perplexing difficulty—to wit, the white man's power to enslave the black man. It was a grand achievement, and I prized it highly. From that moment, I understood the path-way from slavery to freedom. It was just what I wanted, and I got it at a time when I the least expected it. Whilst I was saddened by the thought of losing the aid of my kind mistress, I was gladdened by the invaluable instruction which, by the merest accident, I had gained from my master. Though conscious of the difficulty of learning without a teacher, I set out with high hope, and a fixed purpose, at whatever cost of trouble, to learn how to read. The very decided manner with which he spoke, and strove to impress his wife with the evil consequences of giving me instruction, served to convince me that he was deeply sensible of the truths he was uttering. It gave me the best assurance that I might rely with the utmost confidence on the results which, he said, would flow from teaching me to read. What he most dreaded, that I most desired. What he most loved, that I most hated. That which to him was great evil, to be carefully shunned, was to me a great good, to be diligently sought; and the argument which he so warmly urged, against my learning to read, only served to inspire me with a desire and determination to learn. In learning to read, I owe almost as much to the bitter opposition of my master, as to the kindly aid of my mistress. I acknowledge the benefit of both.

Source: *Narrative of the Life of Frederick Douglass, An American Slave,* Frederick Douglass, 1845.

Analyzing Primary Sources

1. Who first taught Frederick Douglass how to read?
   A. Mr. Auld
   B. Mrs. Auld
   C. his mother
   D. another slave

2. According to Douglass, Mrs. Auld changed as a result of her
   F. power over her slaves.
   G. disagreement with her husband.
   H. inability to teach Douglass to read.
   J. fear of a slave revolt.

3. **Critical Thinking   Recognizing Points of View** According to the excerpt, how did Frederick Douglass view his master's opposition to educating slaves?

Historical Critique

To gain support for what cause did Douglass write his autobiography? What made him an effective witness?

Introduction In 1848, Elizabeth Cady Stanton and Lucretia Mott led a women's rights convention in Seneca Falls, New York. The event marked the beginning of an organized women's rights movement in the United States. The women and men attending the convention adopted the following Declaration of Sentiments and a number of resolutions.

Vocabulary Before you read the selection, find the meanings of these words in a dictionary: **impel, endowed, inalienable, allegiance, prudence, transient, usurpations, evinces, despotism, constrains, tyranny, franchise, facilities, zealous.**

★ ★ ★ ★ ★ ★ ★ ★ ★

Declaration of Sentiments

When, in the course of human events, it becomes necessary for one portion of the family of man to assume among the people of the earth a position different from that which they have hitherto occupied, but one to which the laws of nature and of nature's God entitle them, a decent respect to the opinions of mankind requires that they should declare the causes that impel them to such a course.

We hold these truths to be self-evident that all men and women are created equal; that they are endowed by their Creator with certain inalienable rights; that among these are life, liberty, and the pursuit of happiness; that to secure these rights governments are instituted, deriving their just powers from the consent of the governed. Whenever any form of government becomes destructive of these ends, it is the right of those who suffer from it to refuse allegiance to it, and to insist upon the institution of a new government, laying its foundation on such principles, and organizing its powers in such form, as to them shall seem most likely to effect their safety and happiness. Prudence, indeed, will dictate that governments long established should not be changed for light and transient causes; and accordingly all experience hath shown that mankind are more disposed to

suffer while evils are sufferable, than to right themselves by abolishing the forms to which they are accustomed. But when a long train of abuses and usurpations, pursuing invariably the same object, evinces a design to reduce them under absolute despotism, it is their duty to throw off such government, and to provide new guards for their future security. Such has been the patient sufferance of the women under this government, and such is now the necessity which constrains them to demand the equal station to which they are entitled.

The history of mankind is a history of repeated injuries and usurpations on the part of man toward woman, having in direct object the establishment of an absolute tyranny over her. To prove this, let facts be submitted to a candid world.

He has never permitted her to exercise her inalienable right to the elective franchise.

He has compelled her to submit to laws, in the formation of which she had no voice.

He has withheld from her rights which are given to the most ignorant and degraded men—both natives and foreigners.

Having deprived her of this first right of a citizen, the elective franchise, thereby leaving her without representation in the halls of legislation, he has oppressed her on all sides.

He has made her, if married, in the eye of the law, civilly dead.

He has taken from her all right in property, even to the wages she earns....

He has denied her the facilities for obtaining a thorough education, all colleges being closed against her....

Resolutions

Resolved, That all laws which prevent woman from occupying such a station in society as her conscience shall dictate, or which place her in a position inferior to that of man, are contrary to the great precept of nature, and therefore of no force or authority.

Resolved, That woman is man's equal—was intended to be so by the Creator, and the

Viewing History

Education for Women

In the early 1800s, American colleges and universities admitted only men. Still, a few women did receive an education at "seminaries for young ladies." This picture by an unknown student shows women studying geography at a seminary, somewhere between 1810 and 1820. ★ **Why did many men think it was not important for women to receive an education?**

highest good of the race demands that she should be recognized as such.

Resolved, That the women of this country ought to be enlightened in regard to the laws under which they live, that they may no longer publish their degradation by declaring themselves satisfied with their present position, nor their ignorance, by asserting that they have all the rights they want....

Resolved, That the speedy success of our cause depends on the zealous and untiring efforts of both men and women....

Source: *Words That Made American History,* Volume 1, edited by Richard N. Current, 1972.

Analyzing Primary Sources

1. What is the main point of this document?
   A. Men should have more rights than women.
   B. Our laws are unfair to both men and women.
   C. Women should have the same rights as men.
   D. All men should be allowed to hold public office.

2. According to this document, women did not have the right to
   F. work.
   G. vote.
   H. travel to a foreign country.
   J. speak out against injustice.

3. **Critical Thinking   Making Inferences** Why do you think that the women at the Seneca Falls Convention used the wording of the Declaration of Independence when they wrote their Declaration of Sentiments?

Historical Critique

For what purpose was this document written? Do you think it was intended to be read primarily by women, by men, or by both?

Unit 5 Division and Reunion

★ Chapter 16 ★ A Dividing Nation

★ 16–1 ★ Caleb's Choice

Introduction G. Clifton Wisler's novel *Caleb's Choice* is set in the late 1850s. Young Caleb Delaney goes to northern Texas to live with his grandmother and his cousins Edith and Micah. In Caleb's new home, people are divided over the Fugitive Slave Law. Caleb is not sure how he feels about the law. In the following excerpt, Caleb helps feed two captured fugitives.

Vocabulary Before you read the selection, find the meanings of these words in a dictionary: **shackled, bounty, wretch.**

★ ★ ★ ★ ★ ★ ★ ★ ★

ou had to admit that they were good at their work. They captured the two runaways from Waco not a half mile from Spring Creek, and they located three others off a Smith County plantation.

"Already wired their owners," Ulysses boasted. "Mr. Francis Leighton will meet us in Dallas to take delivery of his two. Promised us a fifty-dollar bonus, too. We'll leave the other three with Sheriff Rutherford at McKinney. They're worth two hundred dollars altogether."

I thought about that. Papa needed five hundred dollars, and here the Fitches had earned almost that much capturing runaways! The notion had a powerful pull to it. But when I followed Edith out to the well with some food for the prisoners, I realized that I would never have the heart to be a slave catcher. I recognized the two Waco slaves from the sketches on their posters, but

I wasn't prepared for the other three. One was a sad-eyed girl no older than Edith, and the other two were slight-shouldered boys only a little taller than me. Not since departing Dallas had I seen people with such hollow eyes. Their feet were shackled, and their hands were bound with coarse rope that bit into the dark flesh of their wrists. The younger boy bled from the left side of his mouth. Edith gasped when she looked at the backs of the Waco runaways. The Fitches had used a whip on both.

"Fetch some water from the well," Edith told me.

"Already done," Polk Harrison announced, carrying a bucket over. "Spied them on the road."

Edith and Harrison exchanged an odd glance, and I sensed they wanted to say more. The runaways accepted cups of water gratefully, although with downcast eyes. The older ones managed to mumble a thank you when Edith promised to find some salve for their cuts. She placed slices of bread and chunks of ham in their fingers. They ate with considerable difficulty.

"We should notify the sheriff," Edith stormed. "Slaves or not, they don't deserve ill treatment."

"Its not illegal," Harrison argued. "There are slave catchers who do far worse. Fitches know better than to cut off a limb or hamstring a valuable hand. Takes away from the profit."

"They're getting a bonus," I pointed out. "Three hundred and fifty dollars in all."

"A man can always use money," Harrison admitted. "Me, I wouldn't take money earned from another man's bleeding."

"Even a slave?" I asked.

"Especially," Harrison said. "You accept a bounty for a killer, a man likely to hurt somebody else and capable of defending himself, that's one thing. But hunting down some poor wretch who only wants to be left alone?"

"That's pretty strong talk, mister," Ulysses said, walking over, rifle in hand. "You know, it wouldn't surprise me to learn somebody hereabouts hid those older ones. We looked mighty hard for 'em."

"That why you whipped them?" I asked, "To find out?"

"Oh, that was just a little message from Mr. Leighton," Ulysses explained. "Most likely they hid in a slave house at one of the big farms east of here. White men would know better than to help after that trouble on the Colorado River."

"What trouble?" I asked.

"Two years ago the authorities discovered a plot," Harrison told me. "Four hundred slaves were supposed to rise and kill their masters...."

I shivered. Gazing into the eyes of those prisoners, though, I found it hard to imagine myself in much danger. Halfway starved and dressed in rags, they looked more like survivors off a Gulf shipwreck than bloodthirsty killers.

"Don't let 'em fool you, boy," Ulysses said to me in particular. "They hate us...."

"Can't much blame them," Edith said, drawing me away from the well. "Lord knows they've got reason enough."

"I suppose," I said, sighing. "I saw an auction in Dallas. I wouldn't want to be a slave. Desperate like that, they *could* be dangerous, though."

Viewing HISTORY — Human Beings for Sale

In 1853, British artist Eyre Crowe visited Richmond, Virginia, a leading center of the slave trade. Crowe then painted After the Sale: South From Richmond. *It shows newly sold African Americans in a wagon, waiting to be transported to their new owner. In the lower right, two slave traders argue over the price.* ★ **Identify three details in this painting that create sympathy for the enslaved African Americans.**

"I would be," she whispered. "Let's get away from here. I can't bear seeing them that way."

All that afternoon I thought about the slaves. I couldn't get them off my mind.

When I sat at the loft table composing letters to my parents for Polk Harrison to carry back south, I tried to free myself from the runaways' ghostly faces. I couldn't.

Source: *Caleb's Choice*, G. Clifton Wisler, 1996.

Analyzing Literature

1. Who were the Fitches?
   A. slave catchers
   B. Caleb's parents
   C. Caleb's grandparents
   D. abolitionists
2. Who helped the fugitives?
   F. Mr. Leighton
   G. Ulysses
   H. Sheriff Rutherford
   J. Edith

3. **Critical Thinking   Drawing Conclusions** Why do you think that slave catchers were so well paid?

Historical Critique

If you were writing a report about the attitudes of white Texans toward fugitive slaves in the 1800s, could you use *Caleb's Choice* as a historical source? Why or why not?

★ 16–2 ★   **Two Views of the War in Kansas**

Eyewitness Account

Introduction   In 1856, proslavery forces attacked Lawrence, Kansas. An antislavery group led by John Brown attacked Pottawatomie Creek and killed a number of southern settlers. In the following letters, John Lawrie, a northerner, and Axalla John Hoole, a southerner, express their views of the fighting in Kansas.

Vocabulary   Before you read the selection, find the meanings of these words in a dictionary: **endeavors, vengeance, propriety, molest.**

★ ★ ★ ★ ★ ★ ★ ★ ★

John Lawrie:

Dear Art,

When I left home on the fifteenth of last June I had no intention of making a home in Kansas. I intended in case I could find any organization ready to take the field against the Missourians [the proslavery settlers], to use my utmost endeavors to change the attitude of the Free-State [antislavery] settlers from a defensive to an offensive warfare. When I reached Leavenworth, I was unable to find any organization of free-state men,

and could only tell one when I met him by his hanging head and subdued tone of voice....

Hearing that people held up their heads and spoke what they thought in Lawrence, I started for that point and soon found myself at home as far as a hatred of tyranny and a thirst for vengeance for the insult of the 21st of May was concerned. The people had concluded to try whether there was truth in the Border Ruffian assertion *The...Yankees won't fight!* There was quite a stir among the young men in the way of target fighting and drilling in order to prepare themselves for any emergency that might arise requiring them *to contend with superior numbers,* the only thing that thus far has held them back. I found that arms were really scarce. I expected to find plenty of improved fire-arms, and it was with the greatest difficulty I succeeded in getting an old condemned musket. I was looked upon with distrust by a great many persons in Lawrence, having the appearance of a spy in their eyes. It was complimentary, for my appearance seemed above my position to them; but it was very disagreeable. The only military company in town (the Stubbs) expected to attend the convention at Topeka on the second and third of July and the opening of the [antislavery] legislature on the Fourth, when it was expected they would be needed to defend the legislature against the Ruffians and troops of the U.S. I applied for admission into the company and was put off with rather evasive answers. I went up to Topeka, however, resolved to prove myself a true man when the trying time came. I found the people discussing the propriety of defending the legislature against all who might attempt to disperse it....

★ ★ ★ ★ ★ ★ ★ ★ ★

Axalla John Hoole:

Dear Sister,

I fear, Sister, that coming here will do no good at last, as I begin to think that this will be made a free state at last. 'Tis true we have elected proslavery men to draft a state Constitution, but I feel pretty certain, if it is put to the vote of the people, it will be rejected, as I feel pretty confident they have a majority here at this time. The South has ceased all efforts, while the North is redoubling her exertions. We nominated a candidate for Congress last Friday—Ex-Gov. Ransom of Michigan. I must confess I have not much faith in him, though he professes to hate the abolitionists bitterly, and I have heard him say that Negroes were a great deal better off with masters. Still, I fear him, but it was the best we could do.

Viewing HISTORY **A Violent Abolitionist**

Abolitionist John Brown favored violent solutions to the evil of slavery. In 1856, he and his followers murdered five proslavery settlers in Kansas. Three years later, Brown led a raid on a gun warehouse in Harpers Ferry, Virginia. This painting shows Brown being led to his execution, as northerners imagined the scene. ★ **Why do you think many abolitionists did not support John Brown?**

Source: *America Firsthand,* Volume 1, *From Settlement to Reconstruction,* edited by Robert D. Marcus and David Burner, 1989.

Analyzing Primary Sources

1. The proslavery settlers mentioned in Lawrie's letter were from
   A. Ohio.
   B. Missouri.
   C. Kansas.
   D. Indiana.

2. Free-state settlers were supported by
   F. Border Ruffians.
   G. United States troops.
   H. southerners.
   J. northerners.

3. **Critical Thinking** **Recognizing Points of View** What was the point of view of each author on the issue of slavery in Kansas?

Historical Critique

Why are both of these letters reliable sources of information, even though they are written from opposing points of view?

★ 17–1 ★ **A Nurse in the Civil War**

Introduction Louisa May Alcott is best known as the author of the classic novel *Little Women*. During the Civil War, Alcott worked at the Union Hospital in the Georgetown area of Washington. She wrote letters home about her experiences as a volunteer nurse. The letters were later published under the title *Hospital Sketches*.

Vocabulary Before you read the selection, find the meanings of these words in a dictionary: **vilest, chronic, premises, fortitude, feebly, comrade, draughts, admonished, tenanted.**

★ ★ ★ ★ ★ ★ ★ ★ ★

The first thing I met was a regiment of the vilest odors that ever assaulted the human nose . . . and the worst of this affliction was, everyone had assured me that it was a chronic weakness of all hospitals, and I must bear it. I did, armed with lavender water, with which I so besprinkled myself and premises, that, like my friend, Sairy, I was soon known among my patients as "the nurse with the bottle." . . . I progressed by slow stages up stairs and down, till the main hall was reached, and I paused to take breath and a survey. There they were! "our brave boys," as the papers justly call them, for cowards could hardly have been so riddled with shot and shell, so torn and shattered, nor have borne suffering for which we have no name, with an uncomplaining fortitude, which made one glad to cherish each as a brother. In they came, some on stretchers, some in men's arms, some feebly staggering along propped on rude crutches, and one lay stark and still with covered face, as a comrade gave his name to be recorded before they carried him away to the dead house. All was hurry and confusion; the hall was full of these wrecks of humanity, for the most exhausted could not reach a bed till duly ticketed and registered; the walls were lined with rows of such as could sit, the floor covered with the more disabled, the steps and doorways filled with helpers and lookers on; the sound of many feet and voices made that usually quiet hour as noisy as noon; and, in the midst of it all, the matron's motherly face brought more comfort to many a poor soul, than the cordial draughts she administered, or the cheery words that welcomed all, making of the hospital a home.

The sight of several stretchers, each with its legless, armless, or desperately wounded occupant, entering my ward, admonished me that I was there to work, not to wonder or weep; so I corked up my feelings, and returned to the path of duty, which was rather

Viewing **HISTORY** **Nurse and Patient**

This detail is from an engraving honoring the United States Sanitary Commission. It shows a Union nurse comforting a wounded soldier by reading to him. In the Confederacy, too, dedicated women volunteered their time to care for the wounded and the sick. ★ **In what other ways did women help the war effort?**

"a hard road to travel" just then. The house had been a hotel before hospitals were needed, and many of the doors still bore their old names; some not so inappropriate as might be imaged, for my ward was in truth a *ball-room,* if gunshot wounds could christen it. Forty beds were prepared, many already tenanted by tired men who fell down anywhere, and drowsed till the smell of food roused them. Round the great stove was gathered the dreariest group I ever saw— ragged, gaunt and pale, mud to the knees, with bloody bandages untouched since put on days before; many bundled up in blankets, coats being lost or useless; and all wearing that disheartened look which proclaimed defeat.... I pitied them so much, I dared not speak to them, though, remembering all they had been through since the roust at Fredericksburg, I yearned to serve the dreariest of them all. Presently, Miss Blank tore me from my refuge behind piles of one-sleeved shirts, odd socks, bandages and lint; put basin, sponge, towels and a block of brown soap into my hands, with these appalling directions:

"Come, my dear, begin to wash as fast as you can. Tell them to take off socks, coats, and shirts, scrub them well, put on clean shirts, and the attendants will finish them off, and lay them in bed."

Source: *Hospital Sketches,* Louisa May Alcott, 1864.

Analyzing Primary Sources

1. What did Miss Blank instruct Louisa May Alcott to do?
   A. make beds
   B. wash patients
   C. change bandages
   D. move patients
2. To handle the terrible odors, Miss Alcott
   F. used lavender water.
   G. opened windows.
   H. washed the floors.
   J. used disinfectant.

3. **Critical Thinking   Recognizing Points of View** How did Louisa May Alcott view the soldiers in the hospital?

Historical Critique

Alcott was writing a letter home to her family. Do you think she included all the details of what she witnessed at the hospital? Why or why not?

★ 17–2 ★   *The Gettysburg Address*

Historical Document ★★★★★

Introduction   At the Battle of Gettysburg in July 1863, the Union army lost more than 23,000 soldiers. The Confederates lost 28,000 men. On November 19, 1863, President Abraham Lincoln visited Gettysburg to dedicate the battlefield cemetery. The brief but stirring speech President Lincoln gave on that day became known as the "Gettysburg Address."

Vocabulary   Before you read the selection, find the meanings of these words in a dictionary: **score, proposition, consecrate, hallow, detract, vain, perish.**

★ ★ ★ ★ ★ ★ ★ ★

Four score and seven years ago our fathers brought forth on this continent, a new nation, conceived in liberty, and dedicated to the proposition that all men are created equal. Now we are engaged in a great civil war, testing whether that nation, or any nation so conceived and so dedicated, can long endure. We are met on a great battlefield of that war. We have come to dedicate a portion of that field, as a final resting place for those

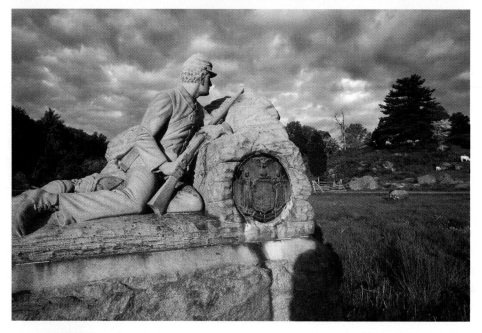

Honoring the Dead

This statue stands at the Gettysburg National Military Park in Pennsylvania. This soldier looks over the now-peaceful field, where a bloody battle took place in July 1863. ★ **What was the outcome of the Battle of Gettysburg?**

who here gave their lives that that nation might live. It is altogether fitting and proper that we should do this. But, in a larger sense, we can not dedicate—we can not consecrate—we can not hallow—this ground. The brave men, living and dead, who struggled here, have consecrated it, far above our poor power to add or detract. The world will little note, nor long remember what we say here, but it can never forget what they did here. It is for us the living, rather, to be dedicated here to the unfinished work which they who fought here have thus far so nobly advanced.

It is rather for us to be here dedicated to the great task remaining before us—that from these honored dead we take increased devotion to that cause for which they gave the last full measure of devotion—that we here highly resolve that these dead shall not have died in vain—that this nation, under God, shall have a new birth of freedom—and that government of the people, by the people, for the people, shall not perish from the earth.

Source: *The Annals of America,* Volume 9, *The Crisis of the Union,* 1976.

Analyzing Primary Sources

1. What is this speech mainly about?
   A. the Declaration of Independence
   B. our nation's founders
   C. the Civil War
   D. President Lincoln

2. At what occasion was this speech given?
   F. the dedication of a cemetery
   G. the Battle of Gettysburg
   H. President Lincoln's inauguration
   J. the end of the Civil War

3. Critical Thinking   Analyzing Ideas
Give examples of how Lincoln uses this speech to try to remind people of the ideals upon which the United States was founded.

Historical Critique

In addition to honoring the dead, is Lincoln trying to gain support for a particular cause? Explain.

★ 18–1 ★ **A Southerner Looks to the Future**

Introduction Susan Bradford was the daughter of a Florida planter. In November 1866, she married Nicholas Eppes, who had fought in the Confederate army. His family owned a plantation near Tallahassee. Before her marriage, she kept a diary. Later, Susan Bradford Eppes used her diary and her experiences before and after the war to write books about the South.

Vocabulary Before you read the selection, find the meanings of these words in a dictionary: **fret, invalid, dispatch, proffer, proposition, recoup, impoverished.**

★ ★ ★ ★ ★ ★ ★ ★ ★

January 1st, 1866.—A New Year but a Happy New Year? No indeed. We got up this morning to find ourselves the only occupants of Pine Hill plantation. It was a clean sweep, all were gone.... Not a servant, not one and we unused to work....

January 2nd, 1866.—I have slept well and I feel decidedly better. I am not going to fret because the negroes are gone, nor will I bother my brains as to their whereabouts. I am going to learn to do all these things that need doing and bye and bye I shall do them well....

February 17th, 1866.—The house party is a thing of the past and will be long remembered.... Mrs. Miller is a sweet old lady, a South Carolinian by birth, who married a Northern man. Her invalid son, Lieutenant Charles Miller, excited my pity to such an extent that I have tried to forget his blue [Yankee] uniform and remember only that he suffers. I think the almost constant contact with the sick and wounded soldiers in our own army has automatically made me tender of those who are ill....

Our own boys tease me about my "sick Yankee," but I think it is right or I would not do it....

March 1st, 1866.—Little Diary, I have tried hard to tell you my secret but there are some things too sacred to write about. My Soldier in Gray has held by promise for many months and, before the year is out, we expect to be married....

March 14th, 1866.—Riding horse-back with My Soldier this afternoon I told him...I had heard Mr. Coolidge [a Yankee officer] was related to him and if that was so I wanted to know why he did not make friends with him? He looked very serious and I was beginning to fear I had hurt him in some unknown way.

At last he spoke, "I have never mentioned my cousin, Sidney Coolidge to you; he came to Florida to visit our family prior to the war....I loved my cousin Sidney and looked forward to the visit, which he had promised us at some future time.

"The war came on and during the whole four years of war, I was in the thickest of the fighting. After Gettysburg I was promoted and assigned to the Army of the West. One day I was sent to carry a dispatch for my general. Crossing the field of Chickamauga, I was hit by a bullet;...I was stunned but soon recovered, delivered the dispatch and turned to go. An officer who knew me, laid his hand on my arm and said:

"'Your cousin, Colonel Coolidge, lies dead in that tent, don't you want to go and look at him?'....

"Now, this young lieutenant you like so much, is probably a relative...but this is the way I feel about it; if the Confederates had been the victorious army and I had been occupying the conquered country, if, in fact, our positions could be reversed, I should look him up, claim the tie of blood and proffer the hand of friendship. As things stand, he is the conqueror, I am the conquered and if any advances are made they must come from him...."

July 21st, 1866.—This is the anniversary of the Battle of Manassas. How hopeful we were then and it seems ages ago, so much has crowded into life in these last years....

August 26th, 1866.—We have to look ahead and plan for the fall wedding which My Soldier pleads for.... I do not want a grand wedding such as my sisters had; circumstances are so different now. Father's fortune has been swept away by the results of the war. It is true, he still has his land but that is almost valueless at present and it may never bring in anything again as land without labor is a poor proposition.

Father has aged since the surrender and he will never be able to recoup his losses. All this show and expense is wholly unnecessary. What I would like would be a pretty wedding dress, every girl wants that, but I want a quiet wedding with my family and his family present and some of his friends and some of my friends for attendants....

October 5th, 1866.—My dress has been bought....[Mother] has let all our friends know that "no wedding presents must be sent." She says the South is impoverished, there are few who can afford to give a handsome gift and yet almost every one will spend that which they can ill-afford, rather than be outdone in general giving. I am well satisfied with this arrangement....

November 1st, 1866.—My dear little friend...I am telling you goodbye. Whatever the future may bring me of weal or woe will not be recorded. This is MY DAY, my wedding day.

Source: *Through Some Eventful Years,* Susan Bradford Eppes, 1926.

Viewing History — The End of the Confederacy

In Richard Brooke's painting Furling the Flag, *Confederate soldiers weep as they roll up their flag for the last time. The end of the Civil War was a difficult time for southerners. Black and white, they had to adjust to a new world.*

★ **Compare the mood of this painting to the feelings Susan Bradford Eppes expressed in her diary. How are they similar? How are they different?**

1. Why did Susan Bradford Eppes want a simple wedding?
   A. She was marrying a Yankee officer.
   B. She was sad about the South's defeat.
   C. The family's servants had all left.
   D. The war left her family poor.

2. This passage is mainly about the
   F. effects of the Civil War on the author's life.
   G. major battles of the Civil War.
   H. author's plans for her wedding.
   J. conflicts between Yankee and Confederate officers.

3. **Critical Thinking   Recognizing Points of View** How does Susan Bradford Eppes reveal her feelings about the South after the war?

Historical Critique

Eppes did not publish her diary at the time it was written. She selected certain passages to include in a book nearly 60 years later. What information would help you judge the reliability of the published diary as a source of information?

★ 18–2 ★   Out From This Place

Introduction   *Out From This Place* by Joyce Hansen is a novel about African American life at the start of Reconstruction. In the final chapter, Easter, a freed slave, writes a letter to Miss Grantley, the woman who taught her how to read. Easter describes what she finally decided to do with her life. The letter also describes what life was like for freedmen in a small South Carolina town.

★ ★ ★ ★ ★ ★ ★ ★ ★

March 31, 1866

Dear Miss Grantley,

I hope this letter finds you enjoying the best of health. Please forgive me for taking so long to write to you, but it took me this long to make another decision. First, let me tell you how our town is coming along. We call it New Canaan. We have a church, a school, and we are building a molasses mill and a general store. Some of the people still work for the Williams family to make extra money for the land they purchased.

Miss Fortune moved to the cabin that was built next to the school especially for the teacher. We call it the teacher's house. The men and women take turns keeping guard, though, to make certain that the buckra don't come and burn down our school as they

try to do last week. Miss Fortune smelled the smoke and saw the men who set the fire riding away. She say it looked like they was wearing some kind of hood. Thank God we put the fire out before it made much damage. And to think we told her to come and live among us because we thought she would be safer with us than in the cottage near the big house!

Some bad news. Miriam and several other children died from a terrible fever. Brother Thomas still cannot talk and cannot walk by himself. But we pray that one day he'll be better.

Now for my life. I have decided, first, not to marry Julius but to go back to the old Rebel camp and find Mariah and Gabriel. Remember I tell you about them? If Obi is searching for me, he'll go to them because that's where he last left me. I went to the Freedmen's Bureau even though I said I wasn't going again, and I was told that they have a list from a colored regiment. They will write to me when they get more information.

Jason joined a medicine show. I got a letter from him and he says he is happy and fine. I miss him so much.

Now for the big news and decision: I want to go to the school in Philadelphia. We don't

Many northern teachers, both black and white, went to the South during Reconstruction. Their first task was to teach freedmen to read and write. This engraving shows a classroom in Vicksburg, Mississippi. ★ **Why are there so many adults in this classroom?**

PRIMARY SCHOOL FOR FREEDMEN, IN CHARGE OF Mrs. GREEN, AT VICKSBURG, MISSISSIPPI.

have enough schools or teachers to go around. Our small schoolhouse is full to overflowing, with some of the children coming from the Riverview plantation. Rose and Miss Fortune helped me to make up my mind to go to Philadelphia. Also, Miss Fortune said that I could live with her family while I attended the school. That made me feel less afraid about going. I have a welcome letter from her family already saying that I do not have to worry about my room and board.

So, my dear Miss Grantley, I hope you are happy and excited about my decision as I am. I hope it's not too late for me to attend the school. I saved a little bit of money, and Rose and a few of the other people want to help pay some of the costs too. I look forward to hearing from you soon. I am, as always,

Your Friend and Student,
Easter

Source: *Out From This Place,* Joyce Hansen, 1988.

Analyzing Literature

1. What decision does Easter make about her future?
   A. She wants to work for the Freedmen's Bureau.
   B. She wants to buy some land.
   C. She wants to go to school.
   D. She wants to work for the Williams family.

2. Where is Easter planning to go and live?
   F. Philadelphia
   G. the Williams plantation
   H. the Riverview plantation
   J. New Canaan

3. **Critical Thinking   Drawing Conclusions** Based on this reading, what impression does the author want to create about freed slaves in the South during Reconstruction?

Historical Critique

Could you use this letter as an authentic historical document about Reconstruction in the South? Why or why not?

Reference Section

★ The Declaration of Independence ★

On June 7, 1776, the Continental Congress approved the resolution that "these United Colonies are, and of right ought to be, free and independent States." Congress then appointed a committee to write a declaration of independence. The committee members were John Adams, Benjamin Franklin, Robert Livingston, Roger Sherman, and Thomas Jefferson.

Jefferson actually wrote the Declaration, but he got advice from the others. On July 2, Congress discussed the Declaration and made some changes. On July 4, 1776, it adopted the Declaration of Independence in its final form.

The Declaration is printed in black. The headings have been added to show the parts of the Declaration. They are not part of the original text. Annotations, or explanations, are on the tan side of the page. Page numbers in the annotations show where a subject is discussed in the text. Difficult words are defined.

dissolve: break **powers of the earth:** other nations **station:** place **impel:** force

The colonists feel that they must explain to the world the reasons why they are breaking away from England.

endowed: given **unalienable rights:** so basic that they cannot be taken away *secure:* protect *instituted:* set up *deriving:* getting *alter:* change *effect:* bring about

People set up governments to protect their basic rights. Governments get their power from the consent of the governed. If a government takes away the basic rights of the people, the people have the right to change the government.

prudence: wisdom *transient:* temporary, passing *disposed:* likely *usurpations:* taking and using powers that do not belong to a person *invariably:* always *evinces a design to reduce them under absolute despotism:* makes a clear plan to put them under complete and unjust control *sufferance:* endurance

When in the course of human events it becomes necessary for one people to dissolve the political bands which have connected them with another and to assume, among the powers of the earth, the separate and equal station to which the laws of nature and of nature's God entitle them, a decent respect to the opinions of mankind requires that they should declare the causes which impel them to the separation.

The Purpose of Government Is to Protect Basic Rights

We hold these truths to be self-evident, that all men are created equal; that they are endowed by their Creator with certain unalienable rights; that among these are life, liberty, and the pursuit of happiness. That, to secure these rights, governments are instituted among men, deriving their just powers from the consent of the governed; that, whenever any form of government becomes destructive of these ends, it is the right of the people to alter or to abolish it, and to institute a new government, laying its foundation on such principles and organizing its powers in such form, as to them shall seem most likely to effect their safety and happiness. Prudence, indeed, will dictate that governments long established should not be changed for light and transient causes; and, accordingly, all experience hath shown that mankind are more disposed to suffer, while evils are sufferable, than to right themselves by abolishing the forms to which they are accustomed. But when a long train of abuses and usurpations, pursuing invariably the same object, evinces a design to reduce them under absolute despotism, it is their right, it is their duty, to throw off such government and to provide new guards for their future security. Such has been the patient sufferance of these colonies, and such is now the necessity which constrains them to alter their former systems of government. The history of the present King of Great Britain is a history of repeated injuries and usurpations, all having, in direct object, the establishment of an absolute tyranny over these States. To prove this, let facts be submitted to a candid world:

Wrongs Done by the King

He has refused his assent to laws the most wholesome and necessary for the public good.

He has forbidden his governors to pass laws of immediate and pressing importance, unless suspended in their operation till his assent should be obtained; and, when so suspended, he has utterly neglected to attend to them.

He has refused to pass other laws for the accommodation of the large districts of people, unless those people would relinquish the right of representation in the legislature; a right inestimable to them and formidable to tyrants only.

He has called together legislative bodies at places unusual, uncomfortable, and distant from the depository of their public records, for the sole purpose of fatiguing them into compliance with his measures.

He has dissolved representative houses, repeatedly for opposing, with manly firmness, his invasions on the rights of the people.

He has refused, for a long time after such dissolutions, to cause others to be elected: whereby the legislative powers, incapable of annihilation, have returned to the people at large for their exercise; the state remaining, in the meantime, exposed to all the danger of invasion from without and convulsions within.

He has endeavored to prevent the population of these States; for that purpose, obstructing the laws for naturalization of foreigners, refusing to pass others to encourage their migration hither, and raising the conditions of new appropriations of lands.

He has obstructed the administration of justice by refusing his assent to laws for establishing judiciary powers.

He has made judges dependent on his will alone for the tenure of their offices and the amount and payment of their salaries.

He has erected a multitude of new offices and sent hither swarms of officers to harass our people and eat out their substance.

He has kept among us, in time of peace, standing armies, without the consent of our legislatures.

He has affected to render the military independent of, and superior to, the civil power.

He has combined with others to subject us to a jurisdiction foreign to our Constitution and unacknowledged by our laws, giving his assent to their acts of pretended legislation—

For quartering large bodies of armed troops among us;

constrains: forces *absolute tyranny:* harsh and unjust government *candid:* free from prejudice

People do not change governments for slight reasons. But they are forced to do so when a government becomes tyrannical. King George III has a long record of abusing his power.

assent: approval *relinquish:* give up *inestimable:* too great a value to be measured *formidable:* causing fear

This part of the Declaration spells out three sets of wrongs that led the colonists to break with Britain.

The first set of wrongs is the king's unjust use of power. The king refused to approve laws that are needed. He has tried to control the colonial legislatures.

depository: storehouse *fatiguing:* tiring out *compliance:* giving in *dissolved:* broken up *annihilation:* total destruction *convulsions:* disturbances

The king has tried to force colonial legislatures into doing his will by wearing them out. He has dissolved legislatures (such as those of Massachusetts). (See page 90.)

endeavored: tried *obstructing:* blocking *naturalization:* process of becoming a citizen *migration:* moving *hither:* here *appropriations:* grants *obstructed the administration of justice:* prevented justice from being done *judiciary powers:* system of law courts *tenure:* term (of office) *erected:* set up *multitude:* large number *swarms:* huge crowds *harass:* cause trouble *render:* make

Among other wrongs, he has refused to let settlers move west to take up new land. He has prevented justice from being done. Also, he has sent large numbers of customs officials to cause problems for the colonists.

jurisdiction: authority

quartering: housing

mock: false

The king has joined with others, meaning Parliament, to make laws for the colonies. The Declaration then lists the second set of wrongs—unjust acts of Parliament.

imposing: forcing **depriving:** taking away **transporting us beyond seas:** sending colonists to England for trial **neighboring province:** Quebec **arbitrary government:** unjust rule **fit instrument:** suitable tool **invested with power:** having the power

During the years leading up to 1776, the colonists claimed that Parliament had no right to make laws for them because they were not represented in Parliament. Here, the colonists object to recent laws of Parliament, such as the Quartering Act and the blockade of colonial ports (page 90), which cut off their trade. They also object to Parliament's claim that it had the right to tax them without their consent.

abdicated: given up **plundered:** robbed **ravaged:** attacked **mercenaries:** hired soldiers **desolation:** misery **perfidy:** falseness **barbarous:** uncivilized **constrained:** forced **brethren:** brothers **domestic insurrections:** internal revolts

Here, the Declaration lists the third set of wrongs—warlike acts of the king. Instead of listening to the colonists, the king has made war on them. He has hired soldiers to fight in America.

oppressions: harsh rule **petitioned:** asked **redress:** relief **unwarrantable jurisdiction over:** unfair authority **magnanimity:** generosity **conjured:** called upon **common kindred:** relatives **disavow:** turn away from **consanguinity:** blood relationships, kinship **acquiesce:** agree **denounces:** speaks out against

During this time, colonists have repeatedly asked for relief. But their requests have brought only more suffering. They have appealed to the British people but received no help. So they are forced to separate.

For protecting them by a mock trial from punishment for any murders which they should commit on the inhabitants of these States;

For cutting off our trade with all parts of the world;

For imposing taxes on us without our consent;

For depriving us, in many cases, of the benefit of trial by jury;

For transporting us beyond seas to be tried for pretended offences;

For abolishing the free system of English laws in a neighboring province, establishing therein an arbitrary government, and enlarging its boundaries, so as to render it at once an example and fit instrument for introducing the same absolute rule into these colonies;

For taking away our charters, abolishing our most valuable laws, and altering, fundamentally, the powers of our governments;

For suspending our own legislatures and declaring themselves invested with power to legislate for us in all cases whatsoever.

He has abdicated government here by declaring us out of his protection and waging war against us.

He has plundered our seas, ravaged our coasts, burnt out towns, and destroyed the lives of our people.

He is, at this time, transporting large armies of foreign mercenaries to complete the works of death, desolation, and tyranny already begun with circumstances of cruelty and perfidy scarcely paralleled in the most barbarous ages, and totally unworthy, the head of a civilized nation.

He has constrained our fellow citizens, taken captive on the high seas, to bear arms against their country, to become the executioners of their friends and brethren, or to fall themselves by their hands.

He has excited domestic insurrections amongst us and has endeavored to bring on the inhabitants of our frontiers, the merciless Indian savages, whose known rule of warfare is an undistinguished destruction of all ages, sexes, and conditions.

In every state of these oppressions, we have petitioned for redress in the most humble terms; our repeated petitions have been answered only by repeated injury. A prince whose character is thus marked by every act which may define a tyrant is unfit to be the ruler of a free people.

Nor have we been wanting in attention to our British brethren. We have warned them, from time to time, of attempts made by their legislature to extend an unwarrantable jurisdiction over us. We have reminded them of the circumstances of our emigration and settlement here. We have appealed to their native justice and magnanimity, and we have conjured them, by the ties of our common kindred, to disavow these usurpations, which would inevitably interrupt our connections and correspondence. They, too, have been deaf to the voice of justice and consanguinity. We must, therefore, acquiesce in the necessity which denounces our separation, and hold them, as we hold the rest of mankind, enemies in war, in peace, friends.

Colonies Declare Independence

We, therefore, the representatives of the United States of America, in general Congress assembled, appealing to the Supreme Judge of the world for the rectitude of our intentions, do, in the name and by the authority of the good people of these colonies, solemnly publish and declare, that these united colonies are, and of right ought to be, free and independent states: that they are absolved from all allegiance to the British Crown, and that all political connection between them and the state of Great Britain is, and ought to be, totally dissolved; and that, as free and independent states, they have full power to levy war, conclude peace, contract alliances, establish commerce, and to do all other acts and things which independent states may of right do. And, for the support of this declaration, with a firm reliance on the protection of Divine Providence, we mutually pledge to each other our lives, our fortunes, and our sacred honor.

appealing: calling on **rectitude of our intentions:** moral rightness of our plans **absolved from all allegiance:** freed from loyalty **levy war:** declare war **contract alliances:** make treaties

As the representatives of the United States, they declare that the colonies are free and independent states.

The states need no longer be loyal to the British king. They are an independent nation that can make war and sign treaties.

Relying on help from Divine Providence, the signers of the Declaration promise their lives, money, and honor to fight for independence.

★ Signers of the Declaration of Independence ★

John Hancock, President
Charles Thomson,
Secretary

New Hampshire
Josiah Bartlett
William Whipple
Matthew Thornton

Massachusetts
Samuel Adams
John Adams
Robert Treat Paine
Elbridge Gerry

Rhode Island
Stephen Hopkins
William Ellery

Connecticut
Roger Sherman
Samuel Huntington
William Williams
Oliver Wolcott

Delaware
Caesar Rodney
George Read
Thomas McKean

New York
William Floyd
Philip Livingston
Francis Lewis
Lewis Morris

New Jersey
Richard Stockton
John Witherspoon
Francis Hopkinson
John Hart
Abraham Clark

Georgia
Button Gwinnett
Lyman Hall
George Walton

Maryland
Samuel Chase
William Paca
Thomas Stone
Charles Carroll

North Carolina
William Hooper
Joseph Hewes
John Penn

Virginia
George Wythe
Richard Henry Lee
Thomas Jefferson
Benjamin Harrison
Thomas Nelson, Jr.
Francis Lightfoot Lee
Carter Braxton

South Carolina
Edward Rutledge
Thomas Heyward, Jr.
Thomas Lynch, Jr.
Arthur Middleton

Pennsylvania
Robert Morris
Benjamin Rush
Benjamin Franklin
John Morton
George Clymer
James Smith
George Taylor
James Wilson
George Ross

★ The Constitution ★
of the United States of America

The Constitution is printed in black. The titles of articles, sections, and clauses are not part of the original document. They have been added to help you find information in the Constitution. Some words or lines are crossed out because they have been changed by amendments or no longer apply. Annotations, or explanations, are on the tan side of the page. Page numbers in the annotations show where a subject is discussed in the text. Difficult words are defined.

The Preamble describes the purpose of the government set up by the Constitution. Americans expect their government to defend justice and liberty and provide peace and safety from foreign enemies.

The Constitution gives Congress the power to make laws. Congress is divided into the Senate and the House of Representatives.

Clause 1 *Electors* refers to voters. Members of the House of Representatives are elected every two years. Any citizen allowed to vote for members of the larger house of the state legislature can also vote for members of the House.

Clause 2 A member of the House of Representatives must be at least 25 years old, an American citizen for 7 years, and a resident of the state he or she represents.

Clause 3 The number of representatives each state elects is based on its population. An *enumeration,* or census, must be taken every 10 years to determine population. Today, the number of representatives in the House is fixed at 435.

This is the famous Three-Fifths Compromise worked out at the Constitutional Convention (page 124). *Persons bound to service* meant indentured servants. *All other persons* meant slaves. All free people in a state were counted. However, only three fifths of the slaves were included in the population count. This three-fifths clause became meaningless when slaves were freed by the Thirteenth Amendment.

Preamble

We the people of the United States, in order to form a more perfect Union, establish justice, insure domestic tranquillity, provide for the common defense, promote the general welfare, and secure the blessings of liberty to ourselves and our posterity, do ordain and establish this Constitution for the United States of America.

Article 1. The Legislative Branch

Section 1. A Two-House Legislature

All legislative powers herein granted shall be vested in a Congress of the United States, which shall consist of a Senate and House of Representatives.

Section 2. House of Representatives

1. Election of Members The House of Representatives shall be composed of members chosen every second year by the people of the several states, and the electors in each state shall have the qualifications requisite for electors of the most numerous branch of the state legislature.

2. Qualifications No person shall be a Representative who shall not have attained to the age of twenty-five years, and been seven years a citizen of the United States, and who shall not, when elected, be an inhabitant of that state in which he shall be chosen.

3. Determining Representation Representatives and direct taxes shall be apportioned among the several states which may be included within this Union, according to their respective numbers which shall be determined by adding to the whole number of free persons, including those bound to service for a term of years, and excluding Indians not taxed, three-fifths of all other persons. The actual enumeration shall be made within three years after the first meeting of the Congress of the United States, and within every subsequent term of ten years, in such manner as they shall by law direct. The number of Representatives shall not exceed one for every 30,000, but each state shall have at least one Representative; and until such enumeration shall be made, the state of New Hampshire shall be entitled to choose three; Massachusetts, eight; Rhode Island and Providence Plantations, one; Connecticut, five; New York, six; New Jersey, four; Pennsylvania, eight; Delaware, one; Maryland, six; Virginia, ten; North Carolina, five; South Carolina, five; and Georgia, three.

4. Filling Vacancies When vacancies happen in the representation from any state, the executive authority thereof shall issue writs of election to fill such vacancies.

5. Selection of Officers; Power of Impeachment The House of Representatives shall choose their Speaker and other officers; and shall have the sole power of impeachment.

Section 3. The Senate

1. Selection of Members The Senate of the United States shall be composed of two Senators from each state chosen by the legislature thereof, for six years, and each Senator shall have one vote.

2. Alternating Terms; Filling Vacancies Immediately after they shall be assembled in consequence of the first election, they shall be divided as equally as may be into three classes. The seats of the Senators of the first class shall be vacated at the expiration of the second year, of the second class at the expiration of the fourth year, and of the third class at the expiration of the sixth year, so that one-third may be chosen every second year; and if vacancies happen by resignation, or otherwise, during the recess of the legislature of any state, the executive thereof may make temporary appointments until the next meeting of the legislature, which shall then fill such vacancies.

3. Qualifications No person shall be a Senator who shall not have attained to the age of thirty years, and been nine years a citizen of the United States, and who shall not, when elected, be an inhabitant of that state for which he shall be chosen.

4. President of the Senate The Vice-President of the United States shall be president of the Senate, but shall have no vote, unless they be equally divided.

5. Election of Senate Officers The Senate shall choose their other officers, and also a president *pro tempore,* in the absence of the Vice-President, or when he shall exercise the office of the President of the United States.

6. Impeachment Trials The Senate shall have the sole power to try all impeachments. When sitting for that purpose, they shall be on oath or affirmation. When the President of the United States is tried, the Chief Justice shall preside; and no person shall be convicted without the concurrence of two-thirds of the members present.

Clause 4 *Executive authority* means the governor of a state. If a member of the House leaves office before his or her term ends, the governor must call a special election to fill the seat.

Clause 5 The House elects a speaker. Today, the speaker is usually chosen by the party that has a majority in the House. Also, only the House has the power to *impeach,* or accuse, a federal official of wrongdoing.

Clause 1 Each state has two senators. Senators serve for six-year terms. The Seventeenth Amendment changed the way senators were elected.

Clause 2 Every two years, one third of the senators run for reelection. Thus, the makeup of the Senate is never totally changed by any one election. The Seventeenth Amendment changed the way of filling *vacancies,* or empty seats. Today, the governor of a state must choose a senator to fill a vacancy that occurs between elections.

Clause 3 A senator must be at least 30 years old, an American citizen for 9 years, and a resident of the state he or she represents.

Clause 4 The Vice President presides over Senate meetings, but he or she can vote only to break a tie.

Clause 5 *Pro tempore* means temporary. The Senate chooses one of its members to serve as president pro tempore when the Vice President is absent.

Clause 6 The Senate acts as a jury if the House impeaches a federal official. The Chief Justice of the Supreme Court presides if the President is on trial. Two thirds of all senators present must vote for *conviction,* or finding the accused guilty. No President has ever been convicted. The House impeached President Andrew Johnson in 1868, but the Senate acquitted him of the charges (page 413). In 1974, President Richard Nixon resigned before he could be impeached.

Clause 7 If an official is found guilty by the Senate, he or she can be removed from office and barred from holding federal office in the future. These are the only punishments the Senate can impose. However, the convicted official can still be tried in a criminal court.

Clause 1 Each state legislature can decide when and how congressional elections take place, but Congress can overrule these decisions. In 1842, Congress required each state to set up congressional districts with one representative elected from each district. In 1872, Congress decided that congressional elections must be held in every state on the same date in even-numbered years.

Clause 2 Congress must meet at least once a year. The Twentieth Amendment moved the opening date of Congress to January 3.

Clause 1 Each house decides whether a member has the qualifications for office set by the Constitution. A *quorum* is the smallest number of members who must be present for business to be conducted. Each house can set its own rules about absent members.

Clause 2 Each house can make rules for the conduct of members. It can only expel a member by a two-thirds vote.

Clause 3 Each house keeps a record of its meetings. *The Congressional Record* is published every day with excerpts from speeches made in each house. It also records the votes of each member.

Clause 4 Neither house can *adjourn,* or stop meeting, for more than three days unless the other house approves. Both houses of Congress must meet in the same city.

Clause 1 *Compensation* means salary. Congress decides the salary for its members. While Congress is in session, a member is free from arrest in civil cases and cannot be sued for anything he or she says on the floor of Congress. This allows for freedom of debate. However, a member can be arrested for a criminal offense.

7. Penalties Upon Conviction Judgment in cases of impeachment shall not extend further than to removal from office, and disqualification to hold and enjoy any office of honor, trust, or profit under the United States; but the party convicted shall nevertheless be liable and subject to indictment, trial, judgment, and punishment, according to law.

Section 4. Elections and Meetings

1. Election of Congress The times, places, and manner of holding elections for Senators and Representatives shall be prescribed in each state by the legislature thereof; but the Congress may at any time by law make or alter such regulations, except as to the places of choosing Senators.

2. Annual Sessions The Congress shall assemble at least once in every year, ~~and such meeting shall be on the first Monday in December, unless they shall by law appoint a different day.~~

Section 5. Rules for the Conduct of Business

1. Organization Each house shall be the judge of the elections, returns, and qualifications of its own members, and a majority of each shall constitute a quorum to do business; but a smaller number may adjourn from day to day, and may be authorized to compel the attendance of absent members, in such manner, and under such penalties, as each house may provide.

2. Procedures Each house may determine the rules of its proceedings, punish its members for disorderly behavior, and with the concurrence of two-thirds, expel a member.

3. A Written Record Each house shall keep a journal of its proceedings, and from time to time publish the same, excepting such parts as may in their judgment require secrecy; and the yeas and nays of the members of either house on any question shall, at the desire of one-fifth of those present, be entered on the journal.

4. Rules for Adjournment Neither house, during the session of Congress, shall, without the consent of the other, adjourn for more than three days, nor to any other place than that in which the two houses shall be sitting.

Section 6. Privileges and Restrictions

1. Salaries and Immunities The Senators and Representatives shall receive a compensation for their services, to be ascertained by law and paid out of the Treasury of the United States. They shall in all cases, except treason, felony, and breach of the peace, be privileged from arrest during their attendance at the session of their respective houses, and in going to and returning from the same; and for any speech or debate in either house, they shall not be questioned in any other place.

2. Restrictions on Other Employment No Senator or Representative shall, during the time for which he was elected, be appointed to any civil office under the authority of the United States, which shall have been created, or the emoluments whereof shall have been increased, during such time; and no person holding any office under the United States shall be a member of either house during his continuance in office.

Section 7. Law-Making Process

1. Tax Bills All bills for raising revenue shall originate in the House of Representatives; but the Senate may propose or concur with amendments as on other bills.

2. How a Bill Becomes a Law Every bill which shall have passed the House of Representatives and the Senate shall, before it become a law, be presented to the President of the United States; if he approve, he shall sign it, but if not, he shall return it, with his objections, to that house in which it shall have originated, who shall enter the objections at large on their journal, and proceed to reconsider it. If after such reconsideration two-thirds of that house shall agree to pass the bill, it shall be sent, together with the objections, to the other house, by which it shall likewise be reconsidered, and, if approved by two-thirds of that house, it shall become a law. But in all such cases the votes of both houses shall be determined by yeas and nays, and the names of the persons voting for and against the bill shall be entered on the journal of each house respectively. If any bill shall not be returned by the President within ten days (Sundays excepted) after it shall have been presented to him, the same bill shall be a law, in like manner as if he had signed it, unless the Congress by their adjournment prevent its return, in which case it shall not be a law.

3. Resolutions Passed by Congress Every order, resolution, or vote to which the concurrence of the Senate and House of Representatives may be necessary (except on a question of adjournment) shall be presented to the President of the United States; and before the same shall take effect, shall be approved by him, or being disapproved by him, shall be repassed by two-thirds of the Senate and House of Representatives, according to the rules and limitations prescribed in the case of a bill.

Section 8. Powers Delegated to Congress

The Congress shall have the power

1. Taxes To lay and collect taxes, duties, imposts, and excises, to pay the debts and provide for the common defense and general welfare of the United States; but all duties, imposts, and excises shall be uniform throughout the United States;

2. Borrowing To borrow money on the credit of the United States;

Clause 2 *Emolument* also means salary. A member of Congress cannot hold another federal office during his or her term. A former member of Congress cannot hold an office created while he or she was in Congress. An official in another branch of government cannot serve at the same time in Congress. This strengthens the separation of powers.

Clause 1 *Revenue* is money raised by the government through taxes. Tax bills must be introduced in the House. The Senate, however, can make changes in tax bills. This clause protects the principle that people can be taxed only with their consent.

Clause 2 A *bill,* or proposed law, that is passed by a majority of the House and Senate is sent to the President. If the President signs the bill, it becomes law.

A bill can also become law without the President's signature. The President can refuse to act on a bill. If Congress is in session at the time, the bill becomes law 10 days after the President receives it.

The President can *veto,* or reject, a bill by sending it back to the house where it was introduced. Or if the President refuses to act on a bill and Congress adjourns within 10 days, then the bill dies. This way of killing a bill without taking action is called the *pocket veto.*

Congress can override the President's veto if each house of Congress passes the bill again by a two-thirds vote. This clause is an important part of the system of checks and balances (page 130).

Clause 3 Congress can pass resolutions or orders that have the same force as laws. Any such resolution or order must be signed by the President (except on questions of adjournment). Thus, this clause prevents Congress from bypassing the President simply by calling a bill by another name.

Clause 1 *Duties* are tariffs. *Imposts* are taxes in general. *Excises* are taxes on the production or sale of certain goods. Congress has the power to tax and spend tax money. Taxes must be the same in all parts of the country.

Clause 2 Congress can borrow money for the United States. The government often borrows money by selling *bonds,* or certificates that promise to pay the holder a certain sum of money on a certain date (page 174).

Clause 3 Only Congress has the power to regulate foreign and *interstate trade,* or trade between states. Disagreement over interstate trade was a major problem with the Articles of Confederation (pages 117–118).

Clause 4 *Naturalization* is the process whereby a foreigner becomes a citizen. *Bankruptcy* is the condition in which a person or business cannot pay its debts. Congress has the power to pass laws on these two issues. The laws must be the same in all parts of the country.

Clause 5 Congress has the power to coin money and set its value. Congress has set up the National Bureau of Standards to regulate weights and measures.

Clause 6 *Counterfeiting* is the making of imitation money. *Securities* are bonds. Congress can make laws to punish counterfeiters.

Clause 7 Congress has the power to set up and control the delivery of mail.

Clause 8 Congress may pass copyright and patent laws. A *copyright* protects an author. A patent makes an inventor the sole owner of his or her work for a limited time.

Clause 9 Congress has the power to set up *inferior,* or lower, federal courts under the Supreme Court.

Clause 10 Congress can punish *piracy,* or the robbing of ships at sea.

Clause 11 Only Congress can declare war. Declarations of war are granted at the request of the President. *Letters of marque and reprisal* were documents issued by a government allowing merchant ships to arm themselves and attack ships of an enemy nation. They are no longer issued.

Clauses 12, 13, 14 These clauses place the army and navy under the control of Congress. Congress decides on the size of the armed forces and the amount of money to spend on the army and navy. It also has the power to write rules governing the armed forces.

Clauses 15, 16 The *militia* is a body of citizen soldiers. Congress can call up the militia to put down rebellions or fight foreign invaders. Each state has its own militia, today called the National Guard. Normally, the militia is under the command of a state's governor. However, it can be placed under the command of the President.

3. Commerce To regulate commerce with foreign nations, and among the several states, and with the Indian tribes;

4. Naturalization; Bankruptcy To establish a uniform rule of naturalization, and uniform laws on the subject of bankruptcies throughout the United States;

5. Coins; Weights; Measures To coin money, regulate the value thereof, and of foreign coin, and fix the standard of weights and measures;

6. Counterfeiting To provide for the punishment of counterfeiting the securities and current coin of the United States;

7. Post Offices To establish post offices and post roads;

8. Copyrights; Patents To promote the progress of science and useful arts by securing for limited times to authors and inventors the exclusive right to their respective writings and discoveries;

9. Federal Courts To constitute tribunals inferior to the Supreme Court;

10. Piracy To define and punish piracies and felonies committed on the high seas and offenses against the law of nations;

11. Declarations of War To declare war, ~~grant letters of marque and reprisal,~~ and make rules concerning captures on land and water;

12. Army To raise and support armies, but no appropriation of money to that use shall be for a longer term than two years;

13. Navy To provide and maintain a navy;

14. Rules for the Military To make rules for the government and regulation of the land and naval forces;

15. Militia To provide for calling forth the militia to execute the laws of the Union, suppress insurrections, and repel invasions;

16. Rules for the Militia To provide for organizing, arming, and disciplining the militia, and for governing such part of them as may be employed in the service of the United States, reserving to the states, respectively, the appointment of the officers, and the authority of training the militia according to the discipline prescribed by Congress;

17. National Capital To exercise exclusive legislation in all cases whatsoever, over such district (not exceeding ten miles square) as may, by cession of particular states, and the acceptance of Congress, become the seat of government of the United States, and to exercise like authority over all places purchased by the consent of the legislature of the state in which the same shall be, for the erection of forts, magazines, arsenals, dock-yards, and other needful buildings;—and

18. Necessary Laws To make all laws which shall be necessary and proper for carrying into execution the foregoing powers, and all other powers vested by this Constitution in the government of the United States, or in any department or officer thereof.

Section 9. Powers Denied to the Federal Government

1. The Slave Trade ~~The migration or importation of such persons as any of the states now existing shall think proper to admit shall not be prohibited by the Congress prior to the year 1808; but a tax or duty may be imposed on such importation, not exceeding $10 for each person.~~

2. Writ of Habeas Corpus The privilege of the writ of habeas corpus shall not be suspended, unless when in cases of rebellion or invasion the public safety may require it.

3. Bills of Attainder and Ex Post Facto Laws No bill of attainder or *ex post facto* law shall be passed.

4. Apportionment of Direct Taxes ~~No capitation or other direct tax shall be laid, unless in proportion to the census or enumeration herein before directed to be taken.~~

5. Taxes on Exports No tax or duty shall be laid on articles exported from any state.

6. Special Preference for Trade No preference shall be given any regulation of commerce or revenue to the ports of one state over those of another; nor shall vessels bound to, or from, one state, be obliged to enter, clear, or pay duties in another.

7. Spending No money shall be drawn from the Treasury, but in consequence of appropriations made by law; and a regular statement and account of the receipts and expenditures of all public money shall be published from time to time.

Clause 17 Congress controls the district around the national capital. In 1790, Congress made Washington, D.C., the nation's capital (page 175). In 1973, it gave residents of the District the right to elect local officials.

Clause 18 Clauses 1–17 list the powers delegated to Congress. The writers of the Constitution added Clause 18 so that Congress could deal with the changing needs of the nation. It gives Congress the power to make laws as needed to carry out the first 17 clauses. Clause 18 is sometimes called the elastic clause because it lets Congress stretch the meaning of its power.

Clause 1 *Such persons* means slaves. This clause resulted from a compromise between the supporters and the opponents of the slave trade (page 125). In 1808, as soon as Congress was permitted to abolish the slave trade, it did so. The $10 import tax was never imposed.

Clause 2 A *writ of habeas corpus* is a court order requiring government officials to bring a prisoner to court and explain why he or she is being held. A writ of habeas corpus protects people from unlawful imprisonment. The government cannot suspend this right except in times of rebellion or invasion.

Clause 3 A *bill of attainder* is a law declaring that a person is guilty of a particular crime. An *ex post facto law* punishes an act which was not illegal when it was committed. Congress cannot pass a bill of attainder or *ex post facto* laws.

Clause 4 A *capitation tax* is a tax placed directly on each person. *Direct taxes* are taxes on people or on land. They can be passed only if they are divided among the states according to population. The Sixteenth Amendment allowed Congress to tax income without regard to the population of the states.

Clause 5 This clause forbids Congress to tax exports. In 1787, southerners insisted on this clause because their economy depended on exports.

Clause 6 Congress cannot make laws that favor one state over another in trade and commerce. Also, states cannot place tariffs on interstate trade.

Clause 7 The federal government cannot spend money unless Congress *appropriates* it, or passes a law allowing it. This clause gives Congress an important check on the President by controlling the money he or she can spend. The government must publish a statement showing how it spends public funds.

Clause 8 The government cannot award titles of nobility, such as Duke or Duchess. American citizens cannot accept titles of nobility from foreign governments without the consent of Congress.

Clause 1 The writers of the Constitution did not want the states to act like separate nations. So they prohibited states from making treaties or coining money. Some powers denied to the federal government are also denied to the states. For example, states cannot pass *ex post facto* laws.

Clauses 2, 3 Powers listed here are forbidden to the states, but Congress can lift these prohibitions by passing laws that give these powers to the states.

Clause 2 forbids states from taxing imports and exports without the consent of Congress. States may charge inspection fees on goods entering the states. Any profit from these fees must be turned over to the United States Treasury.

Clause 3 forbids states from keeping an army or navy without the consent of Congress. States cannot make treaties or declare war unless an enemy invades or is about to invade.

Clause 1 The President is responsible for *executing,* or carrying out, laws passed by Congress.

Clauses 2, 3 Some writers of the Constitution were afraid to allow the people to elect the President directly (page 130). Therefore, the Constitutional Convention set up the electoral college. Clause 2 directs each state to choose electors, or delegates to the electoral college, to vote for President. A state's electoral vote is equal to the combined number of senators and representatives. Each state may decide how to choose its electors. Members of Congress and federal officeholders may not serve as electors. This much of the original electoral college system is still in effect.

Clause 3 called upon each elector to vote for two candidates. The candidate who received a majority of the electoral votes would become President. The runner-up would become Vice President. If no candidate won a majority, the House would choose the President. The Senate would choose the Vice President.

The election of 1800 showed a problem with the original electoral college system (page 189). Thomas Jefferson was the Republican candidate

8. Creation of Titles of Nobility No title of nobility shall be granted by the United States; and no person holding any office of profit or trust under them, shall, without the consent of the Congress, accept of any present, emolument, office, or title, of any kind whatever, from any king, prince, or foreign state.

Section 10. Powers Denied to the States

1. Unconditional Prohibitions No state shall enter into any treaty, alliance, or confederation; grant letters of marque and reprisal; coin money; emit bills of credit; make anything but gold and silver coin a tender in payment of debts; pass any bill of attainder, *ex post facto* law, or law impairing the obligation of contracts, or grant any title of nobility.

2. Powers Conditionally Denied No state shall, without the consent of the Congress, lay any imposts or duties on imports or exports, except what may be absolutely necessary for executing its inspection laws; and the net produce of all duties and imposts, laid by any state on imports or exports, shall be for the use of the Treasury of the United States; and all such laws shall be subject to the revision and control of the Congress.

3. Other Denied Powers No state shall, without the consent of Congress, lay any duty of tonnage, keep troops, or ships of war in time of peace, enter into any agreement or compact with another state, or with a foreign power, or engage in war, unless actually invaded, or in such imminent danger as will not admit of delay.

Article 2. The Executive Branch

Section 1. President and Vice-President

1. Chief Executive The executive power shall be vested in a President of the United States of America. He shall hold his office during the term of four years, and together with the Vice-President, chosen for the same term, be elected as follows:

2. Selection of Electors Each state shall appoint, in such manner as the legislature thereof may direct, a number of electors, equal to the whole number of Senators and Representatives to which the state may be entitled in the Congress; but no Senator or Representative, or person holding an office or trust or profit under the United States, shall be appointed an elector.

3. Electoral College Procedures The electors shall meet in their respective states, and vote by ballot for two persons, of whom one at least shall not be an inhabitant of the same state with themselves. And they shall make a list of all the persons voted for, and of the number of votes for each; which list they shall sign and certify, and transmit sealed to the seat of the government of the United States, directed to the president of the Senate. The president of the Senate shall, in the presence of the Senate and House of Representatives, open all the certificates, and the votes shall then be counted. The person having the greatest number of votes shall be President, if such number be a majority of the whole number of electors appointed; and if there be more than one who have such majority, and have an equal number of votes, then the House of Representatives shall immediately choose by ballot one of them for President; and if no person have a majority, then from the five highest on the list the said House shall in like manner choose the President. But in choosing the President the votes shall be taken by states, the representation from each state having one vote. A quorum for this purpose shall consist of a member or members from two-thirds of the states, and a majority of all the states shall be necessary to a choice. In every case, after the choice of the President, the person having the greatest number of votes of the electors shall be the Vice-President. But if there should remain two or more who have equal votes, the Senate shall choose from them by ballot the Vice-President.

4. Time of Elections The Congress may determine the time of choosing the electors, and the day on which they shall give their votes; which day shall be the same throughout the United States.

5. Qualifications for President No person except a natural-born citizen or a citizen of the United States, at the time of the adoption of this Constitution, shall be eligible to the office of the President; neither shall any person be eligible to that office who shall not have attained to the age of thirty-five years, and been fourteen years a resident within the United States.

6. Presidential Succession In case of the removal of the President from office, or of his death, resignation, or inability to discharge the powers and duties of the said office, the same shall devolve on the Vice-President, and the Congress may by law provide for the case of removal, death, resignation, or inability, both of the President and Vice-President, declaring what officer shall then act as President, and such officer shall act accordingly, until the disability be removed, or a President shall be elected.

7. Salary The President shall, at stated times, receive for his services, a compensation, which shall neither be increased nor diminished during the period for which he shall have been elected, and he shall not receive within that period any other emolument from the United States, or any of them.

8. Oath of Office Before he enter on the execution of his office, he shall take the following oath or affirmation:—"I do solemnly swear (or affirm) that I will faithfully execute the office of President of the United States, and will to the best of my ability, preserve, protect, and defend the Constitution of the United States."

for President, and Aaron Burr was the Republican candidate for Vice President. In the electoral college, the vote ended in a tie. The election was finally decided in the House, where Jefferson was chosen President. The Twelfth Amendment changed the electoral college system so that this could not happen again.

Clause 4 By a law passed in 1792, electors are chosen on the Tuesday after the first Monday of November every four years. Electors from each state meet to vote in December.

Today, voters in each state choose *slates,* or groups, of electors who are pledged to a candidate for President. The candidate for President who wins the popular vote in each state wins that state's electoral vote.

Clause 5 The President must be a citizen of the United States from birth, at least 35 years old, and a resident of the country for 14 years. The first seven Presidents of the United States were born under British rule, but they were allowed to hold office because they were citizens at the time the Constitution was adopted.

Clause 6 The powers of the President pass to the Vice President if the President leaves office or cannot discharge his or her duties. The wording of this clause caused confusion the first time a President died in office. When President William Henry Harrison died, it was uncertain whether Vice President John Tyler should remain Vice President and act as President or whether he should be sworn in as President. Tyler persuaded a federal judge to swear him in. So he set the precedent that the Vice President assumes the office of President when it becomes vacant. The Twenty-fifth Amendment replaced this clause.

Clause 7 The President is paid a salary. It cannot be raised or lowered during his or her term of office. The President is not allowed to hold any other federal or state position while in office. Today, the President's salary is $200,000 a year.

Clause 8 Before taking office, the President must promise to protect and defend the Constitution. Usually, the Chief Justice of the Supreme Court gives the oath of office to the President.

Clause 1 The President is head of the armed forces and the state militias when they are called into national service. So the military is under *civilian,* or nonmilitary, control.

The President can get advice from the heads of executive departments. In most cases, the President has the power to grant a reprieve or pardon. A *reprieve* suspends punishment ordered by law. A *pardon* prevents prosecution for a crime or overrides the judgment of a court.

Clause 2 The President has the power to make treaties with other nations. Under the system of checks and balances, all treaties must be approved by two thirds of the Senate. Today, the President also makes agreements with foreign governments. These executive agreements do not need Senate approval.

The President has the power to appoint ambassadors to foreign countries and to appoint other high officials. The Senate must *confirm,* or approve, these appointments.

Clause 3 If the Senate is in *recess,* or not meeting, the President may fill vacant government posts by making temporary appointments.

The President must give Congress a report on the condition of the nation every year. This report is now called the State of the Union Address. Since 1913, the President has given this speech in person each January.

The President can call a special session of Congress and can adjourn Congress if necessary. The President has the power to receive, or recognize, foreign ambassadors.

The President must carry out the laws. Today, many government agencies oversee the execution of laws.

Civil officers include federal judges and members of the Cabinet. *High crimes* are major crimes. *Misdemeanors* are lesser crimes. The President, Vice President, and others can be forced out of office if impeached and found guilty of certain crimes. Andrew Johnson is the only President to have been impeached.

Judicial power is the right of the courts to decide legal cases. The Constitution creates the Supreme Court but lets Congress decide the size of the Supreme Court. Congress has the power to set up inferior, or lower, courts. The Judiciary Act of 1789 (page 173) set up district and circuit courts, or courts of appeal. Today, there are 94 district courts and 13 courts of appeal. All federal judges serve for life.

Section 2. Powers of the President

1. Commander in Chief of the Armed Forces The President shall be Commander in Chief of the Army and Navy of the United States, and of the militia of the several states, when called into the actual service of the United States; he may require the opinion, in writing, of the principal officer in each of the executive departments, upon any subject relating to the duties of their respective offices, and he shall have power to grant reprieves and pardons for offenses against the United States, except in cases of impeachment.

2. Making Treaties and Nominations He shall have power, by and with the advice and consent of the Senate, to make treaties, provided two-thirds of the Senators present concur; and he shall nominate, and by and with the advice and consent of the Senate, shall appoint ambassadors, other public ministers and consuls, judges of the Supreme Court, and all other officers of the United States, whose appointments are not herein otherwise provided for, and which shall be established by law; but the Congress may by law vest the appointment of such inferior officers, as they think proper, in the President alone, in the courts of law, or in the heads of departments.

3. Temporary Appointments The President shall have power to fill up all vacancies that may happen during the recess of the Senate, by granting commissions which shall expire at the end of their next session.

Section 3. Duties

He shall from time to time give to the Congress information of the state of the Union, and recommend to their consideration such measures as he shall judge necessary and expedient; he may, on extraordinary occasions, convene both houses, or either of them, and in case of disagreement between them, with respect to the time of adjournment, he may adjourn them to such time as he shall think proper; he shall receive ambassadors and other public ministers; he shall take care that the laws be faithfully executed, and shall commission all the officers of the United States.

Section 4. Impeachment and Removal From Office

The President, Vice-President, and all civil officers of the United States, shall be removed from office on impeachment for, and conviction of, treason, bribery, or other high crimes or misdemeanors.

Article 3. The Judicial Branch

Section 1. Federal Courts

The judicial power of the United States shall be vested in one Supreme Court, and in such inferior courts as the Congress may from time to time ordain and establish. The judges, both of the Supreme and inferior courts, shall hold their offices during good behavior, and shall, at stated times, receive for their services a compensation, which shall not be diminished during their continuance in office.

Section 2. Jurisdiction of Federal Courts

1. Scope of Judicial Power The judicial power shall extend to all cases, in law and equity, arising under this Constitution, the laws of the United States, and treaties made or which shall be made, under their authority; to all cases affecting ambassadors, other public ministers and consuls; to all cases of admiralty and maritime jurisdiction; to controversies to which the United States shall be a party; to controversies between two or more states; ~~between a state and citizens of another state;~~ between citizens of the same state claiming lands under grants of different states, and between a state or the citizens thereof, and foreign states, citizens, or subjects.

2. The Supreme Court In all cases affecting ambassadors, other public ministers and consuls, and those in which a state shall be a party, the Supreme Court shall have original jurisdiction. In all the other cases before mentioned, the Supreme Court shall have appellate jurisdiction, both as to law and fact, with such exceptions, and under such regulations as the Congress shall make.

3. Trial by Jury The trial of all crimes, except in cases of impeachment, shall be by jury; and such trial shall be held in the state where the said crimes shall have been committed; but when not committed within any state, the trial shall be at such place or places as the Congress may by law have directed.

Section 3. Treason

1. Definition Treason against the United States shall consist only in levying war against them, or in adhering to their enemies, giving them aid and comfort. No person shall be convicted of treason unless on the testimony of two witnesses to the same overt act, or on confession in open court.

2. Punishment The Congress shall have power to declare the punishment of treason, but no attainder of treason shall work corruption of blood or forfeiture except during the life of the person attainted.

Article 4. Relations Among the States

Section 1. Official Records and Acts

Full faith and credit shall be given in each state to the public acts, records, and judicial proceedings of every other state. And the Congress may by general laws prescribe the manner in which such acts, records, and proceedings shall be proved, and the effect thereof.

Section 2. Privileges of Citizens

1. Privileges The citizens of each state shall be entitled to all privileges and immunities of citizens in the several states.

Clause 1 *Jurisdiction* refers to the right of a court to hear a case. Federal courts have jurisdiction over cases that involve the Constitution, federal laws, treaties, foreign ambassadors and diplomats, naval and maritime laws, disagreements between states or between citizens from different states, and disputes between a state or citizen and a foreign state or citizen.

In *Marbury* v. *Madison,* the Supreme Court established the right to judge whether a law is constitutional (page 197).

Clause 2 *Original jurisdiction* means the power of a court to hear a case where it first arises. The Supreme Court has original jurisdiction over only a few cases, such as those involving foreign diplomats. More often, the Supreme Court acts as an appellate court. An *appellate court* does not decide guilt. It decides whether the lower court trial was properly conducted and reviews the lower court's decision.

Clause 3 This clause guarantees the right to a jury trial for anyone accused of a federal crime. The only exceptions are impeachment cases. The trial must be held in the state where the crime was committed.

Clause 1 Treason is clearly defined. An *overt act* is an actual action. A person cannot be convicted of treason for what he or she thinks. A person can be convicted of treason only if he or she confesses or two witnesses testify to it.

Clause 2 Congress has the power to set the punishment for traitors. Congress may not punish the children of convicted traitors by taking away their civil rights or property.

Each state must recognize the official acts and records of any other state. For example, each state must recognize marriage certificates issued by another state. Congress can pass laws to ensure this.

Clause 1 All states must treat citizens of another state in the same way it treats its own citizens. However, the courts have allowed states to give residents certain privileges, such as lower tuition rates.

THE CONSTITUTION ★ ★

Clause 2 **Extradition** means the act of returning a suspected criminal or escaped prisoner to a state where he or she is wanted. State governors must return a suspect to another state. However, the Supreme Court has ruled that a governor cannot be forced to do so if he or she feels that justice will not be done.

Clause 3 *Persons held to service or labor* refers to slaves or indentured servants. This clause required states to return runaway slaves to their owners. The Thirteenth Amendment replaces this clause.

Clause 1 Congress has the power to admit new states to the Union. Existing states cannot be split up or joined together to form new states unless both Congress and the state legislatures approve. New states are equal to all other states.

Clause 2 Congress can make rules for managing and governing land owned by the United States. This includes territories not organized into states, such as Puerto Rico and Guam, and federal lands within a state.

In a *republic,* voters choose representatives to govern them. The federal government must protect the states from foreign invasion and from *domestic,* or internal, disorder if asked to do so by a state.

The Constitution can be *amended,* or changed, if necessary. An amendment can be proposed by (1) a two-thirds vote of both houses of Congress or (2) a national convention called by Congress at the request of two thirds of the state legislatures. (This second method has never been used.) An amendment must be *ratified,* or approved, by (1) three fourths of the state legislatures or (2) special conventions in three fourths of the states. Congress decides which method will be used.

The United States government promised to pay all debts and honor all agreements made under the Articles of Confederation.

---

2. Extradition A person charged in any state with treason, felony, or other crime, who shall flee from justice, and be found in another state, shall on demand of the executive authority of the state from which he fled, be delivered up, to be removed to the state having jurisdiction of the crime.

3. Return of Fugitive Slaves ~~No person held to service or labor in one state, under the laws thereof, escaping into another, shall in consequence of any law or regulation therein, be discharged from such service or labor, but shall be delivered up on claim of the party to whom such service or labor may be due.~~

Section 3. New States and Territories

1. New States New states may be admitted by the Congress into this Union; but no new state shall be formed or erected within the jurisdiction of any other state; nor any state be formed by the junction of two of more states, or parts of states, without the consent of the legislatures of the states concerned as well as of the Congress.

2. Federal Lands The Congress shall have power to dispose of and make all needful rules and regulations respecting the territory or other property belonging to the United States; and nothing in this Constitution shall be so construed as to prejudice any claims of the United States, or of any particular state.

Section 4. Guarantees to the States

The United States shall guarantee to every state in this Union a republican form of government, and shall protect each of them against invasion; and on application of the legislature, or of the executive (when the legislature cannot be convened) against domestic violence.

Article 5. Amending the Constitution

The Congress, whenever two-thirds of both houses shall deem it necessary, shall propose amendments to this Constitution, or, on the application of the legislatures of two-thirds of the several states, shall call a convention for proposing amendments, which, in either case, shall be valid to all intents and purposes, as part of this Constitution, when ratified by the legislatures of three-fourths of the several states, or by conventions in three-fourths thereof, as the one or the other mode of ratification may be proposed by the Congress; provided that ~~no amendments which may be made prior to the year 1808 shall in any manner affect the first and fourth clauses in the Ninth Section of the First Article; and that~~ no state, without its consent, shall be deprived of its equal suffrage in the Senate.

Article 6. National Supremacy

Section 1. Prior Public Debts

All debts contracted and engagements entered into, before the adoption of this Constitution, shall be as valid against the United States under this Constitution, as under the Confederation.

Section 2. Supreme Law of the Land

This Constitution, and the laws of the United States which shall be made in pursuance thereof, and all treaties made, or which shall be made, under the authority of the United States, shall be the supreme law of the land; and the judges in every state shall be bound thereby, anything in the constitution or laws of any state to the contrary notwithstanding.

The Constitution, federal laws, and treaties that the Senate has ratified are the supreme, or highest, law of the land. Thus, they outweigh state laws. A state judge must overturn a state law that conflicts with the Constitution or with a federal law.

Section 3. Oaths of Office

The Senators and Representatives before mentioned, and the members of the several state legislatures, and all executive and judicial officers, both of the United States and of the several states, shall be bound by oath or affirmation, to support this Constitution; but no religious test shall ever be required as a qualification to any office or public trust under the United States.

State and federal officeholders take an oath, or solemn promise, to support the Constitution. However, this clause forbids the use of religious tests for officeholders. During the colonial period, every colony except Rhode Island required a religious test for officeholders.

Article 7. Ratification

The ratification of the convention of nine states shall be sufficient for the establishment of the Constitution between the states so ratifying the same.

During 1787 and 1788, states held special conventions. By October 1788, the required nine states had ratified the Constitution.

Done in convention, by the unanimous consent of the states present, the seventeenth day of September, in the year of our Lord one thousand seven hundred and eighty-seven, and of the independence of the United States of America the twelfth. In Witness whereof, we have hereunto subscribed our names.

Attest: William Jackson
Secretary

George Washington
President and deputy from Virginia

New Hampshire
John Langdon
Nicholas Gilman

Massachussetts
Nathaniel Gorham
Rufus King

Connecticut
William Samuel Johnson
Roger Sherman

New York
Alexander Hamilton

New Jersey
William Livingston
David Brearley
William Paterson
Jonathan Dayton

Pennsylvania
Benjamin Franklin
Thomas Mifflin
Robert Morris
George Clymer
Thomas Fitzsimons
Jared Ingersoll
James Wilson
Gouverneur Morris

Delaware
George Read
Gunning Bedford, Jr.
John Dickinson
Richard Bassett
Jacob Broom

Maryland
James McHenry
Dan of St. Thomas Jennifer
Daniel Carroll

Virginia
John Blair
James Madison, Jr.

North Carolina
William Blount
Richard Dobbs Spaight
Hugh Williamson

South Carolina
John Rutledge
Charles Cotesworth Pinckney
Charles Pinckney
Pierce Butler

Georgia
William Few
Abraham Baldwin

★ Amendments to the Constitution ★

The first 10 amendments, which were added to the Constitution in 1791, are called the Bill of Rights. Originally, the Bill of Rights applied only to actions of the federal government. However, the Supreme Court has used the due process clause of the Fourteenth Amendment to extend many of the rights to protect individuals against action by the states.

Congress cannot set up an established, or official, church or religion for the nation. During the colonial period, most colonies had established churches. However, the authors of the First Amendment wanted to keep government and religion separate.

Congress may not **abridge,** or limit, the freedom to speak and write freely. The government may not censor, or review, books and newspapers before they are printed. This amendment also protects the right to assemble, or hold public meetings. **Petition** means ask. **Redress** means to correct. **Grievances** are wrongs. The people have the right to ask the government for wrongs to be corrected.

State militias, such as the National Guard, have the right to bear arms, or keep weapons. Courts have generally ruled that the government can regulate the ownership of guns by private citizens.

During the colonial period, the British quartered, or housed, soldiers in private homes without the permission of the owners (page 90). This amendment limits the government's right to use private homes to house soldiers.

This amendment protects Americans from unreasonable searches and seizures. Search and seizure are permitted only if a judge has issued a **warrant,** or written court order. A warrant is issued only if there is probable cause. This means an officer must show that it is probable, or likely, that the search will produce evidence of a crime. A search warrant must name the exact place to be searched and the things to be seized. In some cases, courts have ruled that searches can take place without a warrant. For example, police may search a person who is under arrest. However, evidence found during an unlawful search cannot be used in a trial.

This amendment protects the rights of the accused. **Capital crimes** are those that can be punished with death. **Infamous crimes** are those that can be punished with prison or loss of rights. The federal government must obtain an **indictment,** or formal accusation, from a grand jury to prosecute anyone for such crimes. A **grand jury** is a panel of between 12 and 23 citizens who

Amendment 1

Freedoms of Religion, Speech, Press, Assembly, and Petition

Congress shall make no law respecting an establishment of religion, or prohibiting the free exercise thereof; or abridging the freedom of speech, or of the press; or the right of the people peaceably to assemble, and to petition the government for a redress of grievances.

Amendment 2

Right to Bear Arms

A well-regulated militia, being necessary to the security of a free state, the right of the people to keep and bear arms shall not be infringed.

Amendment 3

Lodging Troops in Private Homes

No soldier shall, in time of peace, be quartered in any house, without the consent of the owner; nor in time of war, but in a manner to be prescribed by law.

Amendment 4

Search and Seizure

The right of the people to be secure in their persons, houses, papers, and effects, against unreasonable searches and seizures, shall not be violated; and no warrants shall issue but upon probable cause, supported by oath or affirmation, and particularly describing the place to be searched, and the persons or things to be seized.

Amendment 5

Rights of the Accused

No person shall be held to answer for a capital, or otherwise infamous, crime, unless on a presentment or indictment of a grand jury, except in cases arising in the land or naval forces, or in the militia, when in actual service in time of war or public danger; nor shall any person be subject for the same offense to be twice put in jeopardy of life and limb; nor shall be compelled, in any criminal case, to be a witness against himself; nor be deprived of life, liberty, or property, without due process of law; nor shall private property be taken for public use, without just compensation.

Amendment 6
Right to Speedy Trial by Jury
In all criminal prosecutions, the accused shall enjoy the right to a speedy and public trial, by an impartial jury of the state and district wherein the crime shall have been committed, which district shall have been previously ascertained by law, and to be informed of the nature and cause of the accusation; to be confronted with the witnesses against him; to have compulsory process for obtaining witnesses in his favor, and to have the assistance of counsel for his defense.

Amendment 7
Jury Trial in Civil Cases
In suits at common law, where the value in controversy shall exceed $20, the right of trial by jury shall be preserved, and no fact tried by a jury shall be otherwise re-examined in any court of the United States than according to the rules of the common law.

Amendment 8
Bail and Punishment
Excessive bail shall not be required, nor excessive fines imposed, nor cruel and unusual punishments inflicted.

Amendment 9
Powers Reserved to the People
The enumeration in the Constitution, of certain rights, shall not be construed to deny or disparage others retained by the people.

Amendment 10
Powers Reserved to the States
The powers not delegated to the United States by the Constitution, nor prohibited by it to the states, are reserved to the states respectively, or to the people.

Amendment 11
Suits Against States
Passed by Congress on March 4, 1794. Ratified on January 23, 1795.

The judicial power of the United States shall not be construed to extend to any suit in law or equity, commenced or prosecuted against one of the United States, by citizens of another state, or by citizens or subjects of any foreign state.

decide if the government has enough evidence to justify a trial. This procedure prevents prosecution with little or no evidence of guilt. (Soldiers and the militia in wartime are not covered by this rule.)

Double jeopardy is forbidden. This means that a person cannot be tried twice for the same crime—unless a court sets aside a conviction because of a legal error. A person on trial cannot be forced to testify, or give evidence, against himself or herself. A person accused of a crime is entitled to **due process of law,** or a fair hearing or trial. Finally, the government cannot seize private property for public use without paying the owner a fair price for it.

In criminal cases, the jury must be **impartial,** or not favor either side. The accused is guaranteed the right to a trial by jury. The trial must be speedy. If the government purposely postpones the trial so that it becomes hard for the person to get a fair hearing, the charge may be dismissed. The accused must be told the charges against him or her and be allowed to question prosecution witnesses. Witnesses who can help the accused can be ordered to appear in court.

The accused must be allowed a lawyer. Since 1942, the federal government has been required to provide a lawyer if the accused cannot afford one. In 1963, the Supreme Court decided that states must also provide lawyers for a defendant too poor to pay for one.

Common law refers to rules of law established by judges in past cases. This amendment guarantees the right to a jury trial in lawsuits where the sum of money at stake is more than $20. An appeals court cannot change a verdict because it disagrees with the decision of the jury. It can set aside a verdict only if legal errors made the trial unfair.

Bail is money the accused leaves with the court as a pledge to appear for trial. If the accused does not appear for trial, the court keeps the money. **Excessive** means too high. This amendment forbids courts to set unreasonably high bail. The amount of bail usually depends on the seriousness of the charge and whether the accused is likely to appear for the trial. The amendment also forbids cruel and unusual punishments such as mental and physical abuse.

People have rights not listed in the Constitution. This amendment was added because some people feared that the Bill of Rights would be used to limit rights to those actually listed.

This amendment limits the power of the federal government. Powers that are not given to the federal government belong to the states. The powers reserved to the states are not listed in the Constitution.

This amendment changed part of Article 3, Section 2, Clause 1. As a result, a private citizen from one state cannot sue the government of another state in federal court. However, a citizen can sue a state government in a state court.

This amendment changed the way the electoral college voted. Before the amendment was adopted, each elector simply voted for two people. The candidate with the most votes became President. The runner-up became Vice President. In the election of 1800, however, a tie vote resulted between Thomas Jefferson and Aaron Burr (page 189).

In such a case, the Constitution required the House of Representatives to elect the President. Federalists had a majority in the House. They tried to keep Jefferson out of office by voting for Burr. It took 35 ballots in the House before Jefferson was elected President.

To keep this from happening again, the Twelfth Amendment was passed and ratified in time for the election of 1804.

This amendment provides that each elector choose one candidate for President and one candidate for Vice President. If no candidate for President receives a majority of electoral votes, the House of Representatives chooses the President. If no candidate for Vice President receives a majority, the Senate elects the Vice President. The Vice President must be a person who is eligible to be President.

This system is still in use today. However, it is possible for a candidate to win the popular vote and lose in the electoral college. This happened in 1876 (pages 419–420).

The Emancipation Proclamation (1863) freed slaves only in areas controlled by the Confederacy (pages 387–388). This amendment freed all slaves. It also forbids *involuntary servitude,* or labor done against one's will. However, it does not prevent prison wardens from making prisoners work.

Section 2 says that Congress can pass laws to carry out this amendment.

Section 1 defines citizenship for the first time in the Constitution, and it extends citizenship to

Amendment 12

Election of President and Vice-President

Passed by Congress on December 9, 1803. Ratified on June 15, 1804.

The electors shall meet in their respective states, and vote by ballot for President and Vice-President, one of whom, at least, shall not be an inhabitant of the same state with themselves; they shall name in their ballots the person voted for as President, and in distinct ballots the person voted for as Vice-President, and they shall make distinct lists of all persons voted for as President, and of all persons voted for as Vice-President, and of the number of votes for each, which lists they shall sign and certify, and transmit, sealed, to the seat of government of the United States, directed to the President of the Senate; the President of the Senate shall, in the presence of the Senate and House of Representatives, open all the certificates and the votes shall then be counted; the person having the greatest number of votes for President shall be the President, if such number be a majority of the whole number of electors appointed; and if no person have such majority, then from the persons having the highest numbers not exceeding three on the list of those voted for as President, the House of Representatives shall choose immediately, by ballot, the President. But in choosing the President, the votes shall be taken by the states, the representation from each state having one vote; a quorum for this purpose shall consist of a member or members from two-thirds of the states, and a majority of all the states shall be necessary to a choice. And if the House of Representatives shall not choose a President whenever the right of choice shall devolve upon them, before the fourth day of March next following, then the Vice-President shall act as President, as in the case of the death or other constitutional disability of the President. The person having the greatest number of votes as Vice-President, shall be the Vice-President, if such number be a majority of the whole number of electors appointed, and if no person have a majority, then, from the two highest numbers on the list, the Senate shall choose the Vice-President; a quorum for the purpose shall consist of two-thirds of the whole number of Senators, and a majority of the whole number shall be necessary to a choice. But no person constitutionally ineligible to the office of President shall be eligible to that of Vice-President of the United States.

Amendment 13

Abolition of Slavery

Passed by Congress on January 31, 1865. Ratified on December 6, 1865.

Section 1. Neither slavery nor involuntary servitude, except as a punishment for crime whereof the party shall have been duly convicted, shall exist within the United States, or any place subject to their jurisdiction.

Section 2. Congress shall have power to enforce this article by appropriate legislation.

Amendment 14

Rights of Citizens

Passed by Congress on June 13, 1866. Ratified on July 9, 1868.

Section 1. Citizenship All persons born or naturalized in the United States and subject to the jurisdiction thereof, are citizens of the United States and of the state wherein they reside. No state shall make or enforce any law which shall abridge the privileges or immunities of citizens of the United States; nor shall any state deprive any person of life, liberty, or property, without due process of law; nor deny to any person within its jurisdiction the equal protection of the laws.

blacks. It also prohibits states from denying the rights and privileges of citizenship to any citizen. This section also forbids states to deny due process of law.

Section 1 guarantees all citizens "equal protection under the law." For a long time, however, the Fourteenth Amendment did not protect blacks from discrimination. After Reconstruction, separate facilities for blacks and whites sprang up (page 423). In 1954, the Supreme Court ruled that separate facilities for blacks and whites were by their nature unequal. This ruling, in the case of *Brown* v. *Board of Education,* made school segregation illegal.

Section 2. Apportionment of Representatives Representatives shall be apportioned among the several states according to their respective numbers, counting the whole number of persons in each state, excluding Indians not taxed. But when the right to vote at any election for the choice of electors for President and Vice-President of the United States, Representatives in Congress, the executive and judicial officers of a state, or the members of the legislature thereof, is denied to any of the male inhabitants of such state, being twenty-one years of age and citizens of the United States, or in any way abridged, except for participation in rebellion, or other crime, the basis of representation therein shall be reduced in the proportion which the number of such male citizens shall bear to the whole number of male citizens twenty-one years of age in such state.

Section 2 replaced the three-fifths clause. It provides that representation in the House of Representatives is decided on the basis of the number of people in the state. It also provides that states which deny the vote to male citizens over age 21 will be punished by losing part of their representation in the House. This provision has never been enforced.

Despite this clause, black citizens were often prevented from voting. In the 1960s, federal laws were passed to end voting discrimination.

Section 3. Former Confederate Officials No person shall be a Senator or Representative in Congress, or elector of President and Vice-President, or hold any office, civil or military, under the United States, or under any state, who, having previously taken an oath, as a member of Congress, or as an officer of the United States, or as a member of any state legislature, or as an executive or judicial officer of any state, to support the Constitution of the United States, shall have engaged in insurrection or rebellion against the same, or given aid or comfort to the enemies thereof. But Congress may, by vote of two-thirds of each house, remove such disability.

This section prohibited people who had been federal or state officials before the Civil War and who had joined the Confederate cause from serving again as government officials. In 1872, Congress restored the rights of former Confederate officials.

Section 4. Government Debt The validity of the public debt of the United States, authorized by law, including debts incurred for payment of pensions and bounties for services in suppressing insurrection or rebellion, shall not be questioned. But neither the United States nor any state shall assume or pay any debt or obligation incurred in aid of insurrection or rebellion against the United States or any claim for the loss or emancipation of any slave; but all such debts, obligations, and claims shall be held illegal and void.

This section recognized that the United States must repay its debts from the Civil War. However, it forbade the repayment of debts of the Confederacy. This meant that people who had loaned money to the Confederacy would not be repaid. Also, states were not allowed to pay former slave owners for the loss of slaves.

Section 5. Enforcement The Congress shall have power to enforce, by appropriate legislation, the provisions of this article.

Congress can pass laws to carry out this amendment.

Amendment 15

Voting Rights

Passed by Congress on February 26, 1869. Ratified on February 2, 1870.

Section 1. Extending the Right to Vote The right of citizens of the United States to vote shall not be denied or abridged by the United States or any state on account of race, color, or previous condition of servitude.

Previous condition of servitude refers to slavery. This amendment gave blacks, both former slaves and free blacks, the right to vote. In the late 1800s, southern states used grandfather clauses, literacy tests, and poll taxes to keep blacks from voting (pages 421–422).

Congress can pass laws to carry out this amendment. The Twenty-fourth Amendment barred the use of poll taxes in national elections. The Voting Rights Act of 1965 gave federal officials the power to register voters in places where there was voting discrimination.

Congress has the power to collect taxes on people's income. An income tax can be collected without regard to a state's population. This amendment changed Article 1, Section 9, Clause 4.

This amendment replaced Article 1, Section 2, Clause 1. Before it was adopted, state legislatures chose senators. This amendment provides that senators are directly elected by the people of each state.

When a Senate seat becomes vacant, the governor of the state must order an election to fill the seat. The state legislature can give the governor power to fill the seat until an election is held.

Senators who had already been elected by the state legislatures were not affected by this amendment.

This amendment, known as **Prohibition,** banned the making, selling, or transporting of alcoholic beverages in the United States. Later, the Twenty-first Amendment **repealed,** or canceled, this amendment.

Both the states and the federal government had the power to pass laws to enforce this amendment.

This amendment had to be approved within seven years. The Eighteenth Amendment was the first amendment to include a time limit for ratification.

Neither the federal government nor state governments can deny the right to vote on account of sex. Thus, women won **suffrage,** or the right to vote. Before 1920, some states had allowed women to vote in state elections.

Congress can pass laws to carry out this amendment.

Section 2. Enforcement   The Congress shall have power to enforce this article by appropriate legislation.

Amendment 16
The Income Tax
Passed by Congress on July 12, 1909. Ratified on February 3, 1913.

The Congress shall have power to lay and collect taxes on incomes, from whatever source derived, without apportionment among the several states, and without regard to any census or enumeration.

Amendment 17
Direct Election of Senators
Passed by Congress on May 13, 1912. Ratified on April 8, 1913.

Section 1. Method of Election   The Senate of the United States shall be composed of two Senators from each state, elected by the people thereof, for six years; and each Senator shall have one vote. The electors in each state shall have the qualifications requisite for electors of the most numerous branch of the state legislatures.

Section 2. Vacancies   When vacancies happen in the representation of any state in the Senate, the executive authority of such state shall issue writs of election to fill such vacancies: *Provided* that the legislature of any state may empower the executive thereof to make temporary appointments until the people fill the vacancies by election as the legislature may direct.

Section 3. Exception   ~~This amendment shall not be so construed as to affect the election or term of any Senator chosen before it becomes valid as part of the Constitution.~~

Amendment 18
Prohibition of Alcoholic Beverages
Passed by Congress on December 18, 1917. Ratified on January 16, 1919.

Section 1. Ban on Alcohol   ~~After one year from the ratification of this article the manufacture, sale, or transportation of intoxicating liquors within, the importation thereof into, or the exportation thereof from, the United States and all territory subject to the jurisdiction thereof for beverage purposes is hereby prohibited.~~

Section 2. Enforcement   ~~The Congress and the several states shall have concurrent power to enforce this article by appropriate legislation.~~

Section 3. Method of Ratification   ~~This article shall be inoperative unless it shall have been ratified as an amendment to the Constitution by the legislatures of the several states, as provided in the Constitution, within seven years from the date of the submission hereof to the states by the Congress.~~

Amendment 19
Women's Suffrage
Passed by Congress on June 4, 1919. Ratified on August 18, 1920.

Section 1. The Right to Vote   The right of citizens of the United States to vote shall not be denied or abridged by the United States or by any state on account of sex.

Section 2. Enforcement   Congress shall have power to enforce this article by appropriate legislation.

Amendment 20

Presidential Terms; Sessions of Congress

Passed by Congress on March 2, 1932. Ratified on January 23, 1933.

Section 1. Beginning of Term   The terms of the President and Vice-President shall end at noon on the 20th day of January, and the terms of Senators and Representatives at noon on the 3rd day of January, of the years in which such terms would have ended if this article had not been ratified; and the terms of their successors shall then begin.

Section 2. Congressional Sessions   The Congress shall assemble at least once in every year, and such meeting shall begin at noon on the 3rd day of January, unless they shall by law appoint a different day.

Section 3. Presidential Succession   If at the time fixed for the beginning of the term of the President, the President-elect shall have died, the Vice-President-elect shall become President. If a President shall not have been chosen before the time fixed for the beginning of his term, or if the President-elect shall have failed to qualify, then the Vice-President-elect shall act as President until a President shall have qualified; and the Congress may by law provide for the case wherein neither a President-elect nor a Vice-President-elect shall have qualified, declaring who shall then act as President, or the manner in which one who is to act shall be selected, and such person shall act accordingly until a President or Vice-President shall have qualified.

Section 4. Elections Decided by Congress   The Congress may by law provide for the case of the death of any of the persons from whom the House of Representatives may choose a President whenever the right of choice shall have devolved upon them, and for the case of the death of any of the persons from whom the Senate may choose a Vice-President whenever the right of choice shall have devolved upon them.

Section 5. Date of Effect   ~~Sections 1 and 2 shall take effect on the 15th day of October following the ratification of this article.~~

Section 6. Ratification Period   ~~This article shall be inoperative unless it shall have been ratified as an amendment to the Constitution by the legislatures of three-fourths of the several states within seven years from the date of its submission.~~

Amendment 21

Repeal of Prohibition

Passed by Congress on February 20, 1933. Ratified on December 5, 1933.

Section 1. Repeal of National Prohibition   The eighteenth article of amendment to the Constitution of the United States is hereby repealed.

Section 2. State Laws   The transportation or importation into any state, territory, or possession of the United States for delivery or use therein of intoxicating liquors, in violation of the laws thereof, is hereby prohibited.

Section 3. Ratification Period   ~~This article shall be inoperative unless it shall have been ratified as an amendment to the Constitution by conventions in the several states, as provided in the Constitution, within seven years from the date of the submission hereof to the states by the Congress.~~

The date for the President and Vice President to take office is January 20. Members of Congress begin their terms of office on January 3. Before this amendment was adopted, these terms of office began on March 4.

Congress must meet at least once a year. The new session of Congress begins on January 3. Before this amendment, members of Congress who had been defeated in November continued to hold office until the following March. Such members were known as *lame ducks.*

By Section 3, if the President-elect dies before taking office, the Vice President-elect becomes President. If no President has been chosen by January 20 or if the elected candidate fails to qualify for office, the Vice President-elect acts as President, but only until a qualified President is chosen.

Finally, Congress can choose a person to act as President if neither the President-elect nor Vice President-elect is qualified to take office.

Congress can pass laws in cases where a presidential candidate dies while an election is being decided in the House. Congress has similar power in cases where a candidate for Vice President dies while an election is being decided in the Senate.

Section 5 sets the date for the amendment to become effective.

Section 6 sets a time limit for ratification.

The Eighteenth Amendment is repealed, making it legal to make and sell alcoholic beverages. Prohibition ended December 5, 1933.

Each state was free to ban the making and selling of alcoholic drink within its borders. This section makes bringing liquor into a "dry" state a federal offense.

Special state conventions were called to ratify this amendment. This is the only time an amendment was ratified by state conventions rather than state legislatures.

Before Franklin Roosevelt became President, no President served more than two terms in office. Roosevelt broke with this custom and was elected to four terms. This amendment provides that no President may serve more than two terms. A President who has already served more than half of someone else's term can serve only one more full term. However, the amendment did not apply to Harry Truman, who had become President after Franklin Roosevelt's death in 1945.

A seven-year time limit is set for ratification.

This amendment gives residents of Washington, D.C., the right to vote in presidential elections. Until this amendment was adopted, people living in Washington, D.C., could not vote for President because the Constitution had made no provision for choosing electors from the nation's capital. Washington, D.C., has three electoral votes.

Congress can pass laws to carry out this amendment.

A *poll tax* is a tax on voters. This amendment bans poll taxes in national elections. Some states used poll taxes to keep blacks from voting. In 1966, the Supreme Court struck down poll taxes in state elections, also.

Congress can pass laws to carry out this amendment.

If the President dies or resigns, the Vice President becomes President. This section clarifies Article 2, Section 1, Clause 6.

Amendment 22
Limit on Number of President's Terms
Passed by Congress on March 12, 1947. Ratified on March 1, 1951.

Section 1. Two-Term Limit No person shall be elected to the office of the President more than twice, and no person who has held the office of President, or acted as President, for more than two years of a term to which some other person was elected President shall be elected to the office of the President more than once. ~~But this Article shall not apply to any person holding the office of President when this Article was proposed by the Congress, and shall not prevent any person who may be holding the office of President, or acting as President, during the term within which this Article becomes operative from holding the office of President or acting as President during the remainder of such term.~~

Section 2. Ratification Period ~~This Article shall be inoperative unless it shall have been ratified as an amendment to the Constitution by the legislatures of three-fourths of the several states within seven years from the date of its submission to the states by the Congress.~~

Amendment 23
Presidential Electors for District of Columbia
Passed by Congress on June 16, 1960. Ratified on April 3, 1961.

Section 1. Determining the Number of Electors The District constituting the seat of Government of the United States shall appoint in such manner as the Congress may direct: A number of electors of President and Vice-President equal to the whole number of Senators and Representatives in Congress to which the District would be entitled if it were a State, but in no event more than the least populous State; they shall be in addition to those appointed by the States, but they shall be considered, for the purposes of the election of President and Vice-President, to be electors appointed by a State; and they shall meet in the District and perform such duties as provided by the twelfth article of amendment.

Section 2. Enforcement The Congress shall have power to enforce this article by appropriate legislation.

Amendment 24
Abolition of Poll Tax in National Elections
Passed by Congress on August 27, 1962. Ratified on January 23, 1964.

Section 1. Poll Tax Banned The right of citizens of the United States to vote in any primary or other election for President or Vice-President, for electors for President or Vice-President, or for Senator or Representative in Congress, shall not be denied or abridged by the United States or any state by reason of failure to pay any poll tax or other tax.

Section 2. Enforcement The Congress shall have the power to enforce this article by appropriate legislation.

Amendment 25
Presidential Succession and Disability
Passed by Congress on July 6, 1965. Ratified on February 11, 1967.

Section 1. President's Death or Resignation In case of the removal of the President from office or his death or resignation, the Vice-President shall become President.

Section 2. Vacancies in Vice-Presidency Whenever there is a vacancy in the office of the Vice-President, the President shall nominate a Vice-President who shall take the office upon confirmation by a majority vote of both houses of Congress.

When a Vice President takes over the office of President, he or she appoints a Vice President who must be approved by a majority vote of both houses of Congress. This section was first applied after Vice President Spiro Agnew resigned in 1973. President Richard Nixon appointed Gerald Ford as Vice President.

Section 3. Disability of the President Whenever the President transmits to the President pro tempore of the Senate and the Speaker of the House of Representatives his written declaration that he is unable to discharge the powers and duties of his office, and until he transmits to them a written declaration to the contrary, such powers and duties shall be discharged by the Vice-President as Acting President.

If the President declares in writing that he or she is unable to perform the duties of office, the Vice President serves as Acting President until the President recovers.

Section 4. Whenever the Vice-President and a majority of either the principal officers of the executive departments or of such other body as Congress may by law provide, transmit to the President *pro tempore* of the Senate and the Speaker of the House of Representatives their written declaration that the President is unable to discharge the powers and duties of his office, the Vice-President shall immediately assume the powers and duties of the office as Acting President.

Thereafter, when the President transmits to the President *pro tempore* of the Senate and the Speaker of the House of Representatives his written declaration that no inability exists, he shall resume the powers and duties of his office unless the Vice-President and a majority of either the principal officers of the executive department or of such other body as Congress may by law provide, transmit within four days to the President *as* of the Senate and the Speaker of the House of Representatives their written declaration that the President is unable to discharge the powers and duties of his office. Thereupon Congress shall decide the issue, assembling within 48 hours for that purpose if not in session. If the Congress, within 21 days after receipt of the latter written declaration, or, if Congress is not in session, within 21 days after Congress is required to assemble, determines by two-thirds vote of both houses that the President is unable to discharge the powers and duties of his office, the Vice-President shall continue to discharge the same as Acting President; otherwise, the President shall assume the powers and duties of his office.

Two Presidents, Woodrow Wilson and Dwight Eisenhower, have fallen gravely ill while in office. The Constitution contained no provision for this kind of emergency.

Section 3 provided that the President can inform Congress that he or she is too sick to perform the duties of office. However, if the President is unconscious or refuses to admit to a disabling illness, Section 4 provides that the Vice President and Cabinet may declare the President disabled. The Vice President becomes Acting President until the President can return to the duties of office. In case of a disagreement between the President and the Vice President and Cabinet over the President's ability to perform the duties of office, Congress must decide the issue. A two-thirds vote of both houses is needed to decide that the President is disabled or unable to fulfill the duties of office.

Amendment 26

Voting Age

Passed by Congress on March 23, 1971. Ratified on July 1, 1971.

Section 1. Lowering of Voting Age The right of citizens of the United States, who are 18 years of age or older, to vote shall not be denied or abridged by the United States or any state on account of age.

In 1970, Congress passed a law allowing 18-year-olds to vote. However, the Supreme Court decided that Congress could not set a minimum age for state elections. So this amendment was passed and ratified.

Section 2. Enforcement The Congress shall have the power to enforce this article by appropriate legislation.

Congress can pass laws to carry out this amendment.

Amendment 27

Congressional Pay Increases

Ratified on May 7, 1992.

No law varying the compensation for the services of the Senators and Representatives shall take effect, until an election of Representatives shall have intervened.

If members of Congress vote themselves a pay increase, it cannot go into effect until after the next congressional election.

★ Presidents of the United States ★

1 **George Washington**
(1732–1799)

Years in office:
1789–1797
Party:
none
Elected from:
Virginia
Vice President:
John Adams

2 **John Adams**
(1735–1826)

Years in office:
1797–1801
Party:
Federalist
Elected from:
Massachusetts
Vice President:
Thomas Jefferson

3 **Thomas Jefferson**
(1743–1826)

Years in office:
1801–1809
Party:
Democratic
   Republican
Elected from:
Virginia
Vice President:
1) Aaron Burr,
2) George Clinton

4 **James Madison**
(1751–1836)

Years in office:
1809–1817
Party:
Democratic
   Republican
Elected from:
Virginia
Vice President:
1) George Clinton,
2) Elbridge Gerry

5 **James Monroe**
(1758–1831)

Years in office:
1817–1825
Party:
Democratic
   Republican
Elected from:
Virginia
Vice President:
Daniel Tompkins

6 **John Quincy Adams**
(1767–1848)

Years in office:
1825–1829
Party:
National
   Republican
Elected from:
Massachusetts
Vice President:
John Calhoun

7 **Andrew Jackson**
(1767–1845)

Years in office:
1829–1837
Party:
Democratic
Elected from:
Tennessee
Vice President:
1) John Calhoun,
2) Martin Van
   Buren

8 **Martin Van Buren**
(1782–1862)

Years in office:
1837–1841
Party:
Democratic
Elected from:
New York
Vice President:
Richard Johnson

9 **William Henry Harrison***
(1773–1841)

Years in office:
1841
Party:
Whig
Elected from:
Ohio
Vice President:
John Tyler

10 **John Tyler**
(1790–1862)

Years in office:
1841–1845
Party:
Whig
Elected from:
Virginia
Vice President:
none

11 **James K. Polk**
(1795–1849)

Years in Office:
1845–1849
Party:
Democratic
Elected from:
Tennessee
Vice President:
George Dallas

12 **Zachary Taylor***
(1784–1850)

Years in office:
1849–1850
Party:
Whig
Elected from:
Louisiana
Vice President:
Millard Fillmore

*Died in office

13 Millard Fillmore
(1800–1874)

Years in office:
1850–1853
Party:
Whig
Elected from:
New York
Vice President:
none

14 Franklin Pierce
(1804–1869)

Years in office:
1853–1857
Party:
Democratic
Elected from:
New Hampshire
Vice President:
William King

15 James Buchanan
(1791–1868)

Years in office:
1857–1861
Party:
Democratic
Elected from:
Pennsylvania
Vice President:
John Breckinridge

16 Abraham Lincoln**
(1809–1865)

Years in office:
1861–1865
Party:
Republican
Elected from:
Illinois
Vice President:
1) Hannibal
   Hamlin,
2) Andrew
   Johnson

17 Andrew Johnson
(1808–1875)

Years in office:
1865–1869
Party:
Republican
Elected from:
Tennessee
Vice President:
none

18 Ulysses S. Grant
(1822–1885)

Years in office:
1869–1877
Party:
Republican
Elected from:
Illinois
Vice President:
1) Schuyler
   Colfax,
2) Henry Wilson

19 Rutherford B. Hayes
(1822–1893)

Years in office:
1877–1881
Party:
Republican
Elected from:
Ohio
Vice President:
William Wheeler

20 James A. Garfield**
(1831–1881)

Years in office:
1881
Party:
Republican
Elected from:
Ohio
Vice President:
Chester A. Arthur

21 Chester A. Arthur
(1830–1886)

Years in office:
1881–1885
Party:
Republican
Elected from:
New York
Vice President:
none

22 Grover Cleveland
(1837–1908)

Years in office:
1885–1889
Party:
Democratic
Elected from:
New York
Vice President:
Thomas
   Hendricks

23 Benjamin Harrison
(1833–1901)

Years in office:
1889–1893
Party:
Republican
Elected from:
Indiana
Vice President:
Levi Morton

24 Grover Cleveland
(1837–1908)

Years in office:
1893–1897
Party:
Democratic
Elected from:
New York
Vice President:
Adlai Stevenson

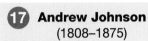

PRESIDENTS OF THE UNITED STATES

**Assassinated

25 William McKinley**
(1843–1901)

Years in office:
1897–1901
Party:
Republican
Elected from:
Ohio
Vice President:
1) Garret Hobart,
2) Theodore
   Roosevelt

26 Theodore Roosevelt
(1858–1919)

Years in office:
1901–1909
Party:
Republican
Elected from:
New York
Vice President:
Charles Fairbanks

27 William Howard Taft
(1857–1930)

Years in office:
1909–1913
Party:
Republican
Elected from:
Ohio
Vice President:
James Sherman

28 Woodrow Wilson
(1856–1924)

Years in office:
1913–1921
Party:
Democratic
Elected from:
New Jersey
Vice President:
Thomas Marshall

29 Warren G. Harding*
(1865–1923)

Years in office:
1921–1923
Party:
Republican
Elected from:
Ohio
Vice President:
Calvin Coolidge

30 Calvin Coolidge
(1872–1933)

Years in office:
1923–1929
Party:
Republican
Elected from:
Massachusetts
Vice President:
Charles Dawes

31 Herbert C. Hoover
(1874–1964)

Years in office:
1929–1933
Party:
Republican
Elected from:
California
Vice President:
Charles Curtis

32 Franklin D. Roosevelt*
(1882–1945)

Years in office:
1933–1945
Party:
Democratic
Elected from:
New York
Vice President:
1) John Garner,
2) Henry Wallace,
3) Harry S Truman

33 Harry S Truman
(1884–1972)

Years in office:
1945–1953
Party:
Democratic
Elected from:
Missouri
Vice President:
Alben Barkley

34 Dwight D. Eisenhower
(1890–1969)

Years in office:
1953–1961
Party:
Republican
Elected from:
New York
Vice President:
Richard M.
Nixon

35 John F. Kennedy**
(1917–1963)

Years in office:
1961–1963
Party:
Democratic
Elected from:
Massachusetts
Vice President:
Lyndon B.
Johnson

36 Lyndon B. Johnson
(1908–1973)

Years in office:
1963–1969
Party:
Democratic
Elected from:
Texas
Vice President:
Hubert
Humphrey

*Died in office
**Assassinated

37 **Richard M. Nixon***
(1913–1994)

Years in office:
1969–1974
Party:
Republican
Elected from:
New York
Vice President:
1) Spiro Agnew,
2) Gerald R. Ford

38 **Gerald R. Ford****
(1913–   )

Years in office:
1974–1977
Party:
Republican
Appointed from:
Michigan
Vice President:
Nelson
  Rockefeller

39 Jimmy Carter
(1924–   )

Years in office:
1977–1981
Party:
Democratic
Elected from:
Georgia
Vice President:
Walter Mondale

40 Ronald W. Reagan
(1911–   )

Years in office:
1981–1989
Party:
Republican
Elected from:
California
Vice President:
George H.W.
  Bush

41 **George H.W. Bush**
(1924–   )

Years in office:
1989–1993
Party:
Republican
Elected from:
Texas
Vice President:
J. Danforth
  Quayle

42 William J. Clinton
(1946–   )

Years in office:
1993–
Party:
Democratic
Elected from:
Arkansas
Vice President:
Albert Gore, Jr.

***Resigned
****Appointed Vice President in
1973 after resignation of Spiro Agnew

★ The Fifty States ★

State	Date of Entry to Union (Order of Entry)	Land Area in Square Miles	Population (In Thousands)	Number of Representatives in House	Capital	Largest City
Alabama	1819 (22)	50,750	4,219	7	Montgomery	Birmingham
Alaska	1959 (49)	570,374	606	1	Juneau	Anchorage
Arizona	1912 (48)	113,642	4,075	6	Phoenix	Phoenix
Arkansas	1836 (25)	52,075	2,453	4	Little Rock	Little Rock
California	1850 (31)	155,973	31,431	52	Sacramento	Los Angeles
Colorado	1876 (38)	103,730	3,656	6	Denver	Denver
Connecticut	1788 (5)	4,845	3,275	6	Hartford	Bridgeport
Delaware	1787 (1)	1,955	706	1	Dover	Wilmington
Florida	1845 (27)	53,997	13,953	23	Tallahassee	Jacksonville
Georgia	1788 (4)	57,919	7,055	11	Atlanta	Atlanta
Hawaii	1959 (50)	6,423	1,179	2	Honolulu	Honolulu
Idaho	1890 (43)	82,751	1,133	2	Boise	Boise
Illinois	1818 (21)	55,593	11,752	20	Springfield	Chicago
Indiana	1816 (19)	35,870	5,752	10	Indianapolis	Indianapolis
Iowa	1846 (29)	55,875	2,829	5	Des Moines	Des Moines
Kansas	1861 (34)	81,823	2,554	4	Topeka	Wichita
Kentucky	1792 (15)	39,732	3,827	6	Frankfort	Louisville
Louisiana	1812 (18)	43,566	4,315	7	Baton Rouge	New Orleans
Maine	1820 (23)	30,865	1,240	2	Augusta	Portland
Maryland	1788 (7)	9,775	5,006	8	Annapolis	Baltimore
Massachusetts	1788 (6)	7,838	6,041	10	Boston	Boston
Michigan	1837 (26)	56,809	9,496	16	Lansing	Detroit
Minnesota	1858 (32)	79,617	4,567	8	St. Paul	Minneapolis
Mississippi	1817 (20)	46,914	2,669	5	Jackson	Jackson
Missouri	1821 (24)	68,898	5,278	9	Jefferson City	Kansas City
Montana	1889 (41)	145,556	856	1	Helena	Billings
Nebraska	1867 (37)	76,878	1,623	3	Lincoln	Omaha
Nevada	1864 (36)	109,806	1,457	2	Carson City	Las Vegas
New Hampshire	1788 (9)	8,969	1,137	2	Concord	Manchester
New Jersey	1787 (3)	7,419	7,904	13	Trenton	Newark
New Mexico	1912 (47)	121,365	1,654	3	Santa Fe	Albuquerque
New York	1788 (11)	47,224	18,169	31	Albany	New York
North Carolina	1789 (12)	48,718	7,070	12	Raleigh	Charlotte
North Dakota	1889 (39)	68,994	638	1	Bismarck	Fargo
Ohio	1803 (17)	40,953	11,102	19	Columbus	Columbus
Oklahoma	1907 (46)	68,679	3,258	6	Oklahoma City	Oklahoma City
Oregon	1859 (33)	96,003	3,086	5	Salem	Portland
Pennsylvania	1787 (2)	44,820	12,052	21	Harrisburg	Philadelphia
Rhode Island	1790 (13)	1,045	997	2	Providence	Providence
South Carolina	1788 (8)	30,111	3,664	6	Columbia	Columbia
South Dakota	1889 (40)	75,898	721	1	Pierre	Sioux Falls
Tennessee	1796 (16)	41,220	5,175	9	Nashville	Memphis
Texas	1845 (28)	261,914	18,378	30	Austin	Houston
Utah	1896 (45)	82,168	1,908	3	Salt Lake City	Salt Lake City
Vermont	1791 (14)	9,249	580	1	Montpelier	Burlington
Virginia	1788 (10)	39,598	6,552	11	Richmond	Virginia Beach
Washington	1889 (42)	66,582	5,343	9	Olympia	Seattle
West Virginia	1863 (35)	24,087	1,822	3	Charleston	Charleston
Wisconsin	1848 (30)	54,314	5,082	9	Madison	Milwaukee
Wyoming	1890 (44)	97,105	476	1	Cheyenne	Cheyenne
District of Columbia		61	570	1 (nonvoting)		

Self-Governing Areas, Possessions, and Dependencies	Land Area in Square Miles	Population (In Thousands)	Capital
Puerto Rico	3,515	3,522	San Juan
Guam	209	133	Agana
U.S. Virgin Islands	132	102	Charlotte Amalie
American Samoa	77	52	Pago Pago

Sources: *Department of Commerce, Bureau of the Census, 1997 Information Please Almanac*

★ State Flags ★

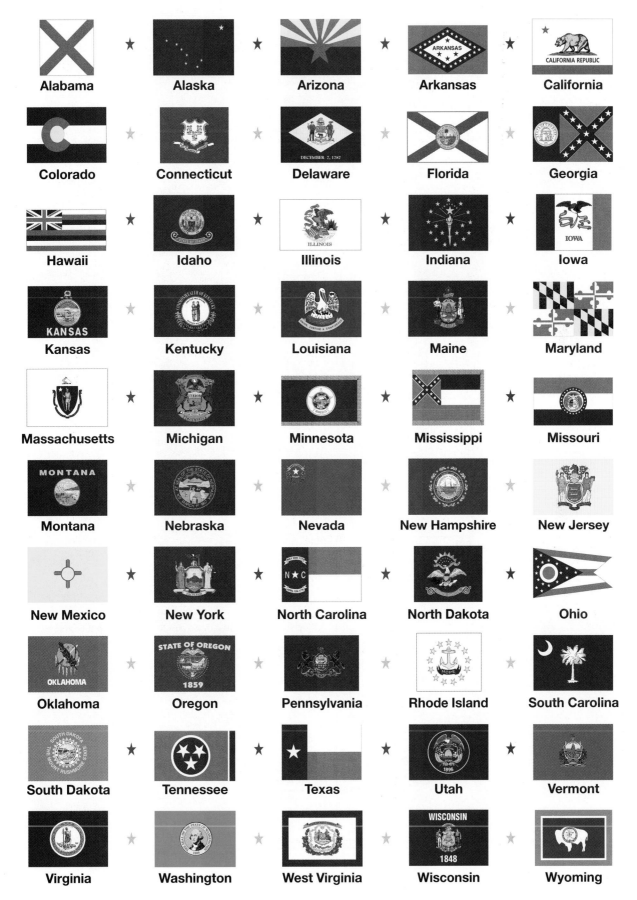

Alabama	Alaska	Arizona	Arkansas	California
Colorado	Connecticut	Delaware	Florida	Georgia
Hawaii	Idaho	Illinois	Indiana	Iowa
Kansas	Kentucky	Louisiana	Maine	Maryland
Massachusetts	Michigan	Minnesota	Mississippi	Missouri
Montana	Nebraska	Nevada	New Hampshire	New Jersey
New Mexico	New York	North Carolina	North Dakota	Ohio
Oklahoma	Oregon	Pennsylvania	Rhode Island	South Carolina
South Dakota	Tennessee	Texas	Utah	Vermont
Virginia	Washington	West Virginia	Wisconsin	Wyoming

★ THE FIFTY STATES ★

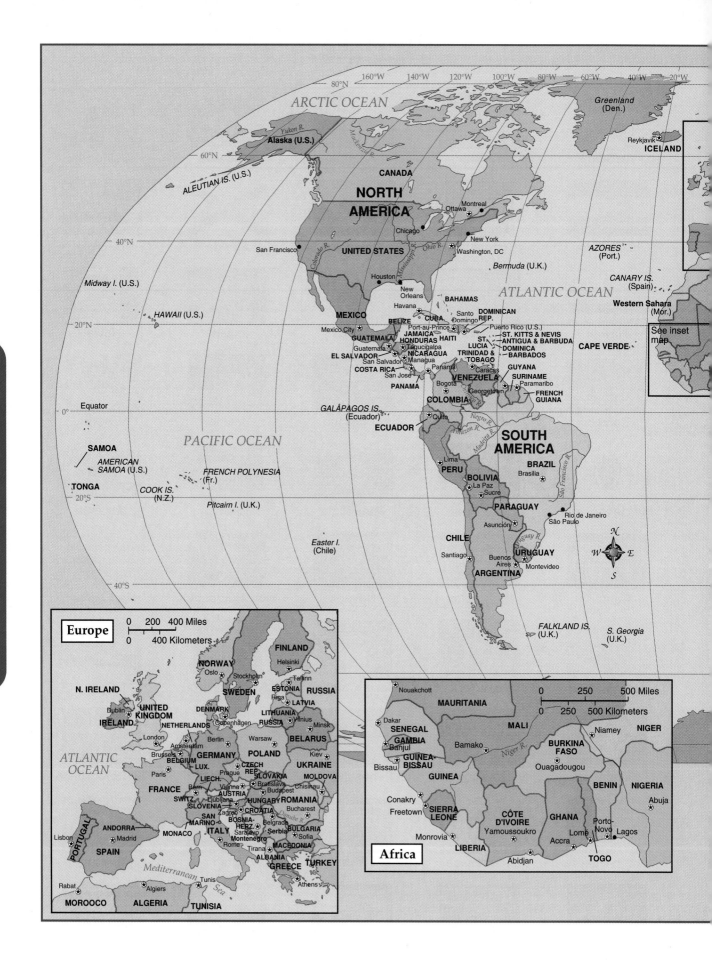

Map Labels

ARCTIC OCEAN

Greenland (Den.)

Reykjavik
ICELAND

Yukon R.

Alaska (U.S.)

60°N

CANADA

ALEUTIAN IS. (U.S.)

NORTH AMERICA

Montreal
Ottawa

Chicago

New York

40°N

San Francisco

UNITED STATES

Washington, DC

AZORES (Port.)

Bermuda (U.K.)

Midway I. (U.S.)

Houston

ATLANTIC OCEAN

CANARY IS. (Spain)

New Orleans

Western Sahara (Mor.)

HAWAII (U.S.)

MEXICO

BAHAMAS

Havana

Santo Domingo

DOMINICAN REP.

20°N

Mexico City

BELIZE

CUBA

Puerto Rico (U.S.)

See inset map

GUATEMALA

Port-au-Prince

JAMAICA

HAITI

ST. KITTS & NEVIS

HONDURAS

ANTIGUA & BARBUDA

CAPE VERDE

Guatemala

Tegucigalpa

ST. LUCIA

DOMINICA

EL SALVADOR

NICARAGUA

TRINIDAD & TOBAGO

BARBADOS

San Salvador

Managua

COSTA RICA

Caracas

GUYANA

SURINAME

Panama

VENEZUELA

PANAMA

Bogota

Georgetown

FRENCH GUIANA

Equator

COLOMBIA

Paramaribo

0°

GALÁPAGOS IS. (Ecuador)

Quito

PACIFIC OCEAN

ECUADOR

Negro R.

SOUTH AMERICA

Amazon R.

Madeira R.

SAMOA

BRAZIL

AMERICAN SAMOA (U.S.)

Lima

Brasilia

São Francisco R.

FRENCH POLYNESIA (Fr.)

PERU

BOLIVIA

TONGA

La Paz

20°S

COOK IS. (N.Z.)

Sucre

Pitcairn I. (U.K.)

PARAGUAY

Rio de Janeiro

São Paulo

Asunción

CHILE

Uruguay R.

Easter I. (Chile)

URUGUAY

N

Santiago

Buenos Aires

W E

ARGENTINA

Montevideo

S

40°S

FALKLAND IS. (U.K.)

S. Georgia (U.K.)

Europe

0   200   400 Miles
0   400 Kilometers

FINLAND

Helsinki

NORWAY

Oslo

Stockholm

ESTONIA

Tallinn

N. IRELAND

SWEDEN

RUSSIA

Riga

LATVIA

Dublin

UNITED KINGDOM

DENMARK

LITHUANIA

Vilnius

IRELAND

NETHERLANDS

Copenhagen

RUSSIA

Minsk

London

Amsterdam

Berlin

Warsaw

BELARUS

ATLANTIC OCEAN

Brussels

GERMANY

POLAND

Kiev

BELGIUM

LUX.

UKRAINE

Paris

Prague

CZECH REP.

SLOVAKIA

MOLDOVA

FRANCE

LIECH.

Vienna

Bratislava

Chisinau

SWITZ.

Bern

AUSTRIA

HUNGARY

ROMANIA

Ljubljana

Budapest

SLOVENIA

Bucharest

SAN MARINO

Zagreb

CROATIA

Danube R.

ANDORRA

BOSNIA-HERZ.

Belgrade

BULGARIA

Lisbon

Madrid

MONACO

Sarajevo

Serbia

Sofia

PORTUGAL

ITALY

Montenegro

MACEDONIA

SPAIN

Rome

Tirana

ALBANIA

TURKEY

GREECE

Mediterranean Sea

Rabat

Tunis

Athens

Algiers

MOROCCO

ALGERIA

TUNISIA

Africa

0   250   500 Miles
0   250   500 Kilometers

Nouakchott

MAURITANIA

Dakar

NIGER

SENEGAL

MALI

Niamey

GAMBIA

Banjul

Bamako

BURKINA FASO

Bissau

GUINEA-BISSAU

Niger R.

GUINEA

Ouagadougou

BENIN

NIGERIA

Conakry

Abuja

Freetown

SIERRA LEONE

CÔTE D'IVOIRE

GHANA

Porto-Novo

Lagos

Monrovia

Yamoussoukro

Lomé

Accra

LIBERIA

Abidjan

TOGO

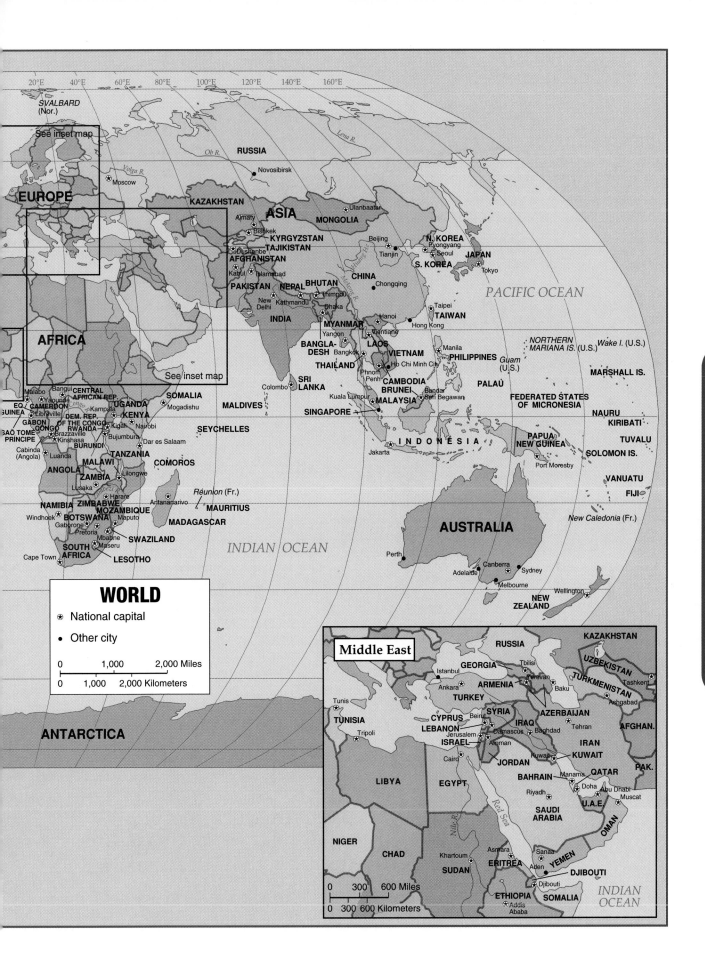

WORLD

⊛ National capital

• Other city

0   1,000   2,000 Miles

0   1,000   2,000 Kilometers

Middle East

0   300   600 Miles

0   300   600 Kilometers

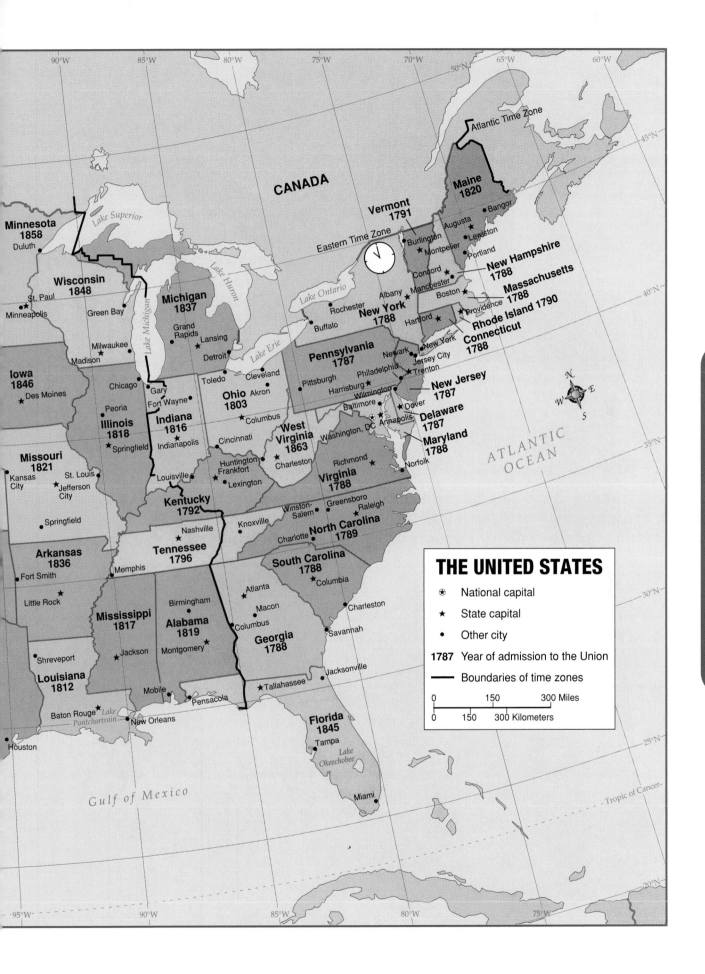

CANADA

Atlantic Time Zone

Maine 1820
● Bangor

Vermont 1791

Eastern Time Zone

Augusta ★
● Lewiston

Burlington ●
★ Montpelier
● Portland

New Hampshire 1788

Concord ★

Minnesota 1858
● Duluth

Lake Superior

Manchester ★

Boston ★
Massachusetts 1788

Wisconsin 1848
★ St. Paul
● Minneapolis

Lake Huron

Albany ●
★
Hartford ●

★ Providence
Rhode Island 1790

Connecticut 1788

Michigan 1837

● Green Bay

● Rochester

New York 1788

Lake Ontario

● Buffalo

Lake Michigan

● Grand Rapids
● Lansing ★

● Milwaukee
★ Madison

Detroit ●

Lake Erie

● Cleveland

Pennsylvania 1787

Newark ●
★
Jersey City ●
Trenton ★
New York ●

Iowa 1846
★ Des Moines

● Chicago
● Gary
● Toledo

Akron ●

Pittsburgh ●

Harrisburg ★
Philadelphia ●

New Jersey 1787

● Peoria
Fort Wayne ●

Ohio 1803

● Columbus

Wilmington ●

● Dover

Delaware 1787

Illinois 1818
★ Springfield

Indiana 1816
★ Indianapolis

● Cincinnati

West Virginia 1863

Baltimore ●
Washington, DC ✪ Annapolis ★

Maryland 1788

Missouri 1821
● Kansas City
● St. Louis
★ Jefferson City

Louisville ●

Huntington ●
Frankfort ★
● Lexington

Charleston ★

Richmond ★

● Norfolk

ATLANTIC OCEAN

Kentucky 1792

Virginia 1788

● Springfield

● Knoxville

Winston-Salem ●
● Greensboro
● Raleigh ★

Arkansas 1836

★ Nashville

Tennessee 1796

● Charlotte
North Carolina 1789

● Fort Smith

Memphis ●

South Carolina 1788
★ Columbia

★ Little Rock

● Atlanta
● Macon

● Charleston

THE UNITED STATES

Mississippi 1817

● Birmingham

Alabama 1819

★ Jackson
Columbus ●
Montgomery ★

Georgia 1788

● Savannah

✪ National capital

★ State capital

● Other city

● Shreveport

Louisiana 1812

Mobile ●

● Jacksonville

1787 Year of admission to the Union

Boundaries of time zones

Baton Rouge ★
Lake Pontchartrain
● New Orleans

Pensacola ●

★ Tallahassee

0	150	300 Miles
0	150	300 Kilometers

● Houston

Florida 1845
● Tampa

Lake Okeechobee

Gulf of Mexico

● Miami

Tropic of Cancer

PHYSICAL FEATURES

Elevations

Above 10,000 feet (3,000 meters)
7,000-10,000 feet (2,000-3,000 meters)
3,000-7,000 feet (1,000-2,000 meters)
700-3,000 feet (200-1,000 meters)
0-700 feet (0-200 meters)
Below sea level

Cape Cod
Long Island
Chesapeake Bay
Cape Hatteras
ATLANTIC COASTAL PLAIN
APPALACHIAN MOUNTAINS
Lake Okeechobee
PLAIN
COASTAL
GULF
Lake Ontario
Lake Erie
Lake Huron
Lake Michigan
Lake Superior
Tennessee R.
Alabama R.
Ohio R.
Mississippi R.
INTERIOR PLAINS
OZARK PLATEAU
OUACHITA MTS.
Mississippi R.
Red R.
Missouri R.
Arkansas R.
Rio Grande
LLANO ESTACADO
GREAT PLAINS
BLACK HILLS
Pikes Peak
Mt. Elbert
ROCKY MOUNTAINS
Platte R.
Missouri R.
Colorado R.
GRAND CANYON
Great Salt Lake
Snake R.
GREAT BASIN
SIERRA NEVADA
Mt. Whitney
CASCADE RANGE
Mt. Rainier
Columbia R.
Rio Grande

N
E
W
S

BROOKS RANGE
Yukon R.
Mt. McKinley

0 250 500 Miles
0 250 500 Kilometers

Kauai
Oahu
Molokai
Maui
Mauna Kea
Hawaii

0 100 Miles
0 100 Kilometers

0 150 300 Miles
0 150 300 Kilometers

NATURAL RESOURCES

Sulphur ○
Tin ■
Uranium ◆
Zinc ✚

Natural gas ◄
Nickel ◆
Oil ✚
Silver ●

Magnesium ✚
Manganese ●
Mercury ○
Molybdenum ◁

Copper ●
Gold ■
Iron ore ◄
Lead ○

Aluminum ◄
Chromium ◁
Coal
Cobalt ◆

★ GEOGRAPHIC ATLAS ★

300 Miles
300 Kilometers

0   150   300

Alaska

0   250   500 Miles
0   250   500 Kilometers

Hawaii

0   100 Miles
0   100 Kilometers

★ Gazetteer of American History ★

This gazetteer, or geographic dictionary, lists places that are important in American history. The approximate latitude and longitude are given for cities, towns, and other specific locations. See text page 10 for information about latitude and longitude. In the Gazetteer, after the description of each place, there are usually two numbers in parentheses. The first number refers to the text page where you can find out more about the place. The second appears in slanted, or *italic*, type and refers to a map *(m)* where the place is shown.

A

Africa Second largest continent in the world. (p. 12, *m10*)

Alabama 22nd state. Nicknamed the Heart of Dixie or the Cotton State. (p. 618, *m622–623*)

Alamo (29°N/99°W) Former mission in San Antonio, Texas, where 255 rebels died during the Texas war for independence. (p. 352, *m352*)

Alaska 49th state. Unofficially nicknamed the Last Frontier. Purchased from Russia in 1867. (p. 618, *m622–623*)

Albany (43°N/74°W) Capital of New York. (p. 171, *m170*)

Andes Rugged mountain chain in South America. (p. 50, *m47*)

Appalachian Mountains Mountain chain that stretches from Georgia to Canada. (p. 16, *m19*)

Appomattox Courthouse (37°N/79°W) Town in Virginia where Lee surrendered to Grant. (p. 473, *m472*)

Argentina Country in South America. (p. 313, *m314*)

Arizona 48th state. Nicknamed the Grand Canyon State. (p. 618, *m622–623*)

Arkansas 25th state. Nicknamed the Land of Opportunity. (p. 618, *m622–623*)

Asia Largest of the world's continents. (p. 12, *m10*)

Atlanta (34°N/84°W) Capital and largest city of Georgia. Burned by Sherman during the Civil War. (p. 472, *m460*)

Atlantic Ocean World's second largest ocean. (p. 14, *m10*)

B

Baltimore (39°N/77°W) Port city in Maryland. (p. 287, *m286*)

Bering Sea Narrow sea between Asia and North America. Scientists think a land bridge was here during the last ice age. *(m31)*

Boston (42°N/71°W) Seaport and industrial city in Massachusetts. (p. 17, *m96*)

Brazil Largest country in South America. (p. 313, *m314*)

Breed's Hill (42°N/71°W) Overlooks Boston harbor. Site of fighting during the Battle of Bunker Hill. (p. 162)

Buena Vista (26°N/101°W) City in Mexico. Site of an American victory in the Mexican War. (p. 362, *m361*)

Buffalo (43°N/79°W) City in New York State on Lake Erie. (p. 307, *m306*)

Bunker Hill (42°N/71°W) Overlooks Boston harbor. Site of first major battle of the Revolution. (p. 162)

C

Cahokia (39°N/90°W) British fort captured by George Rogers Clark during the American Revolution. (p. 174, *m175*)

California 31st state. Nicknamed the Golden State. Ceded to the United States by Mexico in 1848. (p. 618, *m622–623*)

Canada Northern neighbor of the United States. Second largest nation in the world. (p. 141, *m620–621*)

Canadian Shield Lowland region that lies mostly in eastern Canada. (p. 17, *m19*)

Caribbean Sea Tropical sea in the Western Hemisphere. (p. 65, *m67*)

Chancellorsville (38°N/78°W) Site of a Confederate victory in 1863. (p. 458, *m454*)

Charleston (33°N/80°W) City in South Carolina. Site of battles in both the American Revolution and the Civil War. (p. 108, *m107*)

Chesapeake Bay Large inlet of the Atlantic Ocean in Virginia and Maryland. (p. 287, *m286*)

Chicago (42°N/88°W) City in Illinois on Lake Michigan. (p. 5, *m622–623*)

China Country in East Asia. (p. 356, *m620–621*)

Cincinnati (39°N/84°W) City in southern Ohio on the Ohio River. *(m622–623)*

Coastal Plains Region consisting of the Atlantic Plain and the Gulf Plain along the Gulf of Mexico. (p. 17, *m19*)

Colorado 38th state. Nicknamed the Centennial State. (p. 618, *m622–623*)

Colorado River River that begins in the Rocky Mountains and flows into Gulf of California. (p. 18, *m19*)

Columbia River Chief river of the Pacific Northwest. (p. 275, *m273*)

Concord (43°N/71°W) Village in Massachusetts where battle occurred between the British and Americans at the start of the American Revolution. (p. 154, *m162*)

Connecticut One of the original 13 states. Nicknamed the Constitution State or the Nutmeg State. (p. 618, *m622–623*)

Cowpens (35°N/82°W) In South Carolina, site of an American victory in the Revolutionary War. (p. 179, *m179*)

Cumberland Gap (37°N/84°W) Pass in the Appalachian Mountains near the border of Virginia, Kentucky, and Tennessee. (p. 143, *m303*)

Cuzco (14°S/72°W) Capital of the Incan empire. (p. 50, *m47*)

D

Dallas (33°N/97°W) Major city in north central Texas. (*m900–901*)

Delaware One of the original 13 states. Nicknamed the First State or the Diamond State. (p. 618, *m622–623*)

Delaware River Flows into the Atlantic Ocean through Delaware Bay. (p. 82, *m88*)

Detroit (42°N/83°W) Largest city in Michigan. (p. 285, *m286*)

District of Columbia Located on the Potomac River. Seat of the federal government of the United States. (p. 247, *m622–623*)

E

England Part of Great Britain. (p. 78, *m79*)

Equator Line of latitude labeled 0° on maps. Separates the Northern and Southern hemispheres. (p. 10, *m10*)

Erie Canal Linked the Hudson and Mohawk rivers with Buffalo and Lake Erie. Built between 1817 and 1825. (p. 306, *m306*)

Europe World's second smallest continent. (p. 12, *m10*)

F

Florida 27th state. Nicknamed the Sunshine State. (p. 618, *m622–623*)

Fort Donelson (37°N/88°W) Located in Tennessee. Captured by Grant in 1862. (p. 458, *m470*)

Fort Henry (37°N/88°W) Located in Tennessee. Captured by Grant in 1862. (p. 458, *m470*)

Fort McHenry (39°N/77°W) Located in Baltimore harbor. British bombardment there in 1814 inspired Francis Scott Key to write "The Star-Spangled Banner." (p. 287)

Fort Necessity (40°N/79°W) British fort during the French and Indian War. (p. 136, *m138*)

Fort Pitt (40°N/80°W) British fort in the 1700s on the site of present-day Pittsburgh. (p. 140, *m175*)

Fort Sumter (33°N/80°W) Guarded Charleston harbor in South Carolina. First shots of the Civil War fired there in 1861. (p. 443, *m470*)

Fort Ticonderoga (44°N/74°W) Fort at the south end of Lake Champlain. Captured from the British by Ethan Allen in 1775. (p. 140, *m138*)

France Country in Western Europe. (p. 81, *m620–621*)

Fredericksburg (38°N/78°W) Located in eastern Virginia. Site of a Confederate victory in 1862. (p. 457, *m454*)

G

Gadsden Purchase Land purchased from Mexico in 1853. Now part of Arizona and New Mexico. (p. 363, *m363*)

Georgia One of the original 13 states. Nicknamed the Peach State or the Empire State of the South. (p. 618, *m622–623*)

Germany Country in central Europe (p. 381, *m620–621*)

Gettysburg (40°N/77°W) Town in southern Pennsylvania. Site of a Union victory in 1863 and Lincoln's Gettysburg Address. (p. 469, *m454*)

Goliad (29°N//97°W) Texas town where Mexicans killed several hundred Texans during the Texas war for independence. (p. 355, *m355*)

Gonzales (29°N/97°W) City in Texas near San Antonio. Site of the first Texan victory over Mexico in 1835. (p. 352, *m355*)

Great Britain Island nation of Western Europe. Includes England, Scotland, Wales, and Northern Ireland. (p. 135, *m620–621*)

Great Lakes Chain of five lakes in central North America. Lakes Superior, Michigan, Huron, Ontario, and Erie. (p. 18, *m19*)

Great Plains Western part of the Interior Plains. (p. 16, *m19*)

Great Salt Lake (41°N/113°W) Lake in northern Utah with highly saline water. (p. 365, *m366*)

Great Wagon Road Early pioneer route across the Appalachians. (p. 105, *m102*)

Gulf of Mexico Body of water along the southern coast of the United States. (p. 17, *m19*)

H

Haiti Country in the West Indies. The nation won independence from France in the early 1800s. (p. 270, *m620–621*)

Harpers Ferry (39°N/78°W) Town in West Virginia. John Brown raided the arsenal there in 1859. (p. 438, *m454*)

Hawaii Newest of the 50 states. Nicknamed the Aloha State. (p. 618, *m622–623*)

Hawaiian Islands Region in the Pacific Ocean composed of a group of eight large islands and many small islands. (p. 17, *m19*)

Hudson River Largest river in New York State. (p. 78, *m88*)

I

Idaho 43rd state. Nicknamed the Gem State. Acquired as part of the Oregon Territory. (p. 618, *m622–623*)

Illinois 21st state. Nicknamed the Inland Empire. Settled as part of the Northwest Territory. (p. 618, *m622–623*)

Indiana 19th state. Nicknamed the Hoosier State. Settled as part of the Northwest Territory. (p. 618, *m622–623*)

Interior Plains Region of the central United States that stretches from the Rockies to the Appalachians. (p. 16, *m19*)

Intermountain Region Rugged region from the Rocky Mountains to the Sierra Nevada and coastal mountains of the western United States. (p. 15, *m19*)

Iowa 29th state. Nicknamed the Hawkeye State. Acquired as part of the Louisiana Purchase. (p. 618, *m622–623*)

Italy Country in Southern Europe. (p. 502, *m620–621*)

J

Jamestown (37°N/77°W) First successful English colony in North America. (p. 85, *m88*)

K

Kansas 34th state. Nicknamed the Sunflower State. Acquired as part of the Louisiana Purchase. (p. 618, *m622–623*)

Kaskaskia (38°N/90°W) British fort on the Mississippi River captured by George Rogers Clark during the American Revolution. (p. 174, *m175*)

Kentucky 15th state. Nicknamed the Bluegrass State. (p. 618, *m622–623*)

Kilwa (8°S/39°E) East African trading state in the 1400s. (p. 73, *m75*)

King's Mountain (35°N/81°W) In South Carolina, site of an American victory in the Revolutionary War. (p. 178, *m179*)

L

Lancaster Turnpike Road built in the 1790s linking Philadelphia and Lancaster, Pennsylvania. (p. 302, *m303*)

Latin America Name for those parts of the Western Hemisphere where Latin languages such as Spanish, French, and Portuguese are spoken. Includes Mexico, Central America, South America, and the islands of the Caribbean. (p. 312, *m314*)

Lexington (42°N/71°W) Village in Massachusetts. Site of the first clash between minutemen and British troops in 1775. (p. 155, *m162*)

Liberia Country in West Africa. Set up in 1822 as a colony for free African Americans. (p. 403, *m620–621*)

London (51°N/0°) Capital of United Kingdom. (*m898–899*)

Long Island Located in New York. Site of a British victory in the Revolution. (p. 169, *m170*)

Los Angeles (34°N/118°W) City in southern California. First settled by Spanish missionaries. (p. 15, *m67*)

Louisbourg (46°N/60°W) Fort in eastern Canada that played a major role in the French and Indian War. (p. 140, *m138*)

Louisiana 18th state. Nicknamed the Pelican State. First state created out of the Louisiana Purchase. (p. 618, *m622–623*)

Lowell (43°N/83°W) City in Massachusetts. Important site of Industrial Revolution. (p. 296)

M

Maine 23rd state. Nicknamed the Pine Tree State. Originally part of Massachusetts. (p. 618, *m622–623*)

Mali Kingdom in West Africa. Reached its peak between 1200 and 1400. (p. 73, *m75*)

Maryland One of the original 13 states. Nicknamed the Old Line State or the Free State. (p. 618, *m622–623*)

Mason-Dixon Line Boundary between Pennsylvania and Maryland surveyed and marked in the 1760s. (p. 106)

Massachusetts One of the original 13 states. Nicknamed the Bay State or the Old Colony. (p. 618, *m622–623*)

Memphis (35°N/90°W) City in Tennessee on the Mississippi River. Captured by Union forces in 1862. (p. 458, *m470*)

Mexican Cession Lands acquired by the United States from Mexico under the Treaty of Guadalupe Hidalgo in 1848. (p. 363, *m363*)

Mexico Southern neighbor of the United States. Gained independence from Spain in 1821. (p. 312, *m620–621*)

Mexico City (19°N/99°W) Capital of Mexico. (p. 434, *m433*)

Michigan 26th state. Nicknamed the Great Lake State or the Wolverine State. Settled as part of the Northwest Territory. (p. 618, *m622–623*)

Minnesota 32nd state. Nicknamed the Gopher State. Most of it was acquired as part of the Louisiana Purchase from France. (p. 618, *m622–623*)

Mississippi 20th state. Nicknamed the Magnolia State. (p. 618, *m622–623*)

Mississippi River Longest river in the United States. Links the Great Lakes with the Gulf of Mexico. (p. 17, *m19*)

Missouri 24th state. Nicknamed the Show Me State. Acquired as part of the Louisiana Purchase. (p. 618, *m622–623*)

Missouri River Second longest river in the United States. Rises in the northern Rocky Mountains

and joins the Mississippi River near St. Louis, Missouri (p. 17, *m19*)

Mogadishu (2°N/45°E) East African trading state in the 1400s. (p. 73, *m75*)

Montana 41st state. Nicknamed the Treasure State. Acquired in part through the Louisiana Purchase. (p. 618, *m622–623*)

Montreal (46°N/74°W) Major city in Canada. Located in the province of Quebec. (p. 141, *m138*)

N

National Road Early road to the West that began in Cumberland, Maryland, and eventually reached Illinois. (p. 303, *m303*)

Nauvoo (41°N/91°W) Town founded by the Mormons in Illinois in the 1840s. (p. 365, *m366*)

Nebraska 37th state. Nicknamed the Cornhusker State. Acquired as part of the Louisiana Purchase. (p. 618, *m622–623*)

Nevada 36th state. Nicknamed the Sagebrush State or the Battle Born State. Acquired at the end of the Mexican War. (p. 618, *m622–623*)

New Amsterdam (41°N/74°W) Town established by Dutch settlers on Manhattan Island in the early 1600s. Renamed New York by the British. (p. 82)

New France Colony established by France in North America. (p. 81, *m79*)

New Hampshire One of the original 13 states. Nicknamed the Granite State. (p. 618, *m622–623*)

New Jersey One of the original 13 states. Nicknamed the Garden State. (p. 618, *m622–623*)

New Mexico 47th state. Nicknamed the Land of Enchantment. Acquired at the end of the Mexican War. (p. 618, *m622–623*)

New Netherland Dutch colony on the Hudson River. Seized by the English and renamed New York in 1664. (p. 82)

New Orleans (30°N/90°W) Port city in Louisiana near the mouth of the Mississippi River. Settled by the French in the 1600s. (p. 82, *m79*)

New Spain Area in the Americas ruled by Spain for some 300 years. Included much of present-day western United States. (p. 68, *m68*)

New York One of the original 13 states. Nicknamed the Empire State. (p. 618, *m622–623*)

New York City (41°N/74°W) Port city at the mouth of the Hudson River. (p. 101, *m102*)

North America World's third largest continent. (p. 14, *m10*)

North Carolina One of the original 13 states. Nicknamed the Tar Heel State or the Old North State. (p. 618, *m622–623*)

North Dakota 39th state. Nicknamed the Sioux State or the Flickertail State. Acquired as part of the Louisiana Purchase. (p. 618, *m622–623*)

Northwest Territory Name for lands north of the Ohio River. Acquired by the Treaty of Paris in 1783. (p. 190, *m191*)

Nueces River Claimed by Mexico in the Mexican War as the southern border of Texas. (p. 361, *m361*)

O

Ohio 17th state. Nicknamed the Buckeye State. Settled as part of the Northwest Territory. (p. 618, *m622–623*)

Ohio River Important transportation route. Begins at Pittsburgh and flows to the Mississippi River. (p. 133, *m133*)

Oklahoma 46th State. Nicknamed the Sooner State. Acquired as part of the Louisiana Purchase. (p. 618, *m622–623*)

Oregon 33rd state. Nicknamed the Beaver State. Acquired as part of the Oregon Territory. (p. 618, *m622–623*)

Oregon Trail Overland route from Independence, Missouri, to the Columbia River valley. (p. 349, *m347*)

P

Pacific Coast Highest and most rugged region of the United States. Includes the Cascades and the Sierra Nevada. (p. 15, *m19*)

Pacific Ocean World's largest ocean. (p. 14, *m10*)

Panama Country on the isthmus separating North and South America. Gained independence from Colombia in 1903. (p. 516, *m516*)

Panama Canal Canal dug through the Isthmus of Panama to link the Atlantic and Pacific oceans. (p. 517, *m516*)

Paris (49°N/2°E) Capital of France. (p. 172, *m619*)

Pennsylvania One of the original 13 states. Nicknamed the Keystone State. (p. 618, *m622–623*)

Petersburg (37°N/78°W) City in Virginia. Union forces kept the city under siege for nine months during the Civil War. (p. 472, *m472*)

Philadelphia (40°N/75°W) Major port and chief city in Pennsylvania. (p. 247, *m102*)

Philippine Islands Group of islands in the Pacific Ocean. Acquired by the United States in 1898. Gained independence in 1946. (p. 516, *m620–621*)

Pikes Peak (39°N/105°W) Mountain located in the Rocky Mountains of central Colorado. (p. 275, *m273*)

Plymouth (42°N/71°W) New England colony founded in 1620 by Pilgrims. (p. 89, *m88*)

Portugal Country in Western Europe. (p. 61, *m75*)

Potomac River Forms part of the Maryland-Virginia border. Flows through Washington, D.C., and into Chesapeake Bay. (p. 455, *m455*)

Prime Meridian Line of longitude labeled 0° on maps. (p. 10, *m10*)

Princeton (40°N/75°W) City in New Jersey. Site of an American victory during the Revolution. (p. 170, *m170*)

Puerto Rico (18°N/67°W) Island in the Caribbean Sea. A self-governing commonwealth of the United States. (p. 516, *m516*)

Q

Quebec (47°N/71°W) City in eastern Canada. (p. 81, *m79*)

R

Rhode Island One of the original 13 states. Nicknamed Little Rhody or the Ocean State. (p. 618, *m622–623*)

Richmond (38°N/78°W) Capital of Virginia. Capital of the Confederate States of America during the Civil War. (p. 453, *m454*)

Rio Grande River that forms the border between the United States and Mexico. (p. 18, *m19*)

Roanoke Island (36°N/76°W) Island off North Carolina. Site of English "lost colony" founded in 1587. (p. 84, *m88*)

Rocky Mountains Mountains extending through the western United States and Canada. (p. 16, *m19*)

Russia Largest country in the world, spanning Europe and Asia. (p. 502, *m620–621*)

S

Sacramento (39°N/122°W) Capital of California. Developed as a gold rush boom town. (p. 367, *m366*)

St. Augustine (30°N/81°W) City in Florida. Founded by Spain in 1565. Oldest European settlement in the United States. (p. 69, *m67*)

St. Lawrence River Waterway from the Great Lakes to the Atlantic Ocean. Forms part of the border between the United States and Canada. (p. 18, *m79*)

St. Louis (38°N/90°W) City in Missouri on the Mississippi River. Lewis and Clark began their expedition there. (p. 272, *m273*)

Salt Lake City (41°N/112°W) Largest city in Utah. Founded in 1847 by Mormons. (p. 366, *m366*)

San Antonio (29°N/99°W) City in southern Texas. Site of the Alamo. (p. 352, *m352*)

San Diego (33°N/117°W) City in southern California. Founded as the first Spanish mission in California. (p. 357, *m366*)

San Francisco (38°N/122°W) City in northern California. Boom town of the California gold rush. (p. 359, *m366*)

Santa Fe (35°N/106°W) Capital of New Mexico. First settled by the Spanish. (p. 69, *m67*)

Santa Fe Trail Overland trail from Independence to Santa Fe. Opened in 1821. (p. 356, *m366*)

Saratoga (43°N/75°W) City in eastern New York. The American victory there in 1777 was a turning point in the Revolution. (p. 172, *m170*)

Savannah (32°N/81°W) Oldest city in Georgia, founded in 1733. (p. 108, *m107*)

Sierra Nevada Mountain range mostly in California. (p. 15, *m19*)

Songhai West African kingdom in the 1400s. (p. 74, *m75*)

South America World's fourth largest continent. (p. 12, *m10*)

South Carolina One of the original 13 states. Nicknamed the Palmetto State. (p. 618, *m622–623*)

South Dakota 40th state. Nicknamed the Coyote State or the Sunshine State. Acquired as part of the Louisiana Purchase. (p. 618, *m622–623*)

Spain Country in southwestern Europe. (p. 61, *m79*)

Spanish Florida Part of New Spain. Purchased by the United States in 1821. (p. 282, *m283*)

T

Tennessee 16th state. Nicknamed the Volunteer State. Gained statehood after North Carolina ceded its western lands

to the United States. (p. 618, *m622–623*)

Tenochtitlán (19°N/99°W) Capital of the Aztec empire. Now part of Mexico City. (p. 48, *m47*)

Texas 28th state. Nicknamed the Lone Star State. Proclaimed independence from Mexico in 1836. Was a separate republic until 1845. (p. 618, *m622–623*)

Tikal (17°N/90°W) Ancient Mayan city. (p. 47, *m47*)

Timbuktu (17°N/3°W) City on the Niger River in Africa. (p. 74, *m75*)

Trenton (41°N/74°W) Capital of New Jersey. Site of an American victory in the Revolution. (p. 170, *m170*)

U

Utah 45th state. Nicknamed the Beehive State. Settled by Mormons. (p. 618, *m622–623*)

V

Valley Forge (40°N/76°W) Winter headquarters for the Continental Army in 1777–1778. Located near Philadelphia. (p. 173, *m170*)

Veracruz (19°N/96°W) Port city in Mexico on the Gulf of Mexico. (p. 362, *m361*)

Vermont 14th state. Nicknamed the Green Mountain State.(p. 618, *m622–623*)

Vicksburg (42°N/86°W) City in Mississippi. Site of a Union victory in 1863. (p. 468, *m470*)

Vietnam Country in Southeast Asia. Site of a war involving the United States during the Cold War. (p. 517, *m517*)

Vincennes (39°N/88°W) City in Indiana. British fort there was captured by George Rogers Clark in 1779. (p. 174, *m175*)

Virgin Islands (18°N/64°W) Territory of the United States. Purchased from Denmark in 1917. (p. 896, *m898–899*)

Virginia One of the original 13 states. Nicknamed the Old Dominion. (p. 618, *m622–623*)

W

Washington 42nd state. Nicknamed the Evergreen State. Acquired as part of Oregon Territory. (p. 618, *m622–623*)

Washington, D.C. (39°N/77°W) Capital of the United States since 1800. (p. 287, *m214*)

West Indies Islands in the Caribbean Sea. Explored by Columbus. (p. 62, *m68*)

West Virginia 35th state. Nicknamed the Mountain State. Separated from Virginia early in the Civil War. (p. 618, *m622–623*)

Western Hemisphere Western half of the world. Includes North and South America. (p. 12, *m10*)

Wisconsin 30th state. Nicknamed the Badger State. Settled as part of the Northwest Territory. (p. 618, *m622–623*)

Wyoming 44th state. Nicknamed the Equality State. (p. 618, *m622–623*)

Y

Yorktown (37°N/76°W) Town in Virginia. Site of the British surrender in 1781. (p. 180, *m179*)

★ Glossary ★

This glossary defines all vocabulary words and many important historical terms and phrases. These words and terms appear in blue or boldfaced type the first time that they are used in the text. The page number(s) after each definition refers to the page(s) on which the word or phrase is defined in the text. For other references, see the index.

Pronunciation Key

When difficult names or terms first appear in the text, they are respelled to help you with pronunciation. A syllable printed in SMALL CAPITAL LETTERS receives the greatest stress. The pronunciation key below lists the letters and symbols that will help you pronounce the word. It also includes examples of words using each sound and showing how they would be pronounced.

Symbol	Example	Respelling
a	hat	(hat)
ay	pay, late	(pay), (layt)
ah	star, hot	(stahr), (haht)
ai	air, dare	(air), (dair)
aw	law, all	(law), (awl)
eh	met	(meht)
ee	bee, eat	(bee), (eet)
er	learn, sir, fur	(lern), (ser), (fer)
ih	fit	(fiht)
i	mile	(mīl)
ir	ear	(ir)
oh	no	(noh)
oi	soil, boy	(soil), (boi)
oo	root, rule	(root), (rool)
or	born, door	(born), (dor)
ow	plow, out	(plow), (owt)

Symbol	Example	Respelling
u	put, book	(put), (buk)
uh	fun	(fuhn)
yoo	few, use	(fyoo), (yooz)
ch	chill, reach	(chihl), (reech)
g	go, dig	(goh), (dihg)
j	jet, gently bridge	(jeht), (JEHNT lee), (brihj)
k	kite, cup	(kīt), (kuhp)
ks	mix	(mihks)
kw	quick	(kwihk)
ng	bring	(brihng)
s	say, cent	(say), (sehnt)
sh	she, crash	(shee), (krash)
th	three	(three)
y	yet, onion	(yeht), (UHN yuhn)
z	zip, always	(zihp), (AWL wayz)
zh	treasure	(TREH zher)

A

abolitionist person who wanted to end slavery (p. 404)

absolute power total authority by a ruler over the people (p. 49)

adobe sun-dried clay brick (p. 35)

ally nation that works with another nation for a common purpose (p. 172)

altitude height above sea level (p. 19)

amend to change (p. 208)

amendment formal written change (p. 222)

American System plan proposed by Henry Clay that called for high tariffs and internal improvements (p. 310)

amnesty government pardon (pp. 479, 503)

annex to add on (pp. 355, 515)

Antifederalist person who opposed ratification of the Constitution (p. 205)

appeal to ask that a decision be reviewed by a higher court (p. 231)

apprentice (uh PREHN tihs) person who learns a trade or craft from a master (p. 120)

appropriate to set aside money for a special purpose (p. 226)

aqueduct channel for carrying water (p. 50)

archaeology (ahr kee AHL uh jee) study of evidence left by early people in order to find out about their culture (p. 32)

arsenal warehouse for guns and ammunition (p. 438)

Articles of Confederation first constitution of the United States (p. 189)

artifact (AHRT uh fakt) object made by humans and used by archaeologists to learn about past human cultures (p. 32)

artisan worker who has learned a trade, such as carpentry (p. 379)

assembly line method of production in which workers add parts to a product as it moves along on a belt (p. 507)

astrolabe (AS troh layb) instrument to measure the positions of stars and figure out latitude (p. 61)

B

backcountry area of land along the eastern slopes of the Appalachian Mountains (p. 105)

bill proposed law (pp. 203, 221)

bill of rights list of freedoms that a government promises to protect (p. 116)

Bill of Rights first 10 amendments to the Constitution (p. 208)

black codes laws that severely limited the rights of freedmen after the Civil War (p. 482)

blockade shutting off a port by positioning ships to keep people or supplies from moving in or out (p. 164)

bond certificate that promises to repay money loaned, plus interest, on a certain date (p. 246)

Boston Massacre (1770) shooting of five colonists by British soldiers (p. 148)

Boston Tea Party (1773) protest in which colonists dressed as Indians dumped British tea into Boston harbor (p. 151)

boycott to refuse to buy certain goods or services (p. 144)

buffer land between two other lands that reduces the possibility of conflict between the other two (p. 109)

C

Cabinet group of officials who head government departments and advise the President (pp. 224, 245)

canal artificial channel filled with water to allow boats to cross a stretch of land (p. 305)

capitalist person who invests in a business to make a profit (p. 296)

caravel (KAR uh vehl) ship with a steering rudder and triangular sails (p. 62)

carpetbagger name for a northerner who came south after the Civil War seeking personal gain (p. 486)

cartographer person who makes maps (p. 8)

cash crop crop sold for money (p. 103)

caucus private meeting of political party leaders to choose a candidate (p. 327)

causeway raised road across a stretch of water (p. 48)

cavalry troops on horseback (p. 173)

cede to give up, as land (p. 363)

charter legal document giving certain rights to a person or company (p. 85)

checks and balances system by which each branch of government can check, or control, the actions of the other branches (p. 202)

chinampa Aztec floating garden (p. 49)

city-state town that has its own independent government (p. 73)

civil disobedience nonviolent opposition to a government policy or law by refusing to comply with it (p. 510)

civil rights movement the efforts of African Americans and others who worked for equality (p. 510)

civil war war between people of the same country (p. 428)

civilian person not in the military (p. 463)

civilization advanced culture (p. 46)

clan group of related families (p. 45)

climate average weather of a place over a period of 20 to 30 years (p. 19)

clipper ship fast-sailing ship of the mid-1800s (p. 377)

colony group of people who move to a new land and are ruled by the government of their native land (p. 64)

Columbian Exchange worldwide exchange of goods and ideas that began with Columbus's voyages to the Americas (p. 53)

committee of correspondence group of colonists who wrote letters and pamphlets reporting on British actions (p. 149)

common open field where cattle grazed (p. 98)

compromise settlement in which each side gives up some of its demands in order to reach an agreement (p. 194)

Compromise of 1850 agreement over slavery under which California joined the Union as a free state and a strict fugitive slave law was passed (p. 428)

Confederate States of America nation formed in 1861 by the southern states that seceded from the Union (p. 442)

confederation alliance of independent states (p. 189)

conglomerate giant corporation that owns a large number of smaller companies in different fields (p. 508)

conquistador (kahn KEES tuh dor) Spanish word for conqueror (p. 65)

conservative person who wants to keep conditions as they are or return them to the way they used to be (p. 487)

constituent person who elected a representative to office (p. 228)

constitution document that sets out the laws and principles of a government (p. 188)

Constitutional Convention (1787) meeting of delegates from 12 states who wrote the United States Constitution (p. 193)

Continental Army army established by the Second Continental Congress to fight the British (p. 160)

continental divide mountain ridge that separates river systems flowing toward opposite sides of a continent (p. 274)

Copperheads northerners who opposed using force to keep the southern states in the Union (p. 463)

corduroy road road made of logs (p. 302)

corporation business that is owned by investors (p. 508)

cottonocracy name for the wealthy planters who made their money from cotton in the mid-1800s (p. 388)

coureur de bois (koo ruhr duh BWAH) phrase meaning runner of the woods; trapper or trader in New France (p. 81)

creole person born in Spain's American colonies to Spanish parents (pp. 70, 312)

Crusades wars fought by European Christians in the Middle Ages to gain control of the Middle East (p. 60)

culture entire way of life developed by a people (p. 32)

culture area region in which people share a similar way of life (p. 36)

D

dame school private school for girls in the New England colonies (p. 121)

debtor person who owes money (p. 108)

Declaration of Independence (1776) document stating that the colonies were a free and independent nation (p. 166)

democratic ensuring that all people have the same rights (p. 266)

depression period when business slows, prices and wages fall, and unemployment rises (pp. 192, 338)

discrimination policy or attitude that denies equal rights and treatment to certain groups of people (pp. 381, 461)

dissenting opinion statement explaining why a Supreme Court Justice disagrees with the opinion of the majority (p. 231)

domestic tranquillity peace at home (p. 215)

draft law requiring certain people to serve in the military (p. 464)

drought long dry spell (p. 35)

due process principle that government must follow the same fair rules in all cases brought to trial (pp. 209, 232)

dumping selling of goods in another country at very low prices (p. 310)

E

Elastic Clause section of the Constitution that gives Congress the power to make all "necessary and proper" laws (p. 224)

electoral college group of electors from every state who meet every four years to vote for the President and Vice President of the United States (p. 202)

elevation height above sea level (p. 14)

emancipate to set free (p. 459)

Emancipation Proclamation (1863) President Lincoln's declaration freeing slaves in the Confederacy (p. 460)

embargo ban on trade with another country (p. 350)

encomienda (ehn koh mee EHN dah) right given by Spanish government to Spanish settlers to demand labor or taxes from Native Americans (p. 70)

English Bill of Rights (1689) document guaranteeing the basic rights of English citizens (pp. 116, 199)

Enlightenment movement in Europe in the late 1600s and 1700s that emphasized the use of reason (pp. 121, 199)

Equator imaginary line that lies at 0° latitude (p. 8)

execute to carry out (p. 188)

executive agreement informal agreement made by the President with another head of state (p. 229)

executive branch branch of government that carries out laws (p. 194)

expedition long journey or voyage of exploration (p. 272)

export trade product sent to markets outside a country (p. 112)

extended family close-knit family group that includes grandparents, parents, children, aunts, uncles, and cousins (p. 393)

F

faction group inside a political party or other group (p. 253)

factory system method of producing goods that brought workers and machinery together in one place (p. 296)

famine severe food shortage and starvation (p. 381)

federal having to do with the national government (p. 215)

federalism division of power between the states and the national government (p. 200)

feudalism (FYOOD 'l ihz uhm) rule by lords who owe loyalty to a monarch (p. 60)

First Continental Congress (1774) meeting of delegates from 12 colonies in Philadelphia (p. 154)

foreign policy actions that a nation takes in relation to other nations (p. 251)

forty-niner person who headed to California in search of gold during the Gold Rush of 1849 (p. 367)

freedmen men and women who had been slaves (p. 479)

fugitive runaway (p. 428)

G

general welfare well-being of all the people (p. 216)

gentry highest social class in the 13 English colonies (p. 117)

geography the study of people, their environments, and their resources (p. 4)

Gettysburg Address (1863) speech by President Lincoln after the Battle of Gettysburg (p. 470)

glacier thick sheet of ice (p. 30)

globe sphere with a map of Earth printed on it (p. 8)

Glorious Revolution (1688) movement that brought William and Mary to the throne of England and strengthened the rights of English citizens (p. 116)

grandfather clause law that excused a voter from a literacy test if his grandfather had been eligible to vote on January 1, 1867—protected the voting rights of southern whites but not those of southern blacks (p. 493)

Great Awakening religious movement in the English colonies in the early 1700s (p. 119)

Great Compromise plan at the Constitutional Convention that settled the differences between large and small states (p. 196)

Great Depression (1929–1941) worst period of economic decline in United States history (p. 513)

guerrilla soldier who uses hit-and-run tactics (p. 179)

H

habeas corpus right to have charges filed or a hearing before being jailed (p. 464)

hemisphere half of the Earth (p. 8)

hieroglyphics system of writing that uses pictures to represent words and ideas (p. 47)

hill area of raised land that is lower and more rounded than a mountain (p. 14)

history account of what has happened in the lives of different peoples (p. 4)

hogan house made of mud plaster over a framework of wooden poles (p. 41)

House of Burgesses representative assembly in colonial Virginia (pp. 86, 199)

House of Representatives larger house of Congress, in which each state is represented according to its population (p. 225)

Hudson River School group of American artists who painted landscapes of New York's Hudson River region in the mid-1800s (p. 415)

I

igloo house of snow and ice, developed by the Inuits (p. 37)

illegal alien someone who enters a country without legal permission (p. 503)

immigrant person who enters a country in order to settle there (p. 259)

impeach to bring a formal charge of wrongdoing against the President or another public official (pp. 203, 228, 484)

imperialism policy of powerful countries seeking to control the economic and political affairs of weaker countries or regions (p. 515)

import trade product brought into a country (p. 112)

impressment act of forcing someone to serve in the navy (p. 277)

inauguration ceremony at which the President officially takes the oath of office (p. 244)

income tax tax on people's earnings (p. 466)

indentured servant person who agreed to work without wages for some time in exchange for passage to the colonies (p. 117)

Industrial Revolution process by which machines replaced hand tools, and steam and other new sources of power replaced human and animal power (p. 294)

inflation rise in prices and decrease in the value of money (p. 466)

initiative process by which voters can put a bill directly before the state legislature by collecting signatures on a petition (p. 513)

integration bringing together people of different races or ethnic groups (p. 510)

interchangeable parts identical, machine-made parts for a tool or instrument (p. 299)

interstate commerce trade between different states (p. 311)

intervention direct involvement in another country (p. 315)

Intolerable Acts (1774) laws passed by Parliament to punish colonists for the Boston Tea Party (p. 153)

irrigate to bring water to an area (p. 6)

isthmus narrow strip of land (p. 14)

J

jazz music style that developed from blues, ragtime, and other earlier styles (p. 504)

Jim Crow laws laws that separated people of different races in public places in the South (p. 495)

joint committee congressional committee that includes both House and Senate members (p. 226)

judicial branch branch of government that decides if laws are carried out fairly (p. 194)

judicial review power of the Supreme Court to decide whether acts of a President or laws passed by Congress are constitutional (pp. 224, 269)

justice fairness (p. 215)

K

kachina masked dancer at religious ceremonies of the Southwest Indians (p. 41)

kayak (KI ak) small boat made of animal skins (p. 37)

kinship network close ties among family members (p. 74)

kitchen cabinet group of unofficial advisers to President Andrew Jackson (p. 331)

kiva underground chamber where Pueblo men held religious ceremonies (p. 41)

L

laissez faire (lehs ay FAYR) idea that government should play as small a role as possible in economic affairs (pp. 267, 339)

latitude distance north or south from the Equator (p. 4)

lawsuit legal case brought by one person or group against another to settle a dispute (p. 434)

legislative branch branch of government that passes laws (p. 194)

legislature group of people who have the power to make laws (p. 114)

libel publishing a statement that unjustly damages a person's reputation (p. 123)

liberty freedom to live as you please provided you obey the laws and respect the rights of others (p. 217)

literacy test examination to see if a person can read and write, used in the past to restrict voting rights (p. 493)

locomotive engine that uses steam or another power source to pull a railroad train (p. 376)

long house Native American home built of wood poles and bark (p. 44)

longitude distance east or west from the Prime Meridian (p. 4)

Louisiana Purchase (1803) vast territory west of the Mississippi purchased from France (p. 272)

Loyalist colonist who remained loyal to Britain (p.161)

lynching illegal seizure and execution of someone by a mob (p. 495)

M

Magna Carta (1215) document that guaranteed rights to English nobles (pp. 86, 198)

magnetic compass device that shows which direction is North (p. 61)

majority more than half (p. 324)

Manifest Destiny belief that the United States had the right and the duty to expand to the Pacific (p. 359)

manor district ruled by a lord, including the lord's castle, peasants' huts, and surrounding fields (p. 60)

map projection way of drawing the Earth on a flat surface (p. 8)

Marbury v. *Madison* (1803) Supreme Court decison that established the precedent of judicial review (p. 269)

martial law rule by the army instead of the elected government (p. 448)

martyr person who dies for his or her beliefs (p. 438)

Mayflower Compact (1620) agreement for ruling the Plymouth Colony, signed by Pilgrims before they landed at Plymouth (pp. 88, 199)

McCulloch **v.** *Maryland* (1819) Supreme Court ruling that states have no right to interfere with federal institutions within their borders (p. 311)

mercantilism (MER kuhn tihl ihz uhm) economic theory that a nation's strength came from building up its gold supplies and expanding its trade (p. 112)

mercenary soldier who fights merely for pay, often for a foreign country (p. 164)

mestizo in Spanish colonies, person of mixed Spanish and Indian background (p. 70)

Middle Ages period of time in European history from about 500 to 1350 (p. 60)

middle class in the 13 English colonies, class that included skilled craftsworkers, farmers, and some tradespeople (p. 117)

Middle Passage ocean trip from Africa to the Americas in which thousands of enslaved Africans died (p. 77)

militia army of citizens who serve as soldiers in an emergency (p. 154)

minuteman colonial volunteer who trained to fight the British (p. 154)

mission religious settlement run by Catholic priests and friars (p. 69)

missionary person who tries to spread certain religious beliefs among a group of people (p. 81)

Missouri Compromise (1819) plan proposed by Henry Clay to keep the number of slave and free states equal (p. 424)

monarch king or queen (p. 60)

monopoly company that controls all or nearly all the business of an industry (p. 508)

Monroe Doctrine (1823) President Monroe's foreign policy statement warning European nations not to interfere in Latin America (p. 315)

mountain high, steep, rugged land, usually at least 1,000 feet (372 m) above the surrounding land (p. 14)

mountain man fur trapper who lived in the western mountains in the early 1800s (p. 347)

mudslinging political tactic of using insults to attack an opponent's reputation (p. 341)

N

national debt total sum of money a government owes (p. 245)

nationalism pride in one's nation (p. 282)

nativist person who wanted to limit immigration and preserve the United States for native-born white Protestants (p. 381)

natural rights rights that belong to all people from birth (p. 168)

neutral not taking sides in a war (pp. 174, 282)

New Deal program of President Franklin D. Roosevelt to end the Great Depression (p. 514)

nominating convention meeting at which a political party chooses a candidate (p. 327)

North American Free Trade Agreement (NAFTA) treaty among the United States, Canada, and Mexico to gradually remove trade barriers (p. 509)

nullification idea that a state had the right to cancel a federal law it considered unconstitutional (p. 333)

nullify to cancel (p. 260)

O

opinion a judge's official statement regarding the laws bearing on a case (p. 231)

ordinance law (p. 190)

override to overrule or set aside (pp. 203, 221)

P

Parliament representative assembly in England (p. 86)

Patriot colonist who supported independence from British rule (p. 161)

patroon owner of a huge estate in a Dutch colony (p. 100)

penal system system of prisons (p. 399)

peninsulare (puh nihn suh LAH ray) person from Spain who held a position of power in a Spanish colony (p. 70)

pet bank state bank in which President Jackson and Secretary of the Treasury Taney deposited federal money (p. 332)

petition formal request to someone in authority, usually written and signed by a group of people (p. 144)

Pilgrims in the 1600s, English settlers who sought religious freedom in the Americas (p. 88)

plain broad area of fairly level land (p. 14)

plantation large estate farmed by many workers (pp. 72, 109)

plateau raised plain (p. 14)

Plessy **v.** *Ferguson* (1896) Supreme Court ruling that segregation was legal as long as facilities for blacks and whites were equal (p. 505)

poll tax tax required before a person can vote (p. 493)

popular sovereignty idea that the people hold the final authority in government (p. 218), allowing each territory to decide whether to allow slavery (p. 426)

potlatch ceremonial dinner among some Native Americans of the Northwest Coast (p. 38)

preamble opening statement of a declaration, constitution, or other official document (pp. 168, 214)

precedent (PREHS uh dehnt) act or decision that sets an example for others to follow (pp. 224, 244)

precipitation (pree sihp uh TAY shuhn) water that falls as rain, sleet, hail, or snow (p. 19)

predestination belief that God decided in advance which people will gain salvation in heaven (p. 398)

presidio (prih SIHD ee oh) fort where soldiers lived in the Spanish colonies (p. 69)

primary election in which voters choose their party's candidate for the general election (p. 513)

Prime Meridian imaginary line that lies at 0° longitude (p. 8)

profiteer person who takes advantage of a crisis to make money (p. 466)

Progressives reformers who wanted to improve American life in the late 1800s and early 1900s (p. 513)

proprietary colony English colony in which the king gave land to proprietors in exchange for a yearly payment (p. 101)

proprietor owner of a proprietary colony (p. 101)

protective tariff tax on imported goods to protect a country's industry from foreign competition (p. 247)

Protestant Reformation movement to reform the Roman Catholic Church in the 1500s; led to creation of many different Christian churches (p. 79)

public school school supported by taxes (p. 120)

pueblo adobe dwelling of the Anasazis (p. 35); town in the Spanish colonies (p. 69)

Puritans group of English Protestants who settled the Massachusetts Bay Colony (p. 94)

Q

Quakers Protestant reformers who settled in Pennsylvania (p. 101)

quota system system that limited immigration by allowing only a certain number of people from each country to immigrate to the United States (p. 503)

R

racism belief that one race is superior to another (pp. 111, 448)

radical person who wants to make drastic changes in society (p. 482)

ratify to approve (pp. 182, 204)

recall process by which voters can remove an elected official from office (p. 513)

Reconstruction rebuilding of the South after the Civil War (p. 479)

referendum process by which people vote directly on a bill (p. 513)

refugee person who flees his or her homeland to seek safety elsewhere (p. 164)

Renaissance (REHN uh sahns) French word meaning rebirth; burst of learning in Europe from the late 1300s to about 1600 (p. 61)

rendezvous (RAHN day voo) yearly meeting where mountain men traded furs (p. 348)

repeal to cancel or undo (p. 144)

representative government government in which voters elect representatives to make laws for them (pp. 86, 218)

republic nation in which voters elect representatives to govern them (p. 198)

reservation limited area set aside for Native Americans by the government (p. 506)

revival huge meeting held to stir religious feelings (p. 398)

royal colony colony under the control of the English crown (p. 101)

S

Sabbath holy day of rest in some religions (p. 98)

sachem tribal chief of an Eastern Woodlands Native American people (p. 45)

scalawag white southerner who supported the Republicans during Reconstruction (p. 486)

secede to withdraw from membership in a group (pp. 335, 427)

Second Great Awakening religious movement that swept the United States in the early 1800s (p. 398)

sectionalism loyalty to a state or section rather than to the whole country (pp. 310, 425)

sedition stirring up rebellion against a government (p. 259)

segregation separation of people based on racial, ethnic, or other differences (p. 495)

Senate smaller house of Congress, in which each state has two senators (p. 225)

Seneca Falls Convention (1848) meeting at which leaders of the women's rights movement called for equality for women (p. 409)

separation of powers principle by which the powers of government are divided among separate branches (p. 200)

serf peasant who worked for a lord and could not leave without the lord's permission (p. 60)

service industry business in which workers provide a service rather than produce goods (p. 509)

sharecropper person who farms land owned by another in exchange for a share of the crops (p. 490)

Shays' Rebellion (1786) revolt of Massachusetts farmers against increased taxes (p. 192)

siege military blockade of an enemy town or position in order to force it to surrender (pp. 180, 354)

slave code laws that controlled the lives of enslaved African Americans and denied them basic rights (pp. 111, 390)

smuggler person who violates trade laws by illegally taking goods into or out of a country (p. 278)

social reform organized attempt to improve what is unjust or imperfect in society (p. 398)

Sons of Liberty group of colonial men who protested British policies (p. 145)

speculator person who invests in a risky venture in the hope of making a large profit (pp. 246, 338)

spinning jenny machine developed in the 1760s that could spin several threads at once (p. 294)

spoils system practice of rewarding supporters with government jobs (p. 331)

standard time zone one of 24 divisions of the Earth, each an hour apart (p. 12)

standing committee permanent congressional committee assigned to study a specific issue (p. 226)

states' rights idea that states have the right to limit the power of the federal government (p. 333)

stock share in a corporation (p. 508)

strike refusal by workers to do their jobs until their demands are met (p. 379)

suffrage right to vote (p. 326)

suffragist person who campaigned for women's right to vote (p. 512)

Sunbelt name for the southern part of the United States from Florida to southern California (p. 504)

Supreme Court highest court in the United States (p. 231)

surplus an extra amount, more than is needed (p. 50)

T

tariff tax on foreign goods brought into a country (p. 247)

Tariff of Abominatons name southerners gave to the tariff passed in 1828 (p. 333)

telegraph communication device that sends electrical signals along a wire (p. 375)

temperance movement campaign against the sale or drinking of alcohol (p. 401)

tepee (TEE pee) tent made by stretching animal skins on tall poles (p. 42)

terrace level strip of land carved into the side of a hill or mountain for farming (p. 50)

Three-Fifths Compromise agreement at the Constitutional Convention that three fifths of the slaves in any state be counted in its population (p. 196)

toleration willingness to let others practice their own customs and beliefs (p. 96)

total war all-out war that affects civilians at home as well as soldiers in combat (p. 471)

totalitarian state country where a single party controls the government and every aspect of the lives of the people (p. 517)

town meeting session in which citizens discuss and vote on local community issues (p. 98)

trade deficit when a nation buys more goods and services from foreign countries than it sells to them (p. 509)

trade union association of trade workers formed to gain higher wages and better working conditions (p. 379)

Trail of Tears (1838) forced march of Native Americans to lands west of the Mississippi (p. 337)

traitor person who betrays his or her country (p. 166)

transcendentalism belief that the most important truths in life go beyond human reason (p. 413)

transcontinental railroad railroad that stretches across a continent (p. 506)

travois (truh VOI) sled used by Plains people and pulled by a dog or horse (pp. 41, 504)

triangular trade colonial trade route between New England, the West Indies, and Africa (p. 112)

tribe group of Native American people sharing the same customs, languages, and rituals (p. 36)

tributary stream or smaller river that flows into a bigger river (p. 17)

turnpike road built by a private company that charges a toll to use it (p. 302)

tutor private teacher (p. 120)

U

unconstitutional not permitted by the Constitution (pp. 221, 254)

underground railroad network of abolitionists who helped runaway slaves reach freedom in the North or Canada (p. 405)

United Nations international organization formed in 1945 to help solve conflicts between nations (p. 517)

urbanization movement of population from farms to cities (p. 300)

V

veto to reject (pp. 203, 221)

vigilante (vihj uh LAN tee) self-appointed law enforcer who deals out punishment without a trial (p. 368)

W

weather condition of the Earth's atmosphere at any given time and place (p. 19)

Whiskey Rebellion (1794) revolt of farmers to protest the tax on whiskey (p. 249)

women's rights movement campaign to win equality for women (p. 410)

writ of assistance legal document that let a British customs officer inspect a ship's cargo without giving any reason for the search (p. 145)

★ **GLOSSARY** ★

★ Index ★

INDEX

INDEX

prisons, 399, 401; Progressive voting reform, 513; religious freedom, 396; revival movement, *p397,* 398, *q398;* slavery, 403–405, *p403–405, q403, q404,* 407; social reform, 398, *q398,* go*410. See also* Antislavery movement; Civil rights movement; Unions; Women's rights movement

Refugees, 164

Regionalism. *See* North; Sectionalism; Slavery; South; West

Religion: African, 74–75; Aztecs, 49; colonial, 119–120, *q119, p120;* freedom of, *c113,* 188, 205, 209, *c215,* 219, 223, 396; Great Awakening, 119–120, *q119, p120;* of Native Americans, 32–33, *p33,* 36, 37, *p41,* 44, 51; Plymouth settlement, 88, *c113;* predestination, 398; Puritans, 94–95, *p95,* 98, 99, 120; Quakers, 101–102, 111, 177; religious toleration, 96–97, 107; revival movement, *p397,* 398–399, *q398;* of slaves, 393, *q393;* in Texas, 351

Renaissance, 61

Rendezvous, 348, *q348*

Repeal, 144

Representative government, 86, *p86,* 114–116

Republic, 198

Republic of Texas, 352

Republican party, *m496;* formation of, 435; Radical Republicans, 482, 486; slavery and, 435. *See also* Democratic Republican party; Elections, presidential

Reservations, 506

Revels, Hiram, 487

Revere, Paul, 148, 155

Revival movement, *p397,* 398–399, *q398*

Revolutionary War. *See* American Revolution

Rhode Island, 96–97, *m96, c113,* 114, 206, *c210,* 296, *c618*

Rice, *m107,* 108, 109, 111, 118–119

Richmond, VA: American Revolution, *m179,* 180; Civil War, 453, 454, *m454,* 455, 472, *m472;* industry in, 386; Reconstruction, *p477,* 478, *p479;* slavery, 390

Rillieux, Norbert, 390

Rio Grande, 18, 275, 354, 361, *m361,* 362, *m363*

Roads, 51, 123, 301–303, *q301, p302, m303, q304,* 376

Roanoke settlement, 84, *m88*

Robinson projection, 9, *m9*

Rochambeau, Comte de, *m179,* 180

Rock 'n' roll, 504

Rocky Mountains, 16, 22, 38, *m39,* 274–275, 346, *m366*

Rolfe, John, 85

Roman Catholic Church, 351, 352, 381; exploration rivalries and, 80–81; Middle Ages, 60; Protestant Reformation and, 79–80

Roosevelt, Eleanor, *p513*

Roosevelt, Franklin Delano, *p616;* election of 1940, 244; Great Depression, *p513, q513–514;* New Deal, 514; presidential powers, 224

Roosevelt, Theodore, 508, 516–517, *p616*

Rosedown Plantation, *p389*

Ross, Betsy, 176

Royal colony, 101

Rush, Benjamin, 206

Russell, Charles M., 264

Russia: immigrants from, 502; Oregon Country, 346, 347

Russwurm, John, 382, 404

S

Sabbath, 98

Sacajawea, *p265,* 274–275, *p274;* primary source, 555–557

Sachems, 45

St. Augustine, FL, *m67, p69*

St. Lawrence River, 18, 78, *m79,* 81, 82, 132, *m138,* 140–141

St. Leger, Barry, *m170,* 171

St. Louis, MO, *p293*

Salem, MA, *m96,* 99

Salem, Peter, 177

Salt Lake City, UT, 366, *m366*

Samoa, *c618*

Samoset, 89

Samuel, William G., *p345*

San Antonio, TX, *m67,* 344, *p345,* 352–354, *m352, p353, q354,* 355

San Diego, CA, *m67,* 69, 357, 359, 362, *m366*

San Francisco, CA, 15, *m366;* 1906 earthquake, 15; Gold Rush, 367, 368; missions in, *m67,* 69; port of, 359

San Jacinto, Battle of, *m352, p354,* 355

San Juan Capistrano Mission, 357, *p357*

San Martín, José de, 313

Santa Anna, Antonio López de, 352, *p354,* 355, 362

Santa Fe, NM, *m67,* 69, 356, 362, *m366*

Santa Fe Trail, *m366*

Saratoga, Battle of, *m170,* 171–172, go*172*

Satellites, *p3,* 13

Savannah, GA, *m107, p108,* 175, *m179*

Scalawags, 486

Scarlet Letter, The (Hawthorne), 412

Schools. *See* Education

Science. *See* Technology

Science, connections with: botany, Lewis and Clark, 272; corsets vs. bloomers, 408; patents, 383; preserving the Constitution, 204; Roanoke settlement fate, 84; tea myths, 150

Scott, Winfield, 362–363

Secession, 427–428, 440–442

Second Amendment, 209

Second Continental Congress, 160, 188–189; primary source, 543–544

Second Great Awakening, 398–399, *q398*

Sectionalism, 421; agriculture vs. industry, 292; American System,

310–311, *q311;* Mexican War, 362, 425; states' rights, 333, 335. *See also* North; Slavery; South; West

Sedgwick, Catherine, 413

Sedition Act, 243, 259, 267

Segregation, *q495;* Jim Crow Laws, 495, 510; *Plessy* v. *Ferguson,* 495. *See also* Civil rights movement

Seminoles, 314, 335, 337, *m342, q343*

Seminole War, 337

Senate, 194, 201, 225, 226, *c226,* 228, 513

Seneca Falls Convention, 409–410, 511, 576; primary source, 576–577

Senecas, 45, 142, 174

Separation of powers, 200, 201–202, *q201, c202,* 220–221

Separatists, 88

Sequoyah, *p335,* 336

Serfs, 60, *p425*

Seventeenth Amendment, *c215,* 513

Seventh Amendment, 209

Seward, William, 439

Sewing machine, 374

Sharecropping, 490, *p490*

Shawnees, 142, 280, *m280*

Shays' Rebellion, 192, 215

Sheridan, Philip, 471, 472

Sherman, Roger, *p166,* 194, *p194,* 196

Sherman, William Tecumseh, *m470,* 471, 472

Shiloh, Battle of, 458, 467, *m470*

Shoshones, 38, *m39,* 274–275

Shreve, Henry, 305

Siege, 180, 354, 468, 472

Sierra, Junípero, 357, *p357*

Sierra Nevadas, 15, 22, *m366;* primary source, 524–525

Singer, Isaac, 374

Sioux, 270

Sixteenth Amendment, *c215*

Sixth Amendment, 209, *c215,* 223, 232

Sketch Book, The (Irving), 412

Slater, Samuel, *q296*

Slave codes, 111, 390, 404

Slave trade, 75–77, *m75, p76, q76,* 197, *q417;* primary source, 531–532

Slavery: in California, 368, 427, *g427;* in colonies, 87, *q125;* Compromise of 1850, 428–429, *m431;* cotton economy, 372, *p373,* 384, *g385, q392;* Declaration of Independence and, 177; Dred Scott decision, 433–434, *p433,* 483; Emancipation Proclamation, 446, 459–461, *p460, q460,* 481; in Florida, 314; Free Soil party, 426; Fugitive Slave Laws, 428, 429, *q429;* growth of, 108–109, *p110,* 111; John Brown's Raid, 438; Kansas-Nebraska Act, 431–432, *m431, p432;* Mexican War, 362; Missouri Compromise, 424, *m431,* 434; in the North, 381; in Northwest Territory, 191; popular sovereignty, 426, 429, 431, 432–433; resistance against, 393, primary source, 572–573; runaway slaves, 314, 382, 393, *p423,* 428, 429; slave

★ Credits ★

Staff Credits

The people who made up **The American Nation** team—representing editorial, editorial services, design services, field marketing, managing editor, market research, marketing services, on-line services/multimedia development, product marketing, production services, and publishing processes—are listed below. Bold type denotes core team members.

Margaret Antonini, Sarah Carroll, Lynda Cloud, Rhett Conklin, Martha Conway, Carlos Crespo, **Jim Doris,** Libby Forsyth, **Annemarie Franklin, Nancy Gilbert,** Holly Gordon, **Dorshia Johnson, Loretta Moe,** Jim O'Shea, Kirsten Richert, Gerry Schrenk, Anne Shea, Annette Simmons, **Marilyn Stearns,** Frank Tangredi, Elizabeth Torjussen

Acknowledgments

Art and Design: Kathyryn Foot, Karen Vignola, Patty Rodriguez, Rui Camarinha, Anthony Barone, Ernest Albanese, Robert Aleman, Penny Baker, Paul DelSignore, Frances Medico, Doreen Mazur **Editorial:** Mary Aldridge, Gaynor Ellis, Marian Manners, Jeremy Naidus, Andrew Roney **Photo Research:** *Photosearch,* Inc., Lashonda Williams, Vicky Menanteaux, Katarina Gavilanes, Diane Alimena

Text Credits

Grateful acknowledgment is made to the following for copyrighted material:

Page 126 From *American Indian Myths and Legends,* edited by Richard Erdoes and Alfonso Ortiz (New York: Pantheon Books, a division of Random House, 1984). Copyright 1984 by Richard Erdoes and Alfonso Ortiz. **Page 238** Excerpts from "Valley Forge" by Maxwell Anderson from *America on Stage,* edited by Stanley Richards. Copyright © 1976. **Page 418** From *Nightjohn* by Gary Paulsen. Copyright © 1993 by Gary Paulsen. Used by permission of Delacorte Press, a division of Bantam Doubleday Dell Publishing Group, Inc. **Page 527** From "Spider Woman Story" from *Sweet Salt: Navajo Folk Tales and Mythology* by Raymond Friday Locke. Copyright © 1990 by Raymond Friday Locke. Reprinted by permission of the author. **Page 550** From *Who Cares? Millions Do...* by Milton Meltzer. Copyright ©1994 by Milton Meltzer. Reprinted with permission from Walker and Company, 435 Hudson Street, New York, NY 10014. 1-800-289-2553. All Rights Reserved. **Page 566** From *Death Comes for the Archbishop* by Willa Cather. Copyright 1927 by Willa Cather and renewed 1955 by the Executors of the Estate of Willa Cather. Reprinted by permission of Alfred A. Knopf, Inc. **Page 572** From *The Fires of Jubilee, Nat Turner's Fierce Rebellion* by Stephen B. Oates, Harper and Row, Publishers. Copyright ©1975 by Stephen B. Oates. All rights reserved. **Page 578** From *Caleb's Choice* by G. Clifton Wisler. Copyright ©1996 by G. Clifton Wisler. Published by Lodestar Books, an

affiliate of Dutton Children's Books, a division of Penguin Putnam Inc. **Page 587** From *Out From This Place* by Joyce Hansen. Copyright©1988 by Joyce Hansen. Reprinted with permission from Walker and Company, 435 Hudson Street, New York, NY 10014. 1-800-289-2553. All Rights Reserved. **Note:** Every effort has been made to locate the copyright owner of material used in this textbook. Omissions brought to our attention will be corrected in subsequent editions.

Illustration Credits

Cover and Title Page Wolfgang Kaehler; Day Williams/Photo Researchers, Inc. **iv** *t The Puritan,* Augustus Saint-Gaudens, All Rights Reserved, The Metropolitan Museum of Art, Bequest of Jacob Ruppart, 1939 (39.65.53); *b* Jerry Jacka Photography **v** *t* Gallery of the Republic; *b* Courtesy, Independence National Historical Park Collection **vi** *t* Rembrandt Peale, *Thomas Jefferson,* detail, Collection of The New York Historical Society; *bl* O.C. Seltzer, *Lewis and Clark With Sacajawea at the Great Falls of the Missouri,* From the Collection of Gilcrease Museum, Tulsa; *br* American Textile History Museum, Lowell, MA **vii** *t* Museum of Art, Rhode Island School of Design, Gift of Miss Lucy T. Aldrich; *b* Dean Beason, *Settlers' Wagon,* National Gallery of Art, Washington **viii** *t* Photography by Larry Sherer/High Impact Photography, Time-Life Books, Inc.; *mt* Photography by Larry Sherer/High Impact Photography, Time-Life Books, Inc.; *b* Courtesy of the Library of Congress **ix** Courtesy Erie Canal Village **x** ©Robert E. Daemmrich/Tony Stone Images **xi** Lynn Saville **xvi** George Catlin, *LaSalle Claiming Louisiana for France, April 9, 1682,* 1847/1848, Paul Mellon Collection, ©1998 Board of Trustees, National Gallery of Art, Washington **3** NOAA **6** Vito Palmisano/Tony Stone Images **8** Silver Burdett Ginn **12** Map Divison, New York Public Library. Astor, Lenox and Tilden Foundations **14** Daniel J. Cox/Gamma Liaison **15** Jeff Gnass Photography **16** *r* Robert Farber/The Image Bank; *l* ©Francois Gohier/Photo Researchers, Inc. **17** *l* Siegfried Layda/Tony Stone Images; *r* ©Jeff LePore/Photo Researchers, Inc. **18** *r* UPI/CORBIS-BETTMANN; *l* Courtesy National Archives, photo no. NWDNS-79-AA_F09 **20** East Bay Municipal Utility District **21** *l* Duricux/SIPA; *r* Weather Graphics Courtesy of AccuWeather, Inc., 619 West College Avenue, State College, PA 16801, (814) 237-0309; Other Educational Weather Products Available ©1997 **29** Courtesy of the Wheelwright Museum of the American Indian **30** National Museum of American Art, Smithsonian Institution **33** *l* Tom Till/International Stock Photography, Ltd.; *r* Peabody Museum of Archaeology and Ethnology, Harvard University **34** *r* National Park Service; *l* ©Richard J. Green/Photo Researchers, Inc. **35** Jerry Jacka Photography **37** *r* Lee Boltin Picture Library; *l* Grove/ Zuckerman/Index Stock Photography, Inc. **41** *l Kachina Doll,* The Brooklyn Museum, 05.588.7193, Museum Expedition 1905, Museum Collection Fund; *r Butterfly Maiden, Kachina,* Courtesy of the Denver Art Museum, Denver Art Museum, Denver, CO **42** National Museum of American Art, Smithsonian Institution **43** Courtesy of The New York State Museum,

CREDITS ★

Museum **245** *t* Private Collection; *b* The Museum of American Political Life, University of Hartford; photo by Sally Anderson-Bruce **246** Courtesy of the Art Commission of the City of New York **248** David Young Wolff/Tony Stone Images **251** *t* Giraudon/Art Resource, NY; *b* Roger Viollet **252** Courtesy of The Mount Vernon Ladies' Association **254** *l* Unknown, American, Pennsylvania, *He That Tilleth His Land Shall be Satisfied,* detail, Philadelphia Museum of Art: The Edgar William and Bernice Chrysler Garbisch Collection; *r* John Neagle, *Pat Lyon at the Forge,* Henry M. and Zoë Oliver Sherman Fund, Courtesy, Museum of Fine Arts, Boston **255** Corel Professional Photos CD-ROM™ **259** *r* The Granger Collection, New York; *l* The Huntington Library, San Marino, California **260** *r John Adams,* c. 1800, James Sharples, The Museum of Fine Arts, Houston; The Bayou Bend Collection, gift of Miss Ima Hogg; *m* Gilbert Stuart, *Abigail Smith Adams* (Mrs. John Adams), detail, Gift of Mrs. Robert Homans, ©1997 Board of Trustees, National Gallery of Art, Washington, Photo by: Richard Carafelli; *l* National Park Service, Adams National Historic Site **265** *Lewis and Clark on the Lower Columbia,* Charles M. Russell, 1905, 1961.195, gouache, watercolor and graphite on paper, Amon Carter Museum, Forth Worth **267** *r* Rembrandt Peale, *Thomas Jefferson,* detail, Collection of The New-York Historical Society; *l* Robert Llewellyn Photography **268** *t* Silver Burdett Ginn; *b* ©Junebug Clark/Photo Researchers, Inc. **270** Missouri Historical Society, St. Louis **271** Chicago Historical Society **274** *l* John Woodhouse Audubon, *Antelope Americana,* detail, Neg./Trans. no._3267 (2)(Photo by: P. Hollembeak/ Bauer) Courtesy Department of Library Services, American Museum of Natural History; *r* O.C. Seltzer, *Lewis and Clark with Sacajawea at the Great Falls of the Missouri,* From the Collection of Gilcrease Museum, Tulsa **276** The Granger Collection, New York **279** Ohio State Historical Society, Jim Roese, photographer, courtesy Historic Waynesborough **280** Collection of Cranbrook Institute of Science, #CIS 2207. ©Robert Hensleigh, Photographer **281** *r* Courtesy of the Library of Congress; *l* The Field Museum, Neg.# A93851.1c, Chicago **283** Courtesy Scott Baker, Ohio Society War of 1812 **285** U.S. Navy Photos **287** *l* From the collection of Mac G. and Janelle C. Morris; *r* Ted Baker/The Image Bank **288** Courtesy of the Library of Congress **293** Leon Pomarede, *View of St. Louis,* 1835, The Saint Louis Art Museum, Private collection of Dorothy Ziern Hanon & Joseph B. Hanon **295** *r* James Higgins; Use courtesy of Lowell National Historical Park **297** American Textile History Museum, Lowell, MA **298** Reprinted with permission of the News-Press of Fort Myers **301** Dean Beason, *Settlers' Wagon,* National Gallery of Art, Washington **302** Pavel Petrovich Svinin, *Travel by Stagecoach near Trenton, New Jersey,* All rights reserved, The Metropolitan Museum of Art, Rogers Fund, 1942. (42.95.11) **304** Silver Burdett Ginn and Colonial Williamsburg Foundation **305** *l* Courtesy Erie Canal Village; *r* Courtesy Erie Canal Museum **309** *l* Architect of the Capitol; *m* Francis Alexander, *Daniel Webster,* 1835, Hood Museum of Art, Dartmouth College, Hanover, New Hampshire; gift of Dr. George C. Shattuck, Class of 1803; *r* Charles Bird King, *John Caldwell Calhoun,* National Portrait Gallery, Smithsonian Institution, Transfer from the National Gallery of Art; Gift of Andrew W. Mellon, 1942 **313** *t* Anne S.K. Brown Military Collection; *b* Coleccion Museo Nacional de Colombia,

Bogotá **319** John Quidor, *Return of Rip Van Winkle,* 1829, Andrew W. Mellon Collection, ©1998 Board of Trustees, National Gallery of Art, Washington **320** Scotts Bluff National Monument **323** George Caleb Bingham, *The County Election,* 1851–52, oil on canvas, The Saint Louis Art Museum **326** Eunice Pinney, *Two Women,* c. 1815, New York State Historical Association, Cooperstown **327** *l* Courtesy of the Library of Congress; *r* D. Walker/Gamma Liaison **329** Anna Claypoole Peale, *Andrew Jackson,* Yale University Art Gallery **331** The Granger Collection, New York **333** Courtesy of Salem Maritime NHS **334** Lynn Saville **335** Courtesy of the Library of Congress **339** Becker Collection, Division of Political History, National Museum of American History, Smithsonian Institution, #564-97 **340** © Robert E. Daemmrich/Tony Stone Images **345** Courtesy of Bexar County and The Witte Museum, San Antonio, Texas **348** Alfred Jacob Miller, *Fort Laramie,* 1837, Walters Art Gallery, Baltimore **349** *t* Handtinting by Ladleton Studio/Culver Pictures, Inc.; *b* Courtesy of the Lane County Historical Museum **351** Courtesy Local History Programs **353** Corel Professional Photos CD-ROM™ **354** *l* Courtesy of the Texas Memorial Museum; *r* Archives Division, Texas State Library **357** *r* Courtesy of The Oakland Museum History Department; *l* Jim Zuckerman/West Light **360** Bill Pogue/The Stockhouse, Inc. **361** Courtesy of the Costume Department, Chicago Historical Society, 1920.38 **364** *Nuestra Senora del Rosario / Our Lady of the Rosary,* by Santo Nino Santero, New Mexico, 1830–60. Gesso, cloth, tin, wood, and water soluble paint. H: 40 1/2 inches. Courtesy Museum of New Mexico Collections at the Museum of International Folk Art, Santa Fe. Photo by Blair Clark. **368** *l* North Wind Picture Archives; *r* California State Library **373** *b* The Warner Collection of Gulf States Paper Corporation, Tuscaloosa, Alabama; *t* American Steel Foundries **374** National Museum of History and Technology, Smithsonian Institution, Photo No. 90-4210 **379** *l* State Historical Society of Wisconsin; *r* American Textile History Museum, Lowell, MA **380** Michael Newman/PhotoEdit **382** Aaron E. Darling, *John Jones,* 1865, Chicago Historical Society, #1904.0018 **383** National Museum of American History, Smithsonian Institution, Photo No. 73-11287 **384** ©Robert Finken/Photo Researchers, Inc. **387** The Old Print Shop **389** *t* D. Donne Bryant Stock Photography; *b* Courtesy Rosedown Plantation and Historic Garden **391** *t* Maynard Frank Wolfe/Globe Photos; *b* Bob Daemmrich/Stock, Boston/PNI **392** John Antrobus, *Plantation Burial,* 1860, The Historic New Orleans Collection, Museum/Research Center, Acc. No. 1960.46 **397** Museum of Art, Rhode Island School of Design, Gift of Miss Lucy T. Aldrich **399** Courtesy of the Library of Congress **400** Tony Freeman/PhotoEdit **401** *r* Winslow Homer, *Homework,* 1874, watercolor, Canajoharie Library and Art Gallery, Canajoharie, New York; *b* Victor R. Boswell, Jr./National Geographic Society; *m* Richard Nowitz; *l* Richard T. Nowitz, 1991 **403** The Trustees of the Wedgwood Museum, Barlaston, Staffordshire, England **404** *t* Southworth and Hawes, *William Lloyd Garrison,* All Rights Reserved, The Metropolitan Museum of Art, Gift of I.N. Phelps Stokes, Edward S. Hawes, Alice Mary Hawes, Marion Augusta Hawes, 1937 (37.14.37); *b* Courtesy of the Massachusetts Historical Society **405** Sophia Smith Collection, Smith College **406** C.T. Webber, *The Underground Railroad,* Cincinnati Art Museum,

Stop the Presses

Not so long ago, publishers had to stop the presses to get late-breaking information into their books. Today, Prentice Hall can use the Internet to update you quickly and easily on the most recent developments in Social Studies.

Visit Prentice Hall on the Internet at

http://www.phschool.com

for the Prentice Hall Social Studies Update.

There you will find periodic updates in the following areas:

- ★ **United States History**
- ★ **World Studies**
- ★ **American Government**

Each update topic provides you with background information as well as carefully selected links to guide you to related content on the Internet.